Paper 1.1
International Stream

PREPARING FINANCIAL STATEMENTS

For exams in December 2006 and June 2007

Study Text

In this June 2006 new edition

- A new user-friendly format for easy navigation
- Exam-centred topic coverage, directly linked to ACCA's syllabus and study guide
- Exam focus points showing you what the examiner will want you to do
- Regular fast forward summaries emphasising the key points in each chapter
- Questions and quick quizzes to test your understanding
- Exam question bank containing exam standard questions with answers
- A full index

BPP's **i-Learn** and **i-Pass** products also support this paper.

FOR EXAMS IN DECEMBER 2006 AND JUNE 2007

D1697162

PROFESSIONAL EDUCATION

First edition 2001
Sixth edition June 2006

ISBN 0 7517 2676 1 (Previous edition 0 7517 2327 4)

British Library Cataloguing-in-Publication Data
A catalogue record for this book
is available from the British Library

Published by

BPP Professional Education
Aldine House, Aldine Place
London W12 8AW

www.bpp.com

Printed in Great Britain by W M Print
45-47 Frederick Street
Walsall
West Midlands
WS2 9NE.

All our rights reserved. No part of this publication may be reproduced, stored in a retrieval system or transmitted, in any form or by any means, electronic, mechanical, photocopying, recording or otherwise, without the prior written permission of BPP Professional Education.

We are grateful to the Association of Chartered Certified Accountants for permission to reproduce past examination questions. The suggested solutions in the exam answer bank have been prepared by BPP Professional Education.

©
BPP Professional Education
2006

Contents

Page

Introduction

> The introduction pages contain lots of valuable advice and information. They include tips on studying for and passing the exam. Also the content of the syllabus and what has been examined.

The BPP Effective Study Package How the BPP Study Text can help you pass – Help yourself study for your ACCA exams – Syllabus and Study Guide – The exam paper – Current issues – Oxford Brookes BSc (Hons) degree in Applied Accounting – ACCA Professional Development requirements

Part A General framework
1   Introduction to accounting 3

Part B Accounting concepts and principles
2   The accounting equation 21
3   Basic financial statements 33

Part C Double entry bookkeeping and accounting systems
4   Sources, records and the books of original entry 49
5   Ledger accounting and double entry 61
6   From trial balance to financial statements 87
7   Control accounts 101
8   Bank reconciliations 119
9   Correction of errors 131

Part D Accounting treatments
10 Accounting conventions 143
11 The cost of goods sold, accruals and prepayments 163
12 Irrecoverable debts and allowances 181
13 Accounting for inventories 195
14 Non-current assets and depreciation 217
15 Intangible non-current assets 251
16 Events after the balance sheet date and contingencies 263

Part E Financial statements
17 Incomplete records 273
18 Partnership accounts 301
19 Limited liability companies 315
20 Cash flow statements 357
21 Group accounts 375

Part F Interpretation of financial statements
22 Interpretation of financial statements 393

Part G Miscellaneous topics
23 Computer applications in accounting 421
24 The IASB and financial reporting 433

Exam question bank 463
Exam answer bank 507

Index 557
Review form and free prize draw

Computer-based learning products from BPP

If you want to reinforce your studies by **interactive** learning, try BPP's **i-Learn** product, covering major syllabus areas in an interactive format. For **self-testing**, try **i-Pass**, which offers a large number of **objective test questions**, particularly useful where objective test questions form part of the exam.

Learn Online

Learn Online uses BPP's wealth of teaching experience to produce a fully **interactive** e-learning resource **delivered via the Internet**. The site offers comprehensive **tutor support** and features areas such as **study**, **practice**, **email service**, **revision** and **useful resources**.

Visit our website www.bpp.com/acca/learnonline to sample aspects of Learn Online free of charge.

Learning to Learn Accountancy

BPP's ground-breaking **Learning to Learn Accountancy** book is designed to be used both at the outset of your ACCA studies and throughout the process of learning accountancy. It challenges you to consider how you study and gives you helpful hints about how to approach the various types of paper which you will encounter. It can help you **focus your studies on the subject and exam**, enabling you to **acquire knowledge**, **practise and revise efficiently and effectively**.

The BPP Effective Study Package

Recommended period of use	The BPP Effective Study Package
From the outset and throughout	**Learning to Learn Accountancy** Read this invaluable book as you begin your studies and refer to it throughout your studies.
Three to twelve months before the exam	**Study Text and i-Learn** Use the Study Text to acquire knowledge, understanding, skills and the ability to apply techniques. Use BPP's **i-Learn** product to reinforce your learning.
Throughout	**Learn Online** Study, practise, revise and use other helpful resources with BPP's fully interactive e-learning site, including full tutor support.
Throughout	**i-Pass** **i-Pass**, our computer-based testing package, provides objective test questions in a variety of formats and is ideal for self-assessment.
One to six months before the exam	**Practice & Revision Kit** Try the numerous examination-format questions in our Kit and compare your answers with the suggested solutions. Examiners emphasise that tackling exam-standard questions is essential preparation for your exams. Then attempt the two mock exams.
From three months before the exam until the last minute	**Passcards** Work through these short, memorable notes which are focused on the topics most likely to come up in your exam and which you can take anywhere.
One to six months before the exam	**Success CDs** The CDs cover the vital elements of your syllabus in less than 90 minutes per subject. They also contain exam hints to help you fine tune your strategy.

You can purchase these products by visiting www.bpp.com/mybpp

How the BPP Study Text can help you pass

> It provides you with the knowledge and understanding, skills and application techniques that you need to be successful in your exams

This Study Text has been targeted at the **Financial Management and Control** syllabus.

- It is **comprehensive**. It covers the syllabus content. No more, no less.
- It is written at the **right level**. Each chapter is written with ACCA's syllabus and study guide in mind.
- It is aimed at the **exam**. We have taken account of recent exams, guidance the examiner has given and the assessment methodology.

> It allows you to study in the way that best suits your learning style and the time you have available, by following your personal Study Plan (see page (viii))

You may be studying at home on your own or you may be attending a full-time course. You may like to read every word, or you may prefer to skim-read and practise questions the rest of the time. However you study, you will find the BPP Study Text meets your needs in designing and following your personal Study Plan.

> It ties in with the other components of the BPP Effective Study Package to ensure you have the best possible chance of passing the exam (see page (v))

Help yourself study for your ACCA exams

Exams for professional bodies such as ACCA are very different from those you have taken at college or university. You will be under **greater time pressure before** the exam – as you may be combining your study with work. Here are some hints and tips.

The right approach

1 **Develop the right attitude**

Believe in yourself	Yes, there is a lot to learn. But thousands have succeeded before and you can too.
Remember why you're doing it	You are studying for a good reason: to advance your career.

2 **Focus on the exam**

Read through the Syllabus and Study Guide	These tell you what you are expected to know and are supplemented by **Exam focus points** in the text.
Study the Exam paper section	Past papers are likely to be good guides to what you should expect in the exam.

3 **The right method**

See the whole picture	Keeping in mind how all the detail you need to know fits into the whole picture will help you understand it better. • The **Introduction** of each chapter puts the material in context. • The **Syllabus content, Study guide** and **Exam focus points** show you what you need to **grasp**.
Use your own words	To absorb the information (and to practise your written communication skills), you need to **put it into your own words**. • **Take notes.** • Answer the **questions** in each chapter. • Draw **mindmaps**. We have an example for the whole syllabus. • Try **'teaching' a subject** to a colleague or friend.
Give yourself cues to jog your memory	The BPP Study Text uses **bold** to **highlight key points**. • Try **colour coding** with a highlighter pen. • Write **key points** on cards.

4 **The right recap**

Review, review, review	Regularly reviewing a topic in summary form can **fix it in your memory**. The BPP Study Text helps you review in many ways. • **Chapter roundups** summarise the 'Fast forward' key points in each chapter. Use them to recap each study session. • The **Quick quiz** actively tests your grasp of the essentials. • Go through the **Examples** in each chapter a second or third time.

Developing your personal Study Plan

BPP's **Learning to Learn Accountancy** book emphasises the need to use a study plan. Planning and sticking to the plan are key elements of learning successfully.

There are five steps you should work through.

Step 1 How do you learn?

First you need to be aware of your style of learning. BPP's **Learning to Learn Accountancy** book commits a chapter to this **self-discovery**. What types of intelligence do you display when learning? You might be advised to brush up on certain study skills before launching into this Study Text.

BPP's **Learning to Learn Accountancy** book helps you to identify what intelligences you show more strongly and then details how you can tailor your study process to your preferences. It also includes handy hints on how to develop intelligences you exhibit less strongly, but which might be needed as you study accountancy.

Step 2 What do you prefer to do first?

If you prefer to get to grips with a theory before seeing how it is applied, we suggest you concentrate first on the explanations we give in each chapter before looking at the examples and case studies. If you prefer to see first how things work in practice, skim through the detail in each chapter, and concentrate on the examples and case studies, before supplementing your understanding by reading the detail.

Step 3 How much time do you have?

Work out the time you have available per week, given the following.

- The standard you have set yourself
- The time you need to set aside later for work on the Practice & Revision Kit and Passcards
- The other exam(s) you are sitting
- Practical matters such as work, travel, exercise, sleep and social life

		Hours
Note your time available in box A.	A	

Step 4 Allocate your time

- Take the time you have available per week for this Study Text shown in box A, multiply it by the number of weeks available and insert the result in box B.   B
- Divide the figure in box B by the number of chapters in this text and insert the result in box C.   C

Remember that this is only a rough guide. Some of the chapters in this book are longer and more complicated than others, and you will find some subjects easier to understand than others.

Step 5 Implement

Set about studying each chapter in the time shown in box C, following the key study steps in the order suggested by your particular learning style.

This is your personal **Study Plan**. You should try to combine it with the study sequence outlined below. You may want to modify the sequence to adapt it to your **personal style**.

> BPP's **Learning to Learn Accountancy** gives further guidance on developing a study plan, and deciding where and when to study.

Tackling your studies

The best way to approach this Study Text is to tackle the chapters in order. Taking into account your individual learning style, you could follow this sequence for each chapter.

Key study steps	Activity
Step 1 **Topic list**	This topic list helps you navigate each chapter; each numbered topic is a numbered section in the chapter.
Step 2 **Introduction**	This sets your objectives for study by giving you the big picture in terms of the context of the chapter. The content is referenced to the Study Guide, and Exam guidance shows how the topic is likely to be examined. The Introduction tells you **why** the topics covered in the chapter need to be studied.
Step 3 **Knowledge brought forward boxes**	These highlight information and techniques that it is assumed you have 'brought forward' with you from your earlier studies. Remember that you may be tested on these areas in the exam. If you are unsure of these areas, you should consider revising your more detailed study material from earlier papers.
Step 4 **Fast forward**	Fast forward boxes give you a quick summary of the content of each of the main chapter sections. They are listed together in the roundup at the end of each chapter to help you review each chapter quickly.
Step 5 **Explanations**	Proceed methodically through each chapter, particularly focussing on areas highlighted as significant in the chapter introduction, or areas that are frequently examined.
Step 6 **Key terms and Exam focus points**	• Key terms can often earn you **easy marks** if you state them clearly and correctly in an exam answer. They are highlighted in the index at the back of this text. • Exam focus points state how the topic has been or may be examined, difficulties that can occur in questions about the topic, and examiner feedback on common weaknesses in answers.
Step 7 **Note taking**	Take brief notes, if you wish. Don't copy out too much. Remember that being able to record something yourself is a sign of being able to understand it. Your notes can be in whatever format you find most helpful; lists, diagrams, mindmaps.
Step 8 **Examples**	Work through the examples very carefully as they illustrate key knowledge and techniques.
Step 9 **Case studies**	Study each one, and try to add flesh to them from your own experience. They are designed to show how the topics you are studying come alive in the real world.
Step 10 **Questions**	Attempt each one, as they will illustrate how well you've understood what you've read.

INTRODUCTION

Key study steps	Activity
Step 11 **Answers**	Check yours against ours, and make sure you understand any discrepancies.
Step 12 **Chapter roundup**	Review it carefully, to make sure you have grasped the significance of all the important points in the chapter.
Step 13 **Quick quiz**	Use the Quick quiz to check how much you have remembered of the topics covered and to practise questions in a variety of formats.
Step 14 **Question practice**	Attempt the Question(s) suggested at the very end of the chapter. You can find these in the Exam Question Bank at the end of the Study Text, along with the answers so you can see how you did. If you have bought i-Pass, use this too.

Short of time: Skim study technique?

You may find you simply do not have the time available to follow all the key study steps for each chapter, however you adapt them for your particular learning style. If this is the case, follow the **skim study** technique below.

Read the **topic list, chapter introduction** and **knowledge brought forward boxes**.

Skim through the **explanations**, focusing on the points highlighted as important in the **fast forward boxes**.

Read the **key terms** and **exam focus points** carefully.

Go through the **examples** and **case studies**.

Prepare outline **answers** to the **questions**.

Revisit the fast forwards in the **chapter roundups**.

Answer the **quick quiz** and look back at any areas where you got questions wrong.

Do a plan for the **question(s) in the exam question bank** and review our answers carefully.

Brief notes may help you skim study, although you may simply rely on the **passcards** for notes you can use for revision.

Moving on...

When you are ready to start revising, you should still refer back to this Study Text.

- As a source of **reference** (you should find the index particularly helpful for this)
- As a way to **review** (the Fast forwards, Exam focus points, Chapter roundups and Quick quizzes help you here)

Remember to keep careful hold of this Study Text – you will find it invaluable in your work.

> More advice on Study Skills can be found in BPP's **Learning to Learn Accountancy** book.

Paper 1.1

Preparing Financial Statements (INT)

AIM

To develop knowledge and understanding of the techniques used to prepare financial statements, including necessary underlying records, and the interpretation of financial statements for incorporated enterprises, partnerships and sole traders.

OBJECTIVES

On completion of this paper candidates should be able to:

- describe the role and function of external financial reports and identify their users
- explain the accounting concepts and conventions used in preparing financial statements
- record and summarise accounting data
- maintain records relating to non-current asset acquisition and disposal
- prepare basic financial statements for sole traders, partnerships, incorporated enterprises and simple groups
- appraise financial performance and the position of an organisation through the calculation and review of basic ratios
- demonstrate the skills expected in Part 1.

POSITION OF THE PAPER IN THE OVERALL SYLLABUS

No prior knowledge is required before commencing study for Paper 1.1.

The basic financial accounting in Paper 1.1 is developed in Paper 2.5 Financial Reporting and Paper 3.6 Advanced Corporate Reporting. Knowledge from

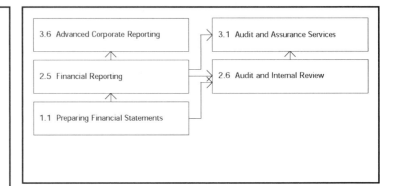

Paper 1.1 provides the background to Paper 2.6 Audit and Internal Review.

SYLLABUS CONTENT

Note: The extent to which accounting standards are examinable is indicated half-yearly in *student accountant* - in February for the June examination and in September for the December examination.

1 **General framework**
   (a) Types of business entity – incorporated entities, partnerships and sole traders.
   (b) Forms of capital and capital structures in incorporated entities.
   (c) The roles of the International Accounting Standards Board (IASB), the Standards Advisory Council (SAC) and the International Financial Reporting Interpretations Committee (IFRIC).
   (d) Application of International Accounting Standards (IASs) and International Financial Reporting Standards (IFRSs) to the preparation and presentation of financial statements.
   (e) The IASB's Framework for the Preparation and Presentation of Financial Statements (paragraphs 1 to 46 only).

2 **Accounting concepts and principles**
   (a) Basic accounting concepts and principles as stated in the IASB's Framework for the Preparation and Presentation of Financial Statements and relevant International Accounting Standards
   (b) Other accounting concepts
       (i) historical cost
       (ii) money measurement
       (iii) entity
       (iv) dual aspect

3 **Double-entry bookkeeping and accounting systems**
   (a) Double-entry bookkeeping and accounting systems

INTRODUCTION

Preparing Financial Statements (INT) – continued

(i) form and content of accounting records (manual and computerised)
(ii) books of original entry, including journals
(iii) accounts receivable and accounts payable ledgers
(iv) cash book
(v) general ledger
(vi) trial balance
(vii) accruals, prepayments and adjustments
(viii) asset registers
(ix) petty cash.

(b) Confirming and correcting mechanisms
(i) control accounts
(ii) bank reconciliations
(iii) suspense accounts and the correction of errors.

(c) General principles of the operation of a sales tax.

(d) Computerised accounting systems.

4 Accounting treatments

(a) Non-current assets, tangible and intangible
(i) distinction between capital and revenue expenditure
(ii) accounting for acquisitions and disposals
(iii) depreciation – definition, reasons for and methods, including straight line, reducing balance and sum of digits
(iv) research and development
(v) elementary treatment of goodwill.

(b) Current assets
(i) inventory

(ii) accounts receivable, including accounting for irrecoverable debts and allowances for receivables
(iii) cash.

(c) Current liabilities and accruals.
(d) Shareholders' equity.
(e) Events after the balance sheet date.
(f) Contingencies.

5 Financial statements

(a) Objectives of financial statements.
(b) Users and their information needs.
(c) Key features of financial statements
(i) balance sheet
(ii) income statement
(iii) cash flow statement
(iv) notes to the financial statements (examined to a limited extent – see d (iii) below).

(d) Preparation of financial statements for:
(i) sole traders, including incomplete records techniques
(ii) partnerships
(iii) limited liability companies, including income statements and balance sheets for internal purposes and for external purposes and preparation of basic cash flow statements for limited liability companies (excluding group cash flow statements), all in accordance with International Accounting Standards. The following notes to the financial statements will be examinable:
   – Statement of changes in equity

   – Non-current assets
   – Events after the balance sheet date
   – Contingent liabilities and contingent assets
   – Research and development expenditure

(iv) groups of companies – preparation of a basic consolidated balance sheet for a company with one subsidiary.

6 Interpretation

(a) Ratio analysis of accounting information and basic interpretation.

EXCLUDED TOPICS

The syllabus content outlines the areas for assessment. No questions will be asked on: clubs and societies, or goodwill arising on change of personnel in partnerships.

KEY AREAS OF THE SYLLABUS

The objective of Paper 1.1, Preparing Financial Statements, is to ensure that candidates have the necessary basic accounting knowledge and skill to progress to the more advanced work of Paper 2.5 Financial Reporting. The two main skills required are:

- The ability to prepare basic financial statements and the underlying accounting records on which they are based.
- An understanding of the principles on which accounting is based.

INTRODUCTION

Preparing Financial Statements (INT) – continued

The key topic areas are as follows:
- preparation of financial statements for limited liability companies for internal purposes or for publication
- preparation of financial statements for partnerships and sole traders (including incomplete records)
- basic group accounts – consolidated balance sheet for a company with one subsidiary
- basic bookkeeping and accounting procedures
- accounting conventions and concepts
- interpretation of financial statements
- cash flow statements
- accounting standards (as listed in the exam notes)

APPROACH TO EXAMINING THE SYLLABUS

The paper based examination is a three hour paper constructed in two sections. Both sections will draw from all parts of the syllabus and will contain both computational and non-computational elements.

	Number of Marks
Section A: 25 compulsory multiple choice questions (2 marks each)	50
Section B: 5 compulsory questions (8 – 12 marks each)	50
	100

Paper 1.1 can also be taken as a three hour computer based examination.

ADDITIONAL INFORMATION

Candidates need to be aware that questions involving knowledge of new examinable regulations will not be set until at least six months after the last day of the month in which the regulation was issued.

The Study Guide provides more detailed guidance on the syllabus. Examinable documents are listed in the 'Exam Notes' section of the *student accountant*, in February for the June examination and in September for the December examination.

Preparing Financial Statements (INT) – continued

STUDY SESSIONS

1 Introduction to Accounting
(a) Define accounting – recording, analysing and summarising transaction data.
(b) Explain types of business entity
   (i) sole trader
   (ii) partnership
   (iii) limited liability company.
(c) Explain users of financial statements and their information needs.
(d) Explain the main elements of financial statements:
   (i) balance sheet
   (ii) income statement.
(e) Explain the purpose of each of the main statements.
(f) Explain the nature, principles and scope of accounting.
(g) Explain the regulatory system: International Accounting Standards Board (IASB), the Standards Advisory Council (SAC) and the International Financial Reporting Interpretations Committee (IFRIC).
(h) Explain the difference between capital and revenue items.

2 Basic balance sheet and income statement
(a) Explain how the balance sheet equation and business entity convention underlie the balance sheet.
(b) Define assets and liabilities.
(c) Explain how and why assets and liabilities are disclosed in the balance sheet.
(d) Draft a simple balance sheet in vertical format.
(e) Explain the matching convention and how it applies to revenue and expenses.
(f) Explain how and why revenue and expenses are disclosed in the income statement.
(g) Illustrate how the balance sheet and income statement are interrelated.
(h) Draft a simple income statement in vertical format.
(i) Explain the significance of gross profit and gross profit as a percentage of sales.

3 & 4 Bookkeeping Principles
(a) Identify the main data sources and records in an accounting system.
(b) Explain the functions of each data source and record.
(c) Explain the concept of double entry and the duality concept.
(d) Outline the form of accounting records in a typical manual system.
(e) Outline the form of accounting records in a typical computerised system.
(f) Explain debit and credit.
(g) Distinguish between asset, liability, revenue and expense accounts.
(h) Explain the meaning of the balance on each type of account.
(i) Illustrate how to balance a ledger account.
(j) Record cash transactions in ledger accounts.
(k) Record credit sale and purchase transactions in ledger accounts.
(l) Explain the division of the ledger into sections.
(m) Record credit sale and purchase transactions using day books.
(n) Explain sales and purchases returns and demonstrate their recording.
(o) Explain the general principles of the operation of a sales tax and prepare the consequent accounting entries.
(p) Explain the need for a record of petty cash transactions.
(q) Illustrate the typical format of the petty cash book.
(r) Explain the importance of using the imprest system to control petty cash.
(s) Extract the ledger balances into a trial balance.
(t) Prepare a simple income statement and balance sheet from a trial balance.
(u) Explain and illustrate the process of closing the ledger accounts in the accounting records when the financial statements have been completed.

INTRODUCTION

Preparing Financial Statements (INT) – continued

5 **The journal; ledger control accounts; bank reconciliations**
   (a) Explain the uses of the journal.
   (b) Illustrate the use of the journal and the posting of journal entries into ledger accounts.
   (c) Explain the types of error which may occur in bookkeeping systems, identifying those which can and those which cannot be detected by preparing a trial balance.
   (d) Illustrate the use of the journal in correcting errors, including the use of a suspense account.
   (e) Prepare statements correcting profit for errors discovered.
   (f) Explain the nature and purpose of control accounts for the accounts receivable and accounts payable ledgers.
   (g) Explain how control accounts relate to the double entry system.
   (h) Construct and agree a ledger control account from given information.
   (i) Explain and prepare bank reconciliation statements including the need for entries in the cash book when reconciling.

6 **Computerised accounting systems**
   (a) Compare manual and computerised accounting systems.
   (b) Identify the advantages and disadvantages of computerised systems.
   (c) Describe the main elements of a computerised accounting system.
   (d) Describe typical data processing work.
   (e) Explain the use of integrated accounting packages.
   (f) Explain the nature and use of micro-computers.
   (g) Explain other business uses of computers.
   (h) Explain the nature and purpose of spreadsheets.
   (i) Explain the nature and purpose of database systems.

7 **The financial statements of a sole trader 1: inventory, accruals and prepayments**
   (a) Revise the format of the income statement and balance sheet from Sessions 1 and 2.
   (b) Explain the need for adjustments for inventory in preparing financial statements.
   (c) Illustrate income statements with opening and closing inventory.
   (d) Explain and demonstrate how opening and closing inventory are recorded in the inventory account.
   (e) Discuss alternative methods of valuing inventory.
   (f) Explain IASB requirements for inventories.
   (g) Explain the use of continuous and period end inventory records.
   (h) Explain the need for adjustments for accruals and prepayments in preparing financial statements.
   (i) Illustrate the process of adjusting for accruals and prepayments in preparing financial statements.
   (j) Prepare financial statements for a sole trader including adjustments for inventory, accruals and prepayments.
   (k) Explain and demonstrate how to calculate the value of closing inventory from given movements in inventory levels, using FIFO (first in first out) and AVCO (average cost).

8 **The financial statements of a sole trader 2: depreciation, irrecoverable debts and allowances for receivables**
   (a) Revise the difference between non-current assets and current assets.
   (b) Define and explain the purpose of depreciation.
   (c) Explain the advantages and disadvantages of the straight line, reducing balance and sum of the digits methods of depreciation and make necessary calculations.
   (d) Explain the relevance of consistency and subjectivity in accounting for depreciation.
   (e) Explain and illustrate how depreciation is presented in the income statement and balance sheet.
   (f) Explain and illustrate how depreciation expense and accumulated depreciation are recorded in ledger accounts.
   (g) Explain the inevitability of irrecoverable debts in most businesses.
   (h) Illustrate the bookkeeping entries to

Preparing Financial Statements (INT) – continued

write off an irrecoverable debt and the effect on the income statement and balance sheet.
(i) Illustrate the bookkeeping entries to record irrecoverable debts recovered.
(j) Explain the difference between writing off an irrecoverable debt and making an allowance for receivables.
(k) Explain and illustrate the bookkeeping entries to create and adjust an allowance for receivables.
(l) Illustrate how to include movements in the allowance for receivables in the income statement and how the closing balance of the allowance may appear in the balance sheet.
(m) Prepare a set of financial statements for a sole trader from a trial balance, after allowing for accruals and prepayments, depreciation, irrecoverable debts and allowances for receivables.

9 & 10 Incomplete records
(a) Explain techniques used in incomplete record situations:
 (i) Calculation of opening capital
 (ii) Use of ledger accounts to calculate missing figures
 (iii) Use of cash and/or bank summaries
 (iv) Use of given gross profit percentage to calculate missing figures.
(b) Explain and illustrate the calculation of profit or loss as the difference between opening and closing net assets.

11 Revise all work to date

12 & 13 Partnership Accounts
(a) Define the circumstances creating a partnership.
(b) Explain the advantages and disadvantages of operating as a partnership, compared with operating as a sole trader or limited liability company.
(c) Explain the typical contents of a partnership agreement, including profit-sharing terms.
(d) Explain the accounting differences between partnerships and sole traders:
 (i) Capital accounts
 (ii) Current accounts
 (iii) Division of profits.
(e) Explain and illustrate how to record partners' shares of profits / losses and their drawings in the accounting records and financial statements.
(f) Explain and illustrate how to account for guaranteed minimum profit share.
(g) Explain and illustrate how to account for interest on drawings.
(h) Draft the income statement, including division of profit, and balance sheet of a partnership from a given trial balance.

Note: Goodwill arising on the admission and retirement of partners, amalgamation and dissolution are not examinable. However, questions on partnership income statements may include the effect of the admission of new partners and the retirement of partners on the profit-sharing arrangements.

14 Accounting concepts and conventions; the IASB's 'Framework for the Preparation and Presentation of Financial Statements' (the Framework) and the IASB standard on the presentation of financial statements
(a) Explain the need for an agreed conceptual framework for financial accounting.
(b) Explain the importance of the following accounting conventions (not mentioned in the Framework):
 (i) Business entity
 (ii) Money measurement
 (iii) Duality
 (iv) Historical cost
 (v) Realisation
 (vi) Time interval.
(c) Revise the users of financial statements from Session 1.
(d) Explain the qualitative characteristics of financial statements as described in paras. 24 to 46 of the Framework (Revision from Session 1).
(e) Explain the IASB requirements relating to accounting policies.

Preparing Financial Statements (INT) – continued

(f) Explain the advantages and disadvantages of historical cost accounting (HCA) in times of changing prices.

(g) Explain in principle the main alternatives to HCA:
(i) Current purchasing power accounting (CPP)
(ii) Current cost accounting (CCA)
Note: computational questions on CPP and CCA will not be set.

(h) Explain the IASB requirements governing revenue recognition

15 Accounting for limited liability companies 1 – basics

Note: The inclusion of an introductory coverage of company accounts at this point is to enable students to practise the work so far on financial statements using questions on limited liability companies, and also to facilitate understanding of reserves referred to in the next Session.

(a) Explain the differences between a sole trader and a limited liability company.
(b) Explain the advantages and disadvantages of operating as a limited liability company rather than as a sole trader.
(c) Explain the capital structure of a limited liability company including:
(i) Authorised share capital
(ii) Issued share capital
(iii) Called up share capital
(iv) Paid up share capital
(v) Ordinary shares
(vi) Preference shares
(vii) Loan notes.
(d) Explain and illustrate the share premium account
(e) Explain and illustrate the other reserves which may appear in a company balance sheet.
(f) Explain why the heading retained earnings appears in a company balance sheet.
(g) Explain and illustrate the recording of dividends
(h) Explain the impact of income tax on company profits and illustrate the ledger account required to record it.
(i) Record income tax in the income statement and balance sheet of a company.
(j) Draft an income statement and balance sheet for a company for internal purposes.

16 Recording and presentation of transactions in non-current assets; liabilities and provisions

(a) Explain and illustrate the ledger entries to record the acquisition and disposal of non-current assets, using separate accounts for non-current asset cost and accumulated depreciation.
(b) Explain and illustrate the inclusion of profits or losses on disposal in the income statement.
(c) Explain and record the revaluation of a non-current asset in ledger accounts and in the balance sheet.
(d) Explain why, after an upward revaluation, depreciation must be based on the revised figure, and for revalued assets sold, the consequent transfer from revaluation reserve to retained earnings as revaluation surplus becomes realised.
(e) Make the adjustments necessary if changes are made in the estimated useful life and/or residual value of a non-current asset.
(f) Explain and illustrate how non-current asset balances and movements are disclosed in company financial statements.
(g) Explain the distinction between current and non-current liabilities.
(h) Explain the difference between liabilities and provisions.
(i) Explain the requirements of International Accounting Standards as regards current assets and current liabilities.

17 Goodwill, Research and Development

(a) Define goodwill.
(b) Explain the factors leading to the creation of non-purchased goodwill.
(c) Explain the difference between purchased and non-purchased

Preparing Financial Statements (INT) – continued

goodwill.
(d) Explain why non-purchased goodwill is not normally recognised in financial statements.
(e) Explain how purchased goodwill arises and is reflected in financial statements.
(f) Adjust the value of purchased goodwill to reflect impairment.
(g) Define "research" and "development".
(h) Classify expenditure as research or development.
(i) Calculate amounts to be capitalised as development expenditure from given information.
(j) Disclose research and development expenditure in the financial statements.

18 Events after the Balance Sheet Date and Contingencies
(a) Define an event after the balance sheet date.
(b) Distinguish between adjusting and non-adjusting events and explain the methods of including them in financial statements.
(c) Classify events as adjusting or non-adjusting.
(d) Draft notes to company financial statements including requisite details of events after the balance sheet date.
(e) Define 'contingent liability' and 'contingent asset'.
(f) Explain the different ways of accounting for contingent liabilities and contingent assets according to their degree of probability.
(g) Draft notes to company financial statements including requisite details of contingent liabilities and contingent assets.

19, 20 & 21 Accounting for Limited Liability Companies 2 – Advanced
(a) Revise the work of Session 15 and the preparation of financial statements for limited liability companies for internal purposes including the treatment of income tax and dividends.
(b) Revise the work of Session 15 on company capital structure, including equity shares, preference shares and loan notes.
(c) Outline the advantages and disadvantages of raising finance by borrowing rather than by the issue of ordinary or preference shares.
(d) Define and illustrate gearing (leverage).
(e) Define a bonus (capitalisation) issue and its advantages and disadvantages.
(f) Record a bonus (capitalisation) issue in ledger accounts and show the effect in the balance sheet.
(g) Define a rights issue and its advantages and disadvantages.
(h) Record a rights issue in ledger accounts and show the effect in the balance sheet.
(i) Revise the definition of reserves and the different types of reserves.
(j) Explain the need for regulation of companies in accounting standards.
(k) Explain the requirements of International Accounting Standards governing financial statements (excluding group aspects):
  (i) Presentation of Financial Statements
  (ii) Accounting policies, changes in accounting estimates and errors
  (iii) Non-current assets held for sale and discontinued operations (basic definitions and disclosure requirements only)
(l) Explain and prepare the notes to financial statements required for the syllabus:
  (i) Statement of changes in equity
  (ii) Details of non-current assets
  (iii) Details of events after the balance sheet date
  (iv) Details of contingent liabilities and contingent assets
  (v) Details of research and development expenditure.
(m) Prepare financial statements for publication complying with relevant accounting standards as detailed above.

22 Revise all work to date

23 Cash flow statements
(a) Explain the differences between profit and cash flow.
(b) Explain the need for management to control cash flow.
(c) Explain the value to users of financial statements of a cash flow statement.
(d) Explain the IASB requirements for cash flow statements (excluding

Preparing Financial Statements (INT) – continued

group aspects).
(e) Explain the inward and outward flows of cash in a typical company.
(f) Calculate the figures needed for the cash flow statement including among others:
   (i) Cash flows from operating activities (indirect method)
   (ii) Cash flows from investing activities.
(g) Calculate cash flow from operating activities using the direct method.
(h) Review of information to be derived by users from the cash flow statement (see also Sessions 26 – 27).
(i) Prepare cash flow statements from given balance sheets with or without an income statement.

24 & 25 Basic consolidated accounts
(a) Define a parent company, subsidiary company and group.
(b) Explain the IASB requirements defining which companies must be consolidated.
(c) Prepare a consolidated balance sheet for a parent with one wholly-owned subsidiary (no goodwill arising).
(d) Explain how to calculate the retained earnings balance for the consolidated balance sheet.
(e) Explain how other reserves (share premium account and revaluation reserve) are dealt with on consolidation.
(f) Introduce the concept of goodwill on acquisition and illustrate the effect on the consolidated balance sheet.
(g) Adjust the value of goodwill on aquisition to reflect impairment.
(h) Explain and illustrate a methodical approach to calculating the necessary figures for the consolidated balance sheet.
(i) Introduce the concept of minority interests in subsidiaries and illustrate the effect on the consolidated balance sheet.
(j) Explain and illustrate how the calculation of the minority interest is made.

26 & 27 Interpretation of Financial Statements
(a) Revise users of financial statements and their information needs.
(b) Explain the advantages and disadvantages of interpretation based on financial statements.
(c) Explain the factors forming the environment in which the business operates.
(d) Explain the uses of ratio analysis.
(e) Explain and calculate the main ratios to be used in interpreting financial statements to appraise:
   (i) Profitability
   (ii) Liquidity
   (iii) Working capital efficiency
   (iv) Financial risk
   (v) Performance from an investor's point of view.
(f) Explain the working capital cycle (or cash operating cycle)
(g) Explain normal levels of certain ratios.
(h) Formulate comments on movements in ratios between one period and another or on differences between ratios for different businesses.
(i) Explain the factors which may distort ratios, leading to unreliable conclusions.
(j) Prepare and comment on a comprehensive range of ratios for a business.

28 Revision

The exam paper

The examination is a **three hour paper** constructed in **two sections**. Both sections will draw from all parts of the syllabus and will contain both computational and discursive elements.

		Number of Marks
Section A:	25 compulsory multiple choice questions of 2 marks each	50
Section B:	5 compulsory questions of 10 marks each	50
		100

Paper 1.1 can also be taken as a three hour computer based examination.

Additional information

Candidates need to be aware that questions involving knowledge of new examinable regulations will not be set until at least six months after the last day of the month in which the regulation was issued.

The Study Guide provides more detailed guidance on the syllabus. Examinable documents are listed in the 'Exam Notes' section of the *Students' Newsletter*.

The examiner continues to be Neil Stein, the current paper 1 examiner.

Analysis of past papers

The analysis below shows the topics which were examined in all sittings of the current syllabus so far and in the Pilot Paper.

Marks

December 2005

Section A

25 MCQs

Section B

		Marks
1	Income statement prepared from incomplete records	50
2	Ledger accounts to show non-current asset transactions	11
3	Consolidated balance sheet	8
4	Four scenarios requiring correct treatment - events after the balance sheet date, provisions, contingencies and non-current asset revaluation	10
5	State and explain four accounting concepts	10
		100

INTRODUCTION

June 2005

Section A

25 MCQs

Section B

1. Limited liability company balance sheet in accordance with IAS 1
2. Journal entries to correct errors and show adjustments to profit
3. Cash flow statement using indirect method
4. Explain risks associated with high gearing and comment on factors which can cause accounting ratios to be misleading
5. Short scenarios involving accounting standards – IAS 37, IAS 10, IAS 2

December 2004

Section A

25 MCQs

Section B

1. Prepare income statement and calculate goods taken from inventory for trader with incomplete records
2. Prepare statement of changes in equity for limited liability company
3. Consolidated balance sheet
4. Accounting entries for R&D expenditure and IAS 38 disclosure note
5. Shortcomings of historical cost accounting in period of rising prices

June 2004

Section A

25 MCQs

Section B

1. Limited liability company income statement, including treatment of proposed dividend
2. Journal entries to clear suspense account balance and deal with vehicle disposal
3. Cash flow statement
4. Interpretation of accounts – working capital ratios and ROCE
5. Explain 'comparability' by reference to the *Framework* and accounting standards

December 2003

Section A

25 MCQs

Section B

1. Limited liability company balance sheet to comply with IAS 1 and disclosure note regarding deferred development costs
2. Ledger account to reflect movement during the year on property, plant and equipment
3. Consolidated balance sheet
4. Inventory valuation, contingent liability, events after the balance sheet date
5. Advantages and disadvantages of historical cost accounting

June 2003

Section A

25 MCQs

Section B

1 Partnership income statement and statement showing division of income. Write up partners' current accounts

2 Cash flow statement with net cash flow from operating activities already given

3 Incomplete records: total profit, purchases figure, sales figure

4 Calculate 5 ratios for each of two years and comment on the movements

5 Explain reserves with examples. Define 'bonus issue' and 'rights issue'

December 2002

Section A

25 MCQs

Section B

1 Income statement for a limited company to comply with IAS 1

2 Prepare journal entries to correct errors. Write up suspense account

3 Consolidated balance sheet

4 Explain depreciation treatment of revalued land and buildings, capitalised development expenditure and quoted equity shares

5 Events after the balance sheet date. Four material items. Advise correct treatment for each and determine financial effect

June 2002

Section A

25 MCQs

Section B

1 Limited liability company's cash flow, using the direct and indirect methods

2 Purchase and sale of non-current assets: accounting and cashflow

3 Limited liability company's balance sheet in accordance with IAS 1

4 Accounting concepts: definition and explanation of going concern, accruals, substance over form and historical cost

5 Ratio analysis: calculation of ratios and commentary on the results

INTRODUCTION

December 2001

Section A

25 MCQs

Section B

1. Limited liability company's income statement to comply with IAS 1
2. Incomplete records: sales revenue figure, purchases figure, closing inventory figure
3. Consolidated balance sheet
4. Explanation and example of materiality and prudence; comparability
5. Overtrading: indication by use of ratios and actions to rectify the position

Pilot paper

Section A

25 MCQs

Section B

1. Explanation of materiality; substance over form; and money measurement concepts
2. Calculation of 6 ratios for each of two years and comment on the movements
3. Cash flow statement using the indirect method
4. Contingent liability; allowance for bad debts; valuation of closing inventory
5. Preparation of a limited liability company's balance sheet

Oxford Brookes BSc (Hons) in Applied Accounting

The standard required of candidates completing Part 2 is that required in the final year of a UK degree. Students completing Parts 1 and 2 will have satisfied the examination requirement for an honours degree in Applied Accounting, awarded by Oxford Brookes University.

To achieve the degree, you must also submit two pieces of work based on a **Research and Analysis Project.**

- A 5,000 word **Report** on your chosen topic, which demonstrates that you have acquired the necessary research, analytical and IT skills.

- A 1,500 word **Key Skills Statement**, indicating how you have developed your interpersonal and communication skills.

BPP was selected by the ACCA and Oxford Brookes University to produce the official text *Success in your Research and Analysis Project* to support students in this task. The book pays particular attention to key skills not covered in the professional examinations.

BPP also offers courses and mentoring services.

For further information, please see BPP's website: www.bpp.com/bsc

ACCA professional development requirements

Soon, you will possess a professional qualification. You know its value by the effort you have put in. To uphold the prestige of the qualification, ACCA, with the other professional bodies that form the International Federation of Accountants (IFAC), requires its members to undertake continuous professional development (CPD). This requirement applies to all members, not just those with a practising certificate. Happily, BPP Professional Education is here to support you in your professional development with materials, courses and qualifications.

> For further information, please see ACCA's website: www.accaglobal.com

Professional development with BPP

You do not have to do exams for professional development (PD) – but you need relevant technical updating and you may also benefit from other work-related training. BPP can provide you with both. Visit our professional development website, www.bpp.com/pd for details of our PD courses in accounting, law, general business skills and other important areas. Offering defined hours of structured CPD, and delivered by top professionals throughout the year and in many locations, our courses are designed to fit around your busy work schedule. Our unique PD passport will give you access to these PD services at an attractive discount.

> For further information, please see BPP's website: www.bpp.com/pd

Oxford Institute of International Finance, (OXIIF) MBA

OXFII is a joint venture between ACCA and Oxford Brookes University, a leading UK university. The MBA, accredited by AMBA (the Association of MBAs), lasts 21 months for ACCA members, and is taught by distance learning with online seminars delivered to a global student base over the Internet. BPP provides the user-friendly materials. As an ACCA member, you will receive credits towards this MBA and you can begin your studies when you have completed your ACCA professional exams. Flexibility, global reach and value for money underpin a high quality learning experience.

The qualification features an introductory module (*Foundations of Management*). Other modules include *Global Business Strategy, Managing Self Development,* and *Organisational Change and Transformation.*

Research Methods are also taught, as they underpin the **research dissertation**.

> For further information, please see the Oxford Institutes's website: www.oxfordinstitute.org
> and BPP's website: www.bpp.com/mba

Diploma in International Financial Reporting

The ACCA's Diploma in International Financial Reporting is designed for those whose country-specific accounting knowledge needs to be supplemented by knowledge of international accounting standards. BPP offers books and courses in this useful qualification – it also earns you valuable CPD points.

> For further information, please see ACCA's website: www.accaglobal.com and BPP's website: www.bpp.com/dipifr

Tax and financial services

If you are interested in tax, BPP offers courses for the ATT (tax technician) and CTA (Chartered Tax Adviser, formerly ATII) qualifications. You can also buy our user-friendly CTA texts to keep up-to-date with tax practice.

> For further information, please see BPP's website: www.bpp.com/att and www.bpp.com/cta

If your role involves selling financial services products, such as pensions, or offering investment advice, BPP provides learning materials and training for relevant qualifications. BPP also offers training for specialist financial markets qualifications (eg CFA®) and insolvency.

> For further information, please see BPP's website: www.bpp.com/financialadvisers

Other business qualifications

BPP supports many business disciplines, such as market research, marketing, human resources management and law. We are the official provider of distance learning programmes for the Market Research Society. We train for the Chartered Institute of Personnel and Development qualification, with a number of other supporting qualifications in training and personnel management. BPP's law school is an industry leader.

> Visit www.bpp.com for further details of all that we can offer you. BPP's personalised online information service, My BPP, will help you keep track of the details you submit to BPP.

Current issues

There are a number of recently issued International Financial Reporting Standards and revisions to existing International Accounting Standards. Those which cover areas with the 1.1 syllabus are examinable for this paper. They are covered at the appropriate points in this Study Text.

The major issue recently has been the requirement for all listed EU companies to report under International standards from 1 January 2005. The IASB's improvements to a number of International standards were intended to help the 'convergence' process by removing some of the differences between local (eg UK) accounting standards and International Accounting Standards.

The first new standard, IFRS1: *First time adoption of International Standards* is intended to help companies make the transition to IFRS. It is explained more fully in Chapter 24.

In past exam papers you will see reference to "allowance for doubtful receivables" or "doubtful debts". ACCA is no longer using this terminology. Your exam will refer to "receivables allowance" or "allowance for receivables" and that terminology has been used in this text.

Part A
General framework

Introduction to accounting

Topic list	Syllabus reference
1 The purpose of accounting information	1(a), 1(c), 5(a) – (b)
2 The main financial statements	1(a) – (e), 5(a)
3 Nature, principles and scope of accounting	1(a) – (e), 5(a) – (b)
4 The desirable qualities of accounting information	1(d), 5(a)
5 The regulatory system	1(c) – (e)
6 Capital and revenue expenditure	1(d)

Introduction

We will begin by looking at the aim of Paper 1.1, as laid out in ACCA's syllabus and Study Guide and discussed already in the introductory pages to this text (if you haven't read through the introductory roman numeral pages, do so now – the information in there is extremely important).

> 'Aim of Paper 1.1
>
> To develop knowledge and understanding of the techniques used to prepare year-end financial statements, including necessary underlying records, and the interpretation of financial statements for incorporated enterprises, partnerships and sole traders.'

Before you learn **how** to prepare accounts, it is important to understand **why** they are prepared. Sections 1 – 3 of this chapter introduce some basic ideas about accounts and give an indication of their purpose. You will also be introduced to the functions which accountants carry out: financial accounting, management accounting, financial management and auditing. All of these functions will be developed in detail in your later studies for the ACCA qualification.

Having identified the main users of financial information, we then go on to look at the characteristics which those users might find desirable in that information in Section 4.

We also consider the present state of international financial accounting, how it has developed and how it is likely develop in the future. In doing so, we touch on the international standard setting process. This is covered in more detail in Chapter 24.

An important distinction is also introduced in this chapter: the distinction between **capital** and **revenue** expenditure. It is very important that you understand this distinction before moving on to the bookkeeping topics in Part C of the Study Text.

PART A   GENERAL FRAMEWORK

Study guide

Section 1 – Introduction to accounting

- Define accounting – recording, analysing and summarising transaction data.
- Explain types of business entity.
    - Sole trader
    - Partnership
    - Limited liability company
- Explain users of financial statements and their information needs.
- Explain the main elements of financial statements.
    - Balance sheet
    - Income statement
- Explain the purpose of each of the main statements.
- Explain the nature, principles and scope of accounting.
- Explain the regulatory system.
    - International Accounting Standards Board (IASB), Standards Advisory Council (SAC) and the International Reporting Interpretations Committee (IFRIC)
- Explain the difference between capital and revenue items.

Exam guide

The ideas discussed in this chapter could be the subject of a MCQ in the exam. In addition, you could be asked to discuss these topics (eg the needs of users of financial statements) in one of the 10 mark questions in section B.

1 The purpose of accounting information

1.1 What is accounting?

> **FAST FORWARD** **Accounting** is a way of recording, analysing and summarising transactions of a business.

The transactions are **recorded** in 'books of original entry' (see Chapter 4).
The transactions are then **analysed** and posted to the ledgers (see Chapter 5).
Finally the transactions are **summarised** in the financial statements (see Chapter 6).

1.2 What is a business?

> **FAST FORWARD** Businesses of whatever size or nature exist to make a **profit**.

There are a number of different ways of looking at a business. Some ideas are listed below.

- A business is a **commercial or industrial concern** which exists to deal in the manufacture, re-sale or supply of goods and services.
- A business is an **organisation which uses economic resources** to create goods or services which customers will buy.

- A business is an **organisation providing jobs** for people.
- A business invests **money in resources** (for example it buys buildings, machinery and so on, it pays employees) in order to make even more money for its owners.

This last definition introduces the important idea of profit. Businesses vary in character, size and complexity. They range from very small businesses (the local shopkeeper or plumber) to very large ones (ICI, Hanson, Shell). However all of them want to earn profits.

Key term

> **Profit** is the excess of revenue over expenditure. When expenditure exceeds revenue, the business is running at a loss.

One of the jobs of an accountant is to measure revenue, expenditure and profit. It is not such a straightforward problem as it may seem and in later chapters we will look at some of the theoretical and practical difficulties involved.

1.3 Types of business entity

There are three main types of business entity.

- Sole traders
- Partnerships
- Limited liability companies

Sole traders are people who work for themselves. Examples include the local shopkeeper, a plumber and a hairdresser. The term sole trader refers to the **ownership** of the business, sole traders can have employees.

Partnerships occur when two or more sole traders decide to share the risks and rewards of a business together. Examples include an accountancy practice, a medical practice and a legal practice.

Limited liability companies are incorporated to take advantage of 'limited liability' for their owners (shareholders). This means that, while sole traders and partners are **personally responsible** for the amounts owed by their businesses, the shareholders of a limited liability company are only responsible for the **amount to be paid for their shares**.

Limited liability companies are dealt with in more detail in Chapter 19.

1.4 The need for accounts

FAST FORWARD

> There are various groups of people who need information about the activities of a business.

Why do businesses need to produce accounts? If a business is being run efficiently, why should it have to go through all the bother of accounting procedures in order to produce financial information?

The International Accounting Standards Board states in its document *Framework for the preparation and presentation of financial statements* (which we will examine in detail later in this Study Text):

> 'The objective of financial statements is to provide information about the **financial position, performance and changes in financial position** of an entity that is useful to a wide range of users in making economic decisions.'

In other words, a business should produce information about its activities because there are various groups of people who want or need to know that information. This sounds rather vague: to make it clearer, we will study the classes of people who need information about a business. We need also to think about what information in particular is of interest to the members of each class.

Large businesses are of interest to a greater variety of people and so we will consider the case of a large public company, whose shares can be purchased and sold on a stock exchange.

1.5 Users of financial statements and accounting information

The following people are likely to be interested in financial information about a large company with listed shares.

(a) **Managers of the company** appointed by the company's owners to supervise the day-to-day activities of the company. They need information about the company's financial situation as it is currently and as it is expected to be in the future. This is to enable them to manage the business efficiently and to make effective decisions.

(b) **Shareholders of the company**, ie the company's owners, want to assess how well the management is performing. They want to know how profitable are the company's operations and how much profit they can afford to withdraw from the business for their own use.

(c) **Trade contacts** include suppliers who provide goods to the company on credit and customers who purchase the goods or services provided by the company. **Suppliers** want to know about the company's ability to pay its debts; **customers** need to know that the company is a secure source of supply and is in no danger of having to close down.

(d) **Providers of finance to the company** might include a bank which allows the company to operate an overdraft, or provides longer-term finance by granting a loan. The bank wants to ensure that the company is able to keep up interest payments, and eventually to repay the amounts advanced.

(e) **The taxation authorities** want to know about business profits in order to assess the tax payable by the company, including sales taxes.

(f) **Employees of the company** should have a right to information about the company's financial situation, because their future careers and the size of their wages and salaries depend on it.

(g) **Financial analysts and advisers** need information for their clients or audience. For example, stockbrokers need information to advise investors; credit agencies want information to advise potential suppliers of goods to the company; and journalists need information for their reading public.

(h) **Government and their agencies** are interested in the allocation of resources and therefore in the activities of enterprises. They also require information in order to provide a basis for national statistics.

(i) **The public**. Enterprises affect members of the public in a variety of ways. For example, enterprises may make a substantial contribution to a local economy by providing employment and using local suppliers. Another important factor is the effect of an enterprise on the environment, for example as regards pollution.

Accounting information is summarised in financial statements to satisfy the **information needs** of these different groups. Not all will be equally satisfied.

Managers of a business need the most information, to help them make their planning and control decisions. They obviously have 'special' access to information about the business, because they are able to demand whatever internally produced statements they require. When managers want a large amount of information about the costs and profitability of individual products, or different parts of their business, they can obtain it through a system of cost and management accounting.

Question | Accounting information (1)

It is easy to see how 'internal' people get hold of accounting information. A manager, for example, can just go along to the accounts department and ask the staff there to prepare whatever accounting statements he needs. But external users of accounts cannot do this. How, in practice, can a business contact or a financial analyst access accounting information about a company?

Answer

The answer is that limited liability companies (though not other forms of business such as partnerships) are usually required to make certain accounting information public. This may be done by filing information centrally, as a government requirement. Alternatively, the public may have the right to apply for such information.

In addition to management information, financial statements are prepared and perhaps published for the benefit of other user groups, which may demand certain information.

(a) The **national laws** of a country may provide for the provision of some accounting information for shareholders and the public.

(b) **National taxation** authorities will receive the information they need to make tax assessments.

(c) A **bank** might demand a forecast of a company's expected future cash flows as a pre-condition of granting an overdraft.

(d) The **International Accounting Standards Board (IASB)** has been responsible for issuing **International Accounting Standards (IASs and IFRSs)** and these require companies to publish certain additional information. Accountants, as members of professional bodies, are placed under a strong obligation to ensure that company accounts conform to the requirements of IAS/IFRS.

(e) Some companies provide, voluntarily, specially prepared financial information for issue to their employees. These statements are known as '**employee reports**'.

1.5.1 Non-commercial undertakings

It is not only businesses that need to prepare accounts. Charities and clubs, for example, prepare financial statements every year. Accounts also need to be prepared for government (public sector) organisations.

2 The main financial statements

 The principle financial statements of a business are the **balance sheet** and the **income statement**.

2.1 Balance sheet

Key term

The **balance sheet** is simply a *list* of all the *assets owned* and all the *liabilities owed* by a business as at a particular date. It is a snapshot of the financial position of the business at a particular moment. Monetary amounts are attributed to each of the assets and liabilities.

Assets and liabilities are explained in more detail in Chapter 2. However, the sum of the assets will always be equal to the sum of the liabilities plus capital.

The amounts invested in a business by the owner are amounts that the business owes to the owner We refer to this as **capital**.

2.2 Income statement

Key term

> An **income statement** is a *record* of *revenue generated* and *expenditure incurred* over a given period. The statement shows whether the business has had more revenue than expenditure (a profit) or vice versa (loss).

The period chosen will depend on the purpose for which the statement is produced. The income statement which forms part of the published annual accounts of a **limited liability company** will usually be for the period of a **year**, commencing from the date of the previous year's accounts. On the other hand, **management** might want to keep a closer eye on a company's profitability by making up **quarterly or monthly** statements.

2.3 Purpose of financial statements

Both the balance sheet and the income statement are **summaries of accumulated data**. For example, the income statement shows a figure for revenue earned from selling goods to customers. This is the total amount of revenue earned from all the individual sales made during the period. One of the jobs of an accountant is to devise methods of recording such individual transactions, so as to produce summarised financial statements from them.

The balance sheet and the income statement form the basis of the accounts of most businesses. For limited liability companies, other information by way of statements and notes may be required by national legislation and/or accounting standards, for example a **cash flow statement**. These are considered in detail later in this Study Text.

2.4 Non-financial statements

FAST FORWARD

> Limited liability companies may produce certain **non-financial statements**, particularly commentaries on the content of financial statements.

Limited liability companies may also be required by local legislation to produce certain **non-financial statements**.

The most important is likely to be some kind of commentary on the contents of the financial sections of the company's report. There may be other information, for example on environmental matters, employees, etc.

In some countries such a commentary is required by law (eg the directors' report in the UK), or by local accounting standards. There is, however, no International Accounting Standard which requires such a commentary, as we will see later.

Many large companies also include a **glossy review** of the business which may include photographs, interviews, bar charts and other diagrams. This is a public relations exercise.

Question   Accounting information (2)

If you work for any kind of organisation it will produce accounting information of some sort. Try to get an example of all the different information it produces, particularly the annual accounts. Look through what you have got carefully. As you work through this Study Text, more and more of it will become understandable.

3 Nature, principles and scope of accounting

FAST FORWARD

You should be able to distinguish the following:

- Financial accounting
- Management accounting
- Financial management
- Auditing

You may have a wide understanding of what accounting is about. Your job may be in one area or type of accounting, but you must understand the breadth of work which an accountant undertakes.

3.1 Management accounting

So far in this chapter we have dealt with **financial** accounts. Financial accounting is mainly a method of reporting the results and financial position of a business. It is not primarily concerned with providing information towards the more efficient running of the business. Although financial accounts are of interest to management, their principal function is to satisfy the information needs of persons not involved in running the business.

This is particularly clear in the context of the published accounts of limited liability companies. **International Accounting Standards** (and national legislation) prescribe that a company should **produce accounts to be presented to the shareholders**. There are usually detailed regulations on what the accounts must contain and this enables shareholders to assess how well management have run the company. Also there are certain outsiders who need information about a company: suppliers, customers, employees, tax authorities, the general public. Their information needs are satisfied, wholly or in part, by the company's published financial statements.

The information needs of management go far beyond those of other account users. Managers have the responsibility of planning and controlling the resources of the business. Therefore they need much more detailed information.

Key term

> **Management (or cost) accounting** is a management information system which analyses data to provide information as a basis for managerial action. The concern of a management accountant is to present accounting information in the form most helpful to management.

You must understand this distinction between management accounting and financial accounting. The accounting statements drawn up by a management accountant are often prepared and presented very differently from those of the financial accountant; for example, they do not need to comply with local law or IASs. You should remember the different reasons for preparing management and financial accounts, and the different users of each.

3.2 Auditing

The annual accounts of a limited liability company must generally be **audited** by a person independent of the company. In practice, this often means that the members of the company appoint a firm of registered auditors to investigate the financial statements and report as to whether or not they show a true and fair view of (or present fairly) the company's results for the year and its financial position at the end of the year.

When the auditors have completed their work they must prepare a **report** explaining the work that they have done and the **opinion** they have formed.

The auditors' report is included as a part of the company's published accounts. It is addressed to the **members** of the company (not to the management).

PART A GENERAL FRAMEWORK

Question
Accountants

They say that America is run by lawyers and Britain is run by accountants, but what do accountants do in your organisation or country? Before moving on to the next section, think of any accountants you know and the kind of jobs they do.

4 The desirable qualities of accounting information

FAST FORWARD You should be able to identify the **desirable qualities** of accounting information.

What type of information should accountants produce? What should its main qualities be from the user's point of view? The following are the characteristics of useful information.

(a) **Relevance**. The information provided satisfies the needs of information users. In the case of company accounts, clearly a wide range of information is needed to satisfy the interested parties already identified.

(b) **Comprehensibility**. Information may be difficult to understand because it is skimpy or incomplete; but too much detail can also cause difficulties of understanding.

(c) **Reliability**. This is enhanced if information is independently verified. Local law usually requires that the accounts published by limited liability companies are verified by an auditor, who must be a person independent of the company and the holder of an approved qualification.

(d) **Completeness**. A company's accounts must present a rounded picture of its economic activities.

(e) **Objectivity**. The usefulness of information is enhanced if it contains a minimum of subjective judgement. This is particularly the case where conflicting interests operate and an unbiased presentation of information is needed. In the context of preparing accounts, where many decisions must be based on judgement rather than objective facts, this problem often arises. Management may paint a rosy picture of a company's profitability to make their own performance look impressive; while the auditor is inclined to take a more prudent view, so that he cannot be held liable by, say, a supplier misled into granting credit to a shaky company.

(f) **Timeliness**. The usefulness of information is reduced if it does not appear until long after the period to which it relates, or at unreasonably long intervals. What constitutes a long interval depends on the circumstances: management of a company may need very frequent (perhaps daily) information to run the business efficiently; but shareholders are normally content to see accounts produced annually.

(g) **Comparability**. Information should be produced on a consistent basis, so that valid comparisons can be made with information from previous periods and with information produced by other sources (for example the accounts of similar companies operating in the same line of business).

Question
Qualities

We will look at the desirable qualities of accounting information again much later, when you have mastered the basics of accounting. In the meantime, can you see any possible conflict arising between some of the above qualities?

10

5 The regulatory system

FAST FORWARD

A number of factors have shaped the **development** of financial accounting.

5.1 Introduction

Although new to the subject, you will be aware from your reading of the press that there have been some considerable upheavals in financial reporting, mainly in response to criticism. The **details** of the regulatory framework of accounting, and the technical aspects of the changes made, will be covered later in this text and in your more advanced studies. The purpose of this section is to give a **general picture** of some of the factors which have shaped financial accounting. We will concentrate on the accounts of limited liability companies, as these are the accounts most closely regulated by statute or otherwise.

The following factors can be identified.

- National/local legislation
- Accounting concepts and individual judgement
- Accounting standards
- Other international influences
- Generally accepted accounting principles (GAAP)
- True and fair view

5.2 National/local legislation

Limited liability companies may be required by law to prepare and publish accounts annually. The form and content of the accounts may be regulated primarily by national legislation, but must also comply with International Accounting Standards (IASs) and International Financial Reporting Standards (IFRSs).

5.3 Accounting concepts and individual judgement

FAST FORWARD

Many figures in financial statements are derived from the **application of judgement** in applying fundamental accounting assumptions and conventions. This can lead to subjectivity.

Financial statements are prepared on the basis of a number of **fundamental accounting assumptions and conventions**. Many figures in financial statements are derived from the application of judgement in putting these assumptions into practice.

It is clear that different people exercising their judgement on the same facts can arrive at very different conclusions.

Case Study

An accountancy training firm has an excellent **reputation** amongst students and employers. How would you value this? The firm may have relatively little in the form of assets that you can touch, perhaps a building, desks and chairs. If you simply drew up a balance sheet showing the cost of the assets owned, then the business would not seem to be worth much, yet its income earning potential might be high. This is true of many service organisations where the people are among the most valuable assets.

Other examples of areas where the judgement of different people may vary are as follows.

(a) Valuation of buildings in times of rising property prices.

(b) Research and development: is it right to treat this only as an expense? In a sense it is an investment to generate future revenue.

(c) Accounting for inflation.

(d) Brands such as 'Snickers' or 'Walkman'. Are they assets in the same way that a fork lift truck is an asset?

Working from the same data, different groups of people produce very different financial statements. If the exercise of judgement is completely unfettered, there will be no comparability between the accounts of different organisations. This will be all the more significant in cases where deliberate manipulation occurs, in order to present accounts in the most favourable light.

5.4 Accounting standards

In an attempt to deal with some of the subjectivity, and to achieve comparability between different organisations, **accounting standards** were developed. These are developed at both a national level (in most countries) and an international level. In this text we are concerned with **International Accounting Standards** (IASs) and **International Financial Reporting** Standards (IFRSs) and a brief summary of the current regime for producing IFRSs is given here. We go into much more depth in Chapter 24.

5.4.1 International Financial Reporting Standards

International Financial Reporting Standards (IFRSs) are produced by the **International Accounting Standards Board (IASB).** The IASC was set up in 1973 to work for the improvement and harmonisation of financial reporting. It has now been replaced by the IASB. The IASB develops IFRSs through an international process that involves the world-wide accountancy profession, the preparers and users of financial statements, and national standard setting bodies. Prior to 2003 standards were issued as International Accounting Standards (IASs). In 2003 IFRS 1 was issued and all new standards are now designated as IFRSs.

The objectives of the IASB are:

(a) To **develop**, in the public interest, a single set of high quality, understandable and enforceable **global accounting standards** that require high quality, transparent and comparable information in financial statements and other financial reporting to help participants in the world's capital markets and other users make economic decisions.

(b) To promote the use and **rigorous application** of those standards.

(c) To bring about **convergence of national accounting standards** and International Financial Reporting Standards to high quality solutions. In the UK the consolidated accounts of listed companies have had to be produced in accordance with IFRS from January 2005.

5.4.2 Standards Advisory Council

The Standards Advisory Council assists the IASB in standard setting. It has about 50 members drawn from organisations all over the world, such as national standard–setting bodies, accountancy firms, the IMF and the World Bank.

The SAC meets the IASB at least three times a year and puts forward the views of its members on current standard–setting projects.

5.4.3 International Financial Reporting Interpretations Committee (IFRIC)

IFRIC was set up in December 2001 and issues guidance in cases where unsatisfactory or conflicting interpretations of accounting standards have developed. In these situations, IFRIC works closely with similar national committees with a view to reaching consensus on the appropriate accounting treatment.

1: INTRODUCTION TO ACCOUNTING

5.4.4 The use and application of IASs and IFRSs

IASs and IFRSs have helped to both improve and harmonise financial reporting around the world. The standards are used in the following ways.

(a) As **national requirements**, often after a national process
(b) As the **basis** for all or some **national requirements**
(c) As an **international benchmark** for those countries which develop their own requirements
(d) By **regulatory authorities** for domestic and foreign companies
(e) **By companies** themselves

As well as the *Framework* document already mentioned, the IASC and IASB have published **over 40 IASs** and **5 IFRSs**, as well as revised standards. There are also various exposure drafts of IFRSs in existence (not on your syllabus). We will deal with the individual IASs and IFRSs which are on your syllabus later in this text. We will also look further into the work of the IASB (in Chapter 24).

5.4.5 Benchmark and allowed alternatives

IASs often allowed more than one accounting treatment. Recent IFRSs and amendments to IASs have sought to disallow alternative treatments.

Ideally there should not be many allowed alternative treatments.

5.5 Generally Accepted Accounting Practice (GAAP)

We also need to consider some important terms which you will meet in your financial accounting studies. GAAP, as a term, has sprung up in recent years and signifies all the rules, from whatever source, which govern accounting.

Key term

> **GAAP** is a set of rules governing accounting. The rules may derive from:
>
> - Local (national) company legislation
> - National and international accounting standards
> - Statutory requirements in other countries (particularly the US)
> - Stock exchange requirements

GAAP will be considered in more detail in Chapter 24.

5.6 True and fair view (or presented fairly)

FAST FORWARD

> Financial statements are required to give a **true and fair view** or **present fairly in all material respects** the financial results of the entity. These terms are not defined and tend to be decided in courts of law on the facts.

It is a requirement of both national legislation (in some countries) and International Standards on Auditing that the financial statements should give a **true and fair view** of (or **'present fairly, in all material respects'**) the financial position of the entity as at the end of the financial year.

5.6.1 True and fair 'override'

The terms 'true and fair view' and 'present fairly, in all material aspects' are not defined in accounting or auditing standards. Despite this, a company's managers may depart from any of the provisions of accounting standards if these are inconsistent with the requirement to give a true and fair view. This is commonly referred to as the 'true and fair override'. It has been treated as an important loophole in the law in different countries and has been the cause of much argument and dissatisfaction within the accounting profession.

PART A   GENERAL FRAMEWORK

6 Capital and revenue expenditure

FAST FORWARD

> **Capital expenditure** is expenditure which results in the **acquisition of non-current assets**.
>
> **Revenue expenditure** is expenditure incurred for the **purpose of the trade** or to **maintain non current assets**.

In the next part of this Study Text you will study the mechanics of preparing financial statements. In order to tackle this subject you need to be familiar with an important distinction, the distinction between **capital and revenue expenditure**.

Key terms

> Capital **expenditure** is expenditure which results in the acquisition of non-current assets, or an improvement in their earning capacity.
>
> (a) Capital expenditure is not charged as an expense in the income statement, although a depreciation charge will usually be made to write off the capital expenditure gradually over time. Depreciation charges are expenses in the income statement.
>
> (b) Capital expenditure on non-current assets results in the appearance of a non-current asset in the balance sheet of the business.
>
> **Revenue expenditure** is expenditure which is incurred for either of the following reasons.
>
> (a) For the purpose of the trade of the business. This includes expenditure classified as selling and distribution expenses, administration expenses and finance charges.
>
> (b) To maintain the existing earning capacity of non-current assets.

Revenue expenditure is charged to the income statement of a period, provided that it relates to the trading activity and sales of that particular period. For example, if a business buys ten steel bars for $200 ($20 each) and sells eight of them during an accounting period, it will have two steel bars left in stock at the end of the period. The full $200 is revenue expenditure but only $160 is a cost of goods sold during the period. The remaining $40 (cost of two units) will be included in the balance sheet in inventory, ie as a current asset valued at $40.

A business purchases a building for $30,000. It then adds an extension to the building at a cost of $10,000. The building needs to have a few broken windows mended, its floors polished and some missing roof tiles replaced. These cleaning and maintenance jobs cost $900.

In this example, the original purchase ($30,000) and the cost of the extension ($10,000) are capital expenditures, because they are incurred to acquire and then improve a non-current asset. The other costs of $900 are revenue expenditure, because these merely maintain the building and thus the 'earning capacity' of the building.

6.1 Capital income and revenue income

Capital income is the proceeds from the sale of non-trading assets (ie proceeds from the sale of non-current assets, including long-term investments). The profits (or losses) from the sale of non-current assets are included in the income statement of a business, for the accounting period in which the sale takes place. For instance, the business may sell vehicles or machinery which it no longer needs – the proceeds will be capital income.

Revenue income is income derived from the following sources.

    (a) The sale of trading assets, such as goods held in stock
    (b) The provision of services
    (c) Interest and dividends received from investments held by the business

6.2 Capital transactions

The categorisation of capital and revenue items given above does not mention raising additional capital from the owner(s) of the business, or raising and repaying loans.

- (a) These transactions add to the cash assets of the business, thereby creating a corresponding liability (capital or loan).
- (b) When a loan is repaid, it reduces the liabilities (loan) and the assets (cash).

None of these transactions would be reported through the income statement.

6.3 Why is the distinction between capital and revenue items important?

Revenue expenditure results from the purchase of goods and services for one of the following reasons.

- (a) To be used fully in the accounting period in which they are purchased, and so be a cost or expense in the income statement.

    OR

- (b) To result in a current asset as at the end of the accounting period because the goods or services have not yet been consumed or made use of. The current asset would be shown in the balance sheet and is not yet a cost or expense in the income statement.

For instance, stock which is purchased for resale will either be sold during the period as per (a) or still be in stock as per (b).

Capital expenditure results in the **purchase or improvement of non-current assets**, which are assets that will provide benefits to the business in more than one accounting period, and which are not acquired with a view to being resold in the normal course of trade. The cost of purchased non-current assets is not charged in full to the income statement of the period in which the purchase occurs. Instead, the non-current asset is gradually depreciated over a number of accounting periods.

Examples of non-current assets are computers for the office, delivery vans, factory machines.

Since revenue items and capital items are accounted for in different ways, the correct and consistent calculation of profit for any accounting period depends on the correct and consistent classification of items as revenue or capital.

This may seem rather confusing at the moment, but things will become clearer in the next few chapters. You must get used to the terminology used as these words appear in the accounting standards themselves, as we will see.

Question — Capital or revenue

State whether each of the following items should be classified as 'capital' or 'revenue' expenditure or income for the purpose of preparing the income statement and the balance sheet of the business.

- (a) The purchase of a property (eg an office building)
- (b) The annual depreciation of such a property
- (c) Solicitors' fees in connection with the purchase of such a property
- (d) The costs of adding extra storage capacity to a mainframe computer used by the business
- (e) Computer repairs and maintenance costs
- (f) Profit on the sale of an office building
- (g) Revenue from sales by credit card

PART A GENERAL FRAMEWORK

(h) The cost of new plant

(i) Customs duty charged on the plant when imported into the country

(j) The 'carriage' costs of transporting the new plant from the supplier's factory to the premises of the business purchasing the plant

(k) The cost of installing the new plant in the premises of the business

(l) The wages of the machine operators

Answer

(a) Capital expenditure

(b) Depreciation of a non-current asset is a revenue expenditure.

(c) The legal fees associated with the purchase of a property may be added to the purchase price and classified as capital expenditure. The cost of the property in the balance sheet of the business will then include the legal fees.

(d) Capital expenditure (enhancing an existing non-current asset)

(e) Revenue expenditure

(f) Capital income (net of the costs of sale)

(g) Revenue income

(h) Capital expenditure

(i) If customs duties are borne by the purchaser of the non-current asset, they may be added to the cost of the machinery and classified as capital expenditure.

(j) Similarly, if carriage costs are paid for by the purchaser of the non-current asset, they may be included in the cost of the non-current asset and classified as capital expenditure.

(k) Installation costs of a non-current asset are also added to the non-current asset's cost and classified as capital expenditure

(l) Revenue expenditure

Exam focus point

Exam questions on the distinction between capital and revenue expenditure come up quite frequently.

Chapter Roundup

- **Accounting** is a way of recording, analysing and summarizing transactions of a business.
- Businesses of whatever size or nature exist to make a **profit**.
- There are **various groups of people** who need information about the activities of a business. You should be fully aware of these different groups and their varying needs.
- The principal financial statements of a business are the **balance sheet** and the **income statement**.
    - The balance sheet is a 'snapshot' of the business position at a given point in time.
    - The income statement is a record of income and expenditure over a period.
- Limited liability companies may produce certain **non-financial statements**, particularly commentaries on the content of financial statements.
- You should be able to distinguish the following.
    - Financial accounting
    - Management accounting
    - Financial management
    - Auditing
- You should be able to identify the **desirable qualities** of accounting information.
- You should also be able to outline the factors which have shaped the **development** of financial accounting. These are as follows.
    - National legislation
    - Accounting concepts and individual judgement
    - Accounting standards (both national and international)
    - Generally accepted accounting practice (GAAP)
- Many figures in financial statements are derived from the **application of judgement** in applying fundamental accounting assumptions and conventions. This can lead to subjectivity.
- Financial statements are required to **give a true and fair view** or to **present fairly in all material respects** the financial results of the entity. These terms are not defined, but tend to be decided in courts of law on the facts.
- **Capital expenditure** is expenditure which results in the **acquisition of non-current assets**.
- **Revenue expenditure** is expenditure incurred **for the purpose of the trade** of the business or for **maintenance of non-current assets**.

Quick Quiz

1. What is the fundamental objective of corporate reports?
2. Identify seven user groups who need accounting information.
3. What are the two main financial statements drawn up by accountants?
4. What are the qualities of useful accounting information?
5. Which of the following factors have not influenced financial accounting?
    A   National legislation
    B   Economic factors
    C   Accounting standards
    D   GAAP

PART A   GENERAL FRAMEWORK

6   What are the objectives of the International Accounting Standards Board?
7   What does GAAP stand for?
8   What is meant by 'true and fair' or 'presented fairly'?
9   Which of the following is an item of capital expenditure?

   A   Cost of goods sold
   B   Purchase of a machine
   C   Repairs to a machine
   D   Wages cost

Answers to Quick Quiz

1   To provide information about the financial position, performance and changes in financial position of an enterprise that is useful to a wide range of users in making economic decisions.

2   See paragraph 1.5.

3   The income statement and the balance sheet.

4   See paragraph 4.

5   B.   Economic factors do not influence the development of financial accounting; all the others do (see paragraph 5.1).

6   See paragraph 5.4.1.

7   Generally accepted accounting practice.

8   See paragraph 5.6.

9   B.   This results in the acquisition of a non-current asset. All the others are revenue expenditure.

Now try the question below from the Exam Question Bank

Number	Level	Marks	Time
Q1	Examination	10	18 mins

Part B
Accounting concepts and principles

The accounting equation

Topic list	Syllabus reference
1 Assets and liabilities and the business entity concept	2(a) – (b)
2 The accounting equation (or balance sheet equation)	2(a) – (b)
3 Payables and receivables	2(a) – (b)

Introduction

Part A of this Study Text gave you a broad overview of accounting information and the uses to which it can be put. Part B should provide you with a understanding of the concepts behind financial accounts preparation.

This chapter introduces a concept which it is important for you to grasp: the **accounting equation**. You may already realise that a balance sheet has to balance. You are about to learn why!

Do not rush this chapter. Without an understanding of these essential points you will find it impossible to master more complex aspects later in your studies.

Study guide

Section 2 – Basic balance sheet and income statement

- Explain how the balance sheet equation and business entity convention underlie the balance sheet.
- Define assets and liabilities.
- Explain the matching convention and how it applies to revenue and expenses.

Exam guide

These topics form the basis of all subsequent accounting treatments. They are likely to be examined as a complete question in Section A or as fundamental knowledge behind a more detailed question in Section B.

1 Assets and liabilities and the business entity concept

Assets are items that the business owns or has the use of. **Liabilities** are items that a business owes to third parties.

1.1 Assets and liabilities

Key term

An **asset** is something valuable which a business owns or has the use of.

Examples of assets are factories, office buildings, warehouses, delivery vans, lorries, plant and machinery, computer equipment, office furniture, cash, goods held in store awaiting sale to customers, and raw materials and components held in store by a manufacturing business for use in production.

Some assets are held and used in operations for a long time. An office building is occupied by administrative staff for years; similarly, a machine has a productive life of many years before it wears out.

Other assets are held for only a short time. The owner of a newsagent shop, for example, has to sell his newspapers on the same day that he gets them. The more quickly a business can sell the goods it has in store, the more profit it is likely to make; provided, of course, that the goods are sold at a higher price than what it cost the business to acquire them.

Key term

A **liability** is something which is owed to somebody else. 'Liabilities' is the accounting term for the debts of a business.

Some examples of liabilities are given below.

- A **bank loan** or bank **overdraft**. The liability is the amount eventually repaid to the bank.
- **Amounts owed to suppliers** for goods purchased but not yet paid for. For example, a boatbuilder buys some timber on credit from a timber merchant, so that the boatbuilder does not pay for the timber until some time after it has been delivered. Until the boatbuilder pays what he owes, the timber merchant is an account payable for the amount owed.
- **Taxation** owed to the government. A business pays tax on its profits but there is a gap in time between when a company declares its profits (and becomes liable to pay tax) and the time when the tax bill is eventually paid.
- **Amounts invested in a business by its shareholders or owners**. This is explained in detail in Paragraph 1.2.

1.2 The business as a separate entity

> **FAST FORWARD**
>
> **The business entity concept** states that a business is treated as a separate entity from its owners for accounting purposes.

So far we have spoken of assets and liabilities 'of a business'. You may have wondered whether an intangible entity, such as a business, can own assets or have liabilities in its own name. There are two aspects to this question: the **strict legal position** and the **convention adopted by accountants**.

Many businesses are carried on in the form of **limited liability companies**. The owners of a limited company are its shareholders, who may be few in number (as with a small, family-owned company) or very numerous (as with a large public company whose shares are quoted on a stock exchange).

The law recognises a company as a legal entity, quite separate from its owners. A company may, in its own name, acquire assets, incur debts, and enter into contracts. If a company's assets became insufficient to meet its liabilities, the company as a separate entity becomes 'bankrupt'. However, the owners of the company are not usually required to pay the debts from their own private resources: the debts are not debts of the shareholders, but of the company.

The case is different, **in law**, when a business is carried on by an individual (a sole trader) or by a group of individuals (a partnership).

Case Study

Rodney Quiff starts business as a hairdresser, trading under the business name 'Quiff's Hair Salon'. The law recognises no distinction between Rodney Quiff, the individual, and the business known as 'Quiff's Hair Salon'. Any debts of the business which cannot be met from business assets must be met from Rodney's private resources.

However, in **accounting** a business is treated as a **separate entity from its owner(s)**. This applies whether or not the business is recognised in law as a separate entity, ie it applies whether the business is carried on by a company or by a sole trader. This is known as the **entity concept**.

Key term

> **Entity concept:** a business is a separate entity from its owner.

At first sight this seems illogical and unrealistic; students often have difficulty in understanding it. Nevertheless, it is an idea which you must try to appreciate. It is the basis of a fundamental rule of accounting, which is that the assets and liabilities of a business must always be equal. We will look at this rule in more detail later in this chapter, but a simple example may clarify the idea of a business as a separate entity from its owners.

Exam focus point

> The entity concept appeared in a question in the June 2005 exam.

1.3 Example: The business as a separate entity

> **FAST FORWARD**
>
> **Capital** is a specific form of liability. It is the amount owed by a business to its owner(s).

On 1 July 20X6, Liza Doolittle opened a flower stall in the market, to sell flowers and potted plants. She had saved up $2,500 to put into her business.

When the business is set up, an accountant's picture can be drawn of what it **owns** and what it **owes**. The business begins by owning the cash that Liza has put into it, $2,500. Does it owe anything? The answer is yes.

PART B ACCOUNTING CONCEPTS AND PRINCIPLES

The business is a separate entity in accounting terms. It has obtained its assets, in this example cash, from its owner Liza Doolittle. It therefore owes this amount of money to its owner. If Liza changed her mind and decided not to go into business after all, the business would be dissolved by the 'repayment' of the cash by the business to Liza.

The amount owed by a business to its owners is often known as **capital**.

2 The accounting equation (or balance sheet equation)

FAST FORWARD

The **accounting equation** emphasises the equality between assets and liabilities (including capital as a liability).

We will start by showing how to account for a business's transactions from the time that trading first begins. We will use an example to illustrate the 'accounting equation', ie the rule that the assets of a business will at all times equal its liabilities. This is also known as the **balance sheet equation.**

2.1 Example: The accounting equation

Let us go back to the example in 1.11 above. The business began by owning the cash that Liza has put into it, $2,500. The business is a separate entity in accounting terms and so it owes the money to Liza as **capital**.

Key term

In accounting, **capital** is an investment of money (funds) with the intention of earning a return. A business proprietor invests capital with the intention of earning profit. As long as that money is invested, accountants will treat the capital as money owed to the proprietor by the business.

Formula to learn

The accounting equation is:

ASSETS = CAPITAL + LIABILITIES

When Liza Doolittle sets up her business:

Capital invested	=	$2,500
Cash	=	$2,500

Capital invested is a form of liability, because it is an amount owed by the business to its owner(s). Adapting this to the idea that assets and liabilities are always equal amounts, we can state the accounting equation as follows.

Assets	=	*Capital*	+	*Liabilities*
For Liza Doolittle, as at 1 July 20X6:				
$2,500 (cash)	=	$2,500	+	$0

2.2 Example continued

Liza Doolittle purchases a market stall from Len Turnip, who is retiring from his fruit and vegetables business. The cost of the stall is $1,800.

She also purchases some flowers and potted plants from a trader in the wholesale market, at a cost of $650.

This leaves $50 in cash, after paying for the stall and goods for resale, out of the original $2,500. Liza keeps $30 in the bank and draws out $20 in small change. She is now ready for her first day of market trading on 3 July 20X6.

The assets and liabilities of the business have now altered, and at 3 July before trading begins, the state of her business is as follows.

Assets		=	Capital	+	Liabilities
	$				
Stall	1,800	=	$2,500	+	$0
Flower and plants	650				
Cash at bank	30				
Cash in hand	20				
	2,500				

The stall and the flowers and plants are physical items, but they must be given a money value. This money value is usually what they cost the business (called **historical cost** in accounting terms).

2.3 Profit introduced into the accounting equation

On 3 July Liza has a very successful day. She sells all of her flowers and plants for $900 cash.

Since Liza has sold goods costing $650 to earn revenue of $900, we can say that she has **earned a profit of $250 on the day's trading.**

Profits belong to the owners of a business. In this case, the $250 belongs to Liza Doolittle. However, so long as the business retains the profits and does not pay anything out to its owners, the **retained profits** are accounted for as an addition to the proprietor's capital.

Assets		=	Capital		+	Liabilities
	$			$		
Stall	1,800		Original investment	2,500		
Flower and plants	0					
Cash in hand and at bank			Retained profit			
(30+20+900)	950		(900 – 650)	250		
	2,750			2,750	+	$0

We can re-arrange the accounting equation to help us to calculate the capital balance.

Assets – liabilities	=	Capital, which is the same as
Net assets	=	Capital

At the beginning and end of 3 July 20X6, Liza Doolittle's financial position was as follows.

		Net assets	Capital
(a)	At the beginning of the day:	$(2,500 – 0) = $2,500 =	$2,500
(b)	At the end of the day:	$(2,750 – 0) = $2,750 =	$2,750

There has been an increase of $250 in net assets, which is the amount of profits earned during the day.

2.4 Drawings

Key term

Drawings are amounts of money taken out of a business by its owner.

Since Liza Doolittle has made a profit of $250 from her first day's work, she might want to withdraw some money from the business. After all, business owners, like everyone else, need income for living expenses. Liza decides to pay herself $180 in 'wages'.

The payment of $180 is regarded by Liza as a fair reward for her day's work and she might think of the sum as wages. However, the $180 is not an expense to be deducted in arriving at the figure of net profit. In other words, it is incorrect to calculate the net profit earned by the business as follows.

	$
Profit on sale of flowers etc	250
Less 'wages' paid to Liza	180
Net profit earned by business (incorrect)	70

This is because any amounts paid by a business to its proprietor are treated by accountants as withdrawals of profit (the usual term is **appropriations of profit**) and not as expenses incurred by the business. In the case of Liza's business, the true position is that the net profit earned is the $250 surplus on sale of flowers.

	$
Net profit earned by business	250
Less profit withdrawn by Liza	180
Net profit retained in the business	70

Profits are capital as long as they are retained in the business. Once they are **appropriated,** the business suffers a reduction in capital.

The withdrawals of profit are taken in cash, and so the business loses $180 of its cash assets. After the withdrawals have been made, the accounting equation would be restated.

(a) **Assets** = **Capital** + **Liabilities**

	$		$		
Stall	1,800	Original investment	2,500		
Flowers and plants	0	Retained profit			
Cash (950 – 180)	770	(250 – 180)	70		
	2,570		2,570	+	$0

(b) Alternatively   Net assets   Capital
                     $(2,570 – 0)   = $2,570

The increase in net assets since trading operations began is now only $(2,570 – 2,500) = $70, which is the amount of the retained profits.

Question
Capital

Fill in the missing words. (Don't cheat!)

Capital = ... less . . . .

Answer

Look back to paragraph 2.1.

2.5 Example continued

FAST FORWARD

You should now be aware that, when business transactions are accounted for it should be possible to **restate the assets and liabilities** of the business after the transactions have taken place.

The next market day is on 10 July and Liza purchases more flowers and plants for cash, at a cost of $740. She is not feeling well, because of a heavy cold, and so she decides to accept help for the day from her cousin Ethel. Ethel is to be paid a wage of $40 at the end of the day.

Trading on 10 July was again very brisk, and Liza and Ethel sold all their goods for $1,100 cash. Liza paid Ethel her wage of $40 and drew out $200 for herself.

2: THE ACCOUNTING EQUATION

Required

(a) State the accounting equation before trading began on 10 July.

(b) State the accounting equation at the end of 10 July, after paying Ethel:

    (i) but before drawings are made.
    (ii) after drawings have been made.

You are reminded that the accounting equation for the business at the end of transactions for 3 July is given in Paragraph 2.4.

Solution

(a) After the purchase of the goods for $740.

Assets		=	Capital	+	Liabilities
	$				
Stall	1,800				
Goods	740				
Cash (770 – 740)	30				
	2,570	=	$ 2,570	+	$0

(b) (i) On 10 July, all the goods are sold for $1,100 cash, and Ethel is paid $40. The profit for the day is $320.

		$	$
Sales			1,100
Less cost of goods sold		740	
Ethel's wage		40	
			780
Profit			320

Assets		=	Capital		+	Liabilities
	$			$		
Stall	1,800		At beginning of 10 July	2,570		
Goods	0		Profits earned on 10 July	320		
Cash						
(30+ 1,100 – 40)	1,090					
	2,890			2,890	+	$0

(ii) After Liza has withdrawn $200 in cash, retained profits will be only $(320 – 200) = $120.

Assets		=	Capital		+	Liabilities
	$			$		
Stall	1,800		At beginning of 10 July	2,570		
Goods	0		Retained profits	120		
Cash			for 10 July			
(1,090 – 200)	890					
	2,690			2,690	+	$0

Tutorial note: It is very important you should understand the principles described so far. Do not read on until you are confident that you understand the solution to this example.

PART B   ACCOUNTING CONCEPTS AND PRINCIPLES

3 Payables and receivables

FAST FORWARD

Trade accounts payable are liabilities. Trade accounts receivable are assets.

3.1 Trade accounts payable (creditors) and trade accounts receivable (debtors)

Key term

> A **creditor** is a person to whom a business owes money.

A **trade creditor** is a person to whom a business owes money for debts incurred in the course of trading operations. In the accounts of a business, debts still outstanding which arise from the purchase from suppliers of materials, components or goods for resale are called **trade accounts payable**, sometimes abbreviated to 'accounts payable' or 'payables'.

A business does not always pay immediately for goods or services it buys. It is a common business practice to make purchases on credit, with a promise to pay within 30 days, or two months or three months, of the date of the bill or 'invoice' for the goods. For example, A buys goods costing $2,000 on credit from B, B sends A an invoice for $2,000, dated 1 March, with credit terms that payment must be made within 30 days. If A then delays payment until 31 March, B will be a creditor of A between 1 and 31 March for $2,000. From A's point of view, the amount owed to B is a **trade account payable.**

A trade account payable is a **liability** of a business.

Key term

> Just as a business might buy goods on credit, so too might it sell goods to customers on credit. A customer who buys goods without paying cash for them straight away is a **debtor** (receivable).

For example, suppose that C sells goods on credit to D for $6,000 on terms that the debt must be settled within two months of the invoice date 1 October. If D does not pay the $6,000 until 30 November, D will be a debtor of C for $6,000 from 1 October until 30 November. In the accounts of the business, amounts owed by debtors are called **trade accounts receivable,** sometimes abbreviated to 'accounts receivable' or 'receivables'.

A trade account receivable is an **asset** of a business. When the debt is finally paid, the trade account receivable 'disappears' as an asset, to be replaced by 'cash at bank and in hand'.

3.2 Example continued

The example of Liza Doolittle's market stall is continued, by looking at the consequences of the following transactions in the week to 17 July 20X6. (See Paragraph 2.5 for the situation as at the end of 10 July.)

(a)   Liza Doolittle realises that she is going to need more money in the business and so she makes the following arrangements.

    (i)   She invests immediately a further $250 of her own capital.

    (ii)   She persuades her Uncle Henry to lend her $500 immediately. Uncle Henry tells her that she can repay the loan whenever she likes, but in the meantime, she must pay him interest of $5 each week at the end of the market day. They agree that it will probably be quite a long time before the loan is eventually repaid.

(b)   She decides to buy a second hand van to pick up flowers and plants from her supplier and bring them to her stall in the market. She finds a car dealer, Laurie Loader, who agrees to sell her a van on credit for $700. Liza agrees to pay for the van after 30 days' trial use.

2: THE ACCOUNTING EQUATION

(c) During the week, Liza's Uncle George telephones her to ask whether she would sell him some garden gnomes and furniture for his garden. Liza tells him that she will look for a supplier. After some investigations, she buys what Uncle George has asked for, paying $300 in cash to the supplier. Uncle George accepts delivery of the goods and agrees to pay $350, but he asks if she can wait until the end of the month for payment. Liza agrees.

(d) Liza buys flowers and plants costing $800. Of these purchases $750 are paid in cash, with the remaining $50 on seven days' credit. Liza decides to use Ethel's services again as an assistant on market day, at an agreed wage of $40.

(e) On 17 July, Liza succeeds in selling all her goods earning revenue of $1,250 (all in cash). She decides to withdraw $240 for her week's work. She also pays Ethel $40 in cash. She decides to make the interest payment to her Uncle Henry the next time she sees him.

(f) We shall ignore any van expenses for the week, for the sake of relative simplicity.

Required

State the accounting equation:

(i) After Liza and Uncle Henry have put more money into the business and after the purchase of the van.

(ii) After the sale of goods to Uncle George.

(iii) After the purchase of goods for the weekly market

(iv) At the end of the day's trading on 17 July, and after withdrawals have been appropriated out of profit.

Solution

There are a number of different transactions to account for here. This solution deals with them one at a time in chronological order. (In practice, it is possible to do one set of calculations which combines the results of all the transactions, but we shall defer such 'shortcut' methods until later.)

(i) *The addition of Liza's extra capital and Uncle Henry's loan*

An investment analyst might call Uncle Henry's loan a capital investment, on the grounds that it will probably be for the long term. Uncle Henry is not the owner of the business, however, even though he has made an investment of a loan in it. He would only become an owner if Liza offered him a partnership in the business, and she has not done so. To the business, Uncle Henry is a long-term creditor, and it is more appropriate to define his investment as a liability of the business and not as business capital.

The accounting equation after $(250 + 500) = $750 cash is put into the business will be:

Assets		=	Capital		+	Liabilities	
	$			$			$
Stall	1,800		As at end of 10 July	2,690		Loan	500
Goods	0		Additional capital put in	250			
Cash (890+750)	1,640						
	3,440	=		2,940	+		500

The purchase of the van (cost $700) on credit

Assets		=	Capital		+	Liabilities	
	$			$			$
Stall	1,800		As at end of 10 July	2,690		Loan	500
Van	700		Additional capital	250		Payables	700
Cash	1,640						
	4,140	=		2,940	+		1,200

PART B   ACCOUNTING CONCEPTS AND PRINCIPLES

(ii) *The sale of goods to Uncle George on credit ($350) which cost the business $300 (cash paid)*

Assets		=	Capital		+	Liabilities	
	$			$			$
Stall	1,800		As at end of 10 July	2,690		Loan	500
Van	700		Additional capital	250		Payables	700
Receivable	350		Profit on sale to				
Cash			Uncle George (350 – 300)	50			
(1,640 – 300)	1,340						
	4,190	=		2,990	+		1,200

(iii) *After the purchase of goods for the weekly market ($750 paid in cash and $50 of purchases on credit)*

Assets		=	Capital		+	Liabilities	
	$			$			$
Stall	1,800		As at end of 10 July	2,690		Loan	500
Van	700		Additional capital	250		Payables	
Goods	800		Profit on sale to			(van)	700
Receivables	350		Uncle George	50		Payables	
Cash						(goods)	50
(1,340 – 750)	590						
	4,240	=		2,990	+		1,250

(iv) *After market trading on 17 July*

Sales of goods costing $800 earned revenues of $1,250. Ethel's wages were $40 (paid), Uncle Henry's interest charge is $5 (not paid yet) and withdrawals on account of profits were $240 (paid). The profit for 17 July may be calculated as follows, taking the full $5 of interest as a cost on that day.

	$	$
Sales		1,250
Cost of goods sold	800	
Wages	40	
Interest	5	
		845
Profit earned on 17 July		405
Profit on sale of goods to Uncle George		50
Profit for the week		455
Drawings		240
Retained profit		215

Assets		=	Capital		+	Liabilities	
	$			$			$
Stall	1,800		As at end of 10 July	2,690		Loan	500
Van	700		Additional capital	250		Payable for	
Goods (800 – 800)	0		Profits retained	215		van	700
Receivables	350					Payable for	
Cash (590+						goods	50
1,250 – 40 – 240)	1,560					Payable for	
						interest	
						payment	5
	4,410			3,155			1,255

3.3 Matching

FAST FORWARD The **matching convention** requires that revenue earned is matched with the expenses incurred in earning it.

In the example above, we have 'matched' the revenue earned with the expenses incurred in earning it. So in part (iv), we included all the costs of the goods sold of $800, even though $50 had not yet been paid in cash. Also the interest of $5 was deducted from revenue, even though it had not yet been paid. This is known as the **matching convention.**

Question — The accounting equation

How would each of these transactions affect the accounting equation?

(a) Purchasing $800 worth of inventory on credit
(b) Paying the telephone bill $25
(c) Selling $450 worth of inventory for $650
(d) Paying $800 to the supplier

Answer

(a)	Increase in liabilities (payables)	$800
	Increase in assets (inventory)	$800
(b)	Decrease in assets (cash)	$25
	Decrease in capital (profit)	$25
(c)	Decrease in assets (inventory)	$450
	Increase in assets (cash)	$650
	Increase in capital (profit)	$200
(d)	Decrease in liabilities (payables)	$800
	Decrease in assets (cash)	$800

Chapter Roundup

- **Assets** are items that a business owns or has the use of.
- **Liabilities** are items that a business owes to third parties.
- The **business entity concept** states that a business is treated as a separate entity from its owners for accounting purposes.
- **Capital** is a specific form of liability. It is the amount owed by a business to its owner(s).
- The **accounting equation** emphasises the equality between assets and liabilities (including capital as a liability).
- You should now be aware that, when business transactions are accounted for, it should be possible to **restate the assets and liabilities** of the business after the transactions have taken place.
- **Trade accounts payable** are **liabilities**. **Trade accounts receivable** are **assets**.
- The **matching convention** requires that revenue earned is matched with the expenses incurred in earning it.

PART B ACCOUNTING CONCEPTS AND PRINCIPLES

Quick Quiz

1. In what sense can a proprietor's capital be regarded as a liability of the business?
2. What is the accounting equation?
3. What are drawings?
4. What does 'matching' mean?
5. Distinguish between an account receivable (a debtor) and an account payable (a creditor).
6. Which ONE of the following is an asset?

    A   The owner's capital
    B   Van
    C   An account payable
    D   A bank overdraft

7. Which ONE of the following is a liability?

    A   Cash
    B   An account receivable
    C   An account payable
    D   Van

Answers to Quick Quiz

1. Due to the business entity concept, a business is treated as being separate from its owner(s). Therefore the capital invested in a business is strictly owed by the business to its owner(s) and so is treated as a liability.

2. Assets = Capital + Liabilities.

3. Amounts of profit withdrawn by the owner in cash and not retained in the business.

4. The matching convention requires that we 'match' revenue earned with the expenses incurred in earning it.

5. An account receivable is an amount owed by a customer to the business eg on a credit sale.

    An account payable is an amount owed by the business to a supplier eg on a credit purchase.

6. B   The van is an asset, all the others are liabilities.

7. C   An account payable is a liability, all the others are assets.

Now try the question below from the Exam Question Bank

Number	Level	Marks	Time
Q2	Examination	10	18 mins

Basic financial statements

Topic list	Syllabus reference
1 The balance sheet	2(a), 5(c)(i)
2 The income statement	2(a), 5(c)(ii)

Introduction

In Chapter 2 you were introduced to the idea of the accounting equation. If you understand this, you will have little difficulty understanding the balance sheet.

You should already have some idea of what is meant by the income statement. In this chapter you will see this in more detail. The income statement matches the revenue earned in a period with the costs incurred in earning it. It is usual to distinguish between a gross profit (sales revenue less the cost of goods sold) and a net profit (being the gross profit less the expenses of selling, distribution, administration, etc).

There is a fair amount to learn before you will be able to prepare these statements yourself, although you will be surprised how quickly you will progress.

It is important to introduce the financial statements now so you can see what you are aiming at. Keep them in your mind as you tackle the 'nuts and bolts' of ledger accounting in the next few chapters.

Study guide

Section 2 – Basic balance sheet and income statement

- Explain how and why assets and liabilities are disclosed in the balance sheet.
- Draft a simple balance sheet in vertical format.
- Explain the matching convention and how it applies to revenue and expenses.
- Explain how and why revenue and expenses are disclosed in the income statement.
- Illustrate how the balance sheet and income statement are interrelated.
- Draft a simple income statement in vertical format.
- Explain the significance of gross profit and the gross profit as a percentage of sales.

Exam guide

Once again this chapter introduces fundamental concepts, which may be examined either by an MCQ in Section A or by production of a basic financial statement in Section B. You are unlikely to be asked to produce both an income statement and a balance sheet in the same question, unless the figures are very straightforward.

1 The balance sheet

FAST FORWARD

A **balance sheet** is a statement of the **financial position** of a business at a given moment in time.

A **balance sheet is a statement of the liabilities, capital and assets of a business at a given moment in time.** It is like a 'snapshot' photograph, since it captures on paper a still image, frozen at a single moment in time, of something which is dynamic and continually changing. Typically, a balance sheet is prepared at the end of the accounting period to which the financial statements relate.

A balance sheet is, therefore, very similar to the accounting equation. In fact, there are only two differences between a balance sheet and an accounting equation as follows.

- The manner or format in which the liabilities and assets are presented
- The extra detail which is usually contained in a balance sheet

The details shown in a balance sheet will not be described in full in this chapter. Instead we will make a start in this chapter and add more detail in later chapters as we go on to look at other ideas and methods in accounting.

A balance sheet is divided into two halves, and presented in either of the following ways.

- **Capital and liabilities** in one half and **assets** in the other.
- **Capital** in one half and **net assets** in the other.

Key term

Net assets = assets less liabilities

In this Study Text we will follow the general format given by IAS 1 *Presentation of financial statements* (discussed in detail in Chapter 19).

NAME OF BUSINESS
BALANCE SHEET AS AT (DATE)

	$
Assets (item by item)	X
Capital	X
Liabilities (item by item)	X
	X

3: BASIC FINANCIAL STATEMENTS

The total value in one half of the balance sheet will equal the total value in the other half. You should readily understand this from the accounting equation.

Since each half of the balance sheet has an equal value, one side balances the other. However, the equal value of the two halves is not the origin of the term balance sheet. A balance sheet is so called because it is a statement of the outstanding balances on the ledger accounts for the capital, liabilities and assets of the business, at a given moment in time. Ledger accounts are described in a later chapter.

Capital, liabilities and assets are usually shown in some detail in a balance sheet. The following paragraphs describe the sort of detail we might expect to find.

1.1 Capital (sole trader)

The proprietor's capital is usually analysed into its component parts.

	$	$
Capital as at the beginning of the accounting period (ie capital 'brought forward')		X
Add additional capital introduced during the period		X
		X
Add profit earned during the period	X	
Less drawings	(X)	
Retained profit for the period		X
Capital as at the end of the accounting period (ie capital 'carried forward')		X

Key terms

> **Brought forward** means 'brought forward from the previous period', and **carried forward** means 'carried forward to the next period'. The carried forward amount at the end of one period is also the brought forward amount of the next period.

1.2 Liabilities

FAST FORWARD

> A distinction is made in the balance sheet between **non-current liabilities** and **current liabilities**. **Current liabilities** are debts which are payable within one year. **Non-current liabilities** are debts which are payable after one year.

The various liabilities should be itemised separately. In addition, a distinction is made between **current liabilities** and **non-current liabilities**.

1.2.1 Current liabilities

Key term

> **Current liabilities** are debts of the business that must be paid within a fairly short period of time; ie they are liabilities that will be liquidated in the near future.

By convention, a 'fairly short period of time' has come to be accepted as one year.

Examples of current liabilities are:

(a) **Loans** repayable within **one year**
(b) A bank **overdraft,** which is usually repayable on demand
(c) Trade accounts **payable**
(d) **Taxation payable**

(e) **'Accrued charges'**. These are expenses already built up by the business, for which no invoice has yet been received, or for which the date of payment by standing order has not yet arrived. An example of accrued charges is the cost of gas or electricity used. If a business ends its accounting year on 31 December, but does not expect its next quarterly gas bill until the end of January, there will be two months of accrued gas charges to record in the balance sheet as a liability. Accruals will be described more fully in a later chapter.

1.2.2 Non-current liabilities

Key term

> A **non-current liability** is a debt which is not payable within the 'short term' (ie it will not be liquidated shortly) and so any liability which is not current must be non-current.

A non-current or deferred liability is a debt due to someone else which has been put off till sometime in the future. Just as 'short-term' by convention means one year or less, 'non-current' means more than one year.

Examples of non-current liabilities are as follows.

(a) **Loans** which are not repayable for more than one year, such as a bank loan or a loan from an individual to a business.

(b) A **mortgage loan**, which is a loan specifically secured against a property. (If the business fails to repay the loan, the lender then has 'first claim' on the property and is entitled to repayment from the proceeds of the enforced sale of the property.)

(c) **Loan stock**. These are common with limited liability companies. Loan stocks are securities issued by a company at a fixed rate of interest. They are repayable on agreed terms by a specified date in the future. Holders of loan stocks are therefore lenders of money to a company. Their interests, including security for the loan, are protected by the terms of a trust deed.

1.3 Assets

> The balance sheet distinguishes between **non-current assets** and **current assets**. **Non-current assets** are acquired for **long-term** use within the business. They are normally valued at cost less depreciation. **Current assets** are expected to be converted into cash within one year.

Assets in the balance sheet are divided into two groups.

(a) *Non-current assets*

 (i) Property, plant and equipment (ie 'tangible' assets)
 (ii) Intangible non-current assets
 (iii) Investments (non-current)

(b) *Current assets*

1.3.1 Non-current assets

Key term

> A **non-current asset** is an **asset acquired for continuing use within the business**, with a view to earning income or making profits from its use, either directly or indirectly.

A non-current asset is not acquired for sale to a customer.

- In a manufacturing industry, a production machine is a non-current asset, because it makes goods which are then sold.

- In a service industry, equipment used by employees giving service to customers is a non-current asset (eg the equipment used in a garage, and furniture in a hotel).
- Less obviously, factory premises, office furniture, computer equipment, company cars, delivery vans or pallets in a warehouse are all non-current assets.

To be classed as a non-current asset in the balance sheet of a business, an item must satisfy two further conditions.

- It must be used by the business. For example, the proprietor's own house would not normally appear on the business balance sheet.
- The asset must have a 'life' in use of more than one year (strictly, more than one 'accounting period' which might be more or less than one year).

Key terms

A **tangible asset** is a physical asset, ie that can be touched. It has a real, 'solid' existence. All of the examples of non-current assets mentioned above are 'tangible' assets. They are often referred to as 'property, plant and equipment'.

Intangible non-current assets are assets which do not have a physical existence. They cannot be 'touched'. An example is a patent, which protects an idea. A description of intangible assets will be deferred until a later chapter.

An **investment** can also be a non-current asset. Investments are commonly found in the published accounts of large limited liability companies. A large company A might invest in another company B by purchasing some of the shares or debentures of B. These investments would earn income for A in the form of dividends or interest paid out by B. If the investments are purchased by A with a view to holding on to them for more than one year, they would be classified as non-current assets of A.

In this chapter, we shall restrict our attention to 'tangible' non-current assets.

Exam focus point

Following the Paper 1.1 Study Guide, this text generally refers to **'non-current' assets/ liabilities**. This is in accordance with IAS 1 (revised). However, this standard states that other terminology, for example **'long-term' asset/liability,** may be used provided the meaning is clear.

1.3.2 Non-current assets and depreciation

Non-current assets can be held and used by a business for a number of years, but they wear out or lose their usefulness in the course of time. Every tangible non-current asset has a limited life. The only exception is land itself, although this can be exhausted if it is used by extractive industries (eg mining).

The accounts of a business try to recognise that the cost of a non-current asset is gradually consumed as the asset wears out. This is done by gradually writing off the asset's cost in the income statement over several accounting periods. For example, in the case of a machine costing $1,000 and expected to wear out after ten years, it might be appropriate to reduce the balance sheet value by $100 each year. This process is known as **depreciation**.

If a balance sheet were drawn up four years after the asset was purchased, the amount of depreciation would be 4 × $100 = $400. The machine would then appear in the balance sheet as follows.

	$
Machine at original cost	1,000
Less accumulated depreciation	400
Net book value*	600

* ie the value of the asset in the books of account, net of depreciation. After ten years the asset would be fully depreciated and would appear in the balance sheet with a net book value of zero.

Question

Residual value

Depreciation is discussed in a later chapter, but in the meantime here is a little test which brings in the concept of *residual value*. Suppose a business buys a car for $10,000. It expects to keep the car for three years and then to trade it in at an estimated value of $3,400. How much depreciation should be accounted for in each year of the car's useful life?

Answer

The point in this case is that the car has a residual value of $3,400. It would be inappropriate to account for depreciation in such a way as to write off the asset completely over three years; the aim should be to account only for its loss of value ($10,000 – $3,400 = $6,600), which suggests depreciation of $2,200 per year.

1.3.3 Current assets

Key terms

Current assets take one of the following forms.

(a) Items owned by the business with the intention of turning them into cash in a short time (usually within one year).

(b) Cash, including money in the bank, owned by the business.

These assets are 'current' in the sense that they are continually flowing through the business; they are always realisable in the near future.

The definition in (a) above needs explaining further. A trader David Wickes runs a business selling motor cars and purchases a showroom, which he stocks with cars for sale. He obtains the cars from a manufacturer and pays for them in cash on delivery.

(a) If he sells a car in a cash sale, the goods are immediately converted into cash. The cash can then be used to buy more cars for re-sale.

(b) If he sells a car in a credit sale, the car will be given to the customer, who then becomes a debtor of the business. Eventually, the debtor will pay what he owes (ie the trade account receivable), and David Wickes will receive cash. Once again, the cash can then be used to buy more cars for sale.

Current assets can be identified in this example as follows.

(a) The cars (goods) held in inventory for re-sale are current assets, because David Wickes intends to sell them within one year in the normal course of trade.

(b) Any receivables are current assets, if they will be paid within one year.

(c) Cash is a current asset.

The transactions described above could be shown as a cash cycle.

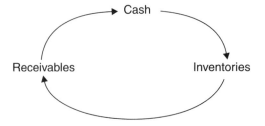

Cash is used to buy goods which are sold. Sales on credit create receivables, but eventually cash is earned from the sales. Some, perhaps most, of the cash will then be used to replenish inventories.

The main items of current assets are therefore as follows.

- Inventories
- Receivables
- Cash

Question — Asset classification

This exercise should ensure you understand asset classification. Cover up the grid in the solution. You should then decide which of the following assets falls into the non-current category and which should be treated as 'current'.

ASSET	BUSINESS	CURRENT OR NON-CURRENT
VAN	DELIVERY FIRM	
MACHINE	MANUFACTURING COMPANY	
CAR	CAR TRADER	
INVESTMENT	ANY	

Answer

ASSET	BUSINESS	CURRENT OR NON-CURRENT
VAN	DELIVERY FIRM	NON-CURRENT
MACHINE	MANUFACTURING COMPANY	NON-CURRENT
CAR	CAR TRADER	CURRENT
INVESTMENT	ANY	EITHER*

* The classification of the investment will depend on the purpose for which it is held. If the intention is to make a non-current investment it will be a non-current asset, but if it is a short term way of investing spare cash it will be a current asset.

It is important to realise that cars are current assets of David Wickes because he is in the business of buying and selling them, ie he is a car trader. If he also has a car which he keeps and uses for business purposes, this car would be a non-current asset. The distinction between a non-current asset and a current asset is not what the asset is physically, but for what **purpose it is obtained and used** by the business.

There are some other categories of current assets.

(a) **Short-term investments**. These are stocks and shares of other businesses, currently owned, but with the intention of selling them in the near future. For example, if a business has a lot of spare cash for a short time, its managers might decide to 'have a flutter' on the stock exchange, and buy shares in one or more large listed companies. The shares will later be sold when the business needs the cash again. If share prices rise in the meantime, the business will make a profit from its short-term investment. Such shares must be readily realisable (ie easy to sell) to be short-term.

(b) **Prepayments**. These are amounts of money already paid by the business for benefits which have not yet been enjoyed, but will be enjoyed within the next accounting period. For example, a business pays an annual insurance premium of $240 to insure its premises against fire and theft, and the premium is payable annually in advance on 1 December. Now, if the business has an accounting year end of 31 December, it will pay $240 on 1 December but only enjoy one month's insurance cover by the end of the year. The remaining 11 months' cover ($220 cost, at $20 per month) will be enjoyed in the next year. The prepayment of $220 is shown in the balance sheet of the business, at 31 December, as a current asset.

A prepayment is a form of receivable. In the example above, at 31 December the insurance company still owes the business 11 months' worth of insurance cover.

1.3.4 Trade accounts receivable and other receivables

Although it is convenient to think of receivables as due from customers who buy goods on credit, it is more accurate to say that a receivables can be due from **anyone** who owes the business money. For example, if a business makes an insurance claim for fire damage, the insurance company is a debtor for the money payable on the claim.

A distinction can be made between two types of receivables.

- **Trade receivables** represent customers who owe money for goods or services bought on credit in the course of the trading activities of the business.

- **Other receivables** are due from anyone else owing money to the business.

1.4 Example: Balance sheet preparation

We shall now look at how the various types of assets and liabilities are shown in the balance sheet of a business. You might like to attempt to prepare a balance sheet yourself before reading the solution which follows.

Question

Balance sheet

You are required to prepare a balance sheet for the Sunken Arches Shoes and Boots Shop as at 31 December 20X6, given the information below.

	$
Capital as at 1 January 20X6	47,600
Profit for the year to 31 December 20X6	8,000
Premises, net book value at 31 December 20X6	50,000
Motor vehicles, net book value at 31 December 20X6	9,000
Fixtures and fittings, net book value at 31 December 20X6	8,000
Non-current loan (mortgage)	25,000
Bank overdraft*	2,000
Goods held for resale (inventories)	16,000
Trade accounts receivable	500
Cash in hand*	100
Trade accounts payable	1,200
Taxation payable	3,500
Drawings	4,000
Accrued costs of rent	600
Prepayment of insurance	300

* A shop might have cash in its cash registers, but an overdraft at the bank.

Answer

SUNKEN ARCHES BALANCE SHEET
AS AT 31 DECEMBER 20X6

	$	$
Assets		
Property, plant and equipment		
Premises	50,000	
Fixtures and fittings	8,000	
Motor vehicles	9,000	
		67,000
Current assets		
Inventories	16,000	
Trade accounts receivable	500	
Prepayment	300	
Cash	100	
		16,900
Total assets		83,900
Capital and liabilities		
Capital		
As at 1 January 20X6	47,600	
Profit for the year	8,000	
Less drawings	(4,000)	
At 31 December 20X6		51,600
Non-current liabilities		
Loan		25,000
Current liabilities		
Bank overdraft	2,000	
Trade accounts payable	1,200	
Taxation payable	3,500	
Accrued costs	600	
		7,300
Total capital and liabilities		83,900

1.5 The order of items in the balance sheet

As we will see later, there are IASs which lay out the required **content**, but there is no IAS which lays out the order of items in the balance sheet. However, the above layout is the preferred format in practice and we will use it throughout this Study Text.

2 The income statement

FAST FORWARD

The **income** statement shows gross profit on trading and net profit after deduction of expenses.

The **income statement** is a statement in which revenues and expenditure are matched to arrive at a figure of profit or loss. Many businesses try to distinguish between a **gross profit** earned on trading, and a **net profit** after other income and expenses.

In the first part of the statement revenue from selling goods is compared with direct costs of acquiring or producing the goods sold to arrive at a gross profit figure. From this, deductions are made in the second half of the statement (which we will call the income and expenses section) in respect of indirect costs (overheads) and additions for non-trading income.

PART B ACCOUNTING CONCEPTS AND PRINCIPLES

Formula to learn

> **Gross profit** = sales less cost of sales
> **Net profit** = gross profit less expenses plus non-trading income.

The income statement shows in detail how the profit (or loss) of a period has arisen. The owners and managers of a business need to know how much profit or loss has been made, but there is only limited information value in the profit figure alone. In order to exercise financial control effectively, managers must know how much income has been earned, what costs have been, and whether the performance of sales or the control of costs appears to be satisfactory. This is the basic reason for preparing the income statement.

We have briefly mentioned the **matching convention** before. The income statement has to **match the revenue earned to the costs of earning that revenue.** This is the reason why prepayments and accrued expenses have to be brought into the financial statements. Prepayments are deducted from expenses and are included in the receivables on the balance sheet, because they related to future periods. Similarly accrued expenses are added to expenses and shown as payables in the balance sheet, because they relate to the current period.

The two parts of the statement are examined in more detail below.

(a) The first part shows the gross profit for the accounting period. Gross profit is the difference between (i) and (ii) below.

   (i) The value of sales (excluding sales taxes)
   (ii) The purchase cost or production cost of the goods sold

   In the retail business, the cost of the goods sold is their purchase cost from the suppliers. In a manufacturing business, the production cost of goods sold is the cost of raw materials in the finished goods, plus the cost of the labour required to make the goods, and often plus an amount of production 'overhead' costs.

(b) The **income and expenses account** shows the net profit of the business. The net profit is:

   (i) the gross profit
   (ii) plus any other income from sources other than the sale of goods
   (iii) minus other expenses of the business, not included in the cost of goods sold

Gross profit is a highly significant figure in the income statements. It represents the profit made from the sale of goods or services. It can be represented as a percentage of sales, called the gross profit margin.

Key term

> **Gross profit margin** = $\dfrac{\text{Gross profit}}{\text{Sales}} \times 100\%$

The gross profit margin will be looked at in more detail later in this Study Text. However it is a very important ratio, as it can be used to compare the results of different periods to see how well the costs of sales are being controlled as sales increase. It can also be used to compare the results of different businesses in the same industry.

2.1 Detail in the income statement

Income from other sources will include the following.

(a) Dividends or interest received from investments

(b) Profits on the sale of non-current assets

(c) Irrecoverable debts written off in a previous accounting period which were unexpectedly paid in the current period (see (a)(vii) below).

Other business expenses that will appear in the income statement are as follows.

(a) **Selling and distribution expenses**. These are expenses associated with the process of selling and delivering goods to customers. They include the following items.

   (i) The salaries of sales management

   (ii) The salaries and commissions of salespeople

   (iii) The travelling and entertainment expenses of salespeople

   (iv) Marketing costs (eg advertising and sales promotion expenses)

   (v) The costs of running and maintaining delivery vans

   (vi) Discounts allowed to customers for early payment of their debt. For example, a business sells goods to a customer for $100 and offers a discount of 5% for payment in cash. If the customer takes the discount, the accounts of the business do not record the sales at $95; they record sales at the full $100, with a cost for discounts allowed of $5. Discounts are described more fully in a later chapter.

   (vii) Bad debts written off. Sometimes customers fail to pay what they owe and a business has to decide at some stage that there is now no prospect of ever being paid. The debt has to be written off as 'bad'. The amount of the debt written off is charged as an expense in the income statement. Bad debts are also described more fully in a later chapter.

(b) **Administration expenses**. These are the expenses of providing management and administration for the business. Examples include the following.

   (i) The salaries of management and office staff
   (ii) Rent and local business or property taxes
   (iii) Insurance
   (iv) Telephone and postage
   (v) Printing and stationery
   (vi) Heating and lighting

(c) **Finance expenses**. These include the following examples.

   (i) Interest on a loan
   (ii) Bank overdraft interest

As far as possible, you should try to group items of expenses (selling and distribution, administration, and finance) but this is not something that you need worry about unnecessarily at this stage.

2.2 Example: Income statement

On 1 June 20X5, Jock Heiss commenced trading as an ice cream salesman, using a van which he drove around the streets of his town.

(a) He rented the van at a cost of $1,000 for three months. Running expenses for the van averaged $300 per month.

(b) He hired a part time helper at a cost of $100 per month.

(c) He borrowed $2,000 from his bank, and the interest cost of the loan was $25 per month.

(d) His main business was to sell ice cream to customers in the street, but he also did some special catering for business customers, supplying ice creams for office parties. Sales to these customers were usually on credit.

(e) For the three months to 31 August 20X5, his total sales were as follows.

(i) Cash sales $8,900
(ii) Credit sales $1,100

(f) He purchased his ice cream from a local manufacturer, Floors Co. The cost of purchases in the three months to 31 August 20X5 was $6,200, and at 31 August he had sold every item. He still owed $700 to Floors Co for unpaid purchases on credit.

(g) One of his credit sale customers has gone bankrupt, owing Jock $250. Jock has decided to write off the debt in full, with no prospect of getting any of the money owed.

(h) He used his own home for his office work. Telephone and postage expenses for the three months to 31 August were $150.

(i) During the period he paid himself $300 per month.

Required

Prepare an income statement for the three months 1 June to 31 August 20X5.

Solution

An income statement can be presented in various formats, but here we will use the vertical format as stipulated in the Study Guide.

JOCK HEISS
INCOME STATEMENT
FOR THE THREE MONTHS ENDED 31 AUGUST 20X5

		$	$
Sales (8,900 + 1,100)			10,000
Less cost of sales			6,200
Gross profit			3,800
Expenses			
Wages (3 × 100)		300	
Van rental		1,000	
Van expenses (3 × 300)	Income &	900	
Bad debt written off	expenses a/c	250	
Telephone and postage		150	
Interest charges (25 × 3)		75	
			2,675
Net profit (transferred to the balance sheet)			1,125

2.3 Relationship between the income statement and the balance sheet

- The net profit is the profit for the period, and it is transferred to the balance sheet of the business as part of the proprietor's capital.

- Drawings are appropriations of profit and not expenses. They must not be included in the income statement. The payments that Jock Heiss makes to himself ($900) are appropriations of profit, which are shown in the capital account detailed on the balance sheet.

- The cost of sales is $6,200, even though $700 of the costs have not yet been paid for. The $700 owed to Floors Co will be shown in the balance sheet as a trade account payable. This is an example of the **matching concept**.

    Under the **matching concept** revenue is **matched** with the expenses incurred in earning it.

2.4 Example: Gross profit margin

FAST FORWARD

> The gross **profit margin** is a means of comparing the cost control between one period and the next.

In the above example, the gross profit margin of Jock Heiss for the three months to 31 August 20X5 is:

$$\frac{3,800}{10,000} \times 100\% = 38\%$$

This can be compared to the gross profit margin for future trading periods to see whether the margin is maintained or improved. If the margin starts to fall, then Jock will need to examine his control of the costs of sales.

Chapter Roundup

- A **balance sheet** is a statement of the **financial position** of a business at a given moment in time.
- A distinction is made in the balance sheet between **non-current liabilities** and **current liabilities**, and between **non-current assets** and **current assets**.
- **'Current'** usually means **'within one year'**. Current assets are expected to be converted into cash within one year. Current liabilities are debts which are payable within one year.
- **Non-current assets** are those acquired for **long-term** use within the business. They are normally valued at cost less depreciation. **Non-current liabilities** are debts which are payable after one year.
- The **income statement** shows gross profit on trading and net profit after deduction of expenses.
- The income statement is prepared under the **matching convention**.
- The **gross profit margin** is a means of comparing the cost control between one period and the next.

Quick Quiz

1. What are the component parts of the item 'proprietor's capital' in a balance sheet?
2. What are 'accrued charges'?
3. Which ONE of the following is a non-current liability?

    A   A bank overdraft
    B   A bank loan repayable within a year
    C   A mortgage repayable in five year's time
    D   A trade payable

4. What is depreciation?
5. What are the main items in current assets in a balance sheet?
6. What are prepayments?
7. What is the difference between gross profit and net profit?
8. Which of the following expenses is included in cost of sales?

    A   Sales people's salaries
    B   Management salaries
    C   Overdraft interest
    D   Cost of raw material

PART B   ACCOUNTING CONCEPTS AND PRINCIPLES

9   A business has sales of $100,000, cost of sales of $60,000 and expenses of $20,000. Which of the following statements is true?

    A   The gross profit margin is 60%
    B   The gross profit margin is 40%
    C   The gross profit margin is 20%
    D   The gross profit margin is 80%

Answers to Quick Quiz

1   See Paragraph 1.1.

2   Expenses already incurred by the business, which have not yet been billed.

3   C   The mortgage is repayable in over a year's time and, therefore, is a non-current liability. The bank overdraft is repayable on demand, a trade payable is usually paid within a year and the bank loan is repayable within one year, so these are all current liabilities.

4   Depreciation is a means of allocating the cost of an asset over the period of its useful life. (This is another example of the matching concept.)

5   - Inventories
    - Receivables
    - Cash

6   Expenses already paid for by the business but which will be used, or the benefits enjoyed, in the next period of trading.

7   Net profit = gross profit less expenses plus non-trading income.

8   D   The others are examples of selling expenses (A), administration expenses (B) and finance expenses (C).

9   B   Gross profit margin = $\frac{\text{Gross profit}}{\text{Sales}} \times 100\% = \frac{(100,000 - 60,000)}{100,000} \times 100\% = 40\%$

Now try the question below from the Exam Question Bank

Number	Level	Marks	Time
Q3	Examination	10	18 mins

Part C

Double entry bookkeeping and accounting systems

Sources, records and the books of original entry

Topic list	Syllabus reference
1 The role of source documents	3(a)
2 The need for books of original entry	3(a)
3 Sales and purchase day books	3(a)
4 Cash book	3(a)

Introduction

From your studies of the first three chapters you should have grasped some important points about the nature and purpose of accounting.

- Most organisations provide products and services in the hope of making a profit for their owners, by receiving payment in money for those goods and services.
- The role of the accounting system is to record these monetary effects and create information about them.

You should also, by now, understand the basic principles underlying the balance sheet and income statement and have an idea of what they look like.

We now turn our attention to the process by which a business transaction works its way through to the financial statements.

It is usual to record a business transaction on a **document**. Such documents include invoices, orders, credit notes and goods received notes, all of which will be discussed in Section 1 of this chapter. In terms of the accounting system these are known as **source documents**. The information on them is processed by the system by, for example, aggregating (adding together) or classifying.

Records of source documents are kept in 'books of original entry', which, as the name suggests, are the first stage at which a business transaction enters into the accounting system. The various types of books of original entry are discussed in Sections 2 to 4.

In the next chapter we consider what happens to transactions after the books of original entry stage.

PART C   DOUBLE ENTRY BOOKKEEPING AND ACCOUNTING SYSTEMS

Study guide

Section 3-4 – Bookkeeping principles

- Identify the main data sources and records in an accounting system.
- Explain the functions of each data source and record.
- Outline the forms of accounting records in a typical manual system.
- Outline the form of accounting records in a typical computerised system.
- Record cash transactions in ledger accounts.
- Record credit sale and purchase transactions using day books.
- Explain sales and purchase returns and demonstrate their recording.
- Explain the need for a record of petty cash transactions.
- Illustrate the typical format of the petty cash book.
- Explain the importance of using the imprest system to control petty cash.

Exam guide

Although these topics may be examined in principle by an MCQ, it is more likely that they will form one of the questions in Section B, where you could be asked to write up a cash book or sales day book, for example.

1 The role of source documents

FAST FORWARD

Business transactions are recorded on **source documents**. Examples are sales and purchase orders, invoices and credit notes.

Whenever a business transaction takes place, involving sales or purchases, receiving or paying money, or owing or being owed money, it is usual for the transaction to be recorded on a document. These documents are the source of all the information recorded by a business.

Documents used to record the business transactions in the 'books of account' of the business include the following.

- **Sales order**. A customer writes out or signs an order for goods or services he requires.
- **Purchase order**. A business orders from another business goods or services, such as material supplies.
- **Invoices** and **credit notes**. These are discussed further below.

Key term

An **invoice** relates to a sales order or a purchase order.

- When a business sells goods or services on credit to a customer, it sends out an invoice. The details on the invoice should match the details on the sales order. The invoice is a request for the customer to pay what he owes.
- When a business buys goods or services on credit it receives an invoice from the supplier. The details on the invoice should match the details on the purchase order.

The invoice is primarily a demand for payment, but it is used for other purposes as well, as we shall see. Since it has several uses, an invoice is often produced on multi-part stationery, or photocopied, or carbon-copied. The top copy will go to the customer and other copies will be used by various people within the business.

1.1 What does an invoice show?

Most invoices are numbered, so that the business can keep track of all the invoices it sends out. Information usually shown on an invoice includes the following.

(a) Name and address of the seller and the purchaser
(b) Date of the sale
(c) Description of what is being sold
(d) Quantity and unit price of what has been sold (eg 20 pairs of shoes at $25 a pair)
(e) Details of trade discount, if any (eg 10% reduction in cost if buying over 100 pairs of shoes)
(f) Total amount of the invoice including (usually) details any of sales tax
(g) Sometimes, the date by which payment is due, and other terms of sale

1.2 The credit note

China Supplies sent out an invoice for 20 dinner plates, but the typist accidentally typed in a total of $162.10, instead of $62.10. The china shop has been **overcharged** by $100. What is China Supplies to do?

Alternatively, when the china shop received the plates it found that they had all been broken in the post and that it was going to send them back. Although the china shop has received an invoice for $62.10, it has no intention of paying it because the plates were useless. Again, what is China Supplies to do?

The answer is that China Supplies sends out a **credit note**. A credit note is sometimes printed in red to distinguish it from an invoice. Otherwise, it will be made out in much the same way as an invoice, but with less detail and 'Credit Note Number' instead of 'Invoice Number'.

Key term

> A **credit note** is a document relating to returned goods or refunds when a customer has been overcharged. It can be regarded as a **negative invoice**.

The following documents are sometimes used in connection with sales and purchases.

(a) Debit notes
(b) Goods received notes

A **debit note** might be issued to **adjust an invoice** already issued. This is also commonly achieved by issuing a revised invoice after raising a credit or debit note purely for internal purposes (ie to keep the records straight).

More commonly, a debit note is issued to a supplier as a means of formally requesting a credit note.

Goods received notes (GRNs) record a receipt of goods, most commonly in a warehouse. They may be used in addition to suppliers' advice notes. Often the accounts department will require to see the relevant GRN before paying a supplier's invoice. Even where GRNs are not routinely used, the details of a consignment from a supplier which arrives without an advice note must always be recorded.

Question — Credit note

Fill in the blanks.

'China Supplies sends out a . . . . to a credit customer in order to correct an error where a customer has been overcharged on an . . . .'

Answer

Credit note; invoice.

2 The need for books of original entry

In the course of business, source documents are created. The details on these source documents need to be summarised, as otherwise the business might forget to ask for some money, or forget to pay some, or even accidentally pay something twice. In other words, it needs to keep records of source documents – of transactions – so that it knows what is going on. Such records are made in **books of original entry**.

Key term

> **Books of original** entry are books in which we first record transactions.

FAST FORWARD

> The main books of original entry are as follows.
>
> (a) Sales day book
> (b) Purchase day book
> (c) Sales returns day book
> (d) Purchases returns day book
> (e) Journal (described in the next chapter)
> (f) Cash book
> (g) Petty cash book

It is worth bearing in mind that, for convenience, this chapter describes books of original entry as if they are actual books written by hand. However, books of original entry are often not books at all, but rather files hidden in the memory of a computer. However, the principles remain the same whether they are manual or computerised.

Exam focus point

> You may not get a question on books of original entry, but you need to know where the entries to the ledger accounts come from and how they are posted.

3 Sales and purchase day books

FAST FORWARD

> Invoices and credit notes are recorded in **day books**.

3.1 The sales day book

Key term

> The **sales day book** is the book of original entry for credit sales.

The sales day book is used to keep a list of all invoices sent out to customers each day. An extract from a sales day book might look like this.

SALES DAY BOOK

Date 20X0	Invoice	Customer	Total amount invoiced $
Jan 10	247	Jones & Co	105.00
	248	Smith Co	86.40
	249	Alex & Co	31.80
	250	Enor College	1,264.60
			1,487.80

Most businesses 'analyse' their sales. For example, this business sells boots and shoes. The sale to Smith was entirely boots, the sale to Alex was entirely shoes, and the other two sales were a mixture of both.

Then the sales day book might look like this.

SALES DAY BOOK

Date 20X0	Invoice	Customer	Total amount invoiced $	Boot sales $	Shoe sales $
Jan 10	247	Jones & Co	105.00	60.00	45.00
	248	Smith Co	86.40	86.40	
	249	Alex & Co	31.80		31.80
	250	Enor College	1,264.60	800.30	464.30
			1,487.80	946.70	541.10

The analysis gives the managers of the business useful information which helps them to decide how best to run the business.

3.2 The purchase day book

A business also keeps a record in the purchase day book of all the invoices it receives.

Key term

The **purchase day book** is the book of original entry for credit purchases.

An extract from a purchase day book might look like this.

PURCHASE DAY BOOK

Date 20X8	Supplier	Total amount Invoiced $	Purchases $	Electricity etc $
Mar 15	Cook & Co	315.00	315.00	
	W Butler	29.40	29.40	
	EEB	116.80		116.80
	Show Fair Co	100.00	100.00	
		561.20	444.40	116.80

- There is no 'invoice number' column, because the purchase day book records **other people's invoices**, which have all sorts of different numbers.
- Like the sales day book, the purchase day book analyses the invoices which have been sent in. In this example, three of the invoices related to goods which the business intends to re-sell (called simply 'purchases') and the fourth invoice was an electricity bill.

3.3 The sales returns day book

When customers return goods for some reason, the returns are recorded in the sales returns day book. An extract from the sales returns day book follows.

SALES RETURNS DAY BOOK

Date 20X8	Customer and goods	Amount $
30 April	Owen Plenty 3 pairs 'Texas' boots	135.00

Key term

> The **sales returns day book** is the book of original entry for goods returned from customers.

Not all sales returns day books analyse what goods were returned, but it makes sense to keep as complete a record as possible.

3.4 The purchase returns day book

Not surprisingly, the purchase returns day book records goods which the business sends back to its suppliers. The business might expect a cash refund for the returns. In the meantime, however, it might receive a credit note from the supplier, indicating the amount by which its total debt to the supplier is to be reduced.

An extract from the purchase returns day book follows.

PURCHASE RETURNS DAY BOOK

Date	Supplier and goods	Amount
20X8		$
29 April	Boxes Co	
	300 cardboard boxes	46.60

Key term

> The **purchase returns day book** is the book of original entry for goods returned to suppliers.

4 Cash book

> The **cash book** may be a manual record or a computer file. It records all transaction that go through the bank account.

4.1 The cash book

The cash book is also a day book, used to keep a record of money received and money paid out by the business. The cash book deals with money paid into and out of the business **bank account**. This could be money received on the business premises in notes, coins and cheques, subsequently paid into the bank. There are also receipts and payments made by bank transfer, standing order, direct debit and bank interest and charges, directly by the bank.

Some cash, in notes and coins, is usually kept on the business premises in order to make occasional payments for odd items of expense. This cash is usually accounted for separately in a **petty cash book** (which we will look at shortly).

One part of the cash book is used to record receipts of cash, and another part is used to record payments. The best way to see how the cash book works is to follow through an example.

Key term

> The **cash book** is the book of original entry for cash receipts and payments.

4.2 Example: Cash book

At the beginning of 1 September, Robin Plenty had $900 in the bank.

During 1 September 20X7, Robin Plenty had the following receipts and payments.

(a) Cash sale: receipt of $80
(b) Payment from credit customer Hay $400 less discount allowed $20
(c) Payment from credit customer Been $720

(d) Payment from credit customer Seed $150 less discount allowed $10
(e) Cheque received for cash to provide a short-term loan from Len Dinger $1,800
(f) Second cash sale: receipt of $150
(g) Cash received for sale of machine $200
(h) Payment to supplier Kew $120
(i) Payment to supplier Hare $310
(j) Payment of telephone bill $400
(k) Payment of gas bill $280
(l) $100 in cash withdrawn from bank for petty cash
(m) Payment of $1,500 to Hess for new plant and machinery

If you look through these transactions, you will see that seven of them are receipts and six of them are payments.

The receipts part of the cash book for 1 September would look like this.

CASH BOOK (RECEIPTS)

Date 20X7	Narrative	Total $
1 Sept	Balance b/d*	900
	Cash sale	80
	Accounts receivable: Hay	380
	Accounts receivable: Been	720
	Accounts receivable: Seed	140
	Loan: Len Dinger	1,800
	Cash sale	150
	Sale of non-current asset	200
		4,370

* 'b/d' = brought down (ie brought forward)

Points to note

- There is space on the right hand side of the cash book so that the receipts can be analysed under various headings – for example, 'cash from receivables', 'cash sales' and 'other receipts'.

- The cash received in the day amounted to $3,470. Added to the $900 at the start of the day, this comes to $4,370. This is not the amount to be carried forward to the next day, because first we have to subtract all the payments made during 1 September.

The payments part of the cash book for 1 September would look like this.

CASH BOOK (PAYMENTS)

Date 20X7	Narrative	Total $
1 Sept	Accounts payable: Kew	120
	Accounts payable: Hare	310
	Telephone	400
	Gas bill	280
	Petty cash	100
	Machinery purchase	1,500
	Balance c/d	1,660
		4,370

As you can see, this is very similar to the receipts part of the cash book. The only points to note are as follows.

(a) The analysis on the right would be under headings like 'payments to payables, 'payments into petty cash', 'wages' and 'other payments'.

(b) Payments during 1 September totalled $2,710. We know that the total of receipts was $4,370. That means that there is a balance of $4,370 − $2,710 = $1,660 to be 'carried down' to the start of the next day. As you can see this 'balance carried down' is noted at the end of the payments column, so that the receipts and payments totals show the same figure of $4,370 at the end of 1 September.

With analysis columns completed, the cash book given in the examples above might look as follows.

CASH BOOK (RECEIPTS)

Date	Narrative	Total $	Accounts receivable $	Cash sales $	Other $
20X7					
1 Sept	Balance b/d	900			
	Cash sale	80		80	
	Accounts receivable: Hay	380	380		
	Accounts receivable: Been	720	720		
	Accounts receivable: Seed	140	140		
	Loan: Len Dinger	1,800			1,800
	Cash sale	150		150	
	Sale of non-current asset	200			200
		4,370	1,240	230	2,000

CASH BOOK (PAYMENTS)

Date	Narrative	Total $	Accounts payable $	Petty cash $	Wages $	Other $
20X7						
1 Sept	Account payable: Kew	120	120			
	Account payable: Hare	310	310			
	Telephone	400				400
	Gas bill	280				280
	Petty cash	100		100		
	Machinery purchase	1,500				1,500
	Balance c/d	1,660				
		4,370	430	100	–	2,180

4.2.1 Bank statements

Weekly or monthly, a business will receive a **bank statement**. Bank statements should be used to check that the amount shown as a balance in the cash book agrees with the amount on the bank statement, and that no cash has 'gone missing'. This agreement or 'reconciliation' of the cash book with a bank statement is the subject of a later chapter.

4.3 Petty cash book

FAST FORWARD

Most businesses keep **petty cash** on the premises, which is topped up from the main bank account. Under the **imprest system**, the petty cash is kept at an agreed sum, so that each topping up is equal to the amount paid out in the period.

Most businesses keep a small amount of cash on the premises to make occasional small payments in cash, eg staff refreshments, postage stamps, to pay the office cleaner, taxi fares, etc. This is often called the cash float or **petty cash** account. The cash float can also be the resting place for occasional small receipts, eg cash paid by a visitor to make a phone call, etc.

Key term

A **petty cash book** is a cash book for small payments.

Although the amounts involved are small, petty cash transactions still need to be recorded; otherwise the cash float could be abused for personal expenses or even stolen.

There are usually more payments than receipts, and petty cash must be 'topped up' from time to time with cash from the business bank account. A typical layout follows.

PETTY CASH BOOK

Receipts $	Date 20X7	Narrative	Total $	Milk $	Postage $	Travel $	Other $
250	1 Sept	Bal b/d					
		Milk bill	25	25			
		Postage stamps	5		5		
		Taxi fare	10			10	
		Flowers for sick staff	15				15
		Bal c/d	195				
250			250	25	5	10	15

Under what is called the **imprest system**, the amount of money in petty cash is kept at an agreed sum or 'float' (say $250). Expense items are recorded on vouchers as they occur, so that at any time:

	$
Cash still held in petty cash	195
Plus voucher payments (25+5+10+15)	55
Must equal the agreed sum or float	250

The total float is made up regularly (to $250, or whatever the agreed sum is) by means of a cash payment from the bank account into petty cash. The amount of the 'top-up' into petty cash will be the total of the voucher payments since the previous top-up.

Key term

The **imprest system** makes a refund of the total paid out in a period.

Try the following exercise on books of original entry.

Question

Books of original entry

State which books of original entry the following transactions would be entered into.

(a) Your business pays A Brown (a supplier) $450.00.
(b) You send D Smith (a customer) an invoice for $650.
(c) Your accounts manager asks you for $12 urgently in order to buy some envelopes.
(d) You receive an invoice from A Brown for $300.
(e) You pay D Smith $500.
(f) F Jones (a customer) returns goods to the value of $250.
(g) You return goods to J Green to the value of $504.
(h) F Jones pays you $500.

Answer

(a) Cash book
(b) Sales day book
(c) Petty cash book
(d) Purchases day book
(e) Cash book
(f) Sales returns day book
(g) Purchase returns day book
(h) Cash book

PART C DOUBLE ENTRY BOOKKEEPING AND ACCOUNTING SYSTEMS

Chapter Roundup

- Business transactions are recorded on **source documents**. These include the following.
    - Sales orders
    - Purchase orders
    - Invoices
    - Credit notes

- These transactions are recorded in **books of original entry** of which there are seven.
    - Sales day book
    - Sales returns day book
    - Purchase day book
    - Purchase returns day book
    - Cash book
    - Petty cash book
    - Journal

- Invoices and credit notes are recorded in day books.

- The **cash book** may be manual record or a computer file. It records all transactions that go through the bank account.

- Most businesses keep **petty cash** on the premises which is topped up from the main bank account. Under the **imprest system** the petty cash is kept at an agreed sum so that each topping up is equal to the amount paid out in the period.

Quick Quiz

1 Name four pieces of information normally shown on an invoice.

2 Name the seven books of original entry.

3 What information is summarised in the sales day book?

4 What is the purchase returns day book used to record?

    A   Supplier's invoices
    B   Customer's invoices
    C   Details of goods returned to suppliers
    D   Details of goods returned by customers

5 What is the difference between the cash book and the petty cash book?

6 Petty cash is controlled under an imprest system. The imprest amount is $100. During a period, payments totalling $53 have been made. How much needs to be reimbursed at the end of the period to restore petty cash to the imprest account?

    A $100
    B $53
    C $47
    D $50

Answers to Quick Quiz

1. **Four** from the following

    - Invoice number
    - Seller's name and address
    - Purchaser's name and address
    - Date of sale
    - Description of goods or services
    - Quantity and unit price
    - Trade discount (if any)
    - Total amount, including sales tax (if any)
    - Any special terms

2.
    - Sales day book
    - Purchase day book
    - Sales returns day book
    - Purchase returns day book
    - Cash book
    - Petty cash book
    - Journal

3. Credit sales invoices, analysed into sales of different products.

4. C   Supplier's invoices (A) are recorded in the purchase day book, customer's invoices (B) are recorded in the sales day book and goods returned by customers (D) are recorded in the sales returns day book.

5. The cash book records amounts paid into or out of the bank account. The petty cash book records payments of small amounts of cash.

6. B   Under the imprest system, a reimbursement is made of the amount of the vouchers (or payments made) for the period.

Now try the questions below from the Exam Question Bank

Number	Level	Marks	Time
Q4	Examination	10	18 mins
Q5	Introductory	–	27 mins

PART C

DOUBLE ENTRY BOOKKEEPING AND ACCOUNTING SYSTEMS

Ledger accounting and double entry

Topic list	Syllabus reference
1 Why do we need ledger accounts?	3(a)
2 The nominal ledger	3(a)
3 Double entry bookkeeping	3(a)
4 The journal	3(a)
5 Day book analysis	3(a)
6 The imprest system	3(a)
7 The receivables and payables ledgers	3(a)
8 Accounting for a sales tax	3(c)

Introduction

In the previous chapter we saw how to organise transactions into lists. It is not easy, however, to see how a business is doing from the information scattered throughout the books of original entry. The lists need to be summarised. This is **ledger accounting**.

The summary is produced in the nominal ledger by a process you may have heard of known as **double entry bookkeeping**. This is the cornerstone of accounts preparation and is surprisingly simple.

PART C   DOUBLE ENTRY BOOKKEEPING AND ACCOUNTING SYSTEMS

Study guide

Sections 3-4 – Bookkeeping principles

- Explain the concept of double entry and the duality concept.
- Explain debit and credit.
- Distinguish between asset, liability, revenue and expense accounts.
- Explain the meaning of the balance on each type of account.
- Illustrate how to balance a ledger account.
- Record cash transactions in ledger accounts.
- Record credit sales and purchase transactions in ledger accounts.
- Explain the division of the ledger into sections.
- Explain the general principles of the operation of a sales tax and prepare the consequent accounting entries.

Section 5 – The journal; ledger control accounts; bank reconciliations

- Explain the uses of the journal.
- Illustrate the use of the journal and the posting of journal entries into ledger accounts.

Exam guide

This chapter is the fundamental background for all accounting. It is, therefore, **extremely important** and is likely to be examined in **both** Section A **and** Section B of the exam.

1 Why do we need ledger accounts?

FAST FORWARD

Ledger accounts **summarise** all the individual transactions listed in the books of original entry.

In earlier chapters we saw how an income statement and balance sheet are presented. We have also seen, by means of the accounting equation, that it is possible to prepare financial statements of a business at any time, at any date and relating to any period of time.

A business is continually making transactions, eg buying and selling, and we do not want to prepare an income statement and a balance sheet on completion of every individual transaction. To do so would be a time-consuming and cumbersome administrative task.

It is common sense that a business should keep a record of the transactions that it makes, the assets it acquires and liabilities it incurs. When the time comes to prepare an income statement and a balance sheet, the relevant information can be taken from those records.

The **records of transactions, assets and liabilities** should be kept in the following ways.

(a) In **chronological order**, and **dated** so that transactions can be related to a particular period of time.

(b) Built up in **cumulative totals**.

    (i) Day by day (eg total sales on Monday, total sales on Tuesday)
    (ii) Week by week
    (iii) Month by month
    (iv) Year by year

We have already seen the first step in this process, which is to list all the transactions in various books of original entry. Now we will look at the method used to summarise these records: **ledger accounting** and **double entry**.

2 The nominal ledger

FAST FORWARD

The principal accounts are contained in a ledger called the **nominal ledger**.

Key term

The **nominal ledger** is an accounting record which summarises the financial affairs of a business.

The nominal ledger is sometimes called the **'general ledger'**.

It contains details of assets, liabilities, capital, income and expenditure, and so profit and loss. It consists of a large number of different accounts, each account having its own purpose or 'name' and an identity or code.

There may be various subdivisions, whether for convenience, ease of handling, confidentiality, security, or to meet the needs of computer software design. For example, the ledger may be split alphabetically, with different clerks responsible for sections A-F, G-M, N-R and S-Z. This can help to stop fraud, as there would have to be collusion between the different section clerks.

Examples of accounts in the nominal ledger include the following.

(a) Plant and machinery at cost (non-current asset)
(b) Motor vehicles at cost (non-current asset)
(c) Plant and machinery, provision for depreciation (liability)
(d) Motor vehicles, provision for depreciation (liability)
(e) Proprietor's capital (liability)
(f) Inventories – raw materials (current asset)
(g) Inventories – finished goods (current asset)
(h) Total trade accounts receivable (current asset)
(i) Total trade accounts payable (current liability)
(j) Wages and salaries (expense item)
(k) Rent and local taxes (expense item)
(l) Advertising expenses (expense item)
(m) Bank charges (expense item)
(n) Motor expenses (expense item)
(o) Telephone expenses (expense item)
(p) Sales (revenue item)
(q) Total cash or bank overdraft (current asset or liability)

When it comes to drawing up the financial statements, the revenue and expense accounts will help to form the income statement; while the asset and liability accounts go into the balance sheet.

2.1 The format of a ledger account

If a ledger account were to be kept in an actual book, rather than as a computer record, it might look like this:

ADVERTISING EXPENSES

Date 20X6	Narrative	Ref.	$	Date	Narrative	Ref.	$
15 April	JFK Agency for quarter to 31 March	PL 348	2,500				

There are two sides to the account, and an account heading on top, and so it is convenient to think in terms of 'T' accounts.

(a) On top of the account is its name.
(b) There is a left hand side, or debit side.
(c) There is a right hand side, or credit side.

NAME OF ACCOUNT			
DEBIT SIDE	$	CREDIT SIDE	$

3 Double entry bookkeeping

FAST FORWARD

Double entry bookkeeping is based on the idea that each transaction has an equal but opposite effect. Every accounting event must be entered in ledger accounts both as a debit and as an equal but opposite credit.

3.1 Dual effect (duality concept)

Double entry bookkeeping is the method used to transfer our weekly/monthly totals from our books of original entry into the nominal ledger.

Central to this process is the idea that every transaction has two effects, the **dual effect**. This feature is not something peculiar to businesses. If you were to purchase a car for $1,000 cash for instance, you would be affected in two ways.

(a) You own a car worth $1,000.
(b) You have $1,000 less cash.

If instead you got a bank loan to make the purchase:

(a) You own a car worth $1,000.
(b) You owe the bank $1,000.

A month later if you pay a garage $50 to have the exhaust replaced:

(a) You have $50 less cash.
(b) You have incurred a repairs expense of $50.

Ledger accounts, with their debit and credit sides, are kept in a way which allows the two-sided nature of every transaction to be recorded. This is known as the **'double entry'** system of bookkeeping, because **every transaction is recorded twice** in the accounts.

3.2 The rules of double entry bookkeeping

FAST FORWARD

A debit entry will:
- increase an asset
- decrease a liability
- increase an expense

A credit entry will:
- decrease an asset
- increase a liability
- increase income

The basic rule, which must always be observed, is that **every financial transaction gives rise to two accounting entries, one a debit and the other a credit**. The total value of debit entries in the nominal ledger is therefore always equal at any time to the total value of credit entries. Which account receives the credit entry and which receives the debit depends on the nature of the transaction.

5: LEDGER ACCOUNTING AND DOUBLE ENTRY

Key terms

- An **increase** in an **expense** (eg a purchase of stationery) or an **increase in an asset** (eg a purchase of office furniture) is a **debit**.
- An **increase** in **revenue** (eg a sale) or an **increase in a liability** (eg buying goods on credit) is a **credit**.
- A **decrease** in an **asset** (eg making a cash payment) is a **credit**.
- A **decrease** in a **liability** (eg paying a creditor) is a **debit**.

In terms of 'T' accounts:

ASSET		LIABILITY		CAPITAL	
DEBIT $	CREDIT $	DEBIT $	CREDIT $	DEBIT $	CREDIT $
Increase	Decrease	Decrease	Increase	Decrease	Increase

For income and expenses, think about profit. Profit retained in the business increases capital. Income increases profit and expenses decrease profit.

INCOME		EXPENSE	
DEBIT $	CREDIT $	DEBIT $	CREDIT $
Decrease	Increase	Increase	Decrease

Have a go at the question below before you learn about this topic in detail.

Question — Debits and credits

Complete the following table relating to the transactions of a bookshop. (The first two are done for you.)

(a) Purchase of books on credit
    (i) accounts payable increase   CREDIT   accounts payable   (increase in liability)
    (ii) purchases expense increases   DEBIT   purchases   (item of expense)

(b) Purchase of cash register
    (i) own a cash register   DEBIT   cash register   (increase in asset)
    (ii) cash at bank decreases   CREDIT   cash at bank   (decrease in asset)

(c) Payment received from a credit customer
    (i) accounts receivable decrease
    (ii) cash at bank increases

(d) Purchase of van
    (i) own a van
    (ii) cash at bank decreases

Answer

(c) Payment received from a credit customer
    (i) accounts receivable decrease   CREDIT   accounts receivable   decrease in asset
    (ii) cash at bank increases   DEBIT   cash at bank   increase in asset

(d) Purchase of van
    (i) own a van   DEBIT   van   increase in asset
    (ii) cash at bank decreases   CREDIT   cash at bank   decrease in asset

How did you get on? Students coming to the subject for the first time often have difficulty in knowing where to begin. A good starting point is the cash account, ie the nominal ledger account in which receipts and payments of cash are recorded. The rule to remember about the cash account is as follows.

(a) A cash **payment** is a **credit** entry in the cash account. Here the **asset is decreasing**. Cash may be paid out, for example, to pay an expense (such as tax) or to purchase an asset (such as a machine). The matching debit entry is therefore made in the appropriate expense or asset account.

(b) A cash **receipt** is a **debit** entry in the cash account. Here the **asset is increasing**. Cash might be received, for example, by a retailer who makes a cash sale. The credit entry would then be made in the sales account.

Key term

> **Double entry bookkeeping** is the method by which a business records financial transactions. An account is maintained for every supplier, customer, asset, liability, and income and expense. Every transaction is recorded twice so that every *debit* is balanced by a *credit*.

3.3 Example: Double entry for cash transactions

In the cash book of a business, the following transactions have been recorded.

(a) A cash sale (ie a receipt) of $250
(b) Payment of a rent bill totalling $150
(c) Buying some goods for cash at $100
(d) Buying some shelves for cash at $200

How would these four transactions be posted to the ledger accounts and to which ledger accounts should they be posted? Don't forget that each transaction will be posted twice, in accordance with the rule of double entry.

Solution

(a) The two sides of the transaction are:

   (i) Cash is received (debit entry in the cash at bank account).
   (ii) Sales increase by $250 (credit entry in the sales account).

CASH AT BANK ACCOUNT

	$		$
Sales a/c	250		

SALES ACCOUNT

	$		$
		Cash a/c	250

(Note how the entry in the cash at bank account is cross-referenced to the sales account and vice-versa. This enables a person looking at one of the accounts to trace where the other half of the double entry can be found.)

(b) The two sides of the transaction are:

   (i) Cash is paid (credit entry in the cash at bank account).
   (ii) Rent expense increases by $150 (debit entry in the rent account).

CASH AT BANK ACCOUNT

	$		$
		Rent a/c	150

RENT ACCOUNT

	$		$
Cash at bank a/c	150		

(c) The two sides of the transaction are:

    (i) Cash is paid (credit entry in the cash at bank account).
    (ii) Purchases increase by $100 (debit entry in the purchases account).

CASH AT BANK ACCOUNT

	$		$
		Purchases a/c	100

PURCHASES ACCOUNT

	$		$
Cash at bank a/c	100		

(d) The two sides of the transaction are:

    (i) Cash is paid (credit entry in the cash at bank account).
    (ii) Assets – in this case, shelves – increase by $200 (debit entry in shelves account).

CASH AT BANK ACCOUNT

	$		$
		Shelves a/c	200

SHELVES (ASSET) ACCOUNT

	$		$
Cash at bank a/c	200		

If all four of these transactions related to the same business, the cash at bank account of that business would end up looking as follows.

CASH AT BANK ACCOUNT

	$		$
Sales a/c	250	Rent a/c	150
		Purchases a/c	100
		Shelves a/c	200

3.4 Credit transactions

FAST FORWARD

Some accounts in the nominal ledger represent the total of very many smaller balances. For example, the **trade accounts receivable** account represents all the balances owed by individual customers of the business while the **trade accounts payable account** represents all money owed by the business to its suppliers.

Not all transactions are settled immediately in cash or by cheque. A business can purchase goods or non-current assets on credit terms, so that the suppliers would be trade accounts payable until settlement was made in cash. Equally, the business might grant credit terms to its customers who would then be trade accounts receivable of the business. Clearly no entries can be made in the cash book when a credit transaction occurs, because no cash has been received or paid, so where can the details of the transactions be entered?

The solution to this problem is to use **trade accounts receivable and trade accounts payable accounts**. When a business acquires goods or services on credit, the credit entry is made in an account designated 'trade accounts payable' instead of in the cash at bank account. The debit entry is made in the appropriate expense or asset account, exactly as in the case of cash transactions. Similarly, when a sale is made to a credit customer the entries made are a debit to the total trade accounts receivable account (instead of cash at bank account) and a credit to sales account.

3.5 Example: Credit transactions

Recorded in the sales day book and the purchase day book are the following transactions.

(a) The business sells goods on credit to a customer Mr A for $2,000.
(b) The business buys goods on credit from a supplier B Inc for $100.

How and where are these transactions posted in the ledger accounts?

Solution

(a)

TRADE ACCOUNTS RECEIVABLE

	$		$
Sales a/c	2,000		

SALES ACCOUNT

	$		$
		Trade accounts receivable account	2,000

(b)

TRADE ACCOUNTS PAYABLE

	$		$
		Purchases a/c	100

PURCHASES ACCOUNT

	$		$
Trade accounts payable a/c	100		

3.5.1 When cash is paid to suppliers or by customers

What happens when a credit transaction is eventually settled? Suppose that, in the example above, the business paid $100 to B Inc one month after the goods were acquired. The two sides of this new transaction are:

(a) Cash is paid (credit entry in the cash at bank account).

(b) The amount owing to trade accounts payable is reduced (debit entry in the trade accounts payable account).

CASH AT BANK ACCOUNT

	$		$
		Trade accounts payable a/c (B Inc)	100

TRADE ACCOUNTS PAYABLE

	$		$
Cash a/c	100		

If we now bring together the two parts of this example, the original purchase of goods on credit and the eventual settlement in cash, we find that the accounts appear as follows.

CASH AT BANK ACCOUNT

	$		$
		Trade accounts payable a/c	100

PURCHASES ACCOUNT

	$		$
Trade accounts payable a/c	100		

TRADE ACCOUNTS PAYABLE

	$		$
Cash at bank a/c	100	Purchases a/c	100

The two entries in trade accounts payable cancel each other out, indicating that no money is owing to suppliers any more. We are left with a credit entry of $100 in the cash at bank account and a debit entry of $100 in the purchases account. These are exactly the same as the entries used to record a **cash** purchase of $100 (compare example above). This is what we would expect: after the business has paid off its trade accounts payable, it is in exactly the same position as if it had made a cash purchase, and the accounting records reflect this similarity.

Similar reasoning applies when a customer settles his debt. In the example above when Mr A pays his debt of $2,000 the two sides of the transaction are:

(a) Cash is received (debit entry in the cash at bank account).

(b) The amount owed by trade accounts receivable is reduced (credit entry in the trade accounts receivable account).

CASH AT BANK ACCOUNT

	$		$
Trade accounts receivable a/c	2,000		

TRADE ACCOUNTS RECEIVABLE

	$		$
		Cash at bank a/c	2,000

The accounts recording this sale to, and payment by, Mr A now appear as follows.

CASH AT BANK ACCOUNT

	$		$
Trade accounts receivable a/c	2,000		

SALES ACCOUNT

	$		$
		Trade accounts receivable a/c	2,000

TRADE ACCOUNTS RECEIVABLE

	$		$
Sales a/c	2,000	Cash at bank a/c	2,000

The two entries in trade accounts receivable cancel each other out; while the entries in the cash at bank account and sales account reflect the same position as if the sale had been made for cash (see above).

Now try the following questions.

Question — Debit and credit

See if you can identify the debit and credit entries in the following transactions.

(a) Bought a machine on credit from A, cost $8,000.
(b) Bought goods on credit from B, cost $500.
(c) Sold goods on credit to C, value $1,200.
(d) Paid D (a credit supplier) $300.
(e) Collected $180 from E, a credit customer.
(f) Paid wages $4,000.
(g) Received rent bill of $700 from landlord G.
(h) Paid rent of $700 to landlord G.
(i) Paid insurance premium $90.

Answer

				$	$
(a)	DEBIT	Machine account (non-current asset)		8,000	
	CREDIT	Trade accounts payable			8,000
(b)	DEBIT	Purchases account		500	
	CREDIT	Trade accounts payable			500
(c)	DEBIT	Trade accounts receivable		1,200	
	CREDIT	Sales			1,200

			$	$
(d)	DEBIT	Trade accounts payable	300	
	CREDIT	Cash at bank		300
(e)	DEBIT	Cash at bank	180	
	CREDIT	Trade accounts receivable		180
(f)	DEBIT	Wages account	4,000	
	CREDIT	Cash at bank		4,000
(g)	DEBIT	Rent account	700	
	CREDIT	Trade accounts payable		700
(h)	DEBIT	Trade accounts payable	700	
	CREDIT	Cash at bank		700
(i)	DEBIT	Insurance costs	90	
	CREDIT	Cash at bank		90

Question — Ledger entries

See now whether you can record the ledger entries for the following transactions. Ron Knuckle set up a business selling keep fit equipment, trading under the name of Buy Your Biceps Shop. He put $7,000 of his own money into a business bank account (transaction A) and in his first period of trading, the following transactions occurred.

		$
Transaction		
B	Paid rent of shop for the period	3,500
C	Purchased equipment (inventories) on credit	5,000
D	Raised loan from bank	1,000
E	Purchase of shop fittings (for cash)	2,000
F	Sales of equipment: cash	10,000
G	Sales of equipment: on credit	2,500
H	Payments for trade accounts payable	5,000
I	Payments from trade accounts receivable	2,500
J	Interest on loan (paid)	100
K	Other expenses (all paid in cash)	1,900
L	Drawings	1,500

Try to do as much of this question as you can by yourself before reading the solution.

Answer

Clearly, there should be an account for cash at bank, trade accounts receivable, trade accounts payable, purchases, a shop fittings account, sales, a loan account and a proprietor's capital account. It is also useful to keep a separate account for **drawings** until the end of each accounting period. Other accounts should be set up as they seem appropriate and in this exercise, accounts for rent, bank interest and other expenses would seem appropriate.

It has been suggested to you that the cash at bank account is a good place to start, if possible. You should notice that cash transactions include the initial input of capital by Ron Knuckle, subsequent drawings, the payment of rent, the loan from the bank, the interest, some cash sales and cash purchases, and payments for trade accounts payable and from trade accounts receivable. (The transactions are identified below by their reference, to help you to find them.)

PART C DOUBLE ENTRY BOOKKEEPING AND ACCOUNTING SYSTEMS

CASH AT BANK

	$		$
Capital – Ron Knuckle (A)	7,000	Rent (B)	3,500
Bank loan (D)	1,000	Shop fittings (E)	2,000
Sales (F)	10,000	Trade trade accounts payable (H)	5,000
Trade accounts receivable (I)	2,500	Bank loan interest (J)	100
		Other expenses (K)	1,900
		Drawings (L)	1,500
			14,000
		Balancing figure – the amount of cash left over after payments have been made	
			6,500
	20,500		20,500

CAPITAL (RON KNUCKLE)

	$		$
		Cash at bank (A)	7,000

BANK LOAN

	$		$
		Cash at bank (D)	1,000

PURCHASES

	$		$
Trade accounts payable (C)	5,000		

TRADE ACCOUNTS PAYABLE

	$		$
Cash at bank (H)	5,000	Purchases (C)	5,000

RENT

	$		$
Cash at bank (B)	3,500		

NON-CURRENT ASSETS

	$		$
Cash at bank (E)	2,000		

SALES

	$		$
		Cash at bank (F)	10,000
		Trade accounts receivable (G)	2,500
			12,500

TRADE ACCOUNTS RECEIVABLE

	$		$
Sales (G)	2,500	Cash at bank (I)	2,500

BANK LOAN INTEREST

	$		$
Cash at bank (J)	100		

OTHER EXPENSES

	$		$
Cash at bank (K)	1,900		

DRAWINGS ACCOUNT

	$		$
Cash at bank (L)	1,500		

(a) If you want to make sure that this solution is complete, you should go through the transactions A to L and tick off each of them twice in the ledger accounts, once as a debit and once as a credit. When you have finished, all transactions in the 'T' account should be ticked, with only totals left over.

(b) In fact, there is an easier way to check that the solution to this sort of problem does 'balance' properly, which we will meet in the next chapter.

(c) On asset and liability accounts, the debit or credit balance represents the amount of the asset or liability outstanding at the period end. For example, on the cash at bank account, debits exceed credits by $6,500 and so there is a debit balance of cash in hand of $6,500. On the capital account, there is a credit balance of $7,000 and so the business owes Ron $7,000.

(d) The balances on the revenue and expense accounts represent the total of each revenue or expense for the period. For example, sales for the period total $12,500.

4 The journal

FAST FORWARD

The **journal** is the record of original entry for transactions which are not recorded in any of the other books of original entry.

You should remember that one of the books of original entry was the **journal**.

Key term

The **journal** keeps a record of unusual movement between accounts. It is used to record any double entries made which do not arise from the other books of original entry. For example, journal entries are made when errors are discovered and need to be corrected.

Whatever type of transaction is being recorded, the **format of a journal entry** is:

Date	Debit	Credit
	$	$
Account to be debited	X	
Account to be credited		X
(Narrative to explain the transaction)		

(Remember: in due course, the ledger accounts will be written up to include the transactions listed in the journal.)

PART C DOUBLE ENTRY BOOKKEEPING AND ACCOUNTING SYSTEMS

A **narrative explanation** must accompany each journal entry. It is required for audit and control, to indicate the purpose and authority of every transaction which is not first recorded in a book of original entry.

> **Exam focus point**
>
> An examination question might ask you to 'journalise' transactions which would not in practice be recorded in the journal at all. If you are faced with such a problem, you should simply record the debit and credit entries for every transaction you can recognise, giving some supporting narrative to each transaction.

4.1 Examples: Journal entries

The following is a summary of the transactions of Hair by Fiona Middleton hairdressing business of which Fiona is the sole proprietor.

1 January	Put in cash of $2,000 as capital
	Purchased brushes and combs for cash $50
	Purchased hair driers from Gilroy Ltd on credit $150
30 January	Paid three months rent to 31 March $300
	Collected and paid in takings $600
31 January	Gave Mrs Sullivan a perm, highlights etc on credit $80

Show the transactions by means of journal entries.

Solution

JOURNAL

			$	$
1 January	DEBIT	Cash at bank	2,000	
	CREDIT	Fiona Middleton – capital account		2,000
	Initial capital introduced			
1 January	DEBIT	Brushes and combs account	50	
	CREDIT	Cash at bank		50
	The purchase for cash of brushes and combs as non-current assets			
1 January	DEBIT	Hair dryer account	150	
	CREDIT	Sundry accounts payable *		150
	The purchase on credit of hair driers as non-current assets			
30 January	DEBIT	Rent account	300	
	CREDIT	Cash at bank		300
	The payment of rent to 31 March			
30 January	DEBIT	Cash at bank	600	
	CREDIT	Sales account		600
	Cash takings			
31 January	DEBIT	Trade accounts receivable	80	
	CREDIT	Sales account		80
	The provision of a hair-do on credit			

* *Note.* Suppliers who have supplied non-current assets are included amongst sundry accounts payable, as distinct from trade suppliers (who have supplied raw materials or goods for resale) who are trade accounts payable. It is quite common to have separate 'total accounts payable' accounts, one for trade accounts payable and another for sundry other accounts payable.

4.2 The correction of errors

The journal is most commonly used to record corrections to errors that have been made in writing up the nominal ledger accounts. Errors corrected by the journal must be **capable of correction by means of a double entry** in the ledger accounts. In other words the error must not have caused total debits and total credits to be unequal.

Special rules, covered in a later chapter, apply when errors are made which break the rule of double entry.

5 Day book analysis

FAST FORWARD

> Entries in the daybooks are totalled and analysed before posting to the nominal ledger.

In the previous chapter, we used the following example of four transactions entered into the sales day book.

SALES DAY BOOK

Date 20X0	Invoice	Customer	Total amount invoiced $	Boot sales $	Shoe sales
Jan 10	247	Jones & Co	105.00	60.00	45.00
	248	Smith Ltd	86.40	86.40	
	249	Alex & Co	31.80		31.80
	250	Enor College	1,264.60	800.30	464.30
			1,487.80	946.70	541.10

We have already seen that in theory these transactions are posted to the ledger accounts as follows.

DEBIT	Trade accounts receivable	$1,487.80	
CREDIT	Sales account		$1,487.80

However a total sales account is not very informative, particularly if the business sells lots of different products. So, using our example, the business might open up a 'sale of shoes' account and a 'sale of boots' account. Then the ledger account postings are:

		$	$
DEBIT	Trade accounts receivable	1,487.80	
CREDIT	Sale of shoes account		541.10
	Sale of boots account		946.70

That is why the analysis of sales is kept. Exactly the same reasoning lies behind the analyses kept in the other books of original entry.

6 The imprest system

FAST FORWARD

> In the last chapter, we saw how the petty cash book was used to operate the imprest system. It is now time to see how the **double entry** works.

A business starts with a cash float on 1.3.20X7 of $250. This will be a payment from cash at bank to petty cash, ie:

DEBIT	Petty cash	$250	
CREDIT	Cash at bank		$250

PART C DOUBLE ENTRY BOOKKEEPING AND ACCOUNTING SYSTEMS

Five payments were made out of petty cash during March 20X7. The petty cash book might look as follows.

Receipts $	Date	Narrative	Total $	Payments Postage $	Travel $
250.00	1.3.X7	Cash			
	2.3.X7	Stamps	12.00	12.00	
	8.3.X7	Stamps	10.00	10.00	
	19.3.X7	Travel	16.00		16.00
	23.3.X7	Travel	5.00		5.00
	28.3.X7	Stamps	11.50	11.50	
250.00			54.50	33.50	21.00

At the end of each month (or at any other suitable interval) the total payments in the petty cash book are **posted** to ledger accounts. For March 20X7, $33.50 would be debited to postage account and $21.00 to travel account. The total payments of $54.50 are credited to the petty cash account. This completes the double entry.

The cash float needs to be topped up by a payment of $54.50 from the main cash book, ie:

		$	$
DEBIT	Petty cash	54.50	
CREDIT	Cash		54.50

So the rules of double entry have been satisfied, and the petty cash book for the month of March 20X7 will look like this.

Receipts $	Date	Narrative	Total $	Payments Postage $	Travel $
250.00	1.3.X7	Cash			
	2.3.X7	Stamps	12.00	12.00	
	8.3.X7	Stamps	10.00	10.00	
	19.3.X7	Travel	16.00		16.00
	23.3.X7	Travel	5.00		5.00
	28.3.X7	Stamps	11.50	11.50	
	31.3.X7	Balance c/d	195.50		
250.00			250.00	33.50	21.00
195.50	1.4.X7	Balance b/d			
54.50	1.4.X7	Cash			

As you can see, the cash float is back up to $250 on 1.4.X7, ready for more payments to be made.

The petty cash account in the ledger will appear as follows.

PETTY CASH

			$				$
1.3.20X7	Cash		250.00	31.3.20X7	Payments		54.50
1.4.20X7	Cash		54.50	1.4.20X7	Balance c/d		250.00
			304.50				304.50
1.4.20X7	Balance b/d		250.00				

Question
Petty cash

Summit Glazing operates an imprest petty cash system. The imprest amount is $150.00. At the end of the period the totals of the four analysis columns in the petty cash book were as follows.

	$
Column 1	23.12
Column 2	6.74
Column 3	12.90
Column 4	28.50

How much cash is required to restore the imprest amount?

Answer

$71.26. This is the total amount of cash that has been used.

7 The receivables and payables ledgers

FAST FORWARD

The receivables and payables ledgers contain the **personal accounts** of individual customers and suppliers. They do not normally form part of the double-entry system.

7.1 Impersonal accounts and personal accounts

The accounts in the nominal ledger (ledger accounts) relate to types of income, expense, asset, liability – rent, sales, trade receivables, payables etc – rather than to the person to whom the money is paid or from whom it is received. They are therefore called **impersonal** accounts. However, there is also a need for **personal** accounts, most commonly for receivables and payables, and these are contained in the receivables ledger and payables ledger.

7.2 The receivables ledger

The sales day book provides a chronological record of invoices sent out by a business to credit customers. For many businesses, this might involve very large numbers of invoices per day or per week. The same customer might appear in several different places in the sales day book, for sales made on credit at different times. So a customer may owe money on several unpaid invoices.

In addition to keeping a chronological record of invoices, a business should also keep a record of how much money each individual credit customer owes, and what this total debt consists of. The need for a **personal account for each customer** is a practical one.

(a) A customer might telephone, and ask how much he currently owes. Staff must be able to tell him.

(b) It is a common practice to send out statements to credit customers at the end of each month, showing how much they still owe, and itemising new invoices sent out and payments received during the month.

(c) The managers of the business will want to keep a check on the credit position of an individual customer, and to ensure that no customer is exceeding his credit limit by purchasing more goods.

(d) Most important is the need to match payments received against debts owed. If a customer makes a payment, the business must be able to set off the payment against the customer's debt and establish how much he still owes on balance.

Key term

> The **receivables ledger** is a ledger for customers' personal accounts.

Receivables ledger accounts are written up as follows.

(a) When entries are made in the sales day book (invoices sent out), they are subsequently also made in the **debit side** of the relevant customer account in the receivables ledger.

(b) Similarly, when entries are made in the cash book (payments received), or in the sales returns day book, they are also made in the **credit side** of the relevant customer account.

Each customer account is given a reference or code number, and it is that reference which appears in the **sales day book**. We say that amounts are **posted** from the sales day book to the receivables ledger.

Here is an example of how a receivables ledger account is laid out.

ENOR COLLEGE

A/c no: RL 9

	$		$
Balance b/f	250.00		
10.1.X0 Sales – SDB 48			
(invoice no 250)	1,264.60	Balance c/d	1,514.60
	1,514.60		1,514.60
11.1.X0 Balance b/d	1,514.60		

The debit side of this personal account, then, shows amounts owed by Enor College. When Enor pays some of the money it owes it will be entered into the cash book (receipts) and subsequently 'posted' to the credit side of the personal account. For example, if the college paid $250 on 10.1.20X0, it would appear as follows.

ENOR COLLEGE

A/c no: RL 9

	$			$
Balance b/f	250.00	10.1.X0	Cash	250.00
10.1.X0 Sales – SDB 48				
(invoice no 250)	1,264.60	Balance c/d		1,264.60
	1,514.60			1,514.60
11.1.X0 Balance b/d	1,264.60			

The opening balance owed by Enor College on 11.1.X0 is now $1,264.60 instead of $1,514.60, because of the $250 receipt which came in on 10.1.X0.

7.3 The payables ledger

The payables ledger, like the receivables ledger, consists of a number of personal accounts. These are separate accounts for **each individual supplier**, and they enable a business to keep a continuous record of how much it owes each supplier at any time.

Key term

> The **payables ledger** is a ledger for suppliers' personal accounts.

After entries are made in the purchase day book, cash book, or purchase returns day book – ie after entries are made in the books of prime entry – they are also made in the relevant supplier account in the payables ledger. Again we say that the entries in the purchase day book are **posted** to the suppliers' personal accounts in the payables ledger.

Here is an example of how a payables ledger account is laid out.

COOK & CO

A/c no: PL 31

	$		$
Balance c/d	515.00	Balance b/f	200.00
		15 Mar 20X8	
		Invoice received	
		PDB 37	315.00
	515.00		515.00
		16 March 20X8	
		Balance b/d	515.00

The credit side of this personal account, then, shows amounts owing to Cook & Co. If the business paid Cook & Co some money, it would be entered into the cash book (payments) and subsequently be posted to the debit side of the personal account. For example, if the business paid Cook & Co $100 on 15 March 20X8, it would appear as follows:

COOK & CO

A/c no: PL 31

		$			$
15.3.X8	Cash	100.00		Balance b/f	200.00
			15.3.X8	Invoice received	
	Balance c/d	415.00		PDB 37	315.00
		515.00			515.00
			16.3.X8	Balance b/d	415.00

The opening balance owed to Cook & Co on 16.3.X8 is now $415.00 instead of $515.00 because of the $100 payment made during 15.3.X8.

8 Accounting for a sales tax

FAST FORWARD

> The business acts as a **collector** of sales tax and so **recoverable amounts** must be excluded from revenue and expenses.

A sales tax is a tax on the supply of goods and services (for example: VAT in the UK, TVA in France). **Tax is collected at each transfer point in the chain from prime producer to final consumer**. Eventually, the consumer bears the tax in full and any tax paid earlier in the chain can be recovered by the trader who paid it.

8.1 Example: Sales tax

A manufacturing company, A Inc, purchases raw materials at a cost of $1,000 plus sales tax at 17½%. From the raw materials A Inc makes finished products which it sells to a retail outlet, B Inc, for $1,600 plus sales tax. B Inc sells the products to customers at a total price of $2,000 plus sales tax. How much sales tax is paid at each stage in the chain?

Solution

	Value of goods sold $	Sales tax at 17½% $
Supplier of raw materials	1,000	175
Value added by A Inc	600	105
Sale to B Inc	1,600	280
Value added by B Inc	400	70
Sales to 'consumers'	2,000	350

8.2 How is a sales tax collected?

Although it is the final consumer who eventually bears the full tax of $350, the sum is **collected and paid by the traders who make up the chain.** Each trader must assume that his customer is the final consumer and must collect and pay over sales tax at the appropriate rate on the full sales value of the goods sold. He is entitled to reclaim sales tax paid on his own purchases and so makes a net payment to the tax authorities equal to the tax on value added by himself.

In the example above, the supplier of raw materials collects from A Inc sales tax of $175, all of which he pays over to the tax authorities. When A Inc sells goods to B Inc, sales tax is charged at the rate of 17½% on $1,600 = $280. Only $105, however, is paid by A Inc to the tax authorities, because the company is entitled to deduct sales tax of $175 suffered on its own purchases. Similarly, B Inc must charge its customers $350 in sales tax, but need only pay over the net amount of $70 after deducting the $280 sales tax suffered on its purchase from A Inc.

8.3 Registered and non-registered persons

Traders whose sales (outputs) are below a certain minimum need not register for sales tax. Such traders neither charge sales tax on their outputs nor are entitled to reclaim sales tax on their inputs (purchases). They are in the same position as a final consumer.

All outputs of registered traders are either taxable or exempt. Traders carrying on exempt activities (such as banks) cannot charge sales tax on their outputs and consequently cannot reclaim sales tax paid on their inputs.

Taxable outputs are usually chargeable at one of **two rates**.

(a) **Lower rate** (which can be zero in the UK)
(b) **Standard rate**

The tax authorities publish lists of supplies falling into each category. **Persons carrying on taxable activities** (even activities taxable at zero per cent) **are entitled to reclaim sales tax paid on their inputs.**

Some traders carry on a **mixture of taxable and exempt activities**. Such traders need to apportion the sales tax suffered on inputs and **can only reclaim the proportion relating to taxable outputs.**

8.4 Accounting for a sales tax

As a general principle the treatment of a sales tax in the accounts of a trader should reflect his role as a collector of the tax and **sales tax should not be included in income or in expenditure whether of a capital or of a revenue nature.**

8.4.1 Irrecoverable sales tax

Where the **trader bears the sales tax** himself, as in the following cases, this should be reflected in the accounts.

(a) **Persons not registered** for sales tax will suffer sales tax on inputs. This will effectively increase the cost of their expenses and their non-current assets and must be so reflected, ie shown **inclusive of sales tax.**

(b) **Registered persons** who also carry on **exempted** activities will have a residue of sales tax which falls directly on them. In this situation the costs to which this residue applies will be inflated by the **irrecoverable sales tax**.

(c) **Non-deductible inputs will be borne** by all traders (examples in the UK are tax on cars bought which are not for resale, entertaining expenses and provision of domestic accommodation for a company's directors).

Exam focus point

> Where a sales tax is not recoverable it must be regarded as an inherent part of the cost of the items purchased and included in the income statement or balance sheet as appropriate.

8.5 Further points

Sales tax is charged on the price net of any discount and this general principle is carried to the extent that where a cash discount is offered, sales tax is charged on the net amount **even where the discount is not taken up.**

Most registered persons are obliged to record a sales tax when a supply is received or made (effectively when a credit sales invoice is raised or a purchase invoice recorded). This has the effect that **the net sales tax liability has on occasion to be paid to the tax authorities before all output tax has been paid by customers**. If a debt is subsequently written off, the sales tax element may not be recoverable from the tax authorities for sometime after the sale, even if the customer becomes insolvent.

8.6 Summary of accounting entries

(a) **Sales revenue** shown in the income statement must **exclude sales tax** on taxable outputs. However trade accounts receivable will **include** sales tax, as it must reflect the total amount due from a customer.

Example of the double entry involved is:

		$	$
DEBIT	Trade account receivable (gross)	587,500	
CREDIT	Sales (net)		500,000
	Sales tax a/c		87,500

(b) **Expenses** shown in the income statement must **exclude recoverable sales tax** on taxable inputs. However any accounts payable will **include** sales tax, as it must reflect the total amount payable. See the following example.

		$	$
DEBIT	Purchases	400	
	Sales tax a/c	70	
CREDIT	Trade accounts payable		470

(c) **Irrecoverable sales tax** allocated to expenses or non-current assets must be **included in their cost** in the income statement or balance sheet.

(d) The net amount due to (or from) the tax authorities should be included in other payables (or receivables) in the balance sheet.

Question — Sales tax

Mussel Inc is preparing accounts for the year ended 31 May 20X9. Included in its balance sheet as at 31 May 20X8 was a balance for sales tax recoverable of $15,000.

Its summary income statement for the year is as follows.

	$'000
Sales (all standard rated)	500
Purchases (all standard rated)	120
Gross profit	380
Expenses	280
Operating profit	100
Interest receivable	20
Profit before tax	120

Note: expenses	$000
Wages and salaries (exempt)	200
Entertainment expenditure (irrecoverable)	10
Other (all standard rated)	70
	280

Payments of $5,000, $15,000 and $20,000 have been made in the year and a repayment of $12,000 was received. What is the balance for sales tax in the balance sheet as at 31 May 20X9? Assume a 17.5% standard rate of sales tax.

Answer

	$		$
Balance b/d	15,000	Sales ($500,000 × 17.5%)	87,500
Purchases ($120,000 × 17.5%)	21,000	Bank	12,000
Expenses ($70,000 × 17.5%)	12,250		
Bank	40,000		
Balance c/d	11,250		
	99,500		99,500

Therefore there is a balance **owing to** the tax authorities of $11,250, which is shown on the balance sheet as a **current liability.**

8.7 Sales tax in the cash book, sales day book and purchase day book

When a business makes a credit sale, the total amount invoiced, including sales tax, will be recorded in the sales day book. The analysis columns will then separate out the sales tax as follows.

Date	Narrative	Total	Sales income	Sales tax
		$	$	$
20.02.X0	A Detter and Sons	235	200	35

A similar analysis will appear in the purchase day book.

When a trade account receivable pays what is due, there is **no need to show the sales tax** in the cash book. This is because it has already been accounted for at the time of sale (see 8.14 (a) above). Similarly sales tax is not recorded when trade accounts payable are paid.

However any **cash sales or expenses** will have to be analysed into sales tax in the cash book. This is because the sales tax has only just arisen from the cash transaction.

Examples of the receipts and payments sides of a cash book follow.

CASH BOOK (RECEIPTS)

Date	Narrative	Total	Receivables ledger	Cash sales	Sales tax on cash sales
		$	$	$	$
20.02.X0	A Detter & Sons	235	235		
	Owen & Co	660	660		
	Cash sales	329		280	49
	Newgate Merchants	184	184		
	Cash sales	94		80	14
		1,502	1,079	360	63

CASH BOOK (PAYMENTS)

Date	Narrative	Total	Payables ledger	Cash purchases and sundries	Sales tax on cash purchases
		$	$	$	$
20.02.X0	A Splier	188	188		
	Telephone bill paid	141		120	21
	Stationery (cash purchase)	47		40	7
	Sales tax paid to tax authorities	1,400		1,400	
		1,776	188	1,560	28

Chapter Roundup

- Ledger accounts **summarise** all the individual transactions listed in the books of original entry.
- **Double entry bookkeeping** is based on the idea that each transaction has an equal but opposite effect.
- Every accounting event must be entered in ledger accounts both as a debit and as an equal but opposite credit. The principal accounts are contained in a ledger called the **nominal ledger**.
- **Debits and credits** are defined as follows.
    - Debit
        - ↑ increase in asset
        - ↓ decrease in liability
        - ↑ increase in expense
    - Credit
        - ↑ increase in liability
        - ↓ decrease in asset
        - ↑ increase in income
- The **journal** is the record of original entry for transactions which are not recorded in any of the other books of original entry.
- Some accounts in the nominal ledger represent the total of very many smaller balances. For example, the **trade accounts receivable account** represents all the balances owed by individual customers of the business, while the **trade accounts payable account** represents all amounts owed by the business to its suppliers.
- Entries in the daybooks are totalled and analysed before posting to the nominal ledger.
- The receivables and payables ledgers contain the **personal accounts** of individual customers and suppliers. They do not normally form part of the double-entry system.

Quick Quiz

1 Give six examples of nominal ledger accounts.

2 What is the double entry to record a cash sale of $50?

3 What is the double entry to record a purchase of office chairs for $1,000?

4 What is the double entry to record a credit sale of $500 + sales tax of $50?

5 Name one reason for making a journal entry.

6 Individual customer accounts are kept in which ledger?

    A   General ledger
    B   Trade accounts receivable
    C   Receivables ledger
    D   Nominal ledger

Answers to Quick Quiz

1 See Section 2.

2

		$	$
DEBIT	Cash a/c	50	
CREDIT	Sales a/c		50

3

		$	$
DEBIT	Non-current assets a/c	1,000	
CREDIT	Cash a/c		1,000

4

		$	$
DEBIT	Accounts receivable a/c	550	
CREDIT	Sales a/c		500
	Sales tax a/c		50

5 Most commonly to correct an error, although it can be used to make any entry that is not recorded in a book of original entry (eg prepayments, accrued expenses, depreciation).

6 C   The receivables ledger contains the individual customer accounts. The general ledger (A) and nominal ledger (D) are different names for the same ledger. This contains the trade accounts receivable account (B) which is the **total** of all the individual customer accounts.

Now try the questions below from the Exam Question Bank

Number	Level	Marks	Time
Q6	Examination	10	18 mins
Q7	Examination	10	18 mins

PART C   DOUBLE ENTRY BOOKKEEPING AND ACCOUNTING SYSTEMS

From trial balance to financial statements

Topic list	Syllabus reference
1 The trial balance	3(a)
2 The income statement	5(c)
3 The balance sheet	5(c)
4 Balancing accounts and preparing financial statements	3(a)

Introduction

In the previous chapter you learned the principles of double entry and how to post to the ledger accounts. The next step in our progress towards the financial statements is the **trial balance**.

Before transferring the relevant balances at the year end to the income statement and putting closing balances carried forward into the balance sheet, it is usual to test the accuracy of double entry bookkeeping records by preparing **a list of account balances**. This is done by taking all the balances on every account; because of the self-balancing nature of the system of double entry, **the total of the debit balances will be exactly equal to the total of the credit balances.**

In very straightforward circumstances, where no complications arise and where the records are complete, it is possible to prepare accounts directly from a trial balance. This is covered in Section 4.

PART C DOUBLE ENTRY BOOKKEEPING AND ACCOUNTING SYSTEMS

Study guide

Section 3-4 – Bookkeeping principles

- Extract the ledger balances into a trial balance.
- Prepare a simple income statement and balance sheet from a trial balance.
- Explain and illustrate the process of closing the ledger accounts in the accounting records when the financial statements have been completed.

Exam guide

Exam questions at all levels in financial accounting can involve preparation of final accounts from a trial balance. Last but not least, you may end up having to do it in 'real life'.

1 The trial balance

FAST FORWARD

At suitable intervals, the entries in each ledger account are totalled and a **balance** is struck. Balances are usually collected in a **trial balance** which is then used as a basis for preparing an income statement and a balance sheet.

You have a list of transactions, and have been asked to post them to the relevant ledger accounts. You do it as quickly as possible and find that you have a little time left over at the end of the day. How do you check that you have posted all the debit and credit entries properly?

There is no foolproof method, but a technique which shows up the more obvious mistakes is to prepare a **trial balance.**

Key term

A **trial balance** is a list of ledger balances shown in debit and credit columns. It can also be called a **list of account balances.**

1.1 The first step

Before you draw up a list of account balances, you must have a collection of ledger accounts. For the sake of convenience, we will use the accounts of Ron Knuckle, which we drew up in the previous chapter.

CASH AT BANK

	$		$
Capital: Ron Knuckle (A)	7,000	Rent	3,500
Bank loan	1,000	Shop fittings	2,000
Sales	10,000	Trade accounts payable	5,000
Trade accounts receivable	2,500	Bank loan interest	100
		Other expenses	1,900
		Drawings	1,500
			14,000
		Balancing figure – the amount of cash left over after payments have been made	6,500
	20,500		20,500

CAPITAL (RON KNUCKLE)

	$		$
		Cash at bank	7,000

BANK LOAN

	$		$
		Cash at bank	1,000

PURCHASES

	$		$
Trade accounts payable	5,000		

TRADE ACCOUNTS PAYABLE

	$		$
Cash at bank	5,000	Purchases	5,000

RENT

	$		$
Cash at bank	3,500		

SHOP FITTINGS

	$		$
Cash at bank	2,000		

SALES

	$		$
		Cash at bank	10,000
		Trade accounts receivable	2,500
			12,500

TRADE ACCOUNTS RECEIVABLE

	$		$
Sales	2,500	Cash at bank	2,500

BANK LOAN INTEREST

	$		$
Cash at bank	100		

OTHER EXPENSES

	$		$
Cash at bank	1,900		

DRAWINGS

	$		$
Cash at bank	1,500		

The next step is to 'balance' each account.

PART C DOUBLE ENTRY BOOKKEEPING AND ACCOUNTING SYSTEMS

1.2 Balancing ledger accounts

At the end of an accounting period, a balance is struck on each account in turn. This means that all the debits on the account are totalled and so are all the credits. **If the total debits exceed the total credits there is said to be a debit balance on the account; if the credits exceed the debits then the account has a credit balance.**

In our simple example, there is very little balancing to do.

(a) Both the trade accounts payable and the trade accounts receivable balance off to zero.
(b) The cash at bank account has a debit balance of $6,500.
(c) The total on the sales account is $12,500, which is a credit balance.

Otherwise, the accounts have only one entry each, so there is no totalling to do to arrive at the balance on each account.

1.3 Collecting the balances

If the basic principle of double entry has been correctly applied throughout the period it will be found that the credit balances equal the debit balances in total. This can be illustrated by collecting together the balances on Ron Knuckle's accounts.

	Debit $	Credit $
Cash at bank	6,500	
Capital		7,000
Bank loan		1,000
Purchases	5,000	
Trade accounts payable		
Rent	3,500	
Shop fittings	2,000	
Sales		12,500
Trade accounts receivable		
Bank loan interest	100	
Other expenses	1,900	
Drawings	1,500	
	20,500	20,500

This is called a **trial balance**. It does not matter in what order the various accounts are listed. It is just a method used to test the accuracy of the double entry bookkeeping.

1.4 What if the trial balance shows unequal debit and credit balances?

FAST FORWARD

A trial balance can be used to test the accuracy of the accounting records. It lists the balances on ledger accounts and totals them. Total debits should equal total credits.

If the two columns of the list are not equal, there must be an error in recording the transactions in the accounts. A list of account balances, however, will **not** disclose the following types of errors.

(a) The **complete omission** of a transaction, because neither a debit nor a credit is made.

(b) The posting of a debit or credit to the correct side of the ledger, but to a **wrong account**.

(c) **Compensating errors** (eg an error of $100 is exactly cancelled by another $100 error elsewhere).

(d) **Errors of principle**, eg cash from debtors being debited to trade accounts receivable and credited to cash at bank instead of the other way round.

6: FROM TRIAL BALANCE TO FINANCIAL STATEMENTS

1.5 Example: Trial balance

As at 30.3.20X7, your business has the following balances on its ledger accounts.

Accounts	Balance $
Bank loan	12,000
Cash at bank	11,700
Capital	13,000
Local business taxes	1,880
Trade accounts payable	11,200
Purchases	12,400
Sales	14,600
Sundry payables	1,620
Trade accounts receivable	12,000
Bank loan interest	1,400
Other expenses	11,020
Vehicles	2,020

During the year the business made the following transactions.

(a) Bought materials for $1,000, half for cash and half on credit
(b) Made $1,040 sales, $800 of which was for credit
(c) Paid wages to shop assistants of $260 in cash

You are required to draw up a trial balance showing the balances as at the end of 31.3.X7.

Solution

First it is necessary to decide which of the original balances are debits and which are credits.

Account	Dr $	Cr $
Bank loan		12,000
Cash at bank	11,700	
Capital		13,000
Local taxes	1,880	
Trade accounts payable		11,200
Purchases	12,400	
Sales		14,600
Sundry payables		1,620
Trade accounts receivable	12,000	
Bank loan interest	1,400	
Other expenses	11,020	
Vehicles	2,020	
	52,420	52,420

Now we must take account of the effects of the three transactions which took place on 31.3.X7.

			$	$
(a)	DEBIT	Purchases	1,000	
	CREDIT	Cash at bank		500
		Trade accounts payable		500
(b)	DEBIT	Cash at bank	240	
	-+	Trade accounts receivable	800	
	CREDIT	Sales		1,040

PART C DOUBLE ENTRY BOOKKEEPING AND ACCOUNTING SYSTEMS

				$	$
(c)	DEBIT	Other expenses		260	
	CREDIT	Cash at bank			260

When these figures are included in the trial balance, it becomes:

Account	Dr $	Cr $
Bank loan		12,000
Cash at bank (11,700 + 240 – 500 – 260)	11,180	
Capital		13,000
Local taxes	1,880	
Trade accounts payable		11,700
Purchases	13,400	
Sales		15,640
Sundry creditors		1,620
Trade accounts receivable	12,800	
Bank loan interest	1,400	
Other expenses	11,280	
Vehicles	2,020	
	53,960	53,960

2 The income statement

FAST FORWARD

> An **income and expense** ledger account is opened up to gather all items relating to income and expenses. When rearranged, these items make up the **income statement**.

The first step in the process of preparing the financial statements is to open up another ledger account, called the **income and expense account**. In it a business summarises its results for the period by gathering together all the ledger account balances relating to the income statement. This account is still part of the double entry system, so the basic rule of double entry still applies: every debit must have an equal and opposite credit entry.

This income and expense account contains the same information as the financial statement we are aiming for, ie the income statement, and in fact there are very few differences between the two. However, the income statement lays the information out differently and it may be much less detailed.

So what do we do with this new ledger account? The first step is to look through the ledger accounts and identify which ones relate to income and expenses. In the case of Ron Knuckle, these accounts consist of purchases, rent, sales, bank loan interest, and other expenses.

The balances on these accounts are transferred to the new income and expense account. For example, the balance on the purchases account is $5,000 DR. To balance this to zero, we write in $5,000 CR. But to comply with the rule of double entry, there has to be a debit entry somewhere, so we write $5,000 DR in the income and expense (I & E) account. Now the balance on the purchases account has been moved to the income and expense account.

If we do the same thing with all the separate accounts of Ron Knuckle dealing with income and expenses, the result is as follows.

PURCHASES

	$		$
Trade account payables	5,000	I & E a/c	5,000

RENT

	$		$
Cash at bank	3,500	I & E a/c	3,500

SALES

	$		$
I & E a/c	12,500	Cash at bank	10,000
		Trade accounts receivable	2,500
	12,500		12,500

BANK LOAN INTEREST

	$		$
Cash at bank	100	I & E a/c	100

OTHER EXPENSES

	$		$
Cash at bank	1,900	I & E a/c	1,900

INCOME AND EXPENSE ACCOUNT

	$		$
Purchases	5,000	Sales	12,500
Rent	3,500		
Bank loan interest	100		
Other expenses	1,900		

(Note that the income and expense account has not yet been balanced off but we will return to that later.)

If you look at the items we have gathered together in the income and expense account, they should strike a chord in your memory. They are the same items that we need to draw up the income statement.

Question — Income statement

Draw up Ron Knuckle's income statement.

Answer

RON KNUCKLE: INCOME STATEMENT

	$	$
Sales		12,500
Cost of sales (= purchases in this case)		(5,000)
Gross profit		7,500
Expenses		
Rent	3,500	
Bank loan interest	100	
Other expenses	1,900	
		(5,500)
Net profit		2,000

PART C DOUBLE ENTRY BOOKKEEPING AND ACCOUNTING SYSTEMS

3 The balance sheet

FAST FORWARD

The balances on all remaining ledger accounts (including the income and expense account) can be listed and rearranged to form the **balance sheet**.

Look back at the ledger accounts of Ron Knuckle. Now that we have dealt with those relating to income and expenses, which ones are left? The answer is that we still have to find out what to do with the cash, capital, bank loan, trade accounts payable, shop fittings, trade accounts receivable and the drawings accounts.

Are these the only ledger accounts left? No: don't forget there is still the last one we opened up, called the **income and expense account**. The balance on this account represents the profit earned by the business, and if you go through the arithmetic, you will find that it has a credit balance – a profit – of $2,000. (Not surprisingly, this is the figure that is shown in the income statement.)

These remaining accounts must also be balanced and ruled off, but since they represent assets and liabilities of the business (not income and expenses) their balances are not transferred to the income and expense account. Instead they are *carried down* in the books of the business. This means that they become opening balances for the next accounting period and indicate the value of the assets and liabilities at the end of one period and the beginning of the next.

The conventional method of ruling off a ledger account at the end of an accounting period is illustrated by the bank loan account in Ron Knuckle's books.

BANK LOAN ACCOUNT

	$		$
Balance carried down (c/d)	1,000	Cash (D)	1,000
		Balance brought down (b/d)	1,000

Ron Knuckle therefore begins the new accounting period with a credit balance of $1,000 on this account. A **credit balance brought down** denotes a liability. An asset would be represented by a **debit balance brought down**.

One further point is worth noting before we move on to complete this example. You will remember that a proprietor's capital comprises any cash introduced by him, plus any profits made by the business, less any drawings made by him. At the stage we have now reached, these three elements are contained in different ledger accounts: cash introduced of $7,000 appears in the capital account; drawings of $1,500 appear in drawings; and the profit made by the business is represented by the $2,000 credit balance on the income and expense account. It is convenient to gather together all these amounts into one **capital account**, in the same way as we earlier gathered together income and expense accounts into one income and expense account.

If we go ahead and gather the three amounts together, the results are as follows.

DRAWINGS

	$		$
Cash at bank	1,500	Capital a/c	1,500

INCOME AND EXPENSE ACCOUNT

	$		$
Purchases	5,000	Sales	12,500
Rent	3,500		
Bank loan interest	100		
Other expenses	1,900		
Capital a/c	2,000		
	12,500		12,500

CAPITAL

	$		$
Drawings	1,500	Cash at bank	7,000
Balance c/d	7,500	I & E a/c	2,000
	9,000		9,000
		Balance b/d	7,500

Question — Balance sheet

You can now complete Ron Knuckle's simple balance sheet.

Answer

RON KNUCKLE
BALANCE SHEET AT END OF FIRST TRADING PERIOD

	$
Assets	
Non-current assets	
Shop fittings	2,000
Current assets	
Cash at bank	6,500
Total assets	8,500
Capital and liabilities	
Proprietor's capital	7,500
Non-current liabilities	
Bank loan	1,000
Total capital and liabilities	8,500

When a balance sheet is drawn up for an accounting period which is not the first one, then it ought to show the capital at the start of the accounting period and the capital at the end of the accounting period. This will be illustrated in the next example.

In an examination question, you might not be given the ledger accounts – you might have to draw them up in the first place. That is the case with the following exercise – see if you can do it by yourself before looking at the solution.

4 Balancing accounts and preparing financial statements

The exercise which follows is by far the most important in this text so far. It uses all the accounting steps from entering up ledger accounts to preparing the financial statements, and is set out in a style which you might well find in an examination. It is **very important that you try the question by yourself:** if you do not, you will be missing out a vital part of this text.

Exam focus point

You are quite likely to get a question requiring you to prepare a balance sheet or income statement from a trial balance.

PART C DOUBLE ENTRY BOOKKEEPING AND ACCOUNTING SYSTEMS

Question

Financial statements

A business is established with capital of $2,000, and this amount is paid into a business bank account by the proprietor. During the first year's trading, the following transactions occurred:

	$
Purchases of goods for resale, on credit	4,300
Payments to trade accounts payable	3,600
Sales, all on credit	5,800
Payments from trade accounts receivable	3,200
Non-current assets purchased for cash	1,500
Other expenses, all paid in cash	900

The bank has provided an overdraft facility of up to $3,000.

Required

Prepare the ledger accounts, an income statement for the year and a balance sheet as at the end of the year.

Answer

The first thing to do is to open ledger accounts so that the transactions can be entered up. The relevant accounts which we need for this example are: cash at bank; capital; trade accounts payable; purchases; non-current assets; sales; trade accounts receivable and other expenses.

The next step is to work out the double entry bookkeeping for each transaction. Normally you would write them straight into the accounts, but to make this example easier to follow, they are first listed below.

		Debit	*Credit*
(a)	Establishing business ($2,000)	Cash at bank	Capital
(b)	Purchases ($4,300)	Purchases	Trade accounts payable
(c)	Payments to trade accounts payable ($3,600)	Trade accounts payable	Cash at bank
(d)	Sales ($5,800)	Trade accounts receivable	Sales
(e)	Payments from trade accounts receivable ($3,200)	Cash at bank	Trade accounts receivable
(f)	Non-current assets ($1,500)	Non-current assets	Cash at bank
(g)	Other (cash) expenses ($900)	Other expenses	Cash at bank

So far, the ledger accounts will look like this.

CASH AT BANK

	$		$
Capital	2,000	Trade accounts payable	3,600
Trade account receivables	3,200	Non-current assets	1,500
		Other expenses	900

CAPITAL

	$		$
		Cash at bank	2,000

TRADE ACCOUNTS PAYABLE

	$		$
Cash at bank	3,600	Purchases	4,300

PURCHASES

	$		$
Trade accounts payable	4,300		

NON-CURRENT ASSETS

	$		$
Cash at bank	1,500		

SALES

	$		$
		Trade accounts receivable	5,800

TRADE ACCOUNTS RECEIVABLE

	$		$
Sales	5,800	Cash at bank	3,200

OTHER EXPENSES

	$		$
Cash at bank	900		

The next thing to do is to balance all these accounts. It is at this stage that you could, if you wanted to, draw up a trial balance to make sure the double entry is accurate. There is not very much point in this simple example, but if you did, it would look like this.

	Dr $	Cr $
Cash at bank		800
Capital		2,000
Trade accounts payable		700
Purchases	4,300	
Non-current assets	1,500	
Sales		5,800
Trade accounts receivable	2,600	
Other expenses	900	
	9,300	9,300

After balancing the accounts, the income and expense account should be opened. Into it should be transferred all the balances relating to income and expense (ie purchases, other expenses, and sales). At this point, the ledger accounts will be as follows.

CASH AT BANK

	$		$
Capital	2,000	Trade accounts payable	3,600
Trade accounts receivable	3,200	Non-current assets	1,500
Balance c/d	800	Other expenses	900
	6,000		6,000
		Balance b/d	800*

PART C DOUBLE ENTRY BOOKKEEPING AND ACCOUNTING SYSTEMS

* A credit balance b/d means that this cash item is a liability, not an asset. This indicates a bank overdraft of $800, with cash income of $5,200 falling short of payments of $6,000 by this amount.

CAPITAL

	$		$
Balance c/d	2,600	Cash at bank	2,000
		I & E a/c	600
	2,600		2,600

TRADE ACCOUNTS PAYABLE

	$		$
Cash at bank	3,600	Purchases	4,300
Balance c/d	700		
	4,300		4,300
		Balance b/d	700

PURCHASES ACCOUNT

	$		$
Trade accounts payable	4,300	I & E a/c	4,300

NON-CURRENT ASSETS

	$		$
Cash at bank	1,500	Balance c/d	1,500
Balance b/d	1,500		

SALES

	$		$
I & E a/c	5,800		5,800

TRADE ACCOUNTS RECEIVABLE

	$		$
Sales	5,800	Cash at bank	3,200
		Balance c/d	2,600
	5,800		5,800
Balance b/d	2,600		

OTHER EXPENSES

	$		$
Cash at bank	900	I & E a/c	900

INCOME AND EXPENSE ACCOUNT

	$		$
Purchases account	4,300	Sales	5,800
Gross profit c/d	1,500		
	5,800		5,800
Other expenses	900	Gross profit b/d	1,500
Net profit (transferred to capital account)	600		
	1,500		1,500

So the income statement will be:

INCOME STATEMENT
FOR THE ACCOUNTING PERIOD

	$
Sales	5,800
Cost of sales (purchases)	4,300
Gross profit	1,500
Expenses	900
Net profit	600

Listing and then rearranging the balances on the ledger accounts gives the balance sheet as:

BALANCE SHEET AS AT THE END OF THE PERIOD

	$	$
Assets		
Non-current assets		1,500
Current assets		
Trade accounts receivable		2,600
Total assets		4,100
Capital and liabilities		
Capital		
At start of period	2,000	
Net profit for period	600	
At end of period		2,600
Current liabilities		
Bank overdraft	800	
Trade accounts payable	700	
		1,500
Total capital and liabilities		4,100

Exam focus point

In an examination you need not spell out your answer in quite such detail. The detail is given here to help you to work through the example properly, and you may wish to do things this way yourself until you get more practised in accounting techniques and are confident enough to take short cuts.

Chapter Roundup

- At suitable intervals, the entries in each **ledger account** are totalled and a **balance** is struck. Balances are usually collected in a **trial balance** which is then used as a basis for preparing an income statement and a balance sheet.

- A trial balance can be used to **test the accuracy of the double entry accounting** records. It works by listing the balances on ledger accounts, some of which will be debits and some credits. The total debits should equal total credits.

- An **income and expense ledger account** is opened up to gather all items relating to income and expenses. When **rearranged**, the items make up the **income statement**.

- The balances on all **remaining ledger accounts** (including the income and expense account) can be listed and **rearranged** to form the **balance sheet**.

PART C DOUBLE ENTRY BOOKKEEPING AND ACCOUNTING SYSTEMS

Quick Quiz

1   What is the purpose of a trial balance?

2   Give four circumstances in which a trial balance might balance although some of the balances are wrong.

3   In a period, sales are $140,000, purchases $75,000 and other expenses $25,000. What is the figure for net profit to be transferred to the capital account?

   A $40,000
   B $65,000
   C $75,000
   D $140,000

4   What is the difference between balancing off an expense account and balancing off a liability account?

Answers to Quick Quiz

1   To test the accuracy of the double entry bookkeeping.

2   See Para 1.4.

3   A

INCOME & EXPENSE ACCOUNT

	$		$
Purchases	75,000	Sales	140,000
Gross profit c/d	65,000		
	140,000		140,000
Other expenses	25,000	Gross profit b/d	65,000
Net profit – to capital a/c	40,000		
	65,000		65,000

B is the **gross** profit figure, while C is the figure for purchases and D sales.

4   When an expense account is balanced off, the balance is transferred to the income and expense account. When a liability account is balanced off, the balance is carried forward to the next trading period.

Now try the question below from the Exam Question Bank

Number	Level	Marks	Time
Q8	Introductory	n/a	27 mins
Q15	Introductory	n/a	45 mins

Control accounts

Topic list	Syllabus reference
1 What are control accounts?	3(b)(i)
2 Discounts	3(a)(iii)
3 The operation of control accounts	3(b)(i)
4 The purpose of control accounts	3(b)(i)

Introduction

So far in this text we have assumed that the bookkeeping and double entry (and subsequent preparation of financial accounts) has been carried out by a business without any mistakes. This is not likely to be the case in real life: even the bookkeeper of a very small business with hardly any accounting entries to make will be prone to human error. If a debit is written as $123 and the corresponding credit as $321, then the books of the business are immediately out of balance by $198.

Once an error has been detected, it has to be corrected.

In this chapter and in the following two chapters we explain how errors can be **detected**, what kinds of error might **exist**, and how to post **corrections** and adjustments to produce final accounts.

Study guide

Section 5 – The journal; ledger control accounts; bank reconciliations

- Explain the nature and purpose of control accounts for the accounts receivable and accounts payable ledgers.
- Explain how control accounts relate to the double entry system.
- Construct and agree a ledger control account from given information.

Exam guide

These are important topics. You are likely to find questions on control accounts in both Section A and Section B of the exam. The questions could be computational or discursive (eg explain the reasons for keeping a control account).

1 What are control accounts?

FAST FORWARD

A control account keeps a total record of a number of individual items. It is an **impersonal** account which is part of the double entry system.

Key terms

A **control account** is an account in the nominal ledger in which a record is kept of the total value of a number of similar but individual items. Control accounts are used chiefly for trade receivables and payables.

- A **receivables control account** is an account in which records are kept of transactions involving all receivables in total. The balance on the receivables control account at any time will be the total amount due to the business at that time from its receivables.

- A **payables control account** is an account in which records are kept of transactions involving all payables in total, and the balance on this account at any time will be the total amount owed by the business at that time to its payables.

Although control accounts are used mainly in accounting for receivables and payables, they can also be kept for other items, such as inventories, wages and salaries, and cash. The first important idea to remember, however, is that a control account is an account which keeps a total record for a collective item (eg receivables), which in reality consists of many individual items (eg individual trade accounts receivable).

A control account is an (impersonal) ledger account which will appear in the nominal ledger.

1.1 Control accounts and personal accounts

The personal accounts of individual debtors of the business are kept in the receivables ledger, and the amount owed by each debtor will be a balance on his personal account. The amount owed by all the debtors together (ie all the trade account receivables) will be a balance on the receivables control account.

At any time the balance on the receivables control account should be equal to the sum of the individual balances on the personal accounts in the receivables ledger.

For example, a business has three trade accounts receivable: A Arnold owes $80, B Bagshaw owes $310 and C Cloning owes $200. The debit balances on the various accounts would be:

Receivables ledger (personal accounts)

	$
A Arnold	80
B Bagshaw	310
C Cloning	200
Nominal ledger: receivables control account	590

What has happened here is that the three entries of $80, $310 and $200 were first entered into the sales day book. They were also recorded in the three personal accounts of Arnold, Bagshaw and Cloning in the receivables ledger – but remember that this is not part of the double entry system.

Later, the **total** of $590 is posted from the sales day book by a debit into the receivables (control) account and a credit to sales. If you add up all the debit figures on the personal accounts, they also should total $590.

2 Discounts

FAST FORWARD

Discounts can be defined as follows:

- **Trade discount** is a reduction in the list price of an article, given by a wholesaler or manufacturer to a retailer. It is often given in return for bulk purchase orders.

- **Cash discount** is a reduction in the amount payable in return for payment in cash, or within an agreed period

Before looking at control accounts for accounts receivable and payable, we need to consider the accounting treatment for discounts.

2.1 Types of discount

A discount is a reduction in the price of goods below the amount at which those goods would normally be sold to other customers. There are two types of discount.

- **Trade** discount
- **Cash** discount

Key term

Trade discount is a reduction in the cost of goods owing to the nature of the trading transaction. It usually results from buying goods in bulk.

2.1.1 Examples of trade discount

(a) A customer is quoted a price of $1 per unit for a particular item, but a lower price of 95 cents per unit if the item is bought in quantities of 100 units or more at a time.

(b) An important customer or a regular customer is offered a discount on all the goods he buys, regardless of the size of each individual order, because the total volume of his purchases over time is so large.

Key term

Cash discount is a reduction in the amount payable to the supplier, in return for immediate payment in cash, rather than purchase on credit, or for payment within an agreed period.

For example, a supplier charges $1,000 for goods, but offers a discount of 5% if the goods are paid for immediately in cash.

For example, a supplier charges $1,000 to a credit customer for goods purchased, but offers a discount of 5% for payment within so many days of the invoice date.

2.2 Accounting for trade discounts

FAST FORWARD

Trade discounts received are deducted from the cost of purchases. **Cash discounts received** are included as 'other income' of the period. **Trade discounts allowed** are deducted from sales and **cash discounts allowed** are shown as expenses of the period.

A trade discount is a reduction in the amount of money demanded from a customer.

(a) If a trade discount is received by a business for goods purchased from a supplier, the amount of money demanded from the business by the supplier will be net of discount (ie it will be the normal sales value less the discount).

(b) Similarly, if a trade discount is given by a business for goods sold to a customer, the amount of money demanded by the business will be after deduction of the discount.

Trade discounts should therefore be accounted for as follows.

(a) **Trade discounts received** should be deducted from the gross cost of purchases. In other words, the cost of purchases in the trading account will be stated at gross cost minus discount (ie it will be stated at the invoiced amount).

(b) **Trade discounts allowed** should be deducted from the gross sales price, so that sales for the period will be reported in the trading account at their invoice value.

2.3 Cash discounts received

When a business is given the opportunity to take advantage of a cash discount or a settlement discount for prompt payment, the decision as to whether or not to take the discount is a matter of financing policy, not of trading policy.

2.4 Example: Cash discounts received

A buys goods from B, on the understanding that A will be allowed a period of credit before having to pay for the goods. The terms of the transaction are as follows.

(a) Date of sale: 1 July 20X6
(b) Credit period allowed: 30 days
(c) Invoice price of the goods: $2,000
(d) Cash discount offered: 4% discount for prompt payment

A has the following choices.

(a) Holding on to his money for 30 days and then paying the full $2,000.
(b) Paying $2,000 less 4% – ie $1,920 now.

This is a financing decision about whether it is worthwhile for A to save $80 by paying its debts sooner, or whether it can employ its cash more usefully for 30 days, and pay the debt at the latest acceptable moment.

If A decides to take the cash discount, he will pay $1,920, instead of the invoiced amount of $2,000. The cash discount received ($80) will be accounted for in the books of A as follows.

(a) In the purchases account, the cost of purchases will be at the invoiced price (or 'full trade' price) of $2,000. When the invoice for $2,000 is received by A, it will be recorded in his books of account at that price, and the subsequent financing decision about accepting the cash discount is ignored.

(b) In the income and expense part of the income statement (which determines net profit or loss), the cash discount received is shown as though it were income received. There is no expense in the income statement from which the cash discount can be deducted, and so there is no alternative other than to show the discount received as income.

In our example

	$
Cost of purchase from B by A	2,000
Discount received (income in the I & E account)	(80)
Net cost	1,920

Question — Discounts

Soft Supplies Co recently purchased from Hard Imports Co 10 printers originally priced at $200 each. A 10% trade discount was negotiated together with a 5% cash discount if payment was made within 14 days. Calculate the following.

(a) The total of the trade discount
(b) The total of the cash discount

Answer

(a) $200 ($200 × 10 × 10%)
(b) $90 ($200 × 10 × 90% × 5%)

2.5 Cash discounts allowed

The same principle is applied in accounting for cash discounts or settlement discounts allowed to customers. Goods are sold at a trade price, and the offer of a discount on that price is a matter of financing policy for the business and not a matter of trading policy.

2.6 Example: Cash discounts allowed

X sells goods to Y at a price of $5,000. Y is allowed 60 days' credit before payment, but is also offered a discount of 2% for payment within 10 days of the invoice date.

X will issue an invoice to Y for $5,000 when the goods are sold. X has no idea whether or not Y will take advantage of the discount. In trading terms, and in terms of the amount charged in the invoice to Y, Y is a debtor for $5,000.

If Y subsequently decides to take the discount, he will pay $5,000 less 2% – ie $4,900 – ten days later. The discount allowed ($100) will be accounted for by X as follows.

(a) In the trading account, sales will be valued at their full invoice price, $5,000.
(b) In the income and expense account, the discount allowed will be shown as an expense.

In our example

	$
Sales	5,000
Discounts allowed (I & E account)	(100)
Net sales	4,900

PART C DOUBLE ENTRY BOOKKEEPING AND ACCOUNTING SYSTEMS

Question — Discounts

You are required to prepare the income statement of Seesaw Timber Merchants for the year ended 31 March 20X6, given the following information.

	$
Purchases at gross cost	120,000
Trade discounts received	4,000
Cash discounts received	1,500
Cash sales	34,000
Credit sales at invoice price	150,000
Cash discounts allowed	8,000
Selling expenses	32,000
Administrative expenses	40,000
Drawings by proprietor, Tim Burr	22,000

Answer

SEESAW TIMBER MERCHANTS
INCOME STATEMENT
FOR THE YEAR ENDED 31 MARCH 20X6

	$	$
Sales (note 1)		184,000
Purchases (note 2)		116,000
Gross profit		68,000
Discounts received		1,500
		69,500
Expenses		
Selling expenses	32,000	
Administrative expenses	40,000	
Discounts allowed	8,000	
		80,000
Net loss transferred to balance sheet		(10,500)

Notes

1 $(34,000 + 150,000)$
2 $(120,000 – 4,000)$
3 Drawings are not an expense, but an appropriation of profit.

3 The operation of control accounts

FAST FORWARD

The two most important **control accounts** are those for **receivables** and **payables**. They are part of the double entry system.

3.1 Example: accounting for receivables

You might still be uncertain why we need to have control accounts at all. Before turning our attention to this question, it will be useful first of all to see how transactions involving receivables are accounted for by means of an illustrative example. Reference numbers are shown in the accounts to illustrate the cross-referencing that is needed, and in the example reference numbers beginning:

(a) SDB, refer to a page in the sales day book

(b) RL, refer to a particular account in the receivables ledger
(c) NL, refer to a particular account in the nominal ledger
(d) CB, refer to a page in the cash book

At 1 July 20X2, the Outer Business Company had no trade accounts receivable. During July, the following transactions affecting credit sales and customers occurred.

(a) July 3: invoiced A Arnold for the sale on credit of hardware goods: $100

(b) July 11: invoiced B Bagshaw for the sale on credit of electrical goods: $150

(c) July 15: invoiced C Cloning for the sale on credit of hardware goods: $250

(d) July 10: received payment from A Arnold of $90, in settlement of his debt in full, having taken a permitted discount of $10 for payment within seven days

(e) July 18: received a payment of $72 from B Bagshaw in part settlement of $80 of his debt; a discount of $8 was allowed for payment within seven days of invoice

(f) July 28: received a payment of $120 from C Cloning, who was unable to claim any discount

Account numbers are as follows:

RL 4   Personal account: A Arnold
RL 9   Personal account: B Bagshaw
RL 13 Personal account: C Cloning
NL 6   Receivables control account
NL 7   Discounts allowed
NL 21 Sales: hardware
NL 22 Sales: electrical
NL 1   Cash at bank

The accounting entries would be as follows.

SALES DAY BOOK   SDB 35

Date 20X2	Name	Ref.	Total $	Hardware $	Electrical $
July 3	A Arnold	RL 4 Dr	100.00	100.00	
11	B Bagshaw	RL 9 Dr	150.00		150.00
15	C Cloning	RL 13 Dr	250.00	250.00	
			500.00	350.00	150.00
			NL 6 Dr	NL 21 Cr	NL 22 Cr

Note. The personal accounts in the receivables ledger are debited on the day the invoices are sent out. The double entry in the ledger accounts might be made at the end of each day, week or month; here it is made at the end of the month, by posting from the sales day book as follows.

			$	$
DEBIT	NL 6	Receivables control account	500	
CREDIT	NL 21	Sales: hardware		350
	NL 22	Sales: electrical		150

PART C   DOUBLE ENTRY BOOKKEEPING AND ACCOUNTING SYSTEMS

CASH BOOK EXTRACT
RECEIPTS – JULY 20X2
CB 23

Date 20X2	Narrative	Ref.	Total $	Discount allowed $	Accounts receivable $
July 10	A Arnold	RL 4 Cr	90.00	10.00	100.00
18	B Bagshaw	RL 9 Cr	72.00	8.00	80.00
28	C Cloning	RL 13 Cr	120.00	–	120.00
			282.00	18.00	300.00
			NL 1 Dr	NL 7 Dr	NL 6 Cr

At the end of July, the cash book is posted to the nominal ledger.

		$	$
DEBIT	Cash at bank	282.00	
	Discount allowed	18.00	
CREDIT	Receivables control account		300.00

The personal accounts in the receivables ledger are memorandum accounts, because they are not a part of the double entry system.

MEMORANDUM RECEIVABLES LEDGER
ARNOLD   A/c no: RL 4

Date 20X2	Narrative	Ref.	$	Date 20X2	Narrative	Ref.	$
July 3	Sales	SDB 35	100.00	July 10	Cash	CB 23	90.00
					Discount	CB 23	10.00
			100.00				100.00

B BAGSHAW   A/c no: RL 9

Date 20X2	Narrative	Ref.	$	Date 20X2	Narrative	Ref.	$
July 11	Sales	SDB 35	150.00	July 18	Cash	CB 23	72.00
					Discount	CB 23	8.00
				July 31	Balance	c/d	70.00
			150.00				150.00
Aug 1	Balance	b/d	70.00				

C CLONING   A/c no: RL 13

Date 20X2	Narrative	Ref.	$	Date 20X2	Narrative	Ref.	$
July 15	Sales	SDB 35	250.00	July 28	Cash	CB 23	120.00
				July 31	Balance	c/d	130.00
			250.00				250.00
Aug 1	Balance	b/d	130.00				

In the nominal ledger, the accounting entries are made from the books of original entry to the ledger accounts, in this example at the end of the month.

7: CONTROL ACCOUNTS

NOMINAL LEDGER (EXTRACT)

RECEIVABLES LEDGER CONTROL ACCOUNT   A/c no: NL 6

Date 20X2	Narrative	Ref.	$	Date 20X2	Narrative	Ref.	$
July 31	Sales	SDB 35	500.00	July 31	Cash and discount	CB 23	300.00
				July 31	Balance	c/d	200.00
			500.00				500.00
Aug 1	Balance	b/d	200.00				

Note. At 31 July the closing balance on the receivables control account ($200) is the same as the total of the individual balances on the personal accounts in the receivables ledger ($0 + $70 + $130).

DISCOUNT ALLOWED   A/c no: NL 7

Date 20X2	Narrative	Ref.	$	Date	Narrative	Ref.	$
July 31	Receivables	CB 23	18.00				

CASH CONTROL ACCOUNT   A/c no: NL 1

Date 20X2	Narrative	Ref.	$	Date	Narrative	Ref.	$
July 31	Cash received	CB 23	282.00				

SALES: HARDWARE   A/c no: NL 21

Date	Narrative	Ref.	$	Date 20X2	Narrative	Ref.	$
				July 31	Receivables	SDB 35	350.00

SALES: ELECTRICAL   A/c no: NL 22

Date	Narrative	Ref.	$	Date 20X2	Narrative	Ref.	$
				July 31	Receivables	SDB 35	150.00

If we take the balance on the accounts shown in this example as at 31 July 20X2, the trial balance is as follows.

TRIAL BALANCE

	Debit $	Credit $
Cash (all receipts)	282	
Receivables	200	
Discount allowed	18	
Sales: hardware		350
Sales: electrical		150
	500	500

The trial balance is shown here to emphasise the point that a trial balance includes the balances on control accounts, but excludes the balances on the personal accounts in the receivables ledger and payables ledger.

3.2 Accounting for payables

If you are able to follow the example above dealing with the receivables control account, you should have no difficulty in dealing with similar examples relating to purchases/payables. If necessary refer back to revise the entries made in the purchase day book and purchase ledger personal accounts.

3.3 Entries in control accounts

Typical entries in the control accounts are listed below. Reference 'Jnl' indicates that the transaction is first lodged in the journal before posting to the control account and other accounts indicated. References SRDB and PRDB are to sales returns and purchase returns day books.

RECEIVABLES CONTROL ACCOUNT

	Ref.	$		Ref.	$
Opening debit balances	b/d	7,000	Opening credit balances		
Sales	SDB	52,390	(if any)	b/d	200
Dishonoured bills or	Jnl	1,000	Cash received	CB	52,250
cheques			Discounts allowed	CB	1,250
Cash paid to clear credit			Returns inwards from		
balances	CB	110	customers	SRDB	800
Closing credit balances	c/d	120	Bad debts	Jnl	300
			Closing debit balances	C/d	5,820
		60,620			60,620
Debit balances b/d		5,820	Credit balances b/d		120

Note. Opening credit balances are unusual in the receivables control account. They represent debtors to whom the business owes money, probably as a result of the over-payment of debts or for advance payments of debts for which no invoices have yet been sent. Bad debts will be dealt with in a later chapter.

PAYABLES CONTROL ACCOUNT

	Ref.	$		Ref.	$
Opening debit balances			Opening credit balances	b/d	8,300
(if any)	b/d	70	Purchases	PDB	31,000
Cash paid	CB	29,840			
Discounts received	CB	30	Cash received clearing		
Returns outwards to	PRDB		debit balances	CB	20
suppliers		60	Closing debit balances		
Closing credit balances	c/d	9,400	(if any)	c/d	80
		39,400			39,400
Debit balances	b/d	80	Credit balances	b/d	9,400

Note. Opening debit balances in the payables control account would represent suppliers who owe the business money, perhaps because the business has overpaid or because a credit note is awaited for returned goods.

Posting from the journal to the memorandum receivables or payables ledgers and to the nominal ledger may be effected at the same time; as in the following example, where C Cloning has returned goods with a sales value of $50.

Journal entry	Ref.	Dr $	Cr $
Sales	NL 21	50	
To receivables control	NL 6		50
To C Cloning (memorandum)	RL 13	–	50
Return of electrical goods inwards			

7: CONTROL ACCOUNTS

Question — Payables control account

A payables control account contains the following entries:

	$
Bank	79,500
Credit purchases	83,200
Discounts received	3,750
Contra with receivables control account	4,000
Balance c/f at 31 December 20X8	12,920

There are no other entries in the account. What was the opening balance brought forward at 1 January 20X8?

Answer

PAYABLES CONTROL

	$		$
Bank payments	79,500	Balance b/f (balancing figure)	16,970
Discounts received	3,750	Purchases	83,200
Contra with receivables	4,000		
Balance c/f	12,920		
	100,170		100,170

Note: 'Contra with receivables control' can happen when a business is both a customer *and* a supplier. In this case, the supplier owed $4,000 for items bought, which he has asked to be offset against the amounts owed to him.

Question — Receivables control account

The total of the balances in a company's receivables ledger is $800 more than the debit balance on its receivables control account. Which one of the following errors could by itself account for the discrepancy?

A The sales day book has been undercast by $800
B Settlement discounts totalling $800 have been omitted from the nominal ledger
C One receivables ledger account with a credit balance of $800 has been treated as a debit balance
D The cash receipts book has been undercast by $800

Answer

A The total of sales invoices in the day book is debited to the control account. If the total is understated by $800, the debits in the control account will also be understated by $800. Options B and D would have the opposite effect: credit entries in the control account would be understated. Option C would lead to a discrepancy of 2 × $800 = $1,600.

PART C DOUBLE ENTRY BOOKKEEPING AND ACCOUNTING SYSTEMS

It may help you to see how the receivables ledger and receivables control account are used, by means of a flowchart.

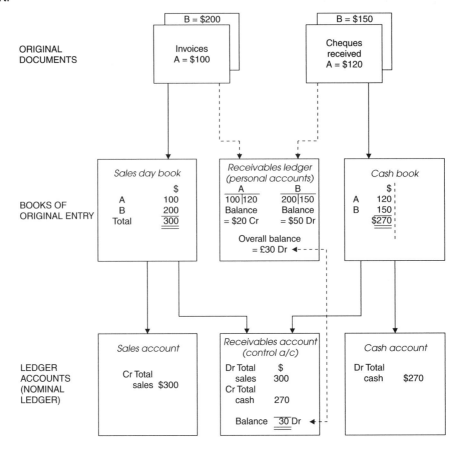

Notes

(a) The receivables ledger is not part of the double entry system (it is not used to post the ledger accounts).

(b) Nevertheless, the total balance on the receivables ledger (ie all the personal account balances added up) should equal the balance on the receivables control account.

See now whether you can do the following question yourself.

Question — Receivables and payables control accounts

On examining the books of Exports Co, you ascertain that on 1 October 20X8 the receivables ledger balances were $8,024 debit and $57 credit, and the payables ledger balances on the same date $6,235 credit and $105 debit.

For the year ended 30 September 20X9 the following particulars are available.

	$
Sales	63,728
Purchases	39,974
Cash from trade accounts receivable	55,212
Cash to trade accounts payable	37,307
Discount received	1,475
Discount allowed	2,328
Returns inwards	1,002
Returns outwards	535
Bad debts written off	326
Cash received in respect of debit balances in payables ledger	105

	$
Amount due from customer as shown by receivables ledger, offset against amount due to the same firm as shown by payables ledger (settlement by contra)	434
Allowances to customers on goods damaged in transit	212

On 30 September 20X9 there were no credit balances in the receivables ledger except those outstanding on 1 October 20X8, and no debit balances in the payables ledger.

You are required to write up the following accounts recording the above transactions bringing down the balances as on 30 September 20X9:

(a) Receivables control account
(b) Payables control account

Answer

(a)

RECEIVABLES CONTROL ACCOUNT

20X8		$	20X8		$
Oct 1	Balances b/f	8,024	Oct 1	Balances b/f	57
20X9			20X9		
Sept 30	Sales	63,728	Sept 30	Cash received from credit customers	55,212
	Balances c/f	57		Discount allowed	2,328
				Returns	1,002
				Bad debts written off	326
				Transfer payables control account	434
				Allowances on goods damaged	212
				Balances c/f	12,238
		71,809			71,809

(b)

PAYABLES CONTROL ACCOUNT

20X8		$	20X8		$
Oct 1	Balances b/f	105	Oct 1	Balances b/f	6,235
20X9			20X9		
Sept 30	Cash paid to credit suppliers	37,307	Sept 30	Purchases	39,974
	Discount received	1,475		Cash	105
	Returns outwards	535			
	Transfer receivables control account	434			
	Balances c/f	6,458			
		46,314			46,314

4 The purpose of control accounts

FAST FORWARD

Cash books and day books are totalled periodically and the totals posted to the control accounts. At suitable intervals, the balances on the personal accounts are extracted and totalled. These balance totals should agree to the balance on the control account. In this way, errors can be located and corrected.

4.1 Reasons for having control accounts

The reasons for having control accounts are as follows.

(a) They provide a **check on the accuracy** of entries made in the personal accounts in the receivables ledger and payables ledger. It is very easy to make a mistake in posting entries, because there might be hundreds of entries to make. Figures can get transposed. Some entries might be omitted altogether, so that an invoice or a payment transaction does not appear in a personal account as it should. By comparing (i) and (ii) below, it is possible to identify that fact that errors have been made.

   (i) The total balance on the receivables control account with the total of individual balances on the personal accounts in the receivables ledger.

   (ii) The total balance on the payables control account with the total of individual balances on the personal accounts in the payables ledger.

(b) The control accounts also assist in the **location of errors**, where postings to the control accounts are made daily or weekly, or even monthly. If a clerk fails to record an invoice or a payment in a personal account, or makes a transposition error, it would be a formidable task to locate the error or errors at the end of a year, say, given the number of transactions. By using the control account, a comparison with the individual balances in the receivables or payables ledger can be made for every week or day of the month, and the error found much more quickly than if control accounts did not exist.

(c) Where there is a separation of clerical (bookkeeping) duties, the control account provides an **internal check**. The person posting entries to the control accounts will act as a check on a different person(s) whose job it is to post entries to the receivables and payables ledger accounts.

(d) To provide total receivables and payables balances more quickly for producing a trial balance or balance sheet. A single balance on a control account is obviously **extracted more simply and quickly** than many individual balances in the receivables or payables ledger. This means also that the number of accounts in the double entry bookkeeping system can be kept down to a manageable size, since the personal accounts are memorandum accounts only.

However, particularly in computerised systems, it may be feasible to use receivables and payables ledgers without the need for operating separate control accounts. In such a system, the receivables or payables ledger printouts produced by the computer constitute the list of individual balances as well as providing a total balance which represents the control account balance.

Exam focus point

You may be asked to explain the purpose of control accounts. However, the most likely type of question is a **control account reconciliation**. This is covered below.

4.2 Balancing and agreeing control accounts with receivables and payables ledgers

The control accounts should be **balanced regularly** (at least monthly), and the balance on the account agreed with the sum of the individual debtors' or suppliers balances extracted from the receivables or payables ledgers respectively. It is one of the sad facts of an accountant's life that more often than not the balance on the control account does not agree with the sum of balances extracted, for one or more of the following reasons.

(a) An **incorrect amount** may be **posted** to the control account because of a **miscast** of the total in the book of original entry (ie adding up incorrectly the total value of invoices or payments). The nominal ledger debit and credit postings will then balance, but the control account balance will not agree with the sum of individual balances extracted from the (memorandum) receivables ledger or payables ledger. A journal entry must then be made in the nominal ledger to correct the control account and the corresponding sales or expense account.

(b) A **transposition error** may occur in posting an individual's balance from the book of prime entry to the memorandum ledger, eg a sale to C Cloning of $250 might be posted to his account as $520. This means that the sum of balances extracted from the memorandum ledger must be corrected. No accounting entry would be required to do this, except to alter the figure in C Cloning's account.

(c) A transaction may be **recorded in the control account** and *not* **in the memorandum ledger**, or vice versa. This requires an entry in the ledger that has been missed out which means a double posting if the control account has to be corrected, and a single posting if it is the individual's balance in the memorandum ledger that is at fault.

(d) The sum of balances extracted from the memorandum ledger may be **incorrectly extracted or miscast**. This would involve simply correcting the total of the balances.

4.3 Example: Agreeing control account balances with the receivables and payables ledgers

Reconciling the control account balance with the sum of the balances extracted from the (memorandum) receivables ledger or payables ledger should be done in two stages.

(a) Correct the total of the balances extracted from the memorandum ledger. (The errors must be located first of course.)

	$	$
Receivables ledger total		
Original total extracted		15,320
Add difference arising from transposition error ($95 written as $59)		36
		15,356
Less		
Credit balance of $60 extracted as a debit balance ($60 × 2)	120	
Overcast of list of balances	90	
		210
		15,146

(b) Bring down the balance before adjustments on the control account, and adjust or post the account with correcting entries.

RECEIVABLES CONTROL ACCOUNT

	$		$
Balance before adjustments	15,091	Petty cash: posting omitted	10
		Returns inwards: individual posting omitted from control Account	35
Undercast of total invoices issued in sales day book	100	Balance c/d (now in agreement with the corrected total of individual balances in (a))	15,146
	15,191		15,191
Balance b/d	15,146		

PART C DOUBLE ENTRY BOOKKEEPING AND ACCOUNTING SYSTEMS

Question — Receivables control account

April Showers sells goods on credit to most of its customers. In order to control its receivables collection system, the company maintains a receivables control account. In preparing the accounts for the year to 30 October 20X3 the accountant discovers that the total of all the personal accounts in the receivables ledger amounts to $12,802, whereas the balance on the receivables control account is $12,550.

Upon investigating the matter, the following errors were discovered.

(a) Sales for the week ending 27 March 20X3 amounting to $850 had been omitted from the control account.

(b) A customer's account balance of $300 had not been included in the list of balances.

(c) Cash received of $750 had been entered in a personal account as $570.

(d) Discounts allowed totalling $100 had not been entered in the control account.

(e) A personal account balance had been undercast by $200

(f) A contra item of $400 with the payables ledger had not been entered in the control account.

(g) An irrecoverable debt of $500 had not been entered in the control account.

(h) Cash received of $250 had been debited to a personal account.

(i) Discounts received of $50 had been debited to Bell's receivables ledger account.

(j) Returns inwards valued at $200 had not been included in the control account.

(k) Cash received of $80 had been credited to a personal account as $8.

(l) A cheque for $300 received from a customer had been dishonoured by the bank, but no adjustment had been made in the control account.

Required

(a) Prepare a corrected receivables control account, bringing down the amended balance as at 1 November 20X3.

(b) Prepare a statement showing the adjustments that are necessary to the list of personal account balances so that it reconciles with the amended receivables control account balance.

Answer

(a)

RECEIVABLES CONTROL ACCOUNT

	$		$
Uncorrected balance b/f	12,550	Discounts omitted (d)	100
Sales omitted (a)	850	Contra entry omitted (f)	400
Bank: cheque dishonoured (l)	300	Irrecoverable debt omitted (g)	500
		Returns inwards omitted (j)	200
		Amended balance c/d	12,500
	13,700		13,700
Balance b/d	12,500		

Note. Items (b), (c), (e), (h), (i) and (k) are matters affecting the personal accounts of customers. They have no effect on the control account.

(b) STATEMENT OF ADJUSTMENTS TO LIST OF PERSONAL ACCOUNT BALANCES

	$	$
Original total of list of balances		12,802
Add: debit balance omitted (b)	300	
debit balance understated (e)	200	
	500	
		500
		13,302
Less: transposition error (c): understatement of cash received	180	
cash debited instead of credited (2 × $250) (h)	500	
discounts received wrongly debited to Bell (i)	50	
understatement of cash received (k)	72	
		802
		12,500

Chapter Roundup

- A control account keeps a total record of a number of individual items. It is an **impersonal** account which is part of the double entry system.

- Discounts can be defined as follows:

    - **Trade discount** is a reduction in the list price of an article, given by a wholesaler or manufacturer to a retailer. It is often given in return for bulk purchase orders.

    - **Cash discounts** is a reduction in the amount payable for the purchase of goods or services in return for payment in cash, or within an agreed period.

- **Trade discounts received** are deducted from the cost of purchases. **Cash discounts received** are included as 'other income' of the period in the income statement. **Trade discounts allowed** are deducted from sales and **cash discounts allowed** are shown as expenses of the period.

- The two most important **control accounts** are those for **receivables** and **payables**. They are part of the double entry system.

- **Cash books and day books are totalled periodically** (say once a month) and the appropriate **totals are posted** to the control accounts.

- The individual entries in cash and day books will have been entered one by one in the appropriate **personal accounts** contained in the receivables ledger and payables ledger. These personal accounts are not part of the double entry system: they are memorandum only.

- At suitable intervals the balances on personal accounts are extracted from the ledgers, listed and totalled. The total of the outstanding balances can then be **reconciled** to the balance on the appropriate control account and any errors located and corrected.

PART C DOUBLE ENTRY BOOKKEEPING AND ACCOUNTING SYSTEMS

Quick Quiz

1   Name five accounting items for which control accounts may be used in the nominal ledger.

2   Give four reasons why a receivables control account is needed as well as a receivables ledger.

3   During a period, A Co has the following transactions on receivables control account. Sales $125,000, cash received $50,000, discounts allowed $2,000. The balance carried forward is $95,000. What was the opening balance at the beginning of the period?

    A $22,000 debit
    B $22,000 credit
    C $18,000 debit
    D $20,000 debit

Answers to Quick Quiz

1   Receivables, payables, inventories, wages and salaries, cash.

2   See Para 4.1.

3   A

RECEIVABLES CONTROL

	$		$
Bal b/f (bal figure)	22,000	Cash	50,000
Sales	125,000	Discounts allowed	2,000
		Bal c/f	95,000
	147,000		147,000

If you had answer B, you reversed the double entry and so produced a payables control account. In answer D, you omitted the discounts allowed figure; while in answer C you put discounts allowed on the debit instead of the credit side of the control account.

Now try the question below from the Exam Question Bank

Number	Level	Marks	Time
Q9	Examination	10	18 mins

Bank reconciliations

Topic list	Syllabus reference
1 Bank statement and cash book	3(b)(ii)
2 The bank reconciliation	3(b)(ii)
3 Worked examples	3(b)(ii)

Introduction

It is very likely that you will have had to do bank reconciliation at work. If not, you will probably have done one on your own bank account without even being aware of it.

The first two sections of this chapter explain why we need a bank reconciliation, and the sort of differences that need to be reconciled.
The third section takes you through some examples of increasing complexity.

PART C DOUBLE ENTRY BOOKKEEPING AND ACCOUNTING SYSTEMS

Study guide

Section 5 – The journal; ledger control accounts; bank reconciliations

- Explain and prepare bank reconciliation statements including the need for entries in the cash book when reconciling.

Exam guide

You are extremely likely to have a bank reconciliation question in the exam. It could appear in Section A or Section B, or it could be examined in both.

1 Bank statement and cash book

FAST FORWARD

In theory, the entries appearing on a business's **bank statement** should be exactly the same as those in the business cash book. The balance shown by the bank statement should be the same as the **cash book** balance on the same date.

The cash book of a business is the record of **how much cash the business believes** that it **has in the bank**. In the same way, you might keep a private record of how much you think you have in your own bank account, perhaps by making a note in your cheque book of income received and the cheques you write. If you do keep such a record, you will probably agree that your bank statement balance is rarely exactly the same as your own figure.

Why might your own estimate of your bank balance be different from the amount shown on your bank statement? There are three common explanations.

(a) **Error**. Errors in calculation, or recording income and payments, are more likely to have been made by you than by the bank, but it is conceivable that the bank has made a mistake too.

(b) **Bank charges or bank interest**. The bank might deduct charges for interest on an overdraft or for its services, which you are not informed about until you receive the bank statement.

(c) **Time differences**

(i) There might be some cheques that you have received and paid into the bank, but which have not yet been **'cleared'** and added to your account. So although your own records show that some cash has been added to your account, it has not yet been acknowledged by the bank – although it will be soon once the cheque has cleared.

(ii) Similarly, you might have made some payments by cheque, and reduced the balance in your account in the record that you keep, but the person who receives the cheque might not bank it for a while. Even when it is banked, it takes a day or two for the banks to process it and for the money to be deducted from your account.

If you do keep a personal record of your cash position at the bank, and if you do check your periodic bank statements against what you think you should have in your account, you will be doing a bank reconciliation.

Key term

A **bank reconciliation** is a comparison of a bank statement (sent monthly, weekly or even daily by the bank) with the cash book. Differences between the balance on the bank statement and the balance in the cash book will be errors or timing differences, and they should be identified and satisfactorily explained.

2 The bank reconciliation

FAST FORWARD

Differences between the cash book and the bank statement arise for three reasons:

- Errors – usually in the cash book
- Omissions – such as bank charges not posted in the cash book
- Timing differences – such as unpresented cheques

2.1 The bank statement

It is a common practice for a business to issue a monthly statement to each credit customer, itemising:

(a) The **balance** owed at the **beginning** of the month
(b) **New debts** incurred during the month
(c) **Payments** made during the month
(d) The **balance** owed at the **end** of the month

In the same way, a bank statement is sent by a bank to its short-term receivables and payables – ie customers with bank overdrafts and customers with money in their account – itemising the balance on the account at the beginning of the period, receipts into the account and payments from the account during the period, and the balance at the end of the period.

It is necessary to remember, however, that if a customer has money in his account, the bank owes him that money, and the customer is therefore a **payable** of the bank (hence the phrase 'to be in credit' means to have money in your account). This means that if a business has $8,000 cash in the bank, it will have a debit balance in its own cash book, but the bank statement, if it reconciles exactly with the cash book, will state that there is a credit balance of $8,000. *(The bank's records are a 'mirror image' of the customer's own records, with debits and credits reversed.)*

2.2 Why is a bank reconciliation necessary?

A bank reconciliation is needed to identify and account for the differences between the cash book and the bank statement.

Question   Differences

These differences fall into three categories. What are they?

Answer

Look back to the beginning of this section.

2.3 What to look for when doing a bank reconciliation

The cash book and bank statement will rarely agree at a given date. If you are doing a bank reconciliation, you may have to look for the following items.

(a) **Corrections and adjustments to the cash book**

   (i) Payments made into the account or from the account by way of standing order, which have not yet been entered in the cash book.

   (ii) Dividends received (on investments held by the business), paid direct into the bank account but not yet entered in the cash book.

PART C   DOUBLE ENTRY BOOKKEEPING AND ACCOUNTING SYSTEMS

(iii) Bank interest and bank charges, not yet entered in the cash book.

(b) **Items reconciling the correct cash book balance to the bank statement**

(i) Cheques drawn (ie paid) by the business and credited in the cash book, which have not yet been presented to the bank, or 'cleared', and so do not yet appear on the bank statement.

(ii) Cheques received by the business, paid into the bank and debited in the cash book, but which have not yet been cleared and entered in the account by the bank, and so do not yet appear on the bank statement.

> **Exam focus point**
>
> You are likely to have a bank reconciliation in Section B. It may be complex and so earn the full 10 marks or it could be part of a larger question.

3 Worked examples

> **FAST FORWARD**
>
> When the differences between the bank statement and the cash book are identified, the cash book must be corrected for any errors or omissions. Any remaining difference can then be shown to be due to timing differences.

3.1 Example: Bank reconciliation

At 30 September 20X6, the balance in the cash book of Wordsworth Co was $805.15 debit. A bank statement on 30 September 20X6 showed Wordsworth Co to be in credit by $1,112.30.

On investigation of the difference between the two sums, it was established that:

(a) The cash book had been undercast by $90.00 on the debit side*.
(b) Cheques paid in not yet credited by the bank amounted to $208.20, called outstanding lodgements.
(c) Cheques drawn not yet presented to the bank amounted to $425.35 called unpresented cheques.

* Note. 'Casting' is an accountant's term for adding up.

Required

(a) Show the correction to the cash book.
(b) Prepare a statement reconciling the balance per bank statement to the balance per cash book.

Solution

(a)

	$
Cash book balance brought forward	805.15
Add	
Correction of undercast	90.00
Corrected balance	895.15

(b)

	$
Balance per bank statement	1,112.30
Add	
Outstanding lodgements	208.20
	1,320.50
Less	
Unpresented cheques	(425.35)
Balance per cash book	895.15

8: BANK RECONCILIATIONS

Question
Reconciliation

On 31 January 20X8 a company's cash book showed a credit balance of $150 on its current account which did not agree with the bank statement balance. In performing the reconciliation the following points come to light.

	$
Not recorded in the cash book	
Bank charges	36
Transfer from deposit account to current account	500
Not recorded on the bank statement	
Unpresented cheques	116
Outstanding lodgements	630

It was also discovered that the bank had debited the company's account with a cheque for $400 in error. What was the original balance on the bank statement?

Answer

CASH ACCOUNT

	$		$
		Balance b/d	150
Transfer from deposit a/c	500	Charges	36
		Balance c/d	314
	500		500

	$
Balance per cash book	314
Add unpresented cheques	116
Less outstanding lodgements	(630)
Less error by bank*	(400)
Balance per bank statement	(600)

*Note that, on the bank statement, a debit is a payment out of the account.

Question
Bank statement

A company's bank statement shows $715 direct debits and $353 investment income not recorded in the cash book. The bank statement does not show a customer's cheque for $875 entered in the cash book on the last day of the accounting period. If the cash book shows a credit balance of $610 what balance appears on the bank statement?

Answer

	$	$
Balance per cash book		(610)
Items on statement, not in cash book		
Direct debits	(715)	
Investment income	353	
		(362)
Corrected balance per cash book		(972)
Item in cash book not on statement:		
Customer's cheque		(875)
Balance per bank statement		(1,847)

3.2 Example: More complicated bank reconciliation

On 30 June 20X0, Cook's cash book showed that he had an overdraft of $300 on his current account at the bank. A bank statement as at the end of June 20X0 showed that Cook was in credit with the bank by $65.

On checking the cash book with the bank statement you find the following.

(a) Cheques drawn, amounting to $500, had been entered in the cash book but had not been presented.

(b) Cheques received, amounting to $400, had been entered in the cash book, but had not been credited by the bank.

(c) On instructions from Cook the bank had transferred interest received on his deposit account amounting to $60 to his current account, recording the transfer on 5 July 20X0. This amount had, however, been credited in the cash book as on 30 June 20X0.

(d) Bank charges of $35 shown in the bank statement had not been entered in the cash book.

(e) The payments side of the cash book had been undercast by $10.

(f) Dividends received amounting to $200 had been paid direct to the bank and not entered in the cash book.

(g) A cheque for $50 drawn on deposit account had been shown in the cash book as drawn on current account.

(h) A cheque issued to Jones for $25 was replaced when out of date. It was entered again in the cash book, no other entry being made. Both cheques were included in the total of unpresented cheques shown above.

Required

(a) Indicate the appropriate adjustments in the cash book.
(b) Prepare a statement reconciling the amended balance with that shown in the bank statement.

Solution

(a) The errors to correct are given in notes (c) (e) (f) (g) and (h) of the problem. Bank charges (note (d)) also call for an adjustment.

(Note that debit entries add to the cash balance and credit entries are deductions from the cash balance)

		Adjustments in cash book Debit $	Credit $
Item			
(c)	Cash book incorrectly credited with interest on 30 June It should have been debited with the receipt	60	
(c)	Debit cash book (current a/c) with transfer of interest from deposit a/c (note 1)	60	
(d)	Bank charges		35
(e)	Undercast on payments (credit) side of cash book		10
(f)	Dividends received should be debited in the cash book	200	
(g)	Cheque drawn on deposit account, not current account. Add cash back to current account	50	
(h)	Cheque paid to Jones is out of date and so cancelled. Cash book should now be debited, since previous credit entry is no longer valid (note 2)	25	
		395	45

	$	$
Cash book: balance on current account as at 30 June 20X0		(300)
Adjustments and corrections:		
Debit entries (adding to cash)	395	
Credit entries (reducing cash balance)	(45)	
Net adjustments		350
Corrected balance in the cash book		50

Notes

1. Item (c) is rather complicated. The transfer of interest from the deposit to the current account was presumably given as an instruction to the bank on or before 30 June 20X0. Since the correct entry is to debit the current account (and credit the deposit account) the correction in the cash book should be to debit the current account with 2 × $60 = $120 – ie to cancel out the incorrect credit entry in the cash book and then to make the correct debit entry. However, the bank does not record the transfer until 5 July, and so it will not appear in the bank statement.

2. Item (h). Two cheques have been paid to Jones, but one is now cancelled. Since the cash book is credited whenever a cheque is paid, it should be debited whenever a cheque is cancelled. The amount of cheques paid but not yet presented should be reduced by the amount of the cancelled cheque.

(b) BANK RECONCILIATION STATEMENT AT 30 JUNE 20X0

	$	$
Balance per bank statement		65
Add: outstanding lodgements	400	
deposit interest not yet credited	60	
		460
		525
Less: unpresented cheques	500	
less cheque to Jones cancelled	(25)	
		475
Balance per corrected cash book		50

Notice that in preparing a bank reconciliation it is good practice to begin with the balance shown by the bank statement and end with the balance shown by the cash book. It is this corrected cash book balance which will appear in the balance sheet as 'cash at bank'. However examination questions sometimes ask for the reverse order: as always, read the question carefully.

You might be interested to see the adjustments to the cash book in part (a) of the problem presented in the 'T' account format, as follows:

CASH BOOK

20X0		$	20X0		$
Jun 30	Bank interest – reversal of incorrect entry	60	Jun 30	Balance brought down	300
	Bank interest account	60		Bank charges	35
	Dividends paid direct to bank	200		Correction of undercast	10
	Cheque drawn on deposit account written back	50		Balance carried down	50
	Cheque issued to Jones cancelled	25			
		395			395

PART C DOUBLE ENTRY BOOKKEEPING AND ACCOUNTING SYSTEMS

Question — Bank reconciliation

From the information given below relating to PWW Co you are required:

(a) to make such additional entries in the cash at bank account of PWW Co as you consider necessary to show the correct balance at 31 October 20X2.

(b) to prepare a statement reconciling the correct balance in the cash at bank account as shown in (a) above with the balance at 31 October 20X2 that is shown on the bank statement from Z Bank Co.

CASH AT BANK ACCOUNT IN THE LEDGER OF PWW CO

20X2 October		$	20X2 October		$
1	Balance b/f	274	1	Wages	3,146
8	Q Manufacturing	3,443	1	Petty Cash	55
8	R Cement	1,146	8	Wages	3,106
11	S Co	638	8	Petty Cash	39
11	T & Sons	512	15	Wages	3,029
11	U & Co	4,174	15	Petty Cash	78
15	V Co	1,426	22	A & Sons	929
15	W Electrical	887	22	B Co	134
22	X and Associates	1,202	22	C & Company	77
26	Y Co	2,875	22	D & E	263
26	Z Co	982	22	F Co	1,782
29	ABC Co	1,003	22	G Associates	230
29	DEE Corporation	722	22	Wages	3,217
29	GHI Co	2,461	22	Petty Cash	91
31	Balance c/f	14	25	H & Partners	26
			26	J Sons & Co	868
			26	K & Co	107
			26	L, M & N	666
			28	O Co	112
			29	Wages	3,191
			29	Petty Cash	52
			29	P & Sons	561
		21,759			**21,759**

Z BANK CO – STATEMENT OF ACCOUNT WITH PWW CO

20X2 October		Payments $	Receipts $		Balance $
1					1,135
1	cheque	55			
1	cheque	3,146			
1	cheque	421		O/D	2,487
2	cheque	73			
2	cheque	155		O/D	2,715
6	cheque	212		O/D	2,927
8	sundry credit		4,589		
8	cheque	3,106			
8	cheque	39		O/D	1,483
11	sundry credit		5,324		3,841
15	sundry credit		2,313		
15	cheque	78			
15	cheque	3,029			3,047
22	sundry credit		1,202		
22	cheque	3,217			
22	cheque	91			941
25	cheque	1,782			
25	cheque	134		O/D	975
26	cheque	929			
26	sundry credit		3,857		
26	cheque	230			1,723
27	cheque	263			
27	cheque	77			1,383
29	sundry credit		4,186		
29	cheque	52			
29	cheque	3,191			
29	cheque	26			
29	dividends on investments		2,728		
29	cheque	666			4,362
31	bank charges	936			3,426

Answer

(a)   CASH BOOK

			$			$
31 Oct	Dividends received		2,728	31 Oct	Unadjusted balance b/f (overdraft)	14
				31 Oct	Bank charges	936
				31 Oct	Adjusted balance c/f	1,778
			2,728			2,728

(b)   BANK RECONCILIATION STATEMENT AT 31 OCTOBER 20X2

	$	$
Corrected balance as per cash book		1,778
Cheques paid out but not yet presented	1,648	
Cheques paid in but not yet cleared by bank	0	
		1,648
Balance as per bank statement		3,426

PART C DOUBLE ENTRY BOOKKEEPING AND ACCOUNTING SYSTEMS

Workings

1. Payments shown on bank statement but not in cash book*
$(421 + 73 + 155 + 212)$ $861

   * Presumably recorded in cash book before 1 October 20X2 but not yet presented for payment as at 30 September 20X2

2. Payments in the cash book and on the bank statement
$(3,146 + 55 + 3,106 + 39 + 78 + 3,029 + 3,217 + 91 + 1,782 + 134 + 929 + 230 + 263 + 77 + 52 + 3,191 + 26 + 666)$ $20,111

3. Payments in the cash book but not on the bank statement = Total payments in cash book $21,759 minus $20,111 = $1,648

		$
(Alternatively	J & Sons	868
	K & Co	107
	O Co	112
	P & Sons	561
		1,648

4. Bank charges, not in the cash book $936

5. Receipts recorded by bank statement but not in cash book: dividends on investments $2,728

6. Receipts in the cash book and also bank statement $21,471
(8 Oct $4,589; 11 Oct $5,324; 15 Oct $2,313; 22 Oct $1,202; 26 Oct $3,857; 29 Oct $4,186)

7. Receipts recorded in cash book but not bank statement   None

8: BANK RECONCILIATIONS

Chapter Roundup

- In theory, the entries appearing on a business's **bank statement** should be exactly the same as those in the business **cash book**. The balance shown by the bank statement as on a particular date should be the same as the cash book balance at the same date.

- It is common (and a very important financial control) to check this at regular intervals, say weekly or monthly. Invariably it will be found that the picture shown by the bank statement differs from that shown by the cash book. There are three reasons for this.

  - **Errors.** Entries on the bank statement may be incorrect, but more commonly, errors may be found in the cash book.

  - **Omissions.** Items may appear on the bank statement which have not yet been entered in the cash book. These may include bank charges and payments made by direct debit.

  - **Timing differences.** Cheques are entered in the cash book as soon as they are written, but there may be a delay before the payee receives them and a further delay while they are processed through the bank clearing system.

- When these discrepancies are noticed, appropriate adjustments must be made. Errors must be corrected; omissions from the cash book must be made good. The balance in the cash book will then be correct and up to date.

- Any remaining difference between the cash book balance and the statement balance should then be explained as the result of identifiable timing differences.

Quick Quiz

1   Name three common reasons for differences between the cash book and the bank statements.

2   Show the standard layout of a bank reconciliation.

3   A bank statement shows a balance of $1,200 in credit. An examination of the statement shows a $500 cheque paid in per the cash book but not yet on the bank statement and a $1,250 cheque paid out but not yet on the statement. In addition the cash book shows deposit interest received of $50 but this is not yet on the statement. What is the balance per the cash book?

    A $1,900 overdrawn
    B $500 overdrawn
    C $1,900 in hand
    D $500 in hand

Answers to Quick Quiz

1 See paragraph 2.

2

	$	$
Balance per bank statement		X
Add: outstanding lodgements	X	
deposit interest not yet credited	X	X
	X	
Less: unpresented cheques		(X)
Balance per corrected cash book		X

3 D

	$	$
Balance per bank statement		1,200
Add: outstanding lodgements	500	
deposit interest not yet credited	50	550
	1,750	
Less: unpresented cheques		(1,250)
Balance per cash book		500

Now try the questions below from the Exam Question Bank

Number	Level	Marks	Time
Q10	Examination	10	18 mins
Q11	Examination	10	18 mins

Correction of errors

Topic list	Syllabus reference
1 Types of error in accounting	3(b)(iii)
2 The correction of errors	3(b)(iii)

Introduction

This chapter continues the subject of errors in accounts. You have already learned about errors which arise in the context of the cash book or the sales and purchase ledgers and receivables and payables control accounts.
Here we deal with errors that may be corrected by means of the journal or a suspense account.

By the end of this chapter you should be able to prepare a set of final accounts for a sole trader from a trial balance after incorporating adjustments to profits for errors.

Study guide

Section 5 – The journal; ledger account controls; bank reconciliations

- Explain the uses of the journal.
- Illustrate the use of the journal and the posting of journal entries into ledger accounts.
- Explain the types of error which may occur in bookkeeping systems, identifying those which can and those which cannot be detected by preparing a trial balance.
- Illustrate the use of the journal in correcting errors, including the use of a suspense account.
- Prepare statements correcting profit for errors discovered.

Exam guide

Errors are more likely to be the subject of a MCQ in Section A. However, the correction of errors is likely to be included in a longer question in Section B.

1 Types of error in accounting

FAST FORWARD

There are five main types of error. Some can be corrected by journal entry, some require the use of a suspense account.

It is not really possible to draw up a complete list of all the errors which might be made by bookkeepers and accountants. Even if you tried, it is more than likely that as soon as you finished, someone would commit a completely new error that you had never even dreamed of! However, it is possible to describe **five types of error** which cover most of the errors which might occur. They are as follows.

- Errors of **transposition**
- Errors of **omission**
- Errors of **principle**
- Errors of **commission**
- **Compensating errors**

Once an error has been detected, it needs to be put right.

- If the correction **involves a double entry** in the ledger accounts, then it is done by using a **journal entry** in the journal.
- When the error **breaks the rule of double entry**, then it is corrected by the use of a **suspense account** as well as a journal entry.

Topics covered in this chapter

- The five common types of error
- Review journal entries (which we briefly looked at earlier in this text)
- Define a **suspense account**, and describe how it is used

1.1 Errors of transposition

Key term

An **error of transposition** is when two digits in an amount are accidentally recorded the wrong way round.

For example, suppose that a sale is recorded in the sales account as $6,843, but it has been incorrectly recorded in the total receivables account as $6,483. The error is the transposition of the 4 and the 8. The consequence is that total debits will not be equal to total credits. You can often detect a transposition error by checking whether the difference between debits and credits can be divided exactly by 9. For example, $6,843 – $6,483 = $360; $360 ÷ 9 = 40.

1.2 Errors of omission

Key term

> An **error of omission** means failing to record a transaction at all, or making a debit or credit entry, but not the corresponding double entry.

Here is an example.

(a) If a business receives an invoice from a supplier for $250, the transaction might be omitted from the books entirely. As a result, both the total debits and the total credits of the business will be out by $250.

(b) If a business receives an invoice from a supplier for $300, the payables control account might be credited, but the debit entry in the purchases account might be omitted. In this case, the total credits would not equal total debits (because total debits are $300 less than they ought to be).

1.3 Errors of principle

Key term

> An **error of principle** involves making a double entry in the belief that the transaction is being entered in the correct accounts, but subsequently finding out that the accounting entry breaks the 'rules' of an accounting principle or concept.

A typical example of such an error is to treat certain revenue expenditure incorrectly as capital expenditure.

(a) For example, repairs to a machine costing $150 should be treated as revenue expenditure, and debited to a repairs account. If, instead, the repair costs are added to the cost of the non-current asset (capital expenditure) an error of principle would have occurred. As a result, although total debits still equal total credits, the repairs account is $150 less than it should be and the cost of the non-current asset is $150 greater than it should be.

(b) Similarly, suppose that the proprietor of the business sometimes takes cash out of the till for his personal use and during a certain year these withdrawals on account of profit amount to $280. The book-keeper states that he has reduced cash sales by $280 so that the cash book could be made to balance. This would be an error of principle, and the result of it would be that the withdrawal account is understated by $280, and so is the total value of sales in the sales account.

1.4 Errors of commission

Key term

> **Errors of commission** are where the bookkeeper makes a mistake in carrying out his or her task of recording transactions in the accounts.

Here are two common types of errors of commission.

(a) **Putting a debit entry or a credit entry in the wrong account**. For example, if telephone expenses of $540 are debited to the electricity expenses account, an error of commission would have occurred. The result is that although total debits and total credits balance, telephone expenses are understated by $540 and electricity expenses are overstated by the same amount.

(b) **Errors of casting (adding up).** The total daily credit sales in the sales day book should be $28,425, but are incorrectly added up as $28,825. The total sales in the sales day book are then used to credit total sales and debit total receivables in the ledger accounts. Although total debits and total credits are still equal, they are incorrect by $400.

1.5 Compensating errors

Key term

Compensating errors are errors which are, coincidentally, equal and opposite to one another.

For example, two transposition errors of $540 might occur in extracting ledger balances, one on each side of the double entry. In the administration expenses account, $2,282 might be written instead of $2,822, while in the sundry income account, $8,391 might be written instead of $8,931. Both the debits and the credits would be $540 too low, and the mistake would not be apparent when the trial balance is cast. Consequently, compensating errors hide the fact that there are errors in the trial balance.

2 The correction of errors

FAST FORWARD

Errors which leave total debits and credits in the ledger accounts in balance can be corrected by using **journal entries**. Otherwise a suspense account has to be opened first, and later cleared by a journal entry.

2.1 Journal entries

Some errors can be corrected by journal entries. To remind you, the format of a journal entry is:

Date	Debit $	Credit $
Account to be debited	X	
Account to be credited		X
(Narrative to explain the transaction)		

Exam focus point

As already indicated, you are often required in an exam to present answers in the form of journal entries.

The journal requires a debit and an equal credit entry for each 'transaction', ie for each correction. This means that if total debits equal total credits before a journal entry is made then they will still be equal after the journal entry is made. This would be the case if, for example, the original error was a debit wrongly posted as a credit and vice versa.

Similarly, if total debits and total credits are unequal before a journal entry is made, then they will still be unequal (by the same amount) after it is made.

For example, a bookkeeper accidentally posts a bill for $40 to the local taxes account instead of to the electricity account. A trial balance is drawn up, and total debits are $40,000 and total credits are $40,000. A journal entry is made to correct the misposting error as follows.

1.7.20X7

DEBIT	Electricity account	$40	
CREDIT	Local taxes account		$40

To correct a misposting of $40 from the local taxes account to electricity account

After the journal has been posted, total debits will still be $40,000 and total credits will be $40,000. Total debits and totals credits are still equal.

Now suppose that, because of some error which has not yet been detected, total debits were originally $40,000 but total credits were $39,900. If the same journal correcting the $40 is put through, total debits will remain $40,000 and total credits will remain $39,900. Total debits were different by $100 **before** the journal, and they are still different by $100 **after** the journal.

This means that journals can only be used to correct errors which require both a credit and (an equal) debit adjustment.

2.2 Example: Journal entries

Listed below are five errors which were used as examples earlier in this chapter. Write out the journal entries which would correct these errors.

(a) A business receives an invoice for $250 from a supplier which was omitted from the books entirely.

(b) Repairs worth $150 were incorrectly debited to the non-current asset (machinery) account instead of the repairs account.

(c) The bookkeeper of a business reduces cash sales by $280 because he was not sure what the $280 represented. In fact, it was a withdrawal on account of profit.

(d) Telephone expenses of $540 are incorrectly debited to the electricity account.

(e) A page in the sales day book has been added up to $28,425 instead of $28,825.

Solution

(a) DEBIT   Purchases $250
      CREDIT   Trade accounts payable $250

A transaction previously omitted

(b) DEBIT   Repairs account $150
      CREDIT   Non-current asset (machinery) a/c $150

The correction of an error of principle: Repairs costs incorrectly added to non-current asset costs

(c) DEBIT   Withdrawals on account $280
      CREDIT   Sales $280

An error of principle, in which sales were reduced to compensate for cash withdrawals not accounted for

(d) DEBIT   Telephone expenses $540
      CREDIT   Electricity expenses $540

Correction of an error of commission: telephone expenses wrongly charged to the electricity account

(e) DEBIT   Trade accounts receivable $400
      CREDIT   Sales $400

The correction of a casting error in the sales day book
($28,825 − $28,425 = $400)

2.3 Use of journal entries in examinations

Occasionally an examination question might ask you to 'journalise' a transaction (ie write it out in the form of a journal entry), even though the transaction is perfectly normal and nothing to do with an error. This is just the examiner's way of finding out whether you know your debits and credits. For example:

Question
Journal

A business sells $500 of goods on credit. Journalise the transaction.

Answer

DEBIT	Trade accounts receivable	$500	
CREDIT	Sales		$500

Goods to the value of $500 sold on credit

No error has occurred here, just a normal credit sale of $500. By asking you to put it in the form of a journal, the examiner can see that you understand the double-entry bookkeeping.

2.4 Suspense accounts

FAST FORWARD

Suspense accounts, as well as being used to correct some errors, are also opened when it is not known immediately where to post an amount. When the mystery is solved, the suspense account is closed and the amount correctly posted using a journal entry.

Key term

A **suspense account** is an account showing a balance equal to the difference in a trial balance.

A suspense account is a **temporary** account which can be opened for a number of reasons. The most common reasons are as follows.

(a) A trial balance is drawn up which does not balance (ie total debits do not equal total credits).

(b) The bookkeeper of a business knows where to post the credit side of a transaction, but does not know where to post the debit (or vice versa). For example, a cash payment might be made and must obviously be credited to cash. But the bookkeeper may not know what the payment is for, and so will not know which account to debit.

In both these cases, a temporary suspense account is opened up until the problem is sorted out. The next few paragraphs explain exactly how this works.

2.5 Use of suspense account: when the trial balance does not balance

When an error has occurred which results in an imbalance between total debits and total credits in the ledger accounts, the first step is to open a suspense account. For example, an accountant draws up a trial balance and finds that total debits exceed total credits by $162.

He knows that there is an error somewhere, but for the time being he opens a suspense account and enters a credit of $162 in it. This serves two purposes.

(a) As the suspense account now exists, the accountant will not forget that there is an error (of $162) to be sorted out.

(b) Now that there is a credit of $162 in the suspense account, the trial balance balances.

When the cause of the $162 discrepancy is tracked down, it is corrected by means of a journal entry. For example, the credit of $162 should be to purchases. The journal entry would be:

DEBIT	Suspense a/c	$162	
CREDIT	Purchases		$162

To close off suspense a/c and correct error

Whenever an error occurs which results in total debits not being equal to total credits, the first step an accountant makes is to open up a suspense account. Three more examples are given below.

2.6 Example: Transposition error

The bookkeeper of Mixem Gladly Co made a transposition error when entering an amount for sales in the sales account. Instead of entering the correct amount of $37,453.60 he entered $37,543.60, transposing the 4 and 5. The trade accounts receivable were posted correctly, and so when total debits and credits on the ledger accounts were compared, it was found that credits exceeded debits by $(37,543.60 − 37,453.60) = $90.

The initial step is to equalise the total debits and credits by posting a debit of $90 to a suspense account.

When the cause of the error is discovered, the double entry to correct it should be logged in the journal as:

DEBIT	Sales	$90	
CREDIT	Suspense a/c		$90

To close off suspense a/c and correct transposition error

2.7 Example: Error of omission

When Guttersnipe Builders paid the monthly salary cheques to its office staff, the payment of $5,250 was correctly entered in the cash account, but the bookkeeper omitted to debit the office salaries account. As a consequence, the total debit and credit balances on the ledger accounts were not equal, and credits exceeded debits by $5,250.

The initial step in correcting the situation is to debit $5,250 to a suspense account, to equalise the total debits and total credits.

When the cause of the error is discovered, the double entry to correct it should be logged in the journal as:

DEBIT	Office salaries account	$5,250	
CREDIT	Suspense a/c		$5,250

To close off suspense account and correct error of omission

2.8 Example: Error of commission

A bookkeeper might make a mistake by entering what should be a debit entry as a credit, or vice versa. For example, a credit customer pays $460 of the $660 he owes to Ashdown Tree Felling Contractors, but Ashdown's bookkeeper debits $460 on the receivables account in the nominal ledger by mistake instead of crediting the payment received.

The total debit balances in Ashdown's ledger accounts would now exceed the total credits by 2 × $460 = $920. The initial step in correcting the error would be to make a credit entry of $920 in a suspense account. When the cause of the error is discovered, it should be corrected as follows.

DEBIT	Suspense a/c	$920	
CREDIT	Trade accounts receivable		$920

To close off suspense account and correct error of commission

In the receivables control account in the nominal ledger, the correction would appear therefore as follows.

RECEIVABLES CONTROL ACCOUNT

	$		$
Balance b/f	660	Suspense a/c: error corrected	920
Payment incorrectly debited	460	Balance c/f	200
	1,120		1,120

2.9 Use of suspense account: not knowing where to post a transaction

Another use of suspense accounts occurs when a bookkeeper does not know where to post one side of a transaction. Until the mystery is sorted out, the entry can be recorded in a suspense account. A typical example is when the business receives cash through the post from a source which cannot be determined. The double entry in the accounts would be a debit in the cash book, and a credit to a suspense account.

2.10 Example: Not knowing where to post a transaction

Windfall Garments received a cheque in the post for $620. The name on the cheque is R J Beasley, but Windfall Garments have no idea who this person is, nor why he should be sending $620. The bookkeeper decides to open a suspense account, so that the double entry for the transaction is:

DEBIT	Cash	$620	
CREDIT	Suspense a/c		$620

Eventually, it transpires that the cheque was in payment for a debt owed by the Haute Couture Corner Shop and paid out of the proprietor's personal bank account. The suspense account can now be cleared, as follows.

DEBIT	Suspense a/c	$620	
CREDIT	Trade accounts receivable		$620

2.11 Suspense accounts might contain several items

If more than one error or unidentifiable posting to a ledger account arises during an accounting period, they will all be merged together in the same suspense account. Indeed, until the causes of the errors are discovered, the bookkeepers are unlikely to know exactly how many errors there are. An examination question might give you a balance on a suspense account, together with enough information to make the necessary corrections, leaving a nil balance on the suspense account and correct balances on various other accounts. In practice, of course, finding these errors is far from easy!

2.12 Suspense accounts are temporary

FAST FORWARD

> **Suspense accounts are only temporary.** None should exist when it comes to drawing up the financial statements at the end of the accounting period.

It must be stressed that a **suspense account can only be temporary**. Postings to a suspense account are only made when the bookkeeper doesn't know yet what to do, or when an error has occurred. Mysteries must be solved, and errors must be corrected. **Under no circumstances should there still be a suspense account when it comes to preparing the balance sheet of a business. The suspense account must be cleared and all the correcting entries made before the final accounts are drawn up.**

This question is quite comprehensive. See if you can tackle it.

Question — Errors

At the year end of T Down & Co, an imbalance in the trial balance was revealed which resulted in the creation of a suspense account with a credit balance of $1,040.

Investigations revealed the following errors.

(i) A sale of goods on credit for $1,000 had been omitted from the sales account.

(ii) Delivery and installation costs of $240 on a new item of plant had been recorded as a revenue expense.

(iii) Cash discount of $150 on paying a supplier, JW, had been taken, even though the payment was made outside the time limit.

(iv) Inventory of stationery at the end of the period of $240 had been ignored.

(v) A purchase of raw materials of $350 had been recorded in the purchases account as $850.

(vi) The purchase returns day book included a sales credit note for $230 which had been entered correctly in the account of the customer concerned, but included with purchase returns in the nominal ledger.

Required

(a) Prepare journal entries to correct *each* of the above errors. Narratives are *not* required.

(b) Open a suspense account and show the corrections to be made.

(c) Prior to the discovery of the errors, T Down & Co's gross profit for the year was calculated at $35,750 and the net profit for the year at $18,500.

Calculate the revised gross and net profit figures after the correction of the errors.

Answer

(a)

				Dr $	Cr $
(i)	DEBIT	Suspense a/c		1,000	
	CREDIT	Sales			1,000
(ii)	DEBIT	Plant		240	
	CREDIT	Delivery cost			240
(iii)	DEBIT	Cash discount received		150	
	CREDIT	JW a/c			150
(iv)	DEBIT	Inventory of stationery		240	
	CREDIT	Stationery expense			240
(v)	DEBIT	Suspense a/c		500	
	CREDIT	Purchases			500
(vi)	DEBIT	Purchase returns		230	
	DEBIT	Sales returns		230	
	CREDIT	Suspense a/c			460

(b)

SUSPENSE A/C

		$			$
(i)	Sales	1,000		End of year balance	1,040
(v)	Purchases	500	(vi)	Purchase returns/sales returns	460
		1,500			1,500

(c)

	$
Gross profit originally reported	35,750
Sales omitted	1,000
Plant costs wrongly allocated	240
Incorrect recording of purchases	500
Sales credit note wrongly allocated	(460)
Adjusted gross profit	37,030
Net profit originally reported	18,500
Adjustments to gross profit $(37,030 – 35,750)	1,280
Cash discount incorrectly taken	(150)
Stationery inventory	240
Adjusted net profit	19,870

Note. It has been assumed that the delivery and installation costs on plant have been included in purchases.

PART C DOUBLE ENTRY BOOKKEEPING AND ACCOUNTING SYSTEMS

Chapter Roundup

- There are five **types of error**.
  - Errors of transposition
  - Errors of omission
  - Errors of principle
  - Errors of commission
  - Compensating errors
- Errors which leave total debits and total credits on the ledger accounts in balance can be corrected by using **journal entries**. Otherwise, a suspense account has to be opened first (and a journal entry used later to record the correction of the error, clearing the suspense account in the process).
- **Suspense accounts**, as well as being used to correct some errors, are also opened when it is not known immediately where to post an amount. When the mystery is solved, the suspense account is closed and the amount correctly posted using a journal entry.
- **Suspense accounts are only temporary**. None should exist when it comes to drawing up the financial statements at the end of the accounting period.

Quick Quiz

1 List five types of error made in accounting.

2 What is the format of a journal entry?

3 Explain what a suspense account is.

4 What must be done with a suspense account before preparing a balance sheet?

5 Sales returns of $460 have inadvertently been posted to the purchase returns, although the correct entry has been made to the accounts receivable control. A suspense account needs to be set up for how much?

    A $460 debit
    B $460 credit
    C $920 debit
    D $920 credit

Answers to Quick Quiz

1 Transposition, omission, principle, commission and compensating errors.

2 See Paragraph 2.1.

3 An account showing a balance equal to the difference on a trial balance.

4 All errors must be identified and the suspense account cleared to nil.

5 C   The sales returns of $460 have been credited to accounts receivable and also $460 has been credited to purchase returns. Therefore the trial balance needs a debit of 2 × $460 = $920 to balance.

Now try the questions below from the Exam Question Bank

Number	Level	Marks	Time
Q12	Introductory	n/a	36 mins
Q34	Examination	10	18 mins

Part D
Accounting treatments

Accounting conventions

Topic list	Syllabus reference
1 Background	1(d), 2(a)
2 IAS 1 *Presentation of financial statements*	1(d), 2(a)
3 Other important concepts and conventions	2(b)
4 IAS 18 *Revenue*	1(d), 2(b)

Introduction

The purpose of this part of the text is to encourage you to think more deeply about the **assumptions** on which financial accounts are prepared.

This chapter deals with the accounting conventions which lie behind accounts preparation and which you may have absorbed subconsciously in the preceding chapters on bookkeeping.

In Chapters 11 and 12 you will see how conventions and assumptions are **put into practice.** Chapters 13 to 16 then deal with certain items which are the subject of accountancy standards.

PART D ACCOUNTING TREATMENTS

Study guide

Section 14 – Accounting concepts and conventions; The IASB's *Framework* and IAS 1

- Explain the importance of the following accounting conventions (not mentioned in the *Framework*).
  - Business entity
  - Money measurement
  - Duality
  - Historical cost
  - Realisation
  - Time interval
- Explain the IASB requirements governing revenue recognition.

Exam guide

Accounting conventions have been called into question and you may be asked to **question them** yourself in an exam. This subject is covered in more detail in Chapter 24 of this Study Text.

1 Background

FAST FORWARD

In preparing financial statements, accountants follow certain **fundamental assumptions**.

Accounting practice has developed gradually over a matter of centuries. Many of its procedures are operated automatically by people who have never questioned whether alternative methods exist which have equal validity. However, the procedures in common use imply the acceptance of certain concepts which are by no means self-evident; nor are they the only possible concepts which could be used to build up an accounting framework.

Our next step is to look at some of the more important concepts which are taken for granted in preparing accounts. In this chapter we shall single out the following assumptions and concepts for discussion.

(a) Going concern
(b) Accruals or matching
(c) Prudence
(d) Consistency concept
(e) Materiality
(f) Substance over form
(g) Business entity
(h) Money measurement
(i) Historical cost convention
(j) Stable monetary unit
(k) Objectivity
(l) Realisation
(m) Duality
(n) Time interval

We begin by considering **accounting policies** and those **fundamental assumptions** which are the subject of IAS 1 *Presentation of financial statements* (items (a) – (f) of the above list).

144

10: ACCOUNTING CONVENTIONS

2 IAS 1 Presentation of financial statements

> **FAST FORWARD**
>
> IAS 1 identifies three fundamental assumptions that must be taken into account when preparing accounts:
> - Going concern
> - Accruals
> - Consistency

IAS 1 *Presentation of financial statements* was published in 1997 and revised in 2004. Here we will look at the general requirements of IAS 1 and what it says about **accounting policies** and **fundamental assumptions**. The rest of the standard, on the format and content of financial statements will be covered in Chapter 19.

2.1 Objectives and scope

The main objective of IAS 1 is:

'to prescribe the basis for presentation of general purpose financial statements, to ensure comparability both with the entity's financial statements of previous periods and with the financial statements of other entities.'

IAS 1 applies to all **general purpose financial statements** prepared and presented in accordance with International Financial Reporting Standards (IFRSs).

2.2 Purpose of financial statements

The **objective of financial statements** is to provide information about the financial position, performance and cash flows of an entity that is useful to a wide range of users in making economic decisions. They also show the result of **management's stewardship** of the resources entrusted to it.

In order to fulfil this objective, financial statements must provide information about the following aspects of an entity's results.

- Assets
- Liabilities
- Equity
- Income and expenses (including gains and losses)
- Other changes in equity
- Cash flows

Along with other information in the notes and related documents, this information will assist users in predicting the entity **future cash flows**.

According to IAS 1, a complete set of financial statements includes the following components.

(a) Balance sheet

(b) Income statement

(c) A statement showing *either* all changes in equity *or* changes in equity other than those arising from capital transactions with and/or distributions to owners.

(d) Cash flow statement

(e) Accounting policies and explanatory notes

The preparation of these statements is the responsibility of the **board of directors**. IAS 1 also encourages a **financial review** by management and the production of any other reports and statements which may aid users.

2.3 Fair presentation and compliance with IASs/IFRSs

Most importantly, financial statements should **present fairly** the financial position, financial performance and cash flows of an entity. **Compliance with IASs/IFRS** will almost always achieve this.

The following points made by IAS 1 expand on this principle.

(a) **Compliance with IASs/IFRSs** should be disclosed

(b) **All relevant IASs/IFRSs** must be followed if compliance with IASs/IFRSs is disclosed

(c) Use of an **inappropriate accounting treatment** cannot be rectified either by disclosure of accounting policies or notes/explanatory material

There may be (very rare) circumstances when management decides that compliance with a requirement of an IAS/IFRS would be misleading. **Departure from the IAS/IFRS** is therefore required to achieve a fair presentation. The following should be disclosed in such an event.

(a) Management confirmation that the financial statements fairly present the entity's financial position, performance and cash flows

(b) Statement that all IASs/IFRSs have been complied with *except* departure from one IAS/IFRS to achieve a fair presentation

(c) Details of the nature of the departure, why the IAS/IFRS treatment would be misleading, and the treatment adopted

(d) Financial impact of the departure

IAS 1 states what is required for a fair presentation.

(a) Selection and application of **accounting policies**

(b) **Presentation of information** in a manner which provides relevant, reliable, comparable and understandable information

(c) **Additional disclosures** where required

2.4 Accounting policies

FAST FORWARD

> IAS 1 also considers three other concepts extremely important. Prudence, substance over form and materiality should govern the selection and application of accounting policies.

Accounting policies should be chosen in order **to comply with International Accounting Standards.** Where there is **no specific requirement** in an IAS or IFRS, policies should be developed so that information provided by the financial statements is:

(a) **Relevant** to the decision-making needs of users.

(b) **Reliable** in that they:

   (i) represent faithfully the **results and financial position** of the entity.
   (ii) reflect the **economic substance** of events and transactions and not merely the legal form.
   (iii) are **neutral**, that is free from bias.
   (iv) are **prudent**.
   (v) are **complete in all material respects**.

(c) **Comparable**

(d) **Understandable**

The IAS then considers certain important assumptions which underpin the preparation and presentation of financial statements.

2.5 Going concern

Key term

> The entity is normally viewed as a **going concern**, that is, as continuing in operation for the foreseeable future. It is assumed that the entity has neither the intention nor the necessity of liquidation or of curtailing materially the scale of its operations.

This concept assumes that, when preparing a normal set of accounts, the business will **continue to operate** in approximately the same manner for the foreseeable future (at least the next 12 months). In particular, the entity will not go into liquidation or scale down its operations in a material way.

The main significance of a going concern is that the assets **should not be valued at their 'break-up' value;** the amount they would sell for if they were sold off piecemeal and the business were broken up.

2.6 Example: Going concern

Emma acquires a T-shirt printing machine at a cost of $60,000. The asset has an estimated life of six years, and it is normal to write off the cost of the asset to the income statement over this time. In this case a depreciation cost of $10,000 per year is charged.

Using the going concern assumption, it is presumed that the business will continue its operations and so the asset will live out its full six years in use. A depreciation charge of $10,000 is made each year, and the value of the asset in the balance sheet is its cost less the accumulated depreciation charged to date. After one year, the **net book value** of the asset is $(60,000 – 10,000) = $50,000, after two years it is $40,000, after three years $30,000 etc, until it is written down to a value of 0 after 6 years.

This asset has no other operational use outside the business and, in a forced sale, it would only sell for scrap. After one year of operation, its scrap value is $8,000.

The net book value of the asset, applying the going concern assumption, is $50,000 after one year, but its immediate sell-off value only $8,000. It can be argued that the asset is over-valued at $50,000, that it should be written down to its break-up value ($8,000) and the balance of its cost should be treated as an expense. However, provided that the going concern assumption is valid, it is appropriate accounting practice to value the asset at its net book value.

Question — Going concern

A retailer commences business on 1 January and buys inventory of 20 washing machines, each costing $100. During the year he sells 17 machines at $150 each. How should the remaining machines be valued at 31 December in the following circumstances?

(a) He is forced to close down his business at the end of the year and the remaining machines will realise only $60 each in a forced sale.

(b) He intends to continue his business into the next year.

Answer

(a) If the business is to be closed down, the remaining three machines must be valued at the amount they will realise in a forced sale, ie 3 × $60 = $180.

(b) If the business is regarded as a going concern, the inventory unsold at 31 December will be carried forward into the following year, when the cost of the three machines will be matched against the eventual sale proceeds in computing that year's profits. The three machines will therefore be valued at cost, 3 × $100 = $300.

PART D   ACCOUNTING TREATMENTS

If the going concern assumption is not followed, that fact must be disclosed, together with the following information.

(a) The basis on which the financial statements have been prepared.
(b) The reasons why the entity is not considered to be a going concern.

2.7 Accruals basis of accounting

Key term

> **Accruals basis of** accounting. Items are recognised as assets, liabilities, equity, income and expenses (the elements of financial statements) when they satisfy the definitions and recognition criteria for those elements in the *Framework*.   IAS 1

Entities should prepare their financial statements on the basis that transactions are recorded in them, not as the cash is paid or received, but as the revenues or expenses are **earned or incurred** in the accounting period to which they relate.

According to the accrual assumption then, in computing profit revenue earned must be **matched against** the expenditure incurred in earning it. This is the **matching convention** that we first met in Chapter 2.

2.8 Example: Accrual

Emma prints 20 T-shirts in her first month of trading (May) at a cost of $5 each. She then sells all of them for $10 each. Emma has therefore made a profit of $100, by matching the revenue ($200) earned against the cost ($100) of acquiring them.

If, however, Emma only sells 18 T-shirts, it is incorrect to charge her income statement with the cost of 20 T-shirts, as she still has two T-shirts in inventory. If she sells them in June, she is likely to make a profit on the sale. Therefore, only the purchase cost of 18 T-shirts ($90) should be matched with her sales revenue ($180), leaving her with a profit of $90.

Her balance sheet will look like this.

	$
Assets	
Inventory (at cost, ie 2 × $5)	10
Accounts receivable (18 × $10)	180
	190
Capital and liabilities	
Proprietor's capital (profit for the period)	90
Accounts payable (20 × $5)	100
	190

However, if Emma had decided to give up selling T-shirts, then the going concern assumption no longer applies and the value of the two T-shirts in the balance sheet is break-up valuation not cost. Similarly, if the two unsold T-shirts are unlikely to be sold at more than their cost of $5 each (say, because of damage or a fall in demand) then they should be recorded on the balance sheet at their *net realisable value* (ie the likely eventual sales price less any expenses incurred to make them saleable) rather than cost. This shows the application of the **prudence concept**, which we will look at shortly.

In this example, the concepts of going concern and accrual are linked. Since the business is assumed to be a going concern, it is possible to carry forward the cost of the unsold T-shirts as a charge against profits of the next period.

2.9 Consistency of presentation

To maintain consistency, the presentation and classification of items in the financial statements should **stay the same from one period to the next**, except as follows.

148

(a) There is a significant change in the **nature of the operations** or a review of the financial statements indicates a **more appropriate presentation.**

(b) A change in presentation is **required by an IAS.**

2.10 Materiality and aggregation

All material items should be **disclosed** in the financial statements.

Amounts which are **immaterial** can be aggregated with amounts of a similar nature or function and need not be presented separately.

Key term

> **Materiality.** Information is material if its omission or misstatement could influence the economic decisions of users taken on the basis of the financial statements. *(IAS 1)*

An error which is too trivial to affect anyone's understanding of the accounts is referred to as **immaterial**. In preparing accounts it is important to assess what is material and what is not, so that time and money are not wasted in the pursuit of excessive detail.

Determining whether or not an item is material is a very **subjective exercise**. There is no absolute measure of materiality. It is common to apply a convenient rule of thumb (for example material items are those with a value greater than 5% of net profits). However some items disclosed in the accounts are regarded as particularly sensitive and even a very small misstatement of such an item is taken as a material error. An example, in the accounts of a limited liability company, is the amount of remuneration paid to directors of the company.

The assessment of an item as material or immaterial may **affect its treatment in the accounts**. For example, the income statement of a business shows the expenses incurred grouped under suitable captions (heating and lighting, rent and local taxes, etc); but in the case of very small expenses it may be appropriate to lump them together as 'sundry expenses', because a more detailed breakdown is inappropriate for such immaterial amounts.

In assessing whether or not an item is material, it is not only the value of the item which needs to be considered. The **context** is also important.

(a) If a balance sheet shows long-term assets of $2 million and inventories of $30,000, an error of $20,000 in the depreciation calculations might not be regarded as material. Whereas an error of $20,000 in the inventory valuation is material. In other words, the total of which the error forms part must be considered.

(b) If a business has a bank loan of $50,000 and a $55,000 balance on bank deposit account, it will be a material misstatement if these two amounts are displayed on the balance sheet as 'cash at bank $5,000'. In other words, incorrect presentation may amount to material misstatement even if there is no monetary error.

Question

Materiality

Would you capitalise the following items in the accounts of a company?

(a) A box file
(b) A computer
(c) A small plastic display stand

Answer

(a) No. You would write it off to the income statement as an expense.

(b) Yes. You would capitalise the computer and charge depreciation on it.

(c) Your answer depends on the size of the company and whether writing off the item has a material effect on its profits. A larger organisation might well write this item off under the heading of advertising expenses, while a small one might capitalise it and depreciate it over time. This is because the item is material to the small company, but not to the large company.

2.11 Offsetting

IAS 1 does not allow **assets and liabilities to be offset** against each other unless such a treatment is required or permitted by another IAS.

Income and expenses can be offset only when one of the following applies.

(a) An IAS requires/permits it.

(b) Gains, losses and related expenses arising from the same/similar transactions are not material.

2.12 Comparative information

IAS 1 requires comparative information to be disclosed for the previous period for all **numerical information**, unless another IAS permits/requires otherwise. Comparatives should also be given in narrative information where helpful.

Comparatives should be **restated** when the presentation or classification of items in the financial statements is amended.

2.13 Prudence

Key term

> **Prudence.** The inclusion of a degree of caution in the exercise of the judgements needed in making the estimates required under conditions of uncertainty, such that assets or income are not overstated and liabilities or expenses are not understated.

Prudence must be exercised when preparing financial statements because of the **uncertainty** surrounding many transactions. It is not permitted, however, to create secret or hidden reserves using prudence as a justification.

There are three important issues to bear in mind.

(a) Where **alternative procedures or valuations** are possible, the one selected should be the one which gives the most cautious result. For example, you may have wondered why the three washing machines in Question 1 were stated in the balance sheet at their cost ($100 each) rather than their selling price ($150 each). This is simply an aspect of prudence: to value the machines at $150 would be to anticipate making a profit before the profit had been realised.

(b) Where a **loss is foreseen,** it should be anticipated and taken into account immediately. Even when the exact amount of the loss is not known, an estimate of the loss should be made, based on the best information available. If a business purchases inventory for $1,200 but, because of a sudden slump in the market, only $900 is likely to be realised when the inventory is sold; the prudence concept dictates that the inventory is valued at $900. It is not enough to wait until the inventory is sold, and then recognise the $300 loss; it must be recognised as soon as it is foreseen.

(c) Profits should only be recognised when **realised** in the form of cash or another asset with a reasonably certain cash value.

2.14 Examples: Prudence

Some examples might help to explain the application of prudence.

(a) A company begins trading on 1 January 20X5 and sells goods worth $100,000 during the year to 31 December. At 31 December there are accounts receivable outstanding of $15,000. Of these, the company is now doubtful whether $6,000 will ever be paid.

The company should make a *provision for doubtful debts* of $6,000. Sales for 20X5 are shown in the income statement at their full value of $100,000, but the provision for doubtful debts is a charge of $6,000. Since there is some uncertainty that the sales will be realised in the form of cash, prudence dictates that the $6,000 should not be included in the profit for the year.

(b) Samson Feeble trades as a carpenter. He undertakes to make a range of kitchen furniture for a customer at an agreed price of $1,000. At the end of Samson's accounting year the job is unfinished (being two thirds complete) and the following data has been assembled.

	$
Costs incurred in making the furniture to date	800
Further estimated costs to completion of the job	400
Total cost	1,200

The incomplete job represents *work in progress* at the end of the year which is an asset, like inventory. Its cost to date is $800, but by the time the job is completed Samson will make a loss of $200.

The full $200 loss should be charged against profits of the current year. The value of work in progress at the year end is its *net realisable value*, which is lower than its cost. The net realisable value can be calculated in either of two ways.

	(i) $		(ii) $
Eventual sales value	1,000	Work in progress at cost	800
Less further costs to completion in order to make the sale	400	Less loss foreseen	200
Net realisable value	600		600

2.15 Substance over form

Key term

Substance over form. The principle that transactions and other events are accounted for and presented in accordance with their substance and economic reality and not merely their legal form.

Substance over form usually applies to transactions which are fairly complicated. It is very important because it acts as a 'catch-all' to stop enterprises distorting their results by following the **letter of the law,** instead of showing what the enterprise has really been doing.

2.16 Presentation of accounting policies

There should be a specific section for accounting policies in the notes to the financial statements and the following should be disclosed there.

(a) **Measurement bases** used in preparing the financial statements

(b) Each **specific accounting policy** necessary for a proper understanding of the financial statements

To be clear and understandable it is essential that financial statements disclose the accounting policies used in their preparation. This is because **policies may vary**, not only from enterprise to enterprise, but also from country to country. As an aid to users, all the major accounting policies used should be disclosed in the same note.

There is a wide range of policies available in many accounting areas. Examples where such differing policies exist are as follows, although the list is not exhaustive and it has been selected from the standard to reflect the limited areas covered in your syllabus.

Area	Policy
General	– Overall valuation policy (eg historical cost, general purchasing power, replacement value) – Events subsequent to the balance sheet date
Assets	– Receivables – Inventories and related cost of goods sold – Depreciable assets and depreciation – Research and development – Patents and trademarks – Goodwill
Liabilities and provisions	– Commitments and contingencies
Profits and losses	– Methods of revenue recognition – Maintenance, repairs and improvements – Gains and losses on disposals of property

3 Other important concepts and conventions

FAST FORWARD

Other important accounting concepts are:
- The business entity concept
- The money measurement concept
- The historical cost convention
- The stable monetary unit
- Objectivity
- The realisation concept
- Duality
- Time interval

3.1 The business entity concept

This concept has already been discussed in Chapter 2. Briefly, the concept is that accountants regard a business as a separate entity, distinct from its owners or managers. The concept applies whether the business is a limited liability company (and so recognised in law as a separate entity) or a sole proprietorship or partnership (in which case the business is not separately recognised by the law).

3.2 The money measurement concept

Key term

> The **money measurement concept** states that accounts will only deal with those items to which a monetary value can be attributed.

In the balance sheet of a business, monetary values can be attributed to such assets as machinery (eg the original cost) and inventories (eg net realisable value).

The money measurement concept introduces limitations to the subject-matter of accounts. A business may have intangible assets, such as the flair of a good manager or the loyalty of its workforce. These may be important enough to give it a clear superiority over an otherwise identical business, but because they cannot be evaluated in monetary terms they do not appear anywhere in the accounts.

3.3 The historical cost convention

A basic principle of accounting (some writers include it in the list of fundamental accounting assumptions) is that items are normally stated in accounts at historical cost, ie at the amount which the business paid to acquire them. An important advantage of this procedure is that the objectivity of accounts is maximised: there is usually documentary evidence to prove the amount paid to purchase an asset or pay an expense.

Key term

> **Historical cost** means that transactions are recorded at the cost when they occurred.

In general, accountants prefer to deal with costs, rather than with 'values'. This is because valuations tend to be subjective and to vary according to what the valuation is for. For example, a company acquires a machine to manufacture its products. The machine has an expected useful life of four years. At the end of two years the company is preparing a balance sheet and has to decide what monetary amount to attribute to the asset.

Numerous possibilities can be considered.

(a) The original cost (historical cost) of the machine
(b) Half of the historical cost, on the ground that half of its useful life has expired
(c) The amount the machine fetches on the secondhand market
(d) The amount needed to replace the machine with an identical machine
(e) The amount needed to replace the machine with a more modern machine incorporating the technological advances of the previous two years
(f) The machine's economic value, ie the amount of the profits it is expected to generate for the company during its remaining life

All of these valuations have something to commend them, but the great advantage of the first two is that they are based on a figure (the machine's historical cost) which is objectively verifiable. (Some authors regard objectivity as an accounting concept in its own right.) The subjective judgement involved in the other valuations, particularly (f), is so great as to lessen the reliability of any accounts in which they are used.

3.4 Stable monetary unit

The financial statements are expressed in terms of a monetary unit (eg in the UK the £, in the USA the $). It is assumed that the value of this unit remains constant.

In practice, of course, the value of the unit varies and comparisons between the accounts of the current year and those of previous years may be misleading (eg in times of inflation).

3.5 Objectivity

An accountant must show objectivity. This means answers must be free of any personal opinion or prejudice, and should be as precise and as detailed as the situation warrants. The result of this should be that any number of accountants will give the same answer independently of each other.

Key term

> **Objectivity** means that accountants must be free from bias.

In practice, objectivity is difficult. Two accountants faced with the same accounting data may come to different conclusions as to the correct treatment. It was to combat subjectivity that accounting standards were developed.

Exam focus point

> 'Objectivity' is sometimes called 'neutrality'.

3.6 The realisation concept

Key term

> The **realisation concept** means that revenue and profits are recognised when realised.

The realisation concept states that revenue and profits are not anticipated, but are recognised by inclusion in the income statement only when **realised** in the form either of **cash** or of other assets, the ultimate cash realisation of which can be assessed with reasonable certainty. Provision is made for all known liabilities (expenses and losses) whether the amount of these is known with certainty or is a best estimate in the light of the information available.

There are some **exceptions** to the rule, notably for land and buildings. With dramatic rises in property prices in some countries, it has been a common practice to **revalue land and buildings** periodically to a current value, to avoid having a misleading balance sheet. Even if the sale of the property is not contemplated, such revaluations create an unrealised profit:

DEBIT   Land and buildings account
CREDIT   Revaluation reserve account

This profit is sometimes known as a *holding gain*, because it is a profit which arises in the course of holding the asset as a result of its increase in value above cost.

In spite of such exceptions, however, the realisation principle has long been accepted by all practising accountants and it is standard practice that only profits realised at the balance sheet date should be included in the income statement.

Unfortunately there is no standard definition of realised profits and losses. It could be said that they are such profits or losses of a company as fall to be treated as realised in accordance with principles generally accepted at the time when the accounts are prepared. One aspect of the problem is the question: **At what point in the business cycle should revenue be recognised as earned?** We will consider this further when we look at IAS 18 in the next section.

3.7 The duality concept

Every transaction has two effects. This convention underpins double entry bookkeeping, and you have seen it at work in your studies from Chapter 5 onwards.

3.8 The time interval concept

The time interval concept is also known as **timeliness,** which we have looked at earlier in your studies.

This concept states that financial statements should be produced within a time interval that enables users to make relevant economic decisions. In other words there is no point in producing information that is so out of date, that no decisions can be based on it.

Question

Accounting concepts

(a) You depreciate your office equipment by 20% each year because it has a useful life, on average, of five years. This year your profitability is down and you think you can squeeze an extra year's life out of your equipment. Is it acceptable not to charge any depreciation this year?

(b) You have recently paid $4.95 for a waste paper bin which should have a useful life of about five years. Should you treat it as a long-term asset?

Answer

(a) No, because of the consistency assumption. Once the depreciation policy has been established, it should not be changed without good cause.

(b) No, because of the materiality concept. The cost of the bin is very small. Rather than cluttering up the balance sheet for five years, treat the $4.95 as an expense in this year's income statement.

4 IAS 18 Revenue

FAST FORWARD

IAS 18 *Revenue* is concerned with the recognition of revenues arising from fairly common transactions:

- The sale of goods
- The rendering of services
- The use of others of assets of the entity yielding interest, royalties and dividends.

Generally revenue is recognised when the entity has transferred to the buyer the **significant risks and rewards** of ownership and when the revenue can be **measured reliably**.

4.1 Introduction

Accruals accounting is based on the **matching of costs with the revenue they generate**. It is crucially important under this convention that we establish the point at which revenue is recognised, so that the correct treatment can be applied to the related costs. For example, the costs of producing an item of finished goods should be carried as an asset in the balance sheet until such time as it is sold; they should then be written off as a charge to the trading account. Which of these two treatments should be applied cannot be decided until it is clear at what moment the sale of the item takes place.

The decision has a **direct impact on profit** since, under the prudence concept, it is unacceptable to recognise the profit on sale until a sale has taken place, in accordance with the criteria of revenue recognition.

Revenue is generally recognised as **earned at the point of sale**, because at that point four criteria will generally have been met.

- The product or service has been **provided to the buyer**.

- The buyer has **recognised his liability** to pay for the goods or services provided. The converse of this is that the seller has recognised that ownership of goods has passed from himself to the buyer.

- The buyer has indicated his **willingness to hand over cash** or other assets in settlement of his liability.
- The **monetary value** of the goods or services has been established.

At earlier points in the business cycle there will not in general be **firm evidence** that the above criteria will be met. Until work on a product is complete, there is a risk that some flaw in the manufacturing process will necessitate its writing off; even when the product is complete there is no guarantee that it will find a buyer.

At later points in the business cycle, for example when cash is received for a credit sale, the recognition of revenue may occur in a period later than that in which the related costs were charged. Revenue recognition then depends on fortuitous circumstances, such as the cash flow of a company's receivables, and can fluctuate misleadingly from one period to another.

However, there are times when revenue is **recognised at other times than at the completion of a sale**. For example, in the recognition of profit on long-term construction contracts. Under IAS 11 *Construction contracts* (not in your syllabus) contract revenue and contract costs are recognised by reference to the stage of completion of the contract activity at the balance sheet date. You will learn about this later in your studies.

4.2 IAS 18 Revenue

IAS 18 governs the recognition of revenue in specific (common) types of transaction. Generally, recognition occurs when it is probable that **future economic benefits** will flow to the entity and when these benefits can be **measured reliably**.

Income, as defined by the IASC's *Framework* document (see Chapter 24), includes both revenues and gains. Revenue is income arising in the ordinary course of an entity's activities, such as sales, fees, interest, dividends or royalties.

4.3 Scope

IAS 18 covers the revenue from specific types of transaction or events.

- **Sale of goods** (manufactured products and items purchased for resale)
- **Rendering of services**
- Use by others of entity assets yielding **interest, royalties and dividends**

Interest, royalties and dividends are included as income because they arise from the use of an entity assets by other parties.

Key terms

> **Interest** is the charge for the use of cash or cash equivalents or amounts due to the entity.
>
> **Royalties** are charges for the use of long-term assets of the entity, eg patents, computer software and trademarks.
>
> **Dividends** are distributions of profit to holders of equity investments, in proportion with their holdings, of each relevant class of capital.

The standard specifically **excludes** various types of revenue arising from leases, insurance contracts, changes in value of financial instruments or other current assets, natural increases in agricultural assets and mineral ore extraction.

4.4 Definitions

The following definitions are given in the standard.

Key terms

> **Revenue** is the gross inflow of economic benefits during the period arising in the course of the ordinary activities of an entity when those inflows result in increases in equity, other than increases relating to contributions from equity participants.
>
> **Fair value** is the amount for which an asset could be exchanged, or a liability settled, between knowledgeable, willing parties in an arm's length transaction. *(IAS 18)*

Revenue **does not include** sales taxes, value added taxes or goods and service taxes which are only collected for third parties, because these do not represent an economic benefit flowing to the entity. The same is true for revenues collected by an agent on behalf of a principal. Revenue for the agent is only the commission received for acting as agent.

4.5 Measurement of revenue

When a transaction takes place, the amount of revenue is usually decided by the **agreement of the buyer and seller**. The revenue is actually measured, however, as the **fair value of the consideration received**, which will take account of any trade discounts and volume rebates.

4.6 Identification of the transaction

Normally, each transaction can be looked at **as a whole**. Sometimes, however, transactions are more complicated, and it is necessary to break a transaction down into its **component parts**. For example, a sale may include the transfer of goods and the provision of future servicing, the revenue for which should be deferred over the period the servicing is performed.

At the other end of the scale, **seemingly separate transactions must be considered together** if apart they lose their commercial meaning. An example would be to sell an asset with an agreement to buy it back at a later date. The second transaction cancels the first and so both must be considered together.

4.7 Sale of goods

Revenue from the sale of goods should only be recognised when *all* these conditions are satisfied.

(a) The entity has transferred the **significant risks and rewards** of ownership of the goods to the buyer

(b) The entity has **no continuing managerial involvement** to the degree usually associated with ownership, and no longer has effective control over the goods sold

(c) The amount of revenue can be **measured reliably**

(d) It is probable that the **economic benefits** associated with the transaction will flow to the entity

(e) The **costs incurred** in respect of the transaction can be measured reliably

The transfer of risks and rewards can only be decided by examining each transaction. Mainly, the transfer occurs at the same time as either the **transfer of legal title**, or the **passing of possession** to the buyer – this is what happens when you buy something in a shop.

If **significant risks and rewards remain with the seller**, then the transaction is *not* a sale and revenue cannot be recognised, for example if the receipt of the revenue from a particular sale depends on the buyer receiving revenue from his own sale of the goods.

It is possible for the seller to retain only an **'insignificant' risk of ownership** and for the sale and revenue to be recognised. The main example here is where the seller retains title only to ensure collection of what is owed on the goods. This is a common commercial situation, and when it arises the revenue should be recognised on the date of sale.

The probability of the entity receiving the revenue arising from a transaction must be assessed. It may only become probable that the economic benefits will be received when an uncertainty is removed, for example government permission for funds to be received from another country. Only when the uncertainty is removed should the revenue be recognised. This is in contrast with the situation where revenue has already been recognised, but where the **collectability of the cash** is brought into doubt. Where recovery has ceased to be probable, the amount should be recognised as an expense, *not* an adjustment of the revenue previously recognised. These points also apply to services and interest, royalties and dividends below.

Matching should take place, ie the revenue and expenses relating to the same transaction should be recognised at the same time. It is usually easy to estimate expenses at the date of sale (eg warranty costs, shipment costs, etc). Where they cannot be estimated reliably, then revenue cannot be recognised; any consideration already received is treated as a liability.

4.8 Rendering of services

When the outcome of a transaction involving the rendering of services can be estimated reliably, the associated revenue should be recognised by reference to the **stage of completion of the transaction** at the balance sheet date. The outcome of a transaction can be estimated reliably when *all* these conditions are satisfied.

(a) The amount of revenue can be **measured reliably**

(b) It is probable that the **economic benefits** associated with the transaction will flow to the entity

(c) The **stage of completion** of the transaction at the balance sheet date can be measured reliably

(d) The **costs incurred** for the transaction and the costs to complete the transaction can be measured reliably

The parties to the transaction will normally have to agree the following before an entity can make reliable estimates.

(a) Each party's **enforceable rights** regarding the service to be provided
(b) The **consideration** to be exchanged
(c) The **manner and terms of settlement**

There are various methods of determining the stage of completion of a transaction, but for practical purposes, when services are performed by an indeterminate number of acts over a period of time, revenue should be recognised on a **straight line basis** over the period, unless there is evidence for the use of a more appropriate method. If one act is of more significance than the others, then the significant act should be carried out *before* revenue is recognised.

In uncertain situations, when the outcome of the transaction involving the rendering of services cannot be estimated reliably, the standard recommends a **no loss/no gain approach**. Revenue is recognised only to the extent of the expenses that are recoverable.

This is particularly likely during the **early stages of a transaction**, but it is still probable that the entity will recover the costs incurred. So the revenue recognised in such a period will be equal to the expenses incurred, with no profit.

Obviously, if the costs are not likely to be reimbursed, then they must be recognised as an expense immediately. **When the uncertainties cease to exist**, revenue should be recognised.

4.9 Interest, royalties and dividends

When others use the entity's assets yielding interest, royalties and dividends, the revenue should be recognised on the bases set out below.

(a) It is probably that the **economic benefits** associated with the transaction will flow to the entity

(b) The amount of the revenue can be **measured reliably**

The revenue is recognised on the following bases.

(a) **Interest** is recognised on a time proportion basis that takes into account the effective yield on the asset

(b) **Royalties** are recognised on an accruals basis in accordance with the substance of the relevant agreement

(c) **Dividends** are recognised when the shareholder's right to receive payment is established

It is unlikely that you would be asked about anything as complex as this in the exam, but you should be aware of the basic requirements of the standard. The **effective yield** on an asset mentioned above is the rate of interest required to discount the stream of future cash receipts expected over the life of the asset.

Royalties are usually recognised on the same basis that they accrue **under the relevant agreement**. Sometimes the true substance of the agreement may require some other systematic and rational method of recognition.

Once again, the points made above about **probability and collectability** on sale of goods also apply here.

4.10 Disclosure

The following items should be disclosed.

(a) The **accounting policies** adopted for the recognition of revenue, including the methods used to determine the stage of completion of transactions involving the rendering of services

(b) The amount of each **significant category of revenue** recognised during the period including revenue arising from the sources below

　　(i) The sale of goods
　　(ii) The rendering of services
　　(iii) Interest
　　(iv) Royalties
　　(v) Dividends

(c) The amount of revenue arising from **exchanges of goods or services** included in each significant category of revenue

Any **contingent gains or losses**, such as those relating to warranty costs, claims or penalties should be treated according to IAS 10 *Events occurring after the balance sheet date* (see Chapter 16).

| Question | Prudence |

Given that prudence is the main consideration, discuss under what circumstances, if any, revenue might be recognised at the following stages of a sale.

(a) Goods are acquired by the business which it confidently expects to resell very quickly.
(b) A customer places a firm order for goods.
(c) Goods are delivered to the customer.
(d) The customer is invoiced for goods.
(e) The customer pays for the goods.
(f) The customer's cheque in payment for the goods has been cleared by the bank.

Answer

(a) A sale must never be recognised before the goods have even been ordered by a customer. There is no certainty about the value of the sale, nor when it will take place, even if it is virtually certain that goods will be sold.

(b) A sale must never be recognised when the customer places an order. Even though the order will be for a specific quantity of goods at a specific price, it is not yet certain that the sale transaction will go through. The customer may cancel the order, the supplier might be unable to deliver the goods as ordered or it may be decided that the customer is not a good credit risk.

(c) A sale will be recognised when delivery of the goods is made only when:

   (i) the sale is for cash, and so the cash is received at the same time.
   (ii) the sale is on credit and the customer accepts delivery (eg by signing a delivery note).

(d) The critical event for a credit sale is usually the despatch of an invoice to the customer. There is then a legally enforceable debt, payable on specified terms, for a completed sale transaction.

(e) The critical event for a cash sale is when delivery takes place and when cash is received; both take place at the same time.

It would be too cautious or 'prudent' to await cash payment for a credit sale transaction before recognising the sale, unless the customer is a high credit risk and there is a serious doubt about his ability or intention to pay. But in that case, why would the business risk dispatching the goods?

(f) It would again be over-cautious to wait for clearance of the customer's cheques before recognising sales revenue. Such a precaution would only be justified in cases where there is a very high risk of the bank refusing to honour the cheque.

10: ACCOUNTING CONVENTIONS

Chapter Roundup

- In preparing financial statements, accountants follow certain *fundamental assumptions*.
- Three such assumptions are identified by IAS 1 *Presentation of financial statements.*
    - **Going concern:** unless there is evidence to the contrary, it is assumed that a business will continue to trade normally for the foreseeable future.
    - **Accruals:** revenue earned must be matched against the expenditure incurred in earning it.
    - **Consistency:** accounting policies are consistent from one period to another.
- IAS 1 also considers three other concepts extremely important: prudence, substance over form and materiality should govern the selection and application of accounting policies.
    - **Prudence:** should be exercised where uncertainty exists.
    - **Substance over form:** financial reality takes precedence over legal form when accounting for a transaction.
    - **Materiality:** all items should be disclosed which are material enough to affect evaluations or decisions.
- A number of other concepts may be regarded as extremely important.
    - The **business entity concept**. A business is an entity distinct from its owner(s).
    - The **money measurement concept**. Accounts only deal with items to which monetary values can be attributed.
    - The **historical cost convention**. Transactions are recorded at the cost when they occurred.
    - The **stable monetary unit**. The value of the unit in which accounting statements are prepared does not change.
    - **Objectivity**. Accountants must be free from bias.
    - The **realisation concept**. Revenue and profits are recognised when realised.
    - **Duality**. Every transaction has two effects.
    - **Time interval**. Financial information must be produced with timeliness.
- IAS 18 *Revenue* is concerned with the recognition of revenues arising from fairly common transactions:
    - The sale of goods
    - The rendering of services
    - The use by others of entity assets yielding interest, royalties and dividends
- Generally revenue is recognised when the entity has transferred to the buyer the **significant risks and rewards** of ownership and when the revenue can be **measured reliably**.

Quick Quiz

1 Which IAS deals with accounting assumptions?

2 Which of the following assumptions are included in IAS 1?

    A   Money measurement
    B   Objectivity
    C   Going concern
    D   Business entity

3 Define 'going concern'.

PART D ACCOUNTING TREATMENTS

4   What is meant by the prudence concept?

5   Only items which have a monetary value can be included in accounts. Which accounting concept is this?

    A   Historical cost
    B   Money measurement
    C   Realisation
    D   Business entity

6   Suggest four possible values which might be attributed to an asset in the balance sheet of a business.

7   Generally, when should revenue be recognised?

8   Define 'revenue'.

9   What are the disclosure requirements of IAS 18?

Answers to Quick Quiz

1   IAS 1 *Presentation of Financial Statements*.

2   C   Only going concern is included in IAS 1, the others are assumptions and concepts generally used in accountancy, but not mentioned in IAS 1.

3   The assumption that a business will continue in operation for the foreseeable future, without going into liquidation or materially scaling down its operations.

4   Prudence means to be cautious when exercising judgement. In particular profits should not be recognised until realised, but a loss should be recognised as soon as it is foreseen.

5   B   This is the definition of the money measurement concept.

6   Any four of the following.

    - Historical cost
    - Historical cost depreciated over its useful life
    - The amount it would fetch if sold second hand
    - Replacement cost of an identical machine
    - Replacement cost of the latest machine
    - Economic value

7   At the point of sale.

8   See Paragraph 4.4 for the IAS 18 definition.

9
    - Accounting policies adopted to recognise revenue
    - The amount of each significant category of revenue
    - The amount of revenue arising from exchanges of goods or services

Now try the question below from the Exam Question Bank			
Number	**Level**	**Marks**	**Time**
Q13	Examination	10	18 mins

11: The cost of goods sold, accruals and prepayments

Topic list	Syllabus reference
1 The cost of goods sold	3(a)(vii), 4(b)(i)
2 Accruals and prepayments	3(a)(vii), 4(b)(ii), 4(c)

Introduction

So far we have calculated profit as follows.

	$
Sales	X
Less cost of goods sold	(X)
Gross profit	X
Less expenses	(X)
Net profit	X

However, the figures for 'cost of sales' and 'expenses' may not always be simple. Some adjustments may need to be made.

Section 1 of this chapter deals with the adjustments which may need to be made to the **cost of goods sold**. Section 2 deals with the adjustments which may need to be made to the **expenses**.

PART D   ACCOUNTING TREATMENTS

Study guide

Section 7 – The financial statements of a sole trader 1: inventory, accruals and prepayments

- Revise the format of the income statement and balance sheet from Sections 1 and 2.
- Explain the need for adjustment for inventory in preparing financial statements.
- Illustrate income statements with opening and closing inventory.
- Explain the need for adjustments for accruals and prepayments in preparing financial statements.
- Illustrate the process of adjusting for accruals and prepayments in preparing financial statements,.
- Prepare financial statements for a sole trader including adjustments for inventory, accruals and prepayments.

Exam guide

You may be examined on these topics in Section A or a question in Section B could include these topics as part of a longer question.

1 The cost of goods sold

FAST FORWARD

The **cost of goods sold** is calculated as:

Opening inventory + purchases – closing inventory.

1.1 Unsold goods in inventory at the end of an accounting period

Goods might be unsold at the end of an accounting period and so still be **held in inventory**. The purchase cost of these goods should not be included therefore in the cost of sales of the period.

1.2 Example: Closing inventory

Perry P Louis, trading as the Umbrella Shop, ends his financial year on 30 September each year. On 1 October 20X4 he had no goods in inventory. During the year to 30 September 20X5, he purchased 30,000 umbrellas costing $60,000 from umbrella wholesalers and suppliers. He resold the umbrellas for $5 each, and sales for the year amounted to $100,000 (20,000 umbrellas). At 30 September there were 10,000 unsold umbrellas left in inventory, valued at $2 each.

What was Perry P Louis's gross profit for the year?

Solution

Perry P Louis purchased 30,000 umbrellas, but only sold 20,000. Purchase costs of $60,000 and sales of $100,000 do not represent the same quantity of goods.

The gross profit for the year should be calculated by 'matching' the sales value of the 20,000 umbrellas sold with the cost of those 20,000 umbrellas. The cost of sales in this example is therefore the cost of purchases minus the cost of goods in inventory at the year end.

	$	$
Sales (20,000 units)		100,000
Purchases (30,000 units)	60,000	
Less closing inventory (10,000 units @ $2)	20,000	
Cost of sales (20,000 units)		40,000
Gross profit		60,000

1.3 Example continued

We shall continue the example of the Umbrella Shop into its next accounting year, 1 October 20X5 to 30 September 20X6. During the course of this year, Perry P Louis purchased 40,000 umbrellas at a total cost of $95,000. During the year he sold 45,000 umbrellas for $230,000. At 30 September 20X6 he had 5,000 umbrellas left in inventory, which had cost $12,000.

What was his gross profit for the year?

Solution

In this accounting year, he purchased 40,000 umbrellas to add to the 10,000 he already had in inventory at the start of the year. He sold 45,000, leaving 5,000 umbrellas in inventory at the year end. Once again, gross profit should be calculated by matching the value of 45,000 units of sales with the cost of those 45,000 units.

The cost of sales is the value of the 10,000 umbrellas in inventory at the beginning of the year, plus the cost of the 40,000 umbrellas purchased, less the value of the 5,000 umbrellas in inventory at the year end.

	$	$
Sales (45,000 units)		230,000
Opening inventory (10,000 units) *	20,000	
Add purchases (40,000 units)	95,000	
	115,000	
Less closing inventory (5,000 units)	12,000	
Cost of sales (45,000 units)		103,000
Gross profit		127,000

* Taken from the closing inventory value of the previous accounting year, see paragraph 1.3.

1.4 The cost of goods sold

The cost of goods sold is found by applying the following formula.

Formula to learn

	$
Opening inventory value	X
Add cost of purchases (or, in the case of a manufacturing company, the cost of production)	X
	X
Less closing inventory value	(X)
Equals cost of goods sold	X

In other words, to match 'sales' and the 'cost of goods sold', it is necessary to adjust the cost of goods manufactured or purchased to allow for increases or reduction in inventory levels during the period.

The 'formula' above is based on a logical idea. You should learn it, because it is fundamental among the principles of accounting.

Test your knowledge of the formula with the following example.

1.5 Example: Cost of goods sold and variations in inventory levels

On 1 January 20X6, the Grand Union Food Stores had goods in inventory valued at $6,000. During 20X6 its proprietor purchased supplies costing $50,000. Sales for the year to 31 December 20X6 amounted to $80,000. The cost of goods in inventory at 31 December 20X6 was $12,500.

Calculate the gross profit for the year.

Solution

GRAND UNION FOOD STORES
TRADING ACCOUNT FOR THE YEAR ENDED 31 DECEMBER 20X6

	$	$
Sales		80,000
Opening inventories	6,000	
Add purchases	50,000	
	56,000	
Less closing inventories	12,500	
Cost of goods sold		43,500
Gross profit		36,500

1.6 The cost of carriage inwards and outwards

> **Carriage inwards** is included in the cost of purchases.
> **Courage outwards** is a selling expense.

'Carriage' refers to the **cost of transporting purchased goods** from the supplier to the premises of the business which has bought them. Someone has to pay for these delivery costs: sometimes the supplier pays, and sometimes the purchaser pays. When the purchaser pays, the cost to the purchaser is carriage inwards (**into** the business). When the supplier pays, the cost to the supplier is known as carriage outwards (**out** of the business).

The **cost of carriage inwards** is usually added to the **cost of purchases**, and is therefore included in the **trading account**.

The **cost of carriage outwards** is a **selling and distribution expense** in the **income statement**.

1.7 Example: Carriage inwards and carriage outwards

Gwyn Tring, trading as Clickety Clocks, imports and resells clocks. He pays for the costs of delivering the clocks from his supplier in Switzerland to his shop in Wales.

He resells the clocks to other traders throughout the country, paying the costs of carriage for the consignments from his business premises to his customers.

On 1 July 20X5, he had clocks in inventory valued at $17,000. During the year to 30 June 20X6 he purchased more clocks at a cost of $75,000. Carriage inwards amounted to $2,000. Sales for the year were $162,100. Other expenses of the business amounted to $56,000 excluding carriage outwards which cost $2,500. Gwyn Tring took drawings of $20,000 from the business during the course of the year. The value of the goods in inventory at the year end was $15,400.

Required

Prepare the income statement of Clickety Clocks for the year ended 30 June 20X6.

Solution

CLICKETY CLOCKS
INCOME STATEMENT FOR THE YEAR ENDED 30 JUNE 20X6

	$	$
Sales		162,100
Opening inventory	17,000	
Purchases	75,000	
Carriage inwards	2,000	
	94,000	
Less closing inventory	15,400	
Cost of goods sold		78,600
Gross profit		83,500
Carriage outwards	2,500	
Other expenses	56,000	
		58,500
Net profit (transferred to balance sheet)		25,000

1.8 Goods written off or written down

A trader might be unable to sell all the goods that he purchases, because a number of things might happen to the goods before they can be sold. For example:

(a) Goods might be lost or stolen.

(b) Goods might be damaged, become worthless and so be thrown away.

(c) Goods might become obsolete or out of fashion. These might be thrown away, or sold off at a very low price in a clearance sale.

When goods are **lost, stolen or thrown away** as worthless, the business will make a loss on those goods because their **'sales value' will be nil**.

Similarly, when goods lose value because they have become **obsolete** or out of fashion, the business will **make a loss** if their clearance sales value is less than their cost. For example, if goods which originally cost $500 are now obsolete and could only be sold for $150, the business would suffer a loss of $350.

If, at the end of an accounting period, a business still has goods in inventory which are either worthless or worth less than their original cost, the value of the inventories should be **written down** to:

(a) Nothing, if they are worthless
(b) Their net realisable value, if this is less than their original cost

This means that the loss will be reported as soon as the loss is foreseen, even if the goods have not yet been thrown away or sold off at a cheap price. This is an application of the prudence concept, which we looked at in Chapter 10.

The costs of inventory written off or written down should not usually cause any problems in calculating the gross profit of a business, because the cost of goods sold will include the cost of inventories written off or written down, as the following example shows.

1.9 Example: Inventories written off and written down

Lucas Wagg, trading as Fairlock Fashions, ends his financial year on 31 March. At 1 April 20X5 he had goods in inventory valued at $8,800. During the year to 31 March 20X6, he purchased goods costing $48,000. Fashion goods which cost $2,100 were still held in inventory at 31 March 20X6, and Lucas Wagg believes that these could only now be sold at a sale price of $400. The goods still held in inventory at 31

PART D ACCOUNTING TREATMENTS

March 20X6 (including the fashion goods) had an original purchase cost of $7,600. Sales for the year were $81,400.

Required

Calculate the gross profit of Fairlock Fashions for the year ended 31 March 20X6.

Solution

Initial calculation of closing inventory values:

INVENTORY COUNT

	At cost $	Realisable value $	Amount written down $
Fashion goods	2,100	400	1,700
Other goods (balancing figure)	5,500	5,500	
	7,600	5,900	1,700

FAIRLOCK FASHIONS
TRADING ACCOUNT FOR THE YEAR ENDED 31 MARCH 20X6

	$	$
Sales		81,400
Value of opening inventory	8,800	
Purchases	48,000	
	56,800	
Less closing inventory	5,900	
Cost of goods sold		50,900
Gross profit		30,500

By using the figure of $5,900 for closing inventories, the cost of goods sold automatically includes the inventory written down of $1,700.

Question — Gross profit

Gross profit for 20X7 can be calculated from:

A purchases for 20X7, plus inventory at 31 December 20X7, less inventory at 1 January 20X7
B purchases for 20X7, less inventory at 31 December 20X7, plus inventory at 1 January 20X7
C cost of goods sold during 20X7, plus sales during 20X7
D net profit for 20X7, plus expenses for 20X7

Answer

The answer is given with the next question, so you won't see it before you've thought about it for yourself!

2 Accruals and prepayments

Accrued expenses, (accruals) are expenses which relate to an accounting period but have not been paid for. They are shown in the balance sheet as a liability.

Prepaid expenses (prepayments) are expenses which have already been paid but relate to a future accounting period. They are shown in the balance sheet as an asset.

2.1 Introduction

It has already been stated that the gross profit for a period should be calculated by **matching** sales and the cost of goods sold. In the same way, the net profit for a period should be calculated by charging the expenses which relate to that period. For example, in preparing the income statement of a business for a period of, say, six months, it would be appropriate to charge six months' expenses for rent and local taxes, insurance costs and telephone costs, etc.

Expenses might not be paid for during the period to which they relate. For example, a business rents a shop for $20,000 per annum and pays the full annual rent on 1 April each year. If we calculate the profit of the business for the first six months of the year 20X7, the correct charge for rent in the income statement is $10,000, even though the rent paid is $20,000 in that period. Similarly, the rent charge in the income statement for the second six months of the year is $10,000, even though no rent was actually paid in that period.

Key terms

> **Accruals** or accrued expenses are expenses which are charged against the profit for a particular period, even though they have not yet been paid for.
>
> **Prepayments** are payments which have been made in one accounting period, but should not be charged against profit until a later period, because they relate to that later period.

Accruals and prepayments might seem difficult at first, but the following examples should help to clarify the principle involved, that expenses should be matched against the period to which they relate. We can regard accruals and prepayments as the means by which we move charges into the correct accounting period. If we pay in this period for something which relates to the next accounting period, we use a prepayment to transfer that charge forward to the next period. If we have incurred an expense in this period which will not be paid for until next period, we use an accrual to bring the charge back into this period.

2.2 Example: Accruals

Horace Goodrunning, trading as Goodrunning Motor Spares, ends his financial year on 28 February each year. His telephone was installed on 1 April 20X6 and he receives his telephone account quarterly at the end of each quarter. On the basis of the following data, you are required to calculate the telephone expense to be charged to the income statement for the year ended 28 February 20X7.

Goodrunning Motor Spares – telephone expense for the three months ended:

	$
30.6.20X6	23.50
30.9.20X6	27.20
31.12.20X6	33.40
31.3.20X7	36.00

Solution

The telephone expenses for the year ended 28 February 20X7 are:

	$
1 March – 31 March 20X6 (no telephone)	0.00
1 April – 30 June 20X6	23.50
1 July – 30 September 20X6	27.20
1 October – 31 December 20X6	33.40
1 January – 28 February 20X7 (two months)	24.00
	108.10

The charge for the period 1 January – 28 February 20X7 is two-thirds of the quarterly bill received on 31 March. As at 28 February 20X7, no telephone bill has been received because it is not due for another month. However, it is inappropriate to ignore the telephone expenses for January and February, and so an accrued charge of $24 is made, being two-thirds of the quarter's bill of $36.

PART D   ACCOUNTING TREATMENTS

The accrued charge will also appear in the balance sheet of the business as at 28 February 20X7, as a current liability.

2.3 Example: Accrual

Cleverley started in business as a paper plate and cup manufacturer on 1 January 20X2, making up accounts to 31 December 20X2. Electricity bills received were as follows.

	20X2	20X3	20X4
	$	$	$
31 January	–	6,491.52	6,753.24
30 April	5,279.47	5,400.93	6,192.82
31 July	4,663.80	4,700.94	5,007.62
31 October	4,117.28	4,620.00	5,156.40

What should the electricity charge be for the year ended 31 December 20X2?

Solution

The three invoices received during 20X2 totalled $14,060.55, but this is not the full charge for the year: the November and December electricity charge was not invoiced until the end of January. To show the correct charge for the year, it is necessary to **accrue** the charge for November and December based on January's bill. The charge for 20X2 is:

	$
Paid in year	14,060.55
Accrual ($^2/_3 \times$ $6,491.52)	4,327.68
	18,388.23

The double entry for the accrual (using the **journal**) will be:

DEBIT	Electricity account	$4,327.68	
CREDIT	Accruals (liability)		$4,327.68

2.4 Example: Prepayment

A business opens on 1 January 20X4 in a shop which is on a 20 year lease. The rent is $20,000 per year and is payable quarterly in advance. Payments were made on what are known as the 'quarter-days' (except the first payment) as follows.

	$
1 January 20X4	5,000.00
25 March 20X4	5,000.00
24 June 20X4	5,000.00
29 September 20X4	5,000.00
25 December 20X4	5,000.00

What will the rental charge be for the year ended 31 December 20X4?

Solution

The total amount paid in the year is $25,000. The yearly rental, however, is only $20,000. The last payment was almost entirely a prepayment (give or take a few days) as it is payment in advance for the first three months of 20X5. The charge for 20X4 is therefore:

	$
Paid in year	25,000.00
Prepayment	(5,000.00)
	20,000.00

The double entry for this prepayment is:

DEBIT	Prepayments (asset)	$5,000.00
CREDIT	Rent account	$5,000.00

2.5 Double entry for accruals and prepayments

You can see from the double entry shown for both these examples that the other side of the entry is taken to an asset or a liability account.

- **Prepayments** are included in **receivables** in current assets in the balance sheet. They are **assets** as they represent money that has been paid out in advance of the expense being incurred.

- **Accruals** are included in **payables** in **current liabilities** as they represent liabilities which have been incurred but for which no invoice has yet been received.

Transaction	DR	CR	Description
Accrual	Expense	Liability	Expense incurred in period, not recorded
Prepayment	Asset	(Reduction in) expense	Expense recorded in period, not incurred until next period

2.5.1 Reversing accruals and prepayments in subsequent periods

In each of the above examples, as with all prepayments and accruals, the double entry will be **reversed** in the following period, otherwise the organisation will charge itself twice for the same expense (accruals) *or* will never charge itself (prepayments). It may help to see the accounts in question.

ELECTRICITY ACCOUNT

20X2			$	20X2		$
30.4	Cash		5,279.47	31.12	Income statement	18,388.23
31.7	Cash		4,663.80			
31.10	Cash		4,117.28			
31.12	Balance c/d (accrual)		4,327.68			
			18,388.23			18,388.23
20X3				20X3		
31.1	Cash		6,491.52	1.1	Balance b/d	
30.4	Cash		5,400.93		(accrual reversed)	4,327.68
31.7	Cash		4,700.94	31.12	Income statement	21,387.87
31.10	Cash		4,620.00			
31.12	Balance c/d (accrual)		4,502.16			
			25,715.55			25,715.55

The income statement charge and accrual for 20X3 can be checked as follows.

Invoice paid		Proportion charged in 20X3	$
31.1.X3	6,491.52	1/3	2,163.84
30.4.X3	5,400.94	all	5,400.93
31.7.X3	4,700.94	all	4,700.94
31.10.X3	4,620.00	all	4,620.00
31.1.X4	6,753.24	2/3	4,502.16
Charge to income statement in 20X3			21,387.87

It should be clear to you here that the $5,000 rent prepaid in 20X2 will be added to by the payments in 20X3, and then reduced at the end of 20X3 in the same way.

PART D   ACCOUNTING TREATMENTS

Question — Accruals

Ratsnuffer is a business dealing in pest control. Its owner, Roy Dent, employs a team of eight who were paid $12,000 per annum each in the year to 31 December 20X5. At the start of 20X6 he raised salaries by 10% to $13,200 per annum each.

On 1 July 20X6, he hired a trainee at a salary of $8,400 per annum.

He pays his work force on the first working day of every month, one month in arrears, so that his employees receive their salary for January on the first working day in February, etc.

Required

(a) Calculate the cost of salaries which would be charged in the income statement of Ratsnuffer for the year ended 31 December 20X6.

(b) Calculate the amount actually paid in salaries during the year (ie the amount of cash received by the work force).

(c) State the amount of accrued charges for salaries which would appear in the balance sheet of Ratsnuffer as at 31 December 20X6.

Answer

(a) Salaries cost in the income statement

	$
Cost of 8 employees for a full year at $13,200 each	105,600
Cost of trainee for a half year	4,200
	109,800

(b) *Salaries actually paid in 20X6*

	$
December 20X5 salaries paid in January (8 employees × $1,000 per month)	8,000
Salaries of 8 employees for January – November 20X6 paid in February – December (8 employees × $1,100 per month × 11 months)	96,800
Salaries of trainee (for July – November paid in August – December 20X6: 5 months × $700 per month)	3,500
Salaries actually paid	108,300

(c) *Accrued salaries costs as at 31 December 20X6*
(ie costs charged in the Income statement, but not yet paid)

	$
8 employees x 1 month x $1,100 per month	8,800
1 trainee x 1 month x $700 per month	700
	9,500

(d) *Summary*

	$
Accrued wages costs as at 31 December 20X5	8,000
Add salaries cost for 20X6 (Income statement)	109,800
	117,800
Less salaries paid	108,300
Equals accrued wages costs as at 31 December 20X6 (liability in balance sheet)	9,500

Note. The answer to Question 1 is D. Remember that: Net profit = Gross profit less expenses.

2.6 Example: Prepayments

The Square Wheels Garage pays fire insurance annually in advance on 1 June each year. The firm's financial year end is 28 February. From the following record of insurance payments you are required to calculate the charge to income statement for the financial year to 28 February 20X8.

Insurance paid

	$
1.6.20X6	600
1.6.20X7	700

Insurance cost for:

		$
(a)	The 3 months, 1 March – 31 May 20X7 (3/12 × $600)	150
(b)	The 9 months, 1 June 20X7 – 28 February 20X8 (9/12 × $700)	525
	Insurance cost for the year, charged to the income statement	675

At 28 February 20X8 there is a prepayment for fire insurance, covering the period 1 March – 31 May 20X8. This insurance premium was paid on 1 June 20X7, but only nine months worth of the full annual cost is chargeable to the accounting period ended 28 February 20X8. The prepayment of (3/12 × $700) $175 as at 28 February 20X8 will appear as a current asset in the balance sheet of the Square Wheels Garage as at that date.

In the same way, there was a prepayment of (3/12 × $600) $150 in the balance sheet one year earlier as at 28 February 20X7.

Summary

	$
Prepaid insurance premiums as at 28 February 20X7	150
Add insurance premiums paid 1 June 20X7	700
	850
Less insurance costs charged to the income statement for the year ended 28 February 20X8	675
Equals prepaid insurance premiums as at 28 February 20X8 (asset in balance sheet)	175

Question — Accruals and prepayments

The Batley Print Shop rents a photocopying machine from a supplier for which it makes a quarterly payment as follows:

(a) Three months rental in advance
(b) A further charge of 2 pence per copy made during the quarter just ended

The rental agreement began on 1 August 20X4 and the first six quarterly bills were as follows.

Bills dated and received	Rental	Costs of copies taken	Total
	$	$	$
1 August 20X4	2,100	0	2,100
1 November 20X4	2,100	1,500	3,600
1 February 20X5	2,100	1,400	3,500
1 May 20X5	2,100	1,800	3,900
1 August 20X5	2,700	1,650	4,350
1 November 20X5	2,700	1,950	4,650

The bills are paid promptly, as soon as they are received.

(a) Calculate the charge for photocopying expenses for the year to 31 August 20X4 and the amount of prepayments and/or accrued charges as at that date.

(b) Calculate the charge for photocopying expenses for the following year to 31 August 20X5, and the amount of prepayments and/or accrued charges as at that date.

PART D   ACCOUNTING TREATMENTS

Answer

(a) Year to 31 August 20X4

	$
One months' rental (1/3 × $2,100) *	700
Accrued copying charges (1/3 × $1,500) **	500
Photocopying expense (Income statement)	1,200

* From the quarterly bill dated 1 August 20X4

** From the quarterly bill dated 1 November 20X4

There is a prepayment for 2 months' rental ($1,400) as at 31 August 20X4.

(b) Year to 31 August 20X5

	$	$
Rental from 1 September 20X4 – 31 July 20X5 (11 months at $2,100 per quarter or $700 per month)		7,700
Rental from 1 August – 31 August 20X5 (1/3 × $2,700)		900
Rental charge for the year		8,600
Copying charges:		
1 September – 31 October 20X4 (2/3 × $1,500)	1,000	
1 November 20X4 – 31 January 20X5	1,400	
1 February – 30 April 20X5	1,800	
1 May – 31 July 20X5	1,650	
Accrued charges for August 20X5 (1/3 × $1,950)	650	
		6,500
Total photocopying expenses (Income statement)		15,100

There is a prepayment for 2 months' rental ($1,800) as at 31 August 20X5.

Summary of year 1 September 20X4 – 31 August 20X5

	Rental charges $	Copying costs $
Prepayments as at 31.8.20X4	1,400	
Accrued charges as at 31.8.20X4		(500)
Bills received during the year		
1 November 20X4	2,100	1,500
1 February 20X5	2,100	1,400
1 May 20X5	2,100	1,800
1 August 20X5	2,700	1,650
Prepayment as at 31.8.20X5	(1,800)	
Accrued charges as at 31.8.20X5		650
Charge to the Income statement for the year	8,600	6,500
Balance sheet items as at 31 August 20X5		
Prepaid rental (current asset)	1,800	
Accrued copying charges (current liability)		650

2.7 Further example: Accruals

Willie Woggle opens a shop on 1 May 20X6 to sell hiking and camping equipment. The rent of the shop is $12,000 per annum, payable quarterly in arrears (with the first payment on 31 July 20X6). Willie decides that his accounting period should end on 31 December each year.

The rent account as at 31 December 20X6 will record only two rental payments (on 31 July and 31 October) and there will be two months' accrued rental expenses for November and December 20X6 ($2,000), since the next rental payment is not due until 31 January 20X7.

The charge to the income statement for the period to 31 December 20X6 will be for 8 months' rent (May-December inclusive) and so it follows that the total rental cost should be $8,000.

So far, the rent account appears as follows.

RENT ACCOUNT

		$			$
20X6			*20X6*		
31 July	Cash	3,000			
31 Oct	Cash	3,000	31 Dec	Income statement	8,000

2.21 To complete the picture, the accrual of $2,000 has to be put in, to bring the balance on the account up to the full charge for the year. At the beginning of the next year the accrual is reversed.

RENT ACCOUNT

		$			$
20X6			*20X6*		
31 July	Cash *	3,000			
31 Oct	Cash *	3,000			
31 Dec	Balance c/d (accruals)	2,000	31 Dec	Income statement	8,000
		8,000			8,000
			20X7		
			1 Jan	Balance b/d (accrual reversed)	2,000

* The corresponding credit entry would be cash if rent is paid without the need for an invoice – eg with payment by standing order or direct debit at the bank. If there is always an invoice where rent becomes payable, the double entry would be:

DEBIT	Rent account	$2,000	
CREDIT	Payables		$2,000

Then when the rent is paid, the ledger entries would be:

DEBIT	Creditors	$2,000	
CREDIT	Payables		$2,000

The rent account for the *next* year to 31 December 20X7, assuming no increase in rent in that year, would be as follows.

RENT ACCOUNT

		$			$
20X7			*20X7*		
31 Jan	Cash	3,000	1 Jan	Balance b/d (accrual reversed)	2,000
30 Apr	Cash	3,000			
31 Jul	Cash	3,000			
31 Oct	Cash	3,000			
31 Dec	Balance c/d (accruals)	2,000	31 Dec	Income statement	12,000
		14,000			14,000
			20X8		
			1 Jan	Balance b/d (accrual reversed)	2,000

A full twelve months' rental charges are taken as an expense to the Income statement.

2.8 Further example: Prepayments

Terry Trunk commences business as a landscape gardener on 1 September 20X5. He immediately decides to join his local trade association, the Confederation of Luton Gardeners, for which the annual membership subscription is $180, payable annually in advance. He paid this amount on 1 September. Terry decides that his account period should end on 30 June each year.

In the first period to 30 June 20X6 (10 months), a full year's membership will have been paid, but only ten twelfths of the subscription should be charged to the period (ie 10/12 × $180 = $150). There is a prepayment of two months of membership subscription (ie 2/12 × $180 = $30).

The prepayment is recognised in the ledger account for subscriptions. This is done in much the same way as accounting for accruals, by using the balance carried down/brought down technique.

CREDIT	Subscriptions account with prepayment as a balance c/d	$30
DEBIT	Subscriptions account with the same balance b/d $30	

The remaining expenses in the subscriptions account should then be taken to the Income statement. The balance on the account will appear as a current asset (prepaid subscriptions) in the balance sheet as at 30 June 20X6.

SUBSCRIPTIONS ACCOUNT

			$			$
20X5				20X6		
1 Sept	Cash		180	30 Jun	Income statement	150
				30 Jun	Balance c/d (prepayment)	30
			180			180
20X6						
1 Jul	Balance b/d (prepayment reversed)		30			

2.27 The subscription account for the next year, assuming no increase in the annual charge, will be:

SUBSCRIPTIONS ACCOUNT

			$			$
20X6				20X7		
1 Jul	Balance b/d		30	30 Jun	Income statement	180
1 Sep	Cash		180	30 Jun	Balance c/d (prepayment)	30
			210			210
20X67						
1 Jul	Balance b/d (prepayment reversed)		30			

Again, the charge to the income statement is for a full year's subscriptions.

Exam focus point

> You will almost certainly have to deal with accruals and/or prepayments in the exam, probably in an MCQ. Make sure you understand the logic, then you will be able to do whatever question comes up.

Question

Income statement and balance sheet

The Umbrella Shop has the following trial balance as at 30 September 20X8.

	$	$
Sales		156,000
Purchases	65,000	
Land & buildings – net book value at 30.9.X8	125,000	
Plant & machinery – net book value at 30.9.X8	75,000	
Inventory at 1.10.X7	10,000	
Cash at bank	12,000	
Trade accounts receivable	54,000	
Trade accounts payable		40,000
Selling expenses	10,000	
Cash in hand	2,000	
Administration expenses	15,000	
Finance expenses	5,000	
Carriage inwards	1,000	
Carriage outwards	2,000	
Capital account at 1.10.X7		180,000
	376,000	376,000

The following information is available:

(a) Closing inventory at 30.9.X8 is $13,000, after writing off damaged goods of $2,000.

(b) Included in administration expenses is machinery rental of $6,000 covering the year to 31 December 20X8.

(c) A late invoice for $12,000 covering rent for the year ended 30 June 20X9 has not been included in the trial balance.

Prepare an income statement and balance sheet for the year ended 30 September 20X8. (*Tutorial note:* This will provide useful revision of the forms of the income statement and balance sheet. If necessary refer back to Chapter 6 of this Study Text).

Answer

THE UMBRELLA SHOP
INCOME STATEMENT FOR THE YEAR END 30 SEPTEMBER 20X8

	$	$
Sales		156,000
Opening inventory	10,000	
Purchases	65,000	
Carriage inwards	1,000	
	76,000	
Closing inventory (W1)	13,000	
Cost of goods sold		63,000
Gross profit		93,000
Selling expenses	10,000	
Carriage outwards	2,000	
Administration expenses (W2)	16,500	
Finance expenses	5,000	33,500
Net profit for the period		59,500

PART D ACCOUNTING TREATMENTS

THE UMBRELLA SHOP
BALANCE SHEET AS AT 30 SEPTEMBER 20X8

	$	$
Assets		
Non-current assets		
Land & buildings		125,000
Plant & machinery		75,000
		200,000
Current assets		
Inventory (W1)	13,000	
Trade accounts receivable	54,000	
Prepayments (W4)	1,500	
Cash at bank and in hand	14,000	82,500
		282,500
Capital and liabilities		
Proprietor's capital		
Balance brought forward	180,000	
Profit for the period	59,500	239,500
Current liabilities		
Trade account payable	40,000	
Accruals (W3)	3,000	43,000
		282,500

Workings

1 **Closing inventory**

As the figure of $13,000 is **after** writing off damaged goods, no further adjustments are necessary. Remember that you are effectively crediting closing inventory to the trading account of the income statement and the corresponding debit is to the balance sheet.

2 **Administration expenses**

	$
Per trial balance	15,000
Add: accrual (W3)	3,000
	18,000
Less: prepayment (W4)	(1,500)
	16,500

3 **Accrual**

	$
Rent for year to 30 June 20X9	12,000
Accrual for period to 30 September 20X8 ($3/12 \times \$12,000$)	3,000

4 **Prepayment**

	$
Machinery rental for the year to 31 December 20X8	6,000
Prepayment for period 1 October to 31 December 20X8 ($3/12 \times \$6,000$)	1,500

Chapter Roundup

- The **cost of goods sold** is calculated as follows:

	$
Opening inventory	X
Plus purchases	X
	X
Less closing inventory	(X)
	X

- Carriage **inwards** is included in the cost of purchases. Carriage **outwards** is a selling expense.

- **Accrued expenses** are expenses which relate to an accounting period but have not yet been paid for. They are a **charge against the profit** for the period and they are shown in the balance sheet as at the end of the period as a current liability.

- **Prepayments** are expenses which have already been paid but relate to a future accounting period. They are **not charged against the profit** of the current period, and they are shown in the balance sheet at the end of the period as a **current asset**.

Quick Quiz

1. How is the cost of goods sold calculated?

2. Distinguish between carriage inwards and carriage outwards.

3. The cost of goods sold is $14,000. The purchases for the period are $14,000, carriage inwards is $1,000, carriage outwards is $1,500 and closing inventory is $13,000. What was the opening inventory figure?

   A $10,500
   B $11,500
   C $12,000
   D $13,000

4. Give three reasons why goods purchased might have to be written off.

5. If a business has paid rates of $1,000 for the year to 31 March 20X9, what is the prepayment in the accounts for the year to 31 December 20X8?

6. Define an accrual.

PART D ACCOUNTING TREATMENTS

Answers to Quick Quiz

1 See formula to learn in Para 1.4.

2 Carriage inwards is paid on goods coming **into** the business and is added to the cost of purchases.

Carriage outwards is paid on goods going **out of** the business to customers and is charged to selling expenses.

3 C

	$
Opening inventory value (balancing figure)	12,000
Add: purchases (incl carriage inwards)	15,000
	27,000
Less: closing inventory	(13,000)
Cost of goods sold	14,000

If you picked A, then you wrongly included carriage outwards in cost of goods sold. If you chose B, then you used the carriage outwards instead of the carriage inwards figure in your calculations. With D, you ignored carriage inwards and outwards altogether!

4
- Goods are stolen or lost
- Goods are damaged
- Goods are obsolete

5 $3/12 \times \$1,000 = \$250$

6 Expenses charged against profit for a period, even though they have not yet been paid or invoiced.

Now try the question below from the Exam Question Bank

Number	Level	Marks	Time
Q14	Introductory	n/a	27 mins

Irrecoverable debts and allowances

Topic list	Syllabus reference
1 Irrecoverable debts	4(b)(ii)
2 Allowances for receivables	4(b)(ii)
3 Accounting for irrecoverable debts and receivables allowances	4(b)(ii)

Introduction

In this chapter we move closer to our goal of preparing the financial statements. We look at two types of adjustment which need to be made in respect of credit sales.

- Irrecoverable debts
- Allowance for receivables

Important note:

In past exam papers you will see reference to 'allowance for doubtful receivables'. ACCA announced that this terminology would no longer be used, starting from the December 2005 sitting. The December 2005 exam referred to 'receivables allowances' or 'allowance for receivables' and that is the terminology used in this text.

PART D   ACCOUNTING TREATMENTS

Study guide

Section 8 – The financial statements of a sole trader 2: Depreciation, irrecoverable debts and allowances for receivables

- Explain the inevitability of irrecoverable debts in most businesses.
- Illustrate the bookkeeping entries to write off an irrecoverable debt and the effect on the income statement and balance sheet.
- Illustrate the bookkeeping entries to record irrecoverable debts recovered.
- Explain the difference between writing off an irrecoverable debt and making an allowance for receivables.
- Explain and illustrate the bookkeeping entries to create and adjust an allowance for receivables.
- Illustrate how to include movements in the allowance for receivables in the income statement and how the closing balance of the allowance may appear in the balance sheet.

Exam guide

You will always get an exam question involving final accounts preparation. Such questions will often involve an adjustment for irrecoverable debts, and receivables allowances.

1 Irrecoverable debts

FAST FORWARD

> Irrecoverable debts are specific debts owed to a business which it decides are never going to be paid. They are written off as an expense in the income statement.

Customers who buy goods on credit might fail to pay for them, perhaps out of dishonesty or because they have gone bankrupt and cannot pay. Customers in another country might be prevented from paying by the unexpected introduction of foreign exchange control restrictions by their country's government during the credit period.

For one reason or another, a business might decide to give up expecting payment and to write the debt off.

Key term

> An **irrecoverable debt** is a debt which is not expected to be paid.

1.1 Writing off irrecoverable debts

When a business decides that a particular debt is unlikely to be paid, the amount of the debt is 'written off' as an expense in the income statement:

DR   IRRECOVERABLE DEBTS
CR   RECEIVABLES LEDGER

Alfred's Mini-Cab Service sends an invoice for $300 to a customer who subsequently does a 'moonlight flit' from his office premises, never to be seen or heard of again. The debt of $300 must be written off. It might seem sensible to record the business transaction as:

Sales $(300 – 300) = $0.

However, irrecoverable debts written off are accounted for as follows.

(a)   **Sales** are shown at their invoice value in the **income statement**. The sale has been made, and gross profit should be earned. The subsequent failure to collect the debt is a separate matter, which is reported in the income statement under expenses.

(b) **Irrecoverable debts** written off are shown as an **expense in the income and expense account**.
(c) The credit entry removes the receivable from the receivables ledger

In our example of Alfred's Mini-Cab Service:

	$
Sale (in the income statement)	300
Irrecoverable debt written off (expense in the I & E account)	300
Net profit on this transaction	0

Obviously, when a debt is written off, the value of the receivable as a current asset falls to zero. If the debt is expected to be uncollectable, its **'net realisable value'** is nil, and so it has a zero balance sheet value.

1.2 Irrecoverable debts written off and subsequently paid

An irrecoverable debt which has been written off might occasionally be unexpectedly paid. If it is paid in the same accounting period, the write-off journal can simply be reversed. The only accounting problem to consider is when a debt written off as irrecoverable in one accounting period is subsequently paid in a later accounting period. The amount paid should be recorded as additional **income** in the income statement of the period in which the payment is received.

For example, an income statement for the Blacksmith's Forge for the year to 31 December 20X5 could be prepared as shown below from the following information.

	$
Inventory, 1 January 20X5	6,000
Purchases of goods	122,000
Inventory, 31 December 20X5	8,000
Cash sales	100,000
Credit sales	70,000
Discounts allowed	1,200
Discounts received	5,000
Irrecoverable debts written off	9,000
Debts paid in 20X5 which were previously written off as irrecoverable in 20X4	2,000
Other expenses	31,800

BLACKSMITH'S FORGE
INCOME STATEMENT FOR THE YEAR ENDED 31.12.20X5

	$	$
Sales		170,000
Opening inventory	6,000	
Purchases	122,000	
	128,000	
Less closing inventory	8,000	
Cost of goods sold		120,000
Gross profit		50,000
Add: discounts received		5,000
debts paid, previously written off as irrecoverable		2,000
		57,000
Expenses		
Discounts allowed	1,200	
Irrecoverable debts written off	9,000	
Other expenses	31,800	
		42,000
Net profit		15,000

PART D ACCOUNTING TREATMENTS

2 Allowances for receivables

FAST FORWARD

Allowances for receivables may be **specific** (an allowance against a particular receivable) or simply a percentage allowance based on past experience of irrecoverable debts. An increase in the allowance for receivables is shown as an expense in the income statement.

Trade receivables in the balance sheet are shown **net** of any receivables allowance.

When irrecoverable debts are written off, specific debts owed to the business are identified as unlikely ever to be collected.

However, because of the risks involved in selling goods on credit, it might be accepted that a certain percentage of outstanding debts at any time are unlikely to be collected. But although it might be estimated that, say, 5% of debts will prove irrecoverable, the business will not know until later which specific debts are irrecoverable.

A business commences operations on 1 July 20X4, and in the twelve months to 30 June 20X5 makes sales of $300,000 (all on credit) and writes off bad debts amounting to $6,000. Cash received from customers during the year is $244,000, so that at 30 June 20X5, the business has outstanding receivables of $50,000.

	$
Credit sales during the year	300,000
Add receivables at 1 July 20X4	0
Total debts owed to the business	300,000
Less cash received from credit customers	244,000
	56,000
Less bad debts written off	6,000
Trade receivables outstanding at 30 June 20X5	50,000

Now, some of these outstanding debts might turn out to be bad. The business does not know on 30 June 20X5 which specific debts in the total $50,000 owed will be bad, but it might guess (from experience perhaps) that 5% of debts will eventually be found to be irrecoverable.

When a business expects irrecoverable debts amongst its current receivables, but does not yet know which specific debts will be irrecoverable, it can make an **allowance for receivables**.

Key term

An **allowance for receivables** is an estimate of the percentage of debts which are not expected to be paid.

An allowance for receivables provides for future irrecoverable debts, as a prudent precaution by the business. The business will be more likely to avoid claiming profits which subsequently fail to materialise because some debts turn out to be irrecoverable.

(a) When an allowance is first made, the amount of this initial allowance is charged as an expense in the income statement, for the period in which the allowance is created.

(b) When an allowance already exists, but is subsequently increased in size, the amount of the **increase** in allowance is charged as an **expense** in the income statement for the period in which the increased allowance is made.

(c) When an allowance already exists, but is subsequently reduced in size, the amount of the **decrease** in allowance is credited back to the income statement for the period in which the reduction in allowance is made.

Exam focus point

In an exam you will often be required, as part of a longer question, to calculate the increase or decrease in the allowance for receivables.

The balance sheet, as well as the income statement of a business, must be adjusted to show the allowance.

12: IRRECOVERABLE DEBTS AND ALLOWANCES

Important! The value of trade accounts receivable in the balance sheet must be shown after deducting the allowance for receivables.

This is because the net realisable value of all the receivables of the business is estimated to be less than their 'sales value'. After all, this is the reason for making the allowance in the first place. The net realisable value of trade accounts receivable is the total value of receivables minus receivables allowance. Such an allowance is an example of the **prudence concept**, discussed in detail in Chapter 10.

In the example above the newly created allowance for receivables at 30 June 20X5 will be 5% of $50,000 = $2,500. This means that although total trade accounts receivable are $50,000, eventual payment of only $47,500 is expected.

(a) In the income statement, the newly created allowance of $2,500 will be shown as an expense.

(b) In the balance sheet, trade accounts receivable will be shown as:

	$
Total receivables at 30 June 20X5	50,000
Less allowance for receivables	2,500
	47,500

2.1 Example: Allowance for receivables

Corin Flakes owns and runs the Aerobic Health Foods Shop in Dundee. He commenced trading on 1 January 20X1, selling health foods to customers, most of whom make use of a credit facility that Corin offers. (Customers are allowed to purchase up to $200 of goods on credit but must repay a certain proportion of their outstanding debt every month.)

This credit system gives rise to a large number of irrecoverable debts, and Corin Flake's results for his first three years of operations are as follows.

Year to 31 December 20X1
Gross profit	$27,000
Irrecoverable debts written off	$8,000
Debts owed by customers as at 31 December 20X1	$40,000
Allowance for receivables	2½% of outstanding receivables
Other expenses	$20,000

Year to 31 December 20X2
Gross profit	$45,000
Irrecoverable debts written off	$10,000
Debts owed by customers as at 31 December 20X2	$50,000
Allowance for receivables	2½% of outstanding receivables
Other expenses	$28,750

Year to 31 December 20X3
Gross profit	$60,000
Irrecoverable debts written off	$11,000
Debts owed by customers as at 31 December 20X3	$30,000
Allowance for receivables	3% of outstanding receivables
Other expenses	$32,850

Required

For each of these three years, prepare the income statement of the business, and state the value of trade accounts receivable appearing in the balance sheet as at 31 December.

PART D ACCOUNTING TREATMENTS

Solution

AEROBIC HEALTH FOOD SHOP
INCOME STATEMENT FOR THE YEARS ENDED 31 DECEMBER

	20X1		20X2		20X3	
	$	$	$	$	$	$
Gross profit		27,000		45,000		60,000
Expenses:						
Irrecoverable debts written off	8,000		10,000		11,000	
Increase/decrease in allowance for receivables*	1,000		250		(350)	
Other expenses	20,000		28,750		32,850	
		29,000		39,000		43,500
Net profit/(loss)		(2,000)		6,000		16,500

*At 1 January 20X1 when Corin began trading the allowance for receivables was nil. At 31 December 20X1 the allowance required was 2½% of $40,000 = $1,000. The increase in the allowance is therefore $1,000. At 31 December 20X2 the allowance required was 2½% of $50,000 = $1,250. The 20X1 allowance must therefore be increased by $250. At 31 December 20X3 the allowance required is 3% × $30,000 = $900. The 20X2 allowance is therefore reduced by $350.

VALUE OF TRADE ACCOUNTS RECEIVABLE IN THE BALANCE SHEET

	As at 31.12.20X1	As at 31.12.20X2	As at 31.12.20X3
	$	$	$
Total value of receivables	40,000	50,000	30,000
Less allowance for receivables	1,000	1,250	900
Balance sheet value	39,000	48,750	29,100

You should now try to use what you have learned to attempt a solution to the following exercise, which involves preparing an income statement and balance sheet.

Question Newbegin Tools

The financial affairs of Newbegin Tools prior to the commencement of trading were as follows.

NEWBEGIN TOOLS
BALANCE SHEET AS AT 1 AUGUST 20X5

	$	$
Assets		
Non-current assets		
Motor vehicle	2,000	
Shop fittings	3,000	
		5,000
Current assets		
Inventories	12,000	
Cash	1,000	
		13,000
		18,000
Equity and liabilities		
Equity		12,000
Current liabilities		
Bank overdraft	2,000	
Trade payables	4,000	
		6,000
Total capital and liabilities		18,000

At the end of six months the business had made the following transactions.

(a) Goods were purchased on credit at a gross amount of $10,000.

(b) Trade discount received was 2% on this gross amount and there was a cash discount received of 5% on settling debts to suppliers of $8,000. These were the only payments to suppliers in the period.

(c) Closing inventories were valued at $5,450.

(d) Cash sales and credit sales together totalled $27,250.

(e) Outstanding trade accounts receivable balances at 31 January 20X6 amounted to $3,250 of which $250 were to be written off.

(f) A further allowance for receivables is to be made amounting to 2% of the remaining outstanding receivables.

(g) Cash payments were made in respect of the following expenses.

		$
(i)	Stationery, postage and wrapping	500
(ii)	Telephone charges	200
(iii)	Electricity	600
(iv)	Cleaning and refreshments	150

(h) Cash drawings by the proprietor, Alf Newbegin, amounted to $6,000.

(i) The outstanding overdraft balance as at 1 August 20X5 was paid off. Interest charges and bank charges on the overdraft amounted to $40.

Alf Newbegin knew the balance of cash on hand at 31 January 20X6 but he wanted to know if the business had made a profit for the six months that it had been trading, and so he asked his friend, Harry Oldhand, if he could tell him.

Prepare the income statement of Newbegin Tools for the six months to 31 January 20X6 and a balance sheet as at that date.

Answer

The income statement should be fairly straightforward.

NEWBEGIN TOOLS
INCOME STATEMENT
FOR THE SIX MONTHS ENDED 31 JANUARY 20X6

	$	$
Sales		27,250
Opening inventories	12,000	
Purchases (note (a))	9,800	
	21,800	
Less closing inventories	5,450	
Cost of goods sold		16,350
Gross profit		10,900
Discounts received (note (b))		400
		11,300
Electricity (note (c))	600	
Stationery, postage and wrapping	500	
Irrecoverable debts written off	250	
Allowance for receivables (note (d))	60	
Telephone charges	200	
Cleaning and refreshments	150	
Interest and bank charges	40	
		1,800
Net profit		9,500

PART D ACCOUNTING TREATMENTS

Notes

(a) Purchases at cost $10,000 less 2% trade discount.

(b) 5% of $8,000 = $400

(c) Expenses are grouped into sales and distribution expenses (here assumed to be electricity, stationery and postage, bad debts and allowance for receivables) administration expenses (here assumed to be telephone charges and cleaning) and finance charges.

(d) 2% of $3,000 = $60.

The preparation of a balance sheet is not so easy, because we must calculate the value of trade accounts payable and cash in hand.

(a) *Trade accounts payable as at 31 January 20X6*

The amount owing on trade accounts is the sum of the amount owing at the beginning of the period, plus the cost of purchases during the period (net of all discounts), less the payments already made for purchases. If you think carefully about this, you might see that this calculation is logical. What is still owed is the total amount of costs incurred less payments already made.

	$
Accounts payable as at 1 August 20X5	4,000
Add purchases during the period, net of trade discount	9,800
	13,800
Less cash discounts received	(400)
	13,400
Less payments to suppliers accounts during the period*	(7,600)
	5,800

* $8,000 less cash discount of $400.

(b) *Cash at bank and in hand at 31 January 20X6*

This too requires a fairly lengthy calculation. You need to identify cash payments received and cash payments made.

(i) Cash received from sales

	$
Total sales in the period	27,250
Add trade accounts receivable as at 1 August 20X5	0
	27,250
Less unpaid debts as at 31 January 20X6	3,250
Cash received	24,000

(ii) Cash paid

	$
Trade accounts payable (see (a))	7,600
Stationery, postage and wrapping	500
Telephone charges	200
Electricity	600
Cleaning and refreshments	150
Bank charges and interest	40
Bank overdraft repaid	2,000
Drawings by proprietor	6,000
	17,090

Note. It is easy to forget some of these payments, especially drawings.

			$
(iii)	Cash in hand at 1 August 20X5		1,000
	Cash received in the period		24,000
			25,000
	Cash paid in the period		(17,090)
	Cash at bank and in hand as at 31 January 20X6		7,910

(c) When irrecoverable debts are written off, the value of outstanding receivables must be reduced by the amount written off. This is because the customers are no longer expected to pay, and it would be misleading to show them in the balance sheet as current assets of the business for which cash payment is expected within one year. Receivables in the balance sheet will be valued at $3,000 less the allowance for receivables of $60 – ie at $2,940.

NEWBEGIN TOOLS
BALANCE SHEET AS AT 31 JANUARY 20X6

	$	$
Assets		
Non-current assets		
Motor vehicles	2,000	
Shop fittings	3,000	
		5,000
Current assets		
Inventory	5,450	
Trade accounts receivable	2,940	
Cash	7,910	
		16,300
		21,300
Equity and liabilities		
Equity		
Capital at 1 August 20X5	12,000	
Net profit for the period	9,500	
Less drawings	(6,000)	
Capital at 31 January 20X6		15,500
Current liabilities		
Trade accounts payable		5,800
Total capital and liabilities		21,300

The bank overdraft has now been repaid and is therefore not shown.

3 Accounting for irrecoverable debts and receivables allowances

3.1 Irrecoverable debts written off: ledger accounting entries

For irrecoverable debts written off, there is an irrecoverable debts account. The double-entry bookkeeping is fairly straightforward, but there are two separate transactions to record.

(a) When it is decided that a particular debt will not be paid, the customer is no longer called an outstanding receivable, and becomes a irrecoverable debt.

DEBIT   Irrecoverable debts account (expense)
CREDIT Trade accounts receivable

(b) At the end of the accounting period, the balance on the irrecoverable debts account is transferred to the I & E ledger account (like all other expense accounts).

PART D ACCOUNTING TREATMENTS

DEBIT   I & E account
CREDIT   Irrecoverable debts account.

Where an irrecoverable debt is subsequently recovered in the same accounting period, you simply reverse the entries in (a) above and so there will be no need to carry out the entries in (b) above.

DEBIT   Trade accounts receivable
CREDIT   Irrecoverable debts account (expense)

However, where an irrecoverable debt is subsequently recovered in a later accounting period the accounting entries will be as follows.

DEBIT   Trade accounts receivable
CREDIT   Irrecoverable debts recovered (income in the I & E A/c)

3.2 Example: Irrecoverable debts written off

At 1 October 20X5 a business had total outstanding debts of $8,600. During the year to 30 September 20X6 the following transaction took place.

(a)   Credit sales amounted to $44,000.
(b)   Payments from various customers (accounts receivable) amounted to $49,000.
(c)   Two debts, for $180 and $420, were declared irrecoverable and the customers are no longer purchasing goods from the company. These are to be written off.

Required

Prepare the trade accounts receivable account and the irrecoverable debts account for the year.

Solution

TRADE ACCOUNTS RECEIVABLE

	$		$
Opening balance b/f	8,600	Cash	49,000
Sales	44,000	Irrecoverable debts	180
		Irrecoverable debts	420
		Closing balance c/d	3,000
	52,600		52,600
Opening balance b/d	3,000		

IRRECOVERABLE DEBTS

	$		$
Receivables	180	I & E a/c: irrecoverable debts written off	600
Receivables	420		
	600		600

In the receivables ledger, personal accounts of the customers whose debts are irrecoverable will be taken off the ledger. The business should then take steps to ensure that it does not sell goods on credit to those customers again.

3.3 Allowance for receivables: ledger accounting entries

FAST FORWARD Only **movement** on the receivables allowance is debited or credited to irrecoverable debts in the income statement.

A business might know from past experience that, say 2% of receivables balances are unlikely to be collected. It would then be considered prudent to make a general allowance of 2%. It may be that no particular customers are regarded as suspect and so it is not possible to write off any individual customer balances as irrecoverable debts. The procedure is then to leave the total receivables balances completely untouched, but to open up an allowance account by the following entries:

DEBIT   Irrecoverable debts account (expense)
CREDIT   Allowance for receivables

Important!

> When preparing a balance sheet, the credit balance on the allowance account is deducted from the total debit balances in the receivables ledger.

In subsequent years, adjustments may be needed to the amount of the allowance. The procedure to be followed then is as follows.

(a) Calculate the new allowance required.

(b) Compare it with the existing balance on the allowance account (ie the balance b/f from the previous accounting period).

(c) Calculate increase or decrease required.

  (i) If a higher allowance is required now:

   CREDIT   Allowance for receivables
   DEBIT   Irrecoverable debts expense

   with the amount of the increase.

  (ii) If a lower allowance is needed now than before:

   DEBIT   Allowance for receivables
   CREDIT   Irrecoverable debts expense

   with the amount of the decrease.

3.4 Example: Accounting entries for allowance for receivables

Alex Gullible has total receivables outstanding at 31 December 20X2 of $28,000. He believes that about 1% of these balances will not be collected and wishes to make an appropriate allowance. Before now, he has not made any allowance for receivables at all.

On 31 December 20X3 his trade accounts receivable amount to $40,000. His experience during the year has convinced him that an allowance of 5% should be made.

What accounting entries should Alex make on 31 December 20X2 and 31 December 20X3, and what figures for trade accounts receivable will appear in his balance sheets as at those dates?

Solution

At 31 December 20X2

Allowance required   = 1% × $28,000
                     = $280

Alex will make the following entries:

DEBIT	Irrecoverable debts expense	$280	
CREDIT	Allowance for receivables		$280

In the balance sheet receivables will appear as follows under current assets.

	$
Receivables ledger balances	28,000
Less allowance for receivables	280
	27,720

PART D ACCOUNTING TREATMENTS

At 31 December 20X3

Following the procedure described above, Alex will calculate as follows.

	$
Allowance required now (5% × $40,000)	2,000
Existing allowance	(280)
∴ Additional allowance required	1,720

He will make the following entries:

DEBIT	Irrecoverable debts expense	$1,720	
CREDIT	Allowance for receivables		$1,720

The allowance account will by now appear as follows.

ALLOWANCE FOR RECEIVABLES

20X2			$	20X2			$
31 Dec	Balance c/d		280	31 Dec	I & E account		280
20X3				20X3			
31 Dec	Balance c/d		2,000	1 Jan	Balance b/d		280
				31 Dec	I & E account		1,720
			2,000				2,000
				20X4			
				1 Jan	Balance b/d		2,000

For the balance sheet trade accounts receivable will be valued as follows.

	$
Receivables ledger balances	40,000
Less allowance for receivables	2,000
	38,000

In practice, it is unnecessary to show the total receivables balances and the allowance as separate items in the balance sheet. A balance sheet would normally show only the net figure ($27,720 in 20X2, $38,000 in 20X3). However, it might be good practice at this stage in your studies to show the allowance in the balance sheet, so that the examiner/marker can see that your accounting procedures are correct.

Now try the following question on allowance for receivables for yourself.

Question   Receivables allowance

Horace Goodrunning fears that his business will suffer an increase in defaulting receivables in the future and so he decides to make an allowance for receivables of 2% of outstanding trade receivables at the balance sheet date from 28 February 20X6. On 28 February 20X8, Horace decides that the allowance has been over-estimated and he reduces it to 1% of outstanding trade receivables. Outstanding receivables balances at the various balance sheet dates are as follows.

	$
28.2.20X6	15,200
28.2.20X7	17,100
28.2.20X8	21,400

You are required to show extracts from the following accounts for each of the three years above.

(a) Trade accounts receivable
(b) Allowance for receivables
(c) Income and expense account

Show how receivables would appear in the balance sheet at the end of each year.

12: IRRECOVERABLE DEBTS AND ALLOWANCES

Answer

The entries for the three years are denoted by (a), (b) and (c) in each account.

TRADE ACCOUNTS RECEIVABLE (EXTRACT)

			$	
(a)	28.2.20X6	Balance	15,200	
(b)	28.2.20X7	Balance	17,100	
(c)	28.2.20X8	Balance	21,400	

ALLOWANCE FOR RECEIVABLES

			$			$
(a)	28.2.20X6	Balance c/d (2% of 15,200)	304	28.2.20X6	I & E account	304
			304			304
(b)	28.2.20X7	Balance c/d (2% of 17,100)	342	1.3.20X6	Balance b/d	304
				28.2.20X7	I & E account (note (i))	38
			342			342
(c)	28.2.20X8	I & E account (note (ii))	128	1.3.20X7	Balance b/d	342
	28.2.20X8	Balance c/d (1% of 21,400)	214			
			342			342
				1.3.20X8	Balance b/d	214

INCOME AND EXPENSE (EXTRACT)

		$			$
28.2.20X6	Allowance for receivables	304			
28.2.20X7	Allowance for receivables	38			
			28.2.20X8	Allowance for receivables	128

Notes

(i) The increase in the allowance is $(342 – 304) = $38
(ii) The decrease in the allowance is $(342 – 214) = $128
(iii) We calculate the net receivables figure for inclusion in the balance sheet as follows.

	20X6	20X7	20X8
	$	$	$
Current assets			
Trade accounts receivable	15,200	17,100	21,400
Less allowance for receivables	304	342	214
	14,896	16,758	21,186

PART D   ACCOUNTING TREATMENTS

Chapter Roundup

- **Irrecoverable debts** are specific debts owed to a business which it decides are never going to be paid.
- **Irrecoverable debts written off** are an expense in the income statement.
- **Allowances for receivables** may be specific (an allowance against a particular receivable) or simply a percentage allowance based on past experience of irrecoverable debts
- An *increase* in the **allowance for receivables** is an expense in the income statement whereas a *decrease* in the allowance for receivables is credited to irrecoverable debt expense.
- **Trade receivables** are valued in the balance sheet **after deducting any allowance** for receivables.
- Only **movement** in the allowance is debited or credited to irrecoverable debts expense.

Quick Quiz

1   An irrecoverable debt arises in which of the following situations?

    A   A customer pays part of the account
    B   An invoice is in dispute
    C   The customer goes bankrupt
    D   The invoice is not yet due for payment

2   An allowance for receivables of 2% is required. Trade accounts receivable at the period end are $200,000 and the allowable for receivables brought forward from the previous period is $2,000. What movement is required this year?

    A   Increase by $4,000
    B   Decrease by $4,000
    C   Increase by $2,000
    D   Decrease by $2,000

3   If a receivables allowance is increased, what is the effect on the income statement?

4   What is the double entry to record an irrecoverable debt written off?

Answers to Quick Quiz

1   C

2   C   2% of $200,000 = $4,000. Therefore the allowable needs to be increased by $2,000.

3   The increase in the allowance is charged as an expense in the income statement.

4   DEBIT   Irrecoverable debts account (expenses)
    CREDIT   Trade accounts receivable

Now try the question below from the Exam Question Bank			
Number	Level	Marks	Time
Q16	Introductory	n/a	27 mins

194

13

Accounting for inventories

Topic list	Syllabus reference
1 Accounting for opening and closing inventories	4(b)(i)
2 Counting inventories	4(b)(i)
3 Valuing inventories	4(b)(i)
4 IAS 2 Inventories	4(b)(i)

Introduction

Inventory is one of the most important assets in a company's balance sheet. As we have seen, it also affects the income statement, having a direct impact on gross profit.

So far you have come across inventories in the preparation of a simple balance sheet and in the calculation of the cost of goods sold. This chapter explores the **difficulties of valuing inventories**.

This is the first time that you will be required to consider the impact of the relevant International Accounting Standard on the valuation and presentation of an item in the accounts: IAS 2 *Inventories*.

PART D ACCOUNTING TREATMENTS

Study guide

Section 7 – The financial statements of a sole trader 1: inventory, accruals and prepayments

- Explain and demonstrate how opening and closing inventory are recorded in the inventory account.
- Discuss alternative methods of valuing inventory.
- Explain IASB requirements for inventories.
- Explain the use of continuous and period end inventory records.
- Explain and demonstrate how to calculate the value of closing inventory from given movements in inventory levels, using FIFO (first in first out) and AVCO (average cost).

Exam guide

You will definitely be examined on inventories. You might have to calculate closing inventory as part of an accounts preparation question or as an MCQ.

1 Accounting for opening and closing inventories

Opening inventories brought forward in the inventory account are transferred to the trading account, and so at the end of the accounting year the balance on the inventory account ceases to be the opening inventory value b/f and becomes instead the closing inventory value c/f.

In Chapter 11, we saw that in order to calculate **gross profit** it is necessary to work out the **cost of goods sold**, and in order to calculate the cost of goods sold it is necessary to have values for the **opening inventory** (ie inventory in hand at the beginning of the accounting period) and **closing inventory** (ie inventory in hand at the end of the accounting period).

You should remember, in fact, that the trading part of an income statement includes:

	$
Opening inventory	X
Plus purchases	X
Less closing inventory	(X)
Equals cost of goods sold	X

However, just writing down this formula hides three basic problems.

(a) How do you manage to get a **precise count** of inventory in hand at any one time?

(b) Even once it has been counted, how do you **value** the inventory?

(c) Assuming the inventory is given a value, how does the **double entry bookkeeping** for inventory work?

The purpose of this chapter is to answer all three of these questions. In order to make the presentation a little easier to follow, it is convenient to take the last one first.

1.1 Ledger accounting for inventories

The value of **closing inventories** is accounted for in the nominal ledger by debiting an inventory account and crediting the trading account at the end of an accounting period. Inventory will therefore have a debit balance at the end of a period, and this balance will be shown in the balance sheet as a current asset.

It has already been shown that purchases are introduced to the trading section of the income statement by means of the double entry:

DEBIT	Trading account	$X	
CREDIT	Purchases account		$X

But what about opening and closing inventories? How are their values accounted for in the double entry bookkeeping system? The answer is that a inventory account must be kept. This inventory account is only ever used *at the end of an accounting period*, when the business counts up and values the inventory in hand, in a inventory count.

(a) When a inventory count is made, the business will have a value for its closing inventory, and the double entry is:

DEBIT	Inventory account (closing inventory value)	$X	
CREDIT	Trading account		$X

However, rather than show the closing inventory as a 'plus' value in the trading account (by adding it to sales) it is usual to show it as a 'minus' figure in arriving at cost of sales. This is illustrated in Paragraph 1.2 above. The debit balance on inventory account represents an asset, which will be shown as part of current assets in the balance sheet.

(b) Closing inventory at the end of one period becomes opening inventory at the start of the next period. The inventory account remains unchanged until the end of the next period, when the value of opening inventory is taken to the trading account:

DEBIT	Trading account	$X	
CREDIT	Inventory account (value of opening inventory)		$X

Partly as an example of how this ledger accounting for inventories works, and partly as revision on ledger accounting in general, try the following exercise. It is an example from an earlier part of this text which has had a closing inventory figure included.

Question — Inventories

A business is established with capital of $2,000 and this amount is paid into a business bank account by the proprietor. During the first year's trading, the following transactions occurred.

	$
Purchases of goods for resale, on credit	4,300
Payments for trade accounts payable	3,600
Sales, all on credit	4,000
Payments from trade accounts receivable	3,200
Non-current assets purchased for cash	1,500
Other expenses, all paid in cash	900

The bank has provided an overdraft facility of up to $3,000.

All 'other expenses' relate to the current year.

Closing inventory is valued at $1,800. (Because this is the first year of the business, there are no opening inventories.)

Ignore depreciation and withdrawals on account of profit.

Required

Prepare the ledger accounts, a trading, income and expense account for the year and a balance sheet as at the end of the year.

PART D ACCOUNTING TREATMENTS

Answer

CASH

	$		$
Capital	2,000	Trade accounts payable	3,600
Trade accounts receivable	3,200	Non-current assets	1,500
Balance c/d	800	Other expenses	900
	6,000		6,000
		Balance b/d	800

CAPITAL

	$		$
Balance c/d	2,600	Cash	2,000
		I & E a/c	600
	2,600		2,600
		Balance b/d	2,600

TRADE ACCOUNTS PAYABLE

	$		$
Cash	3,600	Purchases	4,300
Balance c/d	700		
	4,300		4,300
		Balance b/d	700

PURCHASES ACCOUNT

	$		$
Trade accounts payable	4,300	Trading a/c	4,300

NON-CURRENT ASSETS

	$		$
Cash	1,500	Balance c/d	1,500
Balance b/d	1,500		

SALES

	$		$
Trading a/c	4,000	Trade accounts receivable	4,000

TRADE ACCOUNTS RECEIVABLE

	$		$
Sales	4,000	Cash	3,200
		Balance c/d	800
	4,000		4,000
Balance b/d	800		

OTHER EXPENSES

	$		$
Cash	900	I & E a/c	900

TRADING, INCOME AND EXPENSE ACCOUNT

	$		$
Purchases account	4,300	Sales	4,000
Gross profit c/d	1,500	Closing inventory (inventory a/c)	1,800
	5,800		5,800
Other expenses	900	Gross profit b/d	1,500
Net profit (transferred to capital account)	600		
	1,500		1,500

Alternatively, closing inventory could be shown as a minus value on the debit side of the trading account, instead of a credit entry, giving purchases $4,300 less closing inventory $1,800 equals cost of goods sold $2,500.

INVENTORY ACCOUNT

	$		$
Trading a/c (closing inventory)	1,800	Balance c/d	1,800
Balance b/d (opening inventory)	1,800		

BALANCE SHEET AS AT THE END OF THE PERIOD

	$	$
Assets		
Non-current assets		1,500
Current assets		
Goods in inventory	1,800	
Trade accounts receivable	800	
		2,600
Total assets		4,100
Capital and liabilities		
Capital		
At start of period	2,000	
Profit for period	600	
At end of period		2,600
Current liabilities		
Bank overdraft	800	
Trade accounts payable	700	
		1,500
Total capital and liabilities		4,100

Make sure you can see what has happened here. The balance on the inventory account was $1,800, which appears in the balance sheet as a current asset. As it happens, the $1,800 closing inventory was the only entry in the inventory account – there was no figure for opening inventory.

If there had been, it would have been eliminated by transferring it as a debit balance to the trading account, ie:

DEBIT	Trading account (with value of opening inventory)
CREDIT	Inventory account (with value of opening inventory)

The debit in the trading account would then have increased the cost of sales, ie opening inventory is added to purchases in calculating cost of sales. Again, this is illustrated in Paragraph 1.2 above.

So if we can establish the value of inventories on hand, the above paragraphs and exercise show us how to account for that value. That takes care of one of the problems noted at the beginning of this chapter. But now another of those problems becomes apparent – how do we establish the **value** of inventories on hand? The first step must be to establish **how much inventory is held**.

2 Counting inventories

FAST FORWARD

> The **quantity** of inventories held at the year end is established by means of a **physical court** of inventory in an annual counting exercise, or by a 'continuous' inventory court.

Business trading is a continuous activity, but accounting statements must be drawn up at a particular date. In preparing a balance sheet it is necessary to '**freeze**' the activity of a business so as to determine its assets and liabilities at a given moment. This includes establishing the quantities of inventories on hand, which can create problems.

In simple cases, when a business holds easily counted and relatively small amounts of inventory, quantities of inventories on hand at the balance sheet date can be determined by physically counting them in an **inventory count**.

In more complicated cases, where a business holds considerable quantities of varied inventory, an alternative approach to establishing quantities is to maintain **continuous inventory records**. This means that a card is kept for every item of inventory, showing receipts and issues from the stores, and a running total. A few inventory items are counted each day to make sure their record cards are correct – this is called a 'continuous' count because it is spread out over the year rather than completed in one count at a designated time.

One obstacle is overcome once a business has established how much inventory is on hand. But another of the problems noted in the introduction immediately raises its head. What value should the business place on those inventories?

3 Valuing inventories

FAST FORWARD

> The value of inventories is calculated at the lower **cost** and **net realisable value** for each separate item or group of items. **Cost** can be arrived at by using **FIFO** (first in-first out) or **AVCO** (weighted average costing).

3.1 The basic rule

There are **several methods** which, in theory, might be used for the valuation of inventory.

(a) Inventories might be valued at their *expected selling price*.

(b) Inventories might be valued at their expected selling price, less any costs still to be incurred in getting them ready for sale and then selling them. This amount is referred to as the *net realisable value* (NRV) of the inventories.

(c) Inventories might be valued at their *historical cost* (ie the cost at which they were originally bought).

(d) Inventories might be valued at the amount it would cost to replace them. This amount is referred to as the *current replacement cost* of inventories.

Current replacement costs are not used in the type of accounts dealt with in this syllabus. They will be considered again briefly in Chapter 24.

The use of selling prices in inventory valuation is ruled out because this would create a profit for the business before the inventory has been sold.

A simple example might help to explain this. A trader buys two items of inventory, each costing $100. He can sell them for $140 each, but in the accounting period we shall consider, he has only sold one of them. The other is closing inventory in hand.

Since only one item has been sold, you might think it is common sense that profit ought to be $40. But if closing inventory is valued at selling price, profit would be $80, ie profit would be taken on the closing inventory as well.

This would contradict the accounting concept of **prudence**, ie to claim a profit before the item has actually been sold.

	$	$
Sales		140
Opening inventory	–	
Purchases (2 × $100)	200	
	200	
Less closing inventory (at selling price)	140	
Cost of sale		60
Profit		80

The same objection **usually** applies to the use of NRV in inventory valuation. The item purchased for $100 requires $5 of further expenditure in getting it ready for sale and then selling it (eg $5 of processing costs and distribution costs). If its expected selling price is $140, its NRV is $(140 – 5) = $135. To value it at $135 in the balance sheet would still be to anticipate a $35 profit.

We are left with **historical cost** as the normal basis of inventory valuation. **The only time when historical cost is not used is in the exceptional cases where the prudence concept requires a lower value to be used.**

Staying with the example in Paragraph 3.6, suppose that the market in this kind of product suddenly slumps and the item's expected selling price is only $90. The item's NRV is then $(90 – 5) = $85 and the business has in effect made a loss of $15 ($100 – $85). The prudence concept requires that losses should be recognised as soon as they are foreseen. This can be achieved by valuing the inventory item in the balance sheet at its NRV of $85.

The argument developed above suggests that the rule to follow is that inventories should be valued at cost, or if lower, net realisable value. The accounting treatment of inventory is governed by an accounting standard, IAS 2 *Inventories*. IAS 2 states that **inventory should be valued at the lower of cost and net realisable value** as we will see below. This is an important rule and one which you should learn by heart.

Rule to learn | Inventory should be valued at the lower of cost and net realisable value.

3.2 Applying the basic valuation rule

If a business has many inventory items on hand the comparison of cost and NRV should theoretically be carried out for each item separately. It is not sufficient to compare the total cost of all inventory items with their total NRV. An example will show why.

Suppose a company has four items of inventory on hand at the end of its accounting period. Their cost and NRVs are as follows.

Inventory item	Cost	NRV	Lower of cost/NRV
	$	$	$
1	27	32	27
2	14	8	8
3	43	55	43
4	29	40	29
	113	135	107

It would be incorrect to compare total costs ($113) with total NRV ($135) and to state inventories at $113 in the balance sheet. The company can foresee a loss of $6 on item 2 and this should be recognised. If the four items are taken together in total the loss on item 2 is masked by the anticipated profits on the other items. By performing the cost/NRV comparison for each item separately the prudent valuation of $107 can be derived. This is the value which should appear in the balance sheet.

However, for a company with large amounts of inventory this procedure may be impracticable. In this case it is acceptable to group similar items into categories and perform the comparison of cost and NRV category by category, rather than item by item.

Question — Valuation

The following figures relate to inventory held at the year end.

	A $	B $	C $
Cost	20	9	12
Selling price	30	12	22
Modification cost to enable sale	–	2	8
Marketing costs	7	2	2
Units held	200	150	300

Required

Calculate the value of inventory held.

Answer

Item	Cost $	NRV $	Valuation $	Quantity Units	Total value $
A	20	23	20	200	4,000
B	9	8	8	150	1,200
C	12	12	12	300	3,600
					8,800

So have we now solved the problem of how a business should value its inventories? It seems that all the business has to do is to choose the lower of cost and net realisable value. This is true as far as it goes, but there is one further problem, perhaps not so easy to foresee: for a given item of inventory, **what was the cost**?

3.3 Determining the purchase cost

Inventories may be **raw materials** or components bought from suppliers, **finished goods** which have been made by the business but not yet sold, or work in the process of production, but only part-completed (this type of inventory is called **work in progress** or WIP). It will simplify matters, however, if we think about the historical cost of purchased raw materials and components, which ought to be their purchase price.

A business may be continually purchasing consignments of a particular component. As each consignment is received from suppliers they are stored in the appropriate bin or on the appropriate shelf or pallet, where they will be mingled with previous consignments. When the storekeeper issues components to production he will simply pull out from the bin the nearest components to hand, which may have arrived in the latest consignment or in an earlier consignment or in several different consignments. Our concern is to devise a pricing technique, a rule of thumb which we can use to attribute a cost to each of the components issued from stores.

There are several techniques which are used in practice.

13: ACCOUNTING FOR INVENTORIES

> **Key terms**
>
> - **FIFO (first in, first out)**. Using this technique, we assume that components are used in the order in which they are received from suppliers. The components issued are deemed to have formed part of the oldest consignment still unused and are costed accordingly.
>
> - **LIFO (last in, first out)**. This involves the opposite assumption, that components issued to production originally formed part of the most recent delivery, while older consignments lie in the bin undisturbed. **This is now disallowed**.
>
> - **AVCO (average cost)**. As purchase prices change with each new consignment, the average price of components in the bin is constantly changed. Each component in the bin at any moment is assumed to have been purchased at the average price of all components in the bin at that moment.
>
> - **Standard cost**. A pre-determined standard cost is applied to all inventory items. If this standard price differs from prices actually paid during the period it will be necessary to write off the difference as a 'variance' in the income statement.
>
> - **Replacement cost**. The arbitrary assumption is made that the cost at which an inventory unit was purchased is the amount it would cost to replace it. This is often (but not necessarily) the unit cost of inventories purchased in the next consignment *following* the issue of the component to production. For this reason, a method which produces similar results to replacement costs is called NIFO (next in, first out).

If you are preparing **financial accounts** you would normally expect to use FIFO or average costs for the balance sheet valuation of inventory. **IAS 2 (revised) does not permit the use of LIFO**. Nevertheless, you should know about all of the methods so that you can discuss the differences between them. You should note furthermore that terms such as LIFO and FIFO refer to **pricing techniques** only. The *actual* components can be used in any order.

To illustrate the various pricing methods, the following transactions will be used in each case.

TRANSACTIONS DURING MAY 20X7

	Quantity Units	Unit cost $	Total cost $	Market value per unit on date of transactions $
Opening balance 1 May	100	2.00	200	
Receipts 3 May	400	2.10	840	2.11
Issues 4 May	200			2.11
Receipts 9 May	300	2.12	636	2.15
Issues 11 May	400			2.20
Receipts 18 May	100	2.40	240	2.35
Issues 20 May	100			2.35
Closing balance 31 May	200			2.38
			1,916	

Receipts mean goods are received into store and issues represent the issue of goods from store. The problem is to put a valuation on the following.

(a) The issues of materials
(b) The closing inventory

How would issues and closing inventory be valued using each of the following in turn?

(a) FIFO
(b) AVCO

PART D   ACCOUNTING TREATMENTS

3.4 FIFO (first in, first out)

FIFO assumes that materials are **issued out of inventory in the order in which they were delivered into inventory**, ie issues are priced at the cost of the earliest delivery remaining in inventory.

The cost of issues and closing inventory value in the example, using FIFO, would be as follows (note that OI stands for opening inventory).

Date of issue	Quantity Units	Value issued	Cost of issues $	$
4 May	200	100 OI at $2	200	
		100 at $2.10	210	
				410
11 May	400	300 at $2.10	630	
		100 at $2.12	212	
				842
20 May	100	100 at $2.12		212
				1,464
Closing inventory value	200	100 at $2.12	212	
		100 at $2.40	240	
				452
				1,916

Note that the cost of materials issued plus the value of closing inventory equals the cost of purchases plus the value of opening inventory ($1,916).

3.5 AVCO (average cost)

There are various ways in which average costs may be used in pricing inventory issues. The most common (cumulative weighted average pricing) is illustrated below.

The **cumulative weighted average pricing method** calculates a weighted average price for all units in inventory. Issues are priced at this average cost, and the balance of inventory remaining would have the same unit valuation.

A new weighted average price is calculated whenever a new delivery of materials into store is received. This is the key feature of cumulative weighted average pricing.

In our example, issue costs and closing inventory values would be as follows.

Date	Received Units	Issued Units	Balance Units	Total inventory value $	Unit cost $	Price of issue $
Opening inventory			100	200	2.00	
3 May	400			840	2.10	
			500	1,040	2.08 *	
4 May		200		(416)	2.08 **	416
			300	624	2.08	
9 May	300			636	2.12	
			600	1,260	2.10 *	
11 May		400		(840)	2.10 **	840
			200	420	2.10	
18 May	100			240	2.40	
			300	660	2.20 *	
20 May		100		(220)	2.20 **	220
						1,476
Closing inventory value			200	440	2.20	440
						1,916

* A new unit cost of inventory is calculated whenever a new receipt of materials occurs.

** Whenever inventories are issued, the unit value of the items issued is the current weighted average cost per unit at the time of the issue.

For this method too, the cost of materials issued plus the value of closing inventory equals the cost of purchases plus the value of opening inventory ($1,916).

3.6 Inventory valuations and profit

In the previous descriptions of FIFO and AVCO the example used raw materials as an illustration. Each method of valuation produced different costs both of closing inventories and also of material issues. Since raw material costs affect the cost of production, and the cost of production works through eventually into the cost of sales, it follows that different methods of inventory valuation will provide different profit figures. An example may help to illustrate this point.

3.7 Example: Inventory valuations and profit

On 1 November 20X2 a company held 300 units of finished goods item No 9639 in inventory. These were valued at $12 each. During November 20X2 three batches of finished goods were received into store from the production department, as follows.

Date	Units received	Production cost per unit
10 November	400	$12.50
20 November	400	$14
25 November	400	$15

Goods sold out of inventory during November were as follows.

Date	Units sold	Sale price per unit
14 November	500	$20
21 November	500	$20
28 November	100	$20

What was the profit from selling inventory item 9639 in November 20X2, applying the following principles of inventory valuation?

(a) FIFO
(b) AVCO (using cumulative weighted average costing)

Ignore administration, sales and distribution costs.

Solution

(a) FIFO

Date	Issue costs	Issue cost Total $	Closing inventory $
14 November	300 units × $12 plus		
	200 units × $12.50	6,100	
21 November	200 units × $12.50 plus		
	300 units × $14	6,700	
28 November	100 units × $14	1,400	
Closing inventory	400 units × $15		6,000
		14,200	6,000

PART D ACCOUNTING TREATMENTS

(b) AVCO *(cumulative weighted average cost)*

			Unit cost $	Balance in inventory $	Total cost of issues $	Closing inventory $
1 November	Opening inventory	300	12.000	3,600		
10 November	400		12.500	5,000		
	700		12.286	8,600		
14 November	500		12.286	6,143	6,143	
	200		12.286	2,457		
20 November	400		14.000	5,600		
	600		13.428	8,057		
21 November	500		13.428	6,714	6,714	
	100		13.428	1,343		
25 November	400		15.000	6,000		
	500		14.686	7,343		
28 November	100		14.686	1,469	1,469	
30 November	400		14.686	5,874	14,326	5,874

Summary: profit

	FIFO $	AVCO $
Opening inventory	3,600	3,600
Cost of production	16,600	16,600
	20,200	20,200
Closing inventory	6,000	5,874
Cost of sales	14,200	14,326
Sales (1,100 × $20)	22,000	22,000
Profit	7,800	7,674

Different inventory valuations have produced different cost of sales figures, and therefore different profits. In our example opening inventory values are the same, therefore the difference in the amount of profit under each method is the same as the difference in the valuations of closing inventory.

The profit differences are only temporary. In our example, the opening inventory in December 20X2 will be $6,000 or $5,874, depending on the inventory valuation used. Different opening inventory values will affect the cost of sales and profits in December, so that in the long run inequalities in cost of sales each month will even themselves out.

Exam focus point If you have to work out the closing inventory value using one of the above rules, you must set out your schedule neatly and clearly.

Question FIFO

A firm has the following transactions with its product R.

Year 1
Opening inventory: nil
Buys 10 units at $300 per unit
Buys 12 units at $250 per unit
Sells 8 units at $400 per unit
Buys 6 units at $200 per unit
Sells 12 units at $400 per unit

Year 2
Buys 10 units at $200 per unit
Sells 5 units at $400 per unit
Buys 12 units at $150 per unit
Sells 25 units at $400 per unit

Required

Using FIFO, calculate the following on an item by item basis for both year 1 and year 2.

(i) The closing inventory
(ii) The sales
(iii) The cost of sales
(iv) The gross profit

Answer

Year 1

Purchases (units)	Sales (units)	Balance (units)	Inventory value $	Unit cost $	Cost of sales $	Sales $
10		10	3,000	300		
12			3,000	250		
		22	6,000			
	8		(2,400)		2,400	3,200
		14	3,600			
6			1,200	200		
		20	4,800			
	12		(3,100)*		3,100	4,800
		8	1,700		5,500	8,000

* 2 @ $300 + 10 @ $250 = $3,100

Year 2

Purchases (units)	Sales (units)	Balance (units)	Inventory value $	Unit cost $	Cost of sales $	Sales $
B/f		8	1,700			
10			2,000	200		
		18	3,700			
	5		(1,100)*		1,100	2,000
		13	2,600			
12		25	1,800	150		
			4,400			
	25		(4,400)**		4,400	10,000
		0	0		5,500	12,000

* 2 @ $250 + 3 @ $200 = $1,100
** 13 @ $200 + 12 @ $150 = $4,400

Trading account

	FIFO	
Year 1	$	$
Sales	FIFO	8,000
Opening inventory	$	
Purchases	7,200	
	7,200	
Closing inventory	1,700	
Cost of sales		5,500
Gross profit		2,500

PART D ACCOUNTING TREATMENTS

Year 2

Sales		12,000
Opening inventory	1,700	
Purchases	3,800	
	5,500	
Closing inventory	0	
Cost of sales		5,500
Gross profit		6,500

4 IAS 2 Inventories

IAS 2 lays out the required accounting treatment for inventories (sometimes called stocks) under the historical cost system. The major area of contention is the cost **value of inventory** to be recorded. This is recognised as an asset of the enterprise until the related revenues are recognised (ie the item is sold) at which point the inventory is recognised as an expense (ie cost of sales). Part or all of the cost of inventories may also be expensed if a write-down to **net realisable value** is necessary.

In other words, the fundamental accounting assumption of **accrual** requires costs to be matched with associated revenues. In order to achieve this, costs incurred for goods which remain unsold at the year end must be carried forward in the balance sheet and matched against future revenues.

4.1 Scope

The following items are **excluded** from the scope of the standard.

- Work in progress under **construction contracts** (covered by IAS 11 *Construction contracts*, which you will study in later financial accounting papers).
- **Financial instruments** (ie shares, bonds)
- **Livestock**, agricultural and forest products, and mineral ores

4.2 Definitions

The standard gives the following important definitions.

Key terms

- **Inventories** are assets:
  - held for sale in the ordinary course of business;
  - in the process of production for such sale; or
  - in the form of materials or supplies to be consumed in the production process or in the rendering of services.
- **Net realisable value** is the estimated selling price in the ordinary course of business less the estimated costs of completion and the estimated costs necessary to make the sale. *(IAS 2)*

Inventories can **include** any of the following.

- **Goods purchased and held for resale**, eg goods held for sale by a retailer, or land and buildings held for resale
- **Finished goods** produced
- **Work in progress** being produced
- Materials and supplies awaiting use in the production process (**raw materials**)

4.3 Measurement of inventories

The standard states that '**Inventories should be measured at the lower of cost and net realisable value.**'

Exam focus point

This is a very important rule and you will be expected to apply it in the exam.

4.4 Cost of inventories

The cost of inventories will consist of all the following costs.

(a) **Purchase**
(b) **Costs of conversion**
(c) Other costs incurred in bringing the inventories to their **present location and condition**

4.4.1 Costs of purchase

The standard lists the following as comprising the costs of purchase of inventories.

(a) **Purchase price**; *plus*

(b) **Import duties** and other taxes; *plus*

(c) Transport, handling and any other cost **directly attributable** to the acquisition of finished goods, services and materials; *less*

(d) **Trade discounts**, rebates and other similar amounts.

4.4.2 Costs of conversion

Costs of conversion of inventories consist of two main parts.

(a) Costs **directly related** to the units of production, eg direct materials, direct labour

(b) Fixed and variable **production overheads** that are incurred in converting materials into finished goods, allocated on a systematic basis.

You may have come across the terms 'fixed production overheads' or 'variable production overheads' elsewhere in your studies. The standard defines them as follows.

Key terms

- **Fixed production overheads** are those indirect costs of production that remain relatively constant regardless of the volume of production, eg the cost of factory management and administration.

- **Variable production overheads** are those indirect costs of production that vary directly, or nearly directly, with the volume of production, eg indirect materials and labour. *(IAS 2)*

The standard emphasises that fixed production overheads must be allocated to items of inventory on the basis of the **normal capacity of the production facilities**. This is an important point.

(a) **Normal capacity** is the expected achievable production based on the average over several periods/seasons, under normal circumstances.

(b) The above figure should take account of the capacity lost through **planned maintenance**.

(c) If it approximates to the normal level of activity then the **actual level of production** can be used.

(d) **Low production** or **idle plant** will *not* result in a higher fixed overhead allocation to each unit.

(e) **Unallocated overheads** must be recognised as an expense in the period in which they were incurred.

(f) When production is **abnormally high**, the fixed production overhead allocated to each unit will be reduced, so avoiding inventories being stated at more than cost.

(g) The allocation of variable production overheads to each unit is based on the **actual use** of production facilities.

4.4.3 Other costs

Any other costs should only be recognised if they are incurred in bringing the inventories to their **present location and condition**.

The standard lists types of cost which **would not be included** in cost of inventories. Instead, they should be recognised as an **expense** in the period they are incurred.

- **Abnormal amounts** of wasted materials, labour or other production costs
- **Storage costs** (except costs which are necessary in the production process before a further production stage)
- **Administrative overheads** not incurred to bring inventories to their present location and conditions
- **Selling costs**

4.4.4 Techniques for the measurement of cost

Two techniques are mentioned by the standard, both of which produce results which **approximate to cost**, and so both of which may be used for convenience.

(a) **Standard costs** are set up to take account of normal production values: amount of raw materials used, labour time etc. They are reviewed and revised on a regular basis.

(b) **Retail method**: this is often used in the retail industry where there is a large turnover of inventory items, which nevertheless have similar profit margins. The only practical method of inventory valuation may be to take the total selling price of inventories and deduct an overall average profit margin, thus reducing the value to an approximation of cost. The percentage will take account of reduced price lines. Sometimes different percentages are applied on a department basis.

4.5 Cost formulas

Cost of inventories should be assigned by **specific identification** of their individual costs.

(a) Items that are **not ordinarily interchangeable**
(b) Goods or services produced and segregated for **specific projects**.

Specific costs should be attributed to individual items of inventory when they are segregated for a specific project, but not where inventories consist of a large number of interchangeable (ie identical or very similar) items. In the latter circumstances, one of **two approaches** may be taken.

The cost formula is that the cost of inventories should be assigned by using the **first-in, first-out (FIFO)** or **weighted average** cost formulas.

Under the weighted average cost method, a recalculation can be made after each purchase (as we calculated), **or alternatively only at the period end**.

LIFO is no longer permitted under IAS 2.

Question — Inventory valuation

You are the accountant at Water Pumps Co, and you have been asked to calculate the valuation of the company's inventory at cost at its year end of 30 April 20X5.

Water Pumps manufactures a range of pumps. The pumps are assembled from components bought by Water Pumps (the company does not manufacture any parts).

The company does not use a standard costing system, and work in progress and finished goods are valued as follows.

(a) Material costs are determined from the product specification, which lists the components required to make a pump.

(b) The company produces a range of pumps. Employees record the hours spent on assembling each type of pump, this information is input into the payroll system which prints the total hours spent each week assembling each type of pump. All employees assembling pumps are paid at the same rate and there is no overtime.

(c) Overheads are added to the inventory value in accordance with IAS 2 *Inventories*. The financial accounting records are used to determine the overhead cost, and this is applied as a percentage based on the direct labour cost.

For direct labour costs, you have agreed that the labour expended for a unit in work in progress is half that of a completed unit.

The draft accounts show the following materials and direct labour costs in inventory.

	Raw materials	Work in progress	Finished goods
Materials ($)	74,786	85,692	152,693
Direct labour ($)		13,072	46,584

The costs incurred in April, as recorded in the financial accounting records, were as follows.

	$
Direct labour	61,320
Selling costs	43,550
Depreciation and finance costs of production machines	4,490
Distribution costs	6,570
Factory manager's wage	2,560
Other production overheads	24,820
Purchasing and accounting costs relating to production	5,450
Other accounting costs	7,130
Other administration overheads	24,770

For your calculations assume that all work in progress and finished goods were produced in April 20X5 and that the company was operating at a normal level of activity.

Required

Calculate the value of overheads which should be added to work in progress and finished goods in accordance with IAS 2 *Inventories*.

Note. You should include details and a description of your workings and all figures should be calculated to the nearest $.

PART D   ACCOUNTING TREATMENTS

Answer

Calculation of overheads for inventory

Production overheads are as follows.

	$
Depreciation/finance costs	4,490
Factory manager's wage	2,560
Other production overheads	24,820
Accounting/purchase costs	5,450
	37,320

Direct labour = $61,320

∴ Production overhead rate = $\dfrac{37,320}{61,320}$ = 60.86%

Inventory valuation

	Raw materials $	WIP $	Finished goods $	Total $
Materials	74,786	85,692	152,693	313,171
Direct labour	–	13,072	46,584	59,656
Production overhead (at 60.86% of labour)	–	7,956	28,351	36,307
	74,786	106,720	227,628	409,134

Variable overheads will be included in the cost of inventory.

4.6 Net realisable value (NRV)

As a general rule assets should not be carried at amounts greater than those expected to be realised from their sale or use. In the case of inventories this amount could fall below cost when items are **damaged or become obsolete**, or where the **costs to completion have increased** in order to make the sale.

In fact we can identify the principal situations in which **NRV is likely to be less than cost.**

(a) An **increase in costs** or a **fall in selling price**

(b) A **physical deterioration** in the condition of inventory

(c) **Obsolescence** of products

(d) A decision as part of the company's marketing strategy to manufacture and sell products at a **loss**

(e) **Errors in production or purchasing**

A write down of inventories would normally take place on an item by item basis, but similar or related items may be **grouped together**. This grouping together is acceptable for, say, items in the same product line, but it is not acceptable to write down inventories based on a whole classification (eg finished goods) or a whole business.

The assessment of NRV should take place **at the same time** as estimates are made of selling price, using the most reliable information available. Fluctuations of price or cost should be taken into account if they relate directly to **events after the balance sheet date,** which confirm conditions existing at the end of the period.

The reasons why inventory is held must also be taken into account. Some inventory, for example, may be held to satisfy a firm contract and its NRV will therefore be the **contract price**. Any additional inventory of the same type held at the period end will, in contrast, be assessed according to general sales prices when NRV is estimated.

Net realisable value must be reassessed at the end of each period and compared again with cost. If the NRV has risen for inventories held over the end of more than one period, then the previous write down must be **reversed** to the extent that the inventory is then valued at the lower of cost and the new NRV. This may be possible when selling prices have fallen in the past and then risen again.

On occasion a write down to NRV may be of such size, incidence or nature that it must be **disclosed separately**.

4.7 Recognition as an expense

The following treatment is required **when inventories are sold**.

(a) The **carrying amount** is recognised as an expense in the period in which the related revenue is recognised

(b) The amount of any **write-down of inventories** to NRV and all losses of inventories are recognised as an expense in the period the write-down or loss occurs

(c) The amount of any **reversal of any write-down of inventories**, arising from an increase in NRV, is recognised as a reduction in the amount of inventories recognised as an expense in the period in which the reversal occurs

4.8 Disclosure

The financial statements should disclose the following.

(a) **Accounting policies** adopted in measuring inventories, including the cost formula used

(b) **Total carrying amount of inventories** and the carrying amount in classifications appropriate to the enterprise

(c) **Carrying amount** of inventories carried at NRV

(d) Amount of any **reversal of any write-down** that is recognised as income in the period

(e) **Circumstances or events** that led to the reversal of a write-down of inventories

(f) Carrying amount of inventories **pledged as security for liabilities**

This information is of great relevance to users of financial statements, particularly the change in assets from period to period. The standard lists common **classifications for inventories**.

(a) Merchandise
(b) Production supplies
(c) Materials
(d) Work in progress
(e) Finished goods

The financial statements must also disclose either (a) or (b) below.

(a) The **cost of inventories** recognised as an expense during the period.

(b) The **operating costs**, applicable to revenues, recognised as an expense during the period, classified by their nature.

The choice reflects differences in **the way the income statement can be presented**.

Where the entity discloses the amount of **operating costs** applicable to the revenues of the period, classified by their nature, then the costs recognised as an expense will be disclosed for:

(a) Raw materials and consumables
(b) Labour costs
(c) Other operating costs
(d) The net change in inventories for the period

PART D   ACCOUNTING TREATMENTS

Chapter Roundup

- **Opening inventories** brought forward in the inventory account are **transferred to the trading account**, and so at the end of the accounting year, the balance on the inventory account ceases to be the opening inventory value b/f, and becomes instead the closing inventory value c/f.

- The value of **closing inventories** is accounted for in the **nominal ledger** by debiting an inventory account and crediting the trading account at the end of an accounting period. The inventory will therefore always have a debit balance at the end of a period, and this balance will be shown in the balance sheet as a current asset for inventories.

- The **quantity** of inventories held at the year end is established by means of a **physical count** of inventory in an annual counting exercise, or by a 'continuous' inventory count.

- The **value** of these inventories is then **calculated, taking the lower of cost and net realisable value for each separate item or group of inventory items.**

- In order to value the inventories, some rule of thumb must be adopted. The possibilities include:

    – FIFO
    – Average costs
    – Standard costs

    But remember that in financial accounts FIFO or average cost should normally be used.

    – **NRV** is the selling price less all costs to completion and less selling costs.
    – **Cost** comprises purchase costs and costs of conversion.

Quick Quiz

1. When is an inventory account used?
2. How is closing inventory incorporated in the financial statements?
3. What is 'continuous' inventory counting?
4. An item of inventory was purchased for $10. However, due to a fall in demand, its selling price will be only $8. In addition further costs will be incurred prior to sale of $1. What is the net realisable value?
   - A $7
   - B $8
   - C $10
   - D $11
5. Why is inventory not valued at expected selling price?
6. Give four methods of pricing an inventory item at historical cost.
7. What is included in the cost of purchase of inventories according to IAS 2?
8. What type of costs should be recognised as an expense, not as part of the cost of inventory?
9. What are the most likely situations when the NRV of inventories falls below cost?

Answers to Quick Quiz

1. Only at the end of an accounting period.
2. DEBIT: Inventory in hand (balance sheet)
   CREDIT: Closing inventory (trading account)
3. A card is kept for every item of inventory. It shows receipts and issues, with a running total. A few inventory items are counted each day to test that the cards are correct.
4. A Net realisable value is selling price ($8) less further costs to sale ($1), ie $7.
5. Mainly because this would result in the business taking a profit before the goods have been sold.
6.
   - FIFO
   - AVCO
   - Standard cost
   - Replacement cost
7. Purchase price **plus** import duties and other taxes **plus** transport costs **less** trade discount.
8. See Paragraph.4.4.3.
9.
   - Increase in costs or a fall in selling price
   - Physical deterioration of inventory
   - Obsolescence
   - Marketing strategy
   - Errors in production or purchasing

Now try the question below from the Exam Question Bank

Number	Level	Marks	Time
Q17	Introductory	n/a	27 mins

Non-current assets and depreciation

14

Topic list	Syllabus reference
1 Depreciation accounting	4(a)(iii)
2 Depreciation: the mechanics	4(a)(iii)
3 Revaluation of non-current assets	4(a)(iii)
4 Non-current asset disposals	4(a)(ii)
5 IAS 16 Property, plant and equipment	4(a)(ii), 4(a)(iii), 5(c)(iv), 5(d)(iii)(i)
6 The asset register	3(a)(viii)
7 Preparation of final accounts for a sole trader	5(d)(i)

Introduction

You should by now be familiar with the distinction between **non-current and current assets**, a non-current asset being one bought for ongoing use in the business. If you are unsure of this, look back to Chapter 3 to refresh your memory.

Non-current assets might be held and used by a business for a number of years, but they **wear out** or lose their usefulness in the course of time. Every tangible non-current asset has a limited life; the only exception is land.

The accounts of a business try to recognise that the cost of a non-current asset is gradually consumed as the asset wears out. This is done by gradually **writing off the asset's cost in the income statement over several accounting periods**. For example, in the case of a machine costing $1,000 and expected to wear out after ten years, it might be appropriate to reduce the balance sheet value by $100 each year. This process is known as **depreciation.** We will look at the definitions, before going on to the mechanics in Section 2.

Occasionally, particularly in the case of land or buildings, the market value of a non-current asset will rise with time. The asset may then be **revalued**. The accounting treatment of revaluations and the effect on depreciation are considered in Section 3. Section 4 deals with disposals of non-current assets. A profit may arise on the sale of a non-current asset if too much depreciation has been charged.

Introduction (continued)

The main categories of non-current tangible assets are governed by IAS 16 **Property, plant and equipment**, which codifies much of the information in Sections 1, 3 and 4.

Non-current assets need to be controlled, as they are usually valuable. One way of doing this is by an **assets register**. This is looked at in Section 6. You are now in the position of being able to prepare the **final accounts for a sole trader** and an example is given in Section 7.

Study guide

Section 8 – The financial statements of a sole trader 2: depreciation

- Revise the difference between non-current assets and current assets.
- Define and explain the purpose of depreciation.
- Explain the advantages and disadvantages of the straight line, reducing balance and sum of the digits methods of depreciation and make necessary calculations.
- Explain the relevance of consistency and subjectivity in accounting for depreciation.
- Explain and illustrate how depreciation is presented in the income statement and balance sheet.
- Explain and illustrate how depreciation expense and accumulated depreciation are recorded in ledger accounts.
- Prepare a set of financial statements for a sole trader from a trial balance, after allowing for accruals and prepayments, depreciation, irrecoverable debts and allowances for receivables.

Section 16 – Recording and presentation of transactions in non-current assets; liabilities and provisions

- Explain and illustrate the ledger entries to record the acquisition and disposal of non-current assets, using separate accounts for non-current asset cost and accumulated depreciation.
- Explain and illustrate the inclusion of profits or losses on disposal in the income statement.
- Explain and record the revaluation of a non-current asset in ledger accounts and in the balance sheet.
- Explain why, after an upward revaluation, depreciation must be based on the revised figure and for revalued assets sold, the consequent transfer from revaluation reserve to retained earnings as revaluation surplus becomes realised.
- Make the adjustments necessary if changes are made in the estimated useful life and/or residual value of a non-current asset.
- Explain and illustrate how non-current asset balances and movements are disclosed in company financial statements.

Exam guide

This topic will be examined! Expect something both in Section A and Section B.

For those studying for the Oxford Brookes degree, project topic 7 includes the acquisition and disposal of company assets.

1 Depreciation accounting

FAST FORWARD

The **cost** of a non-current asset, less its **estimated residual value**, is allocated fairly between accounting periods by means of **depreciation**. Depreciation is both:

- charged against profit; and
- deducted from the value of the non-current asset in the balance sheet.

Where assets held by an enterprise have a **limited useful life**, it is necessary to apportion the value of an asset used in a period against the revenue it has helped to create. If an asset's life extends over more than one accounting period, it earns profits over more than one period. It is a **non-current asset**. **Current assets**, such as stock and cash, are continually being used and replaced. **Non-current assets** such as plant and vehicles are intended for long-term use in the business.

With the exception of land held on freehold or very long leasehold, **every non-current asset eventually wears out over time**. Machines, cars and other vehicles, fixtures and fittings, and even buildings do not last for ever. When a business acquires a non-current asset, it will have some idea about how long its useful life will be.

(a) To keep on using the non-current asset until it becomes **completely worn out**, useless, and worthless.

(b) To **sell off** the non-current asset at the end of its useful life, as a second-hand item or as scrap.

Since a non-current asset has a cost, a limited useful life, and its value eventually declines, it follows that a charge should be made in the income statement to reflect the use that is made of the asset by the business. This charge is called **depreciation**.

Depreciation accounting is governed by IAS 16 *Property, plant and equipment*, which will be looked at in detail in Section 5 of this Chapter. However, this section will deal with some of the IAS 16 definitions of depreciation.

Key terms

- **Depreciation** is the allocation of the depreciable amount of an asset over its estimated useful life. Depreciation for the accounting period is charged to net profit or loss for the period either directly or indirectly.

- **Depreciable assets** are assets which:
    - are expected to be used during more than one accounting period;
    - have a limited useful life; and
    - are held by an enterprise for use in the production or supply of goods and service, for rental to others, or for administrative purposes.

- **Useful life** is either:
    - the period over which a depreciable asset is expected to be used by the enterprise; or
    - the number of production or similar units expected to be obtained from the asset by the enterprise.

- **Depreciable amount** of a depreciable asset is the historical cost or other amount substituted for historical cost in the financial statements, less the estimated residual value. *(IAS 16)*

An 'amount substituted for historical cost' will normally be a **current market value** after a revaluation has taken place.

1.1 Depreciation

IAS 16 requires the depreciable amount to be allocated on a **systematic basis** to each accounting period during the useful life of the asset.

One way of defining depreciation is to describe it as a means of **spreading the cost** of a non-current asset over its useful life, and so matching the cost against the full period during which it earns profits for the business. Depreciation charges are an example of the application of the accrual assumption to calculate profits.

There are situations where, over a period, an asset has **increased in value**, ie its current value is greater than the carrying value in the financial statements. You might think that in

such situations it would not be necessary to depreciate the asset. The standard states, however, that this is irrelevant, and that depreciation should still be charged to each accounting period, based on the depreciable amount, irrespective of a rise in value.

1.2 Useful life

The following factors should be considered when **estimating the useful life** of a depreciable asset.

- Expected **physical wear and tear**
- **Obsolescence**
- Legal or other **limits** on the use of the assets

Once decided, the useful life should be **reviewed periodically** and depreciation rates adjusted for the current and future periods if expectations vary significantly from the original estimates. The effect of the change should be disclosed in the accounting period in which the change takes place.

The assessment of useful life requires **judgement** based on previous experience with similar assets or classes of asset. When a completely new type of asset is acquired (ie through technological advancement or through use in producing a brand new product or service) it is still necessary to estimate useful life, even though the exercise will be much more difficult.

The standard also points out that the physical life of the asset might be longer than its useful life to the enterprise in question. One of the main factors to be taken into consideration is the **physical wear and tear** the asset is likely to endure. This will depend on various circumstances, including the number of shifts for which the asset will be used, the enterprise's repair and maintenance programme and so in. Other factors to be considered include obsolescence (due to technological advances/improvements in production/reduction in demand for the product/service produced by the asset) and legal restrictions, eg length of a related lease.

1.3 Residual value

In most cases the residual value of an asset is **likely to be immaterial**. If it is likely to be of any significant value, that value must be estimated at the date of purchase or any subsequent revaluation. The amount of residual value should be estimated based on the current situation with other similar assets, used in the same way, which are now at the end of their useful lives. Any expected costs of disposal should be offset against the gross residual value.

(a) A non-current asset costing $20,000 which has an expected life of five years and an expected residual value of nil should be depreciated by $20,000, in total over the five year period.

(b) A non-current asset costing $20,000 which has an expected life of five years and an expected residual value of $3,000 should be depreciated by $17,000 in total over the five year period.

1.4 Depreciation methods

Consistency is important. The depreciation method selected should be applied consistently from period to period unless altered circumstances justify a change. When the method *is* changed, the effect should be quantified and disclosed and the reason for the change should be stated.

Various methods of allocating depreciation to accounting periods are available, but whichever is chosen must be applied **consistently** (as required by IAS 1: see Chapter 10), to ensure comparability from period to period. Change of policy is not allowed simply because of the profitability situation of the enterprise.

The various accepted methods of allocating depreciation and the relevant calculations and accounting treatments are discussed in the next section.

1.5 Disclosure

An accounting policy note should disclose the **valuation bases** used for determining the amounts at which depreciable assets are stated, along with the other accounting policies: see IAS 1.

IAS 16 also requires the following to be disclosed for each major class of depreciable asset.

- **Depreciation methods** used
- **Useful lives** or the depreciation rates used
- **Total depreciation** allocated for the period
- **Gross amount** of depreciable assets and the related accumulated depreciation

1.6 What is depreciation?

The need to depreciate non-current assets arises from the **accrual assumption**. If money is expended in purchasing an asset then the amount must at some time be charged against profits. If the asset is one which contributes to an enterprise's revenue over a number of accounting periods it would be inappropriate to charge any single period (eg the period in which the asset was acquired) with the whole of the expenditure. Instead, some method must be found of spreading the cost of the asset over its useful economic life.

This view of depreciation as a process of allocation of the cost of an asset over several accounting periods is the view adopted by IAS 16. It is worth mentioning here two **common misconceptions** about the purpose and effects of depreciation.

(a) It is sometimes thought that the net book value (NBV) of an asset is equal to its net realisable value and that the object of charging depreciation is to **reflect the fall in value of an asset over its life**. This misconception is the basis of a common, but incorrect, argument which says that freehold properties (say) need not be depreciated in times when property values are rising. It is true that historical cost balance sheets often give a misleading impression when a property's NBV is much below its market value, but in such a case it is open to a business to incorporate a revaluation into its books, or even to prepare its accounts based on current costs. This is a separate problem from that of allocating the property's cost over successive accounting periods.

(b) Another misconception is that depreciation is provided **so that an asset can be replaced at the end of its useful life**. This is not the case.

  (i) If there is no intention of replacing the asset, it could then be argued that there is no need to provide for any depreciation at all.

  (ii) If prices are rising, the replacement cost of the asset will exceed the amount of depreciation provided.

PART D ACCOUNTING TREATMENTS

2 Depreciation: the mechanics

FAST FORWARD

Three methods of depreciation are specified in your syllabus:

- the straight line method
- the reducing balance method
- the sum of the digits method

When a non-current asset is depreciated, two things must be accounted for.

(a) The **charge for depreciation** is a cost or expense of the accounting period. For the time being, we shall charge depreciation as an expense in the income statement.

(b) At the same time, the non-current asset is wearing out and diminishing in value, and so the value of the non-current asset in the balance sheet must be reduced by the amount of depreciation charged. The balance sheet value of the non-current asset will be its '**net book value**', which is its cost less accumulated depreciation.

The amount of depreciation deducted from the cost of a non-current asset to arrive at its net book value will build up (or 'accumulate') over time, as more depreciation is charged in each successive accounting period. This accumulated depreciation is a 'provision' because it provides for the fall in value of the non-current asset. The term 'provision for depreciation' refers to the 'accumulated depreciation' or 'aggregate depreciation' of a non-current asset.

For example, if a non-current asset costing $40,000 has an expected life of four years and an estimated residual value of nil, it might be depreciated by $10,000 per annum.

	Depreciation charge for the year (I & E a/c) (A) $	Aggregate depreciation at end of year (B) $	Cost of the asset (C) $	Net book value at end of year (C – B) $
At beginning of its life	–	–	40,000	40,000
Year 1	10,000	10,000	40,000	30,000
Year 2	10,000	20,000	40,000	20,000
Year 3	10,000	30,000	40,000	10,000
Year 4	10,000	40,000	40,000	0
	40,000			

At the end of year 4, the full $40,000 of depreciation charges have been made in the income statements of the four years. The net book value of the non-current asset is now nil. In theory (although perhaps not in practice) the business will no longer use the non-current asset, which now needs replacing.

2.1 Methods of depreciation

There are several different methods of depreciation. Of these, the ones which are specified in the Paper 1.1 Study Guide are:

- Straight-line method
- Reducing balance method
- Sum of the digits method

2.2 The straight line method

This is the most commonly used method of all. The total depreciable amount is charged in equal instalments to each accounting period over the expected useful life of the asset. (In this way, the net book value of the non-current asset declines at a steady rate, or in a 'straight line' over time.)

The annual depreciation charge is calculated as:

$$\frac{\text{Cost of asset minus residual value}}{\text{Expected useful life of the asset}}$$

2.3 Example: Straight line depreciation

(a) A non-current asset costing $20,000 with an estimated life of 10 years and no residual value would be depreciated at the rate of:

$$\frac{\$20,000}{10 \text{ years}} = \$2,000 \text{ per annum}$$

(b) A non-current asset costing $60,000 has an estimated life of 5 years and a residual value of $7,000. The annual depreciation charge using the straight line method would be:

$$\frac{\$(60,000 - 7,000)}{5 \text{ years}} = \$10,600 \text{ per annum}$$

The net book value of the non-current asset would be:

	After 1 year $	After 2 years $	After 3 years $	After 4 years $	After 5 years $
Cost of the asset	60,000	60,000	60,000	60,000	60,000
Accumulated depreciation	10,600	21,200	31,800	42,400	53,000
Net book value	49,400	38,800	28,200	17,600	7,000 *

* ie its estimated residual value.

Since the depreciation charge per annum is the same amount every year with the straight line method, it is often convenient to state that depreciation is charged at the rate of x per cent per annum on the cost of the asset. In the example in Paragraph 2.7(a) above, the depreciation charge per annum is 10% of cost (ie 10% of $20,000 = $2,000).

Examination questions often describe straight line depreciation in this way.

The straight line method of depreciation is a fair allocation of the total depreciable amount between the different accounting periods, *provided that* it is reasonable to assume that the business enjoys equal benefits from the use of the asset in every period throughout its life.

2.4 Assets acquired in the middle of an accounting period

A business can purchase new non-current assets at any time during the course of an accounting period. It might seem fair to charge an amount for depreciation, in the period when the purchase occurs, which reflects the limited use the business has had from the asset in that period.

2.5 Example: Assets acquired in the middle of an accounting period

A business which has an accounting year which runs from 1 January to 31 December purchases a new non-current asset on 1 April 20X1, at a cost of $24,000. The expected life of the asset is 4 years, and its residual value is nil. What should be the depreciation charge for 20X1?

Solution

The annual depreciation charge will be $\frac{\$24,000}{4 \text{ years}} = \$6,000$ per annum

PART D ACCOUNTING TREATMENTS

However, since the asset was acquired on 1 April 20X1, the business has only benefited from the use of the asset for 9 months instead of a full 12 months. It would therefore seem fair to charge depreciation in 20X1 of only:

$$\frac{9}{12} \times \$6,000 = \$4,500$$

Exam focus point

> If an examination question gives you the purchase date of a non-current asset, which is in the middle of an accounting period, you should generally assume that depreciation should be calculated in this way as a 'part-year' amount. However, you will only be given such a problem when the straight line method of depreciation is used.

In practice, many businesses ignore the niceties of part-year depreciation, and charge a full year's depreciation on non-current assets in the year of their purchase, regardless of the time of year they were acquired.

2.6 The reducing balance method

The **reducing balance method** of depreciation calculates the annual depreciation charge as a fixed percentage of the net book value of the asset, as at the end of the previous accounting period.

For example, a business purchases a non-current asset at a cost of $10,000. Its expected useful life is 3 years and its estimated residual value is $2,160. The business wishes to use the reducing balance method to depreciate the asset, and calculates that the rate of depreciation should be 40% of the reducing (net book) value of the asset. (The method of deciding that 40% is a suitable annual percentage is a problem of mathematics, not financial accounting, and is not described here.)

The total depreciable amount is $(10,000 – 2,160) = $7,840.

The depreciation charge per annum and the net book value of the asset as at the end of each year will be as follows.

	$	Accumulated depreciation $	
Asset at cost	10,000		
Depreciation in year 1 (40%)	4,000	4,000	
Net book value at end of year 1	6,000		
Depreciation in year 2			
(40% of reducing balance)	2,400	6,400	(4,000 + 2,400)
Net book value at end of year 2	3,600		
Depreciation in year 3 (40%)	1,440	7,840	(6,400 + 1,440)
Net book value at end of year 3	2,160		

You should note that with the reducing balance method, the annual charge for depreciation is higher in the earlier years of the asset's life, and lower in the later years. In the example above, the annual charges for years 1, 2 and 3 are $4,000, $2,400 and $1,440 respectively.

The reducing balance method might therefore be used when it is considered fair to allocate a greater proportion of the total depreciable amount to the earlier years and a lower proportion to later years, on the assumption that the benefits obtained by the business from using the asset decline over time.

2.7 Sum of the digits method

This method is similar to the reducing balance method as it produces higher depreciation charges in the early years of ownership of a non-current asset. An example will show how the method works.

2.8 Example: Sum of the digits method

Icho Co purchases a non-current asset for $10,000 on 1 January 20X0. The useful life of the asset is five years and the residual value is $1,000. What is the depreciation charge for each year of the asset's life?

Solution

The sum of the digits is 5 years + 4 years + 3 years + 2 years + 1 year = 15, and depreciation is allocated as follows.

Year	Calculation	Depreciation charge $	Aggregate depreciation $
20X1	5/15 × $(10,000 − 1,000)	3,000	3,000
20X2	4/15 × $9,000	2,400	5,400
20X3	3/15 × $9,000	1,800	7,200
20X4	2/15 × $9,000	1,200	8,400
20X5	1/15 × $9,000	600	9,000

A formula can be used to produce the sum of the digits. Where n is the number of years:

Sum of the digits = $\dfrac{n(n+1)}{2}$

So, for example, for 5 years the sum of digits is:

$\dfrac{5(5+1)}{2} = 15$

2.9 Applying a depreciation method consistently

It is up to the business concerned to decide which method of depreciation to apply to its non-current assets. Once that decision has been made, however, it should not be changed; the chosen method of depreciation should be applied **consistently from year to year**. This is an instance of the fundamental accounting assumption of consistency, which we looked at in Chapter 10.

Similarly, it is up to the business to decide what a sensible life span for a non-current asset should be. Again, once that life span has been chosen, it should not be changed unless something unexpected happens to the asset.

It is permissible for a business to depreciate different categories of non-current assets in different ways. For example, if a business owns three cars, then each car would normally be depreciated in the same way (eg by the straight line method); but another category of non-current asset, say, photocopiers, might be depreciated using a different method (eg by the reducing balance method).

Question — Depreciation

A lorry bought for a business cost $17,000. It is expected to last for five years and then be sold for scrap for $2,000.

Required

Work out the depreciation to be charged each year under:

(a) The straight line method
(b) The reducing balance method (using a rate of 35%)

> **Answer**
>
> (a) Under the straight line method, depreciation for each of the five years is:
>
> $$\text{Annual depreciation} = \frac{\$(17{,}000 - 2{,}000)}{5} = \$3{,}000$$
>
> (b) Under the reducing balance method, depreciation for each of the five years is:
>
> | Year | Depreciation | |
> |---|---|---|
> | 1 | 35% × $17,000 | = $5,950 |
> | 2 | 35% × ($17,000 − $5,950) = 35% × $11,050 | = $3,868 |
> | 3 | 35% × ($11,050 − $3,868) = 35% × $7,182 | = $2,514 |
> | 4 | 35% × ($7,182 − $2,514) = 35% × $4,668 | = $1,634 |
> | 5 | Balance to bring book value down to $2,000 = $4,668 − $1,634 − $2,000 | = $1,034 |

2.10 Change in method of depreciation

Having made the above comments about consistency, the depreciation method should be reviewed for appropriateness. If there are any changes in the expected pattern of use of the asset (and hence economic benefit), then the method used should be changed. In such cases, the remaining net book value is depreciated under the new method, ie only current and future periods are affected; the change is not retrospective.

2.11 Example: Change in method of depreciation

Jakob Co purchased an asset for $100,000 on 1.1.X1. It had an estimated useful life of 5 years and it was depreciated using the reducing balance method at a rate of 40%. On 1.1.X3 it was decided to change the method to straight line.

Show the depreciation charge for each year (to 31 December) of the asset's life.

Solution

Year		Depreciation charge $	Aggregate depreciation $
20X1	$100,000 × 40%	40,000	40,000
20X2	$60,000 × 40%	24,000	64,000
20X3	$\frac{\$100{,}000 - \$64{,}000}{3}$	12,000	76,000
20X4		12,000	88,000
20X5		12,000	100,000

2.12 A fall in the value of a non-current asset

When the 'market' value of a non-current asset falls so that it is worth less than the amount of its net book value, **and the fall in value is expected to be permanent**, the asset should be **written down to its new low market value**. The charge in the income statement for the diminution in the value of the asset during the accounting period should then be:

	$
Net book value at the beginning of the period	X
Less new reduced value	(X)
Equals the charge for the diminution in the asset's value in the period.	X

2.13 Example: Fall in asset value

A business purchased a building on 1 January 20X1 at a cost of $100,000. The building has a 20 year life. After 5 years' use, on 1 January 20X6, the business decides that since property prices have fallen sharply, the building is now worth only $60,000, and that the value of the asset should be reduced in the accounts of the business.

The building was being depreciated at the rate of 5% per annum on cost.

Before the asset is reduced in value, the annual depreciation charge is:

$$\frac{\$100,000}{20 \text{ years}} = \$5,000 \text{ per annum } (= 5\% \text{ of } \$100,000)$$

After 5 years, the accumulated depreciation would be $25,000 and the net book value of the building $75,000, which is $15,000 more than the new asset value. This $15,000 should be written off as a charge for depreciation (or fall in the asset's value) in year 5, so that the total charge in year 5 is:

	$
Net book value of the leasehold after 4 years $(100,000 – 20,000)	80,000
Revised asset value at end of year 5	60,000
Charge against profit in year 5	20,000

An alternative method of calculation is:

	$
'Normal' depreciation charge per annum	5,000
Further fall in value, from net book value at end of year 5 to revised value	15,000
Charge against profit in year 5	20,000

The building has a further life of 15 years, and its value is now $60,000. From year 6 to year 20, the annual charge for depreciation will be:

$$\frac{\$60,000}{15 \text{ years}} = \$4,000 \text{ per annum}$$

2.14 Change in expected useful life or residual value of an asset

The depreciation charge on a non-current asset depends not only on the cost (or value) of the asset and its estimated residual value, but also on its **estimated useful life**.

A business purchased a non-current asset costing $12,000 with an estimated life of four years and no residual value. If it used the straight line method of depreciation, it would make an annual provision of 25% of $12,000 = $3,000.

Now what would happen if the business decided after two years that the useful life of the asset has been underestimated, and it still had five more years in use to come (making its total life seven years)?

For the first two years, the asset would have been depreciated by $3,000 per annum, so that its net book value after two years would be $(12,000 – 6,000) = $6,000. If the remaining life of the asset is now revised to five more years, the remaining amount to be depreciated (here $6,000) should be spread over the remaining life, giving an annual depreciation charge for the final five years of:

$$\frac{\text{Net book value at time of life readjustment, minus residual value}}{\text{New estimate of remaining useful life}}$$

$$= \frac{\$6,000}{5 \text{ years}} = \$1,200 \text{ per year}$$

Formula to learn

$$\text{New depreciation} = \frac{\text{NBV less residual value}}{\text{Revised useful life}}$$

Similar adjustments are made when there is a change in the expected residual value of the asset.

2.15 Depreciation is not a cash expense

Depreciation spreads the cost of a non-current asset (less its estimated residual value) over the asset's life. The cash payment for the non-current asset will be made when, or soon after, the asset is purchased. Annual depreciation of the asset in subsequent years is not a cash expense – rather it allocates costs to those later years for a cash payment that has occurred previously.

For example, a business purchased some shop fittings for $6,000 on 1 July 20X5 and paid for them in cash on that date.

Subsequently, depreciation may be charged at $600 every year for ten years. So each year $600 is deducted from profits and the net book value of the fittings goes down, but no actual cash is being paid. The cash was all paid on 1 July 20X5. So annual depreciation is not a cash expense, but rather an allocation of the original cost to later years.

Question — Depreciation

(a) What are the purposes of providing for depreciation?

(b) In what circumstances is the reducing balance method more appropriate than the straight-line method? Give reasons for your answer.

Answer

(a) The accounts of a business try to recognise that the cost of a non-current asset is gradually consumed as the asset wears out. This is done by gradually writing off the asset's cost in the income statement over several accounting periods. This process is known as depreciation, and is an example of the accrual assumption. IAS 16 *Property, plant and equipment* requires that depreciation should be allocated on a systematic basis to each accounting period during the useful life of the asset.

With regard to the accrual principle, it is fair that the profits should be reduced by the depreciation charge; this is not an arbitrary exercise. Depreciation is not, as is sometime supposed, an attempt to set aside funds to purchase new non-current assets when required. Depreciation is not generally provided on freehold land because it does not 'wear out' (unless it is held for mining etc).

(b) The reducing balance method of depreciation is used instead of the straight line method when it is considered fair to allocate a greater proportion of the total depreciable amount to the earlier years and a lower proportion to the later years, on the assumption that the benefits obtained by the business from using the asset decline over time.

In favour of this method it may be argued that it links the depreciation charge to the costs of maintaining and running the asset. In the early years these costs are low and the depreciation charge is high, while in later years this is reversed.

2.16 Accumulated depreciation

Key term

Accumulated **depreciation** is the amount set aside as a charge for the wearing out of non-current assets.

There are two basic aspects of accumulated depreciation to remember.

(a) A depreciation charge is made in the income statement in each accounting period for every depreciable non-current asset. Nearly all non-current assets are depreciable, the most important exceptions being freehold land and non-current investments.

(b) The total accumulated depreciation on a non-current asset builds up as the asset gets older. The total accumulated depreciation is always getting larger, until the non-current asset is fully depreciated.

The ledger accounting entries for depreciation are as follows.

(a) There is an accumulated depreciation account for each separate category of non-current assets, for example, plant and machinery, land and buildings, fixtures and fittings.

(b) The depreciation charge for an accounting period is a charge against profit. It is accounted for as follows.

DEBIT   I & E account (depreciation expense)
CREDIT   Accumulated depreciation account (balance sheet)

with the depreciation charge for the period.

(c) The balance on the balance sheet depreciation account is the total accumulated depreciation. This is always a credit balance brought forward in the ledger account for depreciation.

(d) The non-current asset accounts are unaffected by depreciation. Non-current assets are recorded in these accounts at cost (or, if they are revalued, at their revalued amount).

(e) In the balance sheet of the business, the total balance on the accumulated depreciation account is set against the value of non-current asset accounts (ie non-current assets at cost or revalued amount) to derive the net book value of the non-current assets.

This is how the non-current asset accounts might appear in a trial balance:

	DR	CR
Freehold building – cost	2,000,000	
Freehold building – accumulated depreciation		500,000
Motor vehicles – cost	70,000	
Motor vehicles – accumulated depreciation		40,000
Office equipment – cost	25,000	
Office equipment – accumulated depreciation		15,000

And this is how they would be shown in the balance sheet:

Non current assets
Freehold building	1,500,000
Motor vehicles	30,000
Office equipment	10,000

2.17 Example: Depreciation

Brian Box set up his own computer software business on 1 March 20X6. He purchased a computer system on credit from a manufacturer, at a cost of $16,000. The system has an expected life of three years and a residual value of $2,500. Using the straight line method of depreciation, the non-current asset account, accumulated depreciation account and I & E account (extract) and balance sheet (extract) would be as follows, for each of the next three years, 28 February 20X7, 20X8 and 20X9.

PART D ACCOUNTING TREATMENTS

NON-CURRENT ASSET: COMPUTER EQUIPMENT

	Date		$	Date		$
(a)	1.3.X6	Accounts payable	16,000	28.2.X7	Balance c/d	16,000
(b)	1.3.X7	Balance b/d	16,000	28.2.X8	Balance c/d	16,000
(c)	1.3.X8	Balance b/d	16,000	28.2.X9	Balance c/d	16,000
(d)	1.3.X9	Balance b/d	16,000			

In theory, the non-current asset has now lasted out its expected useful life. However, until it is sold off or scrapped, the asset will still appear in the balance sheet at cost (less accumulated depreciation) and it should remain in the ledger account for computer equipment until it is eventually disposed of.

ACCUMULATED DEPRECIATION

	Date		$	Date		$
(a)	28.2.X7	Balance c/d	4,500	28.2.X7	I & E account	4,500
(b)	28.2.X8	Balance c/d	9,000	1.3.X7	Balance b/d	4,500
				28.2.X8	I & E account	4,500
			9,000			9,000
(c)	28.2.X9	Balance c/d	13,500	1.3.X8	Balance b/d	9,000
				28.2.X9	I & E account	4,500
			13,500			13,500
				1.3.X9 Balance b/d		13,500

The annual depreciation charge is $\dfrac{\$(16{,}000 - 2{,}500)}{3 \text{ years}} = \$4{,}500$ pa

At the end of three years, the asset is fully depreciated down to its residual value (16,000 – 13,500 = 2,500). If it continues to be used by Brian Box, it will not be depreciated any further (unless its estimated residual value is reduced).

INCOME STATEMENT (EXTRACT)

	Date		$
(a)	28 Feb 20X7	Depreciation	4,500
(b)	28 Feb 20X8	Depreciation	4,500
(c)	28 Feb 20X9	Depreciation	4,500

BALANCE SHEET (EXTRACT) AS AT 28 FEBRUARY

	20X7	20X8	20X9
	$	$	$
Computer equipment at cost	16,000	16,000	16,000
Less accumulated depreciation	4,500	9,000	13,500
Net book value	11,500	7,000	2,500

2.18 Example: Allowance for depreciation with assets acquired part-way through the year

Brian Box prospers in his computer software business, and before long he purchases a car for himself, and later for his chief assistant Bill Ockhead. Relevant data is as follows.

230

	Date of purchase	Cost	Estimated life	Estimated residual value
Brian Box car	1 June 20X6	$20,000	3 years	$2,000
Bill Ockhead car	1 June 20X7	$8,000	3 years	$2,000

The straight line method of depreciation is to be used.

Prepare the motor vehicles account and motor vehicle depreciation account for the years to 28 February 20X7 and 20X8. (You should allow for the part-year's use of a car in computing the annual charge for depreciation.)

Calculate the net book value of the motor vehicles as at 28 February 20X8.

Solution

(a) (i) Brian Box car Annual depreciation $\dfrac{\$(20,000 - 2,000)}{3 \text{ years}} =$ $6,000 pa

Monthly depreciation = $500
Depreciation 1 June-20X6 – 28 February 20X7 (9 months) $4,500
1 March 20X7 – 28 February 20X8 $6,000

(ii) Bill Ockhead car Annual depreciation $\dfrac{\$(8,000 - 2,000)}{3 \text{ years}} =$ $2,000 pa

Depreciation 1 June 20X7 – 28 February 20X8 (9 months) $1,500

(b)

MOTOR VEHICLES

Date		$	Date		$
1 Jun 20X6	Payables (or cash) (car purchase)	20,000	28 Feb 20X7	Balance c/d	20,000
1 Mar 20X7	Balance b/d	20,000			
1 Jun 20X7	Payables (or cash) (car purchase)	8,000	28 Feb 20X8	Balance c/d	28,000
		28,000			28,000
1 Mar 20X8	Balance b/d	28,000			

MOTOR VEHICLES – ACCUMULATED DEPRECIATION

Date		$	Date		$
28 Feb 20X7	Balance c/d	4,500	28 Feb 20X7	I & E account	4,500
			1 Mar 20X7	Balance b/d	4,500
28 Feb 20X8	Balance c/d	12,000	28 Feb 20X8	I & E account (6,000+1,500)	7,500
		12,000			12,000
			1 Mar 20X8	Balance b/d	12,000

BALANCE SHEET (WORKINGS) AS AT 28 FEBRUARY 20X8

	Brian Box car		Bill Ockhead car		Total
	$	$	$	$	$
Asset at cost		20,000		8,000	28,000
Accumulated depreciation					
Year to 28 Feb 20X7	4,500		–		
Year to 28 Feb 20X8	6,000		1,500		
		10,500		1,500	12,000
Net book value		9,500		6,500	16,000

PART D   ACCOUNTING TREATMENTS

3 Revaluation of non-current assets

FAST FORWARD When a non-current asset is **revalued**, depreciation is charged on the **revalued amount**.

Largely because of inflation, it is now quite common for the market value of certain non-current assets to **go up, in spite of getting older**. The most obvious example of rising market values is land and buildings.

A business which owns non-current assets which are rising in value is not obliged to revalue those assets in its balance sheet. However, in order to give a more 'true and fair view' of the position of the business, it might be decided that some non-current assets should be revalued upwards; otherwise the total value of the assets of the business might seem unrealistically low. When non-current assets are revalued, depreciation should be charged on the *revalued amount*.

3.1 Example: The revaluation of non-current assets

When Ira Vann commenced trading as a car hire dealer on 1 January 20X1, he purchased business premises at a cost of $50,000.

For the purpose of accounting for depreciation, he decided the following.

(a)   The land part of the business premises was worth $20,000; this would not be depreciated.

(b)   The building part of the business premises was worth the remaining $30,000. This would be depreciated by the straight-line method to a nil residual value over 30 years.

After five years of trading on 1 January 20X6, Ira decides that his business premise is now worth $150,000, divided into:

	$
Land	75,000
Building	75,000
	150,000

He estimates that the building still has a further 25 years of useful life remaining.

Calculate the annual charge for depreciation in each of the 30 years of its life, and the balance sheet value of the land and building as at the end of each year.

Solution

Before the revaluation, the annual depreciation charge is $1,000 per annum on the building. This charge is made in each of the first five years of the asset's life.

The net book value of the asset will decline by $1,000 per annum, to:

(a) $49,000 as at 31.12.X1
(b) $48,000 as at 31.12.X2
(c) $47,000 as at 31.12.X3
(d) $46,000 as at 31.12.X4
(e) $45,000 as at 31.12.X5

When the revaluation takes place, the amount of the revaluation is:

	$
New asset value (to be shown in balance sheet)	150,000
Net book value as at end of 20X5	45,000
Amount of revaluation	105,000

The asset will be revalued by $105,000 to $150,000. If you remember the accounting equation, that the total value of assets must be equalled by the total value of capital and liabilities, you should recognise that if assets go up in value by $105,000, capital or liabilities must also go up by the same amount. Since the increased value benefits the owners of the business, the amount of the revaluation is added to capital (a **revaluation reserve**).

This treatment may surprise you at first. However remember the prudence concept, which states that a profit can not be anticipated before it is realised. Therefore the 'profit' can not be dealt with as income in the income statement. **If the building were to be subsequently sold for the revalued amount, the profit would be realised and could be taken to the income statement.**

The accounting treatment for the revaluation above will be:

DEBIT	Non-current asset	$105,000	
CREDIT	Revaluation reserve		$105,000

If the asset were then to be sold for the carrying value of $150,000, the entries would be:

DEBIT	Cash	$150,000	
CREDIT	Non-current asset		$150,000
DEBIT	Revaluation reserve	$105,000	
CREDIT	Profit on sale of non-current asset		$105,000

Exam focus point

> For the purpose of your 1.1 International syllabus, you only need to know how to set up the revaluation reserve., You will learn more about revaluation reserves in your future studies.

After the revaluation, depreciation will be charged on the building at a new rate of:

$$\frac{\$75,000}{25 \text{ years}} = \$3,000 \text{ per year}$$

The net book value of the property will then fall by $3,000 per year over 25 years, from $150,000 as at 1 January 20X6 to only $75,000 at the end of the 25 years, ie the building part of the property value will have been fully depreciated.

The consequence of a revaluation is therefore a higher annual depreciation charge.

IAS 16 requires the residual value and useful economic life of an asset to be reviewed at each financial year end.

4 Non-current asset disposals

When a non-current asset is **sold**, there is likely to be a **profit or loss on disposal**. This is the difference between the net sale price of the asset and its net book value at the time of disposal.

4.1 The disposal of non-current assets

Non-current assets are not purchased by a business with the intention of reselling them in the normal course of trade. However, they might be sold off at some stage during their life, either when their useful life is over or before then. A business might decide to sell off a non-current asset long before its useful life has ended.

Whenever a business sells something, it will make a profit or a loss. When non-current assets are disposed of, there will be a profit or loss on disposal. As it is a capital item being sold, the profit or loss will be a capital gain or a capital loss. These gains or losses are reported in the income and expenses part of the income statement of the business (not as a trading profit in the trading account). They are commonly referred to as '**profit on disposal of non-current assets**' or '**loss on disposal**'.

Examination questions on the disposal of non-current assets are likely to ask for ledger accounts to be prepared, showing the entries in the accounts to record the disposal. But before we look at the ledger accounting for disposing of assets, we had better look at the principles behind calculating the profit (or loss) on disposing of assets.

4.2 The principles behind calculating the profit or loss on disposal

The profit or loss on the disposal of a non-current asset is the difference between (a) and (b) below.

(a) The net book value of the asset at the time of its sale.
(b) Its net sale price, which is the price minus any costs of making the sale.

A profit is made when the sale price exceeds the net book value, and a loss is made when the sale price is less than the net book value.

4.3 Example: Disposal of a non-current asset

A business purchased a non-current asset on 1 January 20X1 for $25,000. It had an estimated life of six years and an estimated residual value of $7,000. The asset was eventually sold after three years on 1 January 20X4 to another trader who paid $17,500 for it.

What was the profit or loss on disposal, assuming that the business uses the straight line method for depreciation?

Solution

Annual depreciation = $\dfrac{\$(25{,}000 - 7{,}000)}{6 \text{ years}}$ = $3,000 per annum

	$
Cost of asset	25,000
Less accumulated depreciation (three years)	9,000
Net book value at date of disposal	16,000
Sale price	17,500
Profit on disposal	1,500

This profit will be shown in the income statement of the business where it will be an item of other income added to the gross profit brought down from the trading account.

4.4 Second example: Disposal of a non-current asset

A business purchased a machine on 1 July 20X1 at a cost of $35,000. The machine had an estimated residual value of $3,000 and a life of eight years. The machine was sold for $18,600 on 31 December 20X4, the last day of the accounting year of the business. To make the sale, the business had to incur dismantling costs and costs of transporting the machine to the buyer's premises. These amounted to $1,200.

The business uses the straight line method of depreciation. What was the profit or loss on disposal of the machine?

Solution

Annual depreciation $\dfrac{\$(35{,}000 - 3{,}000)}{8 \text{ years}}$ = $4,000 per annum

It is assumed that in 20X1 only one-half year's depreciation was charged, because the asset was purchased six months into the year.

	$	$
Non-current asset at cost		35,000
Depreciation in 20X1 (½ year)	2,000	
20X2, 20X3 and 20X4	12,000	
Accumulated depreciation		14,000
Net book value at date of disposal		21,000
Sale price	18,600	
Costs incurred in making the sale	(1,200)	
Net sale price		17,400
Loss on disposal		(3,600)

This loss will be shown as an expense in the income statement of the business. It is a capital loss, not a trading loss, and it should not therefore be shown in the trading account.

4.5 The disposal of non-current assets: ledger accounting entries

We have already seen how the profit or loss on disposal of a non-current asset should be computed. A profit on disposal is an item of 'other income' in the income statement, and a loss on disposal is an item of expense in the income statement

It is customary in ledger accounting to record the disposal of non-current assets in a **disposal of non-current assets account**.

(a) The profit or loss on disposal is the difference between:

 (i) the sale price of the asset (if any); and
 (ii) the net book value of the asset at the time of sale.

(b) The following items must appear in the disposal of non-current assets account:

 (i) The value of the asset (at cost, or revalued amount*)
 (ii) The accumulated depreciation up to the date of sale
 (iii) The sale price of the asset

*To simplify the explanation of the rules, we will assume now that the non-current assets disposed of are valued at cost.

(c) The ledger accounting entries are as follows.

 (i) DEBIT   Disposal of non-current asset account
     CREDIT   Non-current asset account

 with the cost of the asset disposed of.

 (ii) DEBIT   Accumulated depreciation account
      CREDIT   Disposal of non-current asset account

 with the accumulated depreciation on the asset as at the date of sale.

 (iii) DEBIT   Receivable account or cash book
       CREDIT   Disposal of non-current asset account

 with the sale price of the asset. The sale is therefore not recorded in a sales account, but in the disposal of non-current asset account itself. You will notice that the effect of these entries is to remove the asset, and its accumulated depreciation, from the balance sheet.

The balance on the disposal account is the profit or loss on disposal and the corresponding double entry is recorded in the I & E account itself.

4.6 Example: Disposal of assets: Ledger accounting entries

A business has $110,000 worth of machinery at cost. Its policy is to make a provision for depreciation at 20% per annum straight line. The total provision now stands at $70,000. The business sells for $19,000 a machine which it purchased exactly two years ago for $30,000.

Show the relevant ledger entries.

Solution

PLANT AND MACHINERY ACCOUNT

	$		$
Balance b/d	110,000	Plant disposals account	30,000
		Balance c/d	80,000
	110,000		110,000
Balance b/d	80,000		

PLANT AND MACHINERY ACCUMULATED DEPRECIATION

	$		$
Plant disposals (20% of $30,000 for 2 years)	12,000	Balance b/d	70,000
Balance c/d	58,000		
	70,000		70,000
		Balance b/d	58,000

PLANT DISPOSALS

	$		$
Plant and machinery account	30,000	Accumulated depreciation	12,000
I & E a/c (profit on sale)	1,000	Cash	19,000
	31,000		31,000

Check

	$
Asset at cost	30,000
Accumulated depreciation at time of sale	12,000
Net book value at time of sale	18,000
Sale price	19,000
Profit on sale	1,000

4.7 Example continued

Taking the example above assume that, instead of the machine being sold for $19,000, it was exchanged for a new machine costing $60,000, a credit of $19,000 being received upon exchange. In other words $19,000 is the trade-in price of the old machine. Now what are the relevant ledger account entries?

Solution

PLANT AND MACHINERY ACCOUNT

	$		$
Balance b/d	110,000	Plant disposal	30,000
Cash $(60,000 – 19,000)	41,000	Balance c/d	140,000
Plant disposals	19,000		
	170,000		170,000
Balance b/d	140,000		

The new asset is recorded in the non-current asset account at cost $(41,000 + 19,000) = $60,000.

14: NON-CURRENT ASSETS AND DEPRECIATION

PLANT AND MACHINERY ACCUMULATED DEPRECIATION

	$		$
Plant disposals (20% of $30,000 for 2 years)	12,000	Balance b/d	70,000
Balance c/d	58,000		
	70,000		70,000
		Balance b/d	58,000

PLANT DISPOSALS

	$		$
Plant and machinery	30,000	Accumulated depreciation	12,000
Profit transferred to I & E	1,000	Plant and machinery-part exchange	19,000
	31,000		31,000

Question — Non-current asset ledger accounts

A business purchased two rivet-making machines on 1 January 20X5 at a cost of $15,000 each. Each had an estimated life of five years and a nil residual value. The straight line method of depreciation is used.

Owing to an unforeseen slump in market demand for rivets, the business decided to reduce its output of rivets, and switch to making other products instead. On 31 March 20X7, one rivet-making machine was sold (on credit) to a buyer for $8,000.

Later in the year, however, it was decided to abandon production of rivets altogether, and the second machine was sold on 1 December 20X7 for $2,500 cash.

Prepare the machinery account, depreciation of machinery account and disposal of machinery account for the accounting year to 31 December 20X7.

Answer

MACHINERY ACCOUNT

		$			$
20X7			20X7		
1 Jan	Balance b/f	30,000	31 Mar	Disposal of machinery account	15,000
			1 Dec	Disposal of machinery account	15,000
		30,000			30,000

MACHINERY – ACCUMULATED DEPRECIATION

		$			$
20X7			20X7		
31 Mar	Disposal of machinery account*	6,750	1 Jan	Balance b/f	12,000
1 Dec	Disposal of machinery account**	8,750	31 Dec	I & E account***	3,500
		15,500			15,500

* Depreciation at date of disposal = $6,000 + $750
** Depreciation at date of disposal = $6,000 + $2,750
*** Depreciation charge for the year = $750 + $2,750

DISPOSAL OF MACHINERY

20X7		$	20X7		$
31 Mar	Machinery account	15,000	31 Mar	Account receivable (sale price)	8,000
			31 Mar	Accumulated depreciation	6,750
1 Dec	Machinery	15,000	1 Dec	Cash (sale price)	2,500
			1 Dec	Accumulated depreciation	8,750
			31 Dec	I & E a/c (loss on disposal)	4,000
		30,000			30,000

You should be able to calculate that there was a loss on the first disposal of $250, and on the second disposal of $3,750, giving a total loss of $4,000.

Workings

1 At 1 January 20X7, accumulated depreciation on the machines will be:

2 machines × 2 years × $\dfrac{\$15,000}{5}$ per machine pa = $12,000, or $6,000 per machine

2 Monthly depreciation is $\dfrac{\$3,000}{12}$ = $250 per machine per month

3 The machines are disposed of in 20X7.

(a) On 31 March – after 3 months of the year.
Depreciation for the year on the machine = 3 months × $250 = $750.

(b) On 1 December – after 11 months of the year.
Depreciation for the year on the machine = 11 months × $250 = $2,750

5 IAS 16 Property, plant and equipment

FAST FORWARD

IAS 16 covers all aspects of accounting for property, plant and equipment. This represents the bulk of items which are **'tangible' non-current assets**.

5.1 Scope

IAS 16 should be followed when accounting for property, plant and equipment *unless* another international accounting standard requires a **different treatment**.

IAS 16 **does not apply** to the following.

(a) Forests and other regenerative natural resources

(b) Mineral rights, exploration for and extraction of minerals, oil, gas and other non-regenerative resources.

5.2 Definitions

The standard gives a large number of definitions.

Key terms

> - Property, plant and equipment are tangible assets that:
>   - are held by an entity for use in the production or supply of goods or services, for rental to others, or for administrative purposes; and
>   - are expected to be used during more than on period.
> - **Cost** is the amount of cash or cash equivalents paid or the fair value of the other consideration given to acquire an asset at the time of its acquisition or construction.
> - **Residual value** is the estimated amount that an entity would currently obtain from disposal of the asset, after deducting the estimated costs of disposal, if the asset were already of the age and in the conditions expected at the end of its useful life.
> - **Fair value** is the amount for which an asset could be exchanged between knowledgeable, willing parties in an arm's length transaction.
> - **Carrying amount** is the amount at which an asset is recognised after deducting any accumulated depreciation and impairment losses.
> - **Recoverable amount** is the amount which the entity expects to recover from the future use of an asset, including its residual value on disposal. This is the higher of net selling price or value in use.
>
> *(IAS 16)*

5.3 Recognition

In this context, recognition simply means incorporation of the item in the business's accounts, in this case as a non-current asset. The recognition of property, plant and equipment depends on two criteria.

(a) It is probable that **future economic benefits** associated with the asset will flow to the entity.
(b) The cost of the asset to the entity can be **measured reliably**.

Property, plant and equipment can amount to **substantial amounts** in financial statements, affecting both the presentation of the company's financial position in the balance sheet and the profitability of the entity as shown in the income statement. Smaller items such as tools are often written off as expenses of the period. Most companies have their own policy on this – items below a certain value are charged as expenses.

5.4 Initial measurement

Once an item of property, plant and equipment qualifies for recognition as an asset, it will initially be **measured at cost**.

5.4.1 Components of cost

The standard lists the components of the cost of an item of property, plant and equipment.

- **Purchase price**, less any trade discount or rebate
- **Initial estimate of the costs of dismantling and removing the item and restoring the site on which it is located**
- **Directly attributable costs** of bringing the asset to working condition for its intended use, eg:
  - The cost of site preparation
  - Initial delivery and handling costs
  - Installation costs
  - Professional fees (architects, engineers)

The following costs **will not be part of the cost** of property, plant or equipment unless they can be attributed directly to the asset's acquisition, or bringing it into its working condition.

- Expenses of operations that are incidental to the construction or development of the item
- Administration and other general overhead costs
- Start-up and similar pre-production costs
- Initial operating losses before the asset reaches planned performances

All of these will be recognised as an **expense** rather than an asset.

5.4.2 Exchanges of assets

Exchange or part exchange of assets occurs frequently for items of property, plant and equipment. IAS 16 states that the cost of an item obtained through (part)exchange is the **fair value of the asset received (unless this cannot be measured reliably)**.

5.5 Subsequent expenditure

How should we treat any subsequent expenditure on long-term assets, after their purchase and recognition? **Subsequent expenditure is added to the carrying amount** of the asset, but only when it is probable that future economic benefits, in excess of the originally assessed standard of performance of the existing asset, will flow to the enterprise. All other subsequent expenditure is simply recognised as an expense in the period in which it is incurred.

The important point here is whether any subsequent expenditure on an asset **improves** the condition of the asset beyond the previous performance. The standard gives the following examples of such improvements.

(a) **Modification** of an item of plant to extend its useful life, including increased capacity
(b) **Upgrade** of machine parts to improve the quality of output
(c) Adoption of a **new production process** leading to large reductions in operating costs

Normal repairs and maintenance on property, plant and equipment items merely maintain or restore value, they do *not* improve or increase it, so such costs are recognised as an expense when incurred.

5.6 Measurement subsequent to initial recognition

The standard offers two possible treatments here, essentially a choice between keeping an asset recorded at **cost** or revaluing it to **fair value**.

(a) **Cost model.** Carry the asset at its cost less accumulated depreciation and any accumulated impairment losses.

(b) **Revaluation model.** Carry the asset at a revalued amount, being its fair value at the date of the revaluation less any subsequent accumulated depreciation and any accumulated impairment losses. Revaluations should be made regularly enough so that the carrying amount approximates to fair value at the balance sheet date. The revaluation model is only available if the item can be measured reliably.

5.6.1 Revaluations

The **market value** of land and buildings usually represents fair value, assuming existing use and line of business. Such valuations are usually carried out by professionally qualified valuers.

In the case of **plant and equipment**, fair value can also be taken as **market value**. Where a market value is not available, however, depreciated replacement cost should be used. There may be no market value where types of plant and equipment are sold only rarely or because of their specialised nature (ie they would normally only be sold as part of an ongoing business).

The frequency of valuation depends on the **volatility of the fair values** of individual items of property, plant and equipment. The more volatile the fair value, the more frequently revaluations should be carried out. Where the current fair value is very different from the carrying value then a revaluation should be carried out.

Most importantly, when an item of property, plant and equipment is revalued, **the whole class of assets to which it belongs should be revalued.**

All the items within a class should be **revalued at the same time**, to prevent selective revaluation of certain assets and to avoid disclosing a mixture of costs and values from different dates in the financial statements. A rolling basis of revaluation is allowed if the revaluations are kept up to date and the revaluation of the whole class is completed in a short period of time.

How should any **increase in value** be treated when a revaluation takes place? The debit will be the increase in value in the balance sheet, but what about the credit? IAS 16 requires the increase to be credited to a **revaluation surplus** (ie part of owners' equity), *unless* the increase is reversing a previous decrease which was recognised as an expense. To the extent that this offset is made, the increase is recognised as income; any excess is then taken to the revaluation reserve.

IAS 16 makes further statements about revaluation, but these are beyond the scope of your syllabus.

5.7 Depreciation

The standard reflects the following approach to depreciation.

- The **depreciable amount** of an item of property, plant and equipment should be allocated on a systematic basis over its useful life.

- The **depreciation method** used should reflect the pattern in which the asset's economic benefits are consumed by the entity.

- The **depreciation charge** for each period would be recognised as an expense unless it is included in the carrying amount of another asset.

Most of the comments on depreciation in IAS 16 are dealt with in Section 1.

Land and buildings are dealt with separately even when they are acquired together because land normally has an unlimited life and is therefore not depreciated. In contrast buildings do have a limited life and must be depreciated. Any increase in the value of land on which a building is standing will have no impact on the determination of the building's useful life.

Depreciation is usually treated as an **expense**, but not where it is absorbed by the entity in the process of producing other assets. For example, depreciation of plant and machinery is incurred in the production of goods for sale (inventory items). In such circumstances, the depreciation is included in the cost of the new assets produced.

5.7.1 Review of useful life

A review of the **useful life** of property, plant and equipment should be carried out at least **annually** and the depreciation charge for the current and future periods should be adjusted if expectations have changed significantly from previous estimates.

5.7.2 Review of depreciation method

The **depreciation method** should also be reviewed **periodically** and, if there has been a significant change in the expected pattern of economic benefits from those assets, the method should be changed to suit this changed pattern. When such a change in depreciation method takes place the change should be accounted for as a **change in accounting estimate** and the depreciation charge for the current and future periods should be adjusted.

5.7.3 Impairment of asset values

The **carrying amount** of an item or group of identical items of property, plant and equipment should also be reviewed **periodically**. This is to assess whether the recoverable amount has declined below the carrying amount. When there has been such a decline, the carrying amount should be reduced to the **recoverable amount**.

Recoverable amounts should be considered on an **individual asset basis** or for **groups of identical assets**.

5.8 Retirements and disposals

When an asset is permanently **withdrawn from use, or sold or scrapped**, and no future economic benefits are expected from its disposal, it should be withdrawn from the balance sheet.

Gains or losses are the difference between the estimated net disposal proceeds and the carrying amount of the asset. They should be recognised as income or expense in the income statement.

5.9 Disclosure

The standard has a long list of disclosure requirements, only some of which are relevant to your syllabus.

- **Measurement bases** for determining the gross carrying amount (if more than one, the gross carrying amount for that basis in each category)
- **Depreciation methods** used
- **Useful lives** or depreciation rates used
- **Gross carrying amount** and accumulated depreciation at the beginning and end of the period
- **Reconciliation** of the carrying amount at the beginning and end of the period showing:
    - Additions
    - Disposals
    - Increases/decreases from revaluations
    - Reductions in carrying amount
    - Depreciation
    - Any other movements.

The financial statements should also disclose the following.

- Existence and amounts of **restrictions on title**, and items pledged as security for liabilities
- Accounting policy for **restoration costs**
- Amount of expenditures on account of **items in the course of construction**
- Amount of commitments to **acquisitions**

Revalued assets require further disclosures.

- **Basis** used to revalue the assets
- **Effective date** of the revaluation
- Whether an **independent valuer** was involved
- Nature of any **indices** used to determine replacement cost
- **Carrying amount** of each class of property, plant and equipment that would have been included in the financial statements had the assets been carried at cost less depreciation
- **Revaluation surplus**, indicating the movement for the period and any restrictions on the distribution of the balance to shareholders.

The standard also **encourages disclosure** of additional information, which the users of financial statements may find useful.

- The carrying amount of temporarily idle property, plant and equipment
- The gross carrying amount of any fully depreciated property, plant and equipment that is still in use
- The carrying amount of property, plant and equipment retired from active use and held for disposal
- When the benchmark treatment is used, the fair value of property, plant and equipment when this is materially different from the carrying amount

The following format (with notional figures) is commonly used to disclose non-current assets movements.

	Total $	Land and buildings $	Plant and equipment $
Cost or valuation			
At 1 January 20X4	50,000	40,000	10,000
Revaluation surplus	12,000	12,000	–
Additions in year	4,000	–	4,000
Disposals in year	(1,000)	–	(1,000)
At 31 December 20X4	65,000	52,000	13,000
Depreciation			
At 1 January 20X4	16,000	10,000	6,000
Charge for year	4,000	1,000	3,000
Eliminated on disposals	(500)	–	(500)
At 31 December 20X4	19,500	11,000	8,500
Net book value			
At 31 December 20X4	45,500	41,000	4,500
At 1 January 20X4	34,000	30,000	4,000

Note that this format is only required for company accounts.

Question
Net book value

(a) In a balance sheet prepared in accordance with IAS 16, what does the net book value (carrying value) represent?

(b) In a set of financial statements prepared in accordance with IAS 16, is it correct to say that the net book value (carrying value) figure in a balance sheet cannot be greater than the market (net realisable) value of the partially used asset as at the balance sheet date? Explain your reasons for your answer.

Answer

(a) In simple terms the net book value of an asset is the cost of an asset less the 'accumulated depreciation', that is all depreciation charged so far. It should be emphasised that the main purpose of charging depreciation is to ensure that profits are fairly reported. Thus depreciation is concerned with the income statement rather than the balance sheet. In consequence the net book value figure in the balance sheet can be quite arbitrary. In particular, it does not necessarily bear any relation to the market value of an asset and is of little use for planning and decision making.

An obvious example of the disparity between net book value and market value is found in the case of buildings, which may be worth more than ten times as much as their net book value.

(b) Net book value can in some circumstances be higher than market value (net realisable value). IAS 16 *Property, plant and equipment* states that the value of an asset cannot be greater than its 'recoverable amount'. However 'recoverable amount' as defined in IAS 16 is the amount recoverable from further use. This may be higher than the market value.

This makes sense if you think of a specialised machine which could not fetch much on the secondhand market but which will produce goods which can be sold at a profit for many years.

6 The asset register

FAST FORWARD

An **asset register** is used to record all non-current assets and is an **internal check** on the accuracy of the nominal ledger.

Nearly all organisations keep an asset register. This is a listing of all non-current assets owned by the organisation, broken down perhaps by department, location or asset type.

An asset register is maintained primarily for internal purposes. It shows an organisation's investment in capital equipment. The register is also part of the **internal control system**. The asset registers are sometimes called **real accounts**.

6.1 Data kept in an asset register

Details about each non-current asset include the following.

- The internal reference number (for physical identification purposes)
- Manufacturer's serial number (for maintenance purposes)
- Description of asset
- Location of asset
- Department which 'owns' asset
- Purchase date (for calculation of depreciation)
- Cost
- Depreciation method and estimated useful life (for calculation of depreciation)
- Net book value (or written down value)

7 Preparation of final accounts for a sole trader

You have already had practice at preparing an income statement and balance sheet from a simple trial balance. Now see if you can do the same thing but at a more advanced level, taking account of adjustments for depreciation, inventory, accruals, prepayments, irrecoverable debts and receivables allowances. Have a go at the following question.

Question — Final accounts

The following list of account balances was extracted from the ledger of Kevin Webster, a sole trader, as at 31 May 20X1, the end of his financial year.

KEVIN WEBSTER
TRIAL BALANCE AS AT 31 MAY 20X1

	Dr $	Cr $
Property, at cost	120,000	
Equipment, at cost	80,000	
Accumulated depreciation (as at 1 June 20X0)		
– on property		20,000
– on equipment		38,000
Purchases	250,000	
Sales		402,200
Inventory, as at 1 June 20X0	50,000	
Discounts allowed	18,000	
Discounts received		4,800
Returns out		15,000
Wages and salaries	58,800	
Irrecoverable debts	4,600	
Loan interest	5,100	
Other operating expenses	17,700	
Trade accounts payable		36,000
Trade accounts receivable	38,000	
Cash on hand	300	
Bank	1,300	
Drawings	24,000	
Allowance for receivables		500
17% long-term loan		30,000
Capital, as at 1 June 20X0		121,300
	667,800	667,800

The following additional information as at 31 May 20X1 is available.

(a) Inventory as at the close of business has been valued at cost at $42,000.
(b) Wages and salaries need to be accrued by $800.
(c) Other operating expenses are prepaid by $300.
(d) The allowance for receivables is to be adjusted so that it is 2% of trade receivables.
(e) Depreciation for the year ended 31 May 20X1 has still to be charged as follows:

    Property: 1.5% per annum using the straight line method
    Equipment: 25% per annum using the reducing balance method

Required

Prepare Kevin Webster's income statement for the year ended 31 May 20X1 and his balance sheet as at that date.

Answer

KEVIN WEBSTER
INCOME STATEMENT
FOR THE YEAR ENDED 31 MAY 20X1

	$	$
Sales		402,200
Cost of sales		
Opening inventory	50,000	
Purchases	250,000	
Purchases returns	(15,000)	
	285,000	
Closing inventory	42,000	
		243,000
Gross profit		159,200
Other income: discounts received		4,800
		164,000
Expenses		
Wages and salaries ($58,800 + $800)	59,600	
Discounts allowed	18,000	
Irrecoverable debts (W1)	4,860	
Loan interest	5,100	
Depreciation	12,300	
Other operating expenses ($17,700 – $300)	17,400	
		117,260
Net profit for the year		46,740

KEVIN WEBSTER
BALANCE SHEET AS AT 31 MAY 20X1

	$	$
Assets		
Non-current assets		
Property: cost	120,000	
accumulated depreciation (W2)	21,800	
		98,200
Equipment: cost	80,000	
accumulated depreciation (W2)	48,500	
		31,500
Current assets		
Inventory	42,000	
Trade accounts receivable		
(less allowance for receivables: $38,000 less 2%)	37,240	
Prepayments	300	
Bank	1,300	
Cash in hand	300	
		81,140
Total assets		210,840

	$	$
Capital and liabilities		
Capital		
Balance at 1 June 20X0	121,300	
Net profit for the year	46,740	
Drawings	(24,000)	
Balance at 31 May 20X1		144,040
Non-current liabilities		
17% loan		30,000
Current liabilities		
Trade accounts payable	36,000	
Accruals	800	
		36,800
Total capital and liabilities		210,840

Workings

1   *Allowance for receivables*

	$
Previous allowance	500
New allowance (2% × 38,000)	760
Increase	260
Irrecoverable debts per trial balance	4,600
Income statement	4,860

2   *Depreciation*

	$
Property	
Opening balance	20,000
Charge for the year (1.5% × 120,000)	1,800
Closing balance	21,800
Equipment	
Opening balance	38,000
Charge for the year (25% × 42,000)	10,500
Closing balance	48,500

PART D ACCOUNTING TREATMENTS

> **Tips for final accounts questions**
>
> The examination paper will contain a compulsory question involving preparation of final accounts.
>
> - Such a question may involve a sole trader, which is the type of organisation you have dealt with so far.
> - Alternatively, you may have to prepare the final accounts of a limited liability company or a partnership and the accounts may have to be prepared from incomplete records, all topics you will cover later in this Study Text.
>
> Whatever form the final accounts question takes, you should bear in mind the following tips.
>
> - **Annotate the trial balance**. If you are given a trial balance, note the final destination of each item, for example:
>
>   T = Trading account
>   I/E = Income or expenditure account
>   B/S = Balance sheet
>
> - **Show workings clearly**. The workings should be clearly referenced to the final accounts and should enable the marker to follow through your calculations. This is particularly important because if, as often happens under time pressure, you make minor arithmetical mistakes; you will not be heavily penalised if the marker can see that you have used the right method.
>
> - **Present a clear, logical layout of financial accounts**. Allow plenty of space, better too much than too little. For example if you have to do an income statement and balance sheet you should allow at least one page for the income statement, one for the balance sheet and one or more for your workings. Underline any totals for columns and figures, and if you make a mistake, cross it out neatly and clearly. **You do not have time to wait for correcting fluid to dry.**

Chapter Roundup

- The *cost* of a non-current asset, less its estimated residual value, is **allocated fairly** between accounting periods by means of **depreciation**. Depreciation is both:
  - **charged against profit**; and
  - **deducted from the value of the non-current asset in the balance sheet.**

- There are **several different methods** of depreciation, but the straight line method and the reducing balance method are most commonly used in practice. You also need to know how to use the sum of the digits method. Every method described in this chapter allocates the total depreciable amount between accounting periods, although in different ways.

- When a non-current asset is **revalued, depreciation is charged on the revalued amount**.

- When a non-current asset is **sold**, there is likely to be a **profit or loss on disposal**. This is the difference between the net sale price of the asset and its net book value at the time of disposal.

- IAS 16 covers all aspects of accounting for property, plant and equipment.

- An **asset register** is used to record all non-current assets and is an **internal check** on the accuracy of the nominal ledger.

Quick Quiz

1 Which of the following statements regarding non-current asset accounting is correct?

    A   All non-current assets should be revalued each year.

    B   Non-current assets may be revalued at the discretion of management. Once revaluation has occurred it must be repeated regularly for all non-current assets in a class.

    C   Management can choose which non-current assets in a class of non-current assets should be revalued.

    D   Non-current assets should be revalued to reflect rising prices.

2 Which of the following statements regarding depreciation is correct?

    A   All non-current assets must be depreciated.

    B   Straight line depreciation is usually the most appropriate method of depreciation.

    C   A change in the chosen depreciation method is a change in accounting policy which should be disclosed.

    D   Depreciation charges must be based upon the carrying value of an asset (less residual value if appropriate).

3 What is an asset's net book value?

4 Give three common depreciation methods.

5 A non-current asset (cost $10,000, depreciation $7,500) is given in part exchange for a new asset costing $20,500. The agreed trade-in value was $3,500. The income statement will include?

    A   A loss on disposal $1,000
    B   A profit on disposal $1,000
    C   A loss on purchase of a new asset $3,500
    D   A profit on disposal $3,500

6 What details about a non-current asset might be included in an assets register?

7 Why might the assets register not reconcile with the non-current assets?

Answers to Quick Quiz

1. **B** Correct.
   A Non-current assets may be revalued, there is no requirement to do so in IAS 16.
   C Incorrect, all non-current assets in a class must be revalued.
   D Incorrect, non-current assets may be reduced in value as well as being increased.

2. **D** Correct, carrying value is another name for net book value.
   A Incorrect, some non-current assets are not depreciated eg land.
   B Incorrect, management should choose the most appropriate method.
   C Incorrect, a method change is not a change in accounting policy.

3. Its cost less accumulated depreciation.

4. Straight-line, reducing balance and sum of the digits.

5. **B**

	£
Net book value at disposal	2,500
Trade-in allowance	3,500
Profit	1,000

6. - Date of purchase
   - Description
   - Original cost
   - Depreciation rate and method
   - Accumulated depreciation to date
   - Date and amount of any revaluation

7. - Asset stolen or damaged
   - Obsolete
   - New assets, not yet recorded in the register
   - Improvements not yet recorded in the register
   - Errors in the register

Now try the questions below from the Exam Question Bank

Number	Level	Marks	Time
Q18	Examination	10	18 mins
Q19	Introductory	n/a	36 mins
Q20	Introductory	n/a	27 mins

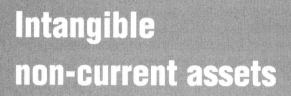

Intangible non-current assets

Topic list	Syllabus reference
1 Goodwill	4(a)(v)
2 Research and development costs	4(a)(iv), 5(c)(iv), 5(d)(iii)

Introduction

Intangible non-current assets are long-term assets which have a value to the business because they have been paid for, but which do not have any physical substance. The most significant of such intangible assets are goodwill and deferred development costs.

The concept of goodwill might be familiar to you already, from common everyday knowledge. It is discussed in Section 1 of this chapter.

In many companies, especially those which produce food or 'scientific' products such as medicines or 'high technology' products, the expenditure on **research and development** is considerable. When R & D is a large item of cost its accounting treatment may have a significant influence on the profits of a business and its balance sheet valuation. Because of this attempts have been made to standardise the treatment, and these are discussed in Section 2 of this chapter.

PART D   ACCOUNTING TREATMENTS

Study guide

Section 17 – Goodwill, research and development

- Define goodwill.
- Explain the factors leading to the creation of non-purchased goodwill.
- Explain the difference between purchased and non-purchased goodwill.
- Explain why non-purchased goodwill is not normally recognised in financial statements.
- Explain how purchased goodwill arises and is reflected in financial statements.
- Adjust the value of purchased goodwill to reflect impairment.
- Define 'research' and 'development'.
- Classify expenditure as research or development.
- Calculate amounts to be capitalised as development expenditure from given information.
- Disclose research and development expenditure in the financial statements.

Exam guide

Calculations of goodwill and R & D expenses are likely to be examined in Section A, although they could feature as part of an accounts preparation question in Section B. Be prepared to discuss these topics in a written question in Section B.

1 Goodwill

FAST FORWARD

> If a business has **goodwill**, it means that the value of the business as a going concern is great than the value of its net assets. The valuation of goodwill is extremely subjective and fluctuates constantly. For this reason, **non-purchased goodwill** is **not** shown as an asset in the balance sheet.

Key term

> If a business has **goodwill** it means that the value of the business as a going concern is greater than the value of its net assets.

Goodwill is created by good relationships between a business and its customers, for example:

(a) By building up a reputation (by word of mouth perhaps) for high quality products or high standards of service

(b) By responding promptly and helpfully to queries and complaints from customers

(c) Through the personality of the staff and their attitudes to customers

The value of goodwill to a business might be extremely significant. However, **goodwill is not usually valued** in the accounts of a business at all, and we should not normally expect to find an amount for goodwill in its balance sheet.

For example, the welcoming smile of the bar staff may contribute more to a wine bar's profits than the fact that a new electronic cash register has recently been acquired; even so, whereas the cash register will be recorded in the accounts as a non-current asset, the value of staff would be ignored for accounting purposes.

On reflection, this omission of goodwill from the accounts of a business might be easy to understand.

(a) The goodwill is inherent in the business but it has not been paid for, and it does not have an 'objective' value. We can guess at what such goodwill is worth, but such guesswork would be a matter of individual opinion, and not based on hard facts.

(b) Goodwill changes from day to day. One act of bad customer relations might damage goodwill and one act of good relations might improve it. Staff with a favourable personality might retire or leave to find another job, to be replaced by staff who need time to find their feet in the job, etc. Since goodwill is continually changing in value, it cannot realistically be recorded in the accounts of the business.

1.1 Purchased goodwill

FAST FORWARD

Goodwill is shown as an asset when someone **purchases a business** as a going concern. In this case the purchaser and vendor will fix an agreed price which includes an element in respect of goodwill. **Purchased goodwill** is then retained in the balance sheet as an **intangible asset**.

There is one exception to the general rule that goodwill has no objective valuation. This is when a business is sold. People wishing to set up in business have a choice of how to do it - they can either buy their own non-current assets and inventory and set up their business from scratch, or they can buy up an existing business from a proprietor willing to sell it.

When a buyer purchases an existing business, he will have to purchase not only its non-current assets and inventories (and perhaps take over its payables and receivables too) but also the goodwill of the business.

1.2 Example: Goodwill

For example, suppose that Tony Tycoon agrees to purchase the business of Clive Dunwell for $30,000. Clive's business has net non-current assets valued at $14,000 and net current assets of $11,000, all of which are taken over by Tony. Tony will be paying **more** for the business than its tangible assets are worth, because he is purchasing the **goodwill** of the business too. The balance sheet of Tony's business when it begins operations (assuming that he does not change the value of the tangible fixed and current assets) will be:

TONY TYCOON
BALANCE SHEET AS AT THE START OF BUSINESS

	$
Intangible non-current asset: goodwill	5,000
Tangible non-current assets: net book value	14,000
Net current assets	11,000
Net assets	30,000
Capital	30,000

Purchased goodwill is shown in this balance sheet because it has been paid for. It has no tangible substance, and so it is an intangible non-current asset.

Key term

Purchased goodwill has been defined as 'the excess of the price paid for a business over the fair market value of the individual assets and liabilities acquired'.

Question

Goodwill

To make sure that you understand goodwill, try a solution to the following quick exercise.

Toad goes into business with $10,000 capital and agrees to buy Thrush's shoe-repair shop in the centre of a busy town for $6,500. Thrush's recent accounts show net assets of $3,500, which Toad values at $4,000.

Required

Prepare the balance sheet of Toad's business at the following times.

(a) Before he purchases Thrush's business
(b) After the purchase

PART D ACCOUNTING TREATMENTS

Answer

(a) Toad's balance sheet before the purchase is:

	$
Cash	10,000
Proprietor's interest	10,000

(b) Thrush's valuation of the assets to be acquired is irrelevant to Toad who sees the situation thus:

	$
Consideration (cash to be paid)	6,500
Less net assets acquired (at Toad's valuation)	4,000
Difference (= goodwill)	2,500

Toad must credit his cash book with the $6,500 paid. He can only debit sundry assets with $4,000. A further debit of $2,500 is thus an accounting necessity and he must open up a goodwill account.

Toad's balance sheet immediately after the transfer would therefore be:

	$
Goodwill	2,500
Sundry assets	4,000
Cash ($10,000 - $6,500)	3,500
	10,000
Proprietor's interest	10,000

(Normally one would have more detail as to the breakdown of the sundry assets into non-current assets, current assets etc, but this is not relevant to the illustration. The main point is that the sundry assets acquired are tangible whereas the goodwill is not.)

This exercise highlights the difference between 'internally generated' goodwill, which (as in Thrush's case above) is not shown in the books and 'purchased' goodwill, which is. The purchased goodwill in this case is simply Thrush's internally generated goodwill, which has changed hands, bought by Toad at a price shown in Toad's accounts.

1.3 The accounting treatment of purchased goodwill

Once purchased goodwill appears in the accounts of a business, we must decide what to do with it. Purchased goodwill is basically a premium paid for the acquisition of a business as a going concern: indeed, it is often referred to as a 'premium on acquisition'. When a purchaser agrees to pay such a premium for goodwill, he does so because he believes that the true value of the business is worth more to him than the value of its tangible assets.

One major reason why he might think so is that the business will earn good profits over the next few years, and so he will pay a premium now to get the business, in the expectation of getting his money back later.

Goodwill, it was suggested earlier, is a continually changing thing. A business cannot last forever on its past reputation; it must create new goodwill as time goes on. Even goodwill created by a favourable location might suddenly disappear, for example, a newsagent's shop by a bus stop will lose its location value if the bus route is axed by the local transport authorities.

If the goodwill loses some or all of its value, it is deemed to have become 'impaired'. Its value in the balance sheet is then written down by the amount of the impairment and the impairment loss is charged against the profit of the period.

Important

> IFRS 3 *Business combinations* requires goodwill to be treated as an **intangible non-current asset**. It is kept at cost in the balance sheet subject to an annual review for impairment.

1.4 How is the value of purchased goodwill decided?

When a business is sold, there is likely to be some purchased goodwill in the selling price. But how is the amount of this purchased goodwill decided?

This is not really a problem for accountants, who must simply record the goodwill in the accounts of the new business. The value of the goodwill is a matter for the purchaser and seller to agree upon in fixing the purchase/sale price. However, two methods of valuation are worth mentioning here.

(a) The seller and buyer agree on a price without specifically quantifying the goodwill. The purchased goodwill will then be the difference between the price agreed and the value of the tangible assets in the books of the new business.

(b) However, the calculation of goodwill often precedes the fixing of the purchase price and becomes a central element of negotiation. There are many ways of arriving at a value for goodwill and most of them are related to the profit record of the business in question. For instance, they may agree to value goodwill as 2 × last year's profit, or a similar calculation.

No matter how goodwill is calculated within the total agreed purchase price, the goodwill shown by the purchaser in his accounts will be the difference between the purchase consideration and **his own valuation** of the tangible net assets acquired. If A values his tangible net assets at $40,000, goodwill is agreed at $21,000 and B agrees to pay $61,000 for the business but values the tangible net assets at only $38,000, then the goodwill in B's books will be $61,000 – $38,000 = $23,000.

2 Research and development costs

FAST FORWARD

Expenditure on **research** must always be written off in the period in which it is incurred.

Development costs are also usually written off. However, if the criteria laid down by IAS 38 are satisfied, development expenditure can be capitalised as an **intangible asset**. If it has a **finite useful life**, it should then be amortised over that life.

Deferred development costs are the other type of intangible non-current asset you need to know about. Large companies may spend significant amounts of money on research and development (R & D) activities. Obviously, any amounts so expended must be credited to cash and debited to an account for research and development expenditure. The accounting problem is **how to treat the debit balance on R & D account** at the balance sheet date.

There are two possibilities.

(a) The debit balance may be classified as an **expense** and transferred to the income statement. This is referred to as 'writing off' the expenditure. The argument here is that it is an expense just like rent or wages and its accounting treatment should be the same.

(b) The debit balance may be classified as an **asset** and included in the balance sheet. This is referred to as 'capitalising' or 'carrying forward' or 'deferring' the expenditure. This argument is based on the accrual assumption. If R & D activity eventually leads to new or improved products which generate revenue, the costs should be carried forward to be matched against that revenue in future accounting periods.

So the main question surrounding research and development (R & D) costs is whether they should be treated as an expense or capitalised as an asset. This question is dealt with in IAS 38 *Intangible assets*.

IAS 38 was published in September 1998 and replaced IAS 9 *Research and development costs*. It was revised in March 2004.

2.1 Definitions

The following definitions are given by the standard.

Key terms

> - An **intangible asset** is an identifiable non-monetary asset without physical substance. The asset must be:
>   - controlled by the entity as a result of events in the past; and
>   - something from which the entity expects future economic benefits to flow
> - **Research** is original and planned investigation undertaken with the prospect of gaining new scientific or technical knowledge and understanding.
> - **Development** is the application of research findings or other knowledge to a plan or design for the production of new or substantially improved materials, devices, products, processes, systems or services prior to the commencement of commercial production or use.
> - **Amortisation** is the systematic allocation of the depreciable amount of an intangible asset over its useful life. Amortisation period and amortisation method should be reviewed at each financial year end.
> - **Depreciable amount** is the cost of an asset, or other amount substituted for cost, less its residual value.
> - **Useful life** is:
>   (a) the period over which an asset is expected to be available for use by an entity; or
>   (b) the number of production or similar units expected to be obtained from the asset by an entity.
>
> *IAS 38* (revised)

Although these definitions are usually well-understood, **in practice** it may not be so easy to identify the activities encompassed by R & D and the dividing line between the categories may be indistinct. Identification often depends on the type of business involved, the projects it undertakes and how it is organised.

The standard gives examples of activities which might be included in either research or development, or which are neither but may be closely associated with both.

- **Research**
  - Activities aimed at obtaining new knowledge
  - The search for applications of research findings or other knowledge
  - The search for product or process alternatives
  - The formulation and design of possible new or improved product or process alternatives

- **Development**
  - The design, construction and testing of pre-production prototypes and models
  - The design of tools, jigs, moulds and dies involving new technology
  - The design, construction and operation of a pilot plant that is not of a scale economically feasible for commercial production
  - The design construction and testing of a chosen alternative for new/improved materials

2.2 Components of research and development costs

Research and development costs will include all costs that are **directly attributable** to research and development activities, or that can be **allocated on a reasonable basis**.

The standard lists the costs which may be included in R & D, where applicable (note that **selling costs are excluded**).

- **Salaries, wages** and other employment related costs of personnel engaged in R & D activities
- Costs of **materials and services** consumed in R & D activities
- **Depreciation** of property, plant and equipment to the extent that these assets are used for R & D activities
- **Overhead costs**, other than general administrative costs, related to R & D activities; these cost are allocated on bases similar to those used in allocating overhead costs to inventories (see IAS 2 *Inventories*)
- **Other costs**, such as the amortisation of patents and licences, to the extent that these assets are used for R & D activities

2.3 Recognition of R & D costs

The relationship between the R & D costs and the **economic benefit** expected to derive from then will determine the allocation of those costs to different periods. Recognition of the costs as an asset will only occur where it is probable that the cost will produce future economic benefits for the entity and where the costs can be measured reliably.

(a) In the case of **research costs**, this will not be the case due to uncertainty about the resulting benefit from them; and so they should be expensed in the period in which they arose.

(b) **Development activities** tend to be much further advanced than the research stage and so it may be possible to determine the likelihood of future economic benefit. Where this can be determined, the development costs should be carried forward as an asset.

2.3.1 Research costs

Research costs should be recognised as an **expense in the period in which they are incurred**. They should not be recognised as an asset in a later period.

2.3.2 Development costs

Alternative treatments are given for development costs, the use of which depends on the situation. Most of the time, development costs will be recognised as an **expense in the period in which they are incurred** unless the criteria for asset recognition identified below are met. Development costs initially recognised as an expense should not be recognised as an asset in a later period.

Development expenditure should be recognised as an asset only when the business can demonstrate **all** of the following. Where the criteria are met, development expenditure *must* be capitalised.

- The technical feasibility of **completing** the intangible asset so that it will be available for use or sale
- Its intention to complete the intangible asset and **use or sell** it
- Its **ability** to use or sell the intangible asset
- How the intangible asset will generate probable **future economic benefits**. Among other things, the entity should demonstrate the existence of a market for the output of the intangible asset itself or, if it is to be used internally, the usefulness of the intangible asset
- The availability of adequate technical, financial and other **resources** to complete the development and to use or sell the intangible asset
- Its ability to **measure reliably** the expenditure attributable to the intangible asset during its development

There is also an important point about the carrying amount of the asset and recoverability. The development costs of a project recognised as an asset should not exceed the amount that it is probable will be **recovered from related future economic benefits**, after deducting further development costs, related production costs, and selling and administrative costs directly incurred in marketing the product.

2.4 Amortisation of development costs

Once capitalised as an asset, development costs must be **amortised** and recognised as an expense to match the costs with the related revenue or cost savings. This must be done on a systematic basis, so as to reflect the pattern in which the related economic benefits are recognised.

It is unlikely to be possible to **match exactly** the economic benefits obtained with the costs which are held as an asset simply because of the nature of development activities. The entity should consider either:

(a) The revenue or other benefits from the sale/use of the product/process
(b) The period of time over which the product/process is expected to be sold/used

Point to note | If the pattern cannot be determined reliably, the straight-line method should be used.

The amortisation will begin when the **asset is available for use**.

If the intangible asset is considered to have an *indefinite* useful life, it should not be amortised but should be subjected to an annual impairment review.

2.5 Impairment of development costs

As with all assets, impairment (fall in value of an asset) is a possibility, but perhaps even more so in cases such as this. The development costs should be **written down** to the extent that the unamortised balance (taken together with further development costs, related production costs, and selling and administrative costs directly incurred in marketing the product) is no longer probable of being recovered from the expected future economic benefit.

2.6 Disclosure

The standard has fairly extensive disclosure requirements for intangible assets. The financial statements should disclose the **accounting policies** for intangible assets that have been adopted.

For **each class of intangible assets** (including development costs), disclosure is required of the following.

- The **method of amortisation** used
- The **useful life** of the assets or the amortisation rate used
- The **gross carrying amount**, the **accumulated amortisation** and the **accumulated impairment losses** as at the beginning and the end of the period
- A **reconciliation of the carrying amount** as at the beginning and at the end of the period (additions, retirements/disposals, revaluations, impairment losses, impairment losses reversed, amortisation charge for the period, net exchange differences, other movements)
- The carrying amount of **internally-generated intangible assets**

Question — Research and development

Y Co is a research company which specialises in developing new materials and manufacturing processes for the furniture industry. The company receives payments from a variety of manufacturers, which pay for the right to use the company's patented fabrics and processes.

15: INTANGIBLE NON-CURRENT ASSETS

Research and development costs for the year ended 30 September 20X5 can be analysed as follows.

	$
Expenditure on continuing research projects	1,420,000
Amortisation of development expenditure capitalised in earlier years	240,000

New projects started during the year:

Project A — 280,000

New flame-proof padding. Expected to cost a total of $800,000 to develop. Expected total revenue $2,000,000 once work completed - probably late 20X6

Project B — 150,000

New colour-fast dye. Expected to cost a total of $3,000,000 to complete. Future revenues are likely to exceed $5,000,000. The completion date is uncertain because external funding will have to be obtained before research work can be completed.

Project C — 110,000

Investigation of new adhesive recently developed in aerospace industry. If this proves effective then Y Co may well generate significant income because it will be used in place of existing adhesives.

Total: 2,200,000

The company has a policy of capitalising all development expenditure where permitted by IAS 38.

Explain how the three research projects A, B and C will be dealt with in Y Co's income statement and balance sheet.

In each case, explain your proposed treatment in terms of IAS 38 *Intangible assets* and, where relevant, in terms of the fundamental accounting assumptions of going concern and accruals, and the prudence concept.

Answer

Project A

This project meets the criteria in IAS 38 for development expenditure to be recognised as an asset. These are as follows.

(a) The product or process is clearly defined and the costs attributable to the product or process can be separately identified and measured reliably.

(b) The technical feasibility of the product or process can be demonstrated.

(c) The enterprise intends to produce and market, or use, the product or process and has the ability to do so.

(d) The existence of a market for the product or process or, if it is to be used internally rather than sold, its usefulness to the enterprise, can be demonstrated.

(e) Adequate resources exist, or their availability can be demonstrated, to complete the project and market or use the product or process.

The capitalisation development costs in a company which is a going concern means that these are accrued in order that they can be matched against the income they are expected to generate.

Hence the costs of $280,000 incurred to date should be transferred from research and development costs to capitalised development expenditure and carried forward until revenues are generated; they should then be matched with those revenues.

PART D ACCOUNTING TREATMENTS

Project B

Whilst this project meets most of the criteria discussed above which would enable the costs to be carried forward it fails on the requirements that 'adequate resources exist, or their availability can be demonstrated, to complete the project'.

Hence it would be prudent to write off these costs. Once funding is obtained the situation can then be reassessed and these and future costs may be capitalised.

Project C

This is a research project according to IAS 38, ie original and planned investigation undertaken with the prospect of gaining new scientific or technical knowledge or understanding.

There is no certainty as to its ultimate success or commercial viability and therefore it cannot be considered to be a development project. IAS 38 therefore requires that costs be written off as incurred.

Question   Y Co (2)

Show how the research and development costs in Question 2 will be disclosed in the accounts of Y Co. Assume the cost of capitalised development expenditure brought forward is $1,480,000, and that accumulated amortisation of $240,000 was brought forward at the beginning of the year.

(a) Income statement
(b) Balance sheet
(c) Notes to the accounts

Answer

(a) INCOME STATEMENT (EXTRACT)

	$
Research expenditure (Project C + 1,420,000)	1,530,000
Development costs (Project B)	150,000
Amortisation of capitalised development costs	240,000

(b) BALANCE SHEET (EXTRACT)

	$
Non current assets	
Intangible assets	
Deferred development costs	1,280,000

NOTE TO ACCOUNTS

Deferred development costs

	$
Cost	
Balance b/f	1,480,000
Additions during year (Project A)	280,000
Balance c/f	1,760,000
Amortisation	
Balance b/f	240,000
Charge during year	240,000
Balance c/f	480,000
Net book value at 30 September 20X5	1,280,000
Net book value at 30 September 20X4	1,240,000

Exam focus point Questions on goodwill and intangible assets appeared in both the June 2005 and December 2005 exams.

15: INTANGIBLE NON-CURRENT ASSETS

Chapter Roundup

- **Intangible long-term assets** are those which have a **value** to the business but which do **not** have any **physical substance**. The most significant intangible assets are **goodwill** and **deferred development costs**.

- If a business has **goodwill**, it means that the **value of the business as a going concern is greater than the value of its net assets**. The valuation of goodwill is extremely subjective and fluctuates constantly. For this reason, **non-purchased goodwill is not shown as an asset** in the balance sheet.

- Goodwill is shown as an asset when someone **purchases a business** as a going concern. In this case the purchaser and vendor will fix an agreed price which includes an element in respect of goodwill.

- **Purchased goodwill** is then retained in the balance sheet as an **intangible asset**.

- Expenditure on **research activities** must always be **written off** in the period in which it is incurred.

- Expenditure on **development activities** will often also be **written off** in the same way. But if the **criteria laid** down by **IAS 38** are **satisfied**, such expenditure **should be capitalised** as an intangible asset. If it has a **finite useful life**, it should then be amortised over that life.

Quick Quiz

1. Why is it unusual to record goodwill as an asset in the accounts?
2. What is purchased goodwill?
3. What method of accounting for purchased goodwill is permitted by IFRS 3?
4. How is the amount of purchased goodwill calculated?
5. What is the required accounting treatment for expenditure on research?
6. In what circumstances may development costs be recognised as an asset?

PART D ACCOUNTING TREATMENTS

Answers to Quick Quiz

1 Because goodwill can not be measured accurately and changes from day to day.

2 When someone purchases a business, they may pay more than the net tangible assets are worth to reflect the 'goodwill' built up by the previous owner. This is purchased goodwill.

3 To treat the goodwill as an intangible non-current asset subject to annual impairment reviews.

4 The purchaser deducts his valuation of the net tangible assets acquired from the price he paid to arrive at the goodwill figure.

5 It is an expense in the period it was incurred.

6 See paragraph 2.3.2.

Now try the question below from the Exam Question Bank

Number	Level	Marks	Time
Q21	Examination	10	18 mins

Events after the balance sheet date and contingencies

Topic list	Syllabus reference
1 IAS 10 (Revised) Events after the balance sheet date	4(e), 5(c)(iv), 5(d)(iii)
2 Contingencies (IAS 37)	4(f), 5(c)(iv), 5(d)(iii)

Introduction

As in the previous chapter you are required here to consider accounting issues which are the subject of international accounting standards IAS 10 and IAS 37.

You will see in IAS 10 the application of the concept of prudence, which you learnt about in Chapter 10. This IAS is very important for your auditing studies. It is more straightforward in theory than in practice. IAS 37 is another important standard that you will meet again later in your studies.

PART D ACCOUNTING TREATMENTS

Study guide

Section 18 – Events after the balance sheet date and contingencies

- Define an event after the balance sheet date.
- Distinguish between adjusting and non-adjusting events and explain the methods of including them in financial statements.
- Classify events as adjusting or non-adjusting.
- Draft notes to company financial statements including requisite details of events after the balance sheet date.
- Define 'contingent liability' and 'contingent asset'.
- Explain the different ways of accounting for contingent liabilities and contingent assets according to their degree of probability.
- Draft notes to company financial statements including requisite details of contingent liabilities and contingent assets.

Exam guide

These are extremely important topics that could be examined in Section A, Section B or **both**.

You will not be expected to refer specifically to the IASes.

1 IAS 10 (Revised) Events after the balance sheet date

FAST FORWARD

> Events after the balance sheet date which provide **additional evidence** of conditions existing at the balance sheet date, will cause **adjustments** to be made to the assets and liabilities in the financial statements.

The financial statements are significant indicators of a company's success or failure. It is important, therefore, that they include all the information necessary for an understanding of the company's position.

IAS 10 *(Revised) Events after the balance sheet date* requires the provision of additional information in order to facilitate such an understanding. IAS 10 deals with events **after** the balance sheet date which may **affect the position at** the balance sheet date.

1.1 Definitions

The standard gives the following definition.

Key terms

> **Events after the balance sheet date** are those events, both favourable and unfavourable, that occur between the balance sheet date and the date on which the financial statements are authorised for issue. Two types of events can be identified:
>
> - those that provide further evidence of conditions that existed at the balance sheet date; and
> - those that are indicative of conditions that arose subsequent to the balance sheet date.   (IAS 10)

1.2 Events after the balance sheet date

Between the balance sheet date and the date the financial statements are authorised (ie for issue outside the organisation), events may occur which show that assets and liabilities at the balance sheet date should be adjusted, or that disclosure of such events should be given.

1.3 Events requiring adjustment

The standard requires adjustment of assets and liabilities in certain circumstances.

> **FAST FORWARD**
>
> An entity shall adjust the amounts recognised in its financial statements to reflect adjusting events after the balance sheet date. (IAS 10)
>
> Where events indicate that the **going concern concept** is no longer appropriate, then the accounts may have to be restated on a break-up basis.

An **example** of additional evidence which becomes available after the balance sheet date is where a **customer goes bankrupt, thus confirming that the trade account receivable balance at the year end is uncollectable.**

In relation to going concern, the standard states that, where operating results and the financial position have deteriorated after the balance sheet date, it may be necessary to reconsider whether the going concern assumption is appropriate in the preparation of the financial statements.

1.4 Events not requiring adjustment

> **FAST FORWARD**
>
> Events which do not affect the situation at the balance sheet date should not be adjusted for, but should be **disclosed** in the financial statements.

The standard then looks at events which do **not** require adjustment.

> An entity shall not adjust the amounts recognised in its financial statements to reflect non-adjusting events after the balance sheet date. (IAS 10)

The **example** given by the standard of such an event is where the **value of an investment falls between the balance sheet date and the date the financial statements are authorised** for issue. The fall in value represents circumstances during the current period, not conditions existing at the previous balance sheet date, so it is not appropriate to adjust the value of the investment in the financial statements. Disclosure is an aid to users, however, indicating 'unusual changes' in the state of assets and liabilities after the balance sheet date.

The rule for **disclosure** of events occurring after the balance sheet date which relate to conditions that arose after that date, is that disclosure should be made if non-disclosure would hinder the user's ability to made **proper evaluations** and decision based on the financial statements. An example might be the acquisition of another business.

1.5 Dividends

Dividends proposed or declared are no longer recognised as a liability and do not appear in the accounts.

1.6 Disclosures

The following **disclosure requirements** are given **for events** which occur after the balance sheet date which do *not* require adjustment. If disclosure of events occurring after the balance sheet date is required by this standard, the following information should be provided:

(a) The nature of the event
(b) An estimate of the financial effect, or a statement that such an estimate cannot be made

PART D   ACCOUNTING TREATMENTS

Question — Events after the balance sheet date

State whether the following events occurring after the balance sheet date require an adjustment to the assets and liabilities of the financial statements.

(a) Purchase of an investment
(b) A change in the rate of tax, applicable to the previous year
(c) An increase in pension benefits
(d) Losses due to fire
(e) A irrecoverable debt suddenly being paid
(f) The receipt of proceeds of sales or other evidence concerning the net realisable value of inventory
(g) A sudden decline in the value of property held as a long-term asset

Answer

(b), (e) and (f) require adjustment.

Of the other items, (a) would not need to be disclosed at all. Item (c) could need a disclosure if the cost to the company is likely to be material. Item (d) again would be disclosed if material, as would (g) if material.

Assuming that item (d) is material, it would be disclosed by way of the following note to the accounts. (The company year end is 31 December 20X8.)

Events after the balance sheet date

On 22 January 20X9, there was a fire at the company's warehouse. As a result, inventories costing a total of $250,000 were destroyed. These inventories are included in assets at the balance sheet date.

2 Contingencies (IAS 37)

2.1 Provisions

FAST FORWARD

A **provision** should be recognised
- When an entity has incurred a **present obligation**
- When it is **probable** that a **transfer of economics benefits** will be required to settle it
- When a **reliable estimate** can be made of the amount involved

Exam focus point

Provisions are not in your syllabus and will be covered in your later studies. However, in order to understand what **contingent assets and liabilities** are you need to distinguish them from **provisions**.

IAS 37 views a provision as a liability.

Key terms

A **provision** is a **liability** of uncertain timing or amount.

A **liability** is an obligation of an enterprise to transfer economic benefits as a result of past transactions or events.   *(IAS 37)*

The IAS distinguishes provisions from other liabilities such as trade creditors and accruals. This is on the basis that for a provision there is **uncertainty** about the timing or amount of the future expenditure. Whilst uncertainty is clearly present in the case of certain accruals the uncertainty is generally much less than for provisions.

Rule of thumb

A provision is made for something which will *probably* happen. It should be recognised when it is probable that a transfer of economic events will take place and when its amount can be estimated reliably.

16: EVENTS AFTER THE BALANCE SHEET DATE AND CONTINGENCIES

Now you are ready to look at contingent assets and liabilities.

FAST FORWARD

> An entity should not recognise a **contingent asset or liability** but they should be disclosed.

2.2 Contingent liabilities

Contingent liabilities are defined as follows.

Key term

> IAS 37 defines a **contingent liability** as:
> - A possible obligation that arises from past events and whose existence will be confirmed only by the occurrence or non-occurrence of one or more uncertain future events not wholly within the entity's control; or
> - A present obligation that arises from past events but is not recognised because:
>   – It is not probable that a transfer of economic benefits will be required to settle the obligation; or
>   – The amount of the obligation cannot be measured with sufficient reliability.

As a rule of thumb, probable means more than 50% likely. **If an obligation is probable, it is not a contingent liability** – instead, a **provision is needed**.

2.3 Treatment of contingent liabilities

Contingent liabilities **should not be recognised in financial statements** but they **should be disclosed**. The required disclosures are:

- A brief description of the nature of the contingent liability
- An estimate of its financial effect
- An indication of the uncertainties that exist
- The possibility of any reimbursement

2.4 Contingent assets

Key term

> IAS 37 defines a **contingent asset** as:
>
> A possible asset that arises from past events and whose existence will be confirmed by the occurrence of one or more uncertain future events not wholly within the enterprise's control.

A contingent asset must not be recognised. Only when the realisation of the related economic benefits is **virtually certain** should recognition take place. At that point, **the asset is no longer a contingent asset**!

2.4.1 Disclosure: contingent liabilities

A **brief description** must be provided of all material contingent liabilities unless they are likely to be remote. In addition, provide

- An estimate of their **financial effect**
- Details of **any uncertainties**

2.4.2 Disclosure: contingent assets

Contingent assets must only be disclosed in the notes if they are **probable**. In that case a brief description of the contingent asset should be provided along with an estimate of its likely financial effect.

You must practise the questions below to get the hang of the IAS 37 rules on contingencies. But first, study the flow chart, taken from IAS 37, which is a good summary of its requirements.

PART D ACCOUNTING TREATMENTS

Exam focus point

If you learn this flow chart you should be able to deal with most questions you are likely to meet in an exam.

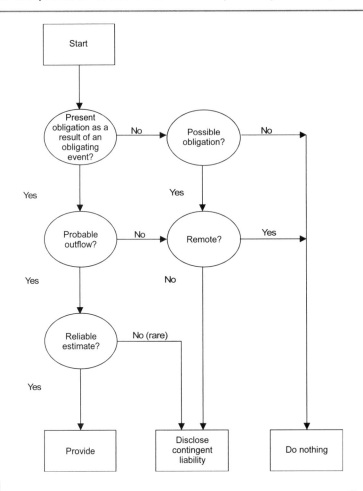

Question Contingencies 1

During 20X9 Smack Co gives a guarantee of certain borrowings of Pony Co, whose financial condition at that time is sound. During 20Y0, the financial condition of Pony Co deteriorates and at 30 June 20Y0 Pony Co files for protection from its creditors.

What accounting treatment is required:

(a) at 31 December 20X9?
(b) at 31 December 20Y0?

Answer

(a) At 31 December 20X9

There is a present obligation as a result of a past obligating event. The obligating event is the giving of the guarantee, which gives rise to a legal obligation. However, at 31 December 20X9 no transfer of economic benefits is probable in settlement of the obligation.

No provision is recognised. The guarantee is disclosed as a contingent liability unless the probability of any transfer is regarded as remote.

An appropriate note to the accounts would be as follows.

Contingent liability

The company has given a guarantee in respect of the bank borrowings (currently $500,000) of Pony Co. At the balance sheet date, Pony Co was sound and it is unlikely that the company will be required to fulfil its guarantee.

(b) At 31 December 20Y0

As above, there is a present obligation as a result of a past obligating event, namely the giving of the guarantee.

At 31 December 20Y0 it is probable that a transfer of economic events will be required to settle the obligation. A provision is therefore recognised for the best estimate of the obligation.

Question — Contingencies 2

After a wedding in 20X0 ten people died, possibly as a result of food poisoning from products sold by Callow Co. Legal proceedings are started seeking damages from Callow but it disputes liability. Up to the date of approval of the financial statements for the year to 31 December 20X0, Callow's lawyers advise that it is probable that it will not be found liable. However, when Callow prepares the financial statements for the year to 31 December 20X1 its lawyers advise that, owing to developments in the case, it is probable that it will be found liable.

What is the required accounting treatment:

(a) at 31 December 20X0?
(b) at 31 December 20X1?

Answer

(a) At 31 December 20X0

On the basis of the evidence available when the financial statements were approved, there is no obligation as a result of past events. No provision is recognised. The matter is disclosed as a contingent liability unless the probability of any transfer is regarded as remote.

(b) At 31 December 20X1

On the basis of the evidence available, there is a present obligation. A transfer of economic benefits in settlement is probable.

A provision is recognised for the best estimate of the amount needed to settle the present obligation.

Question — Contingencies 3

An oil company causes environmental contamination in the course of its operations, but cleans up only when required to do so under the laws of the country in which it is operating. One country in which it has been operating for several years has up to now had no legislation requiring cleaning up. However, there is now an environmental lobby in this country. At the date of the company's year end, it is virtually certain that a draft law requiring clean up of contaminated land will be enacted very shortly. The oil company will then be obliged to deal with the contamination it has caused over the past several years.

What accounting treatment is required at the year end?

Answer

At the year end there is a **present obligation** as a result of a **past obligating event**. Because the passage of the Act is 'virtually certain', the past contamination becomes an obligating event. It is highly probable that an **outflow of economic resources** will be required to settle this. A provision should therefore be made of the best estimate of the costs involved.

Chapter Roundup

- **Events after the balance sheet** date which provide **additional evidence** of conditions existing at the balance sheet date, will cause **adjustments** to be made to the assets and liabilities in the financial statements.

- **Events** which **do not affect the situation at the balance sheet date** should **not be adjusted for**, but should be **disclosed** in the financial statements.

- Where events indicate that the **going concern concept** is no longer appropriate then the **accounts may have to be restated** on a break-up basis.

- A **provision** should be recognised
   - When an entity has a **present obligation**
   - It is **probable** that a **transfer of economic benefits** will be required to settle it
   - A **reliable estimate** can be made of its amount

- An entity **should not recognise a contingent asset or liability**, but they **should be disclosed**.

Quick Quiz

1. When does an event after the balance sheet date require changes to the financial statements?
2. What disclosure is required when it is not possible to estimate the financial effect of an event not requiring adjustment?
3. How does IAS 37 define a contingent liability?
4. When should a contingent liability be recognised?

Answers to Quick Quiz

1. Assets and liabilities should be adjusted for events after the balance sheet date when these provide additional evidence for estimates existing at the balance sheet date.
2. A statement of the nature of the event and the fact that a financial estimate of the event can not be made.
3. See Key Term in paragraph 2.2.
4. They should never be recognised, but disclosed by way of note.

Now try the questions below from the Exam Question Bank

Number	Level	Marks	Time
Q22	Introductory	n/a	36 mins
Q35	Examination	10	18 mins

Part E
Financial statements

Incomplete records

Topic list	Syllabus reference
1 Incomplete records questions	5(d)(i)
2 The opening balance sheet	5(d)(i)
3 Credit sales and trade accounts receivable	5(d)(i)
4 Purchases and trade accounts payable	5(d)(i)
5 Establishing cost of sales	5(d)(i)
6 Stolen goods or goods destroyed	5(d)(i)
7 The cash book	5(d)(i)
8 Accruals and prepayments	5(d)(i)
9 Drawings	5(d)(i)
10 The business equation	5(d)(i)
11 Dealing with incomplete records problems in the examination	5(d)(i)

Introduction

So far in your work on preparing the final accounts for a sole trader we have assumed that a full set of records are kept. In practice many sole traders do not keep a full set of records and you must apply certain techniques to arrive at the necessary figures.

Incomplete records questions are a very good test of your understanding of the way in which a set of accounts is built up.

In most countries, limited liability companies are obliged by national laws to keep proper accounting records.

PART E FINANCIAL STATEMENTS

Study guide

Section 9-10 – Incomplete records

- Explain techniques used in incomplete records situations
    - Calculation of opening capital
    - Use of ledger accounts to calculate missing figures
    - Use of cash and/or bank summaries
    - Use of given gross profit percentage to calculate missing figures
- Explain and illustrate the calculation of profit or loss as the difference between opening and closing net assets

Exam guide

Incomplete records questions appear regularly in the exam. You will certainly get a question on this topic in Section A and possibly Section B as well.

1 Incomplete records questions

FAST FORWARD

Incomplete records questions may test your ability to prepare accounts in the following situations.

- A trader **does not maintain a ledger** and therefore has no continuous double entry record of transactions.
- Accounting records are **destroyed** by accident, such as fire
- Some essential figure is **unknown** and must be calculated as a balancing figure. This may occur as a result of inventory being damaged or destroyed, or because of misappropriation of assets.

Incomplete records problems occur when a business does not have a full set of accounting records, for one of the following reasons.

- The proprietor of the business does not keep a full set of accounts.
- Some of the business accounts are accidentally lost or destroyed.

The problem for the accountant is to prepare a set of year-end accounts for the business; ie an income statement, and a balance sheet. Since the business does not have a full set of accounts, preparing the final accounts is not a simple matter of closing off accounts and transferring balances to the trading, income and expense account, or showing outstanding balances in the balance sheet. The task of preparing the final accounts involves the following.

(a) Establishing the **cost of purchases** and other expenses

(b) Establishing the **total amount of sales**

(c) Establishing the amount of **accounts payable, accruals, accounts receivable and prepayments** at the end of the year

Examination questions often take incomplete records problems a stage further, by introducing an 'incident', such as fire or burglary which leaves the owner of the business uncertain about how much inventory has been destroyed or stolen.

The great merit of incomplete records problems is that they focus attention on the relationship between cash received and paid, sales and accounts receivable, purchases and accounts payable, and inventory, as well as calling for the preparation of final accounts from basic principles.

274

17: INCOMPLETE RECORDS

To understand what incomplete records are about, it will obviously be useful now to look at what exactly might be incomplete. The items we shall consider in turn are:

(a) The opening balance sheet
(b) Credit sales and trade accounts receivable
(c) Purchases and trade accounts payable
(d) Purchases, inventory and the cost of sales
(e) Stolen goods or goods destroyed
(f) The cash book
(g) Accruals and prepayments
(h) Drawings

Exam focus point

> Incomplete records questions are a good test of whether you have a really thorough grasp of double entry. Examiners are fond of them. With practice they become easier and can be very satisfying.

2 The opening balance sheet

In practice there should not be any missing item in the opening balance sheet of the business, because it should be available from the preparation of the previous year's final accounts. However, an examination problem might provide information about the assets and liabilities of the business at the beginning of the period under review, but then leave the balancing figure (ie the proprietor's business capital) unspecified.

2.1 Example: Opening balance sheet

Suppose Joe Han's business has the following assets and liabilities as at 1 January 20X3.

	$
Fixtures and fittings at cost	7,000
Provision for depreciation, fixtures and fittings	4,000
Motor vehicles at cost	12,000
Provision for depreciation, motor vehicles	6,800
Inventory	4,500
Trade accounts receivable	5,200
Cash at bank and in hand	1,230
Trade accounts payable	3,700
Prepayment	450
Accrued rent	2,000

You are required to prepare a balance sheet for the business, inserting a balancing figure for proprietor's capital.

Solution

BALANCE SHEET AS AT 1 JANUARY 20X3

	$	$
Assets		
Non-current assets		
Fixtures and fittings at cost	7,000	
Less accumulated depreciation	4,000	
		3,000
Motor vehicles at cost	12,000	
Less accumulated depreciation	6,800	
		5,200

PART E FINANCIAL STATEMENTS

		$	$
Current assets			
Inventory		4,500	
Trade accounts receivable		5,200	
Prepayment		450	
Cash		1,230	
			11,380
Total assets			19,580
Capital and liabilities			
Proprietor's capital as at 1 January 20X3 (balancing figure)			13,880
Current liabilities			
Trade accounts payable		3,700	
Accrual		2,000	
			5,700
Total capital and liabilities			19,580

3 Credit sales and trade accounts receivable

FAST FORWARD

The approach to incomplete records questions is to build up the information given so as to complete the necessary **double entry**. This may involve reconstructing **control accounts** for:

- cash and bank
- trade accounts receivable and payable

If a business does not keep a record of its sales on credit, the value of these sales can be derived from the opening balance of trade accounts receivable, the closing balance of trade accounts receivable, and the payments received from customers during the period.

Formula to learn: credit sales

	$
Payments from trade accounts receivable	X
Plus closing balance of trade accounts receivable (since these represent sales in the current period for which cash payment has not yet been received)	X
Less opening balance of trade accounts receivable (these represent credit sales in a previous period)	(X)
Credit sales in the period	X

For example, suppose that Joe Han's business had trade accounts receivable of $1,750 on 1 April 20X4 and trade accounts receivable of $3,140 on 31 March 20X5. If payments received from receivables during the year to 31 March 20X5 were $28,490, and if there are no bad debts, then credit sales for the period would be:

	$
Cash from receivables	28,490
Plus closing receivables	3,140
Less opening receivables	(1,750)
Credit sales	29,880

If there are bad debts during the period, the value of sales will be increased by the amount of bad debts written off, no matter whether they relate to opening receivables or credit sales during the current period.

Question   Calculating sales

The calculation above could be made in a T-account, with credit sales being the balancing figure to complete the account. Prepare the T-account.

276

Answer

TRADE ACCOUNTS RECEIVABLE

	$		$
Opening balance b/f	1,750	Cash received	28,490
Credit sales (balancing fig)	29,880	Closing balance c/f	3,140
	31,630		31,630

The same interrelationship between credit sales, cash from receivables, and opening and closing receivables balances can be used to derive a missing figure for cash from receivables, or opening or closing receivables, given the values for the three other items. For example, if we know that opening receivables are $6,700, closing receivables are $3,200 and credit sales for the period are $69,400, then cash from receivables during the period would be as follows.

TRADE ACCOUNTS RECEIVABLE

	$		$
Opening balance	6,700	Cash received (balancing figure)	72,900
Sales (on credit)	69,400	Closing balance c/f	3,200
	76,100		76,100

An alternative way of presenting the same calculation would be:

	$
Opening balance of accounts receivable	6,700
Credit sales during the period	69,400
Total money owed to the business	76,100
Less closing balance of accounts receivable	(3,200)
Equals cash received during the period	72,900

4 Purchases and trade accounts payable

A similar relationship exists between purchases of inventory during a period, the opening and closing balances for trade accounts payable, and amounts paid to suppliers during the period.

If we wish to calculate an unknown amount for purchases, the amount would be derived as follows.

Formula to learn: purchases

	$
Payments to trade accounts payable during the period	X
Plus closing balance of trade accounts payable	X
(since these represent purchases in the current period for which payment has not yet been made)	
Less opening balance of trade accounts payable	(X)
(these debts, paid in the current period, relate to purchases in a previous period)	
Purchases during the period	X

For example, suppose that Joe Han's business had trade payables of $3,728 on 1 October 20X5 and trade payables of $2,645 on 30 September 20X6. If payments to trade payables during the year to 30 September 20X6 were $31,479, then purchases during the year would be:

	$
Payments to trade accounts payable	31,479
Plus closing balance of trade accounts payable	2,645
Less opening balance of trade accounts payable	(3,728)
Purchases	30,396

PART E FINANCIAL STATEMENTS

Question
Calculating purchases 1

Again, the calculation above could be made in a T-account, with purchases being the balancing figure to complete the account. Prepare the T-account.

Answer

TRADE ACCOUNTS PAYABLE

	$		$
Cash payments	31,479	Opening balance b/f	3,728
Closing balance c/f	2,645	Purchases (balancing figure)	30,396
	34,124		34,124

Question
Calculating purchases 2

Mr Harmon does not keep full accounting records, but the following information is available in respect of his accounting year ended 31 December 20X9.

	$
Cash purchases in year	3,900
Cash paid for goods supplied on credit	27,850
Trade accounts payable at 1 January 20X9	970
Trade accounts payable at 31 December 20X9	720

In his trading account for 20X9, what will be Harmon's figure for purchases?

Answer

Credit purchases = $(27,850 + 720 – 970) = $27,600. Therefore total purchases = $(27,600 + 3,900) = $31,500.

5 Establishing cost of sales

FAST FORWARD

Where inventory, sales or purchases is the unknown figure it will be necessary to use information on **gross profit percentages** to construct a working for gross profit in which the unknown figure can be inserted as a balance.

When the value of purchases is not known, a different approach might be required to find out what they were, depending on the nature of the information given to you.

One approach would be to use information about the cost of sales, and opening and closing inventory rather than trade accounts payable to find the cost of purchases.

Formula to learn

		$
Since	opening inventory	X
	plus purchases	X
	less closing inventory	(X)
	equals the cost of goods sold	X
then	the cost of goods sold	X
	plus closing inventory	X
	less opening inventory	(X)
	equals purchases	X

Suppose that the inventory of Joe Han's business on 1 July 20X6 has a balance sheet value of $8,400, and an inventory count at 30 June 20X7 showed inventory to be valued at $9,350. Sales for the year to 30 June 20X7 are $80,000, and the business makes a mark-up of $33^1/_3$% on cost for all the items that it sells. What were the purchases during the year?

The cost of goods sold can be derived from the value of sales, as follows.

		$
Sales	($133^1/_3$%)	80,000
Gross profit (mark-up)	($33^1/_3$%)	20,000
Cost of goods sold	(100%)	60,000

The cost of goods sold is 75% of sales value.

	$
Cost of goods sold	60,000
Plus closing inventory	9,350
Less opening inventory	(8,400)
Purchases	60,950

It is worth mentioning here that two different terms may be given to you in the exam for the calculation of profit.

Key terms

- **Mark-up** is the profit as a percentage of **cost**.
- **Gross profit** is the profit as a percentage of **sales**.

Looking at the above example:

(a) The mark-up on cost is $33^1/_3$%
(b) The gross profit percentage is 25% (ie $33^1/_3$/$133^1/_3$ × 100%)

Question
Calculating purchases 3

Harry has budgeted sales for the coming year of $175,000. He achieves a constant gross mark-up of 40% on cost. He plans to reduce his inventory level by $13,000 over the year.

What will Harry's purchases be for the year?

Answer

Cost of sales = 100/140 × $175,000
 = $125,000

Since the inventory level is being allowed to fall, it means that purchases will be $13,000 less than $125,000 = $112,000.

PART E FINANCIAL STATEMENTS

6 Stolen goods or goods destroyed

A similar type of calculation might be required to derive the value of goods stolen or destroyed. When an unknown quantity of goods is lost, whether they are stolen, destroyed in a fire, or lost in any other way such that the quantity lost cannot be counted, then the cost of the goods lost is the difference between (a) and (b).

(a) The **cost of goods sold**

(b) **Opening inventory of the goods** (at cost) plus **purchases** less **closing inventory of the goods** (at cost)

In theory (a) and (b) should be the same. However, if (b) is a larger amount than (a), it follows that the difference must be the cost of the goods purchased and neither sold nor remaining in inventory, ie the cost of the goods lost.

6.1 Example: Cost of goods destroyed

Orlean Flames is a shop which sells fashion clothes. On 1 January 20X5, it had trade inventory which cost $7,345. During the 9 months to 30 September 20X5, the business purchased goods from suppliers costing $106,420. Sales during the same period were $154,000. The shop makes a gross profit of 40% on cost for everything it sells. On 30 September 20X5, there was a fire in the shop which destroyed most of the inventory in it. Only a small amount of inventory, known to have cost $350, was undamaged and still fit for sale.

How much of the inventory was lost in the fire?

Solution

(a)
	$
Sales (140%)	154,000
Gross profit (40%)	44,000
Cost of goods sold (100%)	110,000

(b)
	$
Opening inventory, at cost	7,345
Plus purchases	106,420
	113,765
Less closing inventory, at cost	350
Equals cost of goods sold and goods lost	113,415

(c)
	$
Cost of goods sold and lost	113,415
Cost of goods sold	110,000
Cost of goods lost	3,415

6.2 Example: Cost of goods stolen

Beau Gullard runs a jewellery shop in the High Street. On 1 January 20X9, his trade inventory, at cost, amounted to $4,700 and his trade payables were $3,950.

During the six months to 30 June 20X9, sales were $42,000. Beau Gullard makes a gross profit of $33^{1}/_{3}\%$ on the sales value of everything he sells.

On 30 June, there was a burglary at the shop, and all the inventory was stolen.

In trying to establish how much inventory had been taken, Beau Gullard was only able to say that:

(a) He knew from his bank statements that he had paid $28,400 to trade account payables in the 6 month period to 30 June 20X9.

(b) He currently had payables due of $5,550.

Required

(a) Calculate the amount of inventory stolen.
(b) Calculate gross profit for the 6 months to 30 June 20X9.

Solution

Step 1 The first 'unknown' is the amount of purchases during the period. This is established by the method previously described in this chapter.

TRADE ACCOUNTS PAYABLE

	$		$
Payments to trade accounts payable	28,400	Opening balance b/f	3,950
Closing balance c/f	5,550	Purchases (balancing figure)	30,000
	33,950		33,950

Step 2 The cost of goods sold is also unknown, but this can be established from the gross profit margin and the sales for the period.

		$
Sales	(100%)	42,000
Gross profit	(33^1/$_3$%)	14,000
Cost of goods sold	(66^2/$_3$%)	28,000

Step 3 The cost of the goods stolen is:

	$
Opening inventory at cost	4,700
Purchases	30,000
	34,700
Less closing inventory (after burglary)	0
Cost of goods sold and goods stolen	34,700
Cost of goods sold (see (b) above)	28,000
Cost of goods stolen	6,700

Step 4 The cost of the goods stolen will not be included in cost of sales, and so the gross profit for the period is as follows.

BEAU GULLARD
GROSS PROFIT FOR THE SIX MONTHS TO 30 JUNE 20X9

	$	$
Sales		42,000
Less cost of goods sold		
Opening inventory	4,700	
Purchases	30,000	
	34,700	
Less inventory stolen	6,700	
		28,000
Gross profit		14,000

6.3 Accounting for inventory destroyed, stolen or otherwise lost

When inventory is stolen, destroyed or otherwise lost, the loss must be accounted for somehow. The procedure was described briefly in the earlier chapter on inventory accounting. Since the loss is not a trading loss, the cost of the goods lost is not included in the cost of sales, as the previous example showed. The accounting double entry is therefore

DEBIT   See below
CREDIT   Cost of sales

The account that is to be debited is one of two possibilities, depending on whether or not the lost goods were insured against the loss.

(a) If the lost goods were not insured, the business must bear the loss, and the loss is shown in the net profit (income and expenses) part of the income statement; ie

DEBIT   I & E a/c
CREDIT   Cost of sales

(b) If the lost goods were insured, the business will not suffer a loss, because the insurance will pay back the cost of the lost goods. This means that there is no charge at all in the income statement, and the appropriate double entry is:

DEBIT   Insurance claim account (receivable account)
CREDIT   Cost of sales

with the cost of the loss. The insurance claim will then be a current asset, and shown in the balance sheet of the business as such. When the claim is paid, the account is then closed by:

DEBIT   Cash
CREDIT   Insurance claim account

7 The cash book

FAST FORWARD

The construction of a cash book, largely from bank statements showing receipts and payments of a business during a given period, is often an important feature of incomplete records problems.

Exam focus point

In an examination, the purpose of an incomplete records question is largely to test the understanding of candidates about how various items of receipts or payments relate to the preparation of a final set of accounts for a business.

We have already seen in this chapter that information about cash receipts or payments might be needed to establish:

(a) The amount of purchases during a period
(b) The amount of credit sales during a period

Other items of receipts or payments might be relevant to establishing:

(a) The amount of cash sales
(b) The amount of certain expenses in the income statement
(c) The amount of withdrawals on account of profit by the business proprietor

It might therefore be helpful, if a business does not keep a cash book day-to-day, to construct a cash book at the end of an accounting period. A business which typically might not keep a day-to-day cash book is a shop.

17: INCOMPLETE RECORDS

(a) Many sales, if not all sales, are cash sales (ie with payment by notes and coins, cheques, or credit cards at the time of sale).

(b) Some payments are made in notes and coins out of the till rather than by payment out of the business bank account by cheque.

Where there appears to be a sizeable volume of receipts and payments in cash (ie notes and coins), then it is also helpful to construct a two column cash book.

Key term

A **two column cash book** is a cash book with one column for receipts and payments, and one column for money paid into and out of the business bank account.

An example will illustrate the technique and the purpose of a two column cash book.

7.1 Example: Two column cash book

Jonathan Slugg owns and runs a shop selling fishing tackle, making a gross profit of 25% on the cost of everything he sells. He does not keep a cash book.

On 1 January 20X7 the balance sheet of his business was as follows.

	$	$
Current assets		
Inventory	10,000	
Cash in the bank	3,000	
Cash in the till	200	
		13,200
Net long-term assets		20,000
		33,200
Trade accounts payable		1,200
Proprietor's capital		32,000
		33,200

In the year to 31 December 20X7:

(a) There were no sales on credit.

(b) $41,750 in receipts were banked.

(c) The bank statements of the period show the payments:

		$
(i)	to trade accounts payable	36,000
(ii)	sundry expenses	5,600
(iii)	to drawings	4,400

(d) Payments were also made in cash out of the till:

		$
(i)	for trade accounts payable	800
(ii)	sundry expenses	1,500
(iii)	to drawings	3,700

At 31 December 20X7, the business had cash in the till of $450 and trade accounts payable of $1,400. The cash balance in the bank was not known and the value of closing inventory has not yet been calculated. There were no accruals or prepayments. No further long-term assets were purchased during the year. The depreciation charge for the year is $900.

Required

(a) Prepare a two column cash book for the period.

(b) Prepare the income statement for the year to 31 December 20X7 and the balance sheet as at 31 December 20X7.

PART E FINANCIAL STATEMENTS

7.2 Discussion and solution

A two column cash book is completed as follows.

Step 1 Enter the opening cash balances.

Step 2 Enter the information given about cash payments (and any cash receipts, if there had been any such items given in the problem).

Step 3 The cash receipts banked are a 'contra' entry, being both a debit (bank column) and a credit (cash in hand column) in the same account.

Step 4 Enter the closing cash in hand (cash in the bank at the end of the period is not known).

CASH BOOK

	Cash in hand $	Bank $		Cash in hand $	Bank $
Balance b/f	200	3,000	Trade accounts payable	800	36,000
Cash receipts banked (contra)		41,750	Sundry expenses	1,500	5,600
Sales*	48,000		Drawings	3,700	4,400
			Cash receipts banked (contra)	41,750	
Balance c/f		*1,250	Balance c/f	450	
	48,200	46,000		48,200	46,000

* Balancing figure

Step 5 The closing balance of money in the bank is a balancing figure.

Step 6 Since all sales are for cash, a balancing figure that can be entered in the cash book is sales, in the cash in hand (debit) column.

It is important to notice that since not all receipts from cash sales are banked, the value of cash sales during the period is:

	$
Receipts banked	41,750
Plus expenses and withdrawals paid out of the till in cash $(800 + 1,500 + 3,700)$	6,000
Plus any cash stolen (here there is none)	0
Plus the closing balance of cash in hand	450
	48,200
Less the opening balance of cash in hand	(200)
Equals cash sales	48,000

The cash book constructed in this way has enabled us to establish both the closing balance for cash in the bank and also the volume of cash sales. The income statement and the balance sheet can also be prepared, once a value for purchases has been calculated.

TRADE ACCOUNTS PAYABLE

	$		$
Cash book: payments from bank	36,000	Balance b/f	1,200
Cash book: payments in cash	800	Purchases (balancing figure)	37,000
Balance c/f	1,400		
	38,200		38,200

The gross profit margin of 25% on cost indicates that the cost of the goods sold is $38,400, ie:

	$
Sales (125%)	48,000
Gross profit (25%)	9,600
Cost of goods sold (100%)	38,400

The closing inventory is now a balancing figure in the trading account.

JONATHAN SLUGG
INCOME STATEMENT
FOR THE YEAR ENDED 31 DECEMBER 20X7

	$	$
Sales		48,000
Less cost of goods sold		
Opening inventory	10,000	
Purchases	37,000	
	47,000	
Less closing inventory (balancing figure)	8,600	
		38,400
Gross profit (25/125 × $48,000)		9,600
Expenses		
Sundry $(1,500 + 5,600)	7,100	
Depreciation	900	
		8,000
Net profit		1,600

JONATHAN SLUGG
BALANCE SHEET AS AT 31 DECEMBER 20X7

	$	$
Assets		
Current assets		
Inventory	8,600	
Cash in the till	450	
		9,050
Net long-term assets $(20,000 – 900)		19,100
Total assets		28,150
Capital and liabilities		
Proprietor's capital		
Balance b/f	32,000	
Net profit for the year	1,600	
Withdrawals on account $(3,700 + 4,400)	(8,100)	
Balance c/f		25,500
Current liabilities		
Bank overdraft	1,250	
Trade payables	1,400	
		2,650
Total capital and liabilities		28,150

7.3 Theft of cash from the till

When cash is stolen from the till, the amount stolen will be a credit entry in the cash book, and a debit in either the net profit section (income and expenses account) of the income statement or insurance claim account, depending on whether the business is insured. The missing figure for cash sales, if this has to be calculated, must not ignore cash received but later stolen – see above.

8 Accruals and prepayments

Where there is an accrued expense or a prepayment, the charge to be made in the income statement for the item concerned should be found from the opening balance b/f, the closing balance c/f, and cash payments for the item during the period. The charge in the income statement is perhaps most easily found as the balancing figure in a T-account.

For example, suppose that on 1 April 20X6 a business had prepaid rent of $700 which relates to the next accounting period. During the year to 31 March 20X7 it pays $9,300 in rent, and at 31 March 20X7 the prepayment of rent is $1,000. The cost of rent in the I&E account for the year to 31 March 20X7 would be the balancing figure in the following T-account. (Remember that a prepayment is a current asset, and so is a debit balance b/f.)

RENT

	$		$
Prepayment: balance b/f	700	I & E a/c (balancing figure)	9,000
Cash	9,300	Prepayment: balance c/f	1,000
	10,000		10,000
Balance b/f	1,000		

8.3 Similarly, if a business has accrued telephone expenses as at 1 July 20X6 of $850, pays $6,720 in telephone bills during the year to 30 June 20X7, and has accrued telephone expenses of $1,140 as at 30 June 20X7, then the telephone expense to be shown in the income statement for the year to 30 June 20X7 is the balancing figure in the following T-account. (Remember that an accrual is a current liability, and so is a credit balance b/f.)

TELEPHONE EXPENSES

	$		$
Cash	6,720	Balance b/f (accrual)	850
Balance c/f (accrual)	1,140	I & E a/c (balancing figure)	7,010
	7,860		7,860
		Balance b/f	1,140

9 Drawings

FAST FORWARD

> **Drawings** often feature as the missing item in an incomplete records problem. The trader has been drawing money but does not know how much.

Drawings would normally represent no particular problem at all in preparing a set of final accounts from incomplete records, but it is not unusual for examination questions to contain complicating situations.

(a) The business owner may pay income into his bank account which has nothing whatever to do with the business operations. For example, the owner might pay dividend income, or other income from investments into the bank, from stocks and shares which he owns personally, separate from the business itself. (In other words, there are no investments in the business balance sheet, and so income from investments cannot possibly be income of the business.) These amounts will be credited to his drawings.

(b) The business owner may pay money out of the business bank account for items which are not business expenses, such as life insurance premiums or a payment for his family's holidays etc. These will be treated as drawings.

17: INCOMPLETE RECORDS

Where such **personal items of receipts or payments** are made the following adjustments should be made.

(a) Receipts should be set off against drawings. For example, if a business owner receives $600 in dividend income and pays it into his business bank account, although the dividends are from investments not owned by the business, then the accounting entry is:

DEBIT   Cash
CREDIT   Drawings

(b) Payments should be charged to drawings on account; ie:

DEBIT   Drawings
CREDIT   Cash

9.1 Beware of the wording in an examination question

You should note that:

(a) If a question states that a proprietor's drawings during a given year are 'approximately $40 per week' then you should assume that drawings for the year are $40 × 52 weeks = $2,080.

(b) However, if a question states that drawings in the year are 'between $35 and $45 per week', do not assume that the drawings average $40 per week and so amount to $2,080 for the year. You could not be certain that the actual withdrawals did average $40, and so you should treat the withdrawals figure as a missing item that needs to be calculated.

10 The business equation

FAST FORWARD

> Where no trading records have been kept, profit can be derived from opening and closing net assets by use of the **business equation.**

The most obvious incomplete records situation is that of a sole trader who has kept no trading records. It may not be possible to reconstruct his whole income statement, but it will be possible to compute his profit for the year using the **business equation**.

Here is the basic balance sheet format:

Assets		XX
Capital	X	
Liabilities	X	XX

This can be rearranged as:

Assets	XX	
Liabilities	(X)	X
Capital		X

So this gives us a figure for capital – assets less liabilities, or **net assets**.

What will increase or decrease capital?

Capital is changed by:

(a) Money paid in by the trader
(b) Drawings by the trader
(c) Profits or losses

So, if we are able to establish the traders net assets at the beginnings and end of the period, we can compute profits as follows:

Profit (loss) = movement in net assets – capital introduced + drawings

We want to eliminate any movement caused by money paid in or taken out for personal use by the trader. So we take out capital introduced and add back in drawings.

10.1 Example: Business equation

Joe starts up his camera shop on 1 January 20X1, from rented premises, with $5,000 inventory and $3,000 in the bank. All of his sales are for cash. He keeps no record of his takings.

At the end of the year he has inventory worth $6,600 and $15,000 in the bank. He owes $3,000 to suppliers. He had paid in $5,000 he won on the lottery and drawn out $2,000 to buy himself a motorbike. The motorbike is not used in the business. He has been taking drawings of $100 per week. What is his profit at 31 December 20X1?

Solution

	$
Opening net assets	
Inventory	5,000
Cash	3,000
	8,000
Closing net assets	
Inventory	6,600
Cash	15,000
Payables	(3,000)
	18,600
Movement in capital (net assets)	10,600
Less capital paid in	(5,000)
Plus drawings ((100 × 52) + 2000)	7,200
Profit	12,800

11 Dealing with incomplete records problems in the examination

A suggested approach to dealing with incomplete records problems brings together the various points described so far in this chapter. The nature of the 'incompleteness' in the records will vary from problem to problem, but the approach, suitably applied, should be successful in arriving at the final accounts whatever the particular characteristics of the problem might be.

The approach is as follows.

Step 1 If possible, and if it is not already known, establish the opening balance sheet and the proprietor's interest.

Step 2 Open up four accounts.

- Income and expense account
- A cash book, with two columns if cash sales are significant and there are payments in cash out of the till
- A trade receivables account
- A trade payables account

Step 3 Enter the opening balances in these accounts.

Step 4 Work through the information you are given line by line; and each item should be entered into the appropriate account if it is relevant to one or more of these four accounts.

You should also try to recognise each item as an 'income or expense item' or a 'closing balance sheet item'.

It may be necessary to calculate an amount for withdrawals on account and an amount for long-term asset depreciation.

Step 5 Look for the balancing figures in your accounts. In particular you might be looking for a value for credit sales, cash sales, purchases, the cost of goods sold, the cost of goods stolen or destroyed, or the closing bank balance. Calculate these missing figures, and make any necessary double entry (eg to the trading account from trade accounts payable for purchases, to the trading account from the cash book for cash sales, and to the trading account from trade accounts receivable for credit sales).

Step 6 Now complete the income statement and balance sheet. Working T-accounts might be needed where there are accruals or prepayments.

Remember

> The business equation [Profit = increase in net assets − capital introduced + drawings] may be useful as a check on the profit figure or to calculate it in a MCQ.

An example will illustrate this approach.

11.1 Example: An incomplete records problem

John Snow is the sole distribution agent in the Branton area for Diamond floor tiles. Under an agreement with the manufacturers, John Snow purchases the Diamond floor tiles at a trade discount of 20% off list price and annually in May receives an agency commission of 1% of his purchases for the year ended on the previous 31 March.

For several years, John Snow has obtained a gross profit of 40% on all sales. In a burglary in January 20X1 John Snow lost inventory costing $4,000 as well as many of his accounting records. However, after careful investigations, the following information has been obtained covering the year ended 31 March 20X1.

(a) Assets and liabilities at 31 March 20X0 were as follows.

		$
Buildings:	at cost	10,000
	accumulated depreciation	6,000
Motor vehicles:	at cost	5,000
	accumulated depreciation	2,000
Inventory: at cost		3,200
Trade accounts receivable (for sales)		6,300
Agency commission due		300
Prepayments (trade expenses)		120
Balance at bank		4,310
Trade accounts payable		4,200
Accrued vehicle expenses		230

(b) John Snow has been notified that he will receive an agency commission of $440 on 1 May 20X1.

(c) Inventory, at cost, at 31 March 20X1 was valued at an amount $3,000 more than a year previously.

(d) In October 20X0 inventory costing $1,000 was damaged by dampness and had to be scrapped as worthless.

PART E FINANCIAL STATEMENTS

(e) Trade accounts payable at 31 March 20X1 related entirely to goods received whose list prices totalled $9,500.

(f) Discounts allowed amounted to $1,620 whilst discounts received were $1,200.

(g) Trade expenses prepaid at 31 March 20X1 totalled $80.

(h) Vehicle expenses for the year ended 31 March 20X1 amounted to $7,020.

(i) Trade accounts receivable (for sales) at 31 March 20X1 were $6,700.

(j) All receipts are passed through the bank account.

(k) Depreciation is charged annually at the following rates.

Buildings 5% on cost
Motor vehicles 20% on cost.

(l) Commissions received are paid directly to the bank account.

(m) In addition to the payments for purchases, the bank payments were:

	$
Vehicle expenses	6,720
Drawings	4,300
Trade expenses	7,360

(n) John Snow is not insured against loss of inventory owing to burglary or damage to inventory caused by damp.

Required

Prepare John Snow's income statement for the year ended 31 March 20X1 and a balance sheet on that date.

11.2 Discussion and solution

This is an incomplete records problem because we are told that John Snow has lost many of his accounting records. In particular we do not know sales for the year, purchases during the year, or all the cash receipts and payments.

The first step is to find the opening balance sheet, if possible. In this case, it is. The proprietor's capital is the balancing figure.

JOHN SNOW
BALANCE SHEET AS AT 31 MARCH 20X0

		$	$
Assets			
Non-current assets			
Buildings: cost		10,000	
accumulated deprecation		6,000	
			4,000
Motor vehicles: cost		5,000	
accumulated depreciation		2,000	
			3,000
Current assets			
Inventory		3,200	
Trade accounts receivable		6,300	
Commission due		300	
Prepayments		120	
Balance of cash at hand		4,310	
			14,230
Total assets			21,230

17: INCOMPLETE RECORDS

Capital and liabilities
Proprietor's capital (balance) 16,800
Current liabilities
  Trade payables 4,200
  Accrued expenses 230
                                                                                                      4,430
Total capital and liabilities 21,230

The next step is to open up an income and expense account, cash book, trade receivables account and trade payables account and to insert the opening balances, if known. Cash sales and payments in cash are not a feature of the problem, and so a single column cash book is sufficient.

The problem should then be read line by line, identifying any transactions affecting those accounts.

I & E ACCOUNT

	$	$
Sales (note (f))		60,000
Opening inventory	3,200	
Purchases (note (a))	44,000	
	47,200	
Less: damaged inventory written off (note (c))	(1,000)	
inventory stolen (note (e))	(4,000)	
	42,200	
Less closing inventory (note (b))	(6,200)	
Cost of goods sold		36,000
Gross profit (note (f))		24,000

CASH BOOK

	$		$
Opening balance	4,310	Trade accounts payable	
Trade accounts receivable (see below)	57,980	(see trade accounts payable)	39,400
Agency commission (note (g))	300	Trade expenses	7,360
		Vehicle expenses	6,720
		Drawings	4,300
		Balance c/f	4,810
	62,590		62,590

TRADE ACCOUNTS RECEIVABLE

	$		$
Opening balance b/f	6,300	Discounts allowed (note (d))	1,620
Sales (note (f))	60,000	Cash received (balancing figure)	57,980
		Closing balance c/f	6,700
	66,300		66,300

TRADE ACCOUNTS PAYABLE

	$		$
Discounts received (note (d))	1,200	Opening balance b/f	4,200
Cash paid (balancing figure)	39,400	Purchases (note (a))	44,000
Closing balance c/f	7,600		
	48,200		48,200

VEHICLE EXPENSES

	$		$
Cash	6,720	Accrual b/f	230
Accrual c/f (balancing figure)	530	I & E account	7,020
	7,250		7,250

PART E FINANCIAL STATEMENTS

The trading account is complete already, but now the income statement and balance sheet can be prepared. Remember not to forget items such as the inventory losses, commission earned on purchases, discounts allowed and discounts received.

JOHN SNOW
INCOME STATEMENT FOR THE YEAR ENDED 31 MARCH 20X1

	$	$
Sales (note (f))		60,000
Opening stock	3,200	
Purchases (note (a))	44,000	
	47,200	
Less: damaged inventory written off (note (c))	(1,000)	
inventory stolen	(4,000)	
	42,200	
Less closing inventory (note (b))	6,200	
Cost of goods sold		36,000
Gross profit (note (f))		24,000
Add: commission on purchases		440
discounts received		1,200
		25,640
Expenses		
Trade expenses (note (h))	7,400	
Inventory damaged	1,000	
Inventory stolen	4,000	
Vehicle expenses	7,020	
Discounts allowed	1,620	
Depreciation		
Buildings	500	
Motor vehicles	1,000	
		22,540
Net profit (to capital account)		3,100

JOHN SNOW
BALANCE SHEET AS AT 31 MARCH 20X1

		$	$
Assets			
Non-current assets			
Buildings:	cost	10,000	
	accumulated depreciation	6,500	
			3,500
Motor vehicles:	cost	5,000	
	accumulated depreciation	3,000	
			2,000
Current assets			
Inventory		6,200	
Trade accounts receivable		6,700	
Commission due		440	
Prepayments (trade expenses)		80	
Balance at bank		4,810	
			18,230
Total assets			23,730

	$	$
Capital and liabilities		
Proprietor's capital		
As at 31 March 20X0	16,800	
Net profit for year to 31 March 20X0	3,100	
Less drawings	(4,300)	
As at 31 March 20X0		15,600
Current liabilities		
Trade accounts payable	7,600	
Accrued expenses	530	
		8,130
Total capital and liabilities		23,730

Notes

(a) The agency commission due on 1 May 20X1 indicates that purchases for the year to 31 March 20X1 were:

100%/1% × $440 = $44,000

(b) Closing inventory at cost on 31 March 20X1 was $(3,200 + 3,000) = $6,200.

(c) Inventory scrapped ($1,000) is accounted for by:

  CREDIT   Cost of sales
  DEBIT   I & E account

(d) Discounts allowed are accounted for by:

  DEBIT   Discounts allowed account
  CREDIT   Trade accounts receivable

Similarly, discounts received are:

  DEBIT   Trade accounts payable
  CREDIT   Discounts received

Note. Discounts received represents settlement discounts, not *trade* discounts, which are not usually accounted for as they are given automatically at source.

(e) Inventory lost in the burglary is accounted for by:

  CREDIT   Cost of sales
  DEBIT   I & E account

(f) The trade discount of 20% has already been deducted in arriving at the value of the purchases. The gross profit is 40% on sales, so with cost of sales = $36,000

		$
Cost	(60%)	36,000
Profit	(40%)	24,000
Sales	(100%)	60,000

(It is assumed that trade expenses are not included in the cost of sales, and so should be ignored in this calculation.)

(g) The agency commission of $300 due on 1 May 20X0 would have been paid to John Snow at that date.

(h) The I & E account expenditure for trade expenses and closing balance on vehicle expenses account are as follows.

TRADE EXPENSES

	$		$
Prepayment	120	I & E account (balancing figure)	7,400
Cash	7,360	Prepayment c/f	80
	7,480		7,480

11.3 Using trade accounts receivable to calculate both cash sales and credit sales

A final point which needs to be considered is how a missing value can be found for cash sales and credit sales, when a business has both, but takings banked by the business are not divided between takings from cash sales and takings from credit sales.

11.4 Example: Using trade accounts receivable

Suppose, for example, that a business had, on 1 January 20X8, trade accounts receivable of $2,000, cash in the bank of $3,000, and cash in hand of $300.

During the year to 31 December 20X8 the business banked $95,000 in takings.

It also paid out the following expenses in cash from the till:

Drawings	$1,200
Sundry expenses	$800

On 29 August 20X8 a thief broke into the shop and stole $400 from the till.

At 31 December 20X8 trade accounts receivable amounted to $3,500, cash in the bank $2,500 and cash in the till $150.

What was the value of sales during the year?

Solution

If we tried to prepare a trade accounts receivable account and a two column cash book, we would have insufficient information, in particular about whether the takings which were banked related to cash sales or credit sales.

TRADE ACCOUNTS RECEIVABLE

	$		$
Balance b/f	2,000	Cash from receivables (credit sales)	Unknown
Credit sales	Unknown	Balance c/f	3,500

CASH BOOK

	Cash	Bank		Cash	Bank
	$	$		$	$
Balance b/f	300	3,000	Drawings	1,200	
			Sundry expenses	800	
Cash from receivables		Unknown	Cash stolen	400	
Cash sales	Unknown		Balance c/f	150	2,500

All we do know is that the combined sums from trade accounts receivable and cash takings banked is $95,000.

The value of sales can be found instead by using the trade receivables account, which should be used to record cash takings banked as well as payments from receivables. The balancing figure in the receivables account will then be a combination of credit sales and some cash sales. The cash book only needs to be a single column.

TRADE ACCOUNTS RECEIVABLE

	$		$
Balance b/f	2,000	Cash banked	95,000
Sales: to trading account	96,500	Balance c/f	3,500
	98,500		98,500

CASH (EXTRACT)

	$		$
Balance in hand b/f	300	*Payments in cash*	
Balance in bank c/f	3,000	Drawings	1,200
Trade receivables a/c	95,000	Expenses	800
		Other payments	?
		Cash stolen	400
		Balance in hand c/f	150
		Balance in bank c/f	2,500

The remaining 'undiscovered' amount of cash sales is now found as follows.

	$	$
Payments in cash out of the till		
Drawings	1,200	
Expenses	800	
		2,000
Cash stolen		400
Closing balance of cash in hand		150
		2,550
Less opening balance of cash in hand		(300)
Further cash sales		2,250

(This calculation is similar to the one described above for calculating cash sales.)

Total sales for the year are:

	$
From trade receivables	96,500
From cash book	2,250
Total sales	98,750

Question

Incomplete records

Mary Grimes, wholesale fruit and vegetable merchant, does not keep a full set of accounting records. However, the following information has been produced from the business's records.

(a) *Summary of the bank account for the year ended 31 August 20X8*

	$		$
1 Sept 20X7 balance b/f	1,970	Payments to suppliers	72,000
Cash from trade receivables	96,000	Purchase of motor van (E471 KBR)	13,000
Sale of private yacht	20,000	Rent and local taxes	2,600
Sale of motor van (A123 BWA)	2,100	Wages	15,100
		Motor vehicle expenses	3,350
		Postages and stationery	1,360
		Drawings	9,200
		Repairs and renewals	650
		Insurances	800
		31 August 20X8 balance c/f	2,010
	120,070		120,070
1 Sept 20X8 balance b/f	2,010		

PART E FINANCIAL STATEMENTS

(b) Assets and liabilities, other than balance at bank

	1 Sept 20X7 $	31 Aug 20X8 $
Trade accounts payable	4,700	2,590
Trade accounts receivable	7,320	9,500
Rent and local taxes accrued	200	260
Motor vans:		
A123 BWA: At cost	10,000	–
Accumulated depreciation	8,000	–
E471 KBR: At cost	–	13,000
Accumulated depreciation	–	To be determined
Inventory	4,900	5,900
Insurance prepaid	160	200

(c) All receipts are banked and all payments are made from the business bank account.

(d) A trade debt of $300 owing by John Blunt and included in the trade accounts receivable at 31 August 20X8 (see (b) above), is to be written off as an irrecoverable debt.

(e) It is Mary Grimes' policy to provide depreciation at the rate of 20% on the cost of motor vans held at the end of each financial year; no depreciation is provided in the year of sale or disposal of a motor van.

(f) Discounts received during the year ended 31 August 20X8 from trade accounts payable amounted to $1,100.

Required

(a) Prepare Mary Grimes' income statement for the year ended 31 August 20X8.
(b) Prepare Mary Grimes' balance sheet as at 31 August 20X8.

Answer

(a) INCOME STATEMENT
FOR THE YEAR ENDED 31 AUGUST 20X8

	$	$
Sales (W1)		98,180
Opening inventory	4,900	
Purchases (W2)	70,990	
	75,890	
Less closing inventory	5,900	
		69,990
Gross profit		28,190
Discounts received		1,100
Profit on sale of motor vehicle ($2,100 – $(10,000 – 8,000))		100
		29,390
Rent and local taxes (W3)	2,660	
Wages	15,100	
Motor vehicle expenses	3,350	
Postages and stationery	1,360	
Repairs and renewals	650	
Insurances (W4)	760	
Irrecoverable debt	300	
Depreciation of van (20% × $13,000)	2,600	
		26,780
		2,610

(b) BALANCE SHEET AS AT 31 AUGUST 20X8

	$	$
Assets		
Non-current assets		
Motor van: cost	13,000	
Depreciation	2,600	
		10,400
Current assets		
Inventory	5,900	
Trade accounts receivable ($9,500 – $300 irrecoverable debt)	9,200	
Prepayment	200	
Cash at bank	2,010	
		17,310
Total assets		27,710
Capital and liabilities		
Capital account		
Balance at 1 September 20X7 (W5)	11,450	
Additional capital: proceeds on sale of yacht	20,000	
Net profit for the year	2,610	
Less drawings	(9,200)	
Balance at 31 August 20X8		24,860
Current liabilities		
Trade accounts payable	2,590	
Accrual	260	
		2,850
Total capital and liabilities		27,710

Workings

1 Sales

	$
Cash received from customers	96,000
Add trade accounts receivable at 31 August 20X8	9,500
	105,500
Less trade accounts receivable at 1 September 20X7	7,320
Sales in year	98,180

2 Purchases

	$	$
Payments to suppliers		72,000
Add: trade accounts payable at 31 August 20X8	2,590	
discounts granted by suppliers	1,100	
		3,690
		75,690
Less trade accounts payable at 1 September 20X7		4,700
		70,990

3 Rent and local taxes

	$
Cash paid in year	2,600
Add accrual at 31 August 20X8	260
	2,860
Less accrual at 1 September 20X7	200
Charge for the year	2,660

PART E FINANCIAL STATEMENTS

4   Insurances

	$
Cash paid in year	800
Add prepayment at 1 September 20X7	160
	960
Less prepayment at 31 August 20X8	200
	760

Workings 1-4 could also be presented in ledger account format as follows.

TRADE ACCOUNTS RECEIVABLE

	$		$
Balance b/f	7,320	Bank	96,000
∴ Sales	98,180	Balance c/f	9,500
	105,500		105,500

TRADE ACCOUNTS PAYABLE

	$		$
Bank	72,000	Balance b/f	4,700
Discounts received	1,100	∴ Purchases	70,990
Balance c/f	2,590		
	75,690		75,690

RENT AND LOCAL TAXES

	$		$
Bank	2,600	Balance b/f	200
Balance c/f	260	∴ I & E charge	2,660
	2,860		2,860

INSURANCES

	$		$
Balance b/f	160	∴ I & E charge	760
Bank	800	Balance c/f	200
	960		960

5   Capital at 1 September 20X7

	$	$
Assets		
Bank balance		1,970
Trade accounts receivable		7,320
Motor van $(10,000 – 8,000)		2,000
Inventory		4,900
Prepayment		160
		16,350
Liabilities		
Trade accounts payable	4,700	
Accrual	200	
		4,900
		11,450

Chapter Roundup

- **Incomplete records** questions may test your ability to prepare accounts in the following situations.
    - A trader **does not maintain a ledger** and therefore has no continuous double entry record of transactions.
    - Accounting records are **destroyed** by accident, such as fire.
    - Some essential figure is **unknown** and must be calculated as a balancing figure. This may occur as a result of inventory being damaged or destroyed, or because of misappropriation of assets.
- The approach to incomplete records questions is to build up the information given so as to complete the necessary **double entry**. This may involve reconstructing **control accounts** for:
    - cash and bank (often in columnar format);
    - trade accounts receivable and payable.
- Where inventory, sales or purchases is the unknown figure it will be necessary to use information on **gross profit percentages** so as to construct a working for gross profit in which the unknown figure can be inserted as a balance.
- The construction of a cashbook, largely from bank statements, showing receipts and payments during the period, is often an important feature of incomplete records problems.
- **Drawings** often feature as the missing item in an incomplete records problem. The trader has been drawing money but does not know how much.
- Where no trading records have been kept, profit can be derived from opening and closing net assets by use of the **business equation**.

Quick Quiz

1. In the absence of a sales account or sales day book, how can a figure of sales for the year be computed?
2. In the absence of a purchase account or purchases day book, how can a figure of purchases for the year be computed?
3. What is the difference between 'mark-up' and 'gross profit percentage'?
4. What is the accounting double entry to record the loss of inventory by fire or burglary?
5. In what circumstances is a two-column cash book useful?
6. If a business proprietor pays his personal income into the business bank account, what is the accounting double entry to record the transaction?

PART E FINANCIAL STATEMENTS

Answers to Quick Quiz

1 By using the trade accounts receivable control account to calculate sales as a balancing figure.

2 By using the trade accounts payable control account to calculate purchases as a balancing figure.

3
- Mark-up is the profit as a percentage of cost.
- Gross profit percentage is the profit as a percentage of sales.

4 DEBIT   I & E a/c
   CREDIT   Cost of sales

   Assuming that the goods were not insured.

5 Where a large amount of receipts and payments are made in cash.

6 DEBIT   Cash
   CREDIT   Drawings

Now try the questions below from the Exam Question Bank

Number	Level	Marks	Time
Q23	Introductory	n/a	36 mins
Q24	Introductory	n/a	45 mins

Partnership accounts

Topic list	Syllabus reference
1 The characteristics of partnerships	5(d)(ii)
2 Preparing partnership accounts	5(d)(ii)

Introduction

So far we have considered businesses owned by one person: sole traders. Now we will consider how we can account for businesses owned by more than one person. This chapter will examine how we can account for partnerships and the next chapter will examine how we can account for companies.

Study guide

Sections 12-13 – Partnership accounts

- Define the circumstances creating a partnership.
- Explain the advantages and disadvantages of operating as a partnership, compared with operating as a sole trader or limited liability company.
- Explain the typical contents of a partnership agreement, including profit-sharing terms.
- Explain the accounting differences between partnerships and sole traders.
    - Capital accounts
    - Current accounts
    - Division of profits
- Explain and illustrate how to record partner's shares of profits/losses and their drawings in the accounting records and financial statements.
- Explain and illustrate how to account for guaranteed minimum profit share.
- Explain and illustrate how to account for interest on drawings.
- Draft the income statement, including division of profit, and balance sheet of a partnership from a given trial balance.

Exam guide

This is an important topic and it is almost certain to appear in the exam.

1 The characteristics of partnerships

Try this exercise to get you thinking.

Question — Partnership

Try to think of reasons why a business should be conducted as a partnership, rather than:

(a) as a sole trader.
(b) as a limited liability company.

Answer

(a) The main problems with trading as a sole trader is the limitation on resources it implies. As the business grows, there will be a need for the following.

   (i) **Additional capital:** although some capital may be provided by a bank, it would not be desirable to have the business entirely dependent on borrowing.

   (ii) **Additional expertise:** a sole trader technically competent in his own field may not have, for example, the financial skills that would be needed in a larger business.

   (iii) **Additional management time:** once a business grows to a certain point, it becomes impossible for one person to look after all aspects of it without help.

(b) The main **disadvantage** of incorporating is the **regulatory burden** faced by limited liability companies in most countries. In addition, there are certain 'businesses' which are not allowed to enjoy limited liability; you may have read about the Lloyd's 'names' who face personal bankruptcy because the option of limited liability was not available to them.

There are also tax factors to consider, but these are beyond the scope of this book.

Key term

> **Partnership** can be defined as the relationship which exists between persons carrying on a business in common with a view of profit.

In other words, a partnership is an arrangement between two or more individuals in which they undertake to share the risks and rewards of a joint business operation.

It is usual for a partnership to be established formally by means of a *partnership agreement*. However, if individuals act as though they are in partnership even if no written agreement exists, then it will be presumed that a partnership does exist and that its terms of agreement are reflected in the way the partners conduct the business, ie the way profits have been divided in the past, etc. In some countries legislation may exist which governs partnerships.

1.1 The partnership agreement

FAST FORWARD

> The terms under which the partnership operates are set out in the **partnership agreement**. The initial capital put into the business by each partner is shown by means of a **capital account** for each partner. The net profit of the partnership is **appropriated** by the partners according to a previously agreed ratio. Each partner also has a current account to which their drawings are charged. Partners may be charged **interest on their drawings** and may receive **interest on capital**.

The partnership agreement is a written agreement in which the terms of the partnership are set out, and in particular the financial arrangements as between partners. The items it should cover include the following.

(a) **Capital**. Each partner puts in a share of the business capital. If there is to be an agreement on how much each partner should put in and keep in the business, as a minimum fixed amount, this should be stated.

(b) **Profit-sharing ratio**. Partners can agree to share profits in any way they choose. For example, if there are three partners in a business, they might agree to share profits equally but on the other hand, if one partner does a greater share of the work, or has more experience and ability, or puts in more capital, the ratio of profit sharing might be different.

(c) **Interest on capital**. Partners might agree to pay themselves interest on the capital they put into the business. If they do so, the agreement will state what rate of interest is to be applied.

(d) **Partners' salaries**. Partners might also agree to pay themselves salaries. These are not salaries in the same way that an employee of the business will be paid a wage or salary, because partners' salaries are an appropriation of profit, and not an expense in the income statement of the business. The purpose of paying salaries is to give each partner a satisfactory basic income before the residual profits are shared out.

(e) **Drawings.** Partners may draw out their share of profits from the business. However, they might agree to put a limit on how much they should draw out in any period. If so, this limit should be specified in the partnership agreement. To encourage partners to delay making withdrawals from the business until the financial year has ended, the agreement might also be that partners should be charged interest on their drawings during the year.

1.2 Example: Partners' salaries and profit-sharing

Bill and Ben are partners sharing profit in the ratio 2:1 and that they agree to pay themselves a salary of $10,000 each. If profits before deducting salaries are $26,000, how much income would each partner receive?

Solution

First, the two salaries are deducted from profit, leaving $6,000 ($26,000 – $20,000).

This $6,000 has to be distributed between Bill and Ben in the ratio 2:1. In other words, Bill will receive twice as much as Ben. You can probably work this out in your head and see that Bill will get $4,000 and Ben $2,000, but we had better see how this is calculated properly.

Add the 'parts' of the ratio together. For our example, 2 + 1 = 3. Divide this total into whatever it is that has to be shared out. In our example, $6,000 ÷ 3 = $2,000. Each 'part' is worth $2,000, so Bill receives 2 × $2,000 = $4,000 and Ben will receive 1 × $2,000 = $2,000.

So the final answer to the question is that Bill receives his salary plus $4,000 and Ben his salary plus $2,000. This could be laid out as follows:

	Bill $	Ben $	Total $
Salary	10,000	10,000	20,000
Share of residual profits (ratio 2:1)	4,000	2,000	6,000
	14,000	12,000	26,000

Question
Profitshare

Suppose Tom, Dick and Harry want to share out $150 in the ratio 7:3:5. How much would each get?

Answer

The sum of the ratio 'parts' is 7 + 3 + 5 = 15. Each part is therefore worth $150 ÷ 15 = $10. So the $150 would be shared as follows.

			$
(a)	Tom:	7 × $10 =	70
(b)	Dick:	3 × $10 =	30
(c)	Harry:	5 × $10 =	50
			150

1.3 Advantages and disadvantages of trading as a partnership

Operating as a partnership entails certain advantages and disadvantages when compared with both sole traders and limited liability companies.

1.3.1 Partnership v sole trader

The advantages of operating as a partnership rather than as a sole trader are practical rather than legal. They include the following.

(a) Risks are spread across a larger number of people.
(b) The trader will have access to a wider network of contacts through the other partners.
(c) Partners should bring to the business not only capital but skills and experience.
(d) It may well be easier to raise finance from external sources such as banks.

Possible disadvantages include the following.

(a) While the risk is spread over a larger number of people, so are the profits!
(b) By bringing in more people the former sole trader dilutes control over his business.
(c) There may be disputes between the partners.

1.3.2 Partnership v limited liability company

Limited liability companies (covered in detail in the next chapter) offer limited liability to their owners. This means that the maximum amount that an owner stands to lose in the event that the company becomes insolvent and must pay off its debts is the capital in the business. In the case of partnerships (and sole traders), liability for the debts of the business is unlimited, which means that if the business runs up debts and is unable to pay, the proprietors will become personally liable for the unpaid debts and would be required, if necessary, to sell their private possessions in order to pay for them.

Limited liability is clearly a significant incentive for a partnership to incorporate (become a company). Other advantages of incorporation are that it is easier to raise capital and that the retirement or death of one of its members does not necessitate dissolution and re-formation of the firm.

In practice, however, particularly for small firms, these advantages are more apparent than real. Banks will normally seek personal guarantees from shareholders before making loans or granting an overdraft facility and so the advantage of limited liability is lost to a small owner managed business.

In addition, a company faces a greater administrative and financial burden.

(a) Compliance with national company legislation, notably in having to prepare annual accounts and have them audited, file annual returns and keep statutory books.
(b) Compliance with national accounting standards and/or IASs.
(c) Formation and annual registration costs.

2 Preparing partnership accounts

FAST FORWARD

If a partner makes a **loan** to the business, he will receive interest on it in the normal way. Loan interest due, interest on capital and partners salaries are deducted and the remaining net profit is apportioned according to the profit sharing ratio.

2.1 How does accounting for partnerships differ from accounting for sole traders?

Partnership accounts are identical in many respects to the accounts of sole traders.

(a) The assets of a partnership are like the assets of any other business, and are accounted for in the same way. The assets side of a partnership balance sheet is no different from what has been shown in earlier chapters of this Study Text.

(b) The net profit of a partnership is calculated in the same way as the net profit of a sole trader. The only minor difference is that if a partner makes a loan to the business (as distinct from capital contribution) then interest on the loan will be an expense in the income statement, in the same way as interest on any other loan from a person or organisation who is not a partner. We will return to partner loans later in the chapter.

There are two respects in which partnership accounts are different, however.

(a) The funds put into the business by each partner are shown differently.

(b) The net profit must be **appropriated** by the partners, ie shared out according to the partnership agreement. This appropriation of profits must be shown in the partnership accounts.

Key term

> **Appropriation of profit** means sharing out profits in accordance with the partnership agreement.

2.2 Funds employed

When a partnership is formed, each partner puts in some capital to the business. These initial capital contributions are recorded in a series of *capital accounts*, one for each partner. (Since each partner is ultimately entitled to repayment of his capital it is clearly vital to keep a record of how much is owed to whom.) The precise amount of initial capital contributed by each partner is a matter for general agreement and there is no question of each partner necessarily contributing the same amount, although this does sometimes happen.

Important!

> The balance for the capital account will always be a brought forward credit entry in the partnership accounts, because the capital contributed by proprietors is a liability of the business.

In addition to a capital account, each partner normally has the following accounts.

(a) A **current account**
(b) A **withdrawals account**

Key term

> A **current account** is used to record the **profits retained in the business** by the partner.

The current account is a sort of capital account, which increases in value when the partnership makes profits, and falls in value when the partner whose current account it is makes drawings out of the business.

The main differences between the capital and current account in accounting for partnerships are as follows.

(a) (i) The balance on the capital account remains static from year to year (with one or two exceptions).

(ii) The current account is continually fluctuating up and down, as the partnership makes profits which are shared out between the partners, and as each partner makes drawings.

(b) A further difference is that when the partnership agreement provides for interest on capital, partners receive interest on the balance in their capital account, but *not on the balance in their current account*.

The drawings accounts serve exactly the same purpose as the drawings account for a sole trader. Each partner's drawings are recorded in a separate account. At the end of an accounting period, each partner's drawings are cleared to his current account.

DEBIT   Current account of partner
CREDIT   Drawings account of partner

(If the amount of the drawings exceeds the balance on a partner's current account, the current account will show a debit balance. However, in normal circumstances, we should expect to find a credit balance on the current accounts.)

The partnership balance sheet will therefore consist of:

(a) the capital accounts of each partner; and
(b) the current accounts of each partner, net of drawings.

This will be illustrated in an example later.

2.3 Loans by partners

In addition, it is sometimes the case that an existing or previous partner will make a loan to the partnership in which case he becomes a creditor of the partnership. On the balance sheet, such a loan is not included as partners' funds, but is shown separately as a long-term liability (unless repayable within twelve months in which case it is a current liability). This is the case whether or not the loan creditor is also an existing partner.

However, **interest on such loans will be credited to the partner's current account**. This is administratively more convenient, especially when the partner does not particularly want to be paid the loan interest in cash immediately it becomes due. You should bear in mind the following.

- (a) Interest on loans from a partner is accounted for as an expense in the income statement, and not as an appropriation of profit, even though the interest is added to the current account of the partners.
- (b) If there is no interest rate specified, national legislation *may* provide for interest to be paid at a specified percentage on loans by partners.

2.4 Appropriation of net profits

The net profit of a partnership is shared out between them according to the terms of their agreement. This sharing out is shown in an **appropriation account**, which follows on from the income statement.

The accounting entries are:

- (a) DEBIT   Income and expense account with net profit c/d
  CREDIT   Appropriation account with net profit b/d
- (b) DEBIT   Appropriation account
  CREDIT   Current accounts of each partner

with an individual share of profits for each partner.

The way in which profit is shared out depends on the terms of the partnership agreement. The steps to take are as follows.

- (a) Establish how much the net profit is.
- (b) Appropriate interest on capital and salaries first. Both of these items are an appropriation of profit and are not expenses in the income statement.
- (c) If partners agree to pay interest on their drawings during the year:

  DEBIT   Current accounts
  CREDIT   Appropriation of profit account

- (d) *Residual profits*: the difference between net profits (plus any interest charged on drawings) and appropriations for interest on capital and salaries is the residual profit. This is shared out between partners in the profit-sharing ratio.
- (e) Each partner's share of profits is credited to his current account.
- (f) The balance on each partner's drawings account is debited to his current account.

In practice each partner's capital account will occupy a separate ledger account, as will his current account etc. The examples which follow in this text use the columnar form; they might also ignore the breakdown of net assets employed (non-current assets, current assets, etc) to help to clarify and simplify the illustrations.

2.4.1 Guaranteed minimum profit share

The partnership agreement may provide that one partner has a guaranteed minimum profit share.

Example:

Tony, John and Gordon are in business sharing profits 4:3:3 after allowing salaries of $30,000 for Tony and John. Tony also has a guaranteed minimum profit share of $120,000. Profit for the year is $260,000. Show the appropriation.

Solution

	Tony $	John $	Gordon $	Total $
Salaries	30,000	30,000	–	60,000
Residual profit share	80,000	60,000	60,000	200,000
4:3:3	110,000	90,000	60,000	260,000
Adjustment to allow for guaranteed minimum profit share	10,000	(5,000)	(5,000)	–
	120,000	85,000	55,000	260,000

> **Exam focus point**
>
> For examination purposes it is customary to represent the details of these accounts side by side, in columnar form, to save time.

2.5 Example: Partnership accounts

Locke, Niece and Munster are in partnership with an agreement to share profits in the ratio 3:2:1. They also agree the following terms.

(a) All three should receive interest at 12% on capital.
(b) Munster should receive a salary of $6,000 per annum.
(c) Interest will be charged on drawings at the rate of 5% (charged on the end of year drawings balances).
(d) The interest rate on the loan by Locke is 5%.

The balance sheet of the partnership as at 31 December 20X5 revealed the following.

	$	$
Capital accounts		
Locke	20,000	
Niece	8,000	
Munster	6,000	
		34,000
Current accounts		
Locke	3,500	
Niece	(700)	
Munster	1,800	
		4,600
Loan account (Locke)		6,000
Capital employed to finance net long-term assets and working capital		44,600

Drawings made during the year to 31 December 20X6 were as follows.

	$
Locke	6,000
Niece	4,000
Munster	7,000

18: PARTNERSHIP ACCOUNTS

The net profit for the year to 31 December 20X6 was $24,530 before deducting loan interest.

Required

Prepare the appropriation account for the year to 31 December 20X6, and the partners' capital accounts, and current accounts.

Solution

The interest payable by each partner on their drawings during the year is:

		$
Locke	5% of $6,000	300
Niece	5% of $4,000	200
Munster	5% of $7,000	350
		850

These payments are debited to the current accounts and credited to the *appropriation* account.

The interest payable to Locke on his loan is:

5% of $6,000 = $300

We can now begin to work out the appropriation of profits.

		$	$
Net profit, less loan interest (deducted in I & E a/c $24,530 – $300)			24,230
Add interest on drawings			850
			25,080
Less Munster salary			6,000
			19,080
Less interest on capital			
Locke	(12% of $20,000)	2,400	
Niece	(12% of $ 8,000)	960	
Munster	(12% of $ 6,000)	720	
			4,080
			15,000
Residual profits			
Locke	(3)	7,500	
Niece	(2)	5,000	
Munster	(1)	2,500	
			15,000

Make sure you remember what the various interest figures represent and that you understand exactly what has been calculated here.

(a) The partners can take drawings out of the business, but if they do they will be charged interest on it.

(b) The partners have capital tied up in the business (of course, otherwise there would be no business) and they have agreed to pay themselves interest on whatever capital each has put in.

(c) Once all the necessary adjustments have been made to net profit, $15,000 remains and is divided up between the partners in the ratio 3:2:1.

Now the financial statements for the partnership can be prepared.

PART E FINANCIAL STATEMENTS

LOCKE NIECE MUNSTER
APPROPRIATION ACCOUNT
FOR THE YEAR ENDED 31 DECEMBER 20X6

	$	$		$	$
			Net profit b/d		24,230
Salaries: Munster		6,000	Interest on drawings		
Interest on capital			Locke	300	
Locke	2,400		Niece	200	
Niece	960		Munster	350	
Munster	720				850
		4,080			
Residual profits					
Locke	7,500				
Niece	5,000				
Munster	2,500				
		15,000			
		25,080			25,080

PARTNERS' CURRENT ACCOUNTS

	Locke	Niece	Munster		Locke	Niece	Munster
	$	$	$		$	$	$
Balance b/f		700		Balance b/f	3,500		1,800
Interest on drawings	300	200	350	Loan interest	300		
Drawings	6,000	4,000	7,000	Interest on capital	2,400	960	720
Balance c/f	7,400	1,060	3,670	Salary			6,000
				Residual profits	7,500	5,000	2,500
	13,700	5,960	11,020		13,700	5,960	11,020
				Balance b/f	7,400	1,060	3,670

PARTNERS' CAPITAL ACCOUNTS

		Locke	Niece	Munster
		$	$	$
	Balance b/f	20,000	8,000	6,000

The balance sheet of the partners as at 31 December 20X6 would be as follows.

	$	$
Capital accounts		
Locke	20,000	
Niece	8,000	
Munster	6,000	
		34,000
Current accounts		
Locke	7,400	
Niece	1,060	
Munster	3,670	
		12,130
Loan account (Locke)		6,000
		52,130
Net assets		
As at 31 December 20X5		44,600
Added during the year (applying the business equation, this is the difference between net profits and drawings = $24,230 − $17,000)		7,230
Add loan interest added to Locke's current account and not paid out		300
As at 31 December 20X6		52,130

Again, make sure you understand what has happened here.

(a) The partners' *capital* accounts have not changed. They were brought forward at $20,000, $8,000 and $6,000, and they are just the same in the new balance sheet.

(b) The partners' *current* accounts have changed. The balances brought forward from last year's balance sheet of $3,500, ($700) and $1,800 have become $7,400, $1,060 and $3,670 in the new balance sheet. How this came about is shown in the partners' current (ledger) accounts.

(c) The events recorded in the current accounts are a reflection of how the partnership has distributed its profit, and this was shown in the appropriation account.

Question — Partnership accounts

Ganatri and Lucifer are in partnership sharing profits and losses in the ratio 7:3 respectively.

The following information has been taken from the partnership records for the financial year ended 31 May 20X9.

Partners' capital account balances:

Ganatri $200,000
Lucifer $140,000

Partners' current accounts, balances as at 1 June 20X8:

Ganatri $15,000 Cr
Lucifer $13,000 Cr

During the year ended 31 May 20X9 the partners made the following withdrawals from the partnership bank account.

Ganatri	$10,000	on 31 August 20X8
	$10,000	on 30 November 20X8
	$10,000	on 28 February 20X9
	$10,000	on 31 May 20X9
Lucifer	$7,000	on 31 August 20X8
	$7,000	on 30 November 20X8
	$7,000	on 28 February 20X9
	$7,000	on 31 May 20X9

Interest is to be charged on drawings at the rate of 12% per annum. Interest is allowed on capital accounts and credit balances on current accounts at the rate of 12% per annum.

Lucifer is to be allowed a salary of $15,000 per annum.

The net profit of the partnership for the year ended 31 May 20X9 is $102,940.

Required

(a) Calculate of the amount of interest chargeable on each partner's drawings for the year ended 31 May 20X9.

(b) Produce the partnership appropriation account for the year ended 31 May 20X9.

(c) Calculate the balance on each partner's current account as at 31 May 20X9.

PART E FINANCIAL STATEMENTS

Answer

(a) *Interest on partners' drawings for the year ended 31 May 20X9*

			$
Ganatri			
31.8.X8	$10,000 \times 12\% \times 9/12$		900
30.11.X8	$10,000 \times 12\% \times 6/12$		600
28.2.X9	$10,000 \times 12\% \times 3/12$		300
			1,800
Lucifer			
31.8.X8	$7,000 \times 12\% \times 9/12$		630
30.11.X8	$7,000 \times 12\% \times 6/12$		420
28.2.X9	$7,000 \times 12\% \times 3/12$		210
			1,260
Total			3,060

(b) GANATRI AND LUCIFER
APPROPRIATION ACCOUNT
FOR THE YEAR ENDED 31 MAY 20X9

	$	$
Net profit b/d		102,940
Add: interest on drawings paid to partnership		3,060
		106,000
Less salary: Lucifer		15,000
Less interest on capital and current accounts		
Ganatri (12% × $215,000)	25,800	
Lucifer (12% × $153,000)	18,360	
		44,160
		46,840
Profit share		
Ganatri (7/10)	32,788	
Lucifer (3/10)	14,052	
		46,840

(c) PARTNERS' CURRENT ACCOUNTS

	Ganatri	Lucifer		Ganatri	Lucifer
	$	$		$	$
Drawings	40,000	28,000	Balances b/d	15,000	13,000
Interest on drawings	1,800	1,260	Salary	–	15,000
Balances c/d	31,788	31,152	Interest on capital		
			and current accounts	25,800	18,360
			Profit share	32,788	14,052
	73,588	60,412		73,588	60,412

2.6 Changes in the partnership

Another aspect to consider is how changes in the partnership will affect the profit sharing arrangements. When a partner retires or a new partner is taken on during the year, the profit for that year will have to be apportioned into the periods before and after the change and the two or more sets of profit sharing arrangements applied. Unless told otherwise, assume that profits were earned evenly throughout the year.

2.7 Example: Profit share

Hook, Line and Sinker have been in partnership for many years, sharing profits in the ratio 3:3:4. On 1 April 20X8 Sinker retires and Hook and Line continue in partnership, sharing the profits equally. On 1 October 20X8, Floater is admitted to the partnership and it is decided that Hook, Line and Floater will now share profits 4:4:2. The net profit for the year to 31 December 20X8 is $150,000. Show how this will be split between the partners.

Solution

There are three distinct periods here – 3 months of Hook, Line and Sinker, 6 months of Hook and Line and 3 months of Hook, Line and Floater. Profits average $12,500 per month. So we apportion as follows:

	Hook	Line	Sinker	Floater	Total
Jan-Mar 20X8					
37,500/3:3:4	11,250	11,250	15,000		37,500
April-Sept 20X8					
75,000/5:5	37,500	37,500	–		75,000
Oct-Dec 20X8					
37,500/4:4:2	15,000	15,000		7,500	37,500
	63,750	63,750	15,000	7,500	150,000

Chapter Roundup

- The terms under which the partnership operates are set out in the **partnership agreement**.
- The initial capital put into the business by each partner is shown by means of a **capital account** for each partner.
- Each partner also has a **current account** to which their drawings are charged.
- The net profit of the partnership is **appropriated** by the partners according to some **previously agreed ratio**.
- Partners may be charged **interest on their drawings**, and may receive interest on capital. If a partner makes a **loan** to the business, he will receive interest on it in the normal way.
- Loan interest due, interest on capital and partners' salaries are deducted and the remaining net profit is apportioned according to the profit sharing ratio.

PART E FINANCIAL STATEMENTS

Quick Quiz

1. What is a partnership?
2. Is a partner's salary an expense of the partnership?
3. Why might a sole trader take on a partner?
4. What is the difference between a partner's capital account and a partner's current account?
5. How is profit shared between partners?
6. A, B and C are in partnership with a profit sharing ratio of 3:2:1. For the year ended 31.12.X9, the partnership profits are $18,000. What is B's share of the profits?

    A $3,000
    B $6,000
    C $9,000
    D $18,000

Answers to Quick Quiz

1. An arrangement between two or more individuals to carry on the risks and rewards of a business together.
2. No. It is an appropriation of profit.
3. See 1.3.
4. The capital account reflects the amount of money invested in the business by each partner. The current account reflects each partner's share of the profits less drawings.
5. According to the terms of the partnership agreements. This may allow interest on capital accounts, charge interest on drawings, allow salaries and then divide the residual profits according to the profit sharing ratio.
6. B. Each 'share' is worth $\frac{\$18,000}{6}$ ($3,000). B's share is, therefore, $6,000.

Now try the questions below from the Exam Question Bank

Number	Level	Marks	Time
Q25	Introductory	n/a	36 mins
Q26	Introductory	n/a	31 mins

Limited liability companies

19

Topic list	Syllabus reference
1 Limited liability and accounting records	5(d)(iii)
2 IAS 1: *Presentation of financial statements*	5(d)(iii)
3 Items in the income statement	5(c)(ii), 5(d)(iii)
4 Items in the balance sheet	4(a), 4(b), 5(c)(i), 5(d)(iii)
5 Shareholders' equity	1(b), 4(d), 5(c)(iv), 5(d)(iii)
6 Bonus and rights issues	4(d), 5(d)(iii)
7 The current/non-current distinction	4(a)-(b), 5(d)(iii)
8 IAS 8 *Accounting policies, changes in accounting estimates and errors*	5(c)(ii), 5(c)(iv), 5(d)(iii)
9 IFRS 5 *Non-current assets held for sale and discontinued operations*	5(d)(iii)
10 Ledger accounts and limited liability companies	5(d)(iii)
11 Company accounts for internal purposes	5(d)(iii)

Introduction

You now come to the point in your studies for Paper 1.1 when you can look at the form and content of the financial statements of **limited liability companies**. Your later financial accounting studies will be concerned almost entirely with company accounts so it is vital that you acquire a sound understanding of the basic concepts now.

We begin this chapter by considering the **status of limited** liability companies and the type of accounting records they maintain in order to prepare financial statements. The financial statements of limited liability companies are usually governed by national legislation and accounting standards. From an international standpoint, however, the **general content** of financial statements is governed by IAS 1 *Presentation of financial statements*. We will look at the standard and explain those items in the financial statements which have not yet appeared in the text.

Introduction (continued)

We will look at another IAS which has a significant impact on the content and form of company accounts, IAS 8 *Accounting policies, changes in accounting estimates and errors*; also an outline of IFRS 5 *Non-current assets held for sale and discontinued operations*.

All these standards are concerned with financial statements produced for external reporting purposes (ie to external users), but companies also produce financial accounts for internal purposes, and we will look at the different approach in preparing accounts for internal rather than external use.

Study guide

Section 15 – Accounting for limited liability companies 1 – basics

- Explain the differences between a sole trader and a limited liability company.
- Explain the advantages and disadvantages of operating as a limited liability company rather than as a sole trader.
- Explain the capital structure of a limited liability company including:
    - Authorised share capital
    - Issued share capital
    - Called up share capital
    - Paid up share capital
    - Ordinary shares
    - Preference shares
    - Loan notes
- Explain and illustrate the share premium account.
- Explain and illustrate the other reserves which may appear in a company balance sheet.
- Explain why the heading retained earnings appears in a company balance sheet.
- Explain and illustrate the recording of dividends.
- Explain the impact of income tax on company profits and illustrate the ledger account required to record it.
- Record income tax in the income statement and balance sheet of a company.
- Draft an income statement and balance sheet for a company for internal purposes.

Section 16 – Recording and presentation of transactions in non-current assets; liabilities and provisions

- Explain the distinction between current and non-current liabilities.
- Explain the difference between liabilities and provisions.
- Explain the requirements of International Accounting Standards as regards current assets and current liabilities.

Section 19, 20 and 21 – Accounting for limited liability companies 2 – Advanced

- Revise the work of Section 15 and the preparation of financial statements for limited liability companies for internal purposes including the treatment of income tax and dividends.
- Revise the work of Section 15 on company capital structure, including equity shares, preference shares and loan notes.
- Outline the advantages and disadvantages of raising finance by borrowing rather than by the issue of ordinary or preference shares.

- Define and illustrate gearing (leverage).
- Define a bonus (capitalisation) issue and its advantages and disadvantages.
- Record a bonus (capitalisation) issue in ledger accounts and show the effect in the balance sheet.
- Define a rights issue and its advantages and disadvantages.
- Record a rights issue in ledger accounts and show the effect in the balance sheet.
- Revise the definition of reserves and the different types of reserves.
- Explain the need for regulation of companies in accounting standards.
- Explain the requirements of International Accounting Standards governing financial statements (excluding group aspects):
    - IAS 1 (Revised) *Presentation of financial statements*:
        - Overall considerations
        - Structure and content
        - Changes in equity
        - Illustrative financial statements
            - Balance sheet
            - Income statement
            - Statement of changes in equity
    - IAS 8 *Accounting policies, changes in accounting estimates and errors*
    - IFRS 5 *Non-current assets held for sale and discontinued operations*
- Explain and prepare the notes to financial statements required for the syllabus:
    - Statements of changes in equity
    - Details of non-current assets
    - Details of events after the balance sheet date
    - Details of contingent liabilities and contingent assets (see Session 18)
    - Details of research and development expenditure
- Prepare financial statements for publication complying with relevant accounting standards as detailed above.

Exam guide

This is the most important topic studied so far. It will form the foundation for all your future studies. You will be examined on it!

For those studying for the Oxford Brookes degree, project topic 7 asks for an analysis of the tax and profit implications of different corporate entities.

1 Limited liability and accounting records

FAST FORWARD

There are some important differences between the accounts of a **limited liability company** and those of sole traders or partnerships.

So far, this Study Text has dealt mainly with the accounts of businesses in general. In this chapter we shall turn our attention to the accounts of limited liability companies. As we should expect, the accounting rules and conventions for recording the business transactions of limited liability companies and then preparing their final accounts are much the same as for sole traders. For example, companies will have a cash book, sales day book, purchase day book, journal, sales ledger, purchase ledger and nominal ledger. They will also prepare an income statement annually and a balance sheet at the end of the accounting year.

There are, however, some **fundamental differences** in the accounts of limited liability companies, of which the following are perhaps the most significant.

(a) The **national legislation** governing the activities of limited liability companies tends to be very extensive. Amongst other things such legislation may define certain minimum accounting records which must be maintained by companies; they may specify that the annual accounts of a company must be filed with a government bureau and so available for public inspection; and they often contain detailed requirements on the minimum information which must be disclosed in a company's accounts. Businesses which are not limited liability companies (non-incorporated businesses) often enjoy comparative freedom from statutory regulation.

(b) The **owners of a company** (its **members** or **shareholders**) may be **very numerous**. Their capital is shown differently from that of a sole trader; and similarly the 'appropriation account' of a company is different.

1.1 Limited liability

Key term

> **Unlimited liability** means that if the business runs up debts that it is unable to pay, the proprietors will become personally liable for the unpaid debts and would be required, if necessary, to sell their private possessions to repay them.

It is worth recapping on the relative **advantages and disadvantages** of limited liability (which we have mentioned in earlier parts of the text). Sole traders and partnerships are, with some significant exceptions, generally fairly small concerns. The amount of capital involved may be modest, and the proprietors of the business usually participate in managing it. Their liability for the debts of the business is unlimited, which means that if the business runs up debts that it is unable to pay, the proprietors will become personally liable for the unpaid debts, and would be required, if necessary, to sell their private possessions in order to repay them. For example, if a sole trader has some capital in his business, but the business now owes $40,000 which it cannot repay, the trader might have to sell his house to raise the money to pay off his business debts.

Limited liability companies offer limited liability to their owners.

Key term

> **Limited liability** means that the maximum amount that an owner stands to lose in the event that the company becomes insolvent and cannot pay off its debts, is his share of the capital in the business.

Thus limited liability is a **major advantage** of turning a business into a limited liability company. However, in practice, banks will normally seek personal guarantees from shareholders before making loans or granting an overdraft facility and so the advantage of limited liability is lost to a small owner managed business.

1.1.1 Disadvantages

(a) Compliance with national legislation
(b) Compliance with national accounting standards and/or IASs
(c) Any formation and annual registration costs

These are needed to avoid the privilege of limited liability being abused.

As a business grows, it needs **more capital** to finance its operations, and significantly more than the people currently managing the business can provide themselves. One way of obtaining more capital is to invite investors from outside the business to invest in the ownership or equity of the business. These new co-owners would not usually be expected to help with managing the business. To such investors, limited liability is very attractive.

Investments are always risky undertakings, but with limited liability the investor knows the maximum amount that he stands to lose when he puts some capital into a company.

1.2 The accounting records of limited companies

There is almost always a **national legal requirement** for companies to keep accounting records which are sufficient to show and explain the company's transactions. The records will probably have the following qualities.

(a) Disclose the company's current financial position at any time.

(b) Contain:

    (i) day-to-day entries of money received and spent.

    (ii) a record of the company's assets and liabilities.

    (iii) where the company deals in goods:

        (1) a statement of inventories held at the year end, and supporting inventory count records.

        (2) with the exception of retail sales, statements of goods bought and sold which identify the sellers and buyers of those goods.

(c) Enable the managers of the company to ensure that the final accounts of the company give a true and fair view of the company's profit or loss and balance sheet position.

The detailed requirements of accounting records which must be maintained will vary from country to country.

Question — Companies

How are limited liability companies regulated in your country?

2 IAS 1: Presentation of financial statements

FAST FORWARD

IAS 1 lists the required contents of a company's income statement and balance sheet. It also give guidance on how items should be presented in the financial statements.

As well as covering accounting policies and other general considerations governing financial statements, IAS 1 *Presentation of financial statements* give substantial guidance on the form and content of published financial statements. The standard looks at the balance sheet and income statement (the cash flow statement is covered by IAS 7). First of all, some general points are made about financial statements.

2.1 Profit or loss for the period

The income statement is the most significant indicator of a company's financial performance. So it is important to ensure that it is not misleading.

The income statement will be misleading if costs incurred in the current year are deducted not from the current year profits but from the balance of accumulated profits brought forward. This presents the current year's results more favourably.

IAS 1 stipulates that all items of income and expense recognised in a period shall be included in profit or loss unless a **standard** or an **interpretation** requires otherwise.

Circumstances where items may be excluded from profit or loss for the current year include the correction of errors and the effect of changes in accounting policies. These are covered in IAS 8.

2.2 How items are disclosed

IAS 1 specifies disclosures of certain items in certain ways.

- Some items must appear on the **face of the balance sheet or income statement**
- Other items can appear in a **note to the financial statements** instead
- **Recommended formats** are given which enterprises may or may not follow, depending on their circumstances

Obviously, disclosures specified by **other standards** must also be made, and we will mention the necessary disclosures when we cover each statement in turn. Disclosures in both IAS 1 and other standards must be made either on the face of the statement or in the notes unless otherwise stated, ie disclosures cannot be made in an accompanying commentary or report.

2.3 Identification of financial statements

As a result of the above point, it is most important that entities **distinguish the financial statements** very clearly from any other information published with them. This is because all IASs apply *only* to the financial statements (ie the main statements and related notes), so readers of the annual report must be able to differentiate between the parts of the report which are prepared under IASs, and other parts which are not.

The entity should **identify each component** of the financial statements very clearly. IAS 1 also requires disclosure of the following information in a prominent position. If necessary it should be repeated wherever it is felt to be of use to the reader in his understanding of the information presented.

- **Name** of the reporting entity (or other means of identification)
- Whether the accounts cover the **single entity** only or a group of entities
- The **balance sheet date** or the period covered by the financial statements (as appropriate)
- The **reporting currency**
- The **level of precision** used in presenting the figures in the financial statements

Judgement must be used to determine the best method of presenting this information. In particular, the standard suggests that the approach to this will be very different when the financial statements are communicated electronically.

The **level of precision** is important, as presenting figures in thousands or millions of units makes the figures more understandable. The level of precision must be disclosed, however, and it should not obscure necessary details or make the information less relevant.

2.4 Reporting period

It is normal for entities to present financial statements **annually** and IAS 1 states that they should be prepared at least as often as this. If (unusually) an entity's balance sheet date is changed, for whatever reason, the period for which the statements are presented will be less or more than one year. In such cases the entity should also disclose:

(a) the **reason(s) why** a period other than one year is used; and

(b) the fact that the comparative figures given **are not in fact comparable** (in particular for the income statement, changes in equity, cash flows and related notes).

For practical purposes, some entities prefer to use a period which **approximates to a year**, eg 52 weeks, and the IAS allows this approach as it will produce statements not materially different from those produced on an annual basis.

2.5 Timeliness

If the publication of financial statements is delayed too long after the balance sheet date, their usefulness will be severely diminished. The standard states that entities should be able to produce their financial statements **within six months of the balance sheet date.** An entity with consistently complex operations cannot use this as a reason for its failure to report on a timely basis. Local legislation and market regulation imposes specific deadlines on certain entities.

IAS 1 looks at the balance sheet and the income statement. We will not give all the detailed disclosures as some are outside the scope of your syllabus. Instead we will look at a **'proforma' set of accounts** based on the Standard and the Pilot Paper.

Exam focus point

> IASs do not set out an **obligatory** format for financial statements but it would be best practice to use the **suggested format** of IAS 1.

2.6 Balance sheet

ABC CO
BALANCE SHEET AS AT 31 DECEMBER 20X2

	20X2		20X1	
	$'000	$'000	$'000	$'000
Assets				
Non-current assets				
Property, plant and equipment	X		X	
Goodwill	X		X	
Other intangible assets	X		X	
		X		X
Current assets				
Inventories	X		X	
Trade and other receivables	X		X	
Other current assets	X		X	
Cash and cash equivalents	X		X	
		X		X
Total assets		X		X
Equity and liabilities				
Equity				
Issued capital	X		X	
Reserves	X		X	
Retained profits/(losses)	X		X	
		X		X
Non-current liabilities				
Long-term borrowings	X		X	
Long-term provisions	X		X	
		X		X
Current liabilities				
Trade and other payables	X		X	
Short-term borrowings	X		X	
Current portion of long-term borrowings	X		X	
Current tax payable	X		X	
		X		X
Total equity and liabilities		X		X

2.7 Income statement

ABC CO
INCOME STATEMENT FOR THE YEAR ENDED 31 DECEMBER 20X2
Illustrating the classification of expenses by function

	20X2	20X1
	$'000	$'000
Revenue	X	X
Cost of sales	(X)	(X)
Gross profit	X	X
Other income	X	X
Distribution costs	(X)	(X)
Administrative expenses	(X)	(X)
Other expenses	(X)	(X)
Finance cost	(X)	(X)
Profit before tax	X	X
Income tax expense	(X)	(X)
Net profit for the period	X	X

NOTES TO THE FINANCIAL STATEMENTS

1 *Accounting policies*

This will generally be the first note to the accounts and is governed by IAS 1 *Presentation of financial statements*. Disclosure of the following policies is likely.

- Depreciation
- Inventories
- Revaluation of long-term assets

2 *General balance sheet disclosures*

- Restrictions on the title to assets
- Security given in respect of liabilities
- Contingent assets and contingent liabilities, quantified if possible
- Amounts committed for future capital expenditure
- Events after the balance sheet date

3 *Property, plant and equipment*

- Land and buildings
- Plant and equipment
- Other categories of assets, suitably identified
- Accumulated depreciation
- Separate disclosure should be made of leaseholds and of assets being acquired on instalment purchase plans.

4 *Other non-current assets*

- Include, if applicable, the method and period of depreciation and any unusual write-offs during the period.
- *Long-term investments* stating the market value of listed investments if different from the carrying amount in the financial statements
- *Long-term receivables*
  - Accounts and notes receivable: trade
  - Receivables from directors
  - Other
- Goodwill
- Patents, trademarks, and similar assets
- Development costs capitalised and their movements during the period

5 *Investments*

For marketable securities, the market value should be disclosed if different from the carrying amount in the financial statements.

6 *Receivables*

- Accounts and notes receivable: trade
- Receivable from directors
- Other receivables and prepaid expenses

7   *Cash*

Cash includes cash on hand and in current and other accounts with banks. Cash which is not immediately available for use, for example balances frozen in foreign banks by exchange restrictions, should be disclosed.

8   *Shareholders' interests*

The following disclosures should be made separately.

- *Share capital*: disclose the following for each class of share capital.
    – Number of shares issued and partly paid, and issued but not fully paid
    – Par value per share or that the shares have not par value
    – Reconciliation of number of shares outstanding at the beginning and end of the year
    – Rights, preferences, and restrictions with respect to the distribution of dividends and to the repayment of capital
    – Shares in the enterprise held by itself or related companies
    – Shares reserved for future issue under options and sales contracts, including the terms and amounts.
    – Description of the nature and purpose of each reserve
    – Dividends proposed but not formally approved for payment
    – Cumulative preferred dividends not recognised
- Statement of changes in equity

9   *Non-current liabilities*

- Exclude the portion repayable within one year.
- Secured loans
- Unsecured loans

A summary of the interest rates, repayment terms, covenants, subordination and conversion features should be shown.

10   *Other liabilities and provisions*

The significant items included in other liabilities and in provisions and accruals should be separately disclosed. You are unlikely to meet any items of this nature in your syllabus.

11   *Payables*

- Accounts and notes payable: trade
- Payables to directors
- Taxes on income
- Other payables and accrued expenses

For the purposes of your syllabus, you need to be able to **produce the following notes** to the accounts.

(a)   Statement of changes in equity (see Section 5 of this Chapter)
(b)   Non-current assets (see Chapter 14 of this Study Text)
(c)   Events after the balance sheet date (Chapter 16)
(d)   Contingent assets and contingent liabilities (Chapter 16)
(e)   Research and development (Chapter 15)

> **Question**   Pro forma
>
> Before we go any further, take a blank sheet of paper and write out the 'pro forma' income statement and balance sheet shown above. Mark which items are likely to require further disclosure, either by note or on the face of the statements.

FAST FORWARD

> You must be able to account for these items when preparing the accounts of limited liability companies.
> - Taxation
> - Ordinary and preference shares
> - Shareholders' equity (share premium, revaluation surplus, reserves and retained earnings)

3 Items in the income statement

3.1 Managers' salaries

The salary of a sole trader or a partner in a partnership is not a charge to the income statement but is an appropriation of profit. The **salary of a manager or member of management board of a limited liability company**, however, is an **expense in the income statement**, even when the manager is a shareholder in the company. Management salaries are included in **administrative expenses.**

3.2 Taxation

Taxation affects both the balance sheet and the income statement.

All companies pay some kind of corporate taxation on the profits they earn, which we will call **income tax** (for the sake of simplicity), but which you may find called 'corporation tax'. The rate of income tax will vary from country to country and there may be variations in rate within individual countries for different types or size of company.

Note that because a company has a **separate legal personality, its tax is included in its accounts**. An unincorporated business would not show personal income tax in its accounts, as it would not be a business expense but the personal affair of the proprietors.

(a) The **charge for income tax on profits for the year** is shown as a **deduction from net profit**, before appropriations.

(b) In the balance sheet, **tax payable** to the government is generally shown as a **current liability** as it is usually due within 12 months of the year end.

(c) For various reasons, the tax on profits in the income statement and the tax payable in the balance sheet are not normally the same amount.

See Section 10 for details of the ledger accounting for income taxes.

4 Items in the balance sheet

There are several items in the balance sheet which you have not come across yet, or which require further explanation. We will deal with these over the course of this and the next three sections.

> **FAST FORWARD**
>
> In preparing a balance sheet you must be able to deal with:
> - ordinary and preference share capital
> - reserves
> - loan stock

4.1 The capital of limited liability companies

The proprietors' capital in a limited liability company consists of **share capital**. When a company is set up for the first time, it issues shares, which are paid for by investors, who then become shareholders of the company. Shares are denominated in units of 25 cents, 50 cents, $1 or whatever seems appropriate. The 'face value' of the shares is called their **par value** or **legal value** (or sometimes the **nominal value**).

For example, when a company is set up with a share capital of, say, $100,000, it may be decided to issue:

(a) 100,000 shares of $1 each par value; or
(b) 200,000 shares of 50c each; or
(c) 400,000 shares of 25c each; or
(d) 250,000 shares of 40c each, etc.

The amount at which the shares are issued may exceed their par value. For example, a company might issue 100,000 $1 shares at a price of $1.20 each. Subscribers will then pay a total of $120,000. The issued share capital of the company would be shown in its accounts at par value, $100,000; the excess of $20,000 is described not as share capital, but as **share premium** or **capital paid-up in excess of par value.**

4.2 Authorised, issued, called-up and paid-up share capital

A distinction must be made between authorised, issued, called-up and paid-up share capital.

(a) **Authorised (or legal) capital** is the maximum amount of share capital that a company is empowered to issue. The amount of authorised share capital varies from company to company, and can change by agreement.

For example, a company's authorised share capital might be 5,000,000 ordinary shares of $1 each. This would then be the maximum number of shares it could issue, unless the maximum were to be changed by agreement.

(b) **Issued capital** is the par amount of share capital that has been issued to shareholders. The amount of issued capital cannot exceed the amount of authorised capital.

Continuing the example above, the company with authorised share capital of 5,000,000 ordinary shares of $1 might have issued 4,000,000 shares. This would leave it the option to issue 1,000,000 more shares at some time in the future.

When share capital is issued, shares are allotted to shareholders. The term 'allotted' share capital means the same thing as issued share capital.

(c) **Called-up capital**. When shares are issued or allotted, a company does not always expect to be paid the full amount for the shares at once. It might instead call up only a part of the issue price, and wait until a later time before it calls up the remainder.

For example, if a company allots 400,000 ordinary shares of $1, it might call up only, say, 75 cents per share. The issued share capital would be $400,000, but the called-up share capital would only be $300,000.

(d) **Paid-up capital**. Like everyone else, investors are not always prompt or reliable payers. When capital is called up, some shareholders might delay their payment (or even default on payment). Paid-up capital is the amount of called-up capital that has been paid.

For example, if a company issues 400,000 ordinary shares of $1 each, calls up 75 cents per share, and receives payments of $290,000, we would have:

	$
Allotted or issued capital	400,000
Called-up capital	300,000
Paid-up capital	290,000
Capital not yet paid-up	10,000

	$
Called-up capital not paid	10,000
Cash (called-up capital paid)	290,000
	300,000
Called-up share capital	
(400,000 ordinary shares of $1, with 75c per share called up)	300,000

The balance sheet of the company would then include called-up capital not paid on the assets side (a receivable).

4.3 Ordinary shares and preference (preferred) shares

At this stage it is relevant to distinguish between the two types of shares most often encountered: **preference shares** and **ordinary shares**.

Key term

> **Preference shares** are shares which confer certain preferential rights on their holder.

Preference shares carry the right to a final dividend which is expressed as a percentage of their par value: eg a 6% $1 preference share carries a right to an annual dividend of 6c. Preference dividends have priority over ordinary dividends; in other words, if the managers of a company wish to pay a dividend (which they are not obliged to do) they must pay any preference dividend first. Otherwise, no ordinary dividend may be paid.

The rights attaching to preference shares are set out in the company's constitution. They may vary from company to company and country to country, but typically:

(a) Preference shareholders have a **priority right** over ordinary shareholders to a return of their capital if the company goes into liquidation.

(b) Preference shares do not **carry a right to vote**.

(c) If the preference shares are **cumulative**, it means that before a company can pay an ordinary dividend it must not only pay the current year's preference dividend, but must also make good any arrears of preference dividends unpaid in previous years.

Ordinary shares are by far the most common. They carry no right to a fixed dividend but are entitled to all profits left after payment of any preference dividend. Generally, however, only a part of such remaining profits is distributed, the rest being kept in reserve (see below).

Key term

> **Ordinary shares** are shares which are not preferred with regard to dividend payments. Thus a holder only receives a dividend after fixed dividends have been paid to preference shareholders.

The amount of ordinary dividends fluctuates although there is a general expectation that it will increase from year to year. Should the company be wound up, any surplus not distributed is shared between the ordinary shareholders. Ordinary shares normally carry voting rights.

Ordinary shareholders are thus the effective **owners** of a company. They own the 'equity' of the business, and any reserves of the business (described later) belong to them. Ordinary shareholders are sometimes referred to as **equity shareholders**. Preference shareholders are in many ways more like creditors of the company (although legally they are members, not creditors). It should be emphasised, however, that the precise rights attached to preference and ordinary shares may vary; the distinctions noted above are generalisations.

4.4 Example: Dividends on ordinary shares and preference shares

Garden Gloves Co has issued 50,000 ordinary shares of 50 cents each and 20,000 7% preference shares of $1 each. Its profits after taxation for the year to 30 September 20X5 were $8,400. The management board has decided to pay an ordinary dividend (ie a dividend on ordinary shares) which is 50% of profits after tax and preference dividend.

Required

Show the amount in total of dividends and of retained profits, and calculate the dividend per share on ordinary shares.

Solution

	$
Profit after tax	8,400
Preference dividend (7% of $1 × 20,000)	1,400
Earnings (profit after tax and preference dividend)	7,000
Ordinary dividend (50% of earnings)	3,500
Retained earnings (also 50% of earnings)	3,500

The ordinary dividend is 7 cents per share ($3,500 ÷ 50,000 ordinary shares).

The appropriation of profit would be as follows:

		$	$
Profit after tax			8,400
Dividends:	preference	1,400	
	ordinary	3,500	
			4,900
Retained profit			3,500

4.5 Deferred shares

Deferred shares are equity shares that have their dividend rights deferred.

(a) Ranking for dividend only after all other classes of share have received a specified rate of dividend; or

(b) Ranking for dividend only after a specified time following issue.

4.6 The market value of shares

The par value of shares will be different from their market value, which is the price at which someone is prepared to purchase shares in the company from an existing shareholder. If Mr A owns 1,000 $1 shares in Z Co he may sell them to B for $1.60 each.

This transfer of existing shares does not affect Z Co's own financial position in any way whatsoever, and apart from changing the register of members, Z Co does not have to bother with the sale by Mr A to Mr B at all. There are certainly no accounting entries to be made for the share sale.

Shares in private companies do not change hands very often, hence their market value is often hard to estimate. Companies listed on a stock exchange are quoted, ie it is the market value of the shares which is quoted.

4.7 Loan stock or bonds

Limited liability companies may issue loan stock or bonds. These are long-term liabilities and in some countries they are described as *loan capital* because they are a means of raising finance, in the same way as issuing share capital raises finance. They are different from share capital in the following ways.

(a) **Shareholders** are **members** of a company, while **providers of loan capital** are **creditors**.

(b) **Shareholders** receive **dividends** (appropriations of profit) whereas the **holders of loan capital** are entitled to a **fixed rate of interest** (an expense charged against revenue).

(c) Loan capital holders can take legal action against a company if their interest is not paid when due, whereas **shareholders cannot enforce the payment of dividends**.

(d) Loan stock is **often secured on company assets**, whereas shares are not.

The holder of loan capital is generally in a less risky position than the shareholder. He has greater security, although his income is fixed and cannot grow, unlike ordinary dividends. As remarked earlier, preference shares are in practice very similar to loan capital, not least because the preference dividend is normally fixed.

Interest is calculated on the par or legal value of loan capital, regardless of its market value. If a company has $700,000 (par value) 12% loan stock in issue, interest of $84,000 will be charged in the income statement per year. Interest is usually paid half-yearly; examination questions often require an accrual to be made for interest due at the year-end.

For example, if a company has $700,000 of 12% loan stock in issue, pays interest on 30 June and 31 December each year, and ends its accounting year on 30 September, there would be an accrual of three months' unpaid interest (3/12 × $84,000) = $21,000 at the end of each accounting year that the loan stock is still in issue.

The issue of loan capital affects a company's gearing. This will be dealt with in detail in Chapter 22.

The next important item on the balance sheet is shareholders' equity and its constituent parts, which we cover in the next section.

Question
Share capital

Distinguish between authorised, issued, called-up and paid-up capital.

Answer

Authorised share capital: the maximum amount of share capital that a company is empowered to issue.

Issued share capital: the amount of share capital that has been issued to shareholders.

Called-up share capital: the amount the company has asked shareholders to pay, for the time being, on shares issued to them.

Paid-up share capital: the amounts actually paid by shareholders on shares issued to them.

5 Shareholders' equity

FAST FORWARD

Share capital and reserves are 'owned' by the shareholders.
They are known collectively as 'shareholders' equity'.

PART E FINANCIAL STATEMENTS

Shareholders' equity consists of the following.

(a) The par value of issued capital (minus any amounts not yet called up on issued shares)
(b) Other equity

The share capital itself might consist of both ordinary shares and preference shares. All reserves, however, are owned by the ordinary shareholders, who own the 'equity' in the company. We looked at share capital in detail above.

'Other equity' consists of four elements.

(a) Capital paid-up in excess of par value (share premium)
(b) Revaluation surplus
(c) Reserves
(d) Retained earnings

We will look at each in turn.

5.1 The share premium account

In this context, 'premium' means the difference between the issue price of the share and its par value. The account is sometimes called 'capital paid-up in excess of par value'. When a company is first incorporated (set up) the issue price of its shares will probably be the same as their par value and so there would be no share premium. If the company does well, the market value of its shares will increase, but not the par value. The price of any new shares issued will be approximately their market value.

The difference between cash received by the company and the par value of the new shares issued is transferred to the **share premium account**. For example, if X Co issues 1,000 $1 ordinary shares at $2.60 each the book entry will be:

		$	$
DEBIT	Cash	2,600	
CREDIT	Ordinary shares		1,000
	Share premium account		1,600

A share premium account only comes into being when a company issues shares at a price in excess of their par value. The market price of the shares, once they have been issued, has no bearing at all on the company's accounts, and so if their market price goes up or down, the share premium account would remain unaltered.

Key term

> A **share premium account** is an account into which sums received as payment for shares in excess of their nominal value must be placed.

Once established, the share premium account constitutes capital of the company which cannot be paid out in dividends, ie it is a capital reserve. The share premium account will increase in value if and when new shares are issued at a price above their par value. The share premium account can be 'used' – and so decrease in value – only in certain very limited ways, which are largely beyond the scope of your basic financial accounting syllabus. One common use of the share premium account, however, is to 'finance' the issue of bonus shares, which are described later in this chapter. Other uses of this account may depend on national legislation.

Important

> The share premium account cannot be distributed as dividend under any circumstances.

The reason for creating such non-distributable reserves is to maintain the capital of the company. This capital 'base' provides some security for the company's creditors, bearing in mind that the liability of shareholders is limited in the event that the company cannot repay its debts. It would be most unjust – and illegal – for a company to pay its shareholders a dividend out of its base capital when it is not even able to pay back its debts.

5.2 Revaluation surplus

We looked at the revaluation of non-current assets in Chapter 14. The result of an upward revaluation is a '**revaluation surplus**'. This is **non-distributable** as it represents unrealised profits on the revalued assets. It is another capital reserve. The relevant part of a revaluation surplus can only become realised if the asset in question is sold, thus realising the gain. The revaluation surplus may fall, however, if an asset which had previously been revalued upwards suffered a fall in value in the next revaluation.

5.3 Reserves

In most countries, a distinction must be made between the following.

(a) **Statutory reserves**, which are reserves which a company is required to set up by law, and which are not available for the distribution of dividends.

(b) **Non-statutory reserves**, which are reserves consisting of profits which are distributable as dividends, if the company so wishes.

Statutory reserves are capital reserves and non-statutory reserves are revenue reserves.

We are concerned here with the latter type, which the company managers may choose to set up. These may have a specific purpose (eg plant and machinery replacement reserve) or not (eg general reserve). The creation of these reserves usually indicates a general intention not to distribute the profits involved at any future date, although legally any such reserves, being non-statutory, remain available for the payment of dividends.

Profits are transferred to these reserves by making an appropriation out of profits, usually profits for the year. Typically, you might come across the following.

	$	$
Profit after taxation		100,000
Appropriations of profit		
Dividend	60,000	
Transfer to general reserve	10,000	
		70,000
Retained earnings for the year		30,000
Retained earnings b/f		250,000
Retained earnings c/f		280,000

5.4 Dividends

Key term

> **Dividends** are appropriations of profit after tax.

Shareholders who are also managers of their company will receive a salary as a manager. They are also entitled to a share of the profits made by the company.

Many companies pay dividends in two stages during the course of their accounting year.

(a) In mid year, after the half-year financial results are known, the company might pay an **interim dividend**.

(b) At the end of the year, the company might propose a further **final dividend**.

The total dividend for the year is the sum of the interim and the final dividend. (Not all companies by any means pay an interim dividend. Interim dividends are, however, commonly paid out by larger limited liability companies.)

At the end of an accounting year, a company's managers may have proposed a final dividend payment, but this will not yet have been paid. The final dividend **does not appear in the accounts** but will be disclosed in the notes.

Exam focus point

Dividends which have been **paid** are shown in the statement of changes in equity (see para 5.7). They are not shown in the income statement, although they are deducted from retained earnings in the balance sheet. **Proposed** dividends are not adjusted for, they are simply disclosed by note.

The terminology of dividend payments can be confusing, since they may be expressed either in the form, as 'x cents per share' or as 'y%'. In the latter case, the meaning is always 'y% of the *par value* of the shares in issue'. For example, suppose a company's issued share capital consists of 100,000 50c ordinary shares which were issued at a premium of 10c per share. The company's balance sheet would include the following.

		$
Ordinary shares:	100,000 50c ordinary shares	50,000
Share premium account	(100,000 × 10c)	10,000

If the managers wish to pay a dividend of $5,000, they may propose either:

(a) a dividend of 5c per share (100,000 × 5c = $5,000); or
(b) a dividend of 10% (10% × $50,000 = $5,000).

Not all profits are distributed as dividends; some will be retained in the business to finance future projects.

Question — Dividend

A company has authorised share capital of 1,000,000 50c ordinary shares and an issued share capital of 800,000 50c ordinary shares. If an ordinary dividend of 5% is declared, what is the amount payable to shareholders?

Answer

800,000 × 50c × 5% = $20,000.

5.5 Retained earnings

This is the **most significant reserve** and is variously described as:

(a) Revenue reserve
(b) Retained profits
(c) Accumulated profits
(d) Undistributed profits
(e) Unappropriated profits

These are **profits** earned by the company and not appropriated by dividends, taxation or transfer to another reserve account.

Provided that a company is earning profits, this reserve generally increases from year to year, as most companies do not distribute all their profits as dividends. Dividends can be paid from it: even if a loss is made in one particular year, a dividend can be paid from previous years' retained earnings.

For example, if a company makes a loss of $100,000 in one year, yet has unappropriated profits from previous years totalling $250,000, it can pay a dividend not exceeding $150,000. One reason for retaining some profit each year is to enable the company to pay dividends even when profits are low (or non-existent). Another reason is usually shortage of cash.

Very occasionally, you might come across a debit balance on the retained earnings account. This would indicate that the company has accumulated losses.

5.6 Distinction between reserves and provisions

Key terms

A **reserve** is an appropriation of distributable profits for a specific purpose (eg plant replacement) while a provision is an amount charged against revenue as an expense. A provision relates either to a diminution in the value of an asset or a known liability (eg audit fees), the amount of which cannot be established with any accuracy.

Provisions or allowances (for depreciation etc) are dealt with in company accounts in the same way as in the accounts of other types of business.

5.7 Statement of changes in equity

In the published accounts, a company has to provide a statement of changes in equity which details the movements on its capital and reserves.

Example: Statement of changes in equity

	Share capital	Share premium	Revaluation reserve	Retained earnings	Total
Balance at 31.12.X0	X	X		X	X
Gain on property revaluation			X		X
Profit for the period				X	X
Dividends				(X)	(X)
Issue of share capital	X	X			X
Balance at 31.12.X1	X	X	X	X	X

Note that the statement of changes in equity simply takes the equity section of the balance sheet and shows the movements during the year. The bottom line shows the amounts for the current balance sheet.

Dividends paid during the year are not shown on the income statement; they are shown in the statement of changes in equity.

6 Bonus and rights issues

A company can increase its share capital by means of a **bonus issue** or a **rights issue**.

6.1 Bonus (capitalisation) issues

A company may wish to increase its share capital without needing to raise additional finance by issuing new shares. For example, a profitable company might expand from modest beginnings over a number of years. Its profitability would be reflected in large balances on its reserves, while its original share capital might look like that of a much smaller business.

It is open to such a company to **re-classify some of its reserves as share capital**. This is purely a paper exercise which raises no funds. Any reserve may be re-classified in this way, including a share premium account or other reserve. Such a re-classification increases the capital base of the company and gives creditors greater protection.

6.2 Example: Bonus issue

BUBBLES CO
BALANCE SHEET (EXTRACT)

	$'000	$'000
Shareholders' equity		
Share capital		
$1 ordinary shares (fully paid)		1,000
Reserves		
Share premium	500	
Retained earnings	2,000	
		2,500
		3,500

Bubbles decided to make a '3 for 2' bonus issue (ie 3 new shares for every 2 already held).

The double entry is:		$'000	$'000
DEBIT	Share premium	500	
	Retained earnings	1,000	
CREDIT	Ordinary share capital		1,500

After the issue the balance sheet is as follows.

	$'000
Share capital: $1 ordinary shares (fully paid)	2,500
Retained earnings	1,000
Shareholders' equity	3,500

1,500,000 new ('bonus') shares are issued to existing shareholders, so that if Mr X previously held 20,000 shares he will now hold 50,000. The total value of his holding should theoretically remain the same however, since the net assets of the company remain unchanged and his share of those net assets remains at 2% (ie 50,000/2,500,000; previously 20,000/1,000,000).

6.3 Rights issues

A **rights issue** (unlike a bonus issue) is **an issue of shares for cash**. The 'rights' are offered to existing shareholders, who can sell them if they wish. This is beneficial for existing shareholders in that the shares are usually issued at a discount to the current market price.

6.4 Example: Rights issue

Bubbles Co (above) decides to make a rights issue, shortly after the bonus issue. The terms are '1 for 5 @ $1.20' (ie one new share for every five already held, at a price of $1.20). Assuming that all shareholders take up their rights (which they are not obliged to) the double entry is:

		$'000	$'000
DEBIT	Cash (2,500 ÷ 5 × $1.20)	600	
CREDIT	Ordinary share capital		500
	Share premium		100

Mr X who previously held 50,000 shares will now hold 60,000, and the value of his holding should increase (all other things being equal) because the net assets of the company will increase. The new balance sheet will show:

	$'000
$1 ordinary shares	3,000
Share premium	100
Retained earnings	1,000
Shareholders' equity	4,100

The increase in funds of $600,000 represents the cash raised from the issue of 500,000 new shares at a price of $1.20 each.

Rights issues are a popular way of raising cash by issuing shares and they are cheap to administer. In addition, shareholders retain control of the business as their holding is not diluted.

Question — Bonus and rights issue

X Co has the following capital structure:

	$
400,000 ordinary shares of 50c	200,000
Share premium account	70,000
Retained earnings	230,000
Shareholders' equity	500,000

Show its capital structure following:

(a) A '1 for 2' bonus issue
(b) A rights issue of '1 for 3' at 75c following the bonus issue, assuming all rights taken up

Answer

(a)

	$
600,000 ordinary shares of 50c	300,000
Retained earnings	200,000
Shareholders equity	500,000

(b)

	$
800,000 ordinary shares of 50c	400,000
Share premium account	50,000
Retained earnings	200,000
Shareholders equity	650,000

The bonus issue was financed by the whole of the share premium account and 30,000 retained earnings. The share premium account has funds again following the rights issue. Note that the bonus issue leaves shareholders equity unchanged. The rights issue will have brought in cash of $150,000 (200,000 x 75c) and shareholders equity is increased by this amount.

7 The current/non-current distinction

FAST FORWARD — You should be aware of the issues surrounding the current/non-current distinction as well as the disclosure requirements laid down in IAS 1.

Current assets and current liabilities of various types have been discussed in earlier parts of this Study Text. You may find it helpful to revise Chapter 3, which gives definitions and examples of assets and liabilities. Users of financial statements need to be able to identify current assets and current liabilities in order to determine the company's financial position. Where current assets are greater than current liabilities, the net excess is often called 'working capital' or 'net current assets'.

7.1 Alternative views of current assets and current liabilities

There is by no means universal agreement over what is meant by 'current' assets and 'current' liabilities, and what should be regarded as 'non-current'.

PART E FINANCIAL STATEMENTS

(a) Is the distinction made to indicate the liquidity position of an entity, ie can it operate from day-to-day without financial difficulties arising?

(b) Is it a way of showing those resources of the entity which are continuously circulating?

These two aspects are incompatible with each other to a great extent and these conflicting views have led to a situation in some countries where items are included in current assets on the basis of arbitrary convention rather than any particular concept. In some circumstances entities may choose not to recognise the current/non-current distinction.

IAS 1 lays down rules for entities which choose to show the current/non-current distinction. It also states what should happen if they do not do so.

Each entity should decide whether it wishes to present current/non-current assets and current/non-current liabilities as **separate classifications** in the balance sheet. This decision should be based on the nature of the entity's options. Where an entity does *not* choose to make this classification, it should present assets and liabilities broadly **in order of their liquidity**.

In either case, the entity should disclose any portion of an asset or liability which is expected to be recovered or settled **after more than twelve months**. For example, for an amount receivable which is due in instalments over 18 months, the portion due after more than twelve months must be disclosed.

The IAS emphasises how helpful information on the **operating cycle** is to users of financial statements. Where there is a clearly defined operating cycle within which the entity supplies goods or services, then information disclosing those net assets that are continuously circulating as **working capital**. This distinguishes them from those net assets used in the long-term operations of the entity. Assets that are expected to be realised and liabilities that are due for settlement within the operating cycle are therefore highlighted.

The liquidity and solvency of an entity is also indicated by information about the **maturity dates** of assets and liabilities. As you will see in your later studies, IAS 32 *Financial instruments: disclosure and presentation* requires disclosure of maturity dates of both financial assets and financial liabilities. (Financial assets include trade and other receivables; financial liabilities include trade and other payables.)

7.2 Current assets

Key term

> An asset should be classified as a **current asset** when it:
>
> - is expected to be realised in, or is held for sale or consumption in, the entity's normal operating cycle; or
> - is held primarily for the purpose of being traded
> - is expected to be realised within twelve months after the balance sheet date
> - is cash or a cash equivalent which is not restricted in its use.
>
> All other assets should be classified as non-current assets. *(IAS 1)*

Non-current includes tangible, intangible operating and financial assets of a long-term nature. Other terms with the same meaning can be used (eg 'fixed', 'long-term').

The term 'operating cycle' has been used several times above and the standard defines it as follows.

Key term

> The **operating cycle** of an entity is the time between the acquisition of assets for processing and their realisation in cash or cash equivalents. *(IAS 1)*

Current assets therefore include assets (such as inventories and trade receivables) that are sold, or realised as part of the normal operating cycle. **This is the case even where they are not expected to be realised within twelve months**.

Current assets will also include **marketable securities** if they are expected to be realised within twelve months of the balance sheet date. If expected to be realised later, they should be included in non-current assets.

7.3 Current liabilities

Key term

> A liability should be classified as a **current liability** when it:
>
> - is expected to be settled in the entity's normal operating cycle; or
> - is due to be settled within twelve months of the balance sheet date
> - is held primarily for the purpose of being traded.
>
> All other liabilities should be classified as non-current liabilities. *(IAS 1)*

The categorisation of current liabilities is very similar to that of current assets. Thus, some current liabilities are part of the **working capital** used in the normal operating cycle of the business (ie trade payables and accruals for employee and other operating costs). Such items will be classed as current liabilities **even where they are due to be settled more than twelve months after the balance sheet date.**

There are also current liabilities which are not settled as part of the normal operating cycle, but which are due to be settled within twelve months of the balance sheet date. These include bank overdrafts, income taxes, other non-trade payables and the current portion of interest-bearing liabilities. Any interest-bearing liabilities that are used to finance working capital on a long-term basis, and that are not due for settlement within twelve months, should be classed as **non-current liabilities**.

In the case of such **long-term interest-bearing securities**, the IAS further states that they should continue to be treated as non-current, even if they are due to be settled within twelve months of the balance sheet date if *all of* the following conditions apply.

(a) The **original term** was for a period of more than twelve months

(b) The entity intends to **refinance** the obligations on a long-term basis

(c) That intention is supported by an **agreement to refinance**, or to reschedule payments, which is completed before the financial statements are approved

Both the amounts thus treated and the information to support the treatment should be **disclosed** as a note to the balance sheet.

Such obligations, which can effectively be 'rolled over' at the discretion of the entity, should not therefore be expected to use any of the entity's working capital. They are therefore part of the entity's **long-term financing** and so are non-current.

There are different situations where the refinancing or 'rolling over' is *not* at the discretion of the entity. In such cases the obligation should be classified as **current** because the refinancing cannot be considered to be automatic.

An obligation could only be classified as **non-current** if a refinancing agreement had been reached before the approval of the financial statements. Only such strong evidence would support treatment of the obligation as non-current at the balance sheet date.

Covenants are often attached to borrowing agreements which represent undertakings by the borrower. Under these covenants, if certain conditions relating to the borrower's financial situation are breached, the amount of the liability becomes repayable on demand. The standard states that such liabilities can only be classified as non-current if both the following circumstances apply.

(a) The lender agrees, before approval of the financial statements, that repayment due to a breach **will not be demanded**.

(b) **Further breaches** are not likely to occur within the next twelve months after the balance sheet date.

For the differences between liabilities and provisions, see Chapter 16 of this Study Text.

8 IAS 8 Accounting policies, changes in accounting estimates and errors

FAST FORWARD

IAS 8 *Accountancy policies, changes in accounting estimates and errors* is an important standard. You should be able to define and deal with:

- changes in accounting policies
- changes in accounting estimates
- errors

IAS 8 lays down the criteria for selecting and changing accounting policies and specifies the accounting treatment and disclosure of changes in accounting policies, changes in accounting estimates, and errors.

8.1 Definitions

The following definitions are given in the standard.

Key terms

- **Accounting policies** are the specific principles, bases, conventions, rules and practices applied by an entity in preparing and presenting financial statements.
- A **change in accounting estimate** is an adjustment of the carrying amount of an asset or a liability, or the amount of the periodic consumption of an asset.
- **Material**: Omissions or misstatements of items are material if they could, individually or collectively, influence the economic decisions of users taken on the basis of the financial statements.
- **Prior period errors** are omissions from, and misstatements in, the entity's financial statements for one or more prior periods.
- **Impracticable**: Applying a requirement is impracticable when the entity cannot apply it after making every reasonable effort to do so.

8.2 Changes in accounting estimates

Estimates arise in relation to business activities because of the **uncertainties inherent within them**. Judgements are made based on the most up to date information and the use of such estimates is a necessary part of the preparation of financial statements. It does *not* undermine their reliability. Here are some examples of accounting estimates.

- A necessary **receivables allowance**
- **Useful lives** of depreciable assets
- Provision for **obsolescence of inventory**

The rule here is that the **effect of a change in an accounting estimate** should be included in the determination of net profit or loss in:

(a) the period of the change, if the change affects that period only; or
(b) the period of the change *and* future periods, if the change affects both.

An example of a change in accounting estimate which affects only the **current period** is the bad debt estimate. However, a revision in the life over which an asset is depreciated would affect both the **current and future periods**, in the amount of the depreciation expense.

Reasonably enough, the effect of a change in an accounting estimate should be included in the **same income statement classification** as was used previously for the estimate. This rule helps to ensure **consistency** between the financial statements of different periods.

The **materiality** of the change is also relevant. The nature and amount of a change in an accounting estimate that has a material effect in the current period (or which is expected to have a material effect in subsequent periods) should be disclosed. If it is not possible to quantify the amount, this impracticability should be disclosed.

8.3 Errors

Errors discovered during a current period which **relate to a prior period** may arise through:

(a) Mathematical mistakes
(b) Mistakes in the application of accounting policies
(c) Misinterpretation of facts
(d) Oversights
(e) Fraud

Most of the time these errors can be **corrected through net profit or loss for the current period**. Where they fulfil the definition of material errors (given above), however, this is not appropriate.

As laid down in IAS 8 the amount of the correction of a material error that relates to prior periods should be reported by **adjusting the opening balance of retained earnings**. Comparative information should be restated (unless this is impracticable).

This treatment means that the financial statements appear as if the material error had been **corrected in the period it was made**. Financial statements include comparatives for the previous period, so any amount relating to the previous period immediately prior to the current one will be included in the net profit or loss for that period. Amounts relating to periods before that will be used to adjust the opening reserves figure of the previous period shown.

Various **disclosures** are required:

(a) **Nature** of the material error
(b) **Amount of the correction** for the current period and for each prior period presented
(c) Amount of the correction relating to periods prior to those included in the **comparative** information
(d) The fact that comparative information has been **restated** or that it is impracticable to do so

PART E FINANCIAL STATEMENTS

 Question — Prior period error

During 20X7 Lubi Co discovered that certain items had been included in inventory at 31 December 20X6, valued at $4.2m, which had in fact been sold before the year end. The following figures for 20X6 (as reported) and 20X7 (draft) are available.

	20X6	20X7 (draft)
	$'000	$'000
Sales	47,400	67,200
Cost of goods sold	(34,570)	(55,800)
Profit before taxation	12,830	11,400
Income taxes	(3,880)	(3,400)
Net profit	8,950	8,000

Reserves at 1 January 20X6 were $13m. The cost of goods sold for 20X7 includes the $4.2m error in opening inventory. The income tax rate was 30% for 20X6 and 20X7.

Required

Show the income statement for 20X7, with the 20X6 comparative, and the adjusted retained earnings.

Answer

INCOME STATEMENT

	20X6	20X7
	$'000	$'000
Sales	47,400	67,200
Cost of goods sold (W1)	(38,770)	(51,600)
Profit before tax	8,630	15,600
Income tax (W2)	(2,620)	(4,660)
Net profit	6,010	10,940

RETAINED EARNINGS

	20X6	20X7
Opening retained earnings		
As previously reported	13,000	21,950
Correction of prior period error (4,200 – 1,260)	–	(2,940)
As restated	13,000	19,010
Net profit for year	6,010	10,940
Closing retained earnings	19,010	29,950

Working

1   Cost of goods sold

	20X6	20X7
	$'000	$'000
As stated in question	34,570	55,800
inventory adjustment	4,200	(4,200)
	38,770	51,600

2   Income tax

	20X6	20X7
	$'000	$'000
As stated in question	3,880	3,400
Inventory adjustment (4,200 × 30%)	1,260	1,260
	2,620	4,660

8.4 Changes in accounting policies

The same accounting policies, are usually adopted from period to period, to allow users to analyse trends over time in profit, cash flows and financial position. **Changes in accounting policy will therefore be rare** and should be made only if required.

(a) By an **standard or an interpretation (of a standard)**

(b) If the change will result in a **more appropriate presentation** of events or transactions in the financial statements of the enterprise

The standard highlights two types of event which do not constitute changes in accounting policy.

(a) Adopting an accounting policy for a **new type of transaction** or event not dealt with previously by the enterprise.

(b) Adopting a **new accounting policy** for a transaction or event which has not occurred in the past or which was not material.

In the case of property, plant and equipment, if a policy of revaluation is adopted for the first time then this is treated, not as a change of accounting policy under IAS 8, but as a revaluation under IAS 16 *Property, plant and equipment* (see Chapter 14). The following paragraphs do not therefore apply to revaluations.

A change in accounting policy should be applied retrospectively. Where an entity cannot determine the effect of applying the new policy to all prior periods, the new policy should be applied prospectively from the start of the earliest period practicable.

(a) **Retrospective application**

The new accounting policy is applied to transactions and events as if it had always been in use. In other words, at the earliest date such transactions or events occurred, the policy is applied from that date.

(b) **Prospective application**

The new policy will be applied only to transactions or events occurring after the date of the change in policy. Existing balances are not recalculated so no change is made to the opening balance on retained reserves or to net profit or loss for the current period relating to prior periods. Only changes caused by the new accounting policy in the existing period are necessary.

Where retrospective application is impracticable, the standard allows prospective application.

8.4.1 Adoption of an IFRS

Where a new IAS or IFRS is adopted, IAS 8 requires any transitional provisions in the new IAS itself to be followed. If none are given in the IFRS which is being adopted, then retrospective application is required.

8.4.2 Other changes in accounting policy:

The IAS requires **retrospective application**, *unless* the amount of any resulting adjustment that relates to prior periods is **not reasonably determinable**. Any resulting adjustment should be reported as an adjustment to the opening balance of retained earnings. Comparative information should be restated unless it is impracticable to do so.

This means that all comparative information must be restated **as if the new policy had always been in force**, with amounts relating to earlier periods reflected in an adjustment to opening reserves of the earliest period presented.

PART E FINANCIAL STATEMENTS

Prospective application is allowed in certain circumstances, when the amount of the adjustment to the opening balance of retained earnings required by the benchmark treatment cannot be reasonably determined.

Certain **disclosures** are required when a change in accounting policy has a material effect on the current period or any prior period presented, or when it may have a material effecting subsequent periods.

(a) Reasons for the change

(b) Amount of the adjustment for the current period and for each period presented

(c) Amount of the adjustment relating to periods prior to those included in the comparative information

(d) The fact that comparative information has been restated or that it is impracticable to do so

Disclosures are required when a change in accounting policy has a material effect on the current period or any prior period presented, or when it may have a material effect in subsequent periods.

(a) Reasons for the change

(b) Amount of the adjustment recognised in net profit/loss in the current period

(c) The amount of the adjustment included in each period for which prior information is presented and the amount of the adjustment relating to periods prior to those included in the financial statements

Question — Change of accounting policy

Wick Co was established on 1 January 20X0. In the first three years' accounts development expenditure was carried forward as an asset in the balance sheet. During 20X3 the managers decided that for the current and future years, all development expenditure should be written off as it is incurred. This decision has not resulted from any change in the expected outcome of development projects on hand, but rather from a desire to favour the prudence concept. The following information is available.

(a) Movements on the development account.

Year	Development expenditure incurred and capitalised during year $'000	Transfer from capitalised development expenditure account to income statement $'000
20X0	525	–
20X1	780	215
20X2	995	360

(b) The 20X2 accounts showed the following.

	$'000
Retained earnings b/f	2,955
Retained earnings for the year	1,825
Retained earnings c/f	4,780

(c) The retained profit for 20X3 after charging the actual development expenditure for the year was $2,030,000.

Required

Show how the change in accounting policy should be reflected in the reserves in the company's 20X3 accounts per IAS 8.

Ignore taxation.

Answer

If the new accounting policy had been adopted since the company was incorporated, the additional income statement charges for development expenditure would have been:

	$'000
20X0	525
20X1 (780 – 215)	565
	1,090
20X2 (995 – 360)	635
	1,725

This means that the reserves brought forward at 1 January 20X3 would have been $1,725,000 less than the reported figure of $4,780,000; while the reserves brought forward at 1 January 20X2 would have been $1,090,000 less than the reported figure of $2,955,000.

The statement of reserves in Wick Co's 20X3 accounts should, therefore, appear as follows.

	20X3 $'000	Comparative (previous year) figures 20X2 $'000	
Retained earnings at the beginning of year			
Previously reported	4,780	2,955	
Retrospective change in accounting policy (note 1)	1,725	1,090	
Restated	3,055	1,865	
Retained earnings for the year	2,030	1,190	(note 2)
Retained earnings at the end of the year	5,085	3,055	

Notes

1. The accounts should include a note explaining the reasons for and consequences of the changes in accounting policy. (See above workings for 20X3 and 20X2.)

2. The retained profit shown for 20X2 is after charging the additional development expenditure of $635,000.

9 IFRS 5 Non-current assets held for sale and discontinued operations

IFRS 5 *Non current assets held for sale and discontinued operations* requires assets and groups of assets that are 'held for sale' to be presented separately on the face of the balance sheet and the results of discontinued operations to be presented separately in the income statement. This is required so that users of financial statements will be better able to make projections about the financial position, profits and cash flows of the entity.

9.1 Definition

It is obviously important to know what does and what does not constitute a 'discontinued operation'.

Key terms

- **Discontinued operation**: a component of an entity that has either been disposed of, or is classified as held for sale, and

    (a) Represents a separate major line of business or geographical area of operations

    (b) Is part of a single co-ordinated plan to dispose of a separate major line of business or geographical area of operations, or

    (c) Is a subsidiary acquired exclusively with a view to resale.

- **Component of an entity**: operations and cash flows that can be clearly distinguished, operationally and for financial reporting purposes, from the rest of the entity.

9.2 Classification of assets held for sale

A non-current asset (or disposal group) should be classified as 'held for sale' if its carrying value will be recovered through a sale transaction rather than through continuing use. A number of detailed criteria must be met:

(a) The asset must be available for immediate sale in its present condition; and
(b) Its sale must be highly probable.

Key term

Disposal group: a group of assets to be disposed of as a group in a single transaction. (This could be a subsidiary or a separate operation within an entity.)

For the sale to be **highly probable**:

(a) Management must be committed to a plan to sell the asset.

(b) There must be an active programme to locate a buyer.

(c) The asset must be marketed for sale at a price that is reasonable in relation to its current fair value.

(d) The sale should be expected to take place within one year from the date of classification, and

(e) It is unlikely that significant changes to the plan will be made or that the plan will be withdrawn.

9.3 Measurement

An entity must measure a non-current asset (or disposal group) classified as held for sale at the lower of its carrying amount and fair value less costs to sell.

9.4 Disclosure

On the face of the income statement, an entity should disclose a single amount comprising.

(a) The post-tax profit or loss of discontinued operations

(b) Any profit or loss on disposal of the discontinued operation and any revaluation gain or impairment loss recognised on the assets in the disposal group

Note: An impairment loss occurs when an assets' recoverable amount falls below its carrying value. This means that the asset has fallen in value. In the exam, you will be told the amount of any impairment loss.

9.5 Presentation of a non-current asset or disposal group classified as held for sale

Non-current assets and disposal groups classified as held for sale should be presented separately from other assets in the balance sheet. The liabilities of a disposal group should be presented separately from other liabilities in the balance sheet.

- (a) Assets and liabilities held for sale should not be offset.
- (b) The major classes of assets and liabilities held for sale should be separately disclosed either on the face of the balance sheet or in the notes.

9.6 Additional disclosures

In the period in which a non-current asset or disposal group has been either classified as held for sale or sold, the following should be disclosed.

- (a) A description of the non-current asset (or disposal group)
- (b) A description of the facts and circumstances of the disposal
- (c) Any gain or loss recognised when the item was classified as held for sale
- (d) The geographical or business **segment** in which it is reported

10 Ledger accounts and limited liability companies

Limited companies keep ledger accounts, and the only difference between the ledger accounts of companies and sole traders is the nature of some of the transactions, assets and liabilities for which accounts need to be kept.

For example, there will be an account for each of the following items:

- (a) *Taxation*

    (i) Tax charged against profits will be accounted for by:

    DEBIT   I & E account
    CREDIT   Taxation account

    (ii) The outstanding balance on the taxation account will be a liability in the balance sheet, until eventually paid, when the accounting entry would be:

    DEBIT   Taxation account
    CREDIT   Cash

- (b) *Dividends*

    A separate account will be kept for the dividends for each different class of shares (eg preference, ordinary).

    (i) Dividends declared out of profits will be disclosed in the notes if they are unpaid at the year end.

    (ii) When dividends are paid, we have:

    DEBIT   Dividends paid account
    CREDIT   Cash

    This applies to the **interim** dividend, which is paid during the year. The **final** dividend will not appear in the accounts until the following year, when it is paid. No dividends payable will be shown at the year end.

PART E FINANCIAL STATEMENTS

(c) *Loan stock*

Loan stock being a long-term liability will be shown as a credit balance in a loan stock account.

Interest payable on such loans is not credited to the loan account, but is credited to a separate payables account for interest until it is eventually paid: ie

DEBIT   Interest account (an expense, chargeable against profits)
CREDIT   Interest payable (a current liability until eventually paid)

(d) *Share capital and reserves*

There will be a separate account for:

(i) each different class of share capital (always a credit balance b/f).
(ii) each different type of reserve (nearly always a credit balance b/f).

Now work through this example to give you practice in preparing financial statements in accordance with IAS 1.

Note that very little detail appears in the income statement – all items of income and expenditure are accumulated under the standard headings. Write out the standard proformas and then go through the workings, inserting figures as you go.

Question — USB

USB, a limited liability company, has the following trial balance at 31 December 20X9.

	Debit $'000	Credit $'000
Cash at bank	100	
Inventory at 1 January 20X9	2,400	
Administrative expenses	2,206	
Distribution costs	650	
Non-current assets at cost:		
Buildings	10,000	
Plant and equipment	1,400	
Motor vehicles	320	
Suspense		1,500
Accumulated depreciation		
Buildings		4,000
Plant and equipment		480
Motor vehicles		120
Retained earnings		560
Trade receivables	876	
Purchases	4,200	
Dividend paid	200	
Sales revenue		11,752
Sales tax payable		1,390
Trade payables		1,050
Share premium		500
$1 ordinary shares		1,000
	22,352	22,352

The following additional information is relevant.

(a) Inventory at 31 December 20X9 was valued at $1,600,000. While doing the inventory count, errors in the previous year's inventory count were discovered. The inventory brought forward at the beginning of the year should have been $2.2m, not $2.4m as above.

(b) Depreciation is to be provided as follows:

    (i) Buildings at 5% straight line, charged to administrative expenses.
    (ii) Plant and equipment at 20% on the reducing balance basis, charged to cost of sales.
    (iii) Motor vehicles at 25% on the reducing balance basis, charged to distribution costs.

(c) No final dividend is being proposed.

(d) A customer has gone bankrupt owing $76,000. This debt is not expected to be recovered and an adjustment should be made. An allowance for receivables of 5% is to be set up.

(e) 1 million new ordinary shares were issued at $1.50 on 1 December 20X9. The proceeds have been left in a suspense account.

REQUIREMENT:

Prepare the income statement for the year to 31 December 20X9, a statement of changes in equity and a balance sheet at that date in accordance with the requirements of International Accounting Standards. Ignore taxation.

Answer

USB
INCOME STATEMENT FOR THE YEAR ENDED 31 DECEMBER 20X9

	$'000
Revenue	11,752
Cost of sales (W2)	4,984
Gross profit	6,768
Administrative expenses (W3)	2,822
Distribution costs (650 + 50 (W1))	700
Profit for the period	3,246

USB
STATEMENT OF CHANGES IN EQUITY FOR THE YEAR ENDED 31 DECEMBER 20X9

	Share capital $'000	Share premium $'000	Retained earnings $'000	Total $'000
Balance at 1 January 20X9	1,000	500	560	2,060
Prior period adjustment			(200)	(200)
Profit for the period			3,246	3,246
Dividend paid			(200)	(200)
Share issue	1,000	500		1,500
Balance at 31 December 20X9	2,000	1,000	3,406	6,406

PART E   FINANCIAL STATEMENTS

USB
BALANCE SHEET AS AT 31 DECEMBER 20X9

	$'000	$'000
Non-current assets		
Property, plant and equipment (W5)		6,386
Current assets		
Inventory	1,600	
Trade receivables (876 – 76 – 40)	760	
Cash	100	
		2,460
Total assets		8,846
Equity and liabilities		
Equity		
Share capital		2,000
Share premium		1,000
Retained earnings (W6)		3,406
Current liabilities		
Sales tax payable	1,390	
Trade payables	1,050	
		2,440
Total equity and liabilities		8,846

Workings

1 Depreciation

	$'000
Buildings (10,000 × 5%)	500
Plant (1,400 – 480) × 20%	184
Motor vehicles (320 – 120) × 25%	50

2 Cost of sales

	$'000
Opening inventory	2,200
Purchases	4,200
Depreciation (W1)	184
Closing inventory	(1,600)
	4,984

3 Administrative expenses

	$'000
Per T/B	2,206
Depreciation (W1)	500
Irrecoverable debt	76
Receivables allowance ((876 – 76) × 5%)	40
	2,822

4 Property, plant and equipment

	Cost	Acc Dep	Dep chg	NBV
	$'000	$'000	$'000	$'000
Buildings	10,000	4,000	500	5,500
Plant	1,400	480	184	736
Motor vehicles	320	120	50	150
	11,720	4,600	734	6,386

5   Retained earnings

	$'000
B/f per T/B	560
Prior period adjustment (inventory)	(200)
Profit for period	3,246
Dividend paid	(200)
	3,406

11 Company accounts for internal purposes

The large amount of information in this chapter so far has really been geared towards the financial statements companies produce for external reporting purposes. In particular, the IASs discussed here are all concerned with external disclosure. **Companies do produce financial accounts for internal purposes, however, and the Paper 1.1 Study Guide states that you should be able to produce such accounts.**

It will often be the case that internal use financial accounts look very similar to those produced for external reporting for various reasons.

(a) The information required by internal users is similar to that required by external users. Any additional information for managers is usually provided by **management accounts**.

(b) Financial accounts produced for internal purposes can be used for external reporting with very little further adjustment.

It remains true, nevertheless, that **financial accounts for internal use can follow whichever format managers wish**. They may be more detailed in some areas than external financial accounts (perhaps giving breakdown of sales and profits by region or by product), but may also exclude some items, for example the taxation charge and dividend may be missed out of the income statement.

You should always read question requirements carefully to discover whether you are being asked to produce accounts for external or internal purposes. Even when producing the latter, however, it is a good idea to stick to the external statement formats as these show best practice.

Now try this exercise. We have avoided the complication of prior period adjustments as these were tested in Section 8.

 Question — Internal accounts

The accountant of Zabit Co has prepared the following trial balance as at 31 December 20X7.

	$'000
50c ordinary shares (fully paid)	350
7% $1 preference shares (fully paid)	100
10% loan stock (secured)	200
Retained earnings 1.1.X7	242
General reserve 1.1.X7	171
Land and buildings 1.1.X7 (cost)	430

PART E FINANCIAL STATEMENTS

	$'000
Plant and machinery 1.1.X7 (cost)	830
Accumulated depreciation	
Buildings 1.1.X7	20
Plant and machinery 1.1.X7	222
Inventory 1.1.X7	190
Sales	2,695
Purchases	2,152
Preference dividend	7
Ordinary dividend (interim)	8
Loan interest	10
Wages and salaries	254
Light and heat	31
Sundry expenses	113
Suspense account	135
Trade accounts receivable	179
Trade accounts payable	195
Cash	126

Notes

(a) Sundry expenses include $9,000 paid in respect of insurance for the year ending 1 September 20X8. Light and heat does not include an invoice of $3,000 for electricity for the three months ending 2 January 20X8, which was paid in February 20X8. Light and heat also includes $20,000 relating to salesmen's commission.

(b) The suspense account is in respect of the following items.

	$'000
Proceeds from the issue of 100,000 ordinary shares	120
Proceeds from the sale of plant	300
	420
Less consideration for the acquisition of Mary & Co	285
	135

(c) The net assets of Mary & Co were purchased on 3 March 20X7. Assets were valued as follows.

	$'000
Investments	231
Inventory	34
	265

All the inventory acquired was sold during 20X7. The investments were still held by Zabit at 31.12.X7.

(d) The property was acquired some years ago. The buildings element of the cost was estimated at $100,000 and the estimated useful life of the assets was fifty years at the time of purchase. As at 31 December 20X7 the property is to be revalued at $800,000.

(e) The plant which was sold had cost $350,000 and had a net book value of $274,000 as on 1.1.X7. $36,000 depreciation is to be charged on plant and machinery for 20X7.

(f) The loan stock has been in issue for some years. The 50c ordinary shares all rank for dividends at the end of the year.

(g) The management wish to provide for:

    (i) loan stock interest due
    (ii) a transfer to general reserve of $16,000
    (iii) audit fees of $4,000

(h) Inventory as at 31 December 20X7 was valued at $220,000 (cost).

(i) Taxation is to be ignored.

Required

Prepare the financial statements of Zabit Co as at 31 December 20X7 including a note showing movement on retained earnings. No other notes are required.

Answer

(a) Normal adjustments are needed for accruals and prepayments (insurance, light and heat, loan interest and audit fees). The loan interest accrued is calculated as follows.

	$'000
Charge needed in income statement (10% × $200,000)	20
Amount paid so far, as shown in list of account balances	10
Accrual: presumably six months' interest now payable	10

The accrued expenses shown in the balance sheet comprise:	$'000
Loan interest	10
Light and heat	3
Audit fee	4
	17

(b) The misposting of $20,000 to light and heat is also adjusted, by reducing the light and heat expense, but charging $20,000 to salesmen's commission.

(c) Depreciation on the building is calculated as $\dfrac{\$100,000}{50} = \$2,000$.

The NBV of the property is then $430,000 − $20,000 − $2,000 = $408,000 at the end of the year. When the property is revalued a reserve of $800,000 − $408,000 = $392,000 is then created.

(d) The profit on disposal of plant is calculated as proceeds $300,000 (per suspense account) less NBV $274,000, ie $26,000. The cost of the remaining plant is calculated at $830,000 − $350,000 = $480,000. The depreciation allowance at the year end is:

	$'000
Balance 1.1.X7	222
Charge for 20X7	36
Less depreciation on disposals (350 − 274)	(76)
	182

(e) Goodwill arising on the purchase of Mary & Co is:

	$'000
Consideration (per suspense account)	285
Assets at valuation	265
Goodwill	20

This is shown as an asset on the balance sheet. The investments, being owned by Zabit at the year end, are also shown on the balance sheet, whereas Mary's inventory, acquired and then sold, is added to the purchases figure for the year.

(f) The other item in the suspense account is dealt with as follows.

	$'000
Proceeds of issue of 100,000 ordinary shares	120
Less nominal value 100,000 × 50c	50
Excess of consideration over par value (= share premium)	70

(g) The transfer to general reserve increases it to $171,000 + $16,000 = $187,000.

We can now prepare the financial statements.

ZABIT CO
INCOME STATEMENT
FOR THE YEAR ENDED 31 DECEMBER 20X7

	$'000	$'000	$'000
Sales			2,695
Less cost of sales			
Opening inventory		190	
Purchases		2,186	
		2,376	
Less closing inventory		220	
			2,156
Gross profit			539
Profit on disposal of plant			26
			565
Expenses			
Wages, salaries and commission		274	
Sundry expenses		107	
Light and heat		14	
Depreciation: buildings		2	
plant		36	
Audit fees		4	
Loan interest		20	
			457
Profit for the period			108

Note:
Movement on retained earnings

	$	$
Profit for the period		108
Transfer to general reserve		(16)
Dividends: preference	7	
ordinary	8	(15)
Retained earnings for the year		77
Retained earnings b/f		242
Retained earnings c/f		319

ZABIT CO
BALANCE SHEET AS AT 31 DECEMBER 20X7

	$'000	$'000
Assets		
Non-current assets		
Property, plant land and equipment		
Property at valuation		800
Plant: cost	480	
depreciation	182	
		298
Goodwill		20
Investments		231
Current assets		
Inventory	220	
Trade accounts receivable	179	
Prepayments	6	
Cash	126	
		531
Total assets		1,880
Equity and liabilities		
Equity		
50c ordinary shares	400	
7% $1 preference shares	100	
Share premium	70	
Revaluation reserve	392	
General reserve	187	
Retained earnings	319	
		1,468
Non-current liabilities		
10% loan stock (secured)		200
Current liabilities		
Trade accounts receivable	195	
Accrued expenses	17	
		212
Total equity and liabilities		1,880

Chapter Roundup

- This chapter is long but extremely important. In it we have explained some important differences between the accounts of a *limited liability company* and those of sole traders or partnerships.

- IAS 1 *Presentation of financial statements* lists the required contents of a company's income statement and balance sheet. These requirements are *in addition* to those disclosures required by other standards (IAS 8, IAS 16, IFRS 5 etc).

- IAS 1 gives substantial guidance on the presentation of financial statements.

- You must be able to account for these items in particular when preparing the accounts of limited liability companies.
    - Taxation
    - Ordinary and preferred shares
    - Shareholders' equity (share premium, revaluation surplus, reserves and retained earnings)

- A company can increase its share capital by means of a **bonus issue** or a **rights issue**.

- You should be aware of the issues surrounding the current/non-current distinction as well as the disclosure requirements laid down in IAS 1.

- IAS 8 *Accounting policies, changes in accounting estimates and errors*, is a very important standard. You should be able to define and deal with:
    - changes in accounting policies
    - changes in accounting estimates
    - material errors

- You should be aware of the disclosures in IFRS 5 *Non-current assets held for sale and discontinued operations*. They are required so that users of financial statements have more useful information about the financial position of the entity.

- IFRS 5 *Non current assets held for sale and discontinued operations* requires assets and groups of assets that are 'held for sale' to be presented separately on the face of the balance sheet and the results of discontinued operations to be presented separately in the income statement.

Quick Quiz

1. What is the meaning of limited liability?
2. What are the general disclosure requirements of IAS 1?
3. What is the difference between issued capital and called-up capital?
4. What are the differences between ordinary shares and preferred shares?
5. What are the differences between loan stock and share capital?
6. A company issues 50,000 $1 shares at a price of $1.25 per share. How much should be posted to the share premium account?

    A $50,000
    B $12,500
    C $62,500
    D $60,000

7. Distinguish between a bonus (capitalisation) issue and a rights issue.

Answers to Quick Quiz

1. The maximum amount that a shareholder has to pay is the amount paid on his shares.
2. Some items have to appear on the face of the income statement or balance sheet, while others are disclosed by way of a note.
3. Issued share capital is the par value of shares issued to shareholders. Called-up share capital is the amount payable to date by the shareholders.
4. Ordinary shares can be paid any or no dividend. The dividend attaching to preferred shares is set from the start.
5. Loan stock are long-term loans, and so loan note holders are long-term payables. Equity shareholders own the company.
6. B. (50,000 × 25c)
7. A bonus issue is financed by capitalising revenue reserves. A rights issue is paid for by the shareholders taking up the shares.

Now try the questions below from the Exam Question Bank

Number	Level	Marks	Time
Q36	Examination	10	18 mins
Q38	Examination	12	22 mins
Q39	Examination	10	18 mins
Q40	Introductory	–	45 mins
Q41	Examination	10	18 mins
Q42	Examination	11	20 mins

PART E FINANCIAL STATEMENTS

Cash flow statements

Topic list	Syllabus reference
1 IAS 7 *Cash flow statements*	5(c)(iii)
2 Preparing a cash flow statement	5(d)(iii)

Introduction

In the long run, a profit will result in an increase in the company's cash balance but, as Keynes observed, 'in the long run we are all dead'. In the short run, **the making of a profit will not necessarily result in an increased cash balance.** The observation leads us to two questions. The first relates to the importance of the distinction between cash and profit. The second is concerned with the usefulness of the information provided by the balance sheet and income statement in the problem of deciding whether the company has, or will be able to generate, sufficient cash to finance its operations.

The importance of the **distinction between cash and profit** and the scant attention paid to this by the income statement has resulted in the development of cash flow statements.

This chapter adopts a systematic approach to the preparation of cash flow statements in examinations; you should learn this method and you will then be equipped for any problems in the exam itself.

PART E   FINANCIAL STATEMENTS

Study guide

Section 23 – Cash flow statements

- Explain the differences between profit and cash flow.
- Explain the need for management to control cash flow.
- Explain the value to users of financial statements of a cash flow statement.
- Explain the IASB requirements for cash flow statements (excluding group aspects).
- Explain the inward and outward flows of cash in a typical company.
- Calculate the figures needed for the cash flow statement including among others:
    - Cash flows from operating activities (indirect method)
    - Cash flows from investing activities
- Calculate cash flow from operating activities using the direct method.
- Review of information to be derived by users from the cash flow statement (see also Sessions 25-26).
- Prepare cash flow statements from given balance sheets with or without an income statement.

Exam guide

This topic is very important. You are certain to be examined on it.

1 IAS 7 Cash flow statements

FAST FORWARD

Cash flow statements are a useful addition to the financial statements of a company because accounting profit is not the only indicator of performance. Cash flow statements concentrate on the sources and uses of cash and are a useful indicator of a company's liquidity and solvency.

It has been argued that 'profit' does not always give a useful or meaningful picture of a company's operations. Readers of a company's financial statements might even be **misled by a reported profit figure**.

(a) Shareholders might believe that if a company makes a profit after tax, of say, $100,000 then this is the amount which it could afford to **pay as a dividend**. Unless the company has **sufficient cash** available to stay in business and also to pay a dividend, the shareholders' expectations would be wrong.

(b) Employees might believe that if a company makes profits, it can afford to **pay higher wages** next year. This opinion may not be correct: the ability to pay wages depends on the **availability of cash**.

(c) Survival of a business entity depends not so much on profits as on its **ability to pay its debts when they fall due**. Such payments might include 'profit and loss' items such as material purchases, wages, interest and taxation etc, but also capital payments for new fixed assets and the repayment of loan capital when this falls due (for example on the redemption of debentures).

From these examples, it may be apparent that a company's performance and prospects depend not so much on the 'profits' earned in a period, but more realistically on liquidity or **cash flows**.

1.1 Funds flow and cash flow

Some countries, either currently or in the past, have required the disclosure of additional statements based on **funds flow** rather than cash flow. However, the definition of 'funds' can be very vague and such statements often simply require a rearrangement of figures already provided in the balance sheet and income statement. By contrast, a statement of cash flows is unambiguous and provides information which is additional to that provided in the rest of the accounts. It also lends itself to organisation by activity and not by balance sheet classification.

Cash flow statements are frequently given as an **additional statement**, supplementing the balance sheet, income statement and related notes. The group aspects of cash flow statements (and certain complex matters) have been excluded as they are beyond the scope of your syllabus.

1.2 Objective of IAS 7

The aim of IAS 7 is to provide information to users of financial statements about an entity's **ability to generate cash and cash equivalents**, as well as indicating the cash needs of the entity. The cash flow statement provides *historical* information about cash and cash equivalents, classifying cash flows between operating, investing and financing activities.

1.3 Scope

A cash flow statement should be presented as an **integral part** of an entity's financial statements. All types of entity can provide useful information about cash flows as the need for cash is universal, whatever the nature of their revenue-producing activities. Therefore **all entities are required by the standard to produce a cash flow statement.**

1.4 Benefits of cash flow information

The use of cash flow statements is very much **in conjunction** with the rest of the financial statements. Users can gain further appreciation of the change in net assets, of the entity's financial position (liquidity and solvency) and the entity's ability to adapt to changing circumstances by adjusting the amount and timing of cash flows. Cash flow statements **enhance comparability** as they are not affected by differing accounting policies used for the same type of transactions or events.

Cash flow information of a historical nature can be used as an indicator of the amount, timing and certainty of future cash flows. Past forecast cash flow information can be **checked for accuracy** as actual figures emerge. The relationship between profit and cash flows can be analysed as can changes in prices over time. All this information helps management to control costs by controlling cash flow.

1.5 Definitions

The standard gives the following definitions, the most important of which are **cash** and **cash equivalents**.

Key terms

- **Cash** comprises cash on hand and demand deposits.
- **Cash equivalents** are short-term, highly liquid investments that are readily convertible to known amounts of cash and which are subject to an insignificant risk of changes in value.
- **Cash flows** are inflows and outflows of cash and cash equivalents.
- **Operating activities** are the principal revenue-producing activities of the enterprise and other activities that are not investing or financing activities.
- **Investing activities** are the acquisition and disposal of non-current assets and other investments not included in cash equivalents.
- **Financing activities** are activities that result in changes in the size and composition of the equity capital and borrowings of the entity. *(IAS 7)*

1.6 Cash and cash equivalents

The standard expands on the definition of cash equivalents: they are not held for investment or other long-term purposes, but rather to meet short-term cash commitments. To fulfil the above definition, an investment's **maturity date should normally be three months from its acquisition date**. It would usually be the case then that equity investments (ie shares in other companies) are *not* cash equivalents. An exception would be where redeemable preference shares were acquired with a very close redemption date.

Loans and other borrowings from banks are classified as investing activities. In some countries, however, **bank overdrafts** are repayable on demand and are treated as part of an enterprise's total cash management system. In these circumstances an overdrawn balance will be included in cash and cash equivalents. Such banking arrangements are characterised by a balance which fluctuates between overdrawn and credit.

Movements between different types of cash and cash equivalent are not included in cash flows. The investment of surplus cash in cash equivalents is part of cash management, not part of operating, investing or financing activities.

1.7 Presentation of a cash flow statement

IAS 7 requires cash flow statements to report cash flows during the period classified by **operating, investing and financing activities.**

The manner of presentation of cash flows from operating, investing and financing activities **depends on the nature of the enterprise**. By classifying cash flows between different activities in this way users can see the impact on cash and cash equivalents of each one, and their relationships with each other. We can look at each in more detail.

1.7.1 Operating activities

This is perhaps the key part of the cash flow statement because it shows whether, and to what extent, companies can **generate cash from their operations**. It is these operating cash flows which must, in the end pay for all cash outflows relating to other activities, ie paying loan interest, dividends and so on.

Most of the components of cash flows from operating activities will be those items which **determine the net profit or loss of the enterprise**, ie they relate to the main revenue-producing activities of the enterprise. The standard gives the following as examples of cash flows from operating activities.

- (a) Cash receipts from the sale of goods and the rendering of services
- (b) Cash receipts from royalties, fees, commissions and other revenue
- (c) Cash payments to suppliers for goods and services
- (d) Cash payments to and on behalf of employees

Certain items may be included in the net profit or loss for the period which do *not* relate to operational cash flows, for example the profit or loss on the sale of a piece of plant will be included in net profit or loss, but the cash flows will be classed as **financing**.

1.7.2 Investing activities

The cash flows classified under this heading show the extent of new investment in **assets which will generate future profit and cash flows**. The standard gives the following examples of cash flows arising from investing activities.

- (a) Cash payments to acquire property, plant and equipment, intangibles and other non-current assets, including those relating to capitalised development costs and self-constructed property, plant and equipment

- (b) Cash receipts from sales of property, plant and equipment, intangibles and other non-current assets
- (c) Cash payments to acquire shares or debentures of other enterprises
- (d) Cash receipts from sales of shares or debentures of other enterprises
- (e) Cash advances and loans made to other parties
- (f) Cash receipts from the repayment of advances and loans made to other parties

1.7.3 Financing activities

This section of the cash flow statement shows the share of cash which the enterprise's capital providers have claimed during the period. This is an indicator of **likely future interest and dividend payments**. The standard gives the following examples of cash flows which might arise under these headings.

- (a) Cash proceeds from issuing shares
- (b) Cash payments to owners to acquire or redeem the enterprise's shares
- (c) Cash proceeds from issuing debentures, loans, notes, bonds, mortgages and other short or long-term borrowings
- (d) Cash repayments of amounts borrowed

1.8 Reporting cash flows from operating activities

The standard offers a choice of method for this part of the cash flow statement.

- (a) **Direct method:** disclose major classes of gross cash receipts and gross cash payments
- (b) **Indirect method**: net profit or loss is adjusted for the effects of transactions of a non-cash nature, any deferrals or accruals of past or future operating cash receipts or payments, and items of income or expense associated with investing or financing cash flows

The **direct method** discloses information, not available elsewhere in the financial statements, which could be of use in estimating future cash flows. However, the **indirect method** is simpler, more widely used and more likely to be examined.

1.8.1 Using the direct method

There are different ways in which the **information about gross cash receipts and payments** can be obtained. The most obvious way is simply to extract the information from the accounting records. This may be a laborious task, however, and the indirect method below may be easier.

1.8.2 Using the indirect method

This method is undoubtedly **easier** from the point of view of the preparer of the cash flow statement. The net profit or loss for the period is adjusted for the following.

- (a) Changes during the period in inventories, operating receivables and payables
- (b) Non-cash items, eg depreciation, provisions, profits/losses on the sales of assets
- (c) Other items, the cash flows from which should be classified under investing or financing activities.

PART E FINANCIAL STATEMENTS

A **proforma** of such a calculation is as follows and this method may be more common in the exam.

	$
Profit before interest and tax (income statement)*	X
Add depreciation	X
Loss (profit) on sale of non-current assets	X
(Increase)/decrease in inventories	(X)/X
(Increase)/decrease in receivables	(X)/X
Increase/(decrease) in payables	X/(X)
Cash generated from operations	X
Interest (paid)/received	(X)
Income taxes paid	(X)
Net cash flows from operating activities	X

* Take profit before tax and add back any interest expense

It is important to understand why **certain items are added and others subtracted**. Note the following points.

(a) Depreciation is not a cash expense, but is deducted in arriving at the profit figure in the income statement. It makes sense, therefore, to eliminate it by adding it back.

(b) By the same logic, a loss on a disposal of a non-current asset (arising through underprovision of depreciation) needs to be added back and a profit deducted.

(c) An increase in inventories means less cash – you have spent cash on buying inventory.

(d) An increase in receivables means the company's receivables have not paid as much, and therefore there is less cash.

(e) If we pay off payables, causing the figure to decrease, again we have less cash.

1.8.3 Indirect versus direct

The direct method is encouraged where the necessary information is not too costly to obtain, but IAS 7 does not demand it. In practice, therefore, the direct method is rarely used. It could be argued that companies ought to monitor their cash flows carefully enough on an ongoing basis to be able to use the direct method at minimal extra cost.

1.9 Interest and dividends

Cash flows from interest and dividends received and paid should each be **disclosed separately**. Each should be classified in a consistent manner from period to period as either operating, investing or financing activities.

Dividends paid by the enterprise can be classified in **one of two ways**.

(a) As a **financing cash flow**, showing the cost of obtaining financial resources.

(b) As a component of **cash flows from operating activities** so that users can assess the enterprise's ability to pay dividends out of operating cash flows.

1.10 Taxes on income

Cash flows arising from taxes on income should be **separately disclosed** and should be classified as cash flows from operating activities *unless* they can be specifically identified with financing and investing activities.

Taxation cash flows are often **difficult to match** to the originating underlying transaction, so most of the time all tax cash flows are classified as arising from operating activities.

1.11 Components of cash and cash equivalents

The components of cash and cash equivalents should be disclosed and a **reconciliation** should be presented, showing the amounts in the cash flow statement reconciled with the equivalent items reported in the balance sheet.

It is also necessary to disclose the **accounting policy** used in deciding the items included in cash and cash equivalents, in accordance with IAS 1 *Presentation of financial statements*, but also because of the wide range of cash management practices worldwide.

1.12 Other disclosures

All enterprises should disclose, together with a **commentary by management**, any other information likely to be of importance, for example:

(a) restrictions on the use of or access to any part of cash equivalents;

(b) the amount of undrawn borrowing facilities which are available; and

(c) Cash flows which increased operating capacity compared to cash flows which merely maintained operating capacity.

1.13 Example of a cash flow statement

In the next section we will look at the procedures for preparing a cash flow statement. First, look at this **example**, adapted from the example given in the standard (which is based on a group and therefore beyond the scope of your syllabus).

1.13.1 Direct method

CASH FLOW STATEMENT (DIRECT METHOD)
YEAR ENDED 20X7

	$m	$m
Cash flows from operating activities		
Cash receipts from customers	30,330	
Cash paid to suppliers and employees	(27,600)	
Cash generated from operations	2,730	
Interest paid	(270)	
Income taxes paid	(900)	
Net cash from operating activities		1,560
Cash flows from investing activities		
Purchase of property, plant and equipment	(900)	
Proceeds from sale of equipment	20	
Interest received	200	
Dividends received	200	
Net cash used in investing activities		(480)
Cash flows from financing activities		
Proceeds from issuance of share capital	250	
Proceeds from long-term borrowings	250	
Dividends paid*	(1,290)	
Net cash used in financing activities		(790)
Net increase in cash and cash equivalents		290
Cash and cash equivalents at beginning of period (Note)		120
Cash and cash equivalents at end of period (Note)		410

* This could also be shown as an operating cash flow

1.13.2 Indirect method

CASH FLOW STATEMENT (INDIRECT METHOD)
YEAR ENDED 20X7

	$m	$m
Cash flows from operating activities		
Net profit before taxation	3,570	
Adjustments for:		
Depreciation	450	
Investment income	(500)	
Interest expense	400	
Operating profit before working capital changes	3,920	
Increase in trade and other receivables	(500)	
Decrease in inventories	1,050	
Decrease in trade payables	(1,740)	
Cash generated from operations	2,730	
Interest paid	(270)	
Income taxes paid	(900)	
Net cash from operating activities		1,560

	$m	$m
Cash flows from investing activities		
Purchase of property, plant and equipment	(900)	
Proceeds from sale of equipment	20	
Interest received	200	
Dividends received	200	
Net cash used in investing activities		(480)
Cash flows from financing activities		
Proceeds from issuance of share capital	250	
Proceeds from long-term borrowings	250	
Dividends paid*	(1,290)	
Net cash used in financing activities		(790)
Net increase in cash and cash equivalents		290
Cash and cash equivalents at beginning of period (Note)		120
Cash and cash equivalents at end of period (Note)		410

* This could also be shown as an operating cash flow

The following note is required to both versions of the statement.

Note: Cash and cash equivalents

Cash and cash equivalents consist of cash on hand and balances with banks, and investments in money market instruments. Cash and cash equivalents included in the cash flow statement comprise the following balance sheet amounts.

	20X7	20X6
	$m	$m
Cash on hand and balances with banks	40	25
Short-term investments	370	95
Cash and cash equivalents	410	120

The company has undrawn borrowing facilities of $2,000 of which only $700 may be used for future expansion.

2 Preparing a cash flow statement

You need to be aware of the **format** of the statement as laid out in IAS 7. Setting out the format is the first step. Then follow the **step-by-step preparation procedure**.

In essence, preparing a cash flow statement is very straightforward. You should therefore simply learn the format and apply the steps noted in the example below. Note that the following items are treated in a way that might seem confusing, but the treatment is logical if you **think in terms of cash**.

(a) **Increase in inventory** is treated as **negative** (in brackets). This is because it represents a cash **outflow**; cash is being spent on inventory.

(b) An **increase in receivables** would be treated as **negative** for the same reasons; more receivables means less cash.

(c) By contrast an **increase in payables is positive** because cash is being retained and not used to settle accounts payable. There is therefore more of it.

PART E FINANCIAL STATEMENTS

2.1 Example: Preparation of a cash flow statement

Colby Co's income statement for the year ended 31 December 20X2 and balance sheets at 31 December 20X1 and 31 December 20X2 were as follows.

COLBY CO
INCOME STATEMENT FOR THE YEAR ENDED 31 DECEMBER 20X2

	$'000	$'000
Sales		720
Raw materials consumed	70	
Staff costs	94	
Depreciation	118	
Loss on disposal of non-current asset	18	
		(300)
		420
Interest payable		(28)
Profit before tax		392
Taxation		(124)
Profit for the period		268

COLBY CO
BALANCE SHEETS AS AT 31 DECEMBER

	20X2		20X1	
	$'000	$'000	$'000	$'000
Assets				
Property, plant and equipment				
Cost	1,596		1,560	
Depreciation	318		224	
		1,278		1,336
Current assets				
Inventory	24		20	
Trade receivables	76		58	
Bank	48		56	
		148		134
Total assets		1,426		1,470
Equity and liabilities				
Capital and reserves				
Share capital	360		340	
Share premium	36		24	
Retained earnings	716		514	
		1,112		878
Non-current liabilities				
Non-current loans		200		500
Current liabilities				
Trade payables	12		6	
Taxation	102		86	
		114		92
		1,426		1,470

During the year, the company paid $90,000 for a new piece of machinery.

Dividends paid during 20X2 totalled $66,000.

Required

Prepare a cash flow statement for Colby Co for the year ended 31 December 20X2 in accordance with the requirements of IAS 7, using the indirect method.

Solution

Step 1 Set out the proforma cash flow statement with the headings required by IAS 7. You should leave plenty of space. Ideally, use three or more sheets of paper, one for the main statement, one for the notes and one for your workings. It is obviously essential to know the formats very well.

Step 2 Begin with the **reconciliation of profit before tax to net cash from operating activities** as far as possible. When preparing the statement from balance sheets, you will usually have to calculate such items as depreciation, loss on sale of non-current assets, profit for the year and tax paid (see Step 4). Note that you may not be given the tax charge in the income statement. You will then have to assume that the tax paid in the year is last year's year-end provision and calculate the charge as the balancing figure.

Step 3 Calculate the cash flow figures for **dividends paid, purchase or sale of non-current assets, issue of shares and repayment of loans** if these are not already given to you (as they may be).

Step 4 If you are not given the profit figure, open up a **working for the trading, income and expense account**. Using the opening and closing balances, the taxation charge and dividends paid and proposed, you will be able to calculate profit for the year as the balancing figure to put in the net profit to net cash flow from operating activities section.

Step 5 You will now be able to **complete the statement** by slotting in the figures given or calculated.

COLBY CO
CASH FLOW STATEMENT FOR THE YEAR ENDED 31 DECEMBER 20X2

	$'000	$'000
Net cash flow from operating activities		
Profit before tax	392	
Depreciation charges	118	
Loss on sale of property, plant and equipment	18	
Interest expense	28	
Increase in inventories	(4)	
Increase in receivables	(18)	
Increase in payables	6	
Cash generated from operations	540	
Interest paid	(28)	
Dividends paid	(66)	
Tax paid (86 + 124 – 102)	(108)	
Net cash flow from operating activities		338
Cash flows from investing activities		
Payments to acquire property, plant and equipment	(90)	
Receipts from sales property, plant and equipment	12	
Net cash outflow from investing activities		(78)
Cash flows from financing activities		
Issues of share capital (360 + 36 – 340 – 24)	32	
Long-term loans repaid (500 – 200)	(300)	
Net cash flows from financing		(268)
Decrease in cash and cash equivalents		(8)
Cash and cash equivalents at 1.1.X2		56
Cash and cash equivalents at 31.12.X2		48

Working: property, plant and equipment

COST

	$'000		$'000
At 1.1.X2	1,560	At 31.12.X2	1,596
Purchases	90	Disposals (balance)	54
	1,650		1,650

ACCUMULATED DEPRECIATION

	$'000		$'000
At 31.1.X2	318	At 1.1.X2	224
Depreciation on disposals (balance)	24	Charge for year	118
	342		342

	$'000
NBV of disposals	30
Net loss reported	(18)
Proceeds of disposals	12

Question

Cash flow statement 2

Set out below are the financial statements of Shabnum Co. You are the financial controller, faced with the task of implementing IAS 7 *Cash flow statements*.

SHABNUM CO
INCOME STATEMENT FOR THE YEAR ENDED 31 DECEMBER 20X2

	$'000
Revenue	2,553
Cost of sales	(1,814)
Gross profit	739
Distribution costs	(125)
Administrative expenses	(264)
	350
Interest received	25
Interest paid	(75)
Profit before taxation	300
Taxation	(140)
Profit for the period	160

SHABNUM CO
BALANCE SHEETS AS AT 31 DECEMBER

	20X2 $'000	20X1 $'000
Assets		
Non-current assets		
Property, plant and equipment	380	305
Intangible assets	250	200
Investments	–	25
Current assets		
Inventories	150	102
Receivables	390	315
Short-term investments	50	–
Cash in hand	2	1
Total assets	1,222	948

20: CASH FLOW STATEMENTS

	$'000	$'000
Equity and liabilities		
Equity		
Share capital ($1 ordinary shares)	200	150
Share premium account	160	150
Revaluation reserve	100	91
Retained earnings	260	180
Non-current liabilities		
Loan	170	50
Current liabilities		
Trade payables	127	119
Bank overdraft	85	98
Taxation	120	110
Total equity and liabilities	1,222	948

The following information is available.

(a) The proceeds of the sale of non-current asset investments amounted to $30,000.

(b) Fixtures and fittings, with an original cost of $85,000 and a net book value of $45,000, were sold for $32,000 during the year.

(c) The following information relates to property, plant and equipment

	31.12.20X2	31.12.20X1
	$'000	$'000
Cost	720	595
Accumulated depreciation	340	290
Net book value	380	305

(d) 50,000 $1 ordinary shares were issued during the year at a premium of 20c per share.

(e) Dividends totalling $80,000 were paid during the year.

Required

Prepare a cash flow statement for the year to 31 December 20X2 using the format laid out in IAS 7.

Answer

SHABNUM CO
CASH FLOW STATEMENT FOR THE YEAR ENDED 31 DECEMBER 20X2

	$'000	$'000
Net cash flows from operating activities		
Profit before tax	300	
Depreciation charge (W1)	90	
Interest expense	50	
Loss on sale of property, plant and equipment (45 – 32)	13	
Profit on sale of non-current asset investments	(5)	
(Increase)/decrease in inventories	(48)	
(Increase)/decrease in receivables	(75)	
Increase/(decrease) in payables	8	
Cash generated from operating activities	333	
Interest received	25	
Interest paid	(75)	
Dividends paid	(80)	
Tax paid (110 + 140 – 120)	(130)	
Net cash flow from operating activities		73

	$'000	$'000
Cash flows from investing activities		
Payments to acquire property, plant and equipment (W2)	(201)	
Payments to acquire intangible non-current assets	(50)	
Receipts from sales of property, plant and equipment	32	
Receipts from sale of non-current asset investments	30	
Net cash flows from investing activities		(189)
Cash flows from financing activities		
Issue of share capital	60	
Long-term loan	120	
Net cash flows from financing		180
Increase in cash and cash equivalents (Note)		64
Cash and cash equivalents at 1.1 X2 (Note)		(97)
Cash and cash equivalents at 31.12.X2 (Note)		(33)

NOTES TO THE CASH FLOW STATEMENT

Note: analysis of the balances of cash and cash equivalents as shown in the balance sheet

	20X2	20X1	Change in year
	$'000	$'000	$'000
Cash in hand	2	1	1
Short term investments	50		50
Bank overdraft	(85)	(98)	13
	(33)	(97)	64

Workings

1   Depreciation charge

	$'000	$'000
Depreciation at 31 December 20X2		340
Depreciation 31 December 20X1	290	
Depreciation on assets sold (85 – 45)	40	
		250
Charge for the year		90

2   Purchase of property, plant and equipment

PROPERTY, PLANT AND EQUIPMENT

	$'000		$'000
1.1.X2 Balance b/d	595	Disposals	85
Revaluation (100 – 91)	9		
Purchases (bal fig)	201	31.12.X2 Balance c/d	720
	805		805

2.2 The advantages of cash flow accounting

The advantages of cash flow accounting are as follows.

(a) Survival in business depends on the **ability to generate** cash. Cash flow accounting directs attention towards this critical issue.

(b) Cash flow is **more comprehensive** than 'profit' which is dependent on accounting conventions and concepts.

(c) **Creditors** (long and short-term) are more interested in an enterprise's ability to repay them than in its profitability. Whereas 'profits' might indicate that cash is likely to be available, cash flow accounting is more direct with its message.

(d) Cash flow reporting provides a better means of **comparing the results** of different companies than traditional profit reporting.

(e) Cash flow reporting **satisfies the needs of all users** better.

 (i) For **management**, it provides the sort of information on which decisions should be taken: (in management accounting, 'relevant costs' to a decision are future cash flows); traditional profit accounting does not help with decision-making.

 (ii) For **shareholders and auditors**, cash flow accounting can provide a satisfactory basis for stewardship accounting.

 (iii) As described previously, the information needs of **creditors and employees** will be better served by cash flow accounting.

(f) Cash flow forecasts are **easier to prepare**, as well as more useful, than profit forecasts.

(g) They can in some respects be **audited more easily** than accounts based on the accruals concept.

(h) The accruals concept is confusing, and cash flows are **more easily understood**.

(i) Cash flow accounting should be both retrospective, and also include a forecast for the future. This is of **great information value** to all users of accounting information.

(j) **Forecasts** can subsequently be **monitored** by the publication of variance statements which compare actual cash flows against the forecast.

Question — Cash flow accounting

Can you think of some possible disadvantages of cash flow accounting?

Answer

The main disadvantages of cash accounting are essentially the advantages of accruals accounting (proper matching of related items). There is also the practical problem that few businesses keep historical cash flow information in the form needed to prepare a historical cash flow statement and so extra record keeping is likely to be necessary.

2.3 Criticisms of IAS 7

The inclusion of **cash equivalents** has been criticised because it does not reflect the way in which businesses are managed: in particular, the requirement that to be a cash equivalent an investment has to be within three months of maturity is considered **unrealistic**.

The management of assets similar to cash (ie 'cash equivalents') is not distinguished from other investment decisions.

Exam focus point: You could be asked to consider the usefulness of a cash flow statement as well as having to prepare one.

PART E   FINANCIAL STATEMENTS

Chapter Roundup

- **Cash flow statements** are a useful addition to the financial statements of companies because it is recognised that accounting profit is not the only indicator of a company's performance.
- Cash flow statements concentrate on the sources and uses of cash and are a useful indicator of a company's **liquidity and solvency**.
- You need to be aware of the **format** of the statement as laid out in **IAS 7**; setting out the format is an essential first stage in preparing the statement, so this format must be learnt.
- Remember the **step-by-step preparation procedure** and use it for all the questions you practise.

Quick Quiz

1   What is the objective of IAS 7?

2   What are the benefits of cash flow information according to IAS 7?

3   Define cash and cash equivalents according to IAS 7.

4   Which of the following headings is not a classification of cash flows in IAS 7?

    A   Operating
    B   Investing
    C   Administration
    D   Financing

5   What is the 'indirect method' of preparing a cash flow statement?

6   Set out the five steps required in preparing a cash flow statement.

7   What are the advantages of cash flow accounting?

Answers to Quick Quiz

1. To provide information to users about the company's ability to generate cash and cash equivalents.

2. Further information is available about liquidation and solvency, of the change in net assets, the ability to adapt to changing circumstances and comparability between enterprises.

3. See Para 1.5, Key Terms.

4. C. Administration costs are a classification in the income statement, not the cash flow statement.

5. The operating cash flow is arrived at by adjusting net profits (or loss) for non-cash items and changes in inventories, operating receivables and operating payables.

6. See Paragraph 2.1.

7. See Paragraph 2.2.

Now try the questions below from the Exam Question Bank

Number	Level	Marks	Time
Q27	Examination	10	18 mins
Q28 (a)	Examination	10	18 mins
Q28 (b)	Examination	10	18 mins
Q29	Examination	10	18 mins

PART E FINANCIAL STATEMENTS

Group accounts

Topic list	Syllabus reference
1 Introduction to group accounts	5(d)(iv)
2 IAS 27: *Summary of consolidation procedures*	5(d)(iv)
3 Cancellation and part cancellation	5(d)(iv)
4 Minority interests	5(d)(iv)
5 Goodwill arising on consolidation	5(d)(iv)
6 A technique of consolidation	5(d)(iv)
7 Summary: consolidated balance sheet	5(d)(iv)

Introduction

This chapter introduces the **basic procedures** required in consolidation and gives a formal step by step plan for carrying out a balance sheet consolidation. This step by step procedure should be useful to you as a starting guide for answering any question, but remember that you cannot rely on it to answer the question for you.

Each question must be approached and **answered on its own merits**. Examiners often put small extra or different problems in because, as they are always reminding students, it is not possible to 'rote-learn' consolidation.

The **method of consolidation** shown here uses schedules for workings (reserves, minority interests etc) rather than the ledger accounts used in some other texts. This is because we believe that ledger accounts lead students to 'learn' the consolidation journals without thinking about what they are doing – always a dangerous practice in consolidation questions.

There are plenty of questions in this chapter – work through *all* of them carefully.

PART E   FINANCIAL STATEMENTS

Study guide

Section 24 – Basic consolidated accounts

- Define parent company, subsidiary company and group.
- Explain the IASB requirements defining which companies must be consolidated.
- Prepare a consolidated balance sheet for a parent with one wholly-owned subsidiary (no goodwill arising).
- Explain how to calculate the retained earnings balance for the consolidated balance sheet.
- Explain how other reserves (share premium account and revaluation reserve) are dealt with on consolidation.
- Introduce the concept of goodwill on acquisition and illustrate the effect on the consolidated balance sheet.
- Adjust the value of goodwill on acquisition to reflect impairment.
- Explain and illustrate a methodical approach to calculating the necessary figures for the consolidated balance sheet.
- Introduce the concept of minority interests in subsidiaries and illustrate the effect on the consolidated balance sheet.
- Explain and illustrate how the calculation of the minority interest is made.

Exam guide

This is a new topic. You have to be able to prepare a simple group balance sheet involving one subsidiary and goodwill. You also need to know about minority interest.

1 Introduction to group accounts

FAST FORWARD

> You will probably know that many large companies actually consist of several companies controlled by one central or administrative company. Together these companies are called a **group**. The controlling company, called the **parent** or **holding company**, will own some or all of the shares in the other companies, called subsidiary and associated companies.

There are many reasons for businesses to operate as groups; for the goodwill associated with the names of the subsidiaries, for tax or legal purposes and so forth. In many countries, company law requires that the results of a group should be presented as a whole. Unfortunately, it is not possible simply to add all the results together and this chapter and those following will teach you how to **consolidate** all the results of companies within a group.

In traditional accounting terminology, a **group of companies** consists of a **parent company** and one or more **subsidiary companies** which are controlled by the holding company.

1.1 Accounting standards

The main accounting standards dealing with consolidated accounts are IAS 27 *Consolidated and separate financial statements* and IFRS 3 *Business combinations*.

IAS 27 covers the basic group definitions and consolidation procedures of a parent-subsidiary relationship. First of all, however, we will look at all the important definitions involved in group accounts, which **determine how to treat each particular type of investment** in group accounts.

21: GROUP ACCOUNTS

Exam focus point

All the definitions relating to group accounts are extremely important. You must **learn them** and **understand** their meaning and application.

1.2 Definitions

We will look at some of these definitions in more detail later, but they are useful here in that they give you an overview of all aspects of group accounts.

- **Control**. The power to govern the financial and operating policies of an entity so as to obtain benefits from its activities.
- **Subsidiary**. An entity that is controlled by another entity (known as the parent).
- **Parent**. An entity that has one or more subsidiaries.
- **Group**. A parent and all its subsidiaries.
- **Minority interest**. That portion of the profit or loss… and the net assets of a subsidiary…which are not owned…by the parent. (IAS 27)

1.3 Investments in subsidiaries

You should be able to tell from the definitions given above that the important point here is **control**. In most cases, this will involve the holding company or parent owning a majority of the ordinary shares in the subsidiary (to which normal voting rights are attached). There are circumstances, however, when the parent may own only a minority of the voting power in the subsidiary, *but* the parent still has control. In terms of group accounts the **minority** refers to the other shareholders in a subsidiary – the owners of shares held outside the group.

IAS 27 states that control can usually be assumed to exist when the parent **owns more than half (ie over 50%) of the voting power** of an enterprise *unless* it can be clearly shown that **such ownership does not constitute control** (these situations will be very rare).

What about situations where this ownership criterion does not exist? IAS 27 lists the following situations where **control exists**, even when the parent owns only 50% or less of the voting power of an enterprise.

(a) The parent has power over more than 50% of the voting rights by virtue of **agreement with other investors**

(b) The parent has power to **govern the financial and operating policies** of the enterprise by statute or under an agreement

(c) The parent has the power to **appoint or remove a majority of members of the board of directors** (or equivalent governing body)

(d) The parent has power to cast a **majority of votes at meetings of the board of directors**

Exam focus point

You should learn the contents of the above paragraph as you may be asked to apply them in the exam.

What does consolidation involve?

Before moving on to the formal definitions, think about what consolidation involves.

Basic principles

- Consolidation means **adding together**.
- Consolidation means **cancellation of like items** internal to the group.
- Consolidate as if you **owned everything** then **show** the **extent to which you do not** own everything.

1.4 Example to show basic principles

There are two companies, Pleasant and Sweet. Pleasant owns 80% of the shares in Sweet. Pleasant has a head office building worth $100,000. Sweet has a factory worth $80,000. Remember that consolidation means presenting the results of two companies as if they were one.

1.4.1 Adding together

You add together the values of the head office building and the factory to get an asset, land and buildings, in the group accounts of $100,000 + $80,000 = £180,000. So far so good; this is what you would expect consolidation to mean.

1.5 Example continued

Suppose Pleasant has receivables of $40,000 and Sweet has receivables of $30,000. Included in the debtors of Pleasant is $5,000 owed by Sweet. Remember again that consolidation means presenting the results of the two companies as if they were one.

Do we then simply add together $40,000 and $30,000 to arrive at the figure for consolidated receivables? We cannot simply do this, because $5,000 of the receivables is owed within the group. This amount is irrelevant when we consider what the group as a whole is owed.

Suppose further that Pleasant has payables of $50,000 and Sweet has payables of $45,000. We already know that $5,000 of Sweet's payables is a balance owed to Pleasant. If we just added the figures together, we would not reflect fairly the amount the group owes to the outside world. The outside world does not care what these companies owe to each other – that is an internal matter for the group.

1.5.1 Cancellation of like items

To arrive at a fair picture we eliminate both the receivable of $5,000 in Pleasant's books and the payable of $5,000 in Sweet's books. Only then do we consolidate by adding together.

Consolidated receivables = $40,000 + $30,000 – $5,000
= £65,000

Consolidated payables = $50,000 + $45,000 – $5,000
= $90,000

1.6 Example continued

So far we have established that consolidation means adding together any items that are not eliminated as internal to the group. Going back to the example, however, we see that Pleasant only owns 80% of Sweet. Should we not then add Pleasant's assets and liabilities to 80% of Sweet's?

1.6.1 Consolidate as if you owned everything

The answer is no. Pleasant **controls** Sweet, its subsidiary. The directors of Pleasant can visit **all** of Sweet's factory, if they wish, not just 80% of it. So the figure for consolidated land and buildings is $100,000 plus $80,000 as stated above.

1.6.2 Show the extent to which you do not own everything

However, if we just add the figures together, we are not telling the whole story. There may well be one or more shareholders who own the remaining 20% of the shares in Sweet Ltd. These shareholders cannot visit 20% of the factory or tell 20% of the workforce what to do, but they do have an **interest** in 20% of the net assets of Sweet. The answer is to show this **minority interest** separately in the bottom half of the consolidated balance sheet.

Now we move onto consider IAS 27.

1.7 Accounting treatment in group accounts

IAS 27 requires a parent to present consolidated financial statements, in which the accounts of the parent and subsidiary (or subsidiaries) are combined and presented **as a single entity**. We will look at how this is accomplished in the next Section.

2 IAS 27: Summary of consolidation procedures

How are consolidated financial statements prepared? IAS 27 lays out the basic procedures and we will consider these in the rest of this chapter.

2.1 Basic procedure

The financial statements of a parent and its subsidiaries are **combined on a line-by-line basis** by adding together like items of assets, liabilities, equity, income and expenses.

The following steps are then taken, in order that the consolidated financial statements should **show financial information about the group as if it was a single entity**.

(a) The carrying amount of the parent's **investment in each subsidiary** and the parent's **portion of equity** of each subsidiary are **eliminated or cancelled** (see Section 3)

(b) **Minority interests in the net income of consolidated subsidiaries** are adjusted against group income, to arrive at the net income attributable to the owners of the parent (see Section 4)

(c) **Minority interests** in the net assets of consolidated subsidiaries should be presented separately in the consolidated balance sheet (see Section 4)

In addition **goodwill on consolidation** should be dealt with according to IFRS 3 (see Section 5).

3 Cancellation and part cancellation

FAST FORWARD

The preparation of a consolidated balance sheet, in a very simple form, consists of two procedures.

(a) Take the individual accounts of the parent company and each subsidiary and **cancel out items** which appear as an asset in one company and a liability in another.

(b) **Add together all the uncancelled assets** and liabilities throughout the group.

Items requiring cancellation may include the following.

(a) The asset **'shares in subsidiary companies'** which appears in the parent company's accounts will be matched with the liability 'share capital' in the subsidiaries' accounts.

(b) There may be **inter-company trading** within the group. For example, S Co may sell goods to P Co. P Co would then be a receivable in the accounts of S Co, while S Co would be a payable in the accounts of P Co.

3.1 Example: Cancellation

P Co regularly sells goods to its one subsidiary company, S Co. The balance sheets of the two companies on 31 December 20X6 are given below.

P CO
BALANCE SHEET AS AT 31 DECEMBER 20X6

	$	$	$
Assets			
Non-current assets			
Property, plant and equipment			35,000
Investment in 40,000 $1 shares in S Co at cost			40,000*
			75,000
Current assets			
Inventories		16,000	
Receivables: S Co	2,000*		
Other	6,000		
		8,000	
Cash at bank		1,000	
			25,000
Total assets			100,000
Equity and liabilities			
Equity			
70,000 $1 ordinary shares		70,000	
Reserves		16,000	
			86,000
Current liabilities			
Payables			14,000
Total equity and liabilities			100,000

S CO
BALANCE SHEET AS AT 31 DECEMBER 20X6

	$	$	$
Assets			
Non-current assets			
Property, plant and equipment			45,000
Current assets			
Inventories		12,000	
Receivables		9,000	
			21,000
Total assets			66,000
Equity and liabilities			
Equity			
40,000 $1 ordinary shares		40,000*	
Reserves		19,000	
			59,000
Current liabilities			
Bank overdraft		3,000	
Payables: P Co		2,000*	
Payables: other		2,000	
			7,000
Total equity and liabilities			66,000

Required

Prepare the consolidated balance sheet of P Co.

Solution

The cancelling items, marked above with asterisks, are:

(a) P Co's asset 'investment in shares of S Co' ($40,000) cancels with S Co's 'share capital' ($40,000);

(b) P Co's asset 'receivables: S Co' ($2,000) cancels with S Co's liability 'payables: P Co' ($2,000).

The remaining assets and liabilities are added together to produce the following consolidated balance sheet.

P CO
CONSOLIDATED BALANCE SHEET AS AT 31 DECEMBER 20X6

	$	$
Assets		
Non-current assets		80,000
Property, plant and equipment (35,000 + 45,000)		
Current assets	28,000	
Inventories (16,000 + 12,000)	15,000	
Receivables (6,000 + 9,000)	1,000	
Cash at bank (P Co)		44,000
		124,000
Total assets		
Equity and liabilities		
Equity	70,000	
70,000 $1 ordinary shares (P Co)	35,000	
Reserves (16,000 + 19,000)		105,000
Current liabilities	3,000	
Bank overdraft (S Co)	16,000	
Payables (14,000 + 2,000)		19,000
		124,000
Total equity and liabilities		

Note the following.

(a) P Co's bank balance is **not netted off** with S Co's bank overdraft. To offset one against the other would be less informative and would conflict with the principle that assets and liabilities should not be netted off.

(b) The share capital in the consolidated balance sheet is the **share capital of the parent company alone**. This must *always* be the case, no matter how complex the consolidation, because the share capital of subsidiary companies must *always* be a wholly cancelling item.

4 Minority interests

Where the holding company does not hold 100% of the shares in the subsidiary, the rest of the shares are held by **minority** shareholders. This **minority interest** must be shown in the balance sheet.

Up to now we have been dealing with cases where the parent owns 100% of the subsidiary. It was mentioned earlier that the total assets and liabilities of subsidiary companies are included in the consolidated balance sheet, even in the case of subsidiaries which are only **partly owned**. A proportion of the net assets of such subsidiaries in fact belongs to investors from outside the group (**minority interests**).

PART E FINANCIAL STATEMENTS

In the consolidated balance sheet it is necessary to distinguish this proportion from those assets attributable to the group and financed by shareholders' equity and reserves.

The net assets of a company are financed by share capital and reserves. The consolidation procedure for dealing with partly owned subsidiaries is to **calculate the proportion of ordinary shares, preference shares and reserves attributable to minority interests.**

4.1 Example: Minority interests

P Co has owned 75% of the share capital of S Co since the date of S Co's incorporation. Their latest balance sheets are given below.

P CO
BALANCE SHEET

	$	$
Assets		
Non-current assets	50,000	
Property, plant and equipment	30,000	
30,000 $1 ordinary shares in S Co at cost		80,000
		45,000
Current assets		125,000
Total assets		
Equity and liabilities		
Equity	80,000	
80,000 $1 ordinary shares	25,000	
Reserves	105,000	
		20,000
Current liabilities		125,000
Total equity and liabilities		

S CO
BALANCE SHEET

	$	$
Assets		
Property, plant and equipment		35,000
Current assets		35,000
Total assets		70,000
Equity and liabilities		
Equity		
40,000 $1 ordinary shares	40,000	
Reserves	10,000	
		50,000
Current liabilities		20,000
Total equity and liabilities		70,000

Required

Prepare the consolidated balance sheet.

Solution

All of S Co's net assets are consolidated despite the fact that the company is only 75% owned. The amount of net assets attributable to minority interests is calculated as follows.

	$
Minority share of share capital (25% × $40,000)	10,000
Minority share of reserves (25% × $10,000)	2,500
	12,500

Of S Co's share capital of $40,000, $10,000 is included in the figure for minority interest, while $30,000 is cancelled with P Co's asset 'investment in S Co'.

The consolidated balance sheet can now be prepared.

P GROUP
CONSOLIDATED BALANCE SHEET

	$	$
Assets		
Property, plant and equipment		85,000
Current assets		80,000
Total assets		165,000
Equity and liabilities		
Equity		
Share capital	80,000	
Reserves $(25,000 + (75% × $10,000))	32,500	
		112,500
Minority interest		12,500
		125,000
Current liabilities		40,000
Total equity and liabilities		165,000

This method of disclosure is required by IAS 1 *Presentation of financial statements*. Follow this example through again and make sure you understand it.

5 Goodwill arising on consolidation

FAST FORWARD

> Where the holding company has paid an amount for shares in a subsidiary which exceeds the fair value of that proportion of its net assets, the excess is deemed to be **goodwill**. Goodwill is accounted for as an intangible asset in the holding company's balance sheet and regularly reviewed for impairment.

In the examples we have looked at so far, the cost of shares acquired by the parent company has always been equal to the par value of those shares. This is seldom the case in practice and we must now consider some more complicated examples. To begin with, **we will examine the entries made by the parent company in its own balance sheet when it acquires shares.**

When a company P Co wishes to **purchase shares** in a company S Co it must pay the previous owners of those shares. The most obvious form of payment would be in **cash**. Suppose P Co purchases all 40,000 $1 shares in S Co and pays $60,000 cash to the previous shareholders in consideration. The entries in P Co's books would be:

DEBIT	Investment in S Co at cost	$60,000	
CREDIT	Bank		$60,000

The amount which P Co records in its books as the cost of its investment in S Co may be more or less than the book value of the assets it acquires. Suppose that S Co in the previous example has nil reserves and nil liabilities, so that its share capital of $40,000 is balanced by total assets with a book value of $40,000. For simplicity, assume that the book value of S Co's assets is the same as their market or fair value.

Now when the directors of P Co agree to pay $60,000 for a 100% investment in S Co they must believe that, in addition to its tangible assets of $40,000, S Co must also have intangible assets worth $20,000. This amount of $20,000 paid over and above the value of the tangible assets acquired is called **goodwill arising on consolidation** (sometimes **premium on acquisition**).

Following the normal cancellation procedure the $40,000 share capital in S Co's balance sheet could be cancelled against $40,000 of the 'investment in S Co' in the balance sheet of P Co. This would leave a $20,000 debit uncancelled in the parent company's accounts and this $20,000 would appear in the consolidated balance sheet under the caption 'Intangible non-current assets: goodwill arising on consolidation'.

5.1 Goodwill and pre-acquisition profits

Up to now we have assumed that S Co had nil reserves when its shares were purchased by P Co. Assuming instead that S Co had earned profits of $8,000 in the period before acquisition, its balance sheet just before the purchase would look as follows.

	$
Total tangible assets	48,000
Share capital	40,000
Reserves	8,000
	48,000

If P Co now purchases all the shares in S Co it will acquire total tangible assets worth $48,000 at a cost of $60,000. Clearly in this case S Co's intangible assets (goodwill) are being valued at $12,000. It should be apparent that any **reserves** earned by the subsidiary **prior to its acquisition** by the parent company must be **incorporated in the cancellation** process so as to arrive at a figure for goodwill arising on consolidation. In other words, not only S Co's share capital, but also its **pre-acquisition reserves**, must be cancelled against the asset 'investment in S Co' in the accounts of the parent company. The uncancelled balance of $12,000 appears in the consolidated balance sheet.

The consequence of this is that **any pre-acquisition reserves of a subsidiary company are not aggregated with the parent company's reserves** in the consolidated balance sheet. The figure of consolidated reserves comprises the reserves of the parent company plus the **post-acquisition reserves only of subsidiary companies**. The post-acquisition reserves are simply reserves now *less* reserves at acquisition.

5.2 Example: Goodwill and pre-acquisition profits

Sing Co acquired the ordinary shares of Wing Co on 31 March when the draft balance sheets of each company were as follows.

SING CO
BALANCE SHEET AS AT 31 MARCH

	$
Assets	
Non-current assets	
Investment in 50,000 shares of Wing Co at cost	80,000
Current assets	40,000
Total assets	120,000

	$
Equity and liabilities	
Equity	
Ordinary shares	75,000
Retained earnings	45,000
Total equity and liabilities	120,000

WING CO
BALANCE SHEET AS AT 31 MARCH

	$
Current assets	60,000
Retained earnings	
50,000 ordinary shares of $1 each	50,000
Revenue reserves	10,000
	60,000

Prepare the consolidated balance sheet as at 31 March.

Solution

The technique to adopt here is to produce a new working: 'Goodwill'. A proforma working is set out below.

Goodwill

	$	$
Cost of investment		X
Share of net assets acquired as represented by:		
Ordinary share capital	X	
Share premium	X	
Reserves on acquisition	X	
Group share %		(X)
Goodwill		X

Applying this to our example the working will look like this.

	$	$
Cost of investment		80,000
Share of net assets acquired as represented by:		
Ordinary share capital	50,000	
Retained earnings on acquisition	10,000	
	60,000	
Group share 100%		60,000
Goodwill		20,000

SING CO
CONSOLIDATED BALANCE SHEET AS AT 31 MARCH

	$	$
Assets		
Equity		
Goodwill arising on consolidation		20,000
Current assets		100,000
		120,000
Capital and reserves		
Ordinary shares		75,000
Retained earnings		45,000
		120,000

5.3 IFRS 3 Business combinations

Goodwill arising on consolidation is one form of **purchased goodwill**, and is governed by IFRS 3. IFRS 3 requires that purchased goodwill should **be capitalised in the consolidated balance sheet**.

The **normal treatment** to deal with goodwill arising on consolidation is therefore to calculate the value of goodwill as in the working shown above, and then show it under 'Intangible non-current assets' in the consolidated balance sheet.

IFRS 3 requires that this goodwill then be reviewed each year for impairment. If the value of goodwill is deemed to have fallen, the amount by which it has become impaired will be written off. In your exam, the amount of any impairment will be given in the question.

Goodwill arising on consolidation is the difference between the cost of an acquisition and the value of the subsidiary's net assets acquired. This difference can be **negative**: the aggregate of the fair values of the separable net assets acquired may exceed what the parent company paid for them. The treatment of this 'negative goodwill' is as follows.

(a) The purchaser should first **re-assess the values of the net assets** acquired to establish that negative goodwill does exist and to confirm its valuation.

(b) Any **negative goodwill** (referred to in IFRS 3 as 'excess') remaining can be treated as **profit in the year**.

6 A technique of consolidation

We have now looked at the topics of cancellation, minority interests and goodwill arising on consolidation. It is time to set out an approach to be used in tackling **consolidated balance sheets**. The approach we recommend consists of five stages.

Stage 1 Cancel items common to both balance sheets.

Stage 2 Produce working for minority interests as shown in Paragraph 4.1.

Stage 3 Produce a goodwill working as shown in Paragraph 5.2 above.

Stage 4 Produce a working for capital and revenue reserves.

Stage 5 Produce the consolidated balance sheet as required by the question. Cross reference all workings and notes.

You should now attempt to apply this technique to the following question.

Question — Consolidation

The draft balance sheets of Ping Co and Pong Co on 30 June 20X4 were as follows.

PING CO
BALANCE SHEET AS AT 30 JUNE 20X4

	$	$
Assets		
Non-current assets		
Property, plant and equipment	50,000	
20,000 ordinary shares in Pong Co at cost	30,000	
		80,000
Current assets		
Inventory	3,000	
Receivables	20,000	
Cash	2,000	
		25,000
Total assets		105,000

Equity and liabilities	$	$
Equity		
Ordinary shares of $1 each	45,000	
Capital reserves	12,000	
Retained earnings	30,000	
		87,000
Current liabilities		
Owed to Pong Co	8,000	
Trade payables	10,000	
		18,000
Total equity and liabilities		105,000

PONG CO
BALANCE SHEET AS AT 30 JUNE 20X4

	$	$
Assets		
Property, plant and equipment		40,000
Current assets		
Inventory	10,000	
Owed by Ping Co	8,000	
Receivables	7,000	
		25,000
Total assets		65,000
Equity and liabilities		
Equity		
Ordinary shares of $1 each	25,000	
Capital reserves	5,000	
Retained earnings	23,000	
		53,000
Current liabilities		
Trade payables		12,000
Total equity and liabilities		65,000

Ping Co acquired its investment in Pong Co on 1 July 20X1 when the revenue reserves (retained earnings) of Pong Co stood at $6,000. There have been no changes in the share capital or capital reserves of Pong Co since that date.

There is no impairment of goodwill.

Prepare the consolidated balance sheet of Ping Co as at 30 June 20X4.

Answer

Stage 1. Agree current accounts. Ping's current liability is $8,000, which agrees to Ping's current asset of $8,000. Cancel common items: these are the current accounts between the two companies of $8,000 each.

Stage 2 Calculate the minority interest.

Minority interest

	$
Ordinary share capital (20% × 25,000)	5,000
Capital reserves (20% × 5,000)	1,000
Retained earnings (20% × 23,000)	4,600
	10,600

PART E FINANCIAL STATEMENTS

Note. In this particular case, where there are no preferred shares or adjustments to Pong Co's retained earnings, the minority interest figure may simply be calculated as 20% of Pong Co's net assets of $(65,000 – 12,000)$, ie 20% × $53,000. Because, however, such adjustments and complications often arise, it is a good idea to get into the habit of producing the working as shown.

Stage 3 Calculate goodwill.

Goodwill

	$	$
Cost of investment		30,000
Share of assets acquired as represented by:		
Ordinary share capital	25,000	
Capital reserves on acquisition	5,000	
Retained earnings on acquisition	6,000	
	36,000	
Group share 80%		28,800
Goodwill		1,200

This goodwill must be shown as an asset in the balance sheet.

Stage 4 Calculate consolidated reserves.

Consolidated capital reserve

	$
Ping Co	12,000
Share of Pong Co's post-acquisition capital reserve	–
	12,000

Consolidated retained earnings

	$
Ping Co	30,000
Share of Pong Co's post-acquisition	
Retained earnings: 80% × (23,000 – 6,000)*	13,600
	43,600

*Note. Post-acquisition retained earnings (reserves) of Pong Co are simply reserves now less reserves at acquisition.

Stage 5 Prepare the consolidated balance sheet.

PING CO
CONSOLIDATED BALANCE SHEET AS AT 30 JUNE 20X4

	$	$
Assets		
Non-current assets		
Intangible asset: goodwill		1,200
Property, plant and equipment ($50,000 + $40,000)		90,000
Current assets		
Inventories ($3,000 + $10,000)	13,000	
Receivables ($20,000 + $7,000)	27,000	
Cash	2,000	
		42,000
Total assets		133,200

		$	$
Equity and liabilities			
Ordinary shares of $1 each		45,000	
Capital reserves		12,000	
Revenue reserves		43,600	
			100,600
Minority interest			10,600
			110,000
Current liabilities			
Trade payables ($10,000 + $12,000)			22,000
Total equity and liabilities			133,200

> **Exam focus point**
>
> A consolidated balance sheet will come up as regularly as clockwork. Make sure you learn the following summary.

7 Summary: Consolidated balance sheet

Purpose	To show the net assets which P controls and the ownership of those assets.
Net assets	Always 100% P plus 100% S providing P holds a majority of voting rights.
Share capital	P only. *Reason.* Simply reporting to the parent company's shareholders in another form.
Reserves (retained earnings)	100% P plus group share of post-acquisition retained reserves of S less consolidation adjustments. *Reason.* To show the extent to which the group actually owns total assets less liabilities.
Minority interest	MI share of S's consolidated net assets. *Reason.* To show the extent to which other parties own net assets that are under the control of the parent company.

PART E FINANCIAL STATEMENTS

Chapter Roundup

- Many large companies consist of several companies controlled by a **parent** or **holding company** which owns some or all of the shares in the other companies. This is known as a **group**.
- The preparation of a consolidated balance sheet consists of two main procedures:
    (a) cancel out items which appear as an asset in one company and a liability in the other
    (b) add together all the uncancelled assets and liabilities
- Where the holding company does not hold 100% of the shares in the subsidiary, the rest of the shares are held by **minority** shareholders. This **minority interest** must be shown in the balance sheet.
- Where the holding company has paid an amount for shares in a subsidiary which exceeds the fair value of that proportion of its net assets, the excess is deemed to be **goodwill**. Goodwill is accounted for as an intangible asset in the holding company's balance sheet and regularly reviewed for impairment.
- This chapter has covered the mechanics of preparing simple **consolidated balance sheets**. In particular, procedures have been described for dealing with:
    - Cancellation
    - Calculation of minority interests
    - Calculation of goodwill arising on consolidation
- A **five-stage drill** has been described and exemplified in a comprehensive example.
- The stages are as follows.
    - Cancel items common to both balance sheets
    - Minority interests
    - Goodwill
    - Reserves
    - Consolidated balance sheet
- It is important that you have a clear understanding of the material in this chapter before you move on to more complicated aspects of consolidation.

Quick Quiz

1 What is the basic objective of consolidation procedures?
2 What are the components making up the figure of minority interest in a consolidated balance sheet?
3 What is 'goodwill arising on consolidation'?

Answers to Quick Quiz

1 To show financial information about the group as if it was a single entity.
2 The proportion of ordinary shares, preferred shares and reserves attributable to minority interests.
3 The amount paid over and above what the net assets of the subsidiary are worth.

Now try the questions below from the Exam Question Bank

Number	Level	Marks	Time
Q30	Examination	10	18 mins
Q31	Examination	10	18 mins

Part F
Interpretation of financial statements

Interpretation of financial statements

Topic list	Syllabus reference
1 The broad categories of ratios	6
2 Profitability and return on capital	6
3 Liquidity, gearing/leverage and working capital	6
4 Shareholders' investment ratios	6
5 Presentation of a ratio analysis report	6

Introduction

So far in this Study Text we have looked at **how** financial statements are prepared and have described their features and contents.

In this chapter we begin to consider the **meaning of the figures in the accounts**, their **relationships with each other** and their **changes over time**. This should lead us to consider how well the figures in the accounts actually represent company performance.

In the final part of the Study Text you will be thinking more broadly about the usefulness of financial statements and other accounting information.

PART F INTERPRETATION OF FINANCIAL STATEMENTS

Study guide

Section 26-27 – Interpretation of financial statements

- Revise users of financial statements and their information needs.
- Explain the advantages and disadvantages of interpretation based on financial statements.
- Explain the factors forming the environment in which the business operates.
- Explain the uses of ratio analysis.
- Explain the main ratios to be used in interpreting financial statements to appraise:
    - Profitability
    - Liquidity
    - Working capital efficiency
    - Financial risk
    - Performance from an investor's point of view
- Explain the working capital cycle (or cash operating cycle).
- Explain normal levels of certain ratios.
- Formulate comments on movements in ratios between one period and another or on differences between ratios for different businesses.
- Explain the factors which may distort ratios, leading to unreliable conclusions.
- Prepare and comment on a comprehensive range of ratios for a business.

Exam guide

Once again this is a key topic. It is most likely to be examined by way of MCQs in Section A. However do not discount the possibility of a full question in Section B. The syllabus has an emphasis on the explanation and discussion of ratios. For those studying for the Oxford Brookes degree, project topic 8 asks for an analysis of the financial situation of your choice of organisation.

1 The broad categories of ratio

If you were to look at a balance sheet or income statement, how would you decide whether the company was doing well or badly? Or whether it was financially strong or financially vulnerable? And what would you be looking at in the figures to help you to make your judgement?

Your syllabus requires you to **appraise and communicate** the position and prospects of a business based on given and prepared statements and ratios.

Ratio analysis involves **comparing one figure against another** to produce a ratio, and assessing whether the ratio indicates a weakness or strength in the company's affairs.

1.1 Ratio analysis

FAST FORWARD

Broadly speaking, basic ratios can be grouped into five categories.

- Profitability and return
- Long-term solvency and stability
- Short-term solvency and liquidity
- Efficiency (turnover ratios)
- Shareholders' investment ratios

Within each heading we will identify a number of standard measures or ratios that are normally calculated and generally accepted as meaningful indicators. One must stress however that each individual business must be considered separately, and a ratio that is meaningful for a manufacturing company may be completely meaningless for a financial institution. **Try not to be too mechanical** when working out ratios and constantly think about what you are trying to achieve.

The key to obtaining meaningful information from ratio analysis is **comparison**. This may involve comparing ratios over time within the same business to establish whether things are improving or declining, and comparing ratios between similar businesses to see whether the company you are analysing is better or worse than average within its specific business sector.

It must be stressed that ratio analysis on its own is not sufficient for interpreting company accounts, and that there are **other items of information** which should be looked at, for example:

(a) The content of any **accompanying commentary** on the accounts and other statements

(b) The age and nature of the **company's assets**

(c) **Current and future developments** in the company's markets, at home and overseas, recent acquisitions or disposals of a subsidiary by the company

(e) Any other **noticeable features** of the report and accounts, such as events after the balance sheet date, contingent liabilities, a qualified auditors' report, the company's taxation position, and so on

1.2 Scenario: Calculating ratios

To illustrate the calculation of ratios, the following balance sheet and income statement figures will be used.

FURLONG CO INCOME STATEMENT
FOR THE YEAR ENDED 31 DECEMBER 20X8

	Notes	20X8 $	20X7 $
Revenue	1	3,095,576	1,909,051
Operating profit	1	359,501	244,229
Interest	2	17,371	19,127
Profit before taxation		342,130	225,102
Taxation		74,200	31,272
Profit for the period		267,930	193,830
Earnings per share		12.8c	9.3c

PART F INTERPRETATION OF FINANCIAL STATEMENTS

FURLONG CO BALANCE SHEET
AS AT 31 DECEMBER 20X8

	Notes	20X8 $	20X8 $	20X7 $	20X7 $
Assets					
Non-current assets					
Property, plant and equipment			802,180		656,071
Current assets					
Inventory		64,422		86,550	
Receivables	3	1,002,701		853,441	
Cash at bank and in hand		1,327		68,363	
			1,068,450		1,008,354
Total assets			1,870,630		1,664,425
Equity and liabilities					
Equity					
Ordinary shares 10c each	5	210,000		210,000	
Share premium account		48,178		48,178	
Retained earnings		630,721		393,791	
			888,899		651,969
Non current liabilities					
10% loan stock 20X4/20X9			100,000		100,000
Current liabilities	4		881,731		912,456
Total equity and liabilities			1,870,630		1,664,425

NOTES TO THE ACCOUNTS

		20X8 $	20X7 $
1	*Sales revenue and profit*		
	Sales revenue	3,095,576	1,909,051
	Cost of sales	2,402,609	1,441,950
	Gross profit	692,967	467,101
	Administration expenses	333,466	222,872
	Operating profit	359,501	244,229
	Depreciation charged	151,107	120,147
2	*Interest*		
	Payable on bank overdrafts and other loans	8,115	11,909
	Payable on loan stock	10,000	10,000
		18,115	21,909
	Receivable on short-term deposits	744	2,782
	Net payable	17,371	19,127
3	*Receivables*		
	Amounts falling due within one year		
	Trade receivables	884,559	760,252
	Prepayments and accrued income	97,022	45,729
		981,581	805,981
	Amounts falling due after more than one year		
	Trade receivables	21,120	47,460
	Total receivables	1,002,701	853,441
4	*Current liabilities*		
	Trade payables	627,018	545,340
	Accruals and deferred income	81,279	280,464
	Corporate taxes	98,000	37,200
	Other taxes	75,434	49,452
		881,731	912,456

		20X8	20X7
		$	$
5	Called up share capital		
	Authorised ordinary shares of 10c each	1,000,000	1,000,000
	Issued and fully paid ordinary shares of 10c each	210,000	210,000

2 Profitability and return on capital

FAST FORWARD

The profitability ratios are:

- Return on capital employed
- Net profit as a percentage of sales
- Asset turnover ratio
- Gross profit as a percentage of sales

In our example, the company made a profit in both 20X8 and 20X7, and there was an increase in profit between one year and the next:

(a) of 52% before taxation.
(b) of 39% after taxation.

Profit before taxation is generally thought to be a better figure to use than profit after taxation, because there might be unusual variations in the tax charge from year to year which would not affect the underlying profitability of the company's operations.

Another profit figure that should be calculated is PBIT, **profit before interest and tax**. This is the amount of profit which the company earned before having to pay interest to the providers of loan capital. By providers of loan capital, we usually mean longer-term loan capital, such as loan stock and medium-term bank loans, which will be shown in the balance sheet as non-current liabilities.

Formula to learn

Profit before interest and tax is therefore:

(a) the profit before taxation; **plus**
(b) interest charges on long-term loan capital.

Published accounts do not always give sufficient detail on interest payable to determine how much is interest on long-term finance. We will assume in our example that the whole of the interest payable ($18,115, note 2) relates to long-term finance.

PBIT in our example is therefore:

	20X8	20X7
	$	$
Profit before tax	342,130	225,102
Interest payable (Note 2 above)	18,115	21,909
PBIT	360,245	247,011

This shows a 46% growth between 20X7 and 20X8.

2.1 Return on capital employed (ROCE)

It is impossible to assess profits or profit growth properly without relating them to the **amount of funds (capital) that were employed in making the profits**. The most important profitability ratio is therefore return on capital employed (ROCE), which states the profit as a percentage of the amount of capital employed.

PART F INTERPRETATION OF FINANCIAL STATEMENTS

Formula to learn

$$\text{ROCE} = \frac{\text{Profit before interest and taxation}}{\text{Capital employed}}$$

Capital employed = Shareholders' equity plus non-current liabilities (*or* total assets less current liabilities)

The underlying principle is that we must **compare like with like**, and so if capital means share capital and reserves plus non-current liabilities and debt capital, profit must mean the profit earned by all this capital together. This is PBIT, since interest is the return for loan capital.

In our example, capital employed = 20X8 $1,870,630 – $881,731 = $988,899
20X7 $1,664,425 – $912,456 = $751,969

These total figures are the total assets less current liabilities figures for 20X8 and 20X7 in the balance sheet.

		20X8	20X7
ROCE	=	$360,245 / $988,899	$247,011 / $751,969
	=	36.4%	32.8%

What does a company's ROCE tell us? What should we be looking for? There are three comparisons that can be made.

(a) The **change in ROCE from one year to the next** can be examined. In this example, there has been an increase in ROCE by about 10% or 11% from its 20X7 level.

(b) The **ROCE being earned by other companies**, if this information is available, can be compared with the ROCE of this company. Here the information is not available.

(c) A comparison of the ROCE with **current market borrowing rates** may be made.

  (i) What would be the cost of extra borrowing to the company if it needed more loans, and is it earning a ROCE that suggests it could make profits to make such borrowing worthwhile?

  (ii) Is the company making a ROCE which suggests that it is getting value for money from its current borrowing?

  (iii) Companies are in a risk business and commercial borrowing rates are a good independent yardstick against which company performance can be judged.

In this example, if we suppose that current market interest rates, say, for medium-term borrowing from banks, is around 10%, then the company's actual ROCE of 36% in 20X8 would not seem low. On the contrary, it might seem high.

However, it is easier to spot a low ROCE than a high one, because there is always a chance that the company's non-current assets, especially property, are **undervalued** in its balance sheet, and so the capital employed figure might be unrealistically low. If the company had earned a ROCE, not of 36%, but of, say only 6%, then its return would have been below current borrowing rates and so disappointingly low.

2.2 Return on equity (ROE)

Return on equity gives a more restricted view of capital than ROCE, but it is based on the same principles.

Formula to learn

$$\text{ROE} = \frac{\text{Profit after interest and preference dividend}}{\text{Ordinary share capital and other equity}}$$

In our example, ROE is calculated as follows.

	20X8	20X7
ROE =	$\dfrac{\$342{,}130}{\$888{,}899} = 38.5\%$	$\dfrac{\$225{,}102}{\$651{,}969} = 34.5\%$

ROE is **not a widely-used ratio**, however, because there are more useful ratios that give an indication of the return to shareholders, such as earnings per share, dividend per share, dividend yield and earnings yield, which are described later.

2.3 Analysing profitability and return in more detail: the secondary ratios

We often sub-analyse ROCE, to find out more about why the ROCE is high or low, or better or worse than last year. There are two factors that contribute towards a return on capital employed, both related to sales turnover.

(a) **Profit margin**. A company might make a high or low profit margin on its sales. For example, a company that makes a profit of 25c per $1 of sales is making a bigger return on its turnover than another company making a profit of only 10c per $1 of sales.

(b) **Asset turnover**. Asset turnover is a measure of how well the assets of a business are being used to generate sales. For example, if two companies each have capital employed of $100,000 and Company A makes sales of $400,000 per annum whereas Company B makes sales of only $200,000 per annum, Company A is making a higher turnover from the same amount of assets (twice as much asset turnover as Company B) and this will help A to make a higher return on capital employed than B. Asset turnover is expressed as 'x times' so that assets generate x times their value in annual turnover. Here, Company A's asset turnover is 4 times and B's is 2 times.

Profit margin and asset turnover together explain the ROCE and if the ROCE is the primary profitability ratio, these other two are the secondary ratios. The relationship between the three ratios can be shown mathematically.

Formula to learn

> Profit margin × Asset turnover = ROCE
>
> $\therefore \quad \dfrac{\text{PBIT}}{\text{Sales}} \times \dfrac{\text{Sales}}{\text{Capital employed}} = \dfrac{\text{PBIT}}{\text{Capital employed}}$

In our example:

		Profit margin		Asset turnover		ROCE
(a)	20X8	$360,245	×	$3,095,576	=	$360,245
		$3,095,576		$988,899		$988,899
		11.64%	×	3.13 times	=	36.4%
(b)	20X7	$247,011	×	$1,909,051	=	$247,011
		$1,909,051		$751,969		$751,969
		12.94%	×	2.54 times	=	32.8%

In this example, the company's improvement in ROCE between 20X7 and 20X8 is attributable to a higher asset turnover. Indeed the profit margin has fallen a little, but the higher asset turnover has more than compensated for this.

It is also worth commenting on the change in sales revenue from one year to the next. You may already have noticed that Furlong achieved sales growth of over 60% from $1.9 million to $3.1 million between 20X7 and 20X8. This is very strong growth, and this is certainly one of the most significant items in the income statement and balance sheet.

2.3.1 A warning about comments on profit margin and asset turnover

It might be tempting to think that a high profit margin is good, and a low asset turnover means sluggish trading. In broad terms, this is so. But there is a trade-off between profit margin and asset turnover, and you cannot look at one without allowing for the other.

(a) A **high profit margin** means a high profit per $1 of sales, but if this also means that sales prices are high, there is a strong possibility that sales turnover will be depressed, and so asset turnover lower.

(b) A **high asset turnover** means that the company is generating a lot of sales, but to do this it might have to keep its prices down and so accept a low profit margin per $1 of sales.

Consider the following.

Company A		Company B	
Sales revenue	$1,000,000	Sales revenue	$4,000,000
Capital employed	$1,000,000	Capital employed	$1,000,000
PBIT	$200,000	PBIT	$200,000

These figures would give the following ratios.

ROCE $= \dfrac{\$200,000}{\$1,000,000} = 20\%$ ROCE $= \dfrac{\$200,000}{\$1,000,000} = 20\%$

Profit margin $= \dfrac{\$200,000}{\$1,000,000} = 20\%$ Profit margin $= \dfrac{\$200,000}{\$4,000,000} = 5\%$

Asset turnover $= \dfrac{\$1,000,000}{\$1,000,000} = 1$ Asset turnover $= \dfrac{\$4,000,000}{\$1,000,000} = 4$

The companies have the same ROCE, but it is arrived at in a very different fashion. Company A operates with a low asset turnover and a comparatively high profit margin whereas company B carries out much more business, but on a lower profit margin. Company A could be operating at the luxury end of the market, whilst company B is operating at the popular end of the market.

2.4 Gross profit margin, net profit margin and profit analysis

Depending on the format of the income statement, you may be able to calculate the gross profit margin as well as the net profit margin. **Looking at the two together** can be quite informative.

For example, suppose that a company has the following summarised income statement for two consecutive years.

	Year 1	Year 2
	$	$
Turnover	70,000	100,000
Cost of sales	42,000	55,000
Gross profit	28,000	45,000
Expenses	21,000	35,000
Net profit	7,000	10,000

Although the net profit margin is the same for both years at 10%, the gross profit margin is not.

In year 1 it is: $\dfrac{\$28,000}{\$70,000} = 40\%$

and in year 2 it is: $\dfrac{\$45,000}{\$100,000} = 45\%$

The improved gross profit margin has not led to an improvement in the net profit margin. This is because expenses as a percentage of sales have risen from 30% in year 1 to 35% in year 2.

3 Liquidity, gearing/leverage and working capital

In this section we look at the **debt** and **gearing/leverage** ratios.
- Debt ratio
- Gearing/leverage ratio
- Interest cover
- Cash flow ratio

3.1 Long-term solvency: debt and gearing ratios

Debt ratios are concerned with **how much the company owes in relation to its size**, whether it is getting into heavier debt or improving its situation, and whether its debt burden seems heavy or light.

(a) When a company is heavily in debt banks and other potential lenders may be unwilling to advance further funds.

(b) When a company is earning only a modest profit before interest and tax, and has a heavy debt burden, there will be very little profit left over for shareholders after the interest charges have been paid. And so if interest rates were to go up (on bank overdrafts and so on) or the company were to borrow even more, it might soon be incurring interest charges in excess of PBIT. This might eventually lead to the liquidation of the company.

These are two big reasons why companies should keep their debt burden under control. There are four ratios that are particularly worth looking at, the debt ratio, gearing ratio, interest cover and cash flow ratio.

3.2 Debt ratio

Formula to learn

The **debt ratio** is the ratio of a company's total debts to its total assets.

(a) Assets consist of fixed assets at their balance sheet value, plus current assets.
(b) Debts consist of all payables, whether they are due within one year or after more than one year.

You can ignore long-term provisions and liabilities, such as deferred taxation.

There is no absolute guide to the maximum safe debt ratio, but as a very general guide, you might regard 50% as a safe limit to debt. In practice, many companies operate successfully with a higher debt ratio than this, but 50% is nonetheless a helpful benchmark. In addition, if the debt ratio is over 50% and getting worse, the company's debt position will be worth looking at more carefully.

In the case of Furlong the debt ratio is as follows.

	20X8	20X7
Total debts	$(881,731 + 100,000)	$(912,456 + 100,000)
Total assets	$1,870,630	$1,664,425
	= 52%	= 61%

In this case, the debt ratio is quite high, mainly because of the large amount of current liabilities. However, the debt ratio has fallen from 61% to 52% between 20X7 and 20X8, and so the company appears to be improving its debt position.

3.3 Gearing/leverage

Capital gearing or leverage is concerned with a company's **long-term capital structure**. We can think of a company as consisting of non-current assets and net current assets (ie working capital, which is current assets minus current liabilities). These assets must be financed by long-term capital of the company, which is either:

(a) shareholders' equity which can be divided into:

  (i) ordinary shares plus other equity; and
  (ii) preference shares; or

(b) long-term debt.

Preference share capital is not debt unless the preference shares are redeemable. However, like loan capital, preference share capital has a prior claim over profits before interest and tax, ahead of ordinary shareholders. Preference dividends must be paid out of profits before ordinary shareholders are entitled to an ordinary dividend, and so we refer to preference share capital and loan capital as **prior charge capital**.

The **capital gearing ratio** is a measure of the proportion of a company's capital that is prior charge capital. It is measured as follows.

Formula to learn

$$\text{Capital gearing} = \frac{\text{Total long-term debt}}{\text{Shareholders' equity} + \text{total long-term debt}}$$

Total long-term debt includes prior charge capital ie capital carrying a right to a fixed return including preference shares and debentures.

As with the debt ratio, there is **no absolute limit** to what a gearing ratio ought to be. A company with a gearing ratio of more than 50% is said to be high-geared (whereas low gearing means a gearing ratio of less than 50%). Many companies are high geared, but if a high geared company is becoming increasingly high geared, it is likely to have difficulty in the future when it wants to borrow even more, unless it can also boost its shareholders' capital, either with retained profits or by a new share issue.

Leverage is the term used to describe the converse of gearing, ie the proportion of total assets financed by equity, and which may be called the equity to assets ratio. It is calculated as follows.

Formula to learn

$$\text{Leverage} = \frac{\text{Shareholders' equity}}{\text{Shareholders' equity plus total long-term debt}}$$

or

$$\frac{\text{Shareholders' equity}}{\text{Total assets less current liabilities}}$$

In the example of Furlong, we find that the company, although having a high debt ratio because of its current liabilities, has a low gearing ratio. It has no preference share capital and its only long-term debt is the 10% loan stock. Leverage is therefore high.

		20X8	20X7
Gearing ratio	=	$\dfrac{\$100{,}000}{\$988{,}899}$	$\dfrac{\$100{,}000}{\$751{,}969}$
		= 10%	= 13%
Leverage	=	$\dfrac{\$888{,}899}{\$988{,}899}$	$\dfrac{\$651{,}969}{\$751{,}969}$
		= 90%	= 87%

As you can see, leverage is the mirror image of gearing.

3.4 The implications of high or low gearing/leverage

We mentioned earlier that **gearing or leverage** is, amongst other things, an attempt to **quantify the degree of risk involved in holding equity shares in a company**, risk both in terms of the company's ability to remain in business and in terms of expected ordinary dividends from the company. The problem with a highly geared company is that by definition there is a lot of debt. Debt generally carries a fixed rate of interest (or fixed rate of dividend if in the form of preference shares), hence there is a given (and large) amount to be paid out from profits to holders of debt before arriving at a residue available for distribution to the holders of equity. The riskiness will perhaps become clearer with the aid of an example.

	Company A $'000	Company B $'000	Company C $'000
Ordinary shares	600	400	300
Revenue reserves	200	200	200
Revaluation reserve	100	100	100
	900	700	600
6% preference shares	–	–	100
10% loan stock	100	300	300
Capital employed	1,000	1,000	1,000
Gearing ratio	10%	30%	40%
Leverage	90%	70%	60%

Now suppose that each company makes a profit before interest and tax of $50,000, and the rate of tax on company profits is 30%. Amounts available for distribution to equity shareholders will be as follows.

	Company A $'000	Company B $'000	Company C $'000
Profit before interest and tax	50	50	50
Interest	10	30	30
Profit before tax	40	20	20
Taxation at 30%	12	6	6
Profit after tax	28	14	14
Preference dividend	–	–	6
Available for ordinary shareholders	28	14	8

If in the subsequent year profit before interest and tax falls to $40,000, the amounts available to ordinary shareholders will become as follows.

	Company A $'000	Company B $'000	Company C $'000
Profit before interest and tax	40	40	40
Interest	10	30	30
Profit before tax	30	10	10
Taxation at 30%	9	3	3
Profit after tax	21	7	7
Preference dividend	–	–	6
Available for ordinary shareholders	21	7	1

Note the following.

	Company A	Company B	Company C
Gearing ratio	10%	30%	40%
Leverage	90%	70%	60%
Change in PBIT	– 20%	– 20%	– 20%
Change in profit available for ordinary shareholders	– 25%	– 50%	– 87.5%

The more highly geared the company, the greater the risk that little (if anything) will be available to distribute by way of dividend to the ordinary shareholders. The example clearly displays this fact in so far as the more highly geared the company, the greater the percentage change in profit available for ordinary shareholders for any given percentage change in profit before interest and tax. The relationship similarly holds when profits increase, and if PBIT had risen by 20% rather than fallen, you would find that once again the largest percentage change in profit available for ordinary shareholders (this means an increase) will be for the highly geared company. This means that there will be greater *volatility* of amounts available for ordinary shareholders, and presumably therefore greater volatility in dividends paid to those shareholders, where a company is highly geared. That is the risk: you may do extremely well or extremely badly without a particularly large movement in the PBIT of the company.

The risk of a company's ability to remain in business was referred to earlier. Gearing or leverage is relevant to this. A highly geared company has a large amount of interest to pay annually (assuming that the debt is external borrowing rather than preferred shares). If those borrowings are **'secured'** in any way (and debentures in particular are secured), then the **holders of the debt are perfectly entitled to force the company** to **realise assets to pay their interest** if funds are not available from other sources. Clearly the more highly geared a company the more likely this is to occur when and if profits fall.

3.5 Interest cover

The interest cover ratio shows whether a company is earning enough profits before interest and tax to pay its interest costs comfortably, or whether its interest costs are high in relation to the size of its profits, so that a fall in PBIT would then have a significant effect on profits available for ordinary shareholders.

Formula to learn

$$\text{Interest cover} = \frac{\text{Profit before interest and tax}}{\text{Interest charges}}$$

An interest cover of 2 times or less would be low, and should really exceed 3 times before the company's interest costs are to be considered within acceptable limits.

Returning first to the example of Companies A, B and C, the interest cover was as follows.

		Company A	Company B	Company C
(a)	When PBIT was $50,000 =	$50,000 / $10,000 = 5 times	$50,000 / $30,000 = 1.67 times	$50,000 / $30,000 = 1.67 times
(b)	When PBIT was $40,000 =	$40,000 / $10,000 = 4 times	$40,000 / $30,000 = 1.33 times	$40,000 / $30,000 = 1.33 times

Note. Although preference share capital is included as prior charge capital for the gearing ratio or leverage, it is usual to exclude preference dividends from 'interest' charges. We also look at all interest payments, even interest charges on short-term debt, and so interest cover and gearing do not quite look at the same thing.

Both B and C have a low interest cover, which is a warning to ordinary shareholders that their profits are highly vulnerable, in percentage terms, to even small changes in PBIT.

Question
Interest cover

Returning to the example of Furlong in Paragraph 2, what is the company's interest cover?

Answer

Interest payments should be taken gross, from the note to the accounts, and not net of interest receipts as shown in the income statement.

	20X8	20X7
PBIT	360,245	247,011
Interest payable	18,115	21,909
	= 20 times	= 11 times

Furlong has more than sufficient interest cover. In view of the company's low gearing, this is not too surprising and so we finally obtain a picture of Furlong as a company that does not seem to have a debt problem, in spite of its high (although declining) debt ratio.

3.6 Cash flow ratio

The cash flow ratio is the ratio of a company's **net cash inflow to its total debts**.

(a) **Net cash inflow** is the amount of cash which the company has coming into the business from its operations. A suitable figure for net cash inflow can be obtained from the cash flow statement.

(b) **Total debts** are short-term and long-term payables, together with provisions for liabilities and charges. A distinction can be made between debts payable within one year and other debts and provisions.

Obviously, a company needs to be earning enough cash from operations to be able to meet its foreseeable debts and future commitments, and the cash flow ratio, and changes in the cash flow ratio from one year to the next, provide a **useful indicator of a company's cash position**.

3.7 Short-term solvency and liquidity

Profitability is of course an important aspect of a company's performance and gearing or leverage is another. Neither, however, addresses directly the key issue of *liquidity*.

Key term

> **Liquidity** is the amount of cash a company can put its hands on quickly to settle its debts (and possibly to meet other unforeseen demands for cash payments too).

FAST FORWARD

> In this section we look at **liquidity** and **working capital** ratios.
>
> - Current ratio
> - Quick ratio (acid test ratio)
> - Accounts receivable collection period
> - Accounts payable payment period
> - Average inventory turnover period

3.7.1 Liquid funds

(a) Cash

(b) Short-term investments for which there is a ready market

(c) Fixed-term deposits with a bank or other financial institution, for example, a six month high-interest deposit with a bank

(d) Trade receivables (because they will pay what they owe within a reasonably short period of time)

(e) Bills of exchange receivable (because like ordinary trade receivables, these represent amounts of cash due to be received within a relatively short period of time)

In summary, **liquid assets are current asset items that will or could soon be converted into cash, and cash itself.** Two common definitions of liquid assets are as follows.

(a) All current assets without exception;

(b) All current assets with the exception of inventories

A company can obtain liquid assets from sources other than sales, such as the issue of shares for cash, a new loan or the sale of fixed assets. But a company cannot rely on these at all times, and in general, obtaining liquid funds depends on making sales and profits. Even so, profits do not always lead to increases in liquidity. This is mainly because funds generated from trading may be immediately invested in non-current assets or paid out as dividends. You should refer back to the chapter on cash flow statements to examine this issue.

The reason why a company needs liquid assets is so that it can meet its debts when they fall due. Payments are continually made for operating expenses and other costs, and so there is a **cash cycle** from trading activities of cash coming in from sales and cash going out for expenses.

3.8 The cash cycle

To help you to understand liquidity ratios, it is useful to begin with a brief explanation of the cash cycle. The cash cycle describes **the flow of cash out of a business and back into it again as a result of normal trading operations.**

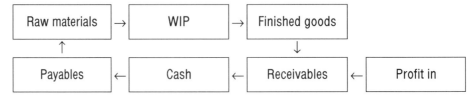

Cash goes out to pay for supplies, wages and salaries and other expenses, although payments can be delayed by taking some credit. A business might hold inventory for a while and then sell it. Cash will come back into the business from the sales, although customers might delay payment by themselves taking some credit.

The main points about the cash cycle are as follows.

(a) The timing of cash flows in and out of a business does not coincide with the time when sales and costs of sales occur. **Cash flows out can be postponed by taking credit. Cash flows in can be delayed by having receivables.**

(b) **The time between making a purchase and making a sale also affects cash flows**. If inventories are held for a long time, the delay between the cash payment for inventory and cash receipts from selling them will also be a long one.

(c) **Holding inventories and having receivables can therefore be seen as two reasons why cash receipts are delayed.** Another way of saying this is that if a company invests in working capital, its cash position will show a corresponding decrease.

(d) Similarly, **taking credit from suppliers can be seen as a reason why cash payments are delayed**. The company's liquidity position will worsen when it has to pay the suppliers, unless it can get more cash in from sales and receivables in the meantime.

The liquidity ratios and working capital turnover ratios are used to test a company's liquidity, length of cash cycle, and investment in working capital.

3.9 Liquidity ratios: current ratio and quick ratio

The 'standard' test of liquidity is the **current ratio**.

Formula to learn

$$\text{Current ratio} = \frac{\text{Current assets}}{\text{Current liabilities}}$$

The idea behind this is that a company should have enough current assets that give a promise of 'cash to come' to meet its future commitments to pay off its current liabilities. Obviously, a **ratio in excess of 1 should be expected**. Otherwise, there would be the prospect that the company might be unable to pay its debts on time. In practice, a ratio comfortably in excess of 1 should be expected, but what is 'comfortable' varies between different types of businesses.

Companies are not able to convert all their current assets into cash very quickly. In particular, some manufacturing companies might hold large quantities of raw material inventories, which must be used in production to create finished goods inventory. These might be warehoused for a long time, or sold on lengthy credit. In such businesses, where inventory turnover is slow, most inventories are not very 'liquid' assets, because the cash cycle is so long. For these reasons, we calculate an additional liquidity ratio, known as the quick ratio or acid test ratio.

The **quick ratio**, or **acid test ratio**, is calculated as follows.

Formula to learn

$$\text{Quick ratio} = \frac{\text{Current assets less inventory}}{\text{Current liabilities}}$$

This ratio should ideally be **at least 1** for companies with a slow inventory turnover. For companies with a fast inventory turnover, a quick ratio can be comfortably less than 1 without suggesting that the company should be in cash flow trouble.

Both the current ratio and the quick ratio offer an indication of the company's liquidity position, but the absolute figures **should not be interpreted too literally**. It is often theorised that an acceptable current ratio is 1.5 and an acceptable quick ratio is 0.8, but these should only be used as a guide. Different businesses operate in very different ways. A supermarket group for example might have a current ratio of 0.52 and a quick ratio of 0.17. Supermarkets have low receivables (people do not buy groceries on credit), low cash (good cash management), medium inventories (high inventories but quick turnover, particularly in view of perishability) and very high payables.

Compare this with a manufacturing and retail organisation, with a current ratio of 1.44 and a quick ratio of 1.03. Such businesses operate with liquidity ratios closer to the standard.

What is important is the **trend** of these ratios. From this, one can easily ascertain whether liquidity is improving or deteriorating. If a supermarket has traded for the last 10 years (very successfully) with current ratios of 0.52 and quick ratios of 0.17 then it should be supposed that the company can continue in business with those levels of liquidity. If in the following year the current ratio were to fall to 0.38 and the quick ratio to 0.09, then further investigation into the liquidity situation would be appropriate. It is the relative position that is far more important than the absolute figures.

Don't forget the other side of the coin either. A current ratio and a quick ratio can get **bigger than they need to be**. A company that has large volumes of inventories and receivables might be over-investing in working capital, and so tying up more funds in the business than it needs to. This would suggest poor management of receivables (credit) or inventories by the company.

3.10 Efficiency ratios: control of receivables, inventories and payables

A rough measure of the average length of time it takes for a company's customers to pay what they owe is the accounts receivable collection period.

Formula to learn

The estimated average accounts receivable collection period is calculated as:

$$\frac{\text{Trade receivables}}{\text{Sales}} \times 365 \text{ days}$$

The figure for sales should be taken as the sales revenue figure in the income statement. The trade receivables are not the total figure for receivables in the balance sheet, which includes prepayments and non-trade receivables. The trade receivables figure will be itemised in an analysis of the receivable total, in a note to the accounts.

The estimate of the accounts receivable collection period is **only approximate**.

(a) The balance sheet value of receivables might be abnormally high or low compared with the 'normal' level the company usually has.

(b) Turnover in the income statement is exclusive of sales taxes, but receivables in the balance sheet are inclusive of sales tax. We are not strictly comparing like with like.

Sales are usually made on 'normal credit terms' of payment within 30 days. A collection period significantly in excess of this might be representative of poor management of funds of a business. However, some companies must allow generous credit terms to win customers. Exporting companies in particular may have to carry large amounts of receivables, and so their average collection period might be well in excess of 30 days.

The **trend of the collection period over time** is probably the best guide. If the collection period is increasing year on year, this is indicative of a poorly managed credit control function (and potentially therefore a poorly managed company).

3.11 Accounts receivable collection period: examples

Using the same types of company as examples, the collection period for each of the companies was as follows.

Company	Trade receivables turnover	Collection period ($\times 365$)	Previous year	Collection period ($\times 365$)
Supermarket	$\dfrac{\$5{,}016K}{\$284{,}986K} =$	6.4 days	$\dfrac{\$3{,}977K}{\$290{,}668K} =$	5.0 days
Manufacturer	$\dfrac{\$458.3m}{\$2{,}059.5m} =$	81.2 days	$\dfrac{\$272.4m}{\$1{,}274.2m} =$	78.0 days
Sugar refiner and seller	$\dfrac{\$304.4m}{\$3{,}817.3m} =$	29.3 days	$\dfrac{\$287.0m}{\$3{,}366.3m} =$	31.1 days

The differences in collection period reflect the differences between the types of business. Supermarkets have hardly any trade receivables at all, whereas the manufacturing companies have far more. The collection periods are fairly constant from the previous year for all three companies.

3.12 Inventory turnover period

Another ratio worth calculating is the inventory turnover period. This is another estimated figure, obtainable from published accounts, which indicates the average number of days that items of inventory are held for. As with the average receivable collection period, however, it is only an approximate estimated figure, but one which should be reliable enough for comparing changes year on year.

Formula to learn

The inventory turnover period is calculated as:

$$\frac{\text{Inventory}}{\text{Cost of sales}} \times 365$$

This is another measure of how vigorously a business is trading. A lengthening inventory turnover period from one year to the next indicates:

(a) a slowdown in trading; or

(b) a build-up in inventory levels, perhaps suggesting that the investment in inventories is becoming excessive.

Generally the **higher the inventory turnover is the better**, but several aspects of inventory holding policy have to balanced.

(a) Lead times
(b) Seasonal fluctuations in orders
(c) Alternative uses of warehouse space
(d) Bulk buying discounts
(e) Likelihood of inventory perishing or becoming obsolete

Presumably if we add together the inventory turnover period and receivables collection period, this should give us an indication of how soon inventory is converted into cash. Both receivables collection period and inventory turnover period therefore give us a further indication of the company's liquidity.

3.13 Examples: Inventory turnover period

The estimated inventory turnover periods for a supermarket are as follows.

Company	Inventory / Cost of sales		Inventory turnover period (days × 365)		Previous year
Supermarket	$15,554K / $254,571K	22.3 days	$14,094K / $261,368K	× 365	= 19.7 days

Question — Liquidity ratios

Calculate liquidity and working capital ratios from the accounts of the TEB Co, a business which provides service support (cleaning etc) to customers worldwide. Comment on the results of your calculations.

	20X7 $m	20X6 $m
Sales revenue	2,176.2	2,344.8
Cost of sales	1,659.0	1,731.5
Gross profit	517.2	613.3
Current assets		
Inventories	42.7	78.0
Receivables (note 1)	378.9	431.4
Short-term deposits and cash	205.2	145.0
	626.8	654.4

	20X7 $m	20X6 $m
Current liabilities		
Loans and overdrafts	32.4	81.1
Tax on profits	79.5	93.9
Payables (note 2)	487.2	467.2
	599.1	642.2
Net current assets	27.7	12.2

Notes
1 Trade receivables   295.2   335.5
2 Trade payables   190.8   188.1

Answer

		20X7			20X6
Current ratio	626.8 / 599.1 =	1.05	654.4 / 642.2 =		1.02
Quick ratio	584.1 / 599.1 =	0.97	576.4 / 642.2 =		0.90
Accounts receivable collection period	295.2 / 2,176.2 × 365 =	49.5 days	335.5 / 2,344.8 × 365		= 52.2 days
Inventory turnover period	42.7 / 1,659.0 × 365 =	9.4 days	78.0 / 1,731.5 × 365		= 16.4 days

The company's current ratio is a little lower than average but its quick ratio is better than average and very little less than the current ratio. This suggests that inventory levels are strictly controlled, which is reinforced by the low inventory turnover period. It would seem that working capital is tightly managed, to avoid the poor liquidity which could be caused by a long receivables collection period and comparatively high payables.

The company in the exercise is a service company and hence it would be expected to have very low inventory and a very short stock turnover period. The similarity of receivables collection period and payables payment period means that the company is passing on most of the delay in receiving payment to its suppliers.

3.14 Accounts payable payment period

Formula to learn

Accounts payable payment period is ideally calculated by the formula:

$$\frac{\text{Trade accounts payable}}{\text{Purchases}} \times 365$$

It is rare to find purchases disclosed in published accounts and so **cost of sales serves as an approximation**. The payment period often helps to assess a company's liquidity; an increase is often a sign of lack of long-term finance or poor management of current assets, resulting in the use of extended credit from suppliers, increased bank overdraft and so on.

Question — Operating cycle

(a) Calculate the operating cycle for Moribund plc for 20X2 on the basis of the following information.

		$
Inventory:	raw materials	150,000
	work in progress	60,000
	finished goods	200,000
Purchases		500,000
Trade accounts receivable		230,000
Trade accounts payable		120,000
Sales		900,000
Cost of goods sold		750,000

Tutorial note. You will need to calculate inventory turnover periods (total year end inventory over cost of goods sold), receivables as daily sales, and payables in relation to purchases, all converted into 'days'.

(b) List the steps which might be taken in order to improve the operating cycle.

PART F   INTERPRETATION OF FINANCIAL STATEMENTS

Answer

(a) The operating cycle can be found as follows.

Inventory turnover period: $\dfrac{\text{Total closing inventory} \times 365}{\text{Cost of goods sold}}$

plus

Accounts receivable collection period: $\dfrac{\text{Closing trade receivables} \times 365}{\text{Sales}}$

less

Accounts payable payment period: $\dfrac{\text{Closing trade payables} \times 365}{\text{Purchases}}$

	20X2
Total closing inventory ($)	410,000
Cost of goods sold ($)	750,000
Inventory turnover period	199.5 days
Closing receivables ($)	230,000
Sales ($)	900,000
Receivables collection period	93.3 days
Closing payables ($)	120,000
Purchases ($)	500,000
Payables payment period	(87.6 days)
Length of operating cycle (199.5 + 93.3 − 87.6)	205.2 days

(b) The steps that could be taken to reduce the operating cycle include the following.

(i) *Reducing the average raw material inventory turnover*

(ii) *Reducing the time taken to produce goods.* However, the company must ensure that quality is not sacrificed as a result of speeding up the production process.

(iii) *Increasing the period of credit taken from suppliers.* The credit period seems very long – the company is allowed three months credit by its suppliers, and probably could not be increased. If the credit period is extended then the company may lose discounts for prompt payment.

(iv) *Reducing the average finished goods inventory turnover.*

(v) *Reducing the average receivables collection period.* The administrative costs of speeding up debt collection and the effect on sales of reducing the credit period allowed must be evaluated. However, the credit period does seem very long by the standards of most industries. It may be that generous terms have been allowed to secure large contracts and little will be able to be done about this in the short term.

4 Shareholders' investment ratios

FAST FORWARD

These are the ratios which help equity shareholders and other investors to assess the value and quality of an investment in the ordinary shares of a company.

(a) Earnings per share
(b) Dividend per share
(c) Dividend cover
(d) P/E ratio
(e) Dividend yield

The value of an investment in ordinary shares in a company **listed on a stock exchange** is its market value, and so investment ratios must have regard not only to information in the company's published accounts, but also to the current price, and the fourth and fifth ratios involve using the share price.

4.1 Earnings per share

It is possible to calculate the return on each ordinary share in the year. This is the earnings per share (EPS). Earnings per share is the amount of net profit for the period that is attributable to each ordinary share which is outstanding during all or part of the period.

Formula to learn

$$\text{Earnings per share} = \frac{\text{Profit after tax and preferred dividends}}{\text{Number of equity shares in issue}}$$

For instance, if profit after tax is $250,000 and preferred dividends are $30,000 and the company has 1 million equity shares in issue, the earnings per share is:

$$\frac{\$250,000 - 30,000}{1,000,000} = 22c$$

4.2 Dividend per share and dividend cover

The **dividend per share** in cents is self-explanatory, and clearly an item of some interest to shareholders.

Formula to learn

$$\text{Dividend cover is a ratio of:} \frac{\text{Earnings per share}}{\text{Net dividend per (ordinary) share}}$$

It shows the **proportion of profit on ordinary activities for the year that is available for distribution to shareholders has been paid (or proposed) and what proportion will be retained in the business to finance future growth.** A dividend cover of 2 times would indicate that the company had paid 50% of its distributable profits as dividends, and retained 50% in the business to help to finance future operations. Retained profits are an important source of funds for most companies, and so the dividend cover can in some cases be quite high.

A **significant change** in the dividend cover from one year to the next would be worth looking at closely. For example, if a company's dividend cover were to fall sharply between one year and the next, it could be that its profits had fallen, but the directors wished to pay at least the same amount of dividends as in the previous year, so as to keep shareholder expectations satisfied.

4.3 P/E ratio

Formula to learn

The **P/E ratio** is the ratio of a company's current share price to the earnings per share.

For instance, if the company in Paragraph 4.1 with an EPS of 22c had a current share price of $2.50, its P/E ratio would be:

$$\frac{250c}{22c} = 11.4$$

A high P/E ratio indicates strong shareholder **confidence** in the company and its future, eg in profit growth, and a lower P/E ratio indicates lower confidence.

The P/E ratio of one company can be compared with the P/E ratios of:

(a) Other companies in the same business sector
(b) Other companies generally

It is often used in **stock exchange reporting** where prices are readily available.

4.4 Dividend yield

Dividend yield is the return a shareholder is currently expecting on the shares of a company.

Formula to learn

$$\text{Dividend yield} = \frac{\text{Dividend on the share for the year}}{\text{Current market value of the share (ex div)}} \times 100\%$$

(a) The dividend per share is taken as the dividend for the previous year.
(b) Ex-div means that the share price does *not* include the right to the most recent dividend.

Shareholders look for **both dividend yield and capital growth**. Obviously, dividend yield is therefore an important aspect of a share's performance.

Question
Interim

In the year to 30 September 20X8, an advertising agency declares an interim ordinary dividend of 7.4c per share and a final ordinary dividend of 8.6c per share. Assuming an ex div share price of 315 cents, what is the dividend yield?

Answer

The net dividend per share is (7.4 + 8.6) = 16 cents

$$\frac{16}{315} \times 100 = 5.1\%$$

5 Presentation of a ratio analysis report

Ratios provide information through **comparison**
- over time
- against a 'norm' or 'standard'
- against the ratios of other companies

However many ratios you calculate, **numbers alone will not answer a question**. You must **interpret** all the information available to you and use ratios to support your answer.

Examination questions on financial performance may try to simulate a real life situation. A set of accounts could be presented and you may be asked to prepare a report on them, addressed to a specific interested party, such as a bank. You should begin your report with a heading showing who it is from, the name of the addressee, the subject of the report and a suitable date.

A good approach is often to head up a **'schedule of ratios and statistics'** which will form an appendix to the main report. Calculate the ratios in a logical sequence, dealing in turn with operating and profitability ratios, use of assets (eg turnover period for inventories, collection period for receivables), liquidity and gearing/leverage.

As you calculate the ratios you are likely to be struck by **significant fluctuations and trends**. These will form the basis of your comments in the body of the report. The report should begin with some introductory comments, setting out the scope of your analysis and mentioning that detailed figures have been included in an appendix. You should then go on to present your analysis under any categories called for by the question (eg separate sections for management, shareholders and creditors, or separate sections for profitability and liquidity).

Finally, look out for opportunities to **suggest remedial action** where trends appear to be unfavourable. Questions sometimes require you specifically to set out your advice and recommendations.

5.1 Planning your answers

This is as good a place as any to stress the importance of planning your answers. This is particularly important for 'wordy' questions. While you may feel like breathing a sigh of relief after all that number crunching, you should not be tempted to 'waffle'. The best way to avoid going off the point is to **prepare an answer plan**. This has the advantage of making you think before you write and structure your answer logically.

The following approach may be adopted when preparing an answer plan.

- (a) Read the question **requirements**.
- (b) **Skim through the question** to see roughly what it is about.
- (c) Read through the question carefully, **underlining any key words**.
- (d) Set out the **headings** for the main parts of your answer. Leave space to insert points within the headings.
- (e) **Jot down points** to make within the main sections, underlining points on which you wish to expand.
- (f) Write your **full answer**.

You should allow yourself the full time allocation for written answers, that is 1.8 minutes per mark. If, however, you run out of time, a clear answer plan with points in note form will earn you more marks than an introductory paragraph written out in full.

PART F INTERPRETATION OF FINANCIAL STATEMENTS

Chapter Roundup

- Broadly speaking, basic ratios can be grouped into five categories.
    - Profitability and return
    - Long-term solvency and stability
    - Short-term solvency and liquidity
    - Efficiency (turnover ratios)
    - Shareholder's investment ratios

- This lengthy chapter has gone into quite a lot of detail about basic ratio analysis. The ratios you should be able to calculate and/or comment on are as follows.

    - **Profitability ratios**
        - Return on capital employed
        - Net profit as a percentage of sales
        - Asset turnover ratio
        - Gross profit as a percentage of sales

    - **Debt and gearing/leverage ratios**
        - Debt ratio
        - Gearing ratio/leverage
        - Interest cover
        - Cash flow ratio

    - **Liquidity and working capital ratios**
        - Current ratio
        - Quick ratio (acid test ratio)
        - Accounts receivable collection period
        - Accounts payable payment period
        - Average inventory turnover period

    - **Ordinary shareholders' investment ratios**
        - Earnings per share
        - Dividend per share
        - Dividend cover
        - P/E ratio
        - Dividend yield

- With the exception of the last two ratios, where the share's market price is required, all of these ratios **can be calculated from information in a company's published accounts**.

- Ratios provide information through **comparison**.
    - **Trends** in a company's ratios from **one year to the next**, indicating an improving or worsening position.
    - In some cases, **against a 'norm' or 'standard'**.
    - In some cases, **against the ratios of other companies**, although differences between one company and another should often be expected.

- You must realise that, however many ratios you can find to calculate, **numbers alone will not answer a question**. You *must* interpret all the information available to you and support your interpretation with ratio calculations.

Quick Quiz

1. Apart from ratio analysis, what other information might be helpful in interpreting a company's accounts?
2. What is the usual formula for ROCE?
3. ROCE can be calculated as the product of two other ratios. What are they?
4. Define the 'debt ratio'.
5. What is the relationship between 'gearing' and 'leverage'?
6. In a period when profits are fluctuating, what effect does a company's level of gearing/leverage have on the profits available for ordinary shareholders?
7. What is a company's cash flow ratio?
8. What is earnings per share?
9. What is the P/E ratio?
10. Write down the best approach to answering an interpretation question.

Answers to Quick Quiz

1. Various other items and notes in the publicised accounts (see Paragraph 1.7).

2. $\dfrac{\text{PBIT}}{\text{Capital employed}}$

3. Profit margin × asset turnover = ROCE

4. $\dfrac{\text{The total of a company's debts}}{\text{Total assets}}$

5. Gearing + Leverage = 100%

6. See Paragraph 3.4.

7. $\dfrac{\text{Net cash inflow}}{\text{Total debts}}$

8. The amount of net profit that is attributable to each ordinary share.

9. $\dfrac{\text{Current share price}}{\text{EPS}}$

10. See Paragraph 5.

Now try the questions below from the Exam Question Bank

Number	Level	Marks	Time
Q32	Examination	10	18 mins
Q37	Examination	10	18 mins

PART F INTERPRETATION OF FINANCIAL STATEMENTS

Part G
Miscellaneous topics

Computer applications in accounting

Topic list	Syllabus reference
1 Accounting packages	3(d)
2 Accounting modules	3(d)
3 Databases	3(d)
4 Spreadsheets	3(d)
5 Practical experience	3(d)

Introduction

We have referred briefly to computerised accounting systems earlier in the text. These days, most accounting systems are computerised and anyone training to be an accountant should be able to work with them.

The most important point to remember is that the principles of computerised accounting are the same as those of manual accounting. You should by now have a good grasp of these principles.

The first section of this chapter talks about accounting **packages**. This is a rather general term, but most of us can probably name the accounting package that we use at work.

An accounting package consists of several accounting **modules**, eg receivables ledger, cash book. An exam question may take one of these modules and ask you to describe inputs, processing and outputs. Alternatively, you may be asked to outline the advantages of computer processing over manual processing, for example, for receivables or payroll.

Questions may ask you to discuss the advantages and disadvantages of **databases** and **spreadsheets**. These are discussed in Sections 3 and 4. It is likely that you will have used a spreadsheet in your workplace.

PART G MISCELLANEOUS TOPICS

Study guide

Section 6 – Computerised accounting systems

- Compare manual and computerised accounting systems.
- Identify the advantages and disadvantages of computerised systems.
- Describe the main elements of a computerised accounting system.
- Describe typical data processing work.
- Explain the use of integrated accounting packages.
- Explain the nature and use of micro-computers.
- Explain other business uses of computers.
- Explain the nature and purpose of spreadsheets.
- Explain the nature and purpose of database systems.

Exam guide

This topic is not a key topic and so it is likely to be examined only in Section A of the exam. However you should be prepared for questions comparing computer systems with manual systems.

1 Accounting packages

FAST FORWARD

Computer software used in accounting may be divided into two types.

- Dedicated accounting packages.
- General software, such as spreadsheets, which can be used for accounting.

The syllabus for this paper requires you to know about the use of computers in financial accounting practice.

Exam focus point

Questions will *not* be set on the technical aspects of how computers work. A typical question might be to give advantages and disadvantages of computerised accounting systems over manual systems.

We shall assume, therefore, that you know that a modern computer generally consists of a keyboard, a television-like screen, a box-like disk drive which contains all the necessary electronic components for data processing, and a printer. This is the computer hardware.

The computer hardware described above is also known as a personal computer (PC), but the technical name is a **micro-computer.**

Key term

Computer programs are the instructions that tell the electronics how to process data. The general term used for these is software.

Software is what we are concerned with in this text, and in particular 'applications software', that is packages of computer programs that carry out specific tasks.

(a) Some applications are devoted specifically to an accounting task, for example a payroll package, a non-current asset register or an inventory control package.

(b) Other applications have many uses in business, including their use for accounting purposes. Packages of this sort that we shall describe are databases and spreadsheets.

1.1 Accounting packages

FAST FORWARD

One of the most important facts to remember about computerised accounting is that **in principle, it is exactly the same as manual accounting.** However, it has certain advantages.

Accounting functions retain the same names in computerised systems as in more traditional written records. Computerised accounting still uses the familiar ideas of day books, ledger accounts, double entry, trial balance and financial statements. The principles of working with computerised sales, purchase and nominal ledgers are exactly what would be expected in the manual methods they replace.

The only difference is that these various books of account have become invisible. Ledgers are now computer files which are held in a computer-sensible form, ready to be called upon.

1.1.1 Advantages

However, the advantages of accounting packages compared with a manual system are as follows.

(a) The packages can be used by **non-specialists**.

(b) A large amount of **data can be processed very quickly**.

(c) Computerised systems are **more accurate** than manual systems.

(d) A computer is capable of handling and processing **large volumes** of data.

(e) Once the data has been input, computerised systems can **analyse data** rapidly to present useful control information for managers such as a trial balance or a trade accounts receivable schedule.

1.1.2 Disadvantages

The advantages of computerised accounting system far outweigh the disadvantages, particularly for large businesses. However, the following may be identified as possible disadvantages.

(a) The initial **time and costs** involved in installing the system, training personnel and so on.

(b) The need for **security checks** to make sure that unauthorised personnel do not gain access to data files.

(c) The necessity to develop a **system of coding** (see below) and checking.

(d) **Lack of 'audit trail'**. It is not always easy to see where a mistake has been made.

(e) Possible **resistance** on the part of staff to the introduction of the system.

1.2 Coding

Computers are used more efficiently if vital information is expressed in the form of codes. For example, nominal ledger accounts will be coded individually, perhaps by means of a two-digit code: eg

00	Ordinary share capital
01	Share premium
05	Income and expenses account
15	Purchases
22	Receivables ledger control account
41	Payables ledger control account
42	Interest
43	Dividends etc

In the same way, individual accounts must be given a unique code number in the sales ledger and purchase ledger.

1.3 Example: Coding

When an invoice is received from a supplier (code 1234) for $3,000 for the purchase of raw materials, the transaction might be coded for input to the computer as:

Supplier Code	Nominal ledger Debit	Nominal ledger Credit	Value	Inventory Code	Quantity
1234	15	41	$3,000	56742	150

Code 15 might represent purchases and code 41 the payables control account. This single input could be used to update the purchase ledger, the nominal ledger, and the inventory ledger. The inventory code may enable further analysis to be carried out, perhaps allocating the cost to a particular department or product. Thus the needs of both financial accounting and cost accounting can be fulfilled at once.

Important!

> If you are not already using one, get some experience between now and the exam, of using an accounting package.

1.4 Modules

Key term

> A **module** is a program which deals with one particular part of a business accounting system.

An accounting package will consist of several modules. A simple accounting package might consist of only one module (in which case it is called a stand-alone module), but more often it will consist of several modules. The name given to a set of several modules is a **suite**. An accounting package, therefore, might have separate modules for some or all of the following.

(a) Invoicing
(b) Inventory
(c) Receivables ledger
(d) Payables ledger
(e) Nominal ledger
(f) Payroll
(g) Cash book
(h) Job costing
(i) Non-current asset register
(j) Report generator

1.5 Integrated software

Each module may be integrated with the others, so that data entered in one module will be passed automatically or by simple operator request through into any other module where the data is of some relevance. For example, if there is an input into the invoicing module authorising the despatch of an invoice to a customer, there might be **automatic links**:

(a) To the sales ledger, to update the file by posting the invoice to the customer's account.

(b) To the inventory module, to update the inventory file by:
   (i) reducing the quantity and value of inventory in hand
   (ii) recording the inventory movement

(c) To the nominal ledger, to update the file by posting the sale to the sales account.

(d) To the job costing module, to record the sales value of the job on the job cost file.

(e) To the report generator, to update the sales analysis and sales totals which are on file and awaiting inclusion in management reports.

23: COMPUTER APPLICATIONS IN ACCOUNTING

A diagram of an **integrated accounting system** is given below.

[Diagram: Decision support system and Executive information system feed into Spreadsheet facilities, which connects (dashed line) to Nominal ledger module. The Nominal ledger module connects to Receivables module, Payables module, Payroll module, Inventory module, and Non-current assets. Receivables, Payables, Payroll, and Inventory modules all feed into Job costing module.]

1.5.1 Advantages

(a) It becomes possible to make just one entry in one of the ledgers which automatically updates the others.

(b) Users can specify reports, and the software will automatically extract the required data from *all* the relevant files.

(c) Both of the above simplify the workload of the user, and the irritating need to constantly load and unload disks is eliminated.

1.5.2 Disadvantages

(a) Usually, it requires more computer memory than separate (stand-alone) systems – which means there is less space in which to store actual data.

(b) Because one program is expected to do everything, the user may find that an integrated package has fewer facilities than a set of specialised modules. In effect, an integrated package could be 'Jack of all trades but master of none'.

2 Accounting modules

FAST FORWARD

> An accountancy package consists of a number of **modules** which perform all the tasks needed to maintain a normal accounting function like payables ledger or payroll. In modern systems the modules are usually integrated with each other.

In this section we shall look at some of the accounting modules in more detail, starting with the receivables ledger.

2.1 Accounting for trade accounts receivable

A computerised receivables ledger will be expected to keep the receivables ledger up-to-date, and also it should be able to produce certain output (eg statements, sales analysis reports, responses to file interrogations etc). The output might be produced daily (eg day book listings), monthly (eg statements), quarterly (eg sales analysis reports) or periodically (eg responses to file interrogations, or customer name and address lists printed on adhesive labels for despatching circulars or price lists).

2.1.1 Inputs to a receivables ledger system

Bearing in mind what we expect to find in a receivables ledger, we can say that typical data input into receivables ledger system is as follows.

(a) **Amendments**
  (i) Amendments to customer details, eg change of address, change of credit limit
  (ii) Insertion of new customers
  (iii) Deletion of old 'non-active' customers

(b) **Transaction data relating to**:
  (i) Sales transactions, for invoicing
  (ii) Customer payments
  (iii) Credit notes
  (iv) Adjustments (debit or credit items)

2.1.2 Outputs from a receivables ledger system

Typical outputs in a computerised receivables ledger are as follows.

(a) **Day book listing**. A list of all transactions posted each day. This provides an audit trail – ie it is information which the auditors of the business can use when carrying out their work. Batch and control totals will be included in the listing.

(b) **Invoices** (if the package is one which is expected to produce invoices.)

(c) **Statements**. End of month statements for customers.

(d) **Aged accounts receivable list**. Probably produced monthly.

(e) **Sales analysis reports**. These will analyse sales according to the sales analysis codes on the receivables ledger file.

(f) **Reminder letters**. Letters can be produced automatically to chase late payers when the due date for payment goes by without payment having been received.

(g) **Customer lists** (or perhaps a selective list). The list might be printed on to adhesive labels, for sending out customer letters or marketing material.

(h) **Responses to enquiries**, perhaps output on to a VDU screen rather than as printed copy, for fast response to customer enquiries.

(i) **Output onto disk file for other modules** – eg to the inventory control module and the nominal ledger module, if these are also used by the organisation, and the package is not an integrated one.

2.1.3 The advantages of a computerised trade accounts receivable system

The advantages of such a system, in addition to the advantages of computerised accounting generally, are its ability to assist in sales administration and marketing by means of outputs such as those listed above.

2.2 Payables ledger

A computerised payables ledger will certainly be expected to keep the payables ledger up-to-date, and also it should be able to output various reports requested by the user. In fact, a computerised payables ledger is much the same as a computerised receivables ledger, except that it is a sort of mirror image as it deals with purchases rather than sales.

Question
Payables ledger

What sort of data would you expect to be held on a payables ledger file?

Answer

The payables ledger will consist of individual records for each supplier account. Just as for customer accounts, some of the data held on record will be *standing* data, and some will be *variable* data.

Standing data will include:		Variable data will include:	
(a)	Account number	(a)	Transaction date
(b)	Name	(b)	Transaction description
(c)	Address	(c)	Transaction code
(d)	Credit details	(d)	Debits
(e)	Bank details (eg method of payment)	(e)	Credits
(f)	Cash discount details, if appropriate	(f)	Balance

2.2.1 Inputs to a payables ledger system

Bearing in mind what we expect to see held on a payables ledger, typical data input into a payables ledger system is:

- (a) Details of purchases recorded on invoices
- (b) Details of returns to suppliers for which credit notes are received
- (c) Details of payments to suppliers
- (d) Adjustments

2.2.2 Processing in a payables ledger system

The primary action involved in updating the payables ledger is adjusting the amounts outstanding on the supplier accounts. These amounts will represent money owed to the suppliers. This processing is identical to updating the accounts in the receivables ledger, except that the receivables ledger balances are debits (receivables) and the payables ledger balances are credits (payables). Again, the open item approach is the best.

2.2.3 Outputs from a payables ledger system

Typical outputs in a computerised payables ledger are as follows.

- (a) **Lists of transactions posted** – produced every time the system is run.
- (b) An **analysis of expenditure** for nominal ledger purposes. This may be produced every time the system is run or at the end of each month.
- (c) **List of payable balances** together with a reconciliation between the total balance brought forward, the transactions for the month and the total balance carried forward.

(d) **Copies of suppliers' accounts**. This may show merely the balance b/f, current transactions and the balance c/f. If complete details of all unsettled items are given, the ledger is known as an **open-ended ledger**. (This is similar to the open item or balance forward methods with a receivables ledger system.)

(e) Any payables ledger system can be used to produce details of payments to be made.

    (i) Remittance advices (usually a copy of the ledger account)
    (ii) Cheques
    (iii) Credit transfer listings

(f) Other special reports may be produced for:

    (i) Costing purposes
    (ii) Updating records about non-current assets
    (iii) Comparisons with budget
    (iv) Aged accounts payable list

2.3 Nominal ledger

The nominal ledger (or general ledger) is an accounting record which summarises the financial affairs of a business. It is the nucleus of an accounting system. It contains details of assets, liabilities and capital, income and expenditure and so profit or loss. It consists of a large number of different accounts, each account having its own purpose or 'name' and an identity or code.

A nominal ledger will consist of a large number of coded accounts. For example, part of a nominal ledger might be as follows.

Account code	Account name
100200	Plant and machinery (cost)
100300	Motor vehicles (cost)
100201	Plant and machinery depreciation
100301	Vehicles depreciation
300000	Total receivables
400000	Total payables
500130	Wages and salaries
500140	Rent and local taxes
500150	Advertising expenses
500160	Bank charges
500170	Motor expenses
500180	Telephone expenses
600000	Sales
700000	Cash

A business will, of course, choose its own codes for its nominal ledger accounts. The codes given in this table are just for illustration.

It is important to remember that a **computerised nominal ledger works in exactly the same way as a manual nominal ledger**, although there are some differences in terminology. For instance, in a manual system, the sales and receivables accounts were posted from the sales day book (not the sales ledger). But in a computerised system, the sales day book is automatically produced as part of the 'receivables ledger module'. So it may **sound** as if you are posting directly from the receivables ledger, but in fact the day book is part of a computerised receivables ledger.

2.3.1 Inputs to the nominal ledger

Inputs depend on whether the accounting system is integrated or not.

(a) If the system is integrated, then as soon as data is put into the sales ledger module (or anywhere else for that matter), the relevant nominal ledger accounts are updated. There is nothing more for the system user to do.

(b) If the system is not integrated then the output from the sales ledger module (and anywhere else) has to be input into the nominal ledger. This is done by using journal entries. For instance.

DEBIT	A/c 300000	$3,000
CREDIT	A/c 600000	$3,000

Where 600000 is the nominal ledger code for sales, and 300000 is the code for receivables.

Regardless of whether the system is integrated or not, the actual data needed by the nominal ledger package to be able to update the ledger accounts includes:

(a) Date
(b) Description
(c) Amount
(d) Account codes (sometimes called distinction codes)

2.3.2 Outputs from the nominal ledger

The main outputs apart from listings of individual nominal ledger accounts are:

(a) trial balance;
(b) financial statements.

3 Databases

FAST FORWARD

A database is a file of data structured in such a way that it can serve a number of applications without its structure being dictated by any particular function.

A database may be described as a 'pool' of data, which can be used by any number of applications. Its use is not restricted to the accounts department. A stricter definition is provided in the *Computing Terminology* of the Chartered Institute of Management Accountants (CIMA).

Key term

'Frequently a much abused term. In its strict sense a **database** is a file of data structured in such a way that it may serve a number of applications without its structure being dictated by any one of those applications, the concept being that programs are written around the database rather than files being structured to meet the needs of specific programs. The term is also rather loosely applied to simple file management software.'

3.1 Objectives of a database

The main virtues of a database are as follow.

(a) There is **common data** for all users to share.
(b) The extra effort of keeping **duplicate files** in different departments is avoided.
(c) Conflicts between departments who use **inconsistent data are avoided**.

A database should have four major objectives.

(a) It should be **shared**. Different users should be able to access the *same data* in the database for their own processing applications (and at the *same time* in some systems) thus removing the need for duplicating data on different files.

(b) The **integrity** of the database must be preserved. This means that one user should not be allowed to alter the data on file so as to spoil the database records for other users. However, users must be able to update the data on file, and so make valid alterations to the data.

(c) The database system should provide for the needs of different users, who each have their own processing requirements and data access methods. In other words, the database should provide for the **operational requirements of all its users**.

(d) The database should be capable of **evolving**, both in the short term (it must be kept updated) and in the longer term (it must be able to meet the future data processing needs of users, not just their current needs).

3.2 Example: Non-current assets and databases

An organisation, especially a large one, may possess a large quantity of non-current assets. Before computerisation these would have been kept in a manual non-current asset register. A database enables this non-current asset register to be stored in an electronic form. A database file for non-current assets might contain most or all of the following categories of information.

(a) Code number to give the asset a unique identification in the database
(b) Type of asset (motor car, leasehold premises), for published accounts purposes
(c) More detailed description of the asset (serial number, car registration number, make)
(d) Physical location of the asset (address)
(e) Organisational location of the asset (accounts department)
(f) Person responsible for the asset (in the case of a company-owned car, the person who uses it)
(g) Original cost of the asset
(h) Date of purchase
(i) Depreciation rate and method applied to the asset
(j) Accumulated depreciation to date
(k) Net book value of the asset
(l) Estimated residual value
(m) Date when the physical existence of the asset was last verified
(n) Supplier

Obviously, the details kept about the asset would depend on the type of asset it is.

Any kind of computerised non-current asset record will improve efficiency in accounting for non-current assets because of the ease and speed with which any necessary calculations can be made. Most obvious is the calculation of the depreciation provision which can be an extremely onerous task if it is done monthly and there are frequent acquisitions and disposals and many different depreciation rates in use.

The particular advantage of using a database for the non-current asset function is its flexibility in generating reports for different purposes. Aside from basic cost and net book value information, a database with fields such as those listed above in the record of each asset could compile reports analysing assets according to location, or by manufacturer. This information could be used to help compare the performance of different divisions, perhaps, or to assess the useful life of assets supplied by different manufacturers. There may be as many more possibilities as there are permutations of the individual pieces of data.

4 Spreadsheets

Spreadsheets are useful in both financial and management accounting.

Key term

A **spreadsheet** is essentially an electronic piece of paper divided into rows and columns with a built in pencil, eraser and calculator. It provides an easy way of performing numerical calculations.

The intersection of each column and row of a spreadsheet is referred to as a cell. A cell can contain text, numbers or formulae. Use of a formula means that the cell which contains the formula will display the results of a calculation based on data in other cells. If the numbers in those other cells change, the result displayed in the formula cell will also change accordingly. With this facility, a spreadsheet is used to create financial models.

Below is a spreadsheet processing budgeted sales figures for three geographical areas for the first quarter of the year.

	A	B	C	D	E
1	BUDGETED SALES FIGURES				
2		Jan	Feb	Mar	Total
3		$'000	$'000	$'000	$'000
4	North	2,431	3,001	2,189	7,621
5	South	6,532	5,826	6,124	18,482
6	West	895	432	596	1,923
7	Total	9,858	9,259	8,909	28,026

4.1 The use of spreadsheets

Spreadsheets have many uses, both for accounting and for other purposes. It is perfectly possible, for example, to create proforma balance sheets and income statements on a spreadsheet, or set up the notes for financial accounts, like the non-current assets note.

5 Practical experience

Reading about computer systems and packages is no substitute for using them, and you should make every effort to gain experience in using an accounting package.

Chapter Roundup

- Computer **software** used in accounting may be divided into two types.
    - Dedicated accounting packages
    - General software, which can be used for accounting.

- In principle computerised accounting is the same as manual accounting, but a computerised approach has certain advantages which you should learn thoroughly.

- An accounting package consists of a number of **'modules'** which perform all the tasks needed to maintain a normal accounting function like payables ledger or payroll. In modern systems the modules are usually integrated with each other.

- A **database** is a file of data structured in such a way that it can serve a number of applications without its structure being dictated by any particular function.

- **Spreadsheets**, too, are often useful both in financial accounting and management accounting.

- **Reading about accounting packages is no substitute for using one.**

PART G MISCELLANEOUS TOPICS

Quick Quiz

1. What are the advantages of computerised accounting?
2. What are the disadvantages?
3. What is an accounting suite?
4. What sort of data is input into a receivables ledger system?
5. What is the open item method of processing?
6. What should be the four major objectives of a database?
7. What are the advantages of using a database to maintain non-current asset records?
8. What is a spreadsheet?

Answers to Quick Quiz

1. See Paragraph 1.1.1.
2. See Paragraph 1.1.2.
3. A set of several different modules.
4. See Paragraph 2.1.1.
5. Payments are credited to specific invoices, so that late payment of invoices can be identified.
6. See Paragraph 3.1.
7. The amount of detail that can be kept about each individual asset and the ease in analysing this information into different reports and calculations (eg depreciation, profit on sale).
8. See Paragraph 4.

The IASB and financial reporting

Topic list	Syllabus reference
1 The International Accounting Standards Board (IASB)	1(c)
2 International Financial Reporting Standards (IFRSs) and International Accounting Standards (IASs)	1(d)
3 Criticisms of accounting conventions	2(a), 2(b)
4 Conceptual framework and GAAP	1(e)
5 The IASB's Framework	1(e), 2(a)

Introduction

We have already discussed the IASB, IASs and IFRSs to some extent, particularly in Chapter 1. Here we are concerned with the **IASB's relationship with other bodies**, and with the way the IASB operates and **how IFRSs are produced**.

Until now, your studies for Paper 1.1 have been almost entirely concerned with the **mechanics** of accounts preparation. This chapter looks at some of the **theory** behind what appears in the accounts.

The most important document in this area is the **IASB's Framework for the preparation and presentation of financial statements**. Since it was published, all IASs have been based on the principles it contains. You only need to know about the first part of the Framework for Paper 1.1; the rest will be introduced in your later studies. This framework was adopted by the IASB when it replaced the IASC.

You must try to understand and appreciate the contents of this chapter. The examiner is not only interested in whether you can add up; he wants to know that you can think about a subject which, after all, is your future career.

PART G MISCELLANEOUS TOPICS

Study guide

Section 14 – Accounting concepts and conventions, the IASB's *Framework* and IAS 1

- Explain the need for an agreed conceptual framework for financial accounting.
- Revise the users of financial statements from Session 1.
- Explain the qualitative characteristics of financial statements as described in paragraphs 24 to 46 of the *Framework* (revision from Session 1).
- Explain the advantages and disadvantages of historical cost accounting (HCA) in times of changing prices.
- Explain in principle the main alternatives to HCA:
    - Current purchasing power accounting (CPP)
    - Current cost accounting (CCA)

    Note: Computational questions on CPP and CCA will not be set.

Exam guide

These ideas are fundamental to your studies and valuable background. However, they are **non-key subjects** for the exam and are likely to be examined by MCQs in Section A. For those studying for the Oxford Brookes degree, project topic 12 asks for an analysis of the effect of any IAS on the accounts of any organisation in terms of profitability or financial stability or balance sheet value.

1 The international accounting standards board (IASB)

FAST FORWARD

> The main objectives of the IASB are to raise the standard of financial reporting and to eventually bring about global harmonisation of accounting standards.

We looked briefly at the IASC in Chapter 1. In April 2001 the IASC was replaced by the IASB which has 12 full-time and 2 part-time members drawn from 9 countries.

The IASB is an **independent private sector body**. Its objective is to achieve uniformity in the accounting principles which are used by businesses and other organisations for financial reporting around the world. The IASB adopted the IASes issued by the IASC and has issued amendments to some of these IASes. Its own standards are known as International Financial Reporting Standards. Five of these have now been issued.

1.1 Objectives of the IASB

Here is a reminder of the formal objectives of the IASB.

(a) To **develop**, in the public interest, a single set of high quality, understandable and enforceable **global accounting standards** that require high quality, transparent and comparable information in financial statements and other financial reporting to help participants in the world's capital markets and other users make economic decisions

(b) To promote the use and **rigorous application** of those standards

(c) To bring about **convergence of national accounting standards** and International Accounting Standards to high quality solutions

Question: International harmonisation

In accounting terms what do you think are:

(a) The advantages to international harmonisation?
(b) The barriers to international harmonisation?

Answer

(a) Advantages of global harmonisation

The advantages of harmonisation will be based on the benefits to users and preparers of accounts, as follows.

(i) Investors, both individual and corporate, would like to be able to compare the financial results of different companies internationally as well as nationally in making investment decisions.

(ii) Multinational companies would benefit from harmonisation for many reasons including the following.

(1) Better access would be gained to foreign investor funds.
(2) Management control would be improved, because harmonisation would aid internal communication of financial information.
(3) Appraisal of foreign enterprises for take-overs and mergers would be more straightforward.
(4) It would be easier to comply with the reporting requirements of overseas stock exchanges.
(5) Preparation of group accounts would be easier.
(6) A reduction in audit costs might be achieved.
(7) Transfer of accounting staff across national borders would be easier.

(iii) Governments of developing countries would save time and money if they could adopt international standards and, if these were used internally, governments of developing countries could attempt to control the activities of foreign multinational companies in their own country. These companies could not 'hide' behind foreign accounting practices which are difficult to understand.

(iv) Tax authorities. It will be easier to calculate the tax liability of investors, including multinationals who receive income from overseas sources.

(v) Regional economic groups usually promote trade within a specific geographical region. This would be aided by common accounting practices within the region.

(vi) Large international accounting firms would benefit as accounting and auditing would be much easier if similar accounting practices existed throughout the world.

(b) Barriers to harmonisation

(i) Different purposes of financial reporting. In some countries the purpose is solely for tax assessment, while in others it is for investor decision-making.

(ii) Different legal systems. These prevent the development of certain accounting practices and restrict the options available.

(iii) Different user groups. Countries have different ideas about who the relevant user groups are and their respective importance. In the USA investor and creditor groups are given prominence, while in Europe employees enjoy a higher profile.

PART G MISCELLANEOUS TOPICS

(iv) Needs of developing countries. Developing countries are obviously behind in the standard setting process and they need to develop the basic standards and principles already in place in most developed countries.

(v) Nationalism is demonstrated in an unwillingness to accept another country's standard.

(vi) Cultural differences result in objectives for accounting systems differing from country to country.

(vii) Unique circumstances. Some countries may be experiencing unusual circumstances which affect all aspects of everyday life and impinge on the ability of companies to produce proper reports, for example hyperinflation, civil war, currency restriction and so on.

(viii) The lack of strong accountancy bodies. Many countries do not have strong independent accountancy or business bodies which would press for better standards and greater harmonisation.

1.2 Current position of the IASB

The IASC published 41 IASs, various exposure drafts of IASs and discussion papers, as well as the *Framework for the preparation and presentation of financial statements*, (which is discussed in Section 6). A substantial number of multinational companies prepare financial statements in accordance with IASs. IASs are also endorsed by many countries as their own standards, either unchanged or with minor amendments. The IASB has adopted the extant IASes and issued 5 IFRSs. **From 1 January 2005 listed companies in the EU have been required to prepare consolidated accounts in accordance with IFRS**

1.2.1 IASB and IOSCO

A great many stock exchanges now accept IAS/IFRS for cross-border listing purposes (ie when a company in one country wishes to list its share on another country's stock exchange), but Canada, Japan and the United states are currently exceptions. The IASB has therefore **produced a comprehensive core set of high quality standards**, aimed at more general acceptance of IFRS for cross-border listings. This work was been reviewed by the Technical Committee of the International Organisation of Securities Commissions (IOSCO).

On 17 May 2000, IOSCO gave its qualified backing to 30 International Accounting Standards. It recommended that its members allow multinationals to use them in cross-border listings. This was a significant step towards global harmonisation. IOSCO and the IASB continue to work together to identify areas where new standards are needed.

Following the publication of the first 5 IFRSs in December 2003 and improvements to existing IASs in March 2004, the IASB has now produced what it considers to be a 'stable platform' for the adoption of IFRS by EU member states.

1.2.2 IASB and the EC/intergovernmental bodies

The European Commission has acknowledged the role of the IASC and IASB in harmonising world-wide accounting rules and EC representatives attend IASB meetings and have joined Steering Committees involved in setting IFRSs. This should bring to an end the idea of a separate layer of European reporting rules.

The EC has also set up a committee to investigate where there are conflicts between EU norms and international standards so that compatibility can be achieved. In turn, the IASC has used EC directives in there work.

The IASB also works closely with the United Nations Commission and Centre on Transnational Reporting Corporations and with the Working Group in Accounting Standards of the Organisation for Economic Co-operation and Development (OECD Working group). These bodies support harmonisation and improvement of financial reporting, but they are not standard-setting bodies and much of their output draws on the work of the IASC and IASB (eg using the IASC's *Framework* document).

1.2.3 IASB and professional accountancy bodies/IFAC

The IASB has become closely connected to the professional accountancy bodies through joining with IFAC. **IFAC represents the worldwide accountancy profession.**

The mission of IFAC is the development and enhancement of the profession to enable it to provide services of a consistently high quality in the pubic interest. It is a non-profit, non-governmental, non-political international organisation of accountancy bodies.

IFAC recognises the IASB as the only body which has the authority to issue accounting standards in its own name. This confers on the IASB the authority to co-operate and negotiate with other organisations and to promote acceptance of IASs worldwide. The IASB and IFAC work together in a number of ways.

1.2.4 The IASB and national standard setting bodies

The IASB's relationships with national standard-setting bodies has improved dramatically over the last few years, as the IASB has attempted to increase comparability between national standards and IASs/IFRSs. FASB (the US standard-setting body) has joined the Consultative Group (along with the EC) and also attends Board meetings. The IASB proposed a regular international conference of standard setting bodies which would look at the possibility of further national/international harmonisation.

Since then, the IASC and IASB have invited comments from national standard setters on exposure drafts of IASs and IFRSs joint work projects have been carried out on specific projects (eg the IASC worked with FASB on earnings per share). Meetings frequently take place between the IASB and national standard setters to discuss future harmonisation.

2 International Financial Reporting Standards (IFRSs) and International Accounting Standards (IASs)

We have already looked at all the IASs covered by the Paper 1.1 syllabus. In this section, we examine the process by which IASs are created and we will list the full range of IASs currently in force, just so you can place the standards you have studied into context. The IASB has adopted all of the current IASs. New standards are now IFRSs.

2.1 Due process

The IASB prepares IFRSs in accordance with **due process**.

Step 1 For each standard, a **Steering Committee** has the responsibility for making recommendations to the Board.

Step 2 The Committee normally publishes a discussion **draft** which sets out the various possible requirements for the standard and the arguments for and against each one.

Step 3 The Board publishes an **exposure draft** for public comment. An exposure draft can be issued only when eight Board members have voted in favour of doing so.

Step 4 It examines the arguments put forward in the comment process before deciding on the **final form** of the standard. A final standard requires eight Board member votes for approval.

For every IFRS the following will be considered.

- All associated accounting issues
- IASC's *Framework* document (see below)
- National and regional accounting requirements
- Steering Committee recommendations
- Board review of the Steering Committee recommendations
- Consultation with Consultative Group and others
- The exposure draft of the standard
- Evaluation of comments received

The procedure can be summarised as follows.

2.1.1 Current IASs/IFRSs

The current list is as follows. Those examinable in Paper 1.1 are highlighted*.

IAS 1*	Presentation of financial statements
IAS 2*	Inventories
IAS 7*	Cash flow statements
IAS 8*	Accounting policies, changes in accounting estimates and errors
IAS 10*	Events after the balance sheet date
IAS 11	Construction contracts
IAS 12	Income taxes
IAS 14	Reporting financial information by segment
IAS 15	Information reflecting the effects of changing prices
IAS 16*	Property, plant and equipment
IAS 17	Leases
IAS 18*	Revenue
IAS 19	Retirement benefit costs
IAS 20	Accounting for government grants and disclosure of government assistance
IAS 21	The effects of changes in foreign exchange rates
IAS 23	Borrowing costs
IAS 24	Related party disclosures
IAS 25	Accounting for investments
IAS 26	Accounting and reporting by retirement benefit plans
IAS 27	Consolidated and separate financial statements
IAS 28	Investments in associates
IAS 29	Financial reporting in hyperinflationary economies
IAS 30	Disclosure in the financial statements of banks and similar financial institutions
IAS 31	Interests in joint ventures
IAS 32	Financial instruments: disclosure and presentation

IAS 33	Earnings per share
IAS 34	Interim financial reporting
IAS 36	Impairment of assets
IAS 37*	Provisions, contingent liabilities and contingent assets
IAS 38*	Intangible assets
IAS 39	Financial instruments: recognition and measurement
IAS 40	Investment property
IAS 41	Agriculture

Notes:

IAS 37	Only paragraphs 10, 27-35, 85-92, Appendices A and B are examinable in so far as they relate to contingent liabilities and contingent assets
IAS 38	Only paragraphs 7, 39-47, 55, 79, 88, 107 and 115 relating to R & D are examinable

IFRS 1	First time adoption of International Financial Reporting Standards
IFRS 2	Share based payment
IFRS 3*	Business combinations
IFRS 4	Insurance contracts
IFRS 5*	Non-current assets held for sale and discontinued operations

(Only paragraphs 6 *Classification*, 15 *Measurement*, 30 and 38 *Presentation* and 30–33(b) *Disclosures*.)

IFRS 6	Exploration for the evaluation of mineral resources
IFRS 7	Financial Instruments: disclosures

Various exposure drafts and discussion papers are currently at different stages within the IAS process, but these are not of concern to you at this stage. By the end of your financial accounting studies, however, you will know *all* the standards, exposure drafts and discussion papers!

Question — Standards 1

Why do you think that those standards highlighted above have been included in your syllabus?

Answer

These standards affect the content and format of almost all financial statements. You therefore need to know about them in order to prepare a basic set of accounts. Most of the other standards will only affect larger and more complex organisations.

Over the last few years the IASB has attempted to **reduce the choice of treatments** available within each standard. The aim was to restrict where possible the permissible accounting treatment to just one, but others are included. Where countries adopt methods other than the IASB preferred method, businesses following the alternative should reconcile their net income and shareholders' interests as reported to the amounts that would be determined using the (benchmark) preferred treatment.

It is interesting to examine the **criteria** used by the board of the IASB to decide whether alternative treatments should be required, preferred or eliminated.

(a) Current world-wide practice and trends in national accounting standards, law and generally accepted accounting principles

(b) Conformity with the *Framework*

(c) The views of regulators and their representative organisation, such as the International Organisation of Securities Commissions (IOSCO)

(d) Consistency within an IFRS and with other IASs/IFRSs. The general trend has been towards eliminating allowed alternative treatments.

2.2 Interpretation of IASs/IFRSs – IFRIC

The IASB has now also developed a procedure for issuing interpretations of its standards. In March 2002 the International Financial Reporting Interpretations Committee (IFRIC) was set up.

The IFRIC will consider accounting issues that are likely to receive divergent or unacceptable treatment in the absence of authoritative guidance. Its review will be within the context of existing IASs/IFRSs and the IASC *Framework*.

The IFRIC will deal with issues of reasonably widespread importance, and not issues of concern to only a small set of enterprises. The interpretations will cover both:

(a) **Mature issues** (unsatisfactory practice within the scope of existing standards).

(b) **Emerging issues** (new topics relating to an existing standard but not actually considered when the standard was developed).

In developing interpretations, the 11-person IFRIC will work closely with similar national committees. If it reached consensus on an interpretation the IFRIC will ask the Board to approve the interpretation for issue. Interpretations will be formally published after approval by the Board.

2.3 Scope and application of IASs and IFRS

2.3.1 Scope

Any limitation of the applicability of a specific IAS or IFRS is made clear within that standard. IASs/IFRSs are **not intended to be applied to immaterial items, nor are they retrospective**. Each individual standard lays out its scope at the beginning of the standard.

2.3.2 Application

Within each individual country **local regulations** govern, to a greater or lesser degree, the issue of financial statements. These local regulations include accounting standards issued by the national regulatory bodies and/or professional accountancy bodies in the country concerned.

The IASB **concentrates on essentials** when producing standards. This means that the IASB tries not to make standards too complex, because otherwise they would be impossible to apply on a worldwide basis.

Question   Standards 2

How far do the accounting standards in force in your country diverge from the IASs you have covered in this text?

If you have the time and energy, perhaps you could find out.

2.4 Worldwide effect of international standards and the IASB

The IASB and before it the IASC has now been in existence for nearly 30 years, and it is worth looking at the effect it has had in that time.

As far as **Europe** is concerned, the consolidated financial statements of many of Europe's top multinationals are prepared in conformity with national requirements, EC directives and IASs/IFRSs. Furthermore, IASs are having a growing influence on national accounting requirements and practices.

Many of these developments have been given added impetus by the internationalisation of capital markets. There was a 2005 deadline for implementation of IASs/IFRSs.

In **Japan**, the influence of the IASC and IASB had, until recently, been negligible. This was mainly because of links in Japan between tax rules and financial reporting. The Japanese Ministry of Finance set up a working committee to consider whether to bring national requirements into line with IASs. The Tokyo Stock Exchange has now announced that it will accept financial statements from foreign issue that conform with home country standards. This was widely seen as an attempt to attract foreign issuers, in particular companies from Hong Kong and Singapore. As these countries base their accounting on international standards, this action is therefore implicit acknowledgement by the Japanese Ministry of Finance of IFRS requirements.

America and Japan have been two of the developed countries which have been most reluctant to accept accounts prepared under IFRSs, but recent developments suggest that such financial statements may soon be acceptable on these important stock exchanges.

In **America**, the Securities and Exchange Commission (SEC) agreed in 1993 to allow foreign issuers (of shares, etc) to follow IASC treatments on certain issues, including cash flow statements under IAS 7. The overall effect is that, where IASB treatments differ from US GAAP, these treatments will now be acceptable. The SEC is now supporting the IASB because it wants to attract foreign listings.

Now that you are aware of the workings and impact of the IASB, we will spend the rest of this chapter looking at some of the problems and criticisms which the IASB is faced with, and how it has tackled some of them. We begin at the end of this section by looking at the problem of choice in IASs/ IFRSs.

2.5 Accounting standards and choice

It is sometimes argued that companies should be given a **choice** in matters of financial reporting on the grounds that accounting standards are detrimental to the quality of such reporting. There are arguments on both sides.

In favour of accounting standards (both national and international), the following points can be made.

(a) They **reduce or eliminate** confusing **variations** in the methods used to prepare accounts.

(b) They provide a **focal point** for debate and discussions about accounting practice.

(c) They oblige companies to **disclose** the accounting policies used in the preparation of accounts.

(d) They are a **less rigid alternative** to enforcing conformity by means of **legislation**.

(e) They have obliged companies to **disclose more accounting information** than they would otherwise have done if accounting standards did not exist, for example IAS 33 *Earnings per share*.

Many companies are reluctant to disclose information which is not required by national legislation. However, the following arguments may be put forward against standardisation and in **favour of choice**.

(a) A **set of rules** which give backing to one method of preparing accounts **might be inappropriate** in some circumstances.

(b) Standards may be **subject to lobbying** or government pressure (in the case of national standards). For example, in the USA, the accounting standard FAS 19 on the accounts of oil and gas companies led to a powerful lobby of oil companies, which persuaded the SEC (Securities and Exchange Commission) to step in. FAS 19 was then suspended.

(c) Many national standards are **not based on a conceptual framework** of accounting, although IASs and IFRSs are (see Section 5 below).

PART G   MISCELLANEOUS TOPICS

(d) There may a **trend towards rigidity**, and away from flexibility in applying the rules.

3 Criticisms of accounting conventions

FAST FORWARD

Accounting conventions are not 'set in stone'. They can be, and have been, criticised.

It is easy to assume that the accounting conventions with which we are familiar from use in this Study Text, are the best ones we could use. However, this is not necessarily the case. This is potentially a vast topic, so we will look at only to two or three examples.

3.1 Criticisms of the prudence concept

'Prudence' and 'accountant' would appear to go together. Surely this bedrock of accounting is unassailable?

Question — Prudence

Before we go any further, can you remember exactly what prudence is?

Answer

The prudence concept lays down that revenue and profits are not anticipated but should only be recorded when earning is reasonably certain. Expenses and liabilities should, however, be recorded when anticipated, as best estimates if no actual figures are available.

Loss in value of assets, whether realised or not, should be recorded when it arises, but a gain in value of an asset should not be recorded except via an unrealised reserve and only then if properly warranted.

An example of the application of the prudence concept is the requirement to value inventory at the lower of cost and net realisable value.

This is all very well, but it can lead to problems, of which the following can be identified as the most significant.

(a) **Prudence** most obviously conflicts with the **accrual** assumption because it requires that the matching of costs and revenues should not take place if there is any doubt about the future recoverability of deferred costs. This conflict has been summarised as 'should we report the worst possible situation (prudence) or the most likely position?

(b) **Prudence** also conflicts with the **going concern** assumption because it may not be prudent to assume that a business is a going concern (although it is realistic).

(c) **Prudence makes it difficult to treat items consistently** because circumstances in one period may require a different treatment from previous periods in order to be prudent.

(d) **Prudence** also undermines several other assumptions. For instance, **objectivity** is regarded as important by most users of accounts but prudence (or conservatism as it is sometimes called) implies a subjectivity in coming to accounting judgements. It is also difficult to reconcile prudence with the use of anything other than the **historical cost convention** for valuing assets (see below).

In the UK, FRS 18 on accounting policies has now downgraded prudence from a **fundamental to a desirable** concept. Accountants are now required to adopt a 'neutral' approach.

442

3.2 Criticisms of the accruals assumption

Try this question before you go any further.

Question
Accruals

Can you remember what the accruals assumption is?.

Answer

Under the accruals assumption, revenue and expenditure are matched and recorded in the accounts when earned or incurred, rather than being dependent on the associated cash movement.

This applies most obviously for credit sales, but also results in the identification of inventory at the end of each accounting period rather than writing all purchases off to the trading account. Only purchases which result in a sale recorded in the period or are used for promotional or similar purposes should be matched with sales for the period. Therefore, if purchased goods still on hand at the period end are of saleable quality and the company will still be trading in the next period (ie the prudence and going concern concepts are satisfied) then any unsold goods can be treated as current assets and their value can be deducted from purchases and opening inventory.

What could possibly be wrong with that? The main criticism relates to the conflict with historical cost accounting.

It can be argued that the accrual assumption is not applied in historical cost accounting. The assumption states that revenue earned must be matched against expenditure incurred in earning it. The cost of goods sold in the income statement is normally computed on the basis of their historical cost. However, a continuing business will want to replace inventories sold and will have to do so at ever higher prices. This means that some of the 'profit' shown by the accounts is not profit at all, but must be spent in restoring the assets of the business to their previous level.

It may be argued that the accrual assumption could be better applied under a system of current cost accounting (see below). This, broadly speaking, values assets at replacement cost. Thus the historical cost profit would be adjusted by the 'cost of sales adjustment' which aims to charge the income statement with the current cost of each item of inventory sold at the date of sale.

Other criticisms of the accrual assumption include the following.

(a) The nature of the matching process is often **arbitrary**, for example in selecting a depreciation method.

(b) The accrual assumption **conflicts with the prudence concept** as indicated above.

(c) The accrual assumption is about getting the income statement figure right. This is an admirable aim in itself, but it may mean that the **balance sheet contains rather arbitrary figures**. For example, when an asset is depreciated, the balance sheet figure is simply the unexpired cost to be allocated to future accounting periods. In other words, it is what is left over after matching has taken place, not in itself a meaningful figure.

3.3 The case for conventional accounting

In view of all the criticisms that have been made of accounting conventions, should we go 'back to the drawing board'? In spite of all these criticisms, there is a great deal to be said for the conventional approach.

(a) **Objectivity**. There is less scope for manipulation of the figures

(b) **Uniformity**. There is less scope for disagreement than with other, more radical approaches

(c) **Familiarity**. The importance of familiarity should not be underestimated. Preparers of accounts are more likely to get them right if they are used to them, and the accounts will mean more to users.

3.4 Criticisms of historical cost accounting

> **FAST FORWARD**
>
> **Historical cost accounts** have a number of deficiencies in times of rising prices. Attempts to deal with the problem have centred mainly on systems based on **current purchasing power** (CPP) or **current cost accounting (CCA)**.

Traditionally, there have been two main reasons for the preparation of accounts.

(a) To fulfil the needs of the owners of a business.

(b) To assist the managers of a business in controlling that business and in making decisions about its future.

Although the information needs of internal and external users differ considerably, it is increasingly clear that accounts prepared on a traditional historical cost basis can present financial information in a misleading manner. The greatest criticisms of traditional accounting concepts are due to their inability to reflect the effects of changing price levels.

Inflation levels vary greatly from country to country over time. When inflation has been high, interest in inflation accounting has risen, only to dwindle as inflation falls. Progress in this area has therefore been slow.

Before mentioning the various alternatives, we should first consider the criticisms of historical cost accounting in more detail.

3.5 Non-current asset values are unrealistic

The most striking example is property. Although some companies have periodically updated the balance sheet values, in general there has been a lack of consistency in the approach adopted and a lack of clarity in the way in which the effects of these changes in value have been expressed.

If non-current assets are retained in the books at their historical cost, **unrealised holding gains are not recognised**. This means that the total holding gain, if any, will be brought into account during the year in which the asset is realised, rather than spread over the period during which it was owned.

There are, in essence, two contradictory points to be considered.

(a) Although it has long been accepted that a balance sheet prepared under the historical cost concept is an historical record and not a statement of current worth, many people now argue that the balance sheet should at least give an indication of the current value of the company's tangible net assets.

(b) The prudence concept requires that profits should only be recognised when realised in the form either of cash or of other assets, the ultimate cash realisation of which can be assessed with reasonable certainty. It may be argued that recognising unrealised holding gains on non-current assets is contrary to this concept.

On balance, the weight of opinion is now in favour of restating asset values. It is felt that the criticism based on prudence can be met by ensuring that valuations are made as objectively as possible (eg in the case of property, by having independent expert valuations) and by not taking unrealised gains through the income statement, but instead through reserves.

3.6 Depreciation is inadequate to finance the replacement of non-current assets

Depreciation is not provided for in order to enforce retention of profits and thus ensure that funds are available for asset replacement. It is intended as a measure of the contribution of non-current assets to the company's activities in the period. However, an incidental effect of providing for depreciation is that not all liquid funds can be paid out to investors and so funds for asset replacement are on hand. What is important is not the replacement of one asset by an identical new one (something that rarely happens) but the replacement of the *operating capability* represented by the old asset.

Another criticism of historical cost depreciation is that it does not fully reflect the value of the asset consumed during the accounting year.

3.7 Holding gains on inventories are included in profit

During a period of high inflation the monetary value of inventory held may increase significantly while they are being processed. The conventions of historical cost accounting lead to the unrealised part of this holding gain (known as *inventory appreciation*) being included in profit for the year.

3.8 Example: Holding gain

This problem can be illustrated using a simple example. At the beginning of the year a company has 100 units of inventory and no other assets. Its trading account for the year is shown below.

TRADING ACCOUNT

	Units	$		Units	$
Opening inventory	100	200	Sales (made 31 December)	100	500
Purchases (made 31 December)	100	400			
	200	600			
Closing inventory (FIFO basis)	100	400			
	100	200			
Gross profit	–	300			
	100	500		100	500

Apparently the company has made a gross profit of $300. But, at the beginning of the year the company owned 100 units of inventory and at the end of the year it owned 100 units of inventory and $100 (sales $500 less purchases $400). From this it would seem that a profit of $100 is more reasonable. The remaining $200 is inventory appreciation arising as the purchase price increased from $2 to $4.

The criticism can be overcome by using a **capital maintenance concept** based on physical units rather than money values.

3.9 Profits (or losses) on holdings of net monetary items are not shown

In periods of inflation the purchasing power, and thus the value, of money falls. It follows that an investment in money will have a lower real value at the end of a period of time than it did at the beginning. A loss has been incurred. Similarly, the real value of a monetary liability will reduce over a period of time and a gain will be made.

3.10 The true effect of inflation on capital maintenance is not shown

To a large extent this follows from the points already mentioned. It is a widely held principle that distributable profits should only be recognised after full allowance has been made for any erosion in the capital value of a business. In historical cost accounts, although capital is maintained in *nominal money terms*, it may not be in *real terms*. In other words, profits may be distributed to the detriment of the long-term viability of the business. This criticism may be made by those who advocate capital maintenance in physical terms and those who prefer money capital maintenance as measured by dollars of current purchasing power (see below).

3.11 Comparisons over time are unrealistic

This will tend to an exaggeration of growth. For example, if a company's profit in 1966 was $100,000 and in 1999 $500,000, a shareholder's initial reaction might be that the company had done rather well. If, however, it was then revealed that with $100,000 in 1966 he could buy exactly the same goods as with $500,000 in 1999, the apparent growth would seem less impressive.

3.12 Alternatives to historical cost accounting

The points given above demonstrate some of the accounting problems which arise in times of severe and prolonged inflation. Of the various possible systems of accounting for price changes, most can be divided into two categories.

(a) **General price change** bases and in particular current purchasing power (CPP)

(b) **Current value bases**: the basic principles of all these are:

    (i) to show balance sheet items at some form of current value rather than historical cost.

    (ii) to compute profits by matching the current value of costs at the date of consumption against revenue.

The current value of an item will normally be based on replacement cost, net realisable value or economic value.

3.13 Current purchasing power

The principal feature of a current purchasing power system is that profit for the year was calculated after an adjustment designed to reflect the effect of general price inflation on the purchasing power of shareholders' equity. All accounts items are restated in terms of a stable monetary unit: the $CPP.

(a) Changes in purchasing power are based on the general level of inflation using a prices index.

(b) CPP measures profits as the increase in the current purchasing power of equity; profits are stated after allowing for the declining purchasing power of money due to price inflation

This is referred to as **real financial capital maintenance.**

3.14 Current cost accounting

A system of current cost accounting (CCA) does not attempt to cater for general price inflation; instead, profit for the year is calculated after allowing for the effects of price increases **specifically** on the operating capability of the particular business.

The principal features of CCA are as follows.

(a) In the balance sheet, assets are stated at their '**value to the business**'. This may be a replacement cost, net realisable value or economic value depending on the circumstances.

(b) In the income statement **holding gains** are **excluded from profit**. A holding gain is the difference between value to the business of an asset and its original cost. If X buys an item for $100 and sells it for $150 there will be an HC profit of $150 − $100 = $50. If the replacement cost of the item at the date of sale is $130, in CC terms there will be an operating gain of $150 − $130 = $20 and a holding gain of $130 − $100 = $30. Current cost accounting recognises operating gains only as profit; historical cost accounting does not differentiate between holding and operating gains, and recognises both as profit.

This is referred to as the **operating capital maintenance concept**.

> **Exam focus point**
>
> You could be asked to discuss the advantages and disadvantages of historical cost accounting.

4 Conceptual framework and GAAP

> **FAST FORWARD**
>
> Attempts to formulate accounting standards in the **absence** of overall conceptual framework have led to:
> - the same issue being treated in more than one standard
> - standards conflicting with each other
> - too many choices of accounting treatment open to preparers of accounts

4.1 The search for a conceptual framework

> **Key term**
>
> A **conceptual framework**, in the field we are concerned with, is a statement of generally accepted theoretical principles which form the frame of reference for financial reporting. These theoretical principles provide the basis for the development of new accounting standards and the evaluation of those already in existence.

The financial reporting process is concerned with providing information that is useful in the business and economic decision-making process. Therefore a conceptual framework will form the theoretical basis for determining which events should be accounted for, how they should be measured and how they should be communicated to the user.

Although it is theoretical in nature, a conceptual framework for financial reporting has highly practical final aims.

The **danger of not having a conceptual framework** is demonstrated in the way some countries' standards have developed over recent years; standards tend to be produced in a **haphazard and fire-fighting approach**. Where an agreed framework exists, the standard-setting body act as an architect or designer, rather than a fire-fighter, building accounting rules on the foundation of sound, agreed basic principles.

The lack of a conceptual framework also means that fundamental principles are tackled more than once in different standards, thereby producing contradictions and inconsistencies in basic concepts, such as those of prudence and matching. This leads to ambiguity and it affects the true and fair concept of financial reporting.

Another problem with the lack of a conceptual framework has become apparent in the USA. The large number of highly detailed standards produced by the Financial Accounting Standards Board (FASB) has created a financial reporting environment governed by specific rules rather than general principles. This would be avoided if a cohesive set of principles were in place.

A conceptual framework can also bolster standard setters against political pressure from various 'lobby groups' and interested parties. Such pressure would only prevail if it was acceptable under the conceptual framework.

4.2 Advantages and disadvantages of a conceptual framework

The **advantages** arising from using a conceptual framework may be summarised as follows.

(a) The situation is **avoided** whereby standards are being developed on a **patchwork** basis, where a particular accounting problem is recognised as having emerged, and resources were then channelled into standardising accounting practice in that area, without regard to whether that particular issue was necessarily the most important issue remaining at that time without standardisation.

(b) As stated above, the development of certain standards (particularly national standards) have been subject to considerable political interference from interested parties. Where there is a conflict of interest between user groups on which policies to choose, policies deriving from a conceptual framework will be **less open** to criticism that the standard-setter buckled to **external pressure**.

(c) Some standards may concentrate on the income statement whereas some may concentrate on the valuation of net assets (balance sheet).

Possible disadvantages of a conceptual framework might be as follows.

(a) Financial statements are intended for a variety of users, and it is not certain that a single conceptual framework can be devised which will suit all users.

(b) Given the diversity of user requirements, there may be a need for a variety of accounting standards, each produced for a different purpose (and with different concepts as a basis).

(c) It is not clear that a conceptual framework makes the task of preparing and then implementing standards any easier than without a framework.

Before we look at the IASC's attempt to produce a conceptual framework, we need to consider another term of importance to this debate: generally accepted accounting practice; or GAAP.

4.3 Generally Accepted Accounting Practice (GAAP)

This term has sprung up in recent years and its signifies all the rules, from whatever source, which govern accounting. In individual countries this is seen primarily as a combination of:

- National corporate law
- National accounting standards
- Local stock exchange requirements

Although those sources are the basis for the GAAP of individual countries, the concept also includes the effects of non-mandatory sources such as:

- International accounting standards
- Statutory requirements in other countries

In many countries, like the UK, GAAP does not have any statutory or regulatory authority or definition, unlike other countries, such as the USA. The term is mentioned rarely in legislation, and only then in fairly limited terms.

There are different views of GAAP in different countries. The UK position can be explained in the following extracts from *UK GAAP* (Davies, Paterson & Wilson, Ernst & Young).

'Our view is that GAAP is a dynamic concept which requires constant review, adaptation and reaction to changing circumstances. We believe that use of the term "principle" gives GAAP an unjustified and inappropriate degree of permanence. GAAP changes in response to changing business and economic needs and developments. As circumstances alter, accounting practices are modified or developed accordingly..... We believe that GAAP goes far beyond mere rules and principles, and encompasses contemporary permissible accounting practice.'

'It is often argued that the term "generally accepted" implies that there must exist a high degree of practical application of a particular accounting practice. However, this interpretation raises certain practical difficulties. For example, what about new areas of accounting which have not, as yet, been generally applied? What about different accounting treatments for similar items – are they all generally accepted?

'It is our view that "generally accepted" does not mean "generally adopted or used". We believe that, in the UK context, GAAP refers to accounting practices which are regarded as permissible by the accounting profession. The extent to which a particular practice has been adopted is, in our opinion, not the overriding consideration. Any accounting practice which is legitimate in the circumstances under which it has been applied should be regarded as GAAP. The decision as to whether or not a particular practice is permissible or legitimate would depend on one or more of the following factors:

- Is the practice addressed either in the accounting standards, statute or other official pronouncements?
- If the practice is not addressed in UK accounting standards, is it dealt with in International Accounting Standards, or the standards of other countries such as the US?
- Is the practice consistent with the needs of users and the objectives of financial reporting?
- Does the practice have authoritative support in the accounting literature?
- Is the practice being applied by other companies in similar situations?
- Is the practice consistent with the fundamental concept of "true and fair"?'

This view is not held in all countries, however. In the USA particularly, the equivalent of a 'true and fair view' is 'fair presentation in accordance with GAAP'. Generally accepted accounting principles are defined as those principles which have 'substantial authoritative support'. Therefore accounts prepared in accordance with accounting principles for which there is not substantial authoritative support are presumed to be misleading or inaccurate.

The effect here is that 'new' or 'different' accounting principles are not acceptable unless they have been adopted by the mainstream accounting profession, usually the standard-setting bodies and/or professional accountancy bodies. This is much more rigid than the UK view expressed above.

4.3.1 GAAP and a conceptual framework

A conceptual framework for financial reporting can be defined as an attempt to codify existing GAAP in order to reappraise current accounting standards and to produce new standards.

5 The IASB's framework

FAST FORWARD

The **IASB's Framework** provides the basis of its **conceptual framework**. IASes and IFRSes are based on this framework. The key elements are:

- Financial statements should provide **useful information** to users.
- **Financial position** is shown in the balance sheet.
- **Financial performance** is shown in the income statement.
- **Changes in financial position** are shown in the cash flow statement.
- The main **underlying assumptions** are **accruals** and **going concern.**
- Financial statements should be:
  – Understandable
  – Relevant
  – Reliable
  – Comparable

In July 1989 the IASC produced a document, *Framework for the preparation and presentation of financial statements* (*'Framework'*) which was adopted by the IASB. The *Framework* is, in effect, the **conceptual** framework upon which all IASs and IFRSs are based and hence which determines how financial statements are prepared and the information they contain.

The *Framework* consists of several sections or chapters, following on after a preface and introduction. These chapters are as follows.

- The objective of financial statements.
- Underlying assumptions
- Qualitative characteristics of financial statements
- The elements of financial statements
- Recognition of the elements of financial statements
- Measurement of the elements of financial statements
- Concepts of capital and capital maintenance

We will look briefly at the preface and introduction to the *Framework* as these will place the document in context with the rest of what you have studied for this paper we will then look only at the first three of the chapters listed above, because the Teaching Guide for Paper 1 states specifically that a detailed knowledge of the remainder of the *Framework* is not examinable. A brief summary of the remaining chapters is given at the end of this section.

5.1 Preface

The preface to the *Framework* points out the fundamental reason why financial statements are produced worldwide, ie to **satisfy the requirements of external users**, but that practice varies due to the individual pressures in each country. These pressures may be social, political, economic or legal, but they result in variations in practice from country to country, including the form of statements, the definition of their component parts (assets, liabilities etc), the criteria for recognition of items and both the scope and disclosure of financial statements.

It is these differences which the IASB wishes to narrow by **harmonising** all aspects of financial statements, including the regulations governing their accounting standards and their preparation and presentation.

The preface emphasises the way **financial statements are used to make economic decisions** and thus financial statements should be prepared to this end. The types of economic decisions for which financial statements are likely to be used include the following.

- Decisions to buy, hold or sell equity investments
- Assessment of management stewardship and accountability
- Assessment of the enterprise's ability to pay employees
- Assessment of the security of amounts lent to the enterprise
- Determination of taxation policies
- Determination of distributable profits and dividends
- Inclusion in national income statistics
- Regulations of the activities of enterprises

Any additional requirements imposed by **national governments** for their own purposes should not affect financial statements produced for the benefit of other users.

The *Framework* recognises that financial statements can be prepared using a **variety of models**. Although the most common is based on historical cost and a nominal unit of currency (ie pound sterling, US dollar etc), the *Framework* can be applied to financial statements prepared under a range of models.

5.2 Introduction

The introduction to the *Framework* lays out the purpose, status and scope of the document. It then looks at different users of financial statements and their information needs.

5.2.1 Purpose and status

The introduction gives a list of the purposes of the *Framework*.

(a) Assist the Board of the IASB in the **development of future** IFRSs and in its review of existing IASs.

(b) Assist the Board of the IASB in **promoting harmonisation** of regulations, accounting standards and procedures relating to the presentation of financial statements by providing a basis for reducing the number of alternative accounting treatments permitted by IASs.

(c) Assist **national standard-setting bodies** in developing national standards.

(d) Assist **preparers of financial statements** in applying IFRSs and in dealing with topics that have yet to form the subject of an IFRS.

(e) Assist **auditors** in forming an opinion as to whether financial statements conform with IASs.

(f) Assist **users of financial statements** in interpreting the information contained in financial statements prepared in conformity with IFRSs.

(g) Provide those who are interested in the work of IASB with **information** about its approach to the **formulation of IFRSs**.

Exam focus point

> The purpose of the IASB *Framework* is highly likely to be tested. It is most likely to be in an MCQ, although do not rule out a written question.

The *Framework* is not an IFRS and so does not overrule any individual IFRS. In the (rare) cases of conflict between an IAS or IFRS and the *Framework*, the IAS or IFRS will prevail. These cases will diminish over time as the *Framework* will be used as a guide in the production of future IASs. The *Framework* itself will be revised occasionally depending on the experience of the IASB in using it.

5.2.2 Scope

The *Framework* deals with:

(a) The **objective** of financial statements

(b) The **qualitative characteristics** that determine the usefulness of information in financial statements

(c) The **definition, recognition and measurement** of the elements from which financial statements are constructed

(d) Concepts of **capital and capital maintenance**

We are only concerned with (a) and (b) here.

The *Framework* is concerned with **'general purpose' financial statements** (ie a normal set of annual statements), but it can be applied to other types of accounts. A complete set of financial statements includes:

(a) A balance sheet
(b) An income statement
(c) A statement of changes in financial position (eg a cash flow statement)
(d) Notes, other statements and explanatory material

Supplementary information may be included, but some items are not included, namely commentaries and reports by the directors, the chairman, management etc.

All types of financial reporting entities are included (commercial, industrial, business; public or private sector).

Key term

> A **reporting entity** is an enterprise for which there are users who rely on the financial statements as their major source of financial information about the entity. *(Framework)*

5.2.3 Users and their information needs

We have already looked at the users of accounting information in Chapter 1. They consist of investors, employees, lenders, suppliers and other trade creditors, customers, government and their agencies and the public. You should be able to remember enough to do the following exercise.

Question — Users' needs

Consider the information needs of the users of financial information listed above.

Answer

(a) **Investors** are the providers of risk capital

   (i) Information is required to help make a decision about buying or selling shares, taking up a rights issue and voting.

   (ii) Investors must have information about the level of dividend, past, present and future and any changes in share price.

   (iii) Investors will also need to know whether the management has been running the company efficiently.

   (iv) As well as the position indicated by the income statements, balance sheet and earnings per share (EPS), investors will want to know about the liquidity position of the company, the company's future prospects, and how the company's shares compare with those of its competitors.

(b) **Employees** need information about the security of employment and future prospects for jobs in the company, and to help with collective pay bargaining.

(c) **Lenders** need information to help them decide whether to lend to a company. They will also need to check that the value of any security remains adequate, that the interest repayments are secure, that the cash is available for redemption at the appropriate time and that any financial restrictions (such as maximum debt/equity ratios) have not been breached.

(d) **Suppliers** need to know whether the company will be a good customer and pay its debts.

(e) **Customers** need to know whether the company will be able to continue producing and supplying goods.

(f) **Government's** interest in a company may be one of creditor or customer, as well as being specifically concerned with compliance with tax and company law, ability to pay tax and the general contribution of the company to the economy.

(g) The **public** at large would wish to have information for all the reasons mentioned above, but it could be suggested that it would be impossible to provide general purpose accounting information which was specifically designed for the needs of the public.

Financial statements cannot meet all these users' needs, but financial statements which meet the **needs of investors** (providers of risk capital) will meet most of the needs of other users.

The *Framework* emphasises that the preparation and presentation of financial statements is primarily the **responsibility of an enterprise's management**. Management also has an interest in the information appearing in financial statements.

5.3 The objective of financial statements

The *Framework* states that:

> 'The objective of financial statements is to provide information about the financial position performance and changes in financial position of an enterprise that is useful to a wide range of users in making economic decisions.'

Such financial statements will meet the needs of most users. The information is, however, restricted.

(a) It is **based on past events** not expected future events.
(b) It does not necessarily contain **non-financial information**.

The statements also show the results of the **management's stewardship**.

5.3.1 Financial position, performance and changes in financial position

It is important for users to assess the **ability of an enterprise to produce cash and cash equivalents** to pay employees, lenders etc.

Financial position (balance sheet) information is affected by the following and information about each one can aid the user.

(a) **Economic resources controlled:** to predict the ability to generate cash

(b) **Financial structure:** to predict borrowing needs, the distribution of future profits/cash and likely success in raising new finance

(c) **Liquidity and solvency:** to predict whether financial commitments will be met as they fall due (liquidity relates to short-term commitments, solvency is longer-term)

In all these areas, the capacity to adapt to changes in the environment in which the enterprise operates is very important.

Financial performance (income statement) information, particularly profitability, is used to assess potential changes in the economic resources the enterprise is likely to control in future. Information about performance variability is therefore important.

Changes in financial position (ie cash flow statement) information is used to assess the enterprise's investing, financing and operating activities. They show the enterprise's ability to produce cash and the needs which utilise those cash flows.

All parts of the financial statements are **interrelated**, reflecting different aspects of the same transactions or events. Each statement provides different information; none can provide all the information required by users.

5.4 Underlying assumptions

We have already met the two assumptions discussed here and you should refer to their definitions in Chapter 10 under IAS 1 (revised).

(a) Accruals basis

Financial statements prepared under the accruals basis show users past transactions involving cash and also obligations to pay cash in the future and resources which represent cash to be received in the future.

(b) Going concern

It is assumed that the enterprise has no intention to liquidate or curtail major operations. If it did, then the financial statements would be prepared on a different (disclosed) basis.

5.5 Qualitative characteristics of financial statements

The *Framework* states that qualitative characteristics are the attributes that make the information provided in financial statements useful to users. The four principal qualitative characteristics are **understandability, relevance, reliability and comparability**.

5.6 Understandability

Users must be able to understand financial statements. They are assumed to have some business, economic and accounting knowledge and to be able to apply themselves to study the information property. **Complex matters should not be left out** of financial statements simply due to its difficulty if it is relevant information.

5.7 Relevance

Only relevant information can be useful. Information is relevant when it helps users evaluate past, present or future events, or it confirms or corrects previous evaluations. The predictive and confirmatory roles of information are interrelated.

Information on financial position and performance is often used to predict future position and performance and other things of interest to the user, eg likely dividend, wage rises. The **manner of showing information** will enhance the ability to make predictions, eg by highlighting unusual items.

The relevance of information is affected by its nature and **materiality**. Information may be judged relevant simply because of its nature (eg remuneration of management). In other cases, both the nature and materiality of the information are important. Materiality is not a primary qualitative characteristic itself (like reliability or relevance), because it is merely a threshold or cut-off point.

5.8 Reliability

Information must also be **reliable** to be useful, ie **free from material error and bias**. The user must be able to depend on it being a faithful representation.

Point to note

> Even if information is relevant, if it is very unreliable it may be misleading to recognise it, eg a disputed claim for damages in a legal action.

5.8.1 Faithful representation

Information must **represent faithfully** the transactions it purports to represent in order to be reliable. There is a risk that this may not be the case, not due to bias, but due to **inherent difficulties in identifying the transactions** or finding an **appropriate method** of measurement or presentation.

Where measurement of the financial effects of an item is so uncertain, enterprises should not recognise such an item, eg internally generated goodwill.

5.8.2 Substance over form

This concept was discussed in Chapter 15. Faithful representation of a transaction is only possible if it is accounted for according to its **substance and economic reality**, not with its legal form.

5.8.3 Neutrality

Information **must be free from bias to be reliable**. Neutrality is lost if the financial statements are prepared so as to influence the user to make a judgement or decision in order to achieve a predetermined outcome.

5.8.4 Prudence

Again, we have already discussed this concept in Chapter 10. Uncertainties exist in the preparation of financial information, eg the collectability of doubtful receivables. These uncertainties are recognised through disclosure and through the application of prudence.

Point to note

> Prudence does not, however, allow the creation of hidden reserves or excessive provisions, understatement of assets or income or overstatement of liabilities or expenses.

5.8.5 Completeness

Financial information must be complete, within the restrictions of materiality and cost, to be reliable. Omission may cause information to be misleading.

5.9 Comparability

Users must be able to compare an enterprise's financial statements:

(a) **through time** to identify trends; and
(b) **with other enterprise's statements**, to evaluate their relative financial position, performance and changes in financial position.

The consistency of treatment is therefore important across like items over time, within the enterprise and across all enterprises.

The **disclosure of accounting policies** is particularly important here. Users must distinguish between different accounting policies to be able to make a valid comparison of similar items in the accounts of different entities.

Comparability is **not the same as uniformity**. Enterprises should change accounting policies if they become inappropriate.

Corresponding information for **preceding** periods should be shown to enable comparison over time.

5.10 Constraints on relevant and reliable information

5.10.1 Timeliness

Information may become irrelevant if there is a delay in reporting it. **There is a balance between timeliness and the provision of reliable information.** Information may be reported on a timely basis when not all aspects of the transaction are known, thus compromising reliability.

Point to note

> If every detail of a transaction is known, it may be too late to publish the information because it has become irrelevant. The overriding consideration is how best to satisfy the economic decision-making needs of the users.

5.10.2 Balance between benefits and cost

This is a pervasive constraint, not a qualitative characteristic. When information is provided, its benefits must exceed the costs of obtaining and presenting it. This is a **subjective** area and there are other difficulties: others than the intended users may gain a benefit; also the cost may be paid by someone other than the users. It is therefore difficult to apply a cost-benefit analysis, but preparers and users should be aware of the constraint.

5.10.3 Balance between qualitative characteristics

A **trade off between qualitative characteristics** of often necessary, the aim being to achieve an appropriate balance to meet the objective of financial statements. It is a matter for professional judgement as to the relative importance of these characteristics in each case.

We have now covered those parts of the IASC's *Framework* which you need to understand in detail. A summary of the rest of the document is given below.

5.11 The elements of financial statements

This section defines the important items which make up the financial statements and looks at their sub-classification.

(a) **Financial position**

    (i) Assets
    (ii) Liabilities
    (iii) Equity

(b) **Performance**

    (i) Income
    (ii) Expenses
    (iii) Capital maintenance adjustments

5.12 Recognition of the elements of financial statements

Having defined the elements, the *Framework* then lays out the criteria for when items should be recognised (ie included in the financial statements). The section looks at the recognition of assets, liabilities, income and expenditure in turn, based on the concept of outflows and inflows of future economic benefit.

5.13 Measurement of the element of financial statements

This brief section simply mentions some of the different measurement bases available, including historical cost and current cost.

5.14 Concepts of capital and capital maintenance

The different concepts are examined briefly, the main two concepts are:

(a) **financial capital maintenance**; and
(b) **physical (or operating) capital maintenance**,

which we discussed briefly in Section 4.

Chapter Roundup

- The main objectives of the IASB are to raise the standard of financial reporting and to eventually bring about global harmonisation of accounting standards.

- **Accounting conventions are not 'set in stone'**. They can be, and have been, criticised.

- **Historical cost accounts** have a **number of deficiencies** in times of rising prices. Attempts to deal with the problem have centred mainly on systems based on current purchasing power (CPP) or current cost (CCA).

- Attempts to formulate accounting standards in the **absence** of an overall conceptual framework have led to:
  - the same issue being treated in more than one standard
  - standards conflicting with each other
  - too many choices of accounting treatment open to preparers of accounts

- The **IASB's Framework** provides the backbone of the IASB's *conceptual framework*. IASs and IFRSs are based on this Framework.

- **Key elements** in the *Framework* are as follows.
  - Financial statements should provide **information that is useful** to a wide range of users in making **economic decisions**.
  - **Financial position** is shown in the balance sheet.
  - **Financial performance** is shown in the income statement.
  - **Changes in financial position** are shown in the cash flow statement.
  - The main underlying assumptions of financial statements are **accruals** and **going concern**.
  - Financial statements should be:
    - Understandable
    - Relevant
    - Reliable
    - Comparable

- You need to be able to express your own ideas on the **usefulness** of financial accounting and to support these ideas with reasoned arguments.

PART G MISCELLANEOUS TOPICS

Quick Quiz

1. What are the objectives of the IASB?
2. What development at the IASB will aid users' interpretation of IFRSs?
3. Which of the following arguments is not in favour of accounting standards, but is in favour of accounting choice?

    A They reduce variations in methods used to produce accounts
    B They oblige companies to disclose their accounting policies
    C They are a less rigid alternative to legislation
    D They may tend towards rigidity in applying the rules

4. What are the criticisms of the prudence concept?
5. What criticisms can be made of traditional historical cost accounting?
6. Why is a conceptual framework necessary?
7. What are the disadvantages of a conceptual framework?
8. Which of the following sections are not included in the IASB's *Framework*?

    A Users of financial statements
    B Underlying assumptions
    C Qualitative characteristics
    D Concept of capital maintenance

9. What does 'reliability' mean in the context of financial statements?
10. What happened in 2005 for listed companies in the EU?

Answers to Quick Quiz

1. See paragraph 1.1.

2. The formation of the International Financial Reporting Interpretations Committee (IFRIC).

3. D   The other arguments are all in favour of accounting standards.

4.
   - Conflicts with the accrual assumption
   - Conflicts with going concern assumption
   - Difficulty in applying consistency
   - Undermines other assumptions eg objectivity

5.
   - Non-current asset values are unrealistic
   - Depreciation is inadequate to finance the replacement of non-current assets
   - Holding gains on inventories are included in profit
   - Profits (or losses) on holdings of net monetary items are not shown
   - Time effect of inflation on capital maintenance is not shown
   - Comparisons over time are unrealistic

6. It forms the theoretical basis for determining what is included in accounts, how they are measured and how they are communicated.

7. See Paragraph 4.2.

8. A

9. Free from material error and bias.

10. The transition to reporting under IFRSs.

Now try the questions below from the Exam Question Bank

Number	Level	Marks	Time
Q33	Examination	10	18 mins

PART G MISCELLANEOUS TOPICS

Exam question bank

EXAM QUESTION BANK

**Examination standard questions are indicated by marks and time allocations.
Introductory questions are indicated by time allocations only**

Exam focus point

> The introductory questions are a lot longer than the 10 mark questions you will find in the exam. However, the idea behind these questions is to **fully practice** all the techniques learnt in each Chapter. It is well worth doing these longer questions, as you will gain confidence in the techniques involved. This, in turn, will help you to take the exam standard questions in your stride.

1 Users of accounting information   18 mins

There are many different user groups of accounting information. Identify those who might be interested in financial information about a large listed company and describe their information needs.

(10 marks)

2 The accounting equation   18 mins

Peter Reid decides he is going to open a bookshop called Easyread, which he does by investing $5,000 on 1 January 20X7. During the first month of Easyread's existence, the following transactions occur.

(a)   Bookshelves are purchased for $1,800.
(b)   Books are purchased for $2,000.
(c)   Half of the books are sold for $1,500 cash.
(d)   Peter draws $200 out of the business for himself.
(e)   Peter's brother John loans $500 to the business.
(f)   Carpets are purchased for $1,000 on credit (to be paid in two months time).
(g)   A bulk order of books worth $400 is sold on credit (to be paid in one month's time) for $600.

Required

Write down the accounting equation after each transaction has occurred.

(10 marks)

3 Financial statements   18 mins

What is the difference between the balance sheet and the income statement? What is the difference between capital and revenue expenditure? Which of the following transactions is capital expenditure and which revenue expenditure?

(a)   A bookseller buys a car for its director for $9,000.
(b)   In the first year, the car is depreciated by $900.
(c)   The business buys books for $1,500.
(d)   The business builds an extension for $7,600.
(e)   The original building is repainted, a job costing $1,200.
(f)   A new sales assistant is taken on and his salary in the first year is $10,000.

(10 marks)

4 Business transactions

18 mins

The following is a list of typical business transactions.

(a) The purchase of goods on credit
(b) Allowance to credit customers upon the return of faulty goods
(c) Refund from petty cash to an employee of an amount spend on entertaining a client
(d) Credit card sales

Required

For each transaction clearly identify the following.

(i) The original document(s) for the data.
(ii) The book of original entry for the transaction.

(10 marks)

5 Weaknesses

27 mins

The managing director of H, a limited liability company, read a newspaper report of a fraud with had recently come to the attention of the police. The perpetrators had sent invoices to several thousand companies. These requested payment for an entry in a trade directory.

The directory did not, however, exist. The newspaper report claimed that approximately 700 companies had paid $2,000 each for an entry in this alleged directory. H's managing director asked whether the company had received one of these invoices. It was discovered that H was one of the companies which had paid the $2,000 charge. The reason for this payment was investigated.

H's accounting system was recently computerised. All invoices are keyed straight into a standard accounting package. The company's accounting department is short staffed and so the default settings on the package have been set to minimise the amount of clerical effort required to process transactions. If, for example, an invoice is received from a new supplier, the program will automatically allocate an account number and open an account in the purchase ledger. At the end of every month, the program calculates the amount which is due to each trade payable; a cheque for each trade payable is automatically printed out for the total of all of the invoices from that trade payable input during the month. When the system was first installed, the accountant used to review accounts payable prior to the cheque run as a check that the system was not being abused. This review was, however, discontinued because of pressure of work and because there were too many invoices to review properly.

The managing director was most disturbed by this description of the purchases system and decided that it was in urgent need of improvement. The company's accountant was ordered to redesign the system. The accountant was authorised to employ additional staff if the extra expense could be justified.

Required

(a) Describe three weaknesses in H's existing purchases system. (6 marks)
(b) How should the purchases and payables system be reorganised? (9 marks)

(15 marks)

6 Beechfield 1   18 mins

Beechfield Co make use of a petty cash book as part of their book-keeping system. The following is a summary of the petty cash transactions for the month of November 20X9.

			$
November	1	Opening petty cash book float received from cashier	350
	2	Cleaning materials	5
	3	Postage stamps	10
	6	Envelopes	12
	8	Taxi fare	32
	10	Petrol for company car	17
	14	Typing paper	25
	15	Cleaning materials	4
	16	Bus fare	2
	20	Visitors' lunches	56
	21	Mops and brushes for cleaning	41
	23	Postage stamps	35
	27	Envelopes	12
	29	Visitors' lunches	30
	30	Photocopying paper	40

Required

Draw up the petty cash book for the month using analysis columns for stationery, cleaning, entertainment, travelling and postage. Show clearly the receipt of the amount necessary to restore the float and the balance brought forward for the start of the following month.

(10 marks)

7 Beechfield 2   18 mins

Using the information in Beechfield 1 above, show how the stationery and postage accounts would appear in the nominal or general ledger. The balance brought on each account being $570 and $630 respectively.

(10 marks)

8 J Ockey   27 mins

Mr J Ockey commenced trading as a wholesale stationer on 1 May 20X4 with a capital of $5,000 with which he opened a bank account for his business.

During May the following transactions took place.

May	1	Bought shop fittings and fixtures for cash from Store Fitments Co for $2,000
	2	Purchased goods on credit from Abel $650
	4	Sold goods on credit to Bruce $700
	9	Purchased goods on credit from Green $300
	11	Sold goods on credit to Hill $580
	13	Cash sales paid intact into bank $200
	16	Received cheque from Bruce in settlement of his account
	17	Purchased goods on credit from Kaye $800
	18	Sold goods on credit to Nailor $360
	19	Sent cheque to Abel in settlement of his account
	20	Paid rent by cheque $200
	21	Paid delivery expenses by cheque $50
	24	Received from Hill $200 on account
	30	Drew cheques for personal expenses $200 and assistant's wages $320
	31	Settled the account of Green.

Required

(a) Record the foregoing in appropriate books of original entry.
(b) Post the entries to the ledger accounts.
(c) Balance the ledger accounts where necessary.
(d) Extract a trial balance at 31 May 20X4.

Note. You are not required to complete any entries in personal accounts.

9 Frontloader   18 mins

Frontloader is a business which acts as a distributor of washing machines entirely on credit terms to a wide range of customers. The following balances were extracted from its ledgers at 30 June 20X5.

	$	$
Sales		723,869
Trade accounts payable: balance at 30 June 20X4		49,781
Trade accounts receivable: balance at 30 June 20X4	84,611	
Purchases of washing machines	342,916	
Discounts allowed	8,214	
Discounts received		6,978
Cash from trade accounts receivable	699,267	
Cash to trade accounts payable		321,853
Returns inwards	36,925	
Overdraft interest	12,748	

A cheque for $1,246 from A Brown, a customer, has been returned by the bank as dishonoured.

You are required to prepare the receivables control account for the year ended 30 June 20X5.

(10 marks)

10 Frank Mercer 1   18 mins

On 10 January 20X9, Frank Mercer received his monthly bank statement for December 20X8. The statement showed the following.

	MIDWEST BANK			
	F Mercer: Statement of Account			
Date	Particulars	Debits	Credits	Balance
20X8		$	$	$
Dec 1	Balance			1,862
Dec 5	417864	243		1,619
Dec 5	Dividend		26	1,645
Dec 5	Bank Giro Credit		212	1,857
Dec 8	417866	174		1,683
Dec 10	417867	17		1,666
Dec 11	Sundry Credit		185	1,851
Dec 14	Standing Order	32		1,819
Dec 20	417865	307		1,512
Dec 20	Bank Giro Credit		118	1,630
Dec 21	417868	95		1,535
Dec 21	416870	161		1,374
Dec 24	Bank charges	18		1,356
Dec 27	Bank Giro Credit		47	1,403
Dec 28	Direct Debit	88		1,315
Dec 29	417873	12		1,303
Dec 29	Bank Giro Credit		279	1,582
Dec 31	417871	25		1,557

His cash book for the corresponding period was as follows.

CASH BOOK

20X8		$	20X8		Cheque no	$
Dec 1	Balance b/d	1,862	Dec 1	Electricity	864	243
Dec 4	J Shannon	212	Dec 2	P Simpson	865	307
Dec 9	M Lipton	185	Dec 5	D Underhill	866	174
Dec 19	G Hurst	118	Dec 6	A Young	867	17
Dec 26	M Evans	47	Dec 10	T Unwin	868	95
Dec 27	J Smith	279	Dec 14	B Oliver	869	71
Dec 29	V Owen	98	Dec 16	Rent	870	161
Dec 30	K Walters	134	Dec 20	M Peters	871	25
			Dec 21	L Philips	872	37
			Dec 22	W Hamilton	873	12
			Dec 31	Balance c/d		1,793
		2,935				2,935

Required

Bring the cash book balance of $1,793 up to date as at 31 December 20X8.

(10 marks)

11 Frank Mercer 2   18 mins

Using the information in Frank Mercer 1 above, draw up a bank reconciliation statement as at 31 December 20X8.

(10 marks)

12 Chi Knitwear   36 mins

Chi Knitwear is an old fashioned firm with a hand-written set of books. A trial balance is extracted at the end of each month, and an income statement and balance sheet are prepared. Control accounts are not maintained. This month however the trial balance will not balance, the credits exceeding debits by $1,536.

You are asked to help and after inspection of the ledgers discover the following errors.

(i) A balance of $87 on a receivables ledger account has been omitted from the schedule of receivables, the total of which was entered as receivables in the trial balance.

(ii) A small piece of machinery purchased for $1,200 had been written off to repairs.

(iii) The receipts side of the cash book had been undercast by $720.

(iv) The total of one page of the sales day book had been carried forward as $8,154, whereas the correct amount was $8,514.

(v) A credit note for $179 received from a supplier had been posted to the wrong side of his account.

(vi) An electricity bill in the sum of $152, not yet accrued for, is discovered in a filing tray.

(vii) Mr Smith paid $731 to clear his account. His personal account has been credited but the cheque has not yet been entered in the cash book.

Required

(a) Write up the suspense account to clear the difference on the trial balance.
(b) State the effect on the accounts of correcting each error.

13 Definitions   18 mins

The observance of the following assumptions is presumed in financial statements unless otherwise stated.

(a) Going concern   (3 marks)
(b) Accruals   (3 marks)
(c) Consistency   (4 marks)

Required

Explain each of the above assumptions giving examples of how each is observed in conventional financial statements.

(10 marks)

14 Rent, local taxes and insurance 27 mins

From the information given below you are required:

(a) To calculate the charge to the income statement for the year ended 30 June 20X6 in respect of rent, local taxes and insurance.

(b) To state the amount of accrual or prepayment for rent, local taxes and insurance as at 30 June 20X6.

The accruals and prepayments as at 30 June 20X5 were as follows.

	$
Rent accrued	2,000
Local taxes prepaid	1,500
Insurance prepaid	1,800

Payments made during the year ended 30 June 20X6 were as follows.

20X5		$
10 August	Rent, three months to 31 July 20X5	3,000
26 October	Insurance, one year to 31 October 20X6	6,000
2 November	Local taxes, six months to 31 March 20X6	3,500
12 December	Rent, four months to 30 November 20X5	4,000
20X6		
17 April	Rent, four months to 31 March 20X6	4,000
9 May	Local taxes, six months to 30 September 20X6	3,500

15 Hacker 45 mins

Hacker commenced business as a food retailer on 1 January 20X0. The following is a summary of the transactions which took place during the first three months of trading.

(a) Cash sales amounted to $3,000, including $500 of sales on credit cards.

(b) Credit sales totalled $1,600 and of this $300 was outstanding at the end of the period.

(c) On the commencement of business Hacker had paid $4,000 into the business, and a full year's rent of $600 had been paid immediately.

(d) A delivery van was purchased on 1 January at a cost of $900.

(e) During the period suppliers had been paid $1,600 for foodstuffs and invoices totalling $400 remained unpaid at 31 March.

(f) The inventory of foodstuffs at the close of business on 31 March was valued at cost at $360.

(g) Sundry expenses (all paid during the period and relating to it) amounted to $400, and during March Hacker withdrew $200 from the business.

Required

(a) Write up the ledger accounts and cash book of Hacker.

(b) Extract a trial balance.

(c) Prepare an income statement for the three months ending 31 March 20X0, and balance sheet at that date.

Tutorial note. Keep firmly in your mind the fact that you are preparing *quarterly* accounts, whereas some expenses are given as an *annual* amount.

16 George
27 mins

George is a wholesaler and the following information relates to his accounting year ending 30 September 20X2.

(a) Goods are sold on credit terms, but some cash sales are also transacted.

(b) At 1 October 20X1 George's trade accounts receivable amounted to $30,000 against which he had set aside a receivables allowance of 5%.

(c) On 15 January 20X2 George was informed the Fall Co had gone into liquidation, owing him $2,000. This debt was outstanding from the previous year.

(d) Cash sales during the year totalled $46,800, whilst credit sales amounted to $187,800.

(e) $182,500 was received from trade accounts receivable.

(f) Cash discounts allowed to credit customers were $5,300.

(g) Apart from Fall Co's irrecoverable debt, other certain irrecoverable debts amounted to $3,500.

(h) George intends to retain the receivables allowance account at 5% of outstanding trade accounts receivable as at the end of the year, and the necessary entry is to be made.

You are required to enter the above transactions in George's ledger accounts and (apart from the cash and income and expense accounts) balance off the accounts and bring down the balances as at 1 October 20X2.

17 After the inventory count
27 mins

After its end of year physical inventory count and valuation, the accounts staff of Caveat Emptor Co have reached a valuation of $153,699 at cost for total inventories held as at the year end.

However, on checking the figures, the chief bookkeeper has come across the following additional facts.

(a) On one of the inventory sheets, a sub-total value of $6,275 had been carried forward on to the next sheet as $6,725.

(b) 260 units of inventory number 73113X which cost $0.60 each have been extended into the total value column at $6 each.

(c) The purchasing department has informed the accounts department that it is in possession of a number of free samples given to them by potential suppliers. Their estimated value, at purchase cost, would be $1,750. They were not included in the inventory referred to above.

(d) The count includes $4,658 of goods bought on credit and still not paid for as at the year end.

(e) The count includes damaged goods which originally cost $2,885. These could be repaired at a cost of $921 and sold for $3,600.

(f) The count excludes 300 units of item 730052 which were sold to a customer Seesaft Co on a sale or return basis, at a price of $8 each. The original cost of the units was $5 each. Seesaft Co has not yet indicated to Caveat Emptor Co whether these goods have been accepted, or whether they will eventually be returned.

(g) The count includes 648 units of item 702422. These cost $7.30 each originally but because of dumping on the market by overseas suppliers, a price war has flared up and the unit price of the item has fallen to $6.50. The price reduction is expected to be temporary, lasting less than a year or so, although some observers of the market predict that the change might be permanent. Caveat Emptor Co has already decided that if the price reduction lasts longer than six months, it will reduce its resale price of the item from $10.90 to about $10.

Required

Calculate the closing inventory figure for inclusion in the annual accounts of Caveat Emptor Co, making whatever adjustments you consider necessary in view of items (a) to (g). Explain your treatment of each item.

18 Plant and equipment — 18 mins

A business's plant and equipment account and depreciation account at 31 December 20X8 show the following:

Year of purchase	Cost $	Accumulated depreciation $
20X5	100,000	80,000
20X6	70,000	42,000
20X7	50,000	20,000
20X8	30,000	6,000
	250,000	148,000

Depreciation is calculated at 20% on a straight line basis with a full year's charge in the year of acquisition and none in the year of disposal.

During 20X9 the following transactions took place:

(a) Purchases of plant and equipment amounted to $150,000
(b) Plant that had been bought in 20X5 for $40,000 was sold for $5,000
(c) Plant that had been bought in 20X7 for $10,000 was damaged and had to be scrapped.

Required

Prepare the following ledger accounts as at 31 December 20X9:

Plant and equipment — cost
— accumulated depreciation
— disposals

(10 marks)

19 Donald Brown   36 mins

Donald Brown, a sole trader, extracted the following trial balance on 31 December 20X0.

	Debit $	Credit $
Capital at 1 January 20X0		26,094
Trade accounts receivable	42,737	
Cash in hand	1,411	
Trade accounts payable		35,404
Fixtures and fittings at cost	42,200	
Discounts allowed	1,304	
Discounts received		1,175
Inventory at 1 January 20X0	18,460	
Sales		491,620
Purchases	387,936	
Motor vehicles at cost	45,730	
Lighting and heating	6,184	
Motor expenses	2,862	
Rent	8,841	
General expenses	7,413	
Balance at bank		19,861
Provision for depreciation		
Fixtures and fitting		2,200
Motor vehicles		15,292
Drawings	26,568	
	591,646	591,646

The following information as at 31 December is also available.

(a) $218 is owing for motor expenses.

(b) $680 has been prepaid for rent.

(c) Depreciation is to be provided of the year as follows.

    Motor vehicles: 20% on cost
    Fixtures and fittings: 10% reducing balance method

(d) Inventory at the close of business was valued at $19,926.

Required

Prepare Donald Brown's income statement for the year ended 31 December 20X0 and his balance sheet at that date.

(20 marks)

20 Brenda Bailey   27 mins

The following list of account balances (trial balance) has been extracted from the accounts of Brenda Bailey, a sole trader.

	Debit $	Credit $
Sales		427,726
Purchases	302,419	
Carriage inwards	476	
Carriage outwards	829	
Wages and salaries	64,210	
Rent and local taxes	12,466	
Heat and light	4,757	
Inventory at 1 July 20X8	15,310	
Drawings	21,600	
Equipment at cost	102,000	
Motor vehicles at cost	43,270	
Provision for depreciation:		
Equipment		22,250
Motor vehicles		8,920
Trade accounts receivable	50,633	
Trade accounts payable		41,792
Bank		3,295
Sundry expenses	8,426	
Cash	477	
Capital		122,890
	626,873	626,873

The following information as at 30 June 20X9 is also available.

(a) $350 is owing for heat and light.

(b) $620 has been prepaid for rent and local taxes.

(c) Depreciation is to be provided for the year as follows.

    Equipment: 10% on cost
    Motor vehicles: 20% on cost.

(d) Inventory at the close of business was valued at $16,480.

Required

Prepare Brenda Bailey's income statement for the year ended 30 June 20X9 and her balance sheet at that date.

(15 marks)

21 Intangible

18 mins

The accounts of Intangible at 1 January 20X6 include capitalised development costs of $26,500. During the year ended 31 December 20X6 Intangible purchased a new business. The consideration paid to the proprietor included $4,800 in respect of goodwill. The company also spent $7,900 in research and $3,500 on development activities.

The directors of Intangible intend to write off $1,200 in respect of impairment of goodwill. They believe that $22,600 of development costs should be carried forward at 31 December 20X6, in accordance with IAS 38.

Show the ledger accounts for goodwill and research and development in the books of Intangible.

(10 marks)

22 Fabricators

36 mins

Fabricators, an engineering company, makes up its financial statements to 31 March in each year. The financial statements for the year ended 31 March 20X1 showed revenue of $3m and trading profit of $400,000.

Before approval of the financial statements by the board of directors on 30 June 20X1 the following events took place.

(a) The financial statements of Patchup for the year ended 28 February 20X1 were received which indicated a permanent decline in that company's financial position. Fabricators had bought shares in Patchup some years ago and this purchase was included in unquoted investments at its cost of $100,000. The financial statements received indicated that this investment was now worth only $50,000.

(b) There was a fire at the company's warehouse on 30 April 20X1 when inventory to the value of $500,000 was destroyed. It transpired that the inventory in the warehouse was under-insured by some 50%.

(c) It was announced on 1 June 20X1 that the company's design for tank cleaning equipment had been approved by the major oil companies and this could result in an increase in the annual turnover of some $1m with a relative effect on profits.

The following points have also to be taken into consideration.

(d) Bills receivable of $150,000 were discounted with the banks on 15 March 20X1 and are due for maturity on 15 September 20X1. If the customer does not pay the bill, Fabricators will be liable to make up the shortfall to the bank.

(e) The company is expecting to receive orders worth up to $2 million for a new item of equipment which is at present on field trials. The equipment is being imported by the company at selling price less a trade discount of 25%. A quantity of this new equipment was held in stock on 31 March 20X1.

You are required to explain how, if at all, items (a) to (e) above should be reflected in the accounts of Fabricators for the year ended 31 March 20X1.

(20 marks)

23 Miss Teek 36 mins

Miss Anne Teek runs a market stall selling old pictures, china, copper goods and curios of all descriptions. Most of her sales are for cash, although regular customers are allowed credit. No double entry accounting records have been kept, but the following information is available.

SUMMARY OF NET ASSETS AT 31 MARCH 20X8

	$	$
Non-current assets		
Motor van: cost	3,000	
Depreciation	2,500	
net book value		500
Current assets		
Inventory	500	
Trade accounts receivable	170	
Cash at bank	2,800	
Cash in hand	55	
		3,525
Current liabilities		
Trade accounts payable		(230)
Net assets		3,795

Additional information

(a) Anne bought a new motor van in January 20X9 receiving a part-exchange allowance of $1,800 for her old van. A full year's depreciation is to be provided on the new van, calculated at 20% on cost.

(b) Anne has taken $50 cash per week for her personal use. She also estimates that petrol for the van, paid in cash, averages $10 per week.

(c) Other items paid in cash were:

Sundry expenses	$24
Repairs to stall canopy	$201

(d) Anne makes a gross profit of 40% on selling prices. She is certain that no goods have been stolen but remembers that she appropriated a set of glasses and some china for her own use. These items had a total selling price of $300.

(e) Trade receivable and payables at 31.3.X9 are $320 and $233 respectively, and cash in hand amounts to $39. No inventory count has been made and there are no accrued or prepaid expenses.

A summary of bank statements for the twelve months in question shows the following.

	$
Credits	
Cash banked (all cash sales)	7,521
Cheques banked (all credit sales)	1,500
Dividend income	210
	9,231

	$
Debits	
Purchase of motor van	3,200
Road fund licence	80
Insurance on van	323
Trade payables for purchases	7,777
Rent	970
Sundry	31
Accountancy fees (re current work)	75
Bank overdraft interest (6 months to 1.10.X8)	20
Returned cheque (bad debt)	29
	12,505

The bank statement for 1 April 20X9 shows an interest charge of $27.

Required

Prepare Anne's income statement for the year to 31 March 20X9 and a balance sheet as at that date.

(Assume a 52 week year.)

(20 marks)

24 Highton   45 mins

A Highton is in business as a general retailer. He does not keep a full set of accounting records; however it has been possible to extract the following details from the few records that are available.

	1 April 20X1	31 March 20X2
	$	$
Freehold land and buildings at cost	10,000	10,000
Motor vehicle (cost $3,000)	2,250	
Inventory, at cost	3,500	4,000
Trade accounts receivable	500	1,000
Prepayments: motor vehicle expenses	200	300
property insurance	50	100
Cash at bank	550	950
Cash in hand	100	450
Loan from Highton's father	10,000	
Accounts payable	1,500	1,800
Accruals: electricity	200	400
motor vehicle expenses	200	100

Extract from a rough cash book for the year to 31 March 20X2

	$
Receipts	
Cash sales	80,400
Payments	$
Cash purchases	17,000
Drawings	7,000
General shop expenses	100
Telephone	100
Wages	3,000

Extract from the bank pass sheets for the year to 31 March 20X2

	$
Receipts	
Cash banked	52,850
Cheques from trade accounts receivable	8,750
Payments	$
Cheques to suppliers	47,200
Loan repayment (including interest)	10,100
Electricity	400
Motor vehicle expenses	1,000
Property insurance	150
Local taxes	300
Telephone	300
Drawings	1,750

Note. Depreciation is to be provided on the motor vehicle at a rate of 25% per annum on cost.

You are required to prepare an income statement for the year to 31 March 20X2, and a balance sheet as at that date.

(25 marks)

25 Alpha, Beta, Gamma   36 mins

Alpha, Beta and Gamma are in partnership. They share profits equally after Alpha has been allowed a yearly salary of $4,000. No interest is charged on drawings or allowed on current accounts or capital accounts. The list of account balances of the partnership at 31 December 20X9 before adjusting for any of the items below, is as follows.

		Dr	Cr
		$'000	$'000
Capital:	Alpha		30
	Beta		25
	Gamma		20
Current:	Alpha		3
	Beta		4
Drawings:	Alpha	4	
	Beta	5	
Sales			200
Inventory 1 January 20X9		30	
Purchases		103	
Operating expenses		64	
Loan:	Beta (10%)		10
Land and buildings		60	
Plant and equipment:	cost	70	
	depreciation to 31 December 20X9		40
Receivables and payables (trade)		40	33
Bank			11
		376	376

(i) Closing inventory on hand at 31 December was $24,000.

(ii) On 31 December it is agreed that in future Alpha, Beta and Gamma will all share profits equally. Alpha will be allowed a salary of $4,000 as before, and Gamma will be allowed a salary of $5,000 per annum.

It is also agreed that land and buildings are to be revalued to a figure of $84,000 and that this revalued figure is to be retained and recorded in the accounts.

(iii) Interest on the loan has not been paid.

(iv) Included in sales are two items sold on 'sale or return' for $3,000 each. Each item had cost the business $1,000. One of these items was in fact returned on 4 January 20Y0 and the other one was one formally accepted by the customer on 6 January 20Y0.

Required

Submit with appropriately labelled headings and subheadings:

(a) Partners' capital accounts in columnar form.
(b) Partners' current accounts in columnar form.
(c) Income statement at 31 December 20X9.
(d) Balance sheet as at 31 December 20X9.

(20 marks)

26 Tripp Stumble and Faull 36 mins

Tripp Stumble and Faull are in partnership, running a mountaineering training school, and sharing residual profits and losses in the ratio 4:3:2 respectively. At 1 October 20X7 their capital and current account balances were as follows.

	Capital account $	Current account $	
Tripp	36,000	1,200	(debit)
Stumble	20,000	1,600	(credit)
Faull	12,000	750	(credit)
	68,000	1,150	

By formal agreement, the partners are entitled to receive interest at 5% on capital. In addition Stumble is paid an annual salary of $4,000 for his part in running the business.

On 1 April 20X8, by mutual agreement, Faull increased his capital by paying a further $3,000 into the partnership bank account. Tripp reduced his capital by $4,000, but kept this in the partnership as a loan bearing interest at 10% per annum. Interest on the loans, by agreement, is credited to Tripp's current account.

The partners are allowed to take drawings at any time during the year, but they have agreed to charge interest on such drawings. The amount withdrawn by each partner, and the interest payable, were as follows during the year to 30 September 20X8.

	Drawings $	Interest on drawings $
Tripp	8,500	450
Stumble	5,500	300
Faull	3,000	150

The trading profit, before interest, of the mountaineering school for the year to 30 September 20X8 was $24,675.

Required

Prepare the appropriation account and the capital and current accounts of the partners for the year ended 30 September 20X8.

(20 marks)

27 Camberwell

18 mins

The following information relates to the transactions of Camberwell Co for the year ended 31 December 20X1.

	$'000
Depreciation	1,320
Cash paid for expenses	3,405
Increase in inventories	555
Cash paid to employees	4,230
Decrease in receivables	420
Cash paid to suppliers	7,410
Decrease in payables	585
Cash received from customers	19,200
Net profit before tax	3,555

Required

Compute Camberwell's net cash flow from operating activities for the company's cash flow statement for the year ended 31 December 20X1 using:

(a) the direct method
(b) the indirect method

(10 marks)

28 Blue

36 mins

The draft financial statements for Blue, a limited liability company, are set out below.

INCOME STATEMENT FOR THE YEAR ENDED 30 SEPTEMBER 20X1

	$'000
Sales revenue	600
Cost of sales	(410)
Gross profit	190
Profit on sale of non-current asset	10
	200
Depreciation	(30)
Operating expenses	(70)
Interest	(15)
Profit for the period	85

Dividends of £35,000 were paid during the year.

BALANCE SHEET AS AT 30 SEPTEMBER

	20X1 $1000	20X1 $1000	20X0 $1000	20X0 $1000
Non-current assets (see note)		450		520
Current assets				
Inventory	65		50	
Receivables	80		30	
Bank and cash	30	175	15	95
		625		615
Share capital		400		400
Retained earnings		95		60
Non-current liability-loan		20		100
Current liabilities				
Payables		110		55
		625		615

Note. The company purchased non-current assets for $40,000 during the year ended 30 September 20X1.

Required

(a) Prepare a cash-flow statement for Blue for the year ended 30 September 20X1. The format need not comply with the accounting standard. Ignore taxation. **(10 marks)**

(b) Discuss whether a cash-flow statement is more important than an income statement to users of accounts. **(10 marks)**

(20 marks)

29 Cat

18 mins

Set out below are the balance sheets of Cat Co as at 30 June 20X1 and 20X2.

CAT CO
BALANCE SHEET AS AT 30 JUNE

	20X1		20X2	
Assets	$	$	$	$
Property, plant and equipment				
Cost	85,000		119,000	
Depreciation	26,000		37,000	
		59,000		82,000
Current assets				
Inventories	34,000		40,000	
Receivables (trade)	26,000		24,000	
Cash at bank	10,000		13,500	
		70,000		77,500
Total assets		129,000		159,500
Equity				
Capital and reserves				
Ordinary $1 shares	26,000		28,000	
Share premium	12,000		13,000	
Retained earnings	31,000		53,500	
		69,000		94,500
Non-current liabilities				
10% loan stock		20,000		10,000
Current liabilities				
Payables (trade)	15,000		23,000	
Taxation	25,000		32,000	
		40,000		55,000
Total equity and liabilities		129,000		159,500

Notes

(a) No property, plant and disposal were disposed of during the year.
(b) Of the 10% loan stock, $10,000 was redeemed on 31 December 20X1.
(c) Dividends of $13,000 were paid during the year.

Required

Prepare a cash flow statement for the year to 30 June 20X2, using the format specified in IAS 7.

(10 marks)

30 Arthur

18 mins

On 1 April 20X0 Arthur acquired 75% of the ordinary share capital of Merlin for $360,000. At that date the balance sheet of Merlin showed the following:

	$
Sundry net assets	320,000
Share capital	
200,000 ordinary shares of $1 each	200,000
Retained earnings	120,000
	320,000

At 31 March 20X3, the balance sheets of the two companies showed the following:

	Arthur $	Merlin $
Sundry net assets	1,120,000	460,000
Investment in Merlin	360,000	
	1,480,000	460,000
Share capital		
Shares of $1 each	1,000,000	200,000
Retained earnings	480,000	260,000
	1,480,000	460,000

Following an impairment review, $72,000 is to be written off goodwill.

Required

Prepare the consolidated balance sheet of Arthur and its subsidiary as at 31 March 20X3.

(10 marks)

31 April and May   18 mins

April Co acquired 75,000 shares in May Co in 20X3, when May Co's retained earnings were 140,000. The draft balance sheets of both companies are given below as at 31 December 20X5.

	April Co $'000	April Co $'000	May Co $'000	May Co $'000
Non-current assets				
Property, plant and equipment	200		200	
Investment in May	250		–	
		450		200
Current assets				
Inventories	60		40	
Receivables	85		54	
Cash	20		10	
		165		104
		615		304
Equity and liabilities				
Ordinary shares: $1	200		100	
Retained earnings	320		180	
		520		280
Current liabilities				
Payables		95		24
		615		304

Required

Prepare the consolidated balance sheet of the April Group. There has been no impairment of goodwill.

(10 marks)

32 Tarquin   18 mins

Tarquin Co is a wholesaler trading in computer games. As the financial controller, you have calculated a number of ratios relating to the years ended 31.12.20X6 and 31.12.20X7. You also have available the industry average for purposes of comparison. There have been no changes in price levels between 20X6 and 20X7. The ratios you have calculated are as follows.

	20X7	20X6	Industry average 20X7
Return on capital employed before tax (ROCE)	19%	19%	19%
Return on owner's equity before tax (ROE)	24%	21%	16%
Gross profit margin	23%	25%	20%
Net profit margin	14%	12%	9%
Leverage	45%	51%	65%
Current ratio	1.6	1.8	1.4
Quick ratio	0.8	0.8	0.8
Accounts receivable collection period	32 days	26 days	29 days
Accounts payable payment period	63 days	42 days	42 days
Inventory turnover	68 days	72 days	72 days

Required

Comment on the significance of these ratios, highlighting their implications for management strategy in 20X7 and for future years. Your commentary should be from the perspective of benefit to the shareholders.

(10 marks)

33 Objectivity 18 mins

It is frequently suggested that accounting information and accounting reports should attempt to be relevant and reliable. These terms could be explained as follows.

'Information has the quality of relevance when it influences the economic decisions of users by helping them evaluate past, present or future events or by confirming, or correcting, their past evaluations.

'Information has the quality of reliability when it is free from material error and bias and can be depended on by users to represent faithfully that which it either purports to represent or could reasonably be expected to represent'.

Required

(a) Explain what accountants mean by the convention of objectivity. (3 marks)

(b) Why do shareholders need to read published accounts of companies in which they own shares? (3 marks)

(c) 'From the viewpoint of shareholders, objectivity will tend to lead to accounts being more reliable, but less relevant.' Do you agree? (4 marks)

(10 marks)

34 Parmagat

18 mins

At the year end the trial balance of Parmagat, a limited liability company, did not balance and the difference of $57,000 was credited to a suspense account.

Further investigation revealed the following:

(a) A new issue of 500,000 $1 shares was made at 30c above par. $500,000 was credited to share capital and the full amount received was debited to the cash account.

(b) Cash of $2,000 was received from an account receivable written off two years previously. The bookkeeper did not know where to post the credit.

(c) The discounts allowed account has been credited with $47,500 discounts allowed to customers paying within 30 days.

Required

(a) Prepare journal entries with narratives to clear the suspense account
(b) Show the suspense account after the journals have been posted

(10 marks)

35 Abacus

18 mins

The directors of Abacus, a limited liability company, are reviewing the draft accounts for the year ended 30 June 20X9. The net profit before tax currently stands at $923,000. The auditors have drawn their attention to the following matters:

(a) An announcement was made on 4 July that one of their customers, Imex, had gone into liquidation. The liquidator is estimating that suppliers will receive 30c in the $. The receivable in Abacus's accounts regarding Imex stands at $325,000 at 30 June.

(b) A line of inventory valued at cost of $150,000 has become obsolete. It can only be disposed of for $200,000 via an agent who will require 20% of selling price. Other disposal costs will amount to $25,000.

(c) An outstanding claim for damages by an ex-employee who was injured in the warehouse is likely to amount to $50,000. No provision has been made for this as it was expected to be covered by insurance. However the insurance company are now claiming that certain safety procedures were not in place, rendering the cover invalid.

Required

Explain how each of these issues should be dealt with and show the effect on the net profit before tax.

(10 marks)

EXAM QUESTION BANK

36 Lewisham

18 mins

Lewisham, a limited liability company, has the following capital structure:

	$'000
Share capital	
50c ordinary shares (fully paid)	15,000
Share premium	3,000
Retained earnings	27,000
	45,000

The following share issues are made:

(a) A '3 for 2' bonus issue, and then
(b) A '1 for 2' rights issue at 80c.

Show the capital structure following these issues, assuming all rights taken up.

(10 marks)

37 Edgeware

18 mins

The financial statements of Edgeware, a limited liability company, for the financial years ended 31 December 20X8 and 20X9 are as follows:

	31 December 20X8		31 December 20X9	
	$'000	$'000	$'000	$'000
INCOME STATEMENT				
Sales revenue		5,327		5,714
Cost of sales: opening inventory	217		314	
Purchases	2,635		2,857	
	2,852		3171	
Less closing inventory	(314)	(2,538)	(417)	(2,754)
Gross profit		2,789		2,960
Expenses		(1,726)		(1,891)
Net profit		1,063		1,069
BALANCE SHEET				
Property, plant and equipment		2,957		3,835
Current assets				
Inventory	314		417	
Receivables	1,331		1,413	
Cash	194	1,839	316	2,146
		4,796		5,981
Issued share capital		2,000		2,000
Retained earnings		1,475		2,544
		3,475		4,544
Current liabilities – payables		1,321		1,437
		4,796		5,981

Required

(a) Compute the following ratios for each of the two years:

   (i) Return on capital employed
   (ii) Gross profit percentage
   (iii) Net profit percentage
   (iv) Asset turnover

(b) Comment briefly on the changes in these ratios and mention possible causes.

(10 marks)

38 Hanoi   22 mins

You are the assistant to the financial controller of Hanoi, a manufacturing company. The company's year end is 31 March. The following balances were extracted as at 1 April 20X3.

	$'000
Freehold land	200
Leasehold premises: cost	150
accumulated amortisation	6
Plant and equipment: cost	120
accumulated depreciation	48
Trade receivables	100
Allowance for receivables	2
Trade payables	76
Operating expenses accrual	10
Inventories	62
Bank balance (positive)	20
10% loan stock	110
8% preference shares (non-redeemable)	100
Share capital (ordinary $1 shares)	200
Retained earnings	100

The following information is also available.

(a) During the year, a boring machine was found to be past its best. It was decided to write down the machine from its net book value of $20,000 to its scrap value of $5,000. The original cost of the machine was $40,000.

(b) On 31 March 20X4 the preference dividend for the year was paid. Loan interest was also all paid on 31 March 20X4.

(c) On 1 April 20X3 50,000 $1 ordinary shares were issued at a premium of 50c per share.

(d) An ordinary dividend of 10c per share was paid on 31 March 20X4.

(e) In the year ended 31 March 20X4, the following transactions took place.

	$
Sales	305,000
Purchases	108,000
Operating expenses paid	58,000
Irrecoverable debts written off	12,000

(f) The lease on the premises, when originally taken out, was for fifty years. The premises are to be amortised over the period of the lease. Plant and equipment is depreciated at 20% pa on the straight line basis.

(g) Inventory at 31 March 20X4 amounted to $45,000.

(h) The following balances were available as at 31 March 20X4.

	$
Accrued operating expenses	15,000
Trade payables	58,000
Trade receivables	96,000
Bank (positive)	164,000

Required

Prepare the income statement of Hanoi for the year ended 31 March 20X4 and a balance sheet at that date.

Note. While you are not required to comply with all statutory disclosure requirements, your financial statements should be clearly and informatively presented and be in accordance with generally accepted principles.

(12 marks)

39 Pride (pilot paper) 18 mins

The following extracts have been taken from the trial balance of Pride Limited at 31 March 20X1:

	$'000	$'000
Issued share capital		
500,000 ordinary shares of 50c each		250
Share premium account 1 April 20X0		180
Retained earnings 31 March 20X1		34
Land at cost	210	
Buildings – cost 1 April 20X0	200	
– accumulated depreciation at 1 April 20X0		120
Plant and equipment – cost	318	
– accumulated depreciation at 1 April 20X0		88
Receivables	146	
Cash at bank	50	
Payables		94
10% loan stock issued 20W5		100
Allowance for receivables		10
Suspense account		166

Notes:

1. The retained earnings balance of $34,000 shown above is the final balance of retained profit for the year and may be incorporated into your answer as such.

2. The balance on the suspense account is made up as follows:

	$'000
Receipt of cash on 8 January 20X1 on the issue of 200,000 ordinary shares of 50c each at a premium of 30c per share	160
Proceeds of sale of plant*	6
	166

   * This plant had originally cost $18,000 and had been written down to $6,000 at 31 March 20X0. The company's policy is to provide depreciation for a full year in the year of acquisition of assets and none in the year of sale.

3. Depreciation is to be provided for on the straight line basis at the following annual rates:

Land	Nil
Buildings	2 per cent
Plant and equipment	20 per cent

4. The allowance for receivables is to be increased to $12,000.

5. Prepayments and accruals at 31 March 20X1 were:

	$000
Prepayments	8,000
Accruals	4,000

6. The closing inventory was $180,000.

Required

Prepare the balance sheet of Pride as at 31 March 20X1 for publication complying as far as possible with the provisions of International Financial Reporting Standards. **(10 marks)**

40 Butthead　　　　　　　　　　　　　　　　　　　　　　　45 mins

Butthead is a small trading company. From the information below, you are required to prepare an income statement and a balance sheet in a form suitable for presentation to the directors. You should show all your workings and your financial statements should provide as much information as is helpful. Taxation is to be ignored.

(a) BUTTHEAD
TRIAL BALANCE AS AT 31 DECEMBER 20X7

	$	$
Sales		160,800
Purchases	82,400	
Inventory at 1 January 20X7	10,800	
Suspense account	2,800	
Freehold building	56,000	
Fixtures and fittings:　cost	52,000	
depreciation 31.12.X7		18,800
Ordinary shares of 25c each		20,000
10% loan stock		16,000
5% preference shares of 25c each		8,000
Retained earnings at 1.1.X7		15,200
Cash at bank	1,200	
Cash in hand	1,200	
Sundry expenses*	37,600	
Share issue account		12,000
Receivables control account	21,200	
Payables control account		14,400
	265,200	265,200

Note. This figure includes depreciation for the year.

(b) The following details relate to the company's bank reconciliation.

　(i) The balance per the bank statement was $1,200 overdrawn.

　(ii) A cheque for $2,000 had been accepted by the bank as being for $2,000, but had been entered in the cash book as $1,600.

　(iii) Bank charges appear on the bank statement, but are not shown in the cash book.

　(iv) On 31 December 20X7 there were unpresented cheques totalling $800, all of which cleared in the first week of the next accounting period.

(c) Inventory at 31 December 20X7 was $13,600.

(d) In January 20X7 12,000 25c shares were issued at $1 each. The cash received was treated correctly, but the corresponding credit was made to a 'share issue account', as the bookkeeper was unsure of the correct treatment.

(e) As at 31 December 20X7, the building is to be revalued to $60,000.

(f) Loan interest for the six months to 30 June 20X7 has been paid and is included in the figure for sundry expenses.

(g) The receivables and payables ledgers do not reconcile with the receivables and payables control accounts. Balance totals are as follows.

Receivables ledger
Debit balances $20,000
Credit balances $1,200

Payables ledger
Credit balances $16,000
Debit balances $800

In reconciling the accounts you discover the following errors.

(i) The total on the receivables control account should be $22,400, not $21,200.

(ii) Contras of $1,600 have been correctly entered in the individual ledger accounts but not in the control accounts.

(iii) The list of debit balances on the receivables ledger has been understated by $400.

(iv) The balance owed to Beavis Co. of $800 has not been included in the list of ledger balances.

(v) During the year, a credit note was issued for $800. This has been treated like an invoice in both the individual ledger account and the control account.

After adjusting for the above errors, any remaining differences should be dealt with by transferring from the control accounts to the suspense account. If there is still a balance on the suspense account, this must be transferred to sundry expenses.

41 Tafford   18 mins

The following is an extract from the trial balance of Tafford a limited liability company, at 30 September 20X1:

	$'000	$'000
Warehouse machinery:		
Cost:	3,000	
Accumulated depreciation at 1 October 20X0		1,700
Motor vehicles:		
Cost	1,180	
Accumulated depreciation at 1 October 20X0		500
Inventory at 1 October 20X0	13,000	
Sales revenue		41,600
Purchases	22,600	
Distribution costs	6,000	
Administrative expenses	5,000	
Allowance for receivables, 1 October 20X0		1,300
Irrecoverable debts written off	600	
10% loan notes (issued 20W9)		10,000
Interest paid on loan notes	500	
Suspense account		100

Notes

1 Closing inventory at 30 September 20X1 was $15,600,000.

2 Irrecoverable debts written off and the movement on the receivables allowance are to be included in administrative costs. The receivables allowance is to be reduced to £500,000.

3   The balance on the suspense account is the proceeds of sale of motor vehicles, entered to the suspense account pending correct treatment in the records.

   The vehicles sold had cost $180,000 and had a written down value at 1 October 20X0 of $60,000. It is the company's policy to provide for a full year's depreciation in the year of purchase of vehicles and none in the year of sale. The vehicles sold were all used in the distribution of the company's sales.

4   Depreciation is to be provided for on the straight line basis as follows:

Warehouse machinery	10%
Motor vehicles	25%

   Depreciation of motor vehicles is to be divided equally between distribution costs and administrative expenses, and depreciation of warehouse machinery charged wholly to distribution costs.

5   Prepayments and accruals at 30 September 20X1 were:

	Prepayments $'000	Accruals $'000
Distribution costs	200	100
Administrative expenses	100	60

6   The estimated income tax expense for the year is $3,000,000

Required

Prepare Tafford's income statement, complying as far as possible with the requirements of IAS 1 Presentation of Financial Statements.

(10 marks)

42 Alpaca   20 mins

The following information is available about the balances and transactions of Alpaca, a limited liability company:

BALANCES AT 30 APRIL 20X1	$
Non-current assets – cost	1,000,000
- accumulated depreciation	230,000
Inventories	410,000
Receivables	380,000
Cash at bank	87,000
Payables	219,000
Issued share capital – ordinary shares of $1 each	400,000
Retained earnings	818,000
10% Loan notes	200,000
Loan note interest owing	10,000

TRANSACTIONS DURING YEAR ENDED 30 APRIL 20X2	$
Sales revenue	4,006,000
Purchases	2,120,000
Expenses	1,640,000
Interest on loan notes paid during year	20,000
Issue of 100,000 $1 ordinary shares at a premium of 50c per share	

There were no purchases or sales of non-current assets during the year.

Adjustments at 30 April 20X2

(1)   Depreciation of $100,000 is to be allowed for.

(2) Debts totalling $20,000 are to be written off.

BALANCES AT 30 APRIL 20X2

	$
Inventory	450,000
Receivables (**before** writing off debts shown above)	690,000
Cash at bank	114,000
Trade payables	180,000

Required

Prepare the balance sheet of Alpaca as at 30 April 20X2 using the format in IAS 1 Presentation of Financial Statements as far as the information available allows.

Note. No formal income statement is required, but your answer should include a working showing your computation of the retained earnings figure in the balance sheet. This working carries 4 of the 11 marks available in all.

(11 marks)

MULTIPLE CHOICE QUESTIONS

1 MCQs   90 mins

(i) In an accounts receivable control account, which of the following lists is composed only of items which would appear on the credit side of the account?

   A   Cash received from customers, sales returns, bad debts written off, contras against amounts due to suppliers in the accounts payable ledger

   B   Sales, cash refunds to customers, bad debts written off, discounts allowed

   C   Cash received from customers, discounts allowed, interest charged on overdue accounts, bad debts written off

   D   Sales, cash refunds to customers, interest charged on overdue accounts, contras against amounts due to suppliers in the accounts payable ledger.

(ii) Y purchased some plant on 1 January 2000 for $38,000. The payment for the plant was correctly entered in the cash book but was entered on the debit side of plant repairs account.

   Y charges depreciation on the straight line basis at 20% per year, with a proportionate charge in the year of acquisition and assuming no scrap value at the end of the life of the asset.

   How will Y's profit for the year ended 31 March 2000 be affected by the error?

   A   Understated by $30,400
   B   Understated by $36,100
   C   Understated by $38,000
   D   Overstated by $1,900

(iii) The trial balance of Z failed to agree, the totals being: debit $836,200
                                                                    credit $819,700

   A suspense account was opened for the amount of the difference and the following errors were found and corrected:

   1   The totals of the cash discount columns in the cash book had not been posted to the discount accounts. The figures were discount allowed $3,900 and discount received $5,100.

   2   A cheque for $19,000 received from a customer was correctly entered in the cash book but was posted to the customer's account as $9,100.

   What will be the remaining balance on the suspense be *after* the correction of these errors?

   A $25,300 credit
   B $7,700 credit
   C $27,700 debit
   D $5,400 credit

(iv) The trial balance of C, a limited liability company, did not agree, and a suspense account was opened for the difference. Checking in the bookkeeping system revealed a number of errors.

   1   $4,600 paid for motor van repairs was correctly treated in the cash book but was credited to motor vehicles asset account

   2   $360 received from B, a customer, was credited in error to the account of BB

   3   $9,500 paid for rent was debited to the rent account as $5,900

   4   The total of the discount allowed column in the cash book had been debited in error to the discounts received account

   5   No entries have been made to record a cash sale of $100.

Which of the errors above would require an entry to the suspense account as part of the process of correcting them?

- A 3 and 4
- B 1 and 3
- C 2 and 5
- D 2 and 3

(v) B acquired a lorry on 1 May 2000 at a cost of $30,000. The lorry has an estimated useful life of four years, and an estimated resale value at the end of that time of $6,000. B charges depreciation on the straight line basis, with a proportionate charge in the period of acquisition.

What will the depreciation charge for the lorry be in B's accounting period to 30 September 2000?

- A $3,000
- B $2,500
- C $2,000
- D $5,000

(vi) IAS 2 *inventories* defines the items that may be included in computing the value of an inventory of finished goods manufactured by a business.

Which one of the following lists consists only of items which may be included in the balance sheet value of such inventories, according to IAS 2?

- A Foreman's wages, carriage inwards, carriage outwards, raw materials
- B Raw materials, carriage inwards, costs of storage of finished goods, plant depreciation
- C Plant depreciation, carriage inwards, raw materials, foreman's wages
- D Carriage outwards, raw materials, foreman's wages, plant depreciation

(vii) The closing inventory of X amounted to $116,400 *excluding* the following two inventory lines:

1. 400 items which had cost $4 each. All were sold after the balance sheet date for $3 each, with selling expenses of $200 for the batch.

2. 200 different items which had cost $30 each. These items were found to be defective at the balance sheet date. Rectification work after the balance sheet amounted to $1,200, after which they were sold for $35 each, with selling expenses totalling $300.

Which of the following total figures should appear in the balance sheet of X for inventory?

- A $122,300
- B $121,900
- C $122,900
- D $123,300

(viii) The IASB's *Framework* gives five qualitative characteristics which make financial information reliable. These five characteristics are:

- A Prudence, consistency, understandability, faithful representation, substance over form
- B Accruals basis, going concern concept, consistency, prudence, true and fair view
- C Faithful representation, neutrality, substance over form, completeness, consistency
- D Substance over form, faithful representation, neutrality, prudence, completeness

(ix) The following attempt at a bank reconciliation statement has been prepared by Q Co:

	$
Overdraft per bank statement	38,600
Add: deposits not credited	41,200
	79,800
Less: outstanding cheques	3,300
Overdraft per cash book	76,500

MULTIPLE CHOICE QUESTIONS

Assuming the bank statement balance of $38,600 to be correct, what *should* the cash book balance be?

- A $76,500 overdrawn, as stated
- B $5,900 overdrawn
- C $700 overdrawn
- D $5,900 cash at bank

(x) After checking a business cash book against the bank statement, which of the following items could require an entry in the cash book?

1. Bank charges
2. A cheque from a customer which was dishonoured
3. Cheque not presented
4. Deposits not credited
5. Credit transfer entered in bank statement
6. Standing order entered in bank statement.

- A 1, 2, 5 and 6
- B 3 and 4
- C 1, 3, 4 and 6
- D 3, 4, 5 and 6

(xi) The following information is relevant to the calculation of the sales figure for Alpha, a sole trader who does not keep proper accounting records:

	$
Opening accounts receivable	29,100
Cash received from credit customers and paid into the bank	381,600
Expenses paid out of cash received from credit customers before banking	6,800
Bad debts written off	7,200
Refunds to credit customers	2,100
Discounts allowed to credit customers	9,400
Cash sales	112,900
Closing accounts receivable	38,600

The figure which should appear in Alpha's trading account for sales is:

- A $525,300
- B $511,700
- C $529,500
- D $510,900

(xii) A sole trader who does not keep full accounting records wishes to calculate her sales revenue for the year.

The information available is:

1	Opening inventory	$17,000
2	Closing inventory	$24,000
3	Purchases	$91,000
4	Standard gross profit percentage on sales revenue	40%

Which of the following is the sales figure for the year calculated from these figures?

- A $117,600
- B $108,000
- C $210,000
- D $140,000

(xiii) A business compiling its accounts for the year to 31 January each year pays rent quarterly in advance on 1 January, 1 April, 1 July and 1 October each year. After remaining unchanged for some years, the rent was increased from $24,000 per year to $30,000 per year as from 1 July 2000.

Which of the following figures is the rent expense which should appear in the income statement for year ended 31 January 2001?

A $27,500
B $29,500
C $28,000
D $29,000

(xiv) On 31 December 2000 the inventory of V was completely destroyed by fire. The following information is available:

1   Inventory at 1 December 2000 at cost $28,400
2   Purchases for December 2000 $49,600
3   Sales for December 2000 $64,800
4   Standard gross profit percentage on sales revenue 30%

Based on this information, which of the following is the amount of inventory destroyed?

A $45,360
B $32,640
C $40,971
D $19,440

(xv) Which of the following statements concerning the accounting treatment of research and development expenditure are true, according to IAS 38 *Intangible assets*?

1   If certain criteria are met, research expenditure may be recognised as an asset.

2   Research expenditure, other than capital expenditure on research facilities, should be recognised as an expense as incurred.

3   In deciding whether development expenditure qualifies to be recognised as an asset, it is necessary to consider whether there will be adequate finance available to complete the project.

4   Development expenditure recognised as an asset must be amortised over a period not exceeding five years.

5   The financial statements should disclose the total amount of research and development expenditure recognised as an expense during the period.

A   1, 4 and 5
B   2, 4 and 5
C   2, 3 and 4
D   2, 3 and 5

(xvi) D, E and F are in partnership, sharing profits in the ratio 5:3:2 respectively, after charging salaries for E and F of $24,000 each per year.

On 1 July 2000 they agreed to change the profit-sharing ratio 3:1:1 and to increase E's salary to $36,000 per year, F's salary continuing unchanged.

For the year ended 31 December 2000 the partnership profit amounted to $480,000.

MULTIPLE CHOICE QUESTIONS

Which of the following correctly states the partners' total profit shares for the year?

	D	E	F
A	$234,000	$136,800	$109,200
B	$213,000	$157,800	$109,200
C	$186,000	$171,600	$122,400
D	$237,600	$132,000	$110,400

(xvii) At 1 January 2000 the capital structure of Q, a limited liability company, was as follows:

	$
Issued share capital 1,000,000 ordinary shares of 50c each	500,000
Share premium account	300,000

On 1 April 2000 the company made an issue of 200,000 50c shares at $1.30 each, and on 1 July the company made a bonus (capitalisation) issue of one share for every four in issue at the time, using the share premium account for the purpose.

Which of the following correctly states the company's share capital and share premium account at 31 December 2000?

	Share capital	Share premium account
A	$750,000	$230,000
B	$875,000	$285,000
C	$750,000	$310,000
D	$750,000	$610,000

(xviii) According to the illustrative financial structure in IAS 1 (revised) *Presentation of financial statements*, dividends paid during the year should be disclosed in:

- A Income statement
- B Statement of changes in equity
- C Balance sheet
- D None of these

(xix) IAS 7 *Cash flow statements* requires the cash flow statement to open with the calculation of net cash from operating activities, arrived at by adjusting net profit before taxation.

Which of the following lists consists only of items which could appear in such a calculation?

- A Depreciation, increase in receivables, decrease in payables, proceeds from sale of equipment, increase in inventories
- B Increase in payables, decrease in inventories, profit on sale of plant, depreciation, decrease in receivables
- C Increase in payables, proceeds from sale of equipment, depreciation, decrease in receivables, increase in inventories
- D Depreciation, interest paid, proceeds from sale of equipment, decrease in inventories.

(xx) IAS 10 *Events after the balance sheet date* regulates the extent to which events after the balance sheet date should be reflected in financial statements.

Which of the following lists of such events consists only of items that, according to IAS 10, should normally be classified as non-adjusting?

- A Insolvency of an account receivable which was outstanding at the balance sheet date, issue of shares or loan notes, a major merger with another company
- B Issue of shares or loan notes, changes in foreign exchange rates, major purchases of non-current assets
- C A major merger with another company, destruction of a major non-current asset by fire, discovery of fraud or error which shows that the financial statements were incorrect

D Sale of inventory, giving evidence about its value at the balance sheet date, issue of shares or loan notes, destruction of a major non-current asset by fire

(xxi) An analysis of its financial statements revealed that the accounts receivable collection period of R, a limited liability company, was 100 days, when 60 days is a reasonable figure.

Which one of the following could NOT account for the high level of 100 days?

A Poor performance in R's credit control department
B A large credit sale made just before the balance sheet date
C R's trade is seasonal
D A downturn in R's trade in the last quarter of the year

(xxii) Which of the following correctly defines working capital?

A Non-current assets plus current assets minus current liabilities
B Current assets minus current liabilities
C Non-current assets plus current assets
D Share capital plus reserves

(xxiii) At 1 January 20X0 H acquired 80% of the share capital of S for $160,000. At that date the share capital of S consisted of 100,000 ordinary shares of $1 each and its reserves totalled $80,000.

In the consolidated balance sheet of H and its subsidiary S at 31 December 20X2 the amount appearing for goodwill should be:

A $16,000
B $19,200
C $28,800
D $4,000

(xxiv) At 1 January 20X0 H Co acquired 60% of the share capital of S for $180,000. At that date the share capital of S consisted of 200,000 shares of 50c each. The reserves of H and S are stated below:

	At 1 January 20X0 $	At 31 December 20X2 $
H	280,000	240,000
S	50,000	180,000

In the consolidated balance sheet of H and its subsidiary S at 31 December 20X2, what amount should appear for the minority interest in S?

A $92,000
B $280,000
C $152,000
D $112,000

(xxv) H acquired 75% of the share capital of S for $280,000 on 1 January 20X0. Goodwill arising on consolidation has been written off as impaired.

Details of the share capital and reserves of S are as follows:

	At 1 January 20X0 $	At 31 December 20X6 $
Share capital	200,000	200,000
Retained earnings	120,000	180,000

At 31 December 2000 the retained earnings of H amounted to $480,000.

MULTIPLE CHOICE QUESTIONS

What figure should appear in the consolidated balance sheet of H and S for the retained earnings at 31 December 20X6?

A $530,000
B $525,000
C $485,000
D $575,000

2 MCQs

(i) Who issues International Accounting Standards?

A   The auditing practices board
B   The stock exchange
C   The IASB
D   The government

(ii) Which of the following is *not* an accounting concept?

A   Prudence
B   Consistency
C   Depreciation
D   Accruals

(iii) When preparing financial statements in periods of inflation, directors

A   Must reduce asset values
B   Must increase asset values
C   Must reduce dividends
D   Need make no adjustments

(iv) The following information relates to a bank reconciliation.

(i) The bank balance in the cashbook before taking the items below into account was $8,970 overdrawn.

(ii) Bank charges of $550 on the bank statement have not been entered in the cashbook.

(iii) The bank has credited the account in error with $425 which belongs to another customer.

(iv) Cheque payments totalling $3,275 have been entered in the cashbook but have not been presented for payment.

(v) Cheques totalling $5,380 have been correctly entered on the debit side of the cashbook but have not been paid in at the bank.

What was the balance as shown by the bank statement *before* taking the items above into account?

A $8,970 overdrawn
B $11,200 overdrawn
C $12,050 overdrawn
D $17,750 overdrawn

(v) W bought a new printing machine from abroad. The cost of the machine was $80,000. The installation costs were $5,000 and the employees received specific training on how to use this particular machine, at a cost of $2,000. Before using the machine to print customers' orders, a test was undertaken and the paper and ink cost $1,000.

What should be the cost of the machine in the company's balance sheet?

A $80,000
B $85,000
C $87,000
D $88,000

(vi) The electricity account for the year ended 30 June 20X1 was as follows.

	$
Opening balance for electricity accrued at 1 July 20X0	300
Payments made during the year	
1 August 20X0 for three months to 31 July 20X0	600
1 November 20X0 for three months to 31 October 20X0	720
1 February 20X1 for three months to 31 January 20X1	900
30 June 20X1 for three months to 30 April 20X1	840

Which of the following is the appropriate entry for electricity?

	Accrued At 30 June 20X1	Charge to income statement year ended 30 June 20X1
A	$Nil	$3,060
B	$460	$3,320
C	$560	$3,320
D	$560	$3,420

(vii) The year end of M Inc is 30 November 20X0. The company pays for its gas by a standing order of $600 per month. On 1 December 20W9, the statement from the gas supplier showed that M Inc had overpaid by $200. M Inc received gas bills for the four quarters commencing on 1 December 20W9 and ending on 30 November 20X0 for $1,300, $1,400, $2,100 and $2,000 respectively.

Which of the following is the correct charge for gas in M Inc's income statement for the year ended 30 November 20X0.

A $6,800
B $7,000
C $7,200
D $7,400

(viii) S sells three products – Basic, Super and Luxury. The following information was available at the year end.

	Basic $ per unit	Super $ per unit	Luxury $ per unit
Original cost	6	9	18
Estimated selling price	9	12	15
Selling and distribution costs	1	4	5
	units	units	units
Units of inventory	200	250	150

The value of inventory at the year end should be

A $4,200
B $4,700
C $5,700
D $6,150

(ix) A car was purchased by a newsagent business in May 20W7 for:

	$
Cost	10,000
Road tax	150
Total	10,150

The business adopts a date of 31 December as its year end.

The car was traded in for a replacement vehicle in August 20X0 at an agreed value of $5,000.

It has been depreciated at 25% per annum on the reducing-balance method, charging a full year's depreciation in the year of purchase and none in the year of sale.

MULTIPLE CHOICE QUESTIONS

What was the profit or loss on disposal of the vehicle during the year ended December 20X0?

A   Profit: $718
B   Profit: $781
C   Profit: $1,788
D   Profit: $1,836

(x)   A summary of the balance sheet of M at 31 March 20X0 was as follows

	$000
Total assets less current liabilities	120
Ordinary share capital	40
Share premium account	10
Accumulated profits	10
5% loan stock 20Y0	60
	120

If the operating profit for the year ended 31 March 20X0 was $15,000, what is the return on capital employed?

A   12.5%
B   25%
C   30%
D   37.5%

(xi)   The annual sales of a company are $235,000 including sales tax at 17.5%. Half of the sales are on credit terms; half are cash sales. The receivables in the balance sheet are $23,500.

What are the receivable days (to the nearest day)?

A   37 days
B   43 days
C   73 days
D   86 days

(xii)   The concept of capital maintenance is important for

A   The sources of finance
B   The measurement of profit
C   The relationship of debt to equity
D   The purchase of non-current assets

(xiii)   An inventory record card shows the following details.

February   1   50 units in stock at a cost of $40 per unit
                7   100 units purchased at a cost of $45 per unit
                14   80 units sold
                21   50 units purchased at a cost of $50 per unit
                28   60 units sold

What is the value of inventory at 28 February using the FIFO method?

A $2,450
B $2,700
C $2,950
D $3,000

(xiv) A particular source of finance has the following characteristics: a fixed return, a fixed repayment date, it is secured and the return is classified as an expense.

Is the source of finance

- A   Ordinary share
- B   Hire purchase
- C   Loan stock
- D   Preference share

(xv) Which of the following statements gives the best definition of the objective of accounting?

- A   To provide useful information to users
- B   To record, categorise and summarise financial transactions
- C   To calculate the taxation due to the government
- D   To calculate the amount of dividend to pay to shareholders

(xvi) A company has been notified that a receivable has been declared bankrupt. The company had previously made a specific allowance for this debt. Which of the following is the correct double entry?

	DR	CR
A	Irrecoverable debts account	Account receivable
B	Account receivable	Irrecoverable debts account
C	Allowance for receivables	Account receivable
D	Account receivable	Allowable for receivables

(xvii) W is registered for sales tax. The managing director has asked four staff in the accounts department why the output tax for the last quarter does not equal 17.5% of sales (17.5% is the rate of tax). Which one of the following four replies she received was *not* correct?

- A   The company had some exports that were not liable to sales tax
- B   The company made some sales of zero-rated products
- C   The company made some sales of exempt products
- D   The company sold some products to businesses not registered for sales tax

(xviii) Which of the following is *not* the purpose of a receivables ledger control account?

- A   A receivables ledger control account provides a check on the arithmetical accuracy of the personal ledger
- B   A receivables ledger control account helps to locate errors in the trial balance
- C   A receivables ledger control account ensures that there are no errors in the personal ledger
- D   Control accounts deter fraud

(xix) The net book value of a company's non-current assets was $200,000 at 1 August 20X0. During the year ended 31 July 20X1, the company sold non-current assets for $25,000 on which it made a loss of $5,000. The depreciation charge of the year was $20,000. What was the net book value of non-current assets at 31 July 20X1?

- A $150,000
- B $155,000
- C $160,000
- D $180,000

MULTIPLE CHOICE QUESTIONS

(xx) The draft balance sheet of B at 31 March 20X1 is set out below.

	$	$
Non-current assets		450
Current assets		
Inventories	65	
Receivables	110	
Prepayments	30	
	205	
Current liabilities		
Payables	30	
Bank overdraft (Note 1)	50	
	80	
		125
		575
Non-current liability		
Loan		(75)
		500
Ordinary share capital		400
Retained earnings		100
		500

Note 1: The bank overdraft first occurred on 30 September 20X0.

What is the gearing of the company?

A   13%
B   16%
C   20%
D   24%

(xxi) According to the IASB *Framework* which of the following is *not* an objective of financial statements?

A   Providing information regarding the financial position of a business
B   Providing information regarding the performance of a business
C   Enabling users to assess the performance of management to aid decision making
D   Helping to assess the going concern status of a business

(xxii) The IASB *Framework* identifies user groups. Which of the following is *not* an information need for the 'Investor' group?

A   Assessment of repayment ability of an entity
B   Measuring performance, risk and return
C   Taking decisions regarding holding investments
D   Taking buy/sell decisions

(xxiii) The role of the IASB is to?

A   Oversee the standard setting and regulatory process
B   Formulate accounting standards
C   Review defective accounts
D   Control the accountancy profession

(xiv) Which of the following items does not appear under the heading 'reserves' on a company balance sheet?

A   Share premium account
B   Retained earnings
C   Revaluation surpluses
D   Loan stock

(xxv) Which of the following statements regarding a limited liability company income statement is correct?

    A   Accounting standards define the expenses which are reported under 'cost of sales'

    B   'Depreciation' appears as a separate heading

    C   Interest payable is deducted from profit after taxation

    D   Irrecoverable debts will be included under one of the statutory expense headings (usually administrative expenses)

MULTIPLE CHOICE QUESTIONS

Exam answer bank

1 Users of accounting information

The people who might be interested in financial information about a large public company may be classified as follows.

(a) *Managers of the company*. These are people appointed by the company's owners to supervise the day-to-day activities of the company. They need information about the company's financial situation as it is currently and as it is expected to be in the future. This is to enable them to manage the business efficiently and to take effective control and planning decisions.

(b) *Shareholders of the company*, ie the company's owners. These will want to assess how effectively management is performing its stewardship function. They will want to know how profitably management is running the company's operations and how much profit they can afford to withdraw from the business for their own use.

(c) *Trade contacts*, including suppliers who provide goods to the company on credit and customers who purchase the goods or services provided by the company. *Suppliers* will want to know about the company's ability to pay its debts; *customers* need to know that the company is a secure source of supply and is in no danger of having to close down.

(d) *Providers of finance to the company*. These might include a bank which permits the company to operate an overdraft, or provides longer-term finance by granting a loan. The bank will want to ensure that the company is able to keep up with interest payments, and eventually to repay the amounts advanced.

(e) *The taxation authorities* will want to know about business profits in order to assess the income tax payable by the company, and also any *sales taxes*.

2 The accounting equation

Transaction	Assets		=	Capital		+	Liabilities	
		$			$			$
Start of business	Cash	5,000	=		5,000	+		0
(a)	Cash	3,200	=		5,000	+		0
	Shelves	1,800						
		5,000						
(b)	Cash	1,200	=		5,000	+		0
	Shelves	1,800						
	Books	2,000						
		5,000						
(c)	Cash	2,700	=		5,000	+		0
	Shelves	1,800		Profit(1,500-1,000)	500			
	Books	1,000						
		5,500			5,500			
(d)	Cash	2,500	=		5,000	+		0
	Shelves	1,800		Profit	500			
	Books	1,000		Withdrawals	(200)			
		5,300			5,300			
(e)	Cash	3,000	=		5,000	+	Loan	500
	Shelves	1,800		Profit	500			
	Books	1,000		Withdrawals	(200)			
		5,800			5,300			500
(f)	Cash	3,000	=		5,000	+	Loan	500
	Shelves	1,800		Profit	500		Payables	1,000
	Books	1,000		Withdrawals	(200)			
	Carpets	1,000			5,300			1,500
		6,800						
(g)	Cash	3,000	=		5,000	+	Loan	500
	Shelves	1,800		Profit	700		Payables	1,000
	Books	600		Withdrawals	(200)			
	Carpets	1,000			5,500			1,500
	Receivables	600						
		7,000						

3 Financial statements

A *balance sheet* is a 'snapshot' of the financial position of a business. It is a statement of the liabilities, assets and capital of the business at a given moment in time. It is basically the same as the accounting equation, but written out in more detail.

The *income statement* is not a static picture like the balance sheet, but is a record of income generated and expenditure incurred over the relevant accounting period.

Capital expenditure is expenditure which results in the acquisition of non-current assets (or an improvement in their earning capacity). It is not charged as an expense in the income statement.

Revenue expenditure is any other expenditure such as purchase of goods and expenses incurred to keep the business running (for example repairs, wages, electricity and so on). It is accounted for in the income statement.

Capital expenditure: (a), (d)

Revenue expenditure: (b), (c), (e), (f)

(Note that the value of the transactions is irrelevant.)

4 Business transactions

(a) *Purchase of goods on credit*

　(i)　The supplier's invoice would be the original document.

　(ii)　The original entry would be made in the purchase day book.

(b) *Allowance to credit customers on the return of faulty goods*

　(i)　The usual documentation is a credit note. Occasionally, however, a customer may himself issue a debit note.

　(ii)　The book of original entry would be the sales returns day book.

(c) *Petty cash reimbursement*

　(i)　The original documents for the data would be the receipts for the expenditure and a petty cash voucher.

　(ii)　The transaction would be entered in the petty cash book.

(d) *Credit card sales*

　(i)　The original documents are the credit card sales vouchers.

　(ii)　The original entry would be made in the cash book. This is because a credit card sale is like a cash sale as far as the retailer is concerned. The credit card company pays immediately, or very soon after the transaction has taken place. There is no need to set up a receivables account.

5 Weaknesses

Tutorial note | This is a 'problem' question. You should have resisted the temptation to write all you know about purchases systems.

(a) Weaknesses in H's existing purchase system are as follows.

　(i)　Invoices are not approved before they are input. This could lead to the creation of fictitious liabilities.

　(ii)　New supplier accounts are opened automatically as a result of keying in an invoice without approval from a responsible official. It would thus be possible to create fictitious accounts.

　(iii)　Cheque payments for accounts payable balances are issued without scrutiny of the account and approval. The could lead to inaccuracy in the account or the name of the supplier.

(b) The purchases and trade payables system should be reorganised as follows.

(i) Purchase invoices should only be input after they have been approved by the relevant department/official who should check them to orders and goods received notes.

(ii) New suppliers' accounts should only be opened with written approval from a responsible official. An audit report of new accounts opened in a particular period (eg a month) should be produced and reviewed.

(iii) The batching of invoices and cash payments will allow batch totals to be agreed to output totals.

(iv) Trade payable accounts should be reconciled to suppliers' statements on a regular basis.

(v) Cheque payments should not be made without approval linked to a review of the relevant invoices.

6 Beechfield 1

PETTY CASH BOOK

Receipts $	Date 20X9	Narrative	Total $	Stationery $	Cleaning $	Entertainment $	Travel $	Postage $
	Nov							
350	1	Cash						
	2	Materials	5		5			
	3	Stamps	10					10
	6	Envelopes	12	12				
	8	Taxi fare	32				32	
	10	Petrol	17				17	
	14	Typing paper	25	25				
	15	Materials	4		4			
	16	Bus fare	2				2	
	20	Visitors' lunch	56			56		
	21	Mops and brushes	41		41			
	23	Stamps	35					35
	27	Envelopes	12	12				
	29	Visitors' lunches	30			30		
	30	Photocopying paper	40	40				
			321	89	50	86	51	45
321	30	Cash						
	30	Balance c/d	350					
671			671					
	Dec							
350	1	Balance b/d						

… EXAM ANSWER BANK

7 Beechfield 2

STATIONERY

20X9		$	20X9		$
1.11	Balance b/d	570			
30.11	Petty cash book	89	30.11	Balance c/d	659
		659			659

POSTAGE

20X9		$	20X9		$
1.11	Balance b/d	630			
30.11	Petty cash book	45	30.11	Balance c/d	675
		675			675

8 J Ockey

(a) The relevant books of prime entry are the cash book, the sales day book and the purchase day book.

CASH BOOK (RECEIPTS)

Date	Narrative	Total	Capital	Sales	Trade receivables
		$	$	$	$
May 1	Capital	5,000	5,000		
May 13	Sales	200		200	
May 16	Bruce	700			700
May 24	Hill	200			200
		6,100	5,000	200	900

CASH BOOK (PAYMENTS)

Date	Narrative	Total	Fixtures and fittings	Trade payables	Rent	Delivery expenses	Withdrawals	Wages
May		$	$	$	$	$	$	$
1	Store Fitments Co	2,000	2,000					
19	Abel	650		650				
20	Rent	200			200			
21	Delivery expenses	50				50		
30	Withdrawals	200					200	
30	Wages	320						320
31	Green	300		300				
		3,720	2,000	950	200	50	200	320

SALES DAY BOOK

Date	Customer	Amount
		$
May 4	Bruce	700
May 11	Hill	580
Mat 18	Nailor	360
		1,640

PURCHASE DAY BOOK

Date	Customer	Amount $
May 2	Abel	650
May 9	Green	300
May 17	Kaye	800
		1,750

(b) and (c)

The relevant ledger accounts are for cash, sales, purchases, trade accounts payable, trade accounts receivable, capital, fixtures and fittings, rent, delivery expenses, drawings and wages. Because this is not the end of the accounting period, balances on sales and expense accounts are not transferred to I & E but are simply carried down to be continued in the next month.

CASH ACCOUNT

	$		$
May receipts	6,100	May payments	3,720
		Balance c/d	2,380
	6,100		6,100

SALES ACCOUNT

	$		$
Balance c/d	1,840	Cash	200
		Trade accounts receivable	1,640
	1,840		1,840

PURCHASES ACCOUNT

	$		$
Trade accounts payable	1,750	Balance c/d	1,750

TRADE ACCOUNTS RECEIVABLE

	$		$
Sales	1,640	Cash	900
		Balance c/d	740
	1,640		1,640

TRADE ACCOUNTS PAYABLE

	$		$
Cash	950	Purchases	1,750
Balance c/d	800		
	1,750		1,750

CAPITAL ACCOUNT

	$		$
Balance c/d	5,000	Cash	5,000

FIXTURES AND FITTINGS ACCOUNT

	$		$
Cash	2,000	Balance c/d	2,000

RENT ACCOUNT

	$		$
Cash	200	Balance c/d	200

DELIVERY EXPENSES ACCOUNT

	$		$
Cash	50	Balance c/d	50

DRAWINGS

	$		$
Cash	200	Balance c/d	200

WAGES ACCOUNT

	$		$
Cash	320	Balance c/d	320

(d) *Trial balance as at 31 May 20X4*

Account	Dr	Cr
	$	$
Cash	2,380	
Sales		1,840
Purchases	1,750	
Trade accounts receivable	740	
Trade accounts payable		800
Capital		5,000
Fixtures and fittings	2,000	
Rent	200	
Delivery expenses	50	
Drawings	200	
Wages	320	
	7,640	7,640

9 Frontloader

Tutorial note. One problem you must deal with in answering this question is identifying which items in the ledgers are relevant to the receivables control account. Irrelevant items are trade accounts payable and purchases of washing machines (purchase ledger), discounts received, cash paid to trade accounts payable, and overdraft interest.

Workings

	$
Sales	723,869
Less discounts allowed	8,214
	715,655
Less returns inwards	36,925
Net sales	678,730
Opening receivables	84,611
Opening receivables plus net sales	763,341
Cash received from trade accounts receivable (excluding J Smith)	699,267
Closing receivables before adjustments for the subsequent entries	64,074
Subsequent entries:	
A Brown's cheque dishonoured; A Brown becomes an account receivable again	1,246
Closing receivables	65,320

These items are shown in the receivables control account below.

RECEIVABLES CONTROL ACCOUNT

	$		$
Opening balance	84,611	Cash received (debit bank a/c)	699,267
Sales on credit (credit sales a/c)	723,869	Discounts allowed	8,214
A Brown's dishonoured cheque (credit bank a/c)	1,246	Returns inwards (debit sales a/c)	36,925
		Closing balance c/d	65,320
	809,726		809,726
Opening balance b/d	65,320		

10 Frank Mercer 1

CASH BOOK

20X8		$	20X8		$
Dec 31	Balance b/f	1,793	Dec 31	Bank charges	18
Dec 31	Dividend	26	Dec 31	Standing order	32
			Dec 31	Direct debit	88
				Balance c/d	1,681
		1,819			1,819

11 Frank Mercer 2

BANK RECONCILIATION AS AT 31 DECEMBER 20X8

	$	$
Balance per bank statement		1,557
Add unrecorded lodgements:		
V Owen	98	
K Walters	134	
		232
Less unpresented cheques:		
B Oliver (869)	71	
L Philips (872)	37	
		(108)
Balance per cash book (corrected)		1,681

12 Chi Knitwear

(a) SUSPENSE ACCOUNT

	$		$
Opening balance	1,536	Receivables: balance omitted	87
Sales: under-recorded	360	Cash book: receipts undercast	720
		Payables: credit note posted to wrong side (2 × $179)	358
		Cash book: Mr Smith's debt paid but cash receipt not recorded	731
	1,896		1,896

Notes

(i) Error (ii) is an error of principle, whereby a non-current asset item (capital expenditure) has been accounted for as revenue expenditure. The correction will be logged in the journal, but since the error did not result in an inequality between debits and credits, the suspense account would not have been used.

(ii) The electricity bill (vi) has been omitted from the accounts entirely. The error of omission means that both debits and credits will be logged in the journal, but the suspense account will not be involved, since there is equality between debits and credits in the error.

(b) (i) The error means that trade accounts receivable are understated. The correction of the error will increase the total amount for receivables to be shown in the balance sheet.

(ii) The correction of this error will add $1,200 to non-current assets at cost (balance sheet item) and reduce repair costs by $1,200. The income statement will therefore show an increased profit of $1,200, less any depreciation now charged on the non-current asset.

(iii) The undercasting (ie under-adding) of $720 on the receipts side of the cash book means that debits of cash will be $720 less than they should have been. The correction of the error will add $720 to the cash balance in the balance sheet.

(iv) This transposition error means that total sales would be under-recorded by $8,514 – $8,154 = $360 in the sales account. The correction of the error will add $360 to total sales, and thus add $360 to the profits in the income statement.

(v) The credit note must have been issued for a purchase return to the supplier by the business. It should have been debited to the supplier's account, but instead has been credited. Assuming that the purchase returns account was credited correctly, the effect of the error has been to overstate total accounts payable by 2 × $179 = $358, and this amount should be credited from the suspense account and debited to the supplier's account. The effect will be to reduce the total for trade accounts payable in the balance sheet by $358.

(vi) The electricity bill, when entered in the accounts, will increase payables by $152, and reduce profits (by adding to electricity expenses) by $152, assuming that none of this cost is a prepayment of electricity charges.

(vii) Since the cheque has not yet been recorded in the cash book, the correction of the error will add $731 to the cash balance in the balance sheet. The reduction in gross receivables by $731 has already been accounted for.

13 Definitions

(a) *Going concern* is the assumption that, when preparing accounts, the business will continue trading for the foreseeable future, without closing down or even running down its activities to a significant extent.

If a business is to be closed down, for example, then any inventory on hand will have to be valued at the amount to be realised in a forced sale. But if the business is regarded as a going concern, then the value of any unsold inventory at the end of an accounting period will be carried forward to the next period and will eventually be matched against income earned in that subsequent period.

(b) Under the *accrual assumption,* when profit is being calculated, revenue earned must be matched against the expenditure incurred in earning it. For example, suppose you were calculating profit for the year ended 31 December 20X8 and had got as far as working out that gross profit was $12,000. To calculate net profit, expenses must be deducted. If rent paid in 20X8 was $700, then only that part of the $700 relating to 20X8 should be deducted from the gross profit. $200 was actually a prepayment for rent in 20X9, and so that $200 must be matched against next year's income, not against the $12,000 for 20X8.

(c) Under the *consistency assumption* the same treatment should be applied from one period to another in accounting for similar items. This enables valid comparisons to be made from one period to the next. In addition, similar items within a single set of accounts should all be treated in the same way.

For example, suppose a business owns a fleet of cars. Then the consistency concept rules that each car should be depreciated in the same way (by whatever method the business deems most appropriate) and once that depreciation policy has been set, it should be applied consistently from one year to the next.

A business can change its accounting methods, but it should explain clearly why it is doing so, and it should show the effects of the change on the profits for the relevant year in its financial statements.

14 Rent, local taxes and insurance

(a) *Rent for the year ending 30 June 20X6*

	$
1 July 20X5 to 31 July 20X5 = $3,000/3	1,000
1 August 20X5 to 30 November 20X5	4,000
1 December 20X5 to 31 March 20X6	4,000
Accrued, 1 April 20X6 to 30 June 20X6 = 3/4 × $4,000	3,000
Charge to income for year ending 30 June 20X6	12,000

Local taxes for the year ending 30 June 20X6

	$	$
Local taxes prepaid last year, relating to this year		1,500
1 October 20X5 to 31 March 20X6		3,500
1 April 20X6 to 30 September 20X6	3,500	
Less prepaid July to September (3/6)	1,750	
April to June 20X6		1,750
Charge to income for year ending 30 June 20X6		6,750

Insurance for the year ending 30 June 20X6

	$	$
Insurance prepaid last year, relating to this year		1,800
1 November 20X5 to 31 October 20X6	6,000	
Less prepaid July to October (4/12)	2,000	
		4,000
Charge to income for year ending 30 June 20X6		5,800

(b) The accrual or prepayment for each expense can be summarised from the workings in part (a).

	$
As at 30 June 20X6	
Rent accrued	3,000
Local taxes prepaid	1,750
Insurance prepaid	2,000

15 Hacker

(a)

CASH BOOK

	$		$
Capital	4,000	Rent	600
Trade accounts receivable	1,300	Delivery van	900
Cash sales	3,000	Trade accounts payable	1,600
		Sundry expenses	400
		Drawings	200
		Balance c/d	4,600
	8,300		8,300
Balance b/d	4,600		

SALES

	$		$
Trading a/c *	4,600	Cash book	3,000
		Trade accounts receivable	1,600
	4,600		4,600

TRADE ACCOUNTS RECEIVABLE

	$		$
Sales: on credit	1,600	Cash book	1,300
		Balance c/d	300
	1,600		1,600
Balance b/d	300		

CAPITAL

	$		$
Drawings *	200	Cash book	4,000
Balance c/d *	6,210	I & E *	2,410
	6,410		6,410
		Balance b/d	6,210

RENT

	$		$
Cash book	600	I & E a/c *	150
		Prepayment c/d *	450
	600		600
Balance b/d	450		

DELIVERY VAN

	$		$
Cash book	900		

TRADE ACCOUNTS PAYABLE

	$		$
Cash book	1,600	∴ Purchases	2,000
Balance c/d	400		
	2,000		2,000
		Balance b/d	400

PURCHASES

	$		$
Trade accounts payable	2,000	Trading a/c*	2,000

SUNDRY EXPENSES

	$		$
Cash book	400	I & E*	400

DRAWINGS

	$		$
Cash book	200	Capital a/c*	200

(b) TRIAL BALANCE

	Dr $	Cr $
Cash book	4,600	
Sales		4,600
Trade accounts receivable	300	
Capital		4,000
Rent	600	
Delivery van	900	
Trade accounts payable		400
Purchases	2,000	
Sundry expenses	400	
Drawings	200	
	9,000	9,000

Note. The asterisked entries will be made after the trial balance has been extracted.

The amounts transferred to the trading account and the income and expense (I&E) account now constitute the income statement.

(c) INCOME STATEMENT
FOR THE THREE MONTHS ENDING 31 MARCH

	$	$
Sales		4,600
Purchases	2,000	
Less closing inventory	360	
Cost of sales		1,640
Gross profit		2,960
Rent	150	
Sundry expenses	400	
		550
Net profit (to capital account)		2,410

INVENTORY ON HAND AT END OF THREE MONTHS

	$		$
Trading a/c	360	Bal c/d	360

BALANCE SHEET AS AT 31 MARCH

	$	$
Assets		
Non-current assets		
Van: cost		900
Current assets		
Inventory at cost	360	
Receivables	300	
Prepayments	450	
Cash	4,600	
		5,710
Total assets		6,610
Capital and liabilities		
Hacker's capital		
Original capital	4,000	
Profit	2,410	
Less drawings	(200)	
Closing capital		6,210
Liabilities		
Trade accounts payable		400
Total capital and liabilities		6,610

16 George

TRADE ACCOUNTS RECEIVABLE

		$			$
1.10.X1	Balance b/f (b)	30,000	15.1.X2	Irrecoverable debts: Fall Co (c)	2,000
30.9.X2	Sales (d)	187,800	30.9.X2	Cash (e)	182,500
				Discounts allowed (f)	5,300
				Irrecoverable debts (g)	3,500
				Balance c/d	24,500
		217,800			217,800
1.10.X2	Balance b/d	24,500			

SALES ACCOUNT

		$			$
30.9.X2	I & E a/c	234,600	30.9.X2	Cash (d)	46,800
				Receivables (d)	187,800
		234,600			234,600

IRRECOVERABLE DEBTS ACCOUNT

		$			$
15.1.X2	Receivables: Fall Co (c)	2,000	30.9.X2	I & E a/c	5,500
30.9.X2	Receivables (g)	3,500			
		5,500			5,500

ALLOWANCE FOR RECEIVABLES ACCOUNT

		$			$
30.9.X2	Balance c/d (h)		1.10.X1	Balance b/f (b)	
	5% × $24,500	1,225		5% × $30,000	1,500
	I & E a/c:				
	reduction in allowance	275			
		1,500			1,500
			1.10.X2	Balance b/d	1,225

DISCOUNTS ALLOWED ACCOUNT

			$				$
30.9.X2	Receivables		5,300	30.9.X2	I & E a/c		5,300

CASH ACCOUNT (EXTRACT)

		$
30.9.X2	Receivables	182,500
	Sales	46,800

INCOME AND EXPENSE ACCOUNT (EXTRACT)

		$			$
30.9.X2	Irrecoverable debts	5,500	30.9.X2	Sales	234,600
				Receivables allowance	
	Discounts allowed	5,300			275

17 After the inventory count

Item	Explanation	Adjustment Add to Inventory value $	Adjustment Subtract inventory value $
(a)	The sub-total error has over-valued inventories by $(6,725 – 6,275)		450
(b)	This arithmetical error has over-valued the item by $(6 – 0.6) per unit for 260 units		1,404
(c)	Free samples are not trading items and should be excluded from the valuation		
(d)	Goods held should be included in the valuation regardless of whether or not they have been paid for yet.		
(e)	Cost $2,885. Net realisable value $(3,600 – 921) = $2,679. The inventory should be valued at the lower of cost and NRV. Since NRV is lower, the original valuation of stocks (at cost) will be reduced by $(2,885 – 2,679)		206
(f)	Inventory issued on sale or return and not yet accepted by the customer should be included in the valuation and valued at the lower of cost and NRV, here at $5 each (cost)	1,500	
(g)	The cost ($7.30) is below the current and foreseeable selling price ($10 or more) which is assumed to be the NRV of the item. Since the current valuation is at the lower of cost and NRV, no change in valuation is necessary		
		1,500	2,060

	$	$
Original valuation of inventories, at cost		153,699
Adjustments and corrections:		
to increase valuation	1,500	
to decrease valuation	(2,060)	
		(560)
Valuation of inventories for the annual accounts		153,139

18 Plant and equipment

Plant and equipment – cost

	DR $		CR $
Balance b/f	250,000	Plant 20X5 disposal	40,000
Purchases	150,000	Plant 20X7 disposal	10,000
		Balance c/d	350,000
	400,000		400,000
Balance b/d	350,000		

Plant and Equipment – Accumulated Depreciation

	DR $		CR $
Plant 20X5 disp	32,000	B/f	148,000
Plant 20X7 disp	4,000	Current year chg – 350,000 x 20%	70,000
Balance c/d	182,000		
	218,000		218,000
		Balance b/d	182,000

Plant and equipment – disposals

	DR $		CR $
Plant 20X5	40,000	Plant 20X5 depn	32,000
Plant 20X7	10,000	Plant 20X7 depn	4,000
		Plant 20X5 proceeds	5,000
		Losses on disposals	9,000
	50,000		50,000
Balance b/d – losses	9,000		

19 Donald Brown

> **Tutorial note.** You should note these points.
>
> (a) Discounts allowed are an expense of the business and should be shown as a deduction from gross profit. Similarly, discounts received is a revenue item and should be added to gross profit.
>
> (b) The figure for depreciation in the list of account balances represents accumulated depreciation up to and including 20W9. You have to calculate the charge for the year 20X0 for the income statement and add this to the account balance figure to arrive at the accumulated depreciation figure to be included in the balance sheet.
>
> (c) In the exam, you will be asked to produce either the income statement or the balance sheet, probably not both. However this is good practice for you and reinforces the relationships between the income statement and the balance sheet.

EXAM ANSWER BANK

DONALD BROWN
INCOME STATEMENT
FOR THE YEAR ENDED 31 DECEMBER 20X0

	$	$
Sales		491,620
Less cost of sales		
Opening inventory	18,460	
Purchases	387,936	
	406,396	
Closing inventory	19,926	
		386,470
Gross profit		105,150
Discounts received		1,175
		106,325
Less expenses:		
Discounts allowed	1,304	
Lighting and heating	6,184	
Motor expenses (2,862 + 218)	3,080	
Rent (8,841 – 680)	8,161	
General expenses	7,413	
Depreciation (W)	13,146	
		39,288
Net profit		67,037

Working: depreciation charge

Motor vehicles: $45,730 × 20% = $9,146
Fixtures and fittings: 10% × $(42,200 – 2,200) = $4,000
Total: $4,000 + $9,146 = $13,146.

DONALD BROWN
BALANCE SHEET AS AT 31 DECEMBER 20X0

	$	$
Assets		
Non-current assets		
Fixtures and fittings: cost	42,200	
depreciation	6,200	
		36,000
Motor vehicles: cost	45,730	
depreciation	24,438	
		21,292
Current assets		
Inventory	19,926	
Trade accounts receivable	42,737	
Prepayments	680	
Cash in hand	1,411	
		64,754
Total assets		122,046

	$	$
Capital and liabilities		
Capital		
Brought forward	26,094	
Net profit for year	67,037	
Drawings	(26,568)	
Carried forward		66,563
Current liabilities		
Trade accounts payable	35,404	
Accruals	218	
Bank overdraft	19,861	
		55,483
Total capital and liabilities		122,046

20 Brenda Bailey

INCOME STATEMENT
FOR THE YEAR ENDED 30 JUNE 20X9

	$	$
Sales		427,726
Opening inventory	15,310	
Purchases	302,419	
Carriage inwards	476	
	318,205	
Less closing inventory	16,480	
Cost of sales		301,725
Gross profit		126,001
Carriage outwards	829	
Wages and salaries	64,210	
Rent and local taxes $(12,466 – 620)	11,846	
Heat and light $(4,757 + 350)	5,107	
Depreciation: equipment	10,200	
motor vehicles	8,654	
Sundry expenses	8,426	
		109,272
Net profit for the year		16,729

BRENDA BAILEY
BALANCE SHEET AS AT 30 JUNE 20X9

	$	$
Assets		
Property, plant and equipment		
Equipment: cost	102,000	
depreciation	32,450	
		69,550
Motor vehicles: cost	43,270	
depreciation	17,574	
		25,696
Current assets		
Inventory	16,480	
Trade accounts receivable	50,633	
Prepayments	620	
Cash	477	
		68,210
Total assets		163,456

	$	$
Capital and liabilities		
Capital		
Balance at 1 July 20X8	122,890	
Profit for year	16,729	
Drawings	(21,600)	
Balance at 30 June 20X9		118,019
Current liabilities		
Bank overdraft	3,295	
Trade accounts payable	41,792	
Accruals	350	
		45,437
Total capital and liabilities		163,456

21 Intangible

> **Tutorial note.** The important point is to distinguish between the amounts actually spent during the year and the amounts charged to the income statement.

PURCHASED GOODWILL

	$		$
Cash	4,800	I & E a/c: impairment loss	1,200
		Balance c/d	3,600
	4,800		4,800
Balance b/d	3,600		

RESEARCH AND DEVELOPMENT EXPENDITURE

	$		$
Balance b/f	26,500	∴ I &E a/c (7,900 + (26,500 +	
Cash: research	7,900	3,500 – 22,600))	15,300
development	3,500	Development costs c/d	22,600
	37,900		37,900
Balance b/d	22,600		

22 Fabricators

The treatment of the events arising in the case of Fabricators would be as follows.

(a) The fall in value of the investment in Patchup has arisen over the previous year and that company's financial accounts for the year to 28 February 20X1 provide additional evidence of conditions that existed at the balance sheet date. The loss of $50,000 is material in terms of the trading profit figure and it should therefore be reflected in the financial statements of Fabricators. Due to the size and nature of the loss, it should be disclosed separately (as part of profit or loss from ordinary activities), according to IAS 8.

(b) The destruction of inventory by fire on 30 April (one month after the balance sheet date) must be considered as a new condition which did not exist at the balance sheet date. Since the loss is material, being $250,000, it should be disclosed separately, by way of a note describing the nature of the event and giving an estimate of its financial effect. Non-reporting of this event would prevent users of the financial statements from reaching a proper understanding of the financial position.

(c) The approval on 1 June of the company's design for tank cleaning equipment creates a new condition which did not exist at the balance sheet date. This is, therefore, an event which does not require adjustment under IAS 10. It is not clear, however, that it is of such material significance that non-reporting would prevent a proper understanding of the financial position. Disclosure may therefore be unnecessary.

(d) The bills have been discounted with recourse (ie if they are dishonoured the bank can claim the money off Fabricators) and hence there is a possibility of a liability arising if the bills are not honoured. Under IAS 37, the contingent liability of $150,000 in respect of bills discounted should be disclosed in the financial statements as a note to the accounts, but not provided for because the loss is not probable.

(e) If the field trials are not successful, then there is a possibility that it will be difficult to sell the equipment. Therefore, consideration should be given as to whether the equipment should be written down in the accounts to net realisable value. If the loss is not probable, a write down would not be required but consideration should be given as to whether the contingent liability should be disclosed by way of note. In the circumstances given, it would appear that the possibility of loss is remote and therefore, under IAS 37, no disclosure would be required. The expected future sales which might arise should not be included in the financial statements.

23 Miss Teek

> **Tutorial note.** The opening balance sheet is given and so need not be reconstructed: Miss Teek's capital at 31 March 20X8 is $3,795. Accounts should be opened for the trading account, receivables, payables and cash. Since some payments are in cash from cash takings, a two column cash book should distinguish between cash transactions and bank transactions.

MISS TEEK
INCOME STATEMENT
FOR THE YEAR ENDED 31 MARCH 20X9

	$	$
Sales: cash (W1)		10,850
credit (W2)		1,650
		12,500
Opening inventory	500	
Purchases (W3)	7,600	
	8,100	
Closing inventory (W4)	(600)	
Cost of sales		7,500
Gross profit		5,000
Expenses		
Rent	970	
Repairs to canopy	201	
Van running expenses $(520 + 80 + 323)	923	
Depreciation	1,000	
Sundry expenses $(24 + 31)	55	
Bank interest	47	
Accounting fees	75	
Bad debts	29	
		3,300
		1,700
Profit on disposal of van (W6)		1,300
Profit for the year		3,000

MISS TEEK
BALANCE SHEET AS AT 31 MARCH 20X9

	$	$
Assets		
Non-current assets		
Motor van: cost (W5)	5,000	
depreciation (W5)	1,000	
net book value		4,000
Current assets		
Inventory (W4)	600	
Receivables (W2)	320	
Cash in hand (W1)	39	
		959
Total assets		4,959
Capital and liabilities		
Proprietor's capital		
Balance at 31 March 20X8	3,795	
Profit for the year	3,000	
Less drawings (W7)	(2,570)	
Balance at 31 March 20X9		4,225
Current liabilities		
Bank overdraft (W1)	474	
Bank interest (presumably not paid until 1 April)	27	
Payables (W3)	233	
		734
Total capital and liabilities		4,959

Workings

1

CASH BOOK

	Cash $	Bank $		Cash $	Bank $
Balance b/d	55	2,800	Drawings (52 × $50)	2,600	
Cash takings banked			Petrol (52 × $10)	520	
(contra entry)		7,521	Sundry expenses	24	
Cheques banked		1,500	Repairs to canopy	201	
Dividend income:			Taking banked (contra		
drawings		210	entry)	7,521	
Cash takings (balancing			Purchase of van		3,200
figures)	10,850		Road fund licence		80
			Insurance on van		323
			Payables		7,777
			Rent		970
			Sundry		31
			Accounting work		75
			Bank interest		20
			Returned cheque: bad debt		29
Balance c/d (overdraft)		474	Balance c/d	39	
	10,905	12,505		10,905	12,505
Balance b/d		39	Balance b/d		474

2

TRADE RECEIVABLES

	$		$
Balance b/d	170	Cash	1,500
Credit sales (balancing figure)	1,650	Balance c/d	320
	1,820		1,820

3

TRADE PAYABLES

	$		$
Bank	7,777	Balance b/d	230
Balance c/d	233	Purchases (balancing figure)	7,780
	8,010		8,010

Goods taken as drawings are as follows.

		$
Selling price	(100%)	300
Gross profit	(40%)	120
Cost	(60%)	180

Therefore, purchases taken to the trading account = $7,780 – $180 = $7,600.

4 *Closing inventory*

		$
Sales $(10,850 + 1,650)	(100%)	12,500
Gross profit	(40%)	5,000
Cost of goods sold	(60%)	7,500

	$
Opening inventory	500
Purchases (W3)	7,600
	8,100
Cost of goods sold	7,500
Closing inventory (balancing figure)	600

5 *New van*

The bank statement shows that the cash paid for the new van was $3,200. Since there was a part exchange of $1,800 on the old van, the cost of the new van must be $5,000 with first year depreciation (20%) $1,000.

6 *Disposal of van*

	$		$
Van at cost	3,000	Provision for depreciation at	
Profit on disposal	1,300	date of sale	2,500
		Asset account (trade in value for	
		new van)	1,800
	4,300		4,300

7 *Drawings*

	$		$
Cash	2,600	Dividend income	210
Inventory (glasses taken (W3))	180	Capital account (balance)	2,570
	2,780		2,780

Since there are no investments in the business balance sheet, the dividend income must be separate from the business. However, since it is paid into the business bank account, it should be accounted for, in effect, as a reduction in drawings.

24 Highton

> **Tutorial note.** This question is longer than an examination question. However if practices all the incomplete records techniques that you will need to know and so is very worthwhile doing. If you can make a reasonable attempt at it, you should be able to handle any incomplete records question in the examination very easily.

INCOME STATEMENT
FOR THE YEAR ENDED 31 MARCH 20X2

	$	$
Sales: cash	80,400	
credit (W1)	9,250	
		89,650
Cost of sales		
Opening inventory	3,500	
Purchases: cash	17,000	
credit (W2)	47,500	
	68,000	
Less closing inventory	4,000	
		64,000
Gross profit		25,650
Expenses		
Depreciation of motor vehicle (25% × $3,000)	750	
Motor vehicle expenses (W3)	800	
Property insurance $(50 + 150 – 100)	100	
Loan interest	100	
Electricity $(400 + 400 – 200)	600	
General shop expenses	100	
Telephone $(100 + 300)	400	
Wages	3,000	
Local taxes	300	
		6,150
Net profit		19,500

BALANCE SHEET AS AT 31 MARCH 20X2

	$	$
Assets		
Property, plant and equipment		
Freehold land and buildings at cost		10,000
Motor vehicle: cost	3,000	
accumulated depreciation	1,500	
		1,500
Current assets		
Inventory	4,000	
Trade accounts receivable	1,000	
Prepayments	400	
Cash at bank	950	
Cash in hand	450	
		6,800
Total assets		18,300
Capital and liabilities		
Proprietor's capital		
At 1 April 20X1 (W4)*	5,250	
Net profit for the year	19,500	
Less drawings $(7,000 + 1,750)	(8,750)	
At 31 March 20X2		16,000
Current liabilities		
Trade accounts payable	1,800	
Accruals	500	
		2,300
Total capital and liabilities		18,300

*The opening capital could be inserted as a balancing figure; W4 is included merely to prove the figure.

Workings

1

RECEIVABLES CONTROL ACCOUNT

	$		$
Opening balance	500	Bank	8,750
∴ Credit sales	9,250	Closing balance	1,000
	9,750		9,750

2

PAYABLES CONTROL ACCOUNT

	$		$
Bank	47,200	Opening balance	1,500
Closing balance	1,800	∴ Credit purchases	47,500
	49,000		49,000

3

MOTOR VEHICLE EXPENSES

	$		$
Prepayment b/f	200	Accrual b/f	200
Bank	1,000	∴ I & E account	800
Accrual b/f	100	Prepayment c/f	300
	1,300		1,300

4   PROPRIETOR'S CAPITAL AT 1 APRIL 20X1

	$	$
Assets		
Inventory	3,500	
Receivables and prepayments	750	
Cash at bank and in hand	650	
Freehold land and buildings	10,000	
Motor vehicle	2,250	
		17,150
Liabilities		
Loan	10,000	
Payables and accruals	1,900	
		(11,900)
Net assets		5,250

25 Alpha, Beta, Gamma

(a)   PARTNERS CAPITAL ACCOUNTS

	Alpha $	Beta $	Gamma $		Alpha $	Beta $	Gamma $
				Balances b/d	30	25	20
Balances c/d	38	33	28	Land revaluation surplus	8	8	8
	38	33	28		38	33	28

(b)   PARTNERS' CURRENT ACCOUNTS

	Alpha $	Beta $	Gamma $		Alpha $	Beta $	Gamma $
Drawings	4	5	–	Balances b/d	3	4	–
Balances c/d	9	6	6	Salary	4	–	–
				Residual profit	6	6	6
				Loan interest	–	1	–
	13	11	6		13	11	6

Note. It is assumed that the adjustment for interest is DR Interest expense CR partners' current accounts. Interest could have been a cash payment, in which case you could have credited cash instead. Gamma's salary will not apply until the next year.

(c) INCOME STATEMENT AND APPROPRIATION ACCOUNTS
FOR THE YEAR ENDED 31 DECEMBER 20X9

	$'000	$'000
Sales (200 – 6)		194
Opening inventory	30	
Purchases	103	
	133	
Closing inventory (24 + 2)	26	
Cost of sales		107
Gross profit		87
Operating expenses	64	
Interest (10% × 10,000)	1	
		65
Net profit		22
Salary: Alpha		4
Residual profit		18
Residual profit appropriated		
Alpha		6
Beta		6
Gamma		6
		18

(d) BALANCE SHEET AS AT 31 DECEMBER 20X9

	$'000	$'000
Assets		
Property, plant and equipment		
Land and buildings (revalued amount)		84
Plant and equipment: cost	70	
depreciation	40	
		30
Current assets		
Inventory (W)	26	
Receivables (W)	34	
		60
Total assets		174
Capital and liabilities		
Partners' capital accounts		
Alpha	38	
Beta	33	
Gamma	28	
		99
Partners' current accounts		
Alpha	9	
Beta	6	
Gamma	6	
		21
Non-current liabilities		
10% loan: Beta		10
Current liabilities		
Bank overdraft	11	
Payables	33	
		44
Total capital and liabilities		174

Working

Sales made on sale or return can only be treated as sales once the customer accepts the goods. Up to that point, the goods 'sold' are treated as inventory and valued at the lower of cost and net realisable value, as usual. The goods accepted in January will therefore be treated as sold in the next accounting period.

	$'000
∴ Sales: 200 – 6	194
Inventory: 24 + 2	26
Receivables: 40 – 6	34

26 Tripp Stumble and Faull

Tripp has reduced his capital by $4,000, but has agreed to keep this money in the partnership business as a loan. Interest, formally agreed at 10% per annum, amounts to:

$$10\% \times \frac{6 \text{ months}}{12 \text{ months}} \times \$4,000 = \$200,$$

for the current year. This interest is deducted from the net profit before interest to arrive at the net profit to be carried down into the appropriation account.

	$
Profit before interest	24,675
Loan interest	200
Net profit	24,475

We are told that the loan interest is credited to Tripp's current account.

TRIPP STUMBLE AND FAULL
APPROPRIATION ACCOUNT
FOR THE YEAR ENDED 30 SEPTEMBER 20X8

	$	$		$	$
Salary: Stumble		4,000	Net profit b/d (24,675–200)		24,475
Interest on capital (W1)			Interest on drawings		
Tripp	1,700		Tripp	450	
Stumble	1,000		Stumble	300	
Faull	675		Faull	150	
		3,375			900
Share of residual profits (W2)					
Tripp (4)	8,000				
Stumble (3)	6,000				
Faull (2)	4,000				
		18,000			
		25,375			25,375

Workings

1   *Interest on capital*

			$	$
Tripp	6 months × 5% pa × $36,000		900	
	6 months × 5% pa × $32,000		800	
				1,700
Stumble	5% × $20,000			1,000
Faull	6 months × 5% pa × $12,000		300	
	6 months × 5% pa × $15,000		375	
				675

2   Residual profits are the balancing figure on the account.
     Tripp = 4/9 × $18,000, Stumble = 3/9 × $18,000, Faull = 2/9 × $18,000.

PARTNERS' CURRENT ACCOUNTS

	Tripp $	Stumble $	Faull $		Tripp $	Stumble $	Faull $
Balance b/d	1,200			Balance b/f		1,600	750
Interest on				Salary		4,000	
drawings	450	300	150	Interest on			
Drawings	8,500	5,500	3,000	Loan	200		
				Interest on			
				Capital	1,700	1,000	675
				Residual			
				Profits	8,000	6,000	4,000
Balance c/d		6,800	2,275	Balance c/d	250		
	10,150	12,600	5,425		10,150	12,600	5,425
Balance b/d	250			Balance b/d		6,800	2,275

PARTNERS' CAPITAL ACCOUNTS

	Tripp $	Stumble $	Faull $		Tripp $	Stumble $	Faull $
Loan account	4,000			Balance b/d	36,000	20,000	12,000
Balance c/d	32,000	20,000	15,000	Cash			3,000
	36,000	20,000	15,000		36,000	20,000	15,000
				Balance b/d	32,000	20,000	15,000

(*Note.* Dates of transactions should strictly be included in the accounts, but are excluded here.)

27 Camberwell

(a)   Direct method

	$'000	$'000
Cash receipts from customers		19,200
Cash paid to suppliers	7,410	
Cash paid to employees	4,230	
Cash paid for expenses	3,405	
		15,045
Net cash flow from operating activities		4,155

(b)   Indirect method

	$'000	$'000
Net profit before taxation		3,555
Adjustment for depreciation		1,320
Changes in working capital:		
Increase in inventories	(555)	
Decrease in receivables	420	
Decrease in payables	(585)	
		(720)
		4,155

28 Blue

(a) **Cash-flow statement for the year ended 30 September 20X1**

	$'000	$'000
Cash flow from operating operating activities – see workings		95
Sale of non-current assets – see workings		90
Interest		(15)
Purchase of non-current asset		(40)
Dividends		(35)
Repayment of loan		(80)
		15
Opening bank and cash	15	
Closing bank and cash	30	
Increase in cash		15

Workings

	$'000
Operating activities	
Profit before tax	85
Interest expense	15
Adjustment for non-cash-flow items	
Profit on sale of non-current asset	(10)
Depreciation	30
	120
Adjustment for working capital	
Inventory	(15)
Receivables	(50)
Payables	40
	95
Sale of non-current assets	
Net book value (520 + 40 – 30 – 450)	80
Profit on sale	10
Proceeds on sale	90

(b) A cash-flow statement (CFS) helps users to assess the liquidity, solvency and financial adaptability of an entity. The liquidity of an entity is revealed by the change in the bank/cash balances between the beginning and end of the period. The solvency of an entity, and whether it is a going concern, may be assessed by using the historical cash flow to forecast future cash flows. The financial adaptability of an entity is its ability to use its cash to meet changes in its business environment.

A CFS is easier to understand than the accruals-based concept of an income statement, since it simply records the receipt and payment of cash, and is therefore likely to be more important to the user of accounts than the more complex income statement.

A CFS is more objective than accruals-based financial statements and it is less capable of manipulation. Users are therefore likely to place greater importance on this statement than the more subjective income statement.

Cash is the life-blood of a business and it is, therefore, vital that users of accounts assess cash flow when appraising a business. The CFS shows how finance is raised and where this is invested in the business. It thus provides a link between the income statement and the balance sheet.

Cash flow provides a basis for determining the amount of dividends to pay, and this is of interest to the users of accounts; similarly, cash flow is useful in valuing a business, which is also of interest to users.

Cash flow from operations is a measure of the 'quality' of the profit: the more closely cash approximates to profit, then the higher the quality.

However, although CFS is conceptually easier to understand than an income statement, the information it gives may be less easy to interpret. An increase in profit gives a positive message; a decrease in profit gives a negative message. Such a direct correlation does not apply to the CFS. Cash may increase, but this may be as a result of selling all the non-current assets; it may decrease, although this may be the result of buying non-current assets which will yield long-term advantages.

The CFS focuses on cash, not working capital, and thus there may be a temporary decrease/increase in cash depending on whether a large receivable has paid or inventory has been built up.

The pattern of cash flows may be erratic and these are not smoothed out by the accruals policy as used in the income statement. The CFS is not, therefore, a measure of economic performance.

Thus the income statement and the CFS are both relevant to the users of accounts and neither should be used in isolation.

29 Cat

CAT CO
CASH FLOW STATEMENT FOR THE YEAR ENDED 30 JUNE 20X2

	$'000	$'000
Cash flows from operating activities		
Profit before tax	67,500	
Depreciation	11,000	
Interest expense	1,500	
Increase in inventories	(6,000)	
Decrease in receivables	2,000	
Increase in payables	8,000	
Interest paid	(1,500)	
Dividends paid	(13,000)	
Income tax paid (W2)	25,000	
Net cash inflow from operating activities		44,500
Cash flows from Investing activities		
Payments to acquire property, plant and equipment (W3)		(34,000)
Net cash inflow before financing		10,500
Cash flows from financing activities		
Issue of ordinary share capital	3,000	
Redemption of loan stock	(10,000)	
Net cash outflow from financing activities		(7,000)
Increase in cash and cash equivalents (Note)		3,500

NOTES TO THE CASH FLOW STATEMENT

Note: analysis of the balances of cash and cash equivalents as shown in the balance sheet

	20X1 $'000	20X2 $'000	Change in year $'000
Cash at bank	10,000	13,500	3,500

Workings

1 Profit before tax

INCOME AND EXPENSE ACCOUNT

	$'000		$'000
Taxation	32,000	Balance b/f 1.7.X1	31,000
Dividends	13,000	Profit before tax (bal fig)	67,500
Balance c/f 30.6.X2	53,500		
	98,500		98,500

2 Tax paid

TAXATION

	$'000		$'000
Tax paid*	25,000	Balance b/f 1.7.X1	25,000
Balance c/f 30.6.X2	32,000	I & E a/c	32,000
	57,000		57,000

Note. The tax paid will be last year's year-end provision

3 Property, plant and equipment

PROPERTY, PLANT AND EQUIPMENT

	$'000		$'000
Balance b/f 1.7.X1	85,000		
Purchases (bal fig)	34,000	Balance c/f 30.6.X2	119,000
	119,000		119,000

30 Arthur

Workings

		$
Merlin		
Share capital	200,000	
Retained earnings	120,000	
	320,000 × 75% =	240,000
Paid by Arthur		360,000
Goodwill		120,000
Written off		72,000
Remaining on consolidated balance sheet		48,000
		120,000

Minority interest
460,000 × 25% = 115,000

Retained earnings

Arthur	480,000
Merlin – post acquisition reserves × 75%	105,000
	585,000
Goodwill written off	(72,000)
	513,000

Arthur Group
Balance sheet as at 31 March 20X3

	$
Goodwill	48,000
Sundry net assets	1,580,000
	1,628,000
Share capital	
1,000,000 shares of $1 each	1,000,000
Retained earnings	513,000
Minority interest	115,000
	1,628,000

31 April and May

Stage 1 There are no common items to cancel

Stage 2. *Minority interest*

Ordinary shares	100
Retained earnings	180
	280 × 25% = 70

Stage 3 *Goodwill*

	$	$
Cost of investment		250
Share of net assets acquired:		
Share capital	100	
Retained earnings	140	
	240	
Group share 75%		180
Goodwill		70

Stage 4 *Group consolidated profits*

	$
April	320
May (180 – 140) × 75%	30
	350

Consolidated balance sheet

	$'000	$'000
Non-current assets		250
Goodwill	70	
Property, plant and equipment (200 + 200)	400	
		470
Current assets		
Inventories (60 + 40)	100	
Receivables (85 + 54)	139	
Cash (20 + 10)	30	
		269
		739

	$'000	$'000
Equity and liabilities		
Ordinary shares	200	
Retained earnings	350	
		550
Minority interest		70
Current liabilities		
Payables (95 + 24)		119
		739

32 Tarquin

Tutorial note. Instead of you being asked to calculate ratios, the ratios are calculated for you and you have to concentrate on interpreting them.

Profitability as measured by the gross profit margin has declined slightly, although it is still higher than the industry average. However, from the point of view of the shareholders, it is the net profit margin which is more important, and this, as well as being above the industry average, has increased in 20X7.

The leverage has decreased and is significantly lower than the industry norm. While a low leverage means greater returns to the shareholders (assuming an interest rate lower than the ROCE of 19%), it is also associated with increased risk from the point of view of the lenders. The ROE has increased in 20X7 compared with 20X6, which is consistent with the decrease in leverage. The ROE is higher than the ROCE, which has remained constant.

Turning to liquidity, the current ratio has fallen slightly from that of the previous year, although again it is above the industry average. It is likely, however, that this fall is due to a reduction in inventories, since the quick ratio has remained constant. This would be consistent with the reduction in inventory turnover.

Accounts payable payment period and accounts receivable collection period have both increased, particularly the payment period. Both are above the industry norm. These increases suggest that the company has been expanding rapidly, perhaps allowing customers to take longer to pay in order to gain customers and financing the expansion through holding back payment to suppliers. Such expansion would be consistent with the reduction in gross profit margin; the company may be cutting prices to increase sales. This is putting pressure on liquidity. There may also be problems with bad debts.

Without further information, for example the turnover figure, it is unwise to make absolute predictions. In general profitability is looking favourable, but liquidity and leverage need to be carefully monitored.

33 Objectivity

(a) Objectivity means the lack of bias, an independence from outside influence. For accountants, objectivity means the ability to prepare or audit accounts uninfluenced by the interests of different user groups.

(b) A shareholder's investment in a company does not entitle him to influence or get involved in the day to day running of the business. That is left to the managers. The published accounts are a report on the stewardship of the managers and show the results and financial position for the year to which they relate. Without them the shareholders would have no information as to how the company was faring.

Although a historical document – accounts only deal with past results – they can give an indication of trends over a number of accounting periods and can thus be useful as a guide to investment.

34 Parmagat

Journals

(a)

	DR	CR
Suspense	150,000	
Share premium		150,000

Being premium on 500,000 shares issued at $1.30.

(b)

	DR	CR
Suspense	2,000	
Debts paid – previously written off		2,000

Being cash received in respect of debt written off in prior year

(c)

	DR	CR
Discounts allowed	95,000	
Suspense		95,000

Being correction regarding discounts allowed posted as credit to the account

Suspense

	DR $		CR $
Share premium	150,000	Opening balance	57,000
Bad debt recovered	2,000	Discounts allowed	95,000
	152,000		152,000

35 Abacus

(a) The value of the Imex receivable will have to be written down. If, as appears likely, something can be recovered, then the debt will not need to be written off entirely. It can be written down to 30c in the $. The write-down needed will be $227,500.

(b) NRV of this inventory is now:

	$
Sales proceeds	200,000
Less agents commission 20%	(40,000)
Less disposal costs	(25,000)
	135,000

As this is less than cost, the inventory should be written down by $15,000.

(c) It currently looks *probable* that this liability will not be met by the insurance company, so it should be provided for in full in accordance with IAS 37.

Effect on net profit before tax

	$
Draft net profit	923,000
Imex write-down	(227,500)
Inventory write-down	(15,000)
Provision for damages	(50,000)
Adjusted net profit	630,500

36 Lewisham

(a) '3 for 2' bonus issue

This involves the issue of 45m new 50c shares, financed from the share premium account and the accumulated profits. The capital structure following this issue will be:

	$'000
Share capital (15,000 + 22,500)	37,500
Share premium	–
Retained earnings (27,000 – 22,500)	7,500
	45,000

(b) '1 for 2' rights issue at 80c

37.5m shares are now issued at 80c.

	$'000
Share capital (37,500 + 18,750)	56,250
Share premium (37.5m x 30c)	11,250
Retained earnings	7,500
	75,000

37 Edgeware

(a)

	20X8	20X9	20X8	20X9
ROCE	$\dfrac{1,063}{3,475}$	$\dfrac{1,069}{4,544}$	30.6%	23.5%
GP%	$\dfrac{2,789}{5,327}$	$\dfrac{2,960}{5,714}$	52.3%	51.8%
NP%	$\dfrac{1,063}{5,327}$	$\dfrac{1,069}{5,714}$	19.9%	18.7%
Asset T/O	$\dfrac{5,327}{3,475}$	$\dfrac{5,714}{4,544}$	1.53	1.26

(b) There has been a significant fall in ROCE. Investigating this further we can see that GP% has only fallen by 0.5% whereas NP% has fallen by 1.2%. This suggests that extra costs have been incurred not in the production process but in the overheads and expenses.

There has also been a decline in the rate of asset turnover. This is mainly attributable to the substantial increase in property, plant and equipment. Possibly new assets have been acquired which are not yet functioning at their full earning capacity, certainly the investment has not yet produced a commensurate increase in revenue.

38 Hanoi

HANOI
INCOME STATEMENT
FOR THE YEAR ENDED 31 MARCH 20X4

	$'000	$'000
Sales		305
Cost of sales		
Opening inventory	62	
Purchases	108	
	170	
Closing inventory	45	
		125
Gross profit		180
Operating expenses (W1)	63	
Plant depreciation (W2)	31	
Lease amortisation	3	
Irrecoverable debt expense	12	
		109
Operating profit		71
Loan interest		11
Profit for the period		60

HANOI
BALANCE SHEET AS AT 31 MARCH 20X4

	Cost $'000	Depn $'000	NBV $'000
Fixed assets			
Freehold land	200	–	200
Leasehold premises	150	9	141
Plant and equipment	85 (W3)	44	41
	435	53	382
Current assets			
Inventories		45	
Receivables (96 – 2)		94	
Bank		164	
			303
			685
Equity and liabilities			
Ordinary $1 shares			250
Share premium			25
8% preference shares			100
Retained earnings (W4)			127
			502
10% loan stock			110
Current liabilities			
Trade payables	58		73
Accrual	15		
			685

Workings

1. *Operating expenses*

	$'000
Owed 1.4.X3	10
Paid during year	58
Owed 31.3.X4	15
Charge to income statement	63

2. *Plant cost and depreciation*

	$'000
Plant at cost b/d	120
Less fully depreciated item	40
Depreciable amount	80

Depreciation charge $80,000 × 20% = $16,000

(*Note*. Plant at cost for balance sheet includes fully depreciated item $(80 + 5) = $85,000.)

Write down on machine (20 − 5) = $15,000.

∴ Total depreciation charge on plant (16 + 15) = $31,000.

3. *Plant: accumulated depreciation*

	$'000
B/d	48
Less fully depreciated item	20
	28
Add charge for year	16
	44

4. *Retained earnings*

	$'000
B/F	100
Profit for period	60
Ordinary dividend (250,000 × 10c)	(25)
Preference dividend (100,000 × 8%)	(8)
	127

39 Pride

Tutorial note. This is a straightforward question. Make sure you know the proforma balance sheet well enough to put it down as you start the question. The allowance for receivables increases to $12,000 so you can ignore the original $10,000.

PRIDE
BALANCE SHEET AS AT 31 MARCH 20X1

	Cost $'000	Accumulated depreciation $'000	Net book value $'000
Non-current assets			
Land	210	–	210
Buildings	200	(124)	76
Plant and equipment	300	(136)	164
	710	(260)	450
Current assets			
Inventory		180	
Receivables (146 – 12)		134	
Prepayments		8	
Cash		50	
			372
			822
Equity and liabilities			
Share capital (250 + 100)			350
Share premium account (180 + 60)			240
Retained earnings			34
			624
Non-current liabilities			
10% loan notes			100
Current liabilities			
Trade payables		94	
Accruals		4	98
			822

Workings

1 Plant and equipment

	$'000
Original cost	318
Disposal	(18)
Cost at year end	300
Depreciation @ 20%	60
Accumulated depreciation	88
Disposal (18 – 6)	(12)
	136

40 Butthead

Tutorial note. This is a longer and more complicated question than you will get in the exam. Don't worry about the time constraint, just go methodically through it. Start with the receivables and payables reconciliation, the bank reconciliation and the suspense account balance.

BUTTHEAD
INCOME STATEMENT
FOR THE YEAR ENDED 31 DECEMBER 20X7

	$	$
Sales (160,800 – 1,600)		159,200
Cost of goods sold		
Opening inventory	10,800	
Purchases	82,400	
	93,200	
Closing inventory	(13,600)	
		(79,600)
Gross profit		79,600
Sundry expenses (W1)		(46,400)
Operating profit		33,200
Loan interest		(1,600)
Profit for the period		31,600

BUTTHEAD
BALANCE SHEET AS AT 31 DECEMBER 20X7

	$	$
Non-current assets		
Freehold building		60,000
Fixtures and fittings: cost	52,000	
depreciation	18,800	
		33,200
		93,200
Current assets		
Inventory	13,600	
Receivables	17,600	
Cash in hand	1,200	
		32,400
		125,600
Equity and liabilities		
Ordinary shares of 25p		23,000
5% preference shares of 25p		8,000
Share premium		9,000
Revaluation reserve		4,000
Retained earnings		46,400
		90,400
Non-current liabilities		
10% loan stock		16,000
Current liabilities		
Payables	16,000	
Loan interest ($^6/_{12} \times 1,600$)	800	
Preference dividend	400	
Bank overdraft	2,000	
		19,200
		125,600

Workings

1 *Sundry expenses*

	$
Per trial balance	37,600
Less loan interest (16,000 × 10% × 6/12)	(800)
Suspense account (W4)	6,400
Bank (2,800 + 400)	3,200
	46,400

2 *Receivables control account and receivables ledger*

RECEIVABLES CONTROL ACCOUNT

	$		$
Balance b/d	21,200	Sales	1,600
Suspense	1,200	Contra	1,600
		Suspense	1,600
		Balance c/d	17,600
	22,400		22,400

Receivables ledger

	Dr	Cr
	$	$
Balances b/d	20,000	1,200
Understatement	400	
Sales		1,600
	20,400	2,800

Net corrected balance: $17,600

3 *Payables control account and payables ledger*

PAYABLES CONTROL ACCOUNT

	$		$
Contra	1,600	Balance b/d	14,400
Balance c/d	16,000	Suspense a/c	3,200
	17,600		17,600

Payables ledger

	Dr	Cr
	$	$
	800	16,000
Beavis Co		800
	800	16,800

Net credit balances: $16,000

4 *Suspense account*

SUSPENSE ACCOUNT

	$		$
Balance b/d	2,800	Receivables control	1,200
Payables control	3,200	Sundry expenses (bal fig)	6,400
Receivables control	1,600		
	7,600		7,600

5   Bank

	$	
Balance per bank statement	(1,200)	o/d
Unpresented cheques	(800)	
	(2,000)	o/d
Cash book balance per t/b	1,200	
Cheque difference (to sundry expenses)	(400)	
Bank charges (bal fig)	(2,800)	
	(2,000)	

41 Tafford

TAFFORD LIMITED
INCOME STATEMENT FOR THE YEAR ENDED 30 SEPTEMBER 20X1

	$'000
Revenue	41,600
Cost of sales (W1)	(20,000)
Gross profit	21,600
Distribution costs (W2)	(6,285)
Administrative expenses (W3)	(4,885)
Finance cost (10% × $10,000,000)	(1,000)
Profit before tax	9,430
Income tax expense	(3,000)
Net profit for the period	6,430

Workings

1   Cost of sales

	$'000
Opening inventory	13,000
Purchases	22,600
	35,600
Less: closing inventory	(15,600)
	20,000

2   Distribution costs

	$'000
Distribution costs (6,000 – 200 + 100)	5,900
Depreciation: warehouse machinery (10% × $3,000,000)	300
motor vehicles (25% × ½ × $(1,180,000 – 180,000))	125
Profit on sale of vehicles	(40)
	6,285

3   Administrative expenses

	$'000
Administrative expenses (5,000 – 100 + 60)	4,960
Irrecoverable debts	600
Reduction in allowance for receivables	(800)
Depreciation: motor vehicles (25% × ½ × $1,000,000)	125
	4,885

42 Alpaca

ALPACA
BALANCE SHEET AS AT 30 APRIL 20X2

Assets	$	$
Non-current assets		
Cost	1,000,000	
Accumulated depreciation	330,000	
		670,000
Current assets		
Inventory	450,000	
Receivables	670,000	
Cash at bank	114,000	
		1,234,000
		1,904,000
Equity and liabilities		
Share capital		500,000
Share premium		50,000
Retained earnings (W2)		964,000
		1,514,000
Non-current liabilities		
10% loan notes		200,000
Current liabilities		
Payables	180,000	
Accruals (W1)	10,000	
		190,000
		1,904,000

Workings

1   Accruals

LOAN NOTE INTEREST

	$		$
Bank	20,000	Bal b/f	10,000
Bal c/f	10,000	Income statement	20,000
	20,000		30,000

2   *Retained earnings*

	$	$	$
Bal b/f			818,000
Sales		4,006,000	
Opening inventory	410,000		
Purchases	2,120,000		
Closing inventory	(450,000)		
		2,080,000	
Gross profit		1,926,000	
Expenses	1,640,000		
Depreciation	100,000		
Irrecoverable debts written off	20,000		
Loan note interest payable (W1)	20,000		
		1,780,000	
Net profit for year			146,000
Balance c/f			964,000

Tutorial note. If you were running out of time, you could take the retained earnings as being the balancing figure. However, you would lose 4 marks for not producing the above workings.

1 MCQs

(i) A

(ii) B

DEBIT	Property, plant and equipment	$38,000	
CREDIT	Plant repairs		$38,000
DEBIT	Dep'n expense	$1,900	
CREDIT	Accumulated dep'n		$1,900

Profit is understated by $38,000 − $1,900 = $36,100

(iii) D

	$
Suspense account	16,500
Discount allowed	3,900
Discount received	(5,100)
Transposition of cash received	(9,900)
	5,400

(iv) B Only errors 1 and 3 involve a suspense account entry to correct them.

(v) B $$\frac{\$30,000 - \$6,000}{4 \text{ years}} \times \frac{5 \text{ months}}{12 \text{ months}} = \$2,500$$

(vi) C

(vii) C

	$
	116,400
Line 1: (400 × $3) − $200	1,000
Line 2: (200 × $35) − $300 − $1,200	5,500
	122,900

(viii) D

(ix) C The bank is overdrawn.

	$
Overdraft	(38,600)
Deposits	41,200
	2,600
Unpresented cheques	(3,300)
Overdraft	(700)

(x) A The other two items are part of the bank reconciliation.

(xi) A

	$
Opening receivables	(29,100)
Cash from credit customers	381,600
Cash sales	112,900
Closing receivables	38,600
Expenses paid out of cash	6,800
Bad debts written off	7,200
Discounts allowed	9,400
Refunds	(2,100)
	525,300

MULTIPLE CHOICE ANSWERS

(xii) D Cost of sales: $17,000 + $91,000 − $24,000 = $84,000

Sales	100%
Cost of sales	60%
Gross profit	40%

Sales: $\dfrac{\$84,000}{60\%} = \$140,000$

(xiii) A $\dfrac{5 \text{ months}}{12 \text{ months}} \times \$24,000 = \$10,000$

$\dfrac{7 \text{ months}}{12 \text{ months}} \times \$30,000 = \$17,500$

Total rent: $10,000 + $17,500 = $27,500

(xiv) B

	$
Inventory out: 64,800 × 70%	(45,360)
Inventory in: purchases	49,600
Inventory at 1 December	28,400
Inventory @ 31 December	32,640

(xv) D Research expenditure is never capitalised

(xvi) A

	D $	E $	F $
Salaries	–	30,000	24,000
PSR to 1.7.20X0 (240,000 − 24,000) 5:3:2	108,000	64,800	43,200
PSR to 31.12.20X0 (240,000 − 30,000) 3:1:1	126,000	42,000	42,000
	234,000	136,800	109,200

(xvii) C

	$
Share capital @ 1.1.20X0	500,000
Issue on 1.4.20X0 (200,000 @ 50c)	100,000
Bonus issue (1.2m ÷ 4) @ 50c	150,000
Share capital as at 31.12.20X0	750,000
Share premium @ 1.1.20X0	300,000
1.4.20X0 200,000 shares @ (130c − 50c)	160,000
Bonus issue (as above)	(150,000)
	310,000

(xviii) B The statement of changes in equity

(xix) B Proceeds from sale of equipment are included in investing activities

(xx) B

(xxi) D

(xxii) B

(xxiii) A

	$
Consideration	160,000
Shares and reserves acquired (100,000 + 80,000) @ 80%	(144,000)
Goodwill	16,000

MULTIPLE CHOICE ANSWERS

(xxiv) D

	$
MI	
Shares	100,000
Reserves	180,000
	280,000
MI @ 40%	112,000

(xxv) C

	$
Consideration	280,000
Acquired 320,000 @ 75%	240,000
Goodwill	40,000

Retained earnings	$
H	480,000
S post acq reserves (180,000 – 120,000) @ 75%	45,000
Goodwill written off	(40,000)
	485,000

MULTIPLE CHOICE ANSWERS

2 MCQ

(i) C

(ii) C

(iii) D

(iv) B

	Cash book	$	Bank statement	$
	Balance	(8,970)	Balance	(11,200)
	Bank charges	(550)	Credit in error	(425)
			Unpresented cheques	(3,275)
			Outstanding deposits	5,380
		(9,250)		(9,250)

(v) D

	$
Cost of machine	80,000
Installation	5,000
Training	2,000
Testing	1,000
	88,000

(vi) C ELECTRICITY ACCOUNT

		$		$
			Balance b/fwd	300
20X0:				
1 August	Paid bank	600		
1 November	Paid bank	720		
20X1:				
1 February	Paid bank	900		
30 June	Paid bank	840		
30 June	Accrual c/d $840 \times {}^2/_3$	560	I & E account	3,320
		3,620		3,620

(vii) A GAS SUPPLIER ACCOUNT

	$			$
Balance b/fwd	200			
Bank $600 x 12	7,200	28 February	invoice	1,300
		31 May	invoice	1,400
		31 August	invoice	2,100
		30 November	invoice	2,000
		30 November	bal. c/d	600
	7,400			7,400

GAS ACCOUNT

		$			$
28 February	invoice	1,300			
31 May	invoice	1,400			
31 August	invoice	2,100			
30 November	invoice	2,000	30 November	I & E account	6,800
		6,800			6,800

(viii) B

	Cost $	Net realisable value $	Lower of cost & NRV $	Units	Value $
Basic	6	8	6	200	1,200
Super	9	8	8	250	2,000
Luxury	18	10	10	150	1,500
					4,700

(ix) B

	$
Cost	10,000
20W7 Depreciation	2,500
	7,500
20W8 Depreciation	1,875
	5,625
20W9 Depreciation	1,406
	4,219
20X0 Part exchange	5,000
Profit	781

(x) A $\quad \dfrac{\text{Operating profit}}{\text{Capital employed}} = \dfrac{\$15,000}{\$120,000} \times 100 = 12.5\%$

(xi) C $\quad \dfrac{\text{Receivables including sales tax}}{\text{Credit sales including sales tax}} = \dfrac{\$23,500}{\$117,500} \times 365 \text{ days} = 73 \text{ days}$

(xii) B

(xiii) C

(xiv) C

(xv) A

(xvi) C

(xvii) D

(xviii) C

(xix) A

	$	$
Net book value at 1st August 20X0		200,000
Less depreciation		(20,000)
Proceeds	25,000	
Loss	5,000	
Therefore net book value		(30,000)
		150,000

(xx) A $\quad$ Gearing =

$\dfrac{\text{debt}}{\text{debt + equity}} = \dfrac{75}{75 + 500} = 13\%$

(xxi) D $\quad$ Correct. This is not an objective from the *framework*. Additional data is required to assess this.

$\quad\quad$ A $\quad$ This is a primary objective.

$\quad\quad$ B $\quad$ Again, a major objective.

$\quad\quad$ C $\quad$ All Classes of users require information for decision making.

MULTIPLE CHOICE ANSWERS

(xxii)	A	This information is needed by lenders
(xxiii)	B	
(xxiv)	D	Loan stock is a non-current liability.
	A	This is statutory reserve.
	B	Otherwise known as the revenue reserve.
	C	This is an unrealised reserve.
(xxv)	D	Correct, company will usually include this under distribution costs or administrative expenses.
	A	Incorrect, the contents of cost of sales are not defined by any IAS.
	B	Depreciation will be included under the relevant statutory expense heading (eg office equipment depreciation will go into administrative expenses).
	C	Incorrect, net profit is calculated after interest.

Index

Note: Key Terms are given in **bold**

Accounting concepts, 11
Accounting equation, 24, 62
Accounting information, 4
Accounting policies, 338
Accounting records, 319
Accounting standards, 11, 437
Accruals basis of accounting, 148
Accruals, 168, 169, 174, 244
Accruals and prepayments, 275, 286
Acid test ratio, 403
Administration expenses, 43
Adoption of an IFRS, 341
Advantages and disadvantages of trading as a partnership, 304
Advantages of cash flow accounting, 367
Advantages of global harmonisation, 431
Allowance for receivables, 184
Amortisation of development costs, 258
Appropriation of profit, 306, 307
Asset, 8, 22, 35
Asset turnover, 395
Assets held for sale, 344
Audit trail, 419
Auditing, 10
Authorised (or nominal) capital, 327
AVCO (average cost), 203

Bad debts, 42, 182, 189, 242, 244, 276
Balance between benefits and cost, 451
Balance between qualitative characteristics, 452
Balance sheet, 7, 8, 41, 94, 95, 114, 184, 326
Balance sheet date, 320
Balance sheet disclosures, 323
Balancing ledger accounts, 90, 95
Bank charges, 120
Bank interest, 120
Bank overdraft, 35
Bank reconciliation, 121, 125
Bank statements, 56
Barriers to harmonisation, 431
Benefits of cash flow information, 355
bills of exchange, 35
Bonus (capitalisation) issues, 333
Books of original entry, 52, 73
Brought forward, 35
Business entity concept, 152
Business equation, 62, 287

Calculating ratios, 391
Called-in capital, 327
Capital, 24, 35
Capital account, 306
Capital expenditure, 14
Capital gearing ratio, 398
Capital income, 15
Capital transactions, 15
Carriage inwards, 166
Carriage outwards, 166
Carried forward, 35
Carrying amount, 239
Cash, 38, 39, 324, 355
Cash and cash equivalents, 356
Cash book, 52, 54, 78, 275, 282
Cash cycle, 38, 402
Cash discounts, 104, 105
Cash equivalents, 355
Cash flow ratio, 401
Cash flow statements, 355
Changes in accounting estimates, 338
Changes in accounting policies, 341
Coding, 419
Comparability, 451
Comparative information, 150
Compensating errors, 90, 132, 134
Completeness, 451
Concepts of capital and capital maintenance, 452
Conceptual framework, 443, 444
Consistency of presentation, 148
Contingent asset, 267
Contingent liability, 267
Continuous inventory records, 200
Control, 373
Control accounts, 102, 114
Correction of errors, 75, 134
Cost, 239
Cost formulas, 210
Cost of goods sold, 165
Costing module, 420
Costs of conversion, 209
Costs of purchase, 209
Counting inventories, 200
Covenants, 338
Credit, 64, 90
Credit note, 51
Credit sales and trade accounts receivable, 275, 276

INDEX

Creditors, 28, 68
Criticisms of accounting conventions, 438
Criticisms of historical cost accounting, 440
Criticisms of the accrual assumption, 439
Criticisms of the prudence concept, 438
Cumulative weighted average costing, 205
Current account, 306
Current assets, 36, 38, 39, 336
Current cost accounting (CCA), 442
Current liabilities, 35, 336, 337
Current purchasing power (CPP);, 442
Current ratio, 403
Current replacement cost, 200

Database, 425
Day book analysis, 75
Debit, 64, 90
Debit note, 51
Debt ratio, 397
Debt/equity ratio, 399
Debtor, 28
Depreciable amount, 219, 256
Depreciable assets, 219
Depreciation, 37, 219, 220, 241, 244
Depreciation methods, 221
Desirable qualities of accounting information, 10
Development, 256
Direct method, 359
Disclosures, 320
Discount, 103
Disposal of non-current assets, 233, 234, 235
Dividend per share and dividend cover, 409
Dividend yield, 410
Dividends, 42, 156, 265, 325
Double entry bookkeeping, 64, 90
Drawings, 25, 275, 306
Duality concept, 154
Due process, 433

Earnings per share, 409
Efficiency ratios, 404
Elements of financial statements, 452
Entity concept, 23
Errors, 75
Errors of commission, 132, 133, 137
Errors of omission, 132, 133, 137
Errors of principle, 90, 132, 133
Errors of transposition, 132
Events after the balance sheet date, 264
Exchanges of assets, 240

Fair presentation and compliance with IASs/IFRSs, 146
Fair value, 157, 239
Faithful representation, 450
FIFO (first in, first out), 203, 204, 210
Final accounts questions, 247
Finance expenses, 43
Financial Accounting Standards Board (FASB), 443
Financial accounts, 9
Financing activities, 355, 358
Fixed production overheads, 209
Format of a ledger account, 63
Framework, 156
Framework for the preparation and presentation of Financial Statements, 5

Gearing ratio, 398
General ledger, 63
Generally Accepted Accounting Practice (GAAP), 13, 444
Going concern, 147, 265
Goods destroyed, 280
Goods received notes, 51
Goods sold, 42
Goods stolen, 280
Goods written off, 167
Goodwill, 252
Goodwill and pre-acquisition profits, 380
Goodwill arising on consolidation, 379
Gross profit, 41, 42, 279
Gross profit margin, 396
Group, 373

Historical cost, 153, 200
Historical cost accounting, 440
Historical cost convention, 153
Holding gain, 441

IAS 1 Presentation of financial statements, 145, 319, 379
IAS 2 Inventories, 201, 208
IAS 4 Depreciation accountings, 241
IAS 7 Cash flow statements, 354
IAS 10 Contingencies and events after the balance sheet date, 159, 264
IAS 16 Property, plant and equipment, 233, 238
IAS 18 Revenue, 156
IAS 27 Consolidated and separate financial statements, 372, 375
IAS 38 Intangible assets, 255
IASB, 12

INDEX

IASC and IOSCO, 432
IASC and national standard setting bodies, 433
IASC and professional accountancy bodies/IFAC, 433
IASC and the EC/intergovernmental bodies, 432
IFRS 1 first-time adoption of international financial reporting standards, 452
IFRS 5 Non-current assets held for sale and discontinued operations, 343
Impairment of development costs, 258
Impersonal accounts, 77
Implications of high or low gearing, 399
Imprest system, 57
Income statement, 7, 8, 41
Income tax, 325
Incomplete records, 274, 288
Indirect costs, 42
Indirect method, 359
Indirect versus direct, 360
Intangible non-current assets, 36, 37, 253
Integrated software, 420, 421
Interest, 156
Interest cover, 400
Interest, royalties and dividends, 158
Internal check, 114
International Accounting Standards Board (IASB), 12
International Financial Reporting Standards (IFRSs), 12
International Organisation of Securities Commissions (IOSCO), 435
Interpretation of IASs, 436
Inventories, 39, 196, 208, 244
Inventory destroyed, 282
Investing activities, 355, 358
Investment, 37, 323
Invoice, 50
Issued capital, 327

Journal, 73
Journal entries, 74, 134

Ledger accounts, 64
Level of precision, 320
Leverage, 398
Liabilities, 8, 35
Liability, 22, 28, 266
LIFO (last in, first out), 203
Limited liability, 318
Limited liability companies, 23, 305, 317, 318
Liquidity, 336, 397, 402, 403
List of account balances/trial balance, 88, 114
Loan stock bonds, 330

Loans by partners, 307
Long-term interest-bearing securities, 337
Long-term solvency, 397

Management (or cost) accounting, 9
Management reports, 420
Market value of shares, 329
Mark-up, 279
Materiality, 149
Measurement of revenue, 157
Measurement of the element of financial statements, 452
Minority interests, 377
Modules, 420
Money measurement concept, 153

Need for accounts, 5
Net assets, 34
Net profit, 41, 42
Net profit margin, 396
Net realisable value, 167, 200, 208, 212
Neutrality, 451
Nominal ledger, 63, 424
Nominal value, 331
Non-commercial undertakings, 7
Non-current assets, 36, 37, 217, 323, 426
Non-current liability, 36, 324
Non-financial statements, 8
Normal capacity, 209

Objectivity, 154
Offsetting, 150
Omission of a transaction, 90
Opening and closing inventories, 197
Opening balance sheet, 275
Operating activities, 355, 358
Operating cycle, 337
Ordinary shares, 328

P/E ratio, 409
Paid-in capital, 327
Par value, 327
Parent, 373
Partnership agreement, 303
Partnerships, 302, 303
Payables control account, 102
Payables, 110, 324
Payables ledger, 78, 79, 114, 422
PBIT, profit before interest and tax, 393
Personal accounts, 77
Petty cash book, 52, 56
Preferred shares, 328

INDEX

Prepayments, 40, 168, 171, 173, 176, 244
Presentation of accounting policies, 151
Presented fairly, 14
Primary profitability ratio, 395
Profit, 5, 25
Profit analysis, 396
Profit and loss account, 184
Profit before interest and tax, 393
Profit margin, 395
Profitability, 393
Profit-sharing ratio, 303
Property, plant and equipment, 36, 238, 239, 323
Prospective application, 341
Provision for depreciation, 228
Provisions, 266, 333
Prudence, 150, 185, 438, 451
Purchase day book, 52, 53
Purchase order, 50
Purchase returns day book, 54
Purchased goodwill, 253, 254, 255
Purchases and trade accounts payable, 275, 277
Purchases returns day book, 52
Purchases, inventory and the cost of sales, 275
Purpose of financial statements, 145

Qualitative characteristics of financial statements, 450
Quick ratio, 403

Ratio analysis, 390
Real accounts, 244
Realisation concept, 154
Reasons for the present state of financial accounting, 11
Receivables, 39, 107, 323
Receivables control account, 102, 110
Receivables ledger, 77, 78, 112
Receivables payment period, 404
Recognition, 239
Recognition of the elements of financial statements, 452
Recoverable amount, 239
Reducing balance method, 222, 224
Relevance, 450
Reliability, 450
Rendering of services, 158
Replacement cost, 203
Reporting entity, 448
Reporting period, 321
Research and development (R & D) costs, 255, 256
Reserve, 331, 333

Residual value, 220, 239
Retail method, 210
Retrospective application, 341
Return on capital employed (ROCE), 393
Return on equity (ROE), 394
Revaluation of non-current assets, 232
Revaluation surplus, 332
Revaluations, 240
Revenue, 157
Revenue expenditure, 14
Revenue income, 15
Review of depreciation method, 241
Review of useful life, 241
Rights issues, 334
Royalties, 156

Sale of goods, 157
Sales day book, 52, 77, 78
Sales order., 50
Sales returns day book, 52, 53, 54
Sales tax, 79
Secondary ratios, 395
Selling and distribution expenses, 43
Separate entity, 23
Settlement discounts, 104, 105
Share premium account, 331
Shareholders' interests, 324
Short-term investments, 39
Short-term solvency, 402
Source documents, 50
Spreadsheets, 426
Stable monetary unit, 153
Standard costs, 203, 210
Statement of changes in equity, 333
Statements, 422
Stolen goods, 280
Stolen goods or goods destroyed, 275
Straight line method, 222, 223
Subsidiaries, 373
Substance over form, 151, 450
Sum of the digits method, 224
Suspense account, 136, 138

T accounts, 63
Tangible asset, 37
Taxation, 325
Theft of cash from the till, 285
Time differences, 120
Timeliness, 451
Trade accounts payable (creditors), 28
Trade accounts receivable (debtors), 28, 40
Trade discount, 104
Trading account, 41, 42

Trading, profit and loss account, 92
Transposition error, 115, 137
Trial balance, 88
True and fair view, 14
Two column cash book, 283
Types of error, 132

UK GAAP, 444
Underlying assumptions, 449
Understandability, 450
United Nations Working Groups of Experts on International Standards of Accounting and Reporting (UN IASR group), 433
Unlimited liability, 318
Unpresented cheques, 124
Use and application of IASs and IFRSs, 13

Useful life, 219, 220, 256
Users of accounting information, 6, 448

Valuing inventories, 200
Variable production overheads, 209

Wages and salaries, 102
Weighted average cost, 210
Working capital, 337
Working Group in Accounting Standards of the Organisation for Economic Co-operation and Development (OECD Working group), 433
Worldwide effect of IASs and the IASC, 436
Wrong account, 90

Review Form & Free Prize Draw – Paper 1.1 Preparing Financial Statements (International) (6/06)

All original review forms from the entire BPP range, completed with genuine comments, will be entered into one of two draws on 31 January 2007 and 31 July 2007. The names on the first four forms picked out on each occasion will be sent a cheque for £50.

Name: _____   Address: _____

How have you used this Interactive Text?
(Tick one box only)
- [ ] Home study (book only)
- [ ] On a course: college _____
- [ ] With 'correspondence' package
- [ ] Other _____

Why did you decide to purchase this Interactive Text? *(Tick one box only)*
- [ ] Have used BPP Texts in the past
- [ ] Recommendation by friend/colleague
- [ ] Recommendation by a lecturer at college
- [ ] Saw advertising
- [ ] Saw information on BPP website
- [ ] Other _____

During the past six months do you recall seeing/receiving any of the following?
(Tick as many boxes as are relevant)
- [ ] Our advertisement in *ACCA Student Accountant*
- [ ] Our advertisement in *Pass*
- [ ] Our advertisement in *PQ*
- [ ] Our brochure with a letter through the post
- [ ] Our website www.bpp.com

Which (if any) aspects of our advertising do you find useful?
(Tick as many boxes as are relevant)
- [ ] Prices and publication dates of new editions
- [ ] Information on Text content
- [ ] Facility to order books off-the-page
- [ ] None of the above

Which BPP products have you used?

Text	✓	Success CD	[ ]	Learn Online	[ ]
Kit	[ ]	i-Learn	[ ]	Home Study Package	[ ]
Passcard	[ ]	i-Pass	[ ]	Home Study PLUS	[ ]

Your ratings, comments and suggestions would be appreciated on the following areas.

	Very useful	Useful	Not useful
Introductory section (Key study steps, personal study)	[ ]	[ ]	[ ]
Chapter introductions	[ ]	[ ]	[ ]
Key terms	[ ]	[ ]	[ ]
Quality of explanations	[ ]	[ ]	[ ]
Case studies and other examples	[ ]	[ ]	[ ]
Exam focus points	[ ]	[ ]	[ ]
Questions and answers in each chapter	[ ]	[ ]	[ ]
Fast forwards and chapter roundups	[ ]	[ ]	[ ]
Quick quizzes	[ ]	[ ]	[ ]
Question Bank	[ ]	[ ]	[ ]
Answer Bank	[ ]	[ ]	[ ]
Index	[ ]	[ ]	[ ]
Icons	[ ]	[ ]	[ ]

Overall opinion of this Study Text   Excellent [ ]   Good [ ]   Adequate [ ]   Poor [ ]

Do you intend to continue using BPP products?   Yes [ ]   No [ ]

On the reverse of this page are noted particular areas of the text about which we would welcome your feedback. The BPP author of this edition can be e-mailed at: marymaclean@bpp.com

Please return this form to: Nick Weller, ACCA Publishing Manager, BPP Professional Education, FREEPOST, London, W12 8BR

Review Form & Free Prize Draw (continued)

TELL US WHAT YOU THINK

Please note any further comments and suggestions/errors below

Free Prize Draw Rules

1   Closing date for 31 January 2007 draw is 31 December 2006. Closing date for 31 July 2007 draw is 30 June 2007.

2   Restricted to entries with UK and Eire addresses only. BPP employees, their families and business associates are excluded.

3   No purchase necessary. Entry forms are available upon request from BPP Professional Education. No more than one entry per title, per person. Draw restricted to persons aged 16 and over.

4   Winners will be notified by post and receive their cheques not later than 6 weeks after the relevant draw date.

5   The decision of the promoter in all matters is final and binding. No correspondence will be entered into.